D0202770

Macroeconomics

Sixth Edition

STEPHEN D. WILLIAMSON

330 Hudson Street, NY NY 10013

Vice President, Business Publishing: Donna Battista
Director of Portfolio Management: Adrienne D'Ambrosio
Director, Courseware Portfolio Management: Ashley Dodge
Senior Sponsoring Editor: Neeraj Bhalla
Editorial Assistant: Michelle Zeng
Vice President, Product Marketing: Roxanne McCarley
Director of Strategic Marketing: Brad Parkins
Strategic Marketing Manager: Deborah Strickland
Product Marketer: Tricia Murphy
Field Marketing Manager: Ramona Elmer
Field Marketing Assistant: Kristen Compton
Product Marketing Assistant: Jessica Quazza
Vice President, Production and Digital Studio, Arts and Business: Etain O'Dea
Director of Production, Business: Jeff Holcomb
Managing Producer, Business: Alison Kalil

Operations Specialist: Carol Melville
Creative Director: Blair Brown
Manager, Learning Tools: Brian Surette
Managing Producer, Digital Studio, Arts and Business: Diane Lombardo
Digital Studio Producer: Melissa Honig
Digital Studio Producer: Alana Coles
Digital Content Team Lead: Noel Lotz
Digital Content Project Lead: Courtney Kamauf
Full-Service Project Management and Composition: SPi Global
Interior Design: SPi Global
Cover Design: SPi Global
Cover Art: Vlad Ageshin/Shutterstock
Printer/Binder: LSC Communications Crawfordsville
Cover Printer: Phoenix Colour

The Pearson Series in Economics

Abel/Bernanke/Croushore
*Macroeconomics**
**denotes MyEconLab titles Visit www.
myeconlab.com to learn more.

Acemoglu/Laibson/List
*Economics**

Bade/Parkin
*Foundations of Economics**

Berck/Helfand
The Economics of the Environment

Bierman/Fernandez
*Game Theory with Economic
Applications*

Blanchard
*Macroeconomics**

Boyer
*Principles of Transportation
Economics*

Branson
Macroeconomic Theory and Policy

Bruce
*Public Finance and the American
Economy*

Carlton/Perloff
Modern Industrial Organization

Case/Fair/Oster
*Principles of Economics**

Chapman
*Environmental Economics: Theory,
Application, and Policy*

Daniels/VanHoose
*International Monetary &
Financial Economics*

Downs
*An Economic Theory of
Democracy*

Farnham
Economics for Managers

Froyen
*Macroeconomics: Theories and
Policies*

Fusfeld
The Age of the Economist

Gerber
*International Economics**

Gordon
*Macroeconomics**

Greene
Econometric Analysis

Gregory/Stuart
*Russian and Soviet Economic
Performance and Structure*

Hartwick/Olewiler
*The Economics of Natural
Resource Use*

Heilbroner/Milberg
*The Making of the Economic
Society*

Heyne/Boettke/Prychitko
The Economic Way of Thinking

Hubbard/O'Brien
*Economics**

InEcon
*Money, Banking, and the Financial
System**

Hubbard/O'Brien/Rafferty
*Macroeconomics**

Hughes/Cain
American Economic History

Husted/Melvin
International Economics

Jehle/Reny
Advanced Microeconomic Theory

Keat/Young/Erfle
Managerial Economics

Klein
*Mathematical Methods for
Economics*

Krugman/Obstfeld/Melitz
*International Economics: Theory
& Policy**

Laidler
The Demand for Money

Lynn
*Economic Development: Theory
and Practice for a Divided
World*

Miller
*Economics Today**

Miller/Benjamin
The Economics of Macro Issues

Miller/Benjamin/North
The Economics of Public Issues

Mishkin
*The Economics of Money, Banking,
and Financial Markets**
*The Economics of Money, Banking,
and Financial Markets, Business
School Edition**
*Macroeconomics: Policy and
Practice**

Murray
*Econometrics: A Modern
Introduction*

O'Sullivan/Sheffrin/Perez
*Economics: Principles,
Applications and Tools**

Parkin
*Economics**

Perloff
*Microeconomics**
*Microeconomics: Theory and
Applications with
Calculus**

Perloff/Brander
*Managerial Economics and
Strategy**

Pindyck/Rubinfeld
*Microeconomics**

**Riddell/Shackelford/Stamos/
Schneider**
*Economics: A Tool for Critically
Understanding Society*

CONTENTS

PREFACE

This book follows a modern approach to macroeconomics by building macroeconomic models from microeconomic principles. As such, it is consistent with the way that macroeconomic research is conducted today.

This approach has three advantages. First, it allows deeper insights into economic growth processes and business cycles, the key topics in macroeconomics. Second, an emphasis on microeconomic foundations better integrates the study of macroeconomics with approaches that students learn in courses in microeconomics and in field courses in economics. Learning in macroeconomics and microeconomics thus becomes mutually reinforcing, and students learn more. Third, in following an approach to macroeconomics that is consistent with current macroeconomic research, students will be better prepared for advanced study in economics.

What's New in the Sixth Edition

The first five editions of *Macroeconomics* had an excellent reception in the market. In the sixth edition, I build on the strengths of the first five editions, while producing a framework for students of macroeconomics that captures all of the latest developments in macroeconomic thinking, applied to recent economic events and developments in macroeconomic policy. Previous editions of this text used available macroeconomic models and new ideas to analyze the events of the global financial crisis of 2008-2009. Now, with the financial crisis receding in the rear-view mirror, there are new challenges that macroeconomists and policymakers need to address, and that students should come to terms with. What are the causes and consequences of the low rates of labor force participation and employment in the United States? What is unconventional monetary policy, and why are many central banks in the world engaging in such policies? What are the macroeconomic implications of default on debt by sovereign governments? Why are real rates of interest so low in world? Can inflation be too low, and what should governments do about too-low inflation? What is the role of fiscal policy in a liquidity trap? What is Neo-Fisherism? What is secular stagnation? These questions, and more, are answered in this revised sixth edition. In detail, the key changes in the sixth edition are:

- Chapter 6, "Search and Unemployment," has been revised to include a section on the "one-sided search model," an approach to modeling the behavior of the unemployed. This model determines the reservation wage for an unemployed worker, and shows how unemployment benefits, job offer rates, and separations determine the unemployment rate.

- Chapter 12, "Money, Banking, Prices, and Monetary Policy," includes a new section about unconventional monetary policy and the zero lower bound. Unconventional policies include quantitative easing and negative nominal interest rates.

- In Chapter 13, there is a new section on business cycle theories as they relate to the 2008-2009 recession in particular.

- Chapter 14 address how New Keynesian models fit the data, and the chapter contains new material on the liquidity trap.

- Chapter 15 is entirely new, and analyzes inflation and its causes in a New Keynesian framework. A basic New Keynesian model shows how monetary policy is conducted, in conventional circumstances, and when the zero lower bound on the nominal interest rate is a problem. The chapter discusses how secular stagnation or world savings gluts can lead to low real interest rates, and zero lower bound monetary policies. Finally, a dynamic New Keynesian rational expectations model is used to introduce Neo-Fisherism—the idea that central banks should correct too-low inflation by increasing nominal interest rates.

- New end-of-chapter problems have been added.

- New "Theory Confronts the Data" features include "Government Expenditure Multipliers in the Recovery from the 2008-2009 Recession" (Chapter 11), "The Phillips Curve" (Chapter 15), and "Greece and Sovereign Default" (Chapter 16).

- New "Macroeconomics in Action" features include "Default on Government Debt" (Chapter 9), "Social Security and Incentives" (Chapter 10), and "Quantitative Easing in the United States" (Chapter 12).

Data figures all have been revised to include the most recent data.

Structure

The text begins with Part I, which provides an introduction and study of measurement issues. Chapter 1 describes the approach taken in the book and the key ideas that students should take away. It previews the important issues that will be addressed throughout the book, along with some recent issues in macroeconomics, and the highlights of how these will be studied. Measurement is discussed in Chapters 2 and 3, first with regard to gross domestic product, prices, savings, and wealth, and then with regard to business cycles. In Chapter 3, we develop a set of key business cycle facts that will be used throughout the book, particularly in Chapters 13-15, where we investigate how alternative business cycle theories fit the facts.

Our study of macroeconomic theory begins in Part II. In Chapter 4, we study the behavior of consumers and firms in detail. In the one-period model developed in Chapter 5, we capture the behavior of all consumers and all firms in the economy with a single representative consumer and a single representative firm. The one-period model is used to show how changes in government spending and total factor productivity affect aggregate output, employment, consumption, and the real wage, and we analyze how proportional income taxation matters for aggregate activity and government tax revenue. In Chapter 6, two search models of unemployment are studied, which can capture some important details of labor market behavior in a macroeconomic context. These search models permit an understanding of the determinants of unemployment, and an explanation for some of the recent unusual labor market behavior observed in the United States.

With a basic knowledge of static macroeconomic theory from Part II, we proceed in Part III to the study of the dynamic process of economic growth. In Chapter 7 we discuss a set of economic growth facts, which are then used to organize our thinking in the context of models of economic growth. The first growth model we examine is a Malthusian growth model, consistent with the late-eighteenth century ideas of Thomas Malthus. The Malthusian model predicts well the features of economic growth in the world before the Industrial Revolution, but it does not predict the sustained growth in per capita incomes that occurred in advanced countries after 1800. The Solow growth model, which we examine next, does a good job of explaining some important observations concerning modern economic growth. Finally, Chapter 7 explains growth accounting, which is an approach to disentangling the sources of growth. In Chapter 8, we discuss income disparities across countries in light of the predictions of the Solow model, and introduce a model of endogenous growth.

In Part IV, we first use the theory of consumer and firm behavior developed in Part II to construct (in Chapter 9) a two-period model that can be used to study consumption-savings decisions and the effects of government deficits on the economy. Chapter 10 extends the two-period model to include credit market imperfections, an approach that is important for understanding the recent global financial crisis, fiscal policy, and social security. The two-period model is then further extended to include investment behavior and to address a wide range of macroeconomic issues in the real intertemporal model of Chapter 11. This model will then serve as the basis for much of what is done in the remainder of the book.

In Part V, we include monetary phenomena in the real intertemporal model of Chapter 11, so as to construct a monetary intertemporal model. This model is used in Chapter 12 to study the role of money and alternative means of payment, to examine the effects of changes in the money supply on the economy, and to study the role of monetary policy. Then, in Chapters 13 and 14, we study theories of the business cycle with flexible wages and prices, as well as New Keynesian business cycle theory. These theories are compared and contrasted, and we examine how alternative business cycle theories fit the data and how they help us to understand recent business cycle behavior in the United States. Chapter 15 extends the New Keynesian sticky price model of Chapter 14, so that the causes and consequences of inflation can be studied, along with the control of inflation by central banks. This chapter also introduces Neo-Fisherian theory, which is a provocative alternative to conventional central banking theories of inflation control.

Part VI is devoted to international macroeconomics. In Chapter 16, the models of Chapters 9 and 11 are used to study the determinants of the current account surplus, and the effects of shocks to the macroeconomy that come from abroad. Then, in Chapter 17, we show how exchange rates are determined, and we investigate the roles of fiscal and monetary policy in an open economy that trades goods and assets with the rest of the world.

Finally, Part VII examines some important topics in macroeconomics. In Chapter 18, we study in more depth the role of money in the economy, the effects of money growth on inflation and aggregate economic activity, banking, and deposit insurance.

Features

Several key features enhance the learning process and illuminate critical ideas for the student. The intent is to make macroeconomic theory transparent, accessible, and relevant.

Real-World Applications

Applications to current and historical problems are emphasized throughout in two running features. The first is a set of "Theory Confronts the Data" sections, which show how macroeconomic theory comes to life in matching (or sometimes falling short of matching) the characteristics of real-world economic data. A sampling of some of these sections includes consumption smoothing and the stock market; government expenditure multipliers in the recovery from the 2008-2009 recession; and the Phillips curve.

The second running feature is a series of "Macroeconomics in Action" boxes. These real-world applications relating directly to the theory encapsulate ideas from front-line research in macroeconomics, and they aid students in understanding the core material. For example, some of the subjects examined in these boxes are the default on government debt; business cycle models and the Great Depression; and quantitative easing in the United States.

Art Program

Graphs and charts are plentiful in this book, as visual representations of macroeconomic models that can be manipulated to derive important results, and for showing the key features of important macro data in applications. To aid the student, graphs and charts use a consistent two-color system that encodes the meaning of particular elements in graphs and of shifts in curves.

End-of-Chapter Summary and List of Key Terms

Each chapter wraps up with a bullet-point summary of the key ideas contained in the chapter, followed by a glossary of the chapter's key terms. The key terms are listed in the order in which they appear in the chapter, and they are highlighted in bold typeface where they first appear.

Questions for Review

These questions are intended as self-tests for students after they have finished reading the chapter material. The questions relate directly to ideas and facts covered in the chapter, and answering them will be straightforward if the student has read and comprehended the chapter material.

Problems

The end-of-chapter problems will help the student in learning the material and applying the macroeconomic models developed in the chapter. These problems are intended to be challenging and thought-provoking.

"Working with the Data" Problems

These problems are intended to encourage students to learn to use the FRED database at the St. Louis Federal Reserve Bank, accessible at http://research.stlouisfed.org/fred2/. FRED assembles most important macroeconomic data for the United States (and for some other countries as well) in one place, and allows the student to manipulate the data and easily produce charts. The problems are data applications relevant to the material in the chapter.

Notation

For easy reference, definitions of all variables used in the text are contained on the end papers.

Mathematics and Mathematical Appendix

In the body of the text, the analysis is mainly graphical, with some knowledge of basic algebra required; calculus is not used. However, for students and instructors who desire a more rigorous treatment of the material in the text, a mathematical appendix develops the key models and results more formally, assuming a basic knowledge of calculus and the fundamentals of mathematical economics. The Mathematical Appendix also contains problems on this more advanced material.

Flexibility

This book was written to be user-friendly for instructors with different preferences and with different time allocations. The core material that is recommended for all instructors is the following:

Chapter 1. Introduction

Chapter 2. Measurement

Chapter 3. Business Cycle Measurement

Chapter 4. Consumer and Firm Behavior: The Work-Leisure Decision and Profit Maximization

Chapter 5. A Closed-Economy One-Period Macroeconomic Model

Chapter 9. A Two-Period Model: The Consumption-Savings Decision and Credit Markets

Chapter 11. A Real Intertemporal Model with Investment

Some instructors find measurement issues uninteresting, and may choose to omit parts of Chapter 2, though at the minimum instructors should cover the key national income accounting identities. Parts of Chapter 3 can be omitted if the instructor chooses not to emphasize business cycles, but there are some important concepts introduced here that are generally useful in later chapters, such as the meaning of correlation and how to read scatter plots and time series plots.

Chapter 6 introduces two search models of unemployment: a one-sided search model, and a two-sided search model. These models allow for an explicit treatment of the determinants of unemployment by including a search friction. This allows for an interesting treatment of labor market issues, but it is possible to skip this chapter, or to put it later in the sequence, if the instructor and students prefer to focus on other topics.

Chapters 7 and 8 introduce economic growth at an early stage, in line with the modern role of growth theory in macroeconomics. However, Chapters 7 and 8 are essentially self-contained, and nothing is lost from leaving growth until later in the sequence—for example, after the business cycle material in Chapters 13-15. Though the text has an emphasis on microfoun-dations, Keynesian analysis receives a balanced treatment. For example, we study a Keynesian coordination failure model in Chapter 13, and examine a New Keynesian sticky price model in Chapters 14 and 15. Keynes-ian economics is fully integrated with flexible-wage-and-price approaches to business cycle analysis, and the student does not need to learn a separate modeling framework, as for example the New Keynesian sticky price model is simply a special case of the general modeling framework developed in Chapter 12. Those instructors who choose to ignore Keynesian analysis can do so without any difficulty. Instructors can choose to emphasize economic growth or business cycle analysis, or they can give their course an international focus. As well, it is possible to deemphasize monetary factors. As a guide, the text can be adapted as follows:

Focus on Models with Flexible Wages and Prices. Omit Chapters 14 and 15.

Focus on Economic Growth. Include Chapters 7 and 8, and consider dropping Chapters 12, 13, 14, and 15, depending on time available.

Focus on Business Cycles. Drop Chapters 7 and 8, and include Chapters 6, 12, 13, 14, and 15.

International Focus. Chapters 16 and 17 can be moved up in the sequence. Chapter 16 can follow Chapter 11, and Chapter 17 can follow Chapter 12.

Advanced Mathematical Treatment. Add material as desired from the Mathematical Appendix.

Supplements

The following materials that accompany the main text will enrich the intermediate macroeconomics course for instructors and students alike.

Instructor's Manual/Test Bank

Written by the author, the Instructor's Manual/Test Bank provides strong instructor support. The Instructor's Manual portion contains sections on Teaching Goals, which give an aerial view of the chapters; classroom discussion topics, which explore lecture-launching ideas and questions; chapter outlines; and solutions to all Questions for Review and Problems found in the text. The Test Bank portion contains multiple-choice questions and answers. The Test Bank is also available in Test Generator Software (TestGen-EQ with QuizMaster-EQ). Fully networkable, this software is available for Windows and Macintosh. TestGen-EQ's friendly graphical interface enables instructors to easily view, edit, and add questions; export questions to create tests; and print tests in a variety of fonts and forms. Search and sort features let the instructor quickly locate questions and arrange them in a preferred order. QuizMaster-EQ automatically grades the exams, stores results on a disk, and allows the instructor to view or print a variety of reports. The Instructor's Manual and Test Bank can be found on the instructor's portion of the Web site accompanying this book at www.pearsonhighered. com/williamson.

Powerpoint Slides: A full set of Powerpoint slides is available for instructors. The slides cover the material for each chapter in detail, including the key figures in the text.

Acknowledgments

Special thanks go to Neeraj Bhalla, Nicole Suddeth, and Pavithra Kumari, and the extended team at Pearson, who provided so much help and encouragement. I am also indebted to Dave Andolfatto, Scott Baier, Ken Beauchemin, Edward Kutsoati, Kuhong Kim, Young Sik Kim, Mike Loewy, B. Ravikumar, Ping Wang, and Bradley Wilson, who used early versions of the manuscript in their classes. Key critical input was also provided by the following reviewers, who helped immensely in improving the manuscript: Terry Alexander, Iowa State University; Alaa AlShawa, University of Western Ontario; David Aschauer, Bates College; Irasema Alonso, University of Rochester; David Andolfatto, Simon Fraser University; Scott Baier, Clemson University; Ken Beauchemin, State University of New York at Albany; Joydeep Bhattacharya, Iowa State University; Michael Binder, University of Maryland; William Blankenau, Kansas State University; Marco Cagetti, University of Virginia; Mustafa Caglayan, University of Liverpool; Gabriele Camera, Purdue University; Leo Chan, University of Kansas; Troy Davig, College of William and Mary; Matthias Doepke, UCLA; Ayse Y. Evrensel, Portland State University; Timothy Fuerst, Bowling Green State University; Lisa Geib-Gundersen, University of Maryland; John Graham, Rutgers University; Yu Hsing, Southeastern Louisiana University; Petur O. Jonsson, Fayetteville State University; Bryce Kanago, University of Northern Iowa; George Karras, University of Illinois; John Knowles, University of Pennsylvania; Hsien-Feng Lee, Taiwan University; Igor Livshits, University of Western Ontario; Michael Loewy, University of South Florida; Kathryn Marshall, Ohio State University; Steve McCafferty, Ohio State University; Oliver Morand, University of Connecticut; Douglas Morgan, University of California, Santa Barbara; Giuseppe Moscarini, Yale University; Daniel Mulino, doctoral candidate, Yale University; Liwa Rachel Ngai,

London School of Economics; Christopher Otrok, University of Virginia; Stephen Parente, University of Illinois at Urbana-Champaign; Prosper Raynold, Miami University; Kevin Reffett, Arizona State University; Robert J. Rossana, Wayne State University; Thomas Tallarini, Carnegie Mellon University; Paul Wachtel, Stern School of Business, New York University; Ping Wang, Vanderbilt University; Bradley Wilson, University of Alabama; Paul Zak, Claremont Graduate University; and Christian Zimmermann, University of Connecticut.

Finally, I wish to thank those economists who specifically reviewed material on economic growth for this edition: Laurence Ales, Carnegie Mellon University; Matthew Chambers, Towson University; Roberto E. Duncan, Ohio University; Rui Zhao, Emory University; Marek Kapicka, University of California, Santa Barbara.

About the Author

Stephen Williamson is a Vice President at the Federal Reserve Bank of St. Louis. He received a B.Sc. in Mathematics and an M.A. in Economics from Queen's University in Kingston, Canada, and his Ph.D. from the University of Wisconsin-Madison. He has held academic positions at Queen's University, the University of Western Ontario, the University of Iowa and Washington University in St. Louis, and has worked as an economist at the Federal Reserve Bank of Minneapolis and the Bank of Canada. Professor Williamson has been an academic visitor at the Federal Reserve Banks of Atlanta, Cleveland, Kansas City, Minneapolis, New York, Philadelphia, the Bank of Canada, and the Board of Governors of the Federal Reserve System. He has also been a long-term visitor at the London School of Economics; the University of Edinburgh; Tilburg University, the Netherlands; Victoria University of Wellington, New Zealand; Seoul National University; Hong Kong University; Queen's University; Fudan University; Indiana University; and the University of Sydney. Professor Williamson has published scholarly articles in the *American Economic Review,* the *Journal of Political Economy,* the *Quarterly Journal ofEconomics,* the *Review of Economic Studies,* the *Journal of Economic Theory,* and the *Journal of Monetary Economics,* among other prestigious economics journals. This text reflects the author's views, and does not necessarily reflect the views of the Federal Reserve Bank of St. Louis, the Board of Governors of the Federal Reserve System, or the Federal Reserve System.

Introduction and Measurement Issues

Part I contains an introduction to macroeconomic analysis and a description of the approach in this text of building useful macroeconomic models based on microeconomic principles. We discuss the key ideas that are analyzed in the rest of this text as well as some current issues in macroeconomics. Then, to lay a foundation for what is done later, we explore how the important variables relating to macroeconomic theory are measured in practice. Finally, we analyze the key empirical facts concerning business cycles. The macroeconomic theory developed in Parts II to VII is aimed at understanding the key ideas and issues discussed in the introduction, and in showing the successes and failures of theory in organizing our thinking about empirical facts.

Chapter  1

Introduction

Learning Objectives

After studying Chapter 1, students will be able to:

1.1 State the two focuses of study in macroeconomics, the key differences between microeconomics and macroeconomics, and the similarities between microeconomics and macroeconomics.

1.2 Explain the key features of trend growth and deviations from trend in per capita gross domestic product in the United States from 1900 to 2014.

1.3 Explain why models are useful in macroeconomics.

1.4 Discuss how microeconomic principles are important in constructing useful macroeconomic models.

1.5 Explain why there is disagreement among macroeconomists, and what they disagree about.

1.6 List the 12 key ideas that will be covered in this book.

1.7 List the key observations that motivate questions we will try to answer in this book.

This chapter frames the approach to macroeconomics that we take in this text, and it foreshadows the basic macroeconomic ideas and issues that we develop in later chapters. We first discuss what macroeconomics is, and we then go on to look at the two phenomena that are of primary interest to macroeconomists—economic growth and business cycles—in terms of post–1900 U.S. economic history. Then, we explain the approach this text takes—building macroeconomic models with microeconomic principles as a foundation—and discuss the issue of disagreement in macroeconomics. Finally, we explore the key lessons that we learn from macroeconomic theory, and we discuss how macroeconomics helps us understand recent and current issues.

What Is Macroeconomics?

LO 1.1 State the two focuses of study in macroeconomics, the key differences between microeconomics and macroeconomics, and the similarities between microeconomics and macroeconomics.

Macroeconomists are motivated by large questions and by issues that affect many people and many nations of the world. Why are some countries exceedingly rich while others are exceedingly poor? Why are most Americans so much better off than their parents and grandparents? Why are there fluctuations in aggregate economic activity? What causes inflation? Why is there unemployment?

Macroeconomics is the study of the behavior of large collections of economic agents. It focuses on the aggregate behavior of consumers and firms, the behavior of governments, the overall level of economic activity in individual countries, the economic interactions among nations, and the effects of fiscal and monetary policy. Macroeconomics is distinct from microeconomics in that it deals with the overall effects on economies of the choices that all economic agents make, rather than on the choices of individual consumers or firms. Since the 1970s, however, the distinction between microeconomics and macroeconomics has blurred in that microeconomists and macroeconomists now use much the same kinds of tools. That is, the **economic models** that macroeconomists use, consisting of descriptions of consumers and firms, their objectives and constraints, and how they interact, are built up from microeconomic principles, and these models are typically analyzed and fit to data using methods similar to those used by microeconomists. What continues to make macroeconomics distinct, though, is the issues it focuses on, particularly **long-run growth** and **business cycles**. Long-run growth refers to the increase in a nation's productive capacity and average standard of living that occurs over a long period of time, whereas business cycles are the short-run ups and downs, or booms and recessions, in aggregate economic activity.

An important goal in this text is to consistently build up macroeconomic analysis from microeconomic principles. There is some effort required in taking this type of approach, but the effort is well worth it. The result is that you will understand better how the economy works and how to improve it.

Gross Domestic Product, Economic Growth, and Business Cycles

LO 1.2 Explain the key features of trend growth and deviations from trend in per capita gross domestic product in the United States from 1900 to 2014.

To begin our study of macroeconomic phenomena, we must first understand what facts we are trying to explain. The most basic set of facts in macroeconomics has to do with the behavior of aggregate economic activity over time. One measure of aggregate economic activity is **gross domestic product (GDP)**, which is the quantity of goods and services produced within a country's borders during some specified period of time. GDP also represents the quantity of income earned by those contributing to domestic output. In Figure 1.1 we show real GDP per capita for the United States for the period 1900–2014. This is a measure of aggregate output that adjusts for inflation and population growth, and the unit of measure is thousands of 2009 dollars per person.

The first observation we can make concerning Figure 1.1 is that there has been sustained growth in per capita GDP during the period 1900–2014. In 1900, the average income for an American was $5,188 (2009 dollars), and this grew to $50,051 (2009 dollars) in 2014. Thus, the average American became almost ten times richer in real terms over the course of 114 years, which is quite remarkable! The second important observation from Figure 1.1 is that, while growth in per capita real GDP was sustained over long periods of time in the United States during the period 1900–2014, this growth was certainly not steady. Growth was higher at some times than at others, and there were periods over which per capita real GDP declined. These fluctuations in economic growth are business cycles.

Figure 1.1 Per Capita Real GDP (in 2009 dollars) for the United States, 1900–2014

Per capita real GDP is a measure of the average level of income for a U.S. resident. Two unusual, though key, events in the figure are the Great Depression, when there was a large reduction in living standards for the average American, and World War II, when per capita output increased greatly.

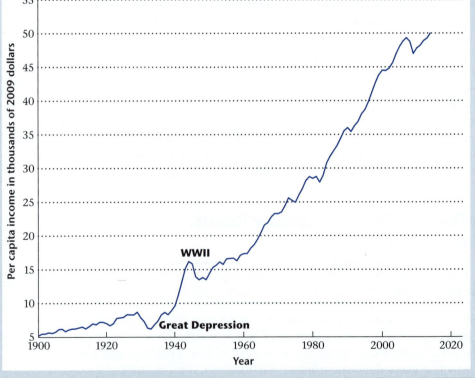

Two key, though unusual, business cycle events in U.S. economic history that show up in Figure 1.1 are the Great Depression and World War II, and these events dwarf any other twentieth-century business cycle events in the United States in terms of the magnitude of the short-run change in economic growth. During the Great Depression, real GDP per capita dropped from a peak of $8,677 (2009 dollars) per person in 1929 to a low of $6,192 (2009 dollars) per person in 1933, a decline of about 29%. At the peak of war production in 1944, GDP had risen to $16,181 (2009 dollars) per person, an increase of 161% from 1933. These wild gyrations in aggregate economic activity over a 15-year period are as phenomenal, and certainly every bit as interesting, as the long-run sustained growth in per capita GDP that occurred from 1900 to 2014. In addition to the Great Depression and World War II, Figure 1.1 shows other business cycle upturns and downturns in the growth of per capita real GDP in the United States that, though less dramatic than the Great Depression or World War II, represent important macroeconomic events in U.S. history.

Figure 1.1, thus, raises the following fundamental macroeconomic questions, which motivate much of the material in this book:

1. What causes sustained economic growth?
2. Could economic growth continue indefinitely, or is there some limit to growth?
3. Is there anything that governments can or should do to alter the rate of economic growth?
4. What causes business cycles?
5. Could the dramatic decreases and increases in economic growth that occurred during the Great Depression and World War II be repeated?
6. Should governments act to smooth business cycles?

In analyzing economic data to study economic growth and business cycles, it often proves useful to transform the data in various ways, so as to obtain sharper insights. For economic time series that exhibit growth, such as per capita real GDP in Figure 1.1, a useful transformation is to take the natural logarithm of the time series. To show why this is useful, suppose that y_t is an observation on an economic time series in period t; for example, y_t could represent per capita real GDP in year t, where $t = 1900, 1901, 1902$, etc. Then, the growth rate from period $t - 1$ to period t in y_t can be denoted by g_t, where

$$g_t = \frac{y_t}{y_{t-1}} - 1.$$

Now, if x is a small number, then $\ln(1 + x) \approx x$, that is, the natural logarithm of $1 + x$ is approximately equal to x. Therefore, if g_t is small,

$$\ln(1 + g_t) \approx g_t,$$

or

$$\ln\left(\frac{y_t}{y_{t-1}}\right) \approx g_t,$$

or

$$\ln y_t - \ln y_{t-1} \approx g_t.$$

Because $\ln y_t - \ln y_{t-1}$ is the slope of the graph of the natural logarithm of y_t between periods $t - 1$ and t, the slope of the graph of the natural logarithm of a time series y_t is a good approximation to the growth rate of y_t when the growth rate is small.

In Figure 1.2, we graph the natural logarithm of real per capita GDP in the United States for the period 1900–2014. As explained above, the slope of the graph is a good approximation to the growth rate of real per capita GDP, so that changes in the slope (e.g., when there is a slight increase in the slope of the graph in the 1950s and 1960s) represent changes in the growth rate of real per capita GDP. It is striking that in Figure 1.2, except for the Great Depression and World War II, a straight line would fit the graph quite well. That is, over the period 1900–2014 (again, except for the Great Depression and World War II), growth in per capita real GDP has been "roughly" constant at about 2.0% per year.

Figure 1.2 Natural Logarithm of Per Capita Real GDP

Here, the slope of the graph is approximately equal to the growth rate of per capita real GDP. Excluding the Great Depression and World War II, the growth rate of per capita real GDP is remarkably close to being constant for the period 1900–2014. That is, a straight line would fit the graph fairly well.

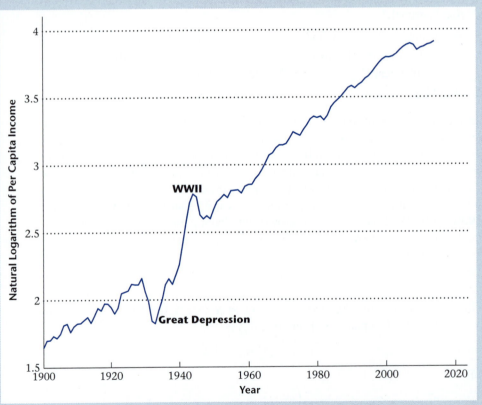

Figure 1.3 Natural Logarithm of Real Per Capita GDP and Trend

Sometimes it is useful to separate long-run growth from business cycle fluctuations. In the figure, the black line is the natural log of per capita real GDP, while the colored line denotes a smooth growth trend fit to the data. The deviations from the smooth trend then represent business cycles.

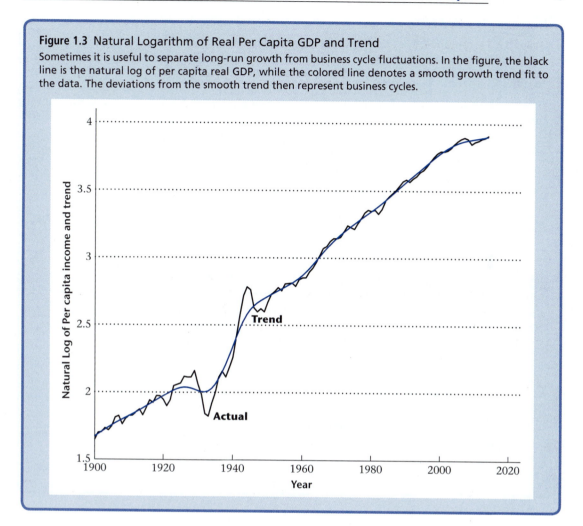

A second useful transformation to carry out on an economic time series is to separate the series into two components: the growth or **trend** component, and the business cycle component. For example, the business cycle component of real per capita GDP can be captured as the deviations of real per capita GDP from a smooth trend fit to the data. In Figure 1.3, we show the trend in the natural log of real per capita GDP as a colored line,[1] while the natural log of actual real per capita GDP is the black line. We then define the business cycle component of the natural log of real per capita GDP to be the difference between the black line and the colored line in Figure 1.3. The logic behind this decomposition of real per capita GDP into trend and business cycle components is that it is often simpler and more productive to consider separately the theory

---

[1] Trend GDP was computed using a Hodrick–Prescott filter, as in E. Prescott, Fall 1986. "Theory Ahead of Business Cycle Measurement," *Federal Reserve Bank of Minneapolis Quarterly Review* 10, 9–22

Figure 1.4 Percentage Deviation from Trend in Real Per Capita GDP
The Great Depression and World War II represent extremely large deviations from trend relative to post–World War II business cycle activity and business cycles before the Great Depression.

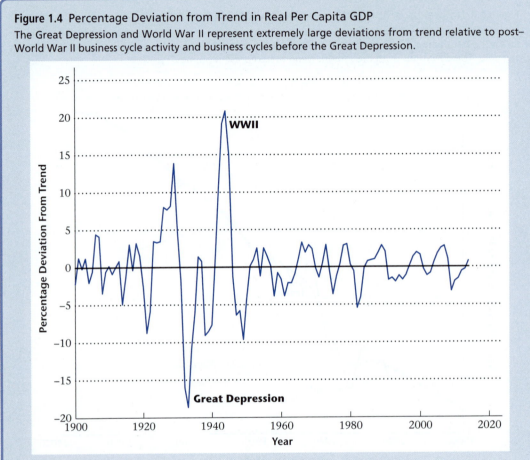

that explains trend growth and the theory that explains business cycles, which are the deviations from trend.

In Figure 1.4, we show only the percentage deviations from trend in real per capita GDP. The Great Depression and World War II represent enormous deviations from trend in real per capita GDP relative to anything else during the time period in the figure. During the Great Depression the percentage deviation from trend in real per capita GDP was close to −20%, whereas the percentage deviation from trend was about 20% during World War II. In the period after World War II, which is the focus of most business cycle analysis, the deviations from trend in real per capita GDP are at most about ±5%.[2]

---

[2]The extremely large deviation from trend in real per capita GNP in the late 1920s is principally a statistical artifact of the particular detrending procedure used here, which is akin to drawing a smooth curve through the time series. The presence of the Great Depression forces the growth rate in the trend to decrease long before the Great Depression actually occurs.

Macroeconomic Models

LO 1.3 Explain why models are useful in macroeconomics.

Economics is a scientific pursuit involving the formulation and refinement of theories that can help us better understand how economies work and how they can be improved. In some sciences, such as chemistry and physics, theories are tested through laboratory experimentation. In economics, experimentation is a new and growing activity, but for most economic theories experimental verification is simply impossible. For example, suppose an economist constructs a theory that implies that U.S. output would drop by half if there were no banks in the United States. To evaluate this theory, we could shut down all U.S. banks for a year to see what would happen. Of course, we know in advance that banks play a very important role in helping the U.S. economy function efficiently, and that shutting them down for a year would likely cause significant irreparable damage. It is extremely unlikely, therefore, that the experiment would be performed. In macroeconomics, most experiments that could be informative are simply too costly to carry out, and in this respect macroeconomics is much like meteorology or astronomy. In predicting the weather or how planets move in space, meteorologists and astronomers rely on **models**, which are artificial devices that can replicate the behavior of real weather systems or planetary systems, as the case may be.

Just like researchers in meteorology or astronomy, macroeconomists use models, which in our case are organized structures to explain long-run economic growth, why there are business cycles, and what role economic policy should play in the macroeconomy. All economic models are abstractions. They are not completely accurate descriptions of the world, nor are they intended to be. The purpose of an economic model is to capture the essential features of the world needed for analyzing a particular economic problem. To be useful then, a model must be simple, and simplicity requires that we leave out some "realistic" features of actual economies. For example, an electronic roadmap is a model of a part of the earth's surface, and it is constructed with a particular purpose in mind, to help motorists guide themselves through the road system from one point to another. A roadmap is hardly a realistic depiction of the earth's surface, as it does not capture the curvature of the earth, and it does not typically include a great deal of information on topography, climate, and vegetation. However, this does not limit the map's usefulness; a roadmap serves the purpose for which it was constructed, and it does so without a lot of extraneous detail.

To be specific, the basic structure of a macroeconomic model is a description of the following features:

1. The consumers and firms that interact in the economy
2. The set of goods that consumers wish to consume
3. Consumers' preferences over goods
4. The technology available to firms for producing goods
5. The resources available

In this text, the descriptions of the above five features of any particular macroeconomic model are provided in mathematical and graphical terms.

Once we have a description of the main economic actors in a model economy (the consumers and firms), the goods consumers want, and the technology available to firms for producing goods from available resources, we want to then use the model to make predictions. This step requires that we specify two additional features of the model. First, we need to know what the goals of the consumers and firms in the model are. How do consumers and firms behave given the environment they live in? In all the models we use in this book, we assume that consumers and firms **optimize**, that is, they do the best they can given the constraints they face. Second, we must specify how consistency is achieved in terms of the actions of consumers and firms. In economic models, this means that the economy must be in **equilibrium**. Several different concepts of equilibrium are used in economic models, but the one that we use most frequently in this book is **competitive equilibrium**. In a competitive equilibrium, we assume that goods are bought and sold on markets in which consumers and firms are price-takers; they behave as if their actions have no effect on market prices. The economy is in equilibrium when market prices are such that the quantity of each good offered for sale (quantity supplied) is equal to the quantity that economic agents want to buy (quantity demanded) in each market.

Once we have a working economic model, with a specification of the economic environment, optimizing firms and consumers, and a notion of equilibrium, we can then begin to ask the model questions.[3] One way to think of this process is that the economic model is an experimental apparatus, and we want to attempt to run experiments using this apparatus. Typically, we begin by running experiments for which we know the answers. For example, suppose that we build an economic model so that we can study economic growth. The first experiment we might like to run is to determine, by working through the mathematics of the model, using graphical analysis, or running the model on a computer, whether in fact the model economy will grow. Further, will it grow in a manner that comes close to matching the data? If it does not, then we want to ask why and to determine whether it would be a good idea to refine the model in some way or to abandon it altogether and start over.

Ultimately, once we are satisfied that a model reasonably and accurately captures the economic phenomenon in which we are interested, we can start running experiments on the model for which we do not know the answers. An experiment we might want to conduct with the economic growth model is to ask, for example, how historical growth performance would have differed in the United States had the level of government spending been higher. Would aggregate economic activity have grown at a higher or a lower rate? How would this have affected the consumption of goods? Would economic welfare have been higher or lower?

In keeping with the principle that models should be simple and designed specifically for the problem at hand, we do not stick to a single all-purpose model in this book.

---

[3]The following description of macroeconomic science is similar to that provided by Robert Lucas in "Methods and Problems in Business Cycle Theory," reprinted in *Studies in Business Cycle Theory*, 1981, MIT Press, pp. 271–296.

Instead, we use an array of different models for different purposes, though these models share a common approach and some of the same principal building blocks. For example, sometimes it proves useful to build models that do not include international trade, macroeconomic growth, or the use of money in economic exchange, whereas at other times it is crucial for the issue at hand that we explicitly model one, two, or perhaps all of these features.

Generally, macroeconomic research is a process whereby we continually attempt to develop better models, along with better methods for analyzing those models. Economic models continue to evolve in a way that helps us better understand the economic forces that shape the world in which we live, so that we can promote economic policies that make society better off.

Microeconomic Principles

LO 1.4 Discuss how microeconomic principles are important in constructing useful macroeconomics models.

This text emphasizes building macroeconomic models on sound microeconomic principles. Because the macroeconomy consists of many consumers and firms, each making decisions at the micro level, macroeconomic behavior is the sum of many microeconomic decisions. It is not immediately obvious, however, that the best way to construct a macroeconomic model is to work our way up from decision making at the microeconomic level. In physics, for example, there is often no loss in ignoring micro behavior. If I throw a brick from the top of a five-story building, and if I know the force that I exert on the brick and the force of gravity on the brick, then Newtonian physics does a very accurate job of predicting when and where the brick lands. However, Newtonian physics ignores micro behavior, which in this case is the behavior of the molecules in the brick.

Why is it that there may be no loss in ignoring the behavior of molecules in a brick, but that ignoring the microeconomic behavior of consumers and firms when doing macroeconomics could be devastating? Throwing a brick from a building does not affect the behavior of the molecules within the brick in any way that would significantly change the trajectory of the brick. Changes in government policy, however, generally alter the behavior of consumers and firms in ways that significantly affect the behavior of the economy as a whole. Any change in government policy effectively alters the features of the economic environment in which consumers and firms must make their decisions. To confidently predict the effects of a policy change on aggregate behavior, we must analyze how the change in policy affects individual consumers and firms. For example, if the federal government changes the income tax rate, and we are interested in the macroeconomic effects of this policy change, the most productive approach is first to use microeconomic principles to determine how a change in the tax rate affects an individual consumer's labor supply and consumption decisions, based on optimizing behavior. Then, we can aggregate these decisions to arrive at a conclusion that is consistent with how the individuals in the economy behave.

Macroeconomists were not always sympathetic to the notion that macro models should be microeconomically sound. Indeed, before the **rational expectations revolution** in the 1970s, which generally introduced more microeconomics into macroeconomics, most macroeconomists worked with models that did not have solid microeconomic foundations, though there were some exceptions.[4] The argument that macroeconomic policy analysis can be done in a sensible way only if microeconomic behavior is taken seriously was persuasively expressed by Robert E. Lucas, Jr. in a journal article published in 1976.[5] This argument is often referred to as the **Lucas critique**.

Disagreement in Macroeconomics

LO 1.5 Explain why there is disagreement among macroeconomists, and what they disagree about.

There is little disagreement in macroeconomics concerning the general approach to be taken to construct models of economic growth. The Solow growth model,[6] studied in Chapters 7 and 8, is a widely accepted framework for understanding the economic growth process, and **endogenous growth models**, which model the economic mechanism determining the rate of economic growth and are covered in Chapter 7, have been well received by most macroeconomists. This is not to say that disagreement has been absent from discussions of economic growth in macroeconomics, only that the disagreement has not generally been over basic approaches to modeling growth.

The study of business cycles in macroeconomics, however, is another story. As it turns out, there is much controversy among macroeconomists concerning business cycle theory and the role of the government in smoothing business cycles over time. In Chapters 13 and 14, we study some competing theories of the business cycle.

Roughly, business cycle theories can be differentiated according to whether they are **Keynesian** or **non-Keynesian**. Traditional Old Keynesian models, in the spirit of J. M. Keynes's *General Theory of Employment, Interest, and Money*, published in 1936, are based on the notion that wages and prices are sticky in the short run, and do not change sufficiently quickly to yield efficient outcomes. In the Old Keynesian world, government intervention through monetary and fiscal policy can correct the inefficiencies that exist in private markets. The rational expectations revolution produced some non-Keynesian theories of the business cycle, including **real business cycle theory**, initiated by Edward Prescott and Finn Kydland in the early 1980s. Real business cycle theory implies that government policy aimed at smoothing business cycles is at best ineffective and at worst detrimental to the economy's performance.

---

[4]See M. Friedman, 1968. "The Role of Monetary Policy," *American Economic Review* 58, 1–17.

[5]See R. E. Lucas, 1976. "Econometric Policy Evaluation: A Critique," *Carnegie-Rochester Conference Series on Public Policy* 1, 19–46.

[6]See R. Solow, 1956. "A Contribution to the Theory of Economic Growth," *Quarterly Journal of Economics* 70, 65–94.

In the 1980s and 1990s, Keynesians used the developments in macroeconomics that came out of the rational expectations revolution to integrate Keynesian economics with modern macroeconomic thought. The result was two new strands of Keynesian thought—**coordination failures** and **New Keynesian economics**. In a coordination failure model of the business cycle, the economy can be stuck in a bad equilibrium, not because of sticky wages and prices, but because economic agents are self-fulfillingly pessimistic. Alternatively, New Keynesian models include sticky wages and prices, as in traditional Old Keynesian models, but New Keynesians use the microeconomic tools that all modern macroeconomists use.

In Chapters 11 through 14, we will study a host of modern business cycle models, which show how changes in monetary factors, changes in productivity, or waves of optimism and pessimism can cause business cycles, and we will show what these models tell us about the conduct of macroeconomic policy. In Chapter 13 we study a Keynesian coordination failure model, and in Chapter 14 we examine a New Keynesian sticky price model. Chapter 13 contains an examination of the real business cycle model.

In this book, we seek an objective view of the competing theories of the business cycle. In Chapters 12 and 13, we study the key features of each of the above theories of the business cycle, and we evaluate the theories in terms of how their predictions match the data.

What Do We Learn from Macroeconomic Analysis?

LO 1.6 List the 12 key ideas that will be covered in this book.

At this stage, it is useful to map out some of the basic insights that can be learned from macroeconomic analysis and which we develop in the remainder of this book. These are the following:

1. *What is produced and consumed in the economy is determined jointly by the economy's productive capacity and the preferences of consumers.* In Chapters 4 and 5, we develop a one-period model of the economy, which specifies the technology for producing goods from available resources, the preferences of consumers over goods, and how optimizing consumers and firms come together in competitive markets to determine what is produced and consumed.

2. *In free market economies, there are strong forces that tend to produce socially efficient economic outcomes.* Social inefficiencies can arise, but for reasons that are well-understood. The notion that an unregulated economy peopled by selfish individuals could result in a socially efficient state of affairs is surprising, and this idea goes back at least as far as Adam Smith's *Wealth of Nations,* written in the eighteenth century. In Chapter 5, we show this result in our one-period model, and we explain the circumstances under which social inefficiencies can arise in practice.

3. *Unemployment is painful for individuals, but it is a necessary evil in modern economies.* There will always be unemployment in a well-functioning

economy. Unemployment is measured as the number of people who are not employed and are actively seeking work. Since all of these people are looking for something they do not have, unemployment might seem undesirable, but the time unemployed people spend searching for jobs is in general well spent from a social point of view. It is economically efficient for workers to be well matched with jobs, in terms of their skills, and if an individual spends a longer time searching for work, this increases the chances of a good match. However, when the average unemployed person needs to spend a longer time searching for work than seems normal, there may be a role for government intervention. In Chapter 6, we explore a modern model of search and matching that can be used to make sense of labor market data and current phenomena.

4. *Improvements in a country's standard of living are brought about in the long run by technological progress.* In Chapters 7 and 8, we study the Solow growth model (along with the Malthusian model of economic growth and an endogenous growth model), which gives us a framework for understanding the forces that account for growth. This model shows that growth in aggregate output is produced by growth in a country's capital stock, growth in the labor force, and technological progress. In the long run, however, growth in the standard of living of the average person comes to a stop unless there are continuous technological improvements. Thus, economic well-being ultimately cannot be improved simply by constructing more machines and buildings; economic progress depends on continuing advances in knowledge.

5. *A tax cut is not a free lunch.* When the government reduces taxes, this increases current incomes in the private sector, and it may seem that this implies that people are wealthier and may want to spend more. However, if the government reduces taxes and holds its spending constant, it must borrow more, and the government will have to increase taxes in the future to pay off this higher debt. Thus, future incomes in the private sector must fall. In Chapter 9, we show that there are circumstances under which a current tax cut has no effects whatsoever; the private sector is no wealthier, and there is no change in aggregate economic activity.

6. *Credit markets and banks play key roles in the macroeconomy.* The advocates of some mainstream economic theories—including theories of economic growth, real business cycle theory, and New Keynesian economics—have sometimes argued that consideration of credit markets, and the underlying frictions that make credit markets and banks work imperfectly, are safely ignored. Macroeconomic events during the global financial crisis of 2008–2009 have shown that this approach is hazardous. Some standard economic tools can be used to make sense of macroeconomic financial events, and to determine the appropriate fiscal and monetary policy responses to a financial crisis. In Chapter 10, we analyze credit market imperfections and show how they matter for financial crises, and we study some of the aggregate implications of financial crises in Chapters 11–14, along with some issues related to banking in Chapter 18.

7. *What consumers and firms anticipate for the future has an important bearing on current macroeconomic events.* In Chapters 9–11, we consider two-period models in

which consumers and firms make dynamic decisions; consumers save for future consumption needs, and firms invest in plant and equipment so as to produce more in the future. If consumers anticipate, for example, that their future incomes will be high, they want to save less in the present and consume more, and this has important implications for current aggregate production, employment, and interest rates. If firms anticipate that a new technological innovation will come on line in the future, this makes them more inclined to invest today in new plant and equipment, and this in turn also affects aggregate production, employment, and interest rates. Consumers and firms are forward-looking in ways that matter for current aggregate economic activity and for government policy.

8. *Money takes many forms, and society is much better off with it than without it. Once we have it, however, changing its quantity ultimately does not matter.* What differentiates money from other assets is its value as a medium of exchange, and having a medium of exchange makes economic transactions much easier in developed economies. Currently in the United States, there are several assets that act as a medium of exchange, including U.S. Federal Reserve notes and transactions deposits at banks. In Chapters 12 and 18, we explore the role of money and banking in the economy. One important result in Chapter 12 is that a one-time increase in the money supply, brought about by the central bank, has no long-run effect on any real economic magnitudes in the economy; it only increases all prices in the same proportion.

9. *Business cycles are similar, but they can have many causes.* In Chapter 3, we show that there are strong regularities in how aggregate macroeconomic variables fluctuate over the business cycle. In Chapters 12–14, we also study some theories that can potentially explain business cycles. The fact that there is more than one business cycle theory to choose from does not mean that only one can be right and all the others are wrong, though some may be more right than others. Potentially, all of these theories shed some light on why we have business cycles and what can be done about them.

10. *Countries gain from trading goods and assets with each other, but trade is also a source of shocks to the domestic economy.* Economists tend to support the lifting of trade restrictions, as free trade allows a country to exploit its comparative advantage in production and, thus, make its citizens better off. However, the integration of world financial and goods markets implies that events in other countries can cause domestic business cycles. In Chapters 16 and 17, we explore how changes in goods prices and interest rates on world markets affect the domestic economy.

11. *In the long run, inflation is caused by growth in the money supply.* **Inflation**, the rate of growth in the average level of prices, can vary over the short run for many reasons. Over the long run, however, the rate at which the central bank (the **Federal Reserve System** in the United States) causes the stock of money to grow determines what the inflation rate is. We study this process in Chapter 18.

12. *If there is a short-run trade-off between output and inflation, that has very different implications relative to the relationship between the nominal interest rate and inflation.* In some countries and for some historical periods, a positive relationship appears

to exist between the deviation of aggregate output from trend and the inflation rate. This relationship is called the **Phillips curve**, and in general the Phillips curve appears to be quite an unstable empirical relationship. Another key relationship observed in the macroeconomic data is the Fisher relation—a positive correlation between nominal interest rates and the inflation rate. So-called Neo-Fisherism takes the theory explaining that observation as a guide for monetary policy. For example, a central bank that wants to increase inflation may want to increase nominal interest rates, rather than reducing them, as Phillips curve reasoning might dictate. We discuss these issues in Chapter 15.

Understanding Recent and Current Macroeconomic Events

LO 1.7 List the key observations that motivate questions we will try to answer in this book.

Part of the excitement of studying macroeconomics is that it can make sense of recent and currently unfolding economic events. In this section, we give an overview of some recent and current issues and how we can understand them better using macroeconomic tools.

Aggregate Productivity

A measure of productivity in the aggregate economy is **average labor productivity**, $\frac{Y}{N}$, where Y denotes aggregate output and N denotes employment. That is, we can measure aggregate productivity as the total quantity of output produced per worker. Aggregate productivity is important, as economic growth theory tells us that growth in aggregate productivity is what determines growth in living standards in the long run. In Figure 1.5, we plot the log of average labor productivity for the United States, measured as the log of real gross domestic product per worker. Here, we show the log of average labor productivity (the blue line), because then the slope of the graph denotes the growth rate in average labor productivity. The key features of Figure 1.5 are that average labor productivity grew at a high rate during the 1950s and most of the 1960s, growth slowed down from the late 1960s until the early 1980s, and then productivity growth increased beginning in the mid-1980s and remained high through the 1990s and into the twenty-first century. Recently, from 2000 to 2015, we appear to have entered another period of low productivity growth, as can be observed in Figure 1.5.

Why has productivity growth declined in the period after the global financial crisis? Is this because all the great elements of technological progress—electrification, running water, antibiotics, and information technology—are well behind us? Is this some lingering effect of the financial crisis, and only temporary? We explore these issues further in Chapters 7 and 8.

Unemployment and Vacancies

As explained previously, the phenomenon of unemployment need not represent a problem, since unemployment is in general a socially useful search activity that is necessary, though sometimes painful to the individuals involved. As macroeconomists, we are interested in what explains the level of unemployment and what the reasons are for

Figure 1.5 Natural Logarithm of Average Labor Productivity

Average labor productivity is the quantity of aggregate output produced per worker. Because the graph is of the log of average labor productivity (the blue line), the slope of the graph is approximately the growth rate in average labor productivity. Productivity growth was high in the 1950s and 1960s, and low from 1970–1980 and from 2010–2015.

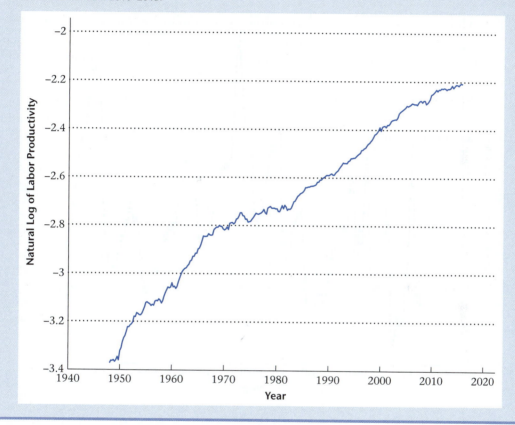

fluctuations in unemployment over time. If we can understand these features, we can go on to determine how macroeconomic policy can be formulated so that labor markets work as efficiently as possible.

In Chapter 6, we introduce two models of search and unemployment, the second of which is based on the work of Nobel Prize winners Peter Diamond, Dale Mortensen, and Christopher Pissarides. These models allow us to explain the determinants of labor force participation, the unemployment rate, the vacancy rate (the fraction of firms searching for workers to hire), and market wages.

Some of the features of labor market data that we would like to explain are in Figures 1.6 and 1.7. Figure 1.6 shows the unemployment rate—the percentage of people in the labor force who are actively searching for work—for the United States, over the period 1948–2015. In the second search model of unemployment studied in Chapter 6, unemployment is explained by the search behavior of firms and workers,

Figure 1.6 The Unemployment Rate for the United States

The unemployment rate is determined by productivity, the generosity of government-provided unemployment insurance, and matching efficiency, among other factors. As the figure shows, the unemployment rate fluctuates significantly.

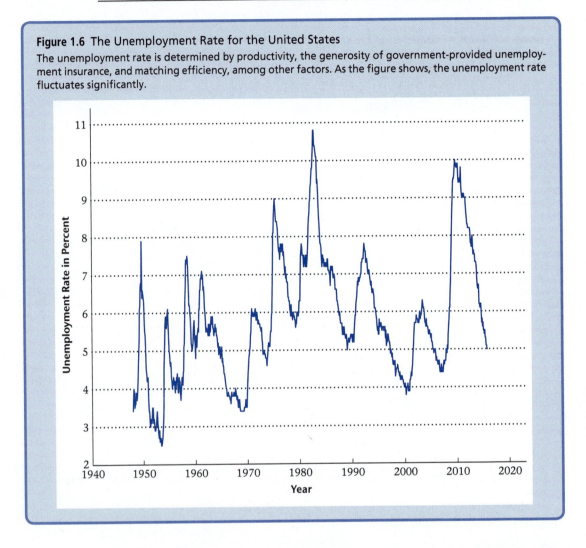

and by how efficiently searching workers and firms are matched. In general, the unemployment rate will be affected by productivity, the generosity of government-provided unemployment insurance, and matching efficiency. All of these factors come into play in explaining both the long-term trends and the fluctuations in the unemployment rate in Figure 1.6.

An interesting feature of the recent labor market data is in Figure 1.7, which is a scatter plot of the vacancy rate (job openings as a percentage of job openings plus total employment) versus the unemployment rate for the period 2000–2015. The dots in the figure represent observations up to the end of 2007 (the beginning of the most recent recession), while the line tracks observations from January 2008 to November 2015. A downward sloping curve—called a **Beveridge curve**—would fit closely the observations from 2000 to 2007, but the last observations—beginning in mid-2009—fall well north of this Beveridge curve. Thus, given the vacancy rates that were observed

Figure 1.7 The Beveridge Curve

The points in the figure denote observations for the period 2000–2007, while the line connects observations from January 2008 to November 2015. The observations from 2000 to 2007 are fit well by an apparently stable downward-sloping Beveridge curve. However, the Beveridge curve appears to have shifted over the period January 2008 to November 2015.

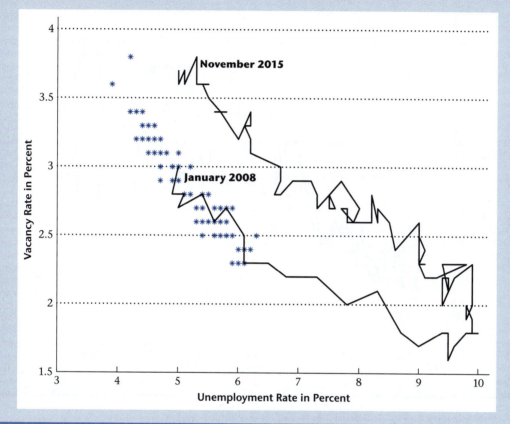

from mid-2009 to November 2015, the unemployment rate would typically have been much lower pre-2008. Our search model of unemployment in Chapter 6 suggests that this shifting of the Beveridge curve could be due to mismatch in the labor market. This mismatch could result from differences between the skills that firms want and what would-be workers possess, or because job vacancies are not in the same geographical regions where the unemployed reside.

Taxes, Government Spending, and the Government Deficit

In Figure 1.8 we show total tax revenues (the black line) and government spending (the colored line) by all levels of government (federal, state, and local) in the United States from 1947 to 2015, as percentages of total GDP. Note the broad upward trend in both taxes and spending. Total taxes were almost 22% of GDP in 1947, and they increased to about 29% of GDP in 2015, while total spending rose from about 23% of

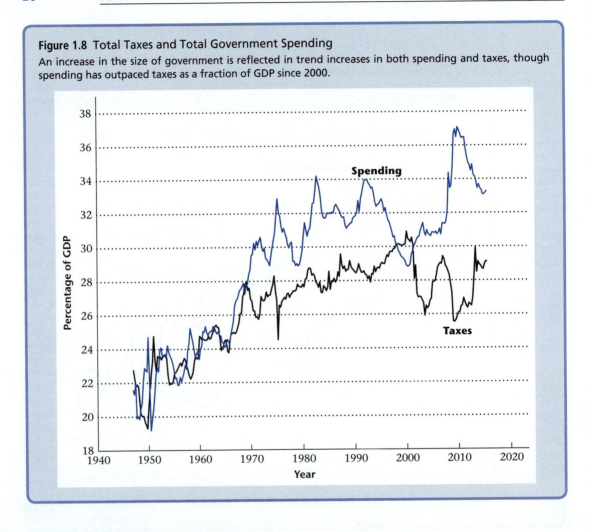

Figure 1.8 Total Taxes and Total Government Spending
An increase in the size of government is reflected in trend increases in both spending and taxes, though spending has outpaced taxes as a fraction of GDP since 2000.

GDP in 1947 to a high of about 33% of GDP in 2015. These trends generally reflect an increase in the size of government in the United States relative to the aggregate economy over this period, though spending has clearly outpaced taxes since 2000.

What ramifications does a larger government have for the economy as a whole? How does higher government spending and taxation affect private economic activity? We show in Chapters 5 and 11 that increased government activity in general causes a **crowding out** of private economic activity. That is, the government competes for resources with the rest of the economy. If the size of the government increases, then through several economic mechanisms there is a reduction in the quantity of spending by private firms on new plant and equipment, and there is a reduction in private consumption expenditures.

An interesting feature of Figure 1.8 is that governments in the United States sometimes spent more than they received in the form of taxes, and sometimes the reverse was true. Just as is the case for private consumers, the government can in principle

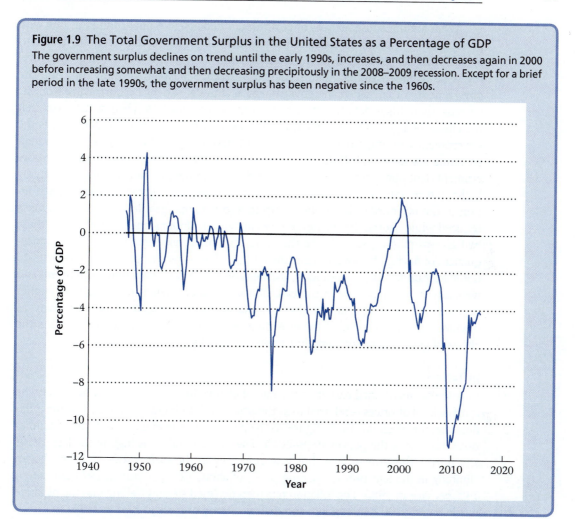

Figure 1.9 The Total Government Surplus in the United States as a Percentage of GDP

The government surplus declines on trend until the early 1990s, increases, and then decreases again in 2000 before increasing somewhat and then decreasing precipitously in the 2008–2009 recession. Except for a brief period in the late 1990s, the government surplus has been negative since the 1960s.

spend more than it earns by borrowing and accumulating debt, and it can earn more than it spends and save the difference, thus reducing its debt. Figure 1.9 shows the total **government surplus** or total **government saving**, which is the difference between taxes and spending, for the period 1947–2015. From Figure 1.9, the government surplus was positive for most of the period from 1948 until 1970, but from 1970 until the late 1990s the surplus was usually negative. When there is a negative government surplus, we say that the government is running a deficit; the **government deficit** is the negative of the government surplus. The largest government deficits over this period were in 1975, when the deficit exceeded 8% of GDP, and in late 2010, when it reached 11% of GDP. There was only a brief period after the late 1970s when governments in the United States ran a surplus; in 1999, the government surplus reached about 2% of GDP. However, the surplus declined dramatically after 1999, reaching −4% of GDP in 2003 before increasing again and then dropping precipitously in the 2008–2009 recession.

What are the consequences of government deficits? We might think, in line with popular conceptions of household finance, that accumulating debt (running a deficit) is bad, whereas reducing debt (running a surplus) is good, but at the aggregate level the issue is not so simple. One principal difference between an individual and the government is that, when the government accumulates debt by borrowing from its citizens, then this is debt that we as a nation owe to ourselves. Then, it turns out that the effects of a government deficit depend on what the source of the deficit is. Is the government running a deficit because taxes have decreased or because government spending has increased? If the deficit is the result of a decrease in taxes, then the government debt that is issued to finance the deficit will have to be paid off ultimately by higher future taxes. Thus, running a deficit in this case implies that there is a redistribution of the tax burden from one group to another; one group has its current taxes reduced while another has its future taxes increased. Under some circumstances, these two groups might essentially be the same, in which case there would be no consequences of having the government run a deficit. This idea, that government deficits do not matter under some conditions, is called the **Ricardian equivalence theorem**, and we study it in Chapter 9. In the case of a government deficit resulting from higher government spending, there are always implications for aggregate economic activity, as discussed earlier in terms of the crowding out of private spending. We examine the effects of government spending in Chapters 5 and 11.

Inflation

Inflation, as mentioned earlier, is the rate of change in the average level of prices. The average level of prices is referred to as the price level. In Figure 1.10 we show the inflation rate, the black line in the figure, as the percentage rate of increase in the consumer price index over the period 1948–2015. The inflation rate was high in the late 1940s and during the Korean War, but was quite low in the early 1960s and then began climbing in the late 1960s, reaching peaks of about 12% per year in 1975 and about 14% per year in 1980. The inflation rate then declined steadily, falling into the negative range in early 2009, increasing, and then declining to close to zero in 2015.

High inflation is economically costly, and the high inflation experienced during the 1970s was seen as a problem for monetary policy in the United States. At the time, monetary policymakers felt that growth in the money supply had been driving this high rate of inflation, and they successfully reduced money growth and inflation during the 1980s. The period from the 1980s until the Great Recession began in late 2007 was one of low inflation. However, in the period after the Great Recession ended in 2009, inflation fell, to the point where the inflation rate was consistently below the Fed's 2% inflation target over the period 2013–2015.

Now, a problem in the United States, and in other countries of the world, is that inflation is viewed by monetary policymakers as being too low—a situation that was perhaps unimaginable in the 1970s. Recently, central banks have failed in their attempts to increase inflation, through various unconventional means. This has caused macroeconomists to rethink theories of inflation, and to introduce newer, alternative theories that can better fit the data and be more useful for economic policy. We discuss these issues in depth in Chapters 12 and 15.

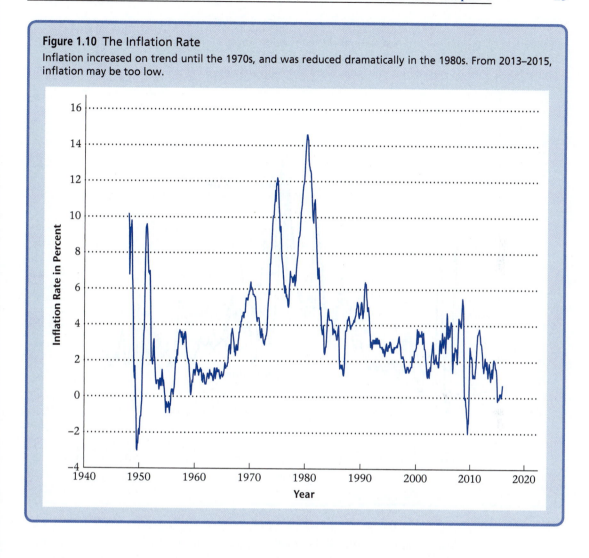

Figure 1.10 The Inflation Rate

Inflation increased on trend until the 1970s, and was reduced dramatically in the 1980s. From 2013–2015, inflation may be too low.

Interest Rates

Interest rates are important, as they affect many private economic decisions, particularly the decisions of consumers as to how much they borrow and lend, and the decisions of firms concerning how much to invest in new plant and equipment. Further, movements in interest rates are an important element in the economic mechanism by which monetary policy affects real magnitudes in the short run. In Figure 1.11 we show the behavior of the short-term **nominal interest rate** (the blue line) in the United States over the period 1947–2015. This is the interest rate in money terms on 91-day U.S. Treasury bills, which are essentially riskless short-term government securities. The short-term nominal interest rate rose on trend through the 1950s, 1960s, and 1970s, reaching a high of more than 15% early in 1980. Since then, the nominal interest rate has declined on trend, and it has been close to 0% since late 2008.

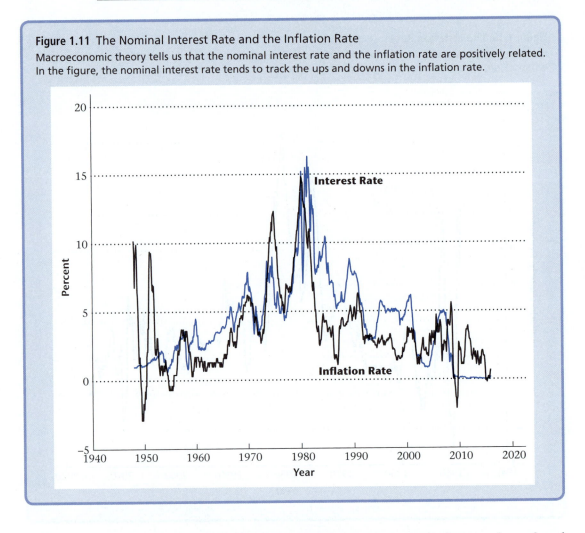

Figure 1.11 The Nominal Interest Rate and the Inflation Rate

Macroeconomic theory tells us that the nominal interest rate and the inflation rate are positively related. In the figure, the nominal interest rate tends to track the ups and downs in the inflation rate.

What explains the level of the nominal interest rate? In the figure we have plotted the inflation rate as the black line, which is measured here by the rate of increase in the consumer price index. The inflation rate tracks the nominal interest rate reasonably closely. Also, several of the peaks in inflation, around 1970, in the mid-1970s, around 1980, around 1990, and in 2001, are coupled with peaks in the nominal interest rate. Thus, the nominal interest rate tends to rise and fall with the inflation rate. Why is this? Economic decisions are based on real rather than nominal interest rates. The **real interest rate**, roughly speaking, is the nominal interest rate minus the expected rate of inflation. That is, the real interest rate is the rate that a borrower expects to have to repay, adjusting for the inflation that is expected to occur over the period of time until the borrower's debt is repaid. If Allen obtains a one-year car loan at an interest rate of 9%, and he expects the inflation rate to be 3% over the next year, then he faces a real interest rate on the car loan of 6%. Because economic decisions are based on real interest rates rather than nominal interest rates, market forces tend to determine the real

Figure 1.12 Real Interest Rate

The figure shows a measure of the real interest rate, which here is the short-term nominal interest rate minus the actual rate of inflation. Monetary policy can have a short-run effect on the real interest rate; for example, the low real interest rates during the 1990–1991, 2001, and 2008–2009 recessions can be attributed to monetary policy actions.

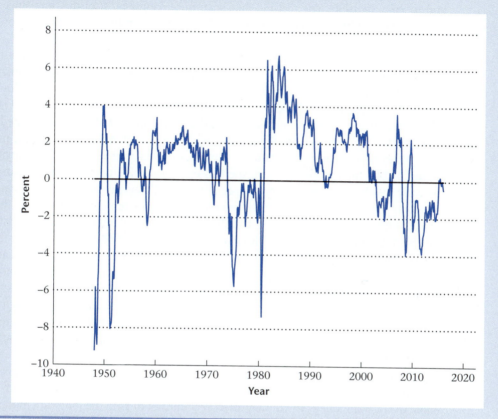

interest rate. Therefore, as the inflation rate rises, the nominal interest rate tends to rise along with it. In Chapters 9–12, we study the determination of real and nominal interest rates, and the relationship between real and nominal rates.

But in Figure 1.11, we can also think of the positive correlation between the nominal interest rate and the inflation rate arising because high (low) nominal interest rates are causing high (low) inflation. Over the medium to long run, the Fisher effect is an important force determining how monetary policy affects inflation. Indeed, in neo-Fisherian theory, a central bank that conducts monetary policy by targeting the nominal interest rate may come to the conclusion that the best way to increase inflation is to increase its nominal interest rate target.

In Figure 1.12 we plot an estimate of the real interest rate, which is the nominal interest rate minus the actual rate of inflation. Thus, this would be the actual real interest rate if consumers and firms could correctly anticipate inflation, so that actual inflation is equal to expected inflation. Consumers and firms cannot correctly anticipate the actual inflation rate. However, given that inflation does not change too much from quarter to quarter, our estimate of the real interest rate has a reasonably small measurement error. The real interest rate fluctuates a great deal over time, and has sometimes been negative, having fallen to about −9% in the late 1940s, to −8% in the early 1950s, and to −7% in 1980. The real rate has been negative for most of the time since the beginning of the financial crisis in late 2008. The period in the mid-1980s was one of particularly high real interest rates.

In the short run, the real interest rate is affected by monetary policy, though there is some disagreement among macroeconomists concerning why the central bank can control the real interest rate, and for how long it can do so. We can give the following interpretation to the path of the real interest rate from the mid-1970s to 2015 in Figure 1.12. First, the real interest rate was low in the mid to late 1970s because the Federal Reserve (the Fed) was causing the money supply to grow at a high rate; that is, monetary policy was expansionary and accommodating. As a result of the high inflation caused by this high money growth, the Fed embarked on a contractionary course in the early 1980s, reducing money supply growth and causing the real interest rate to rise. After the mid-1980s, the Fed remained seriously concerned about the possibility that high inflation could reemerge, and thus caused the real interest rate to be historically high. During the business cycle downturn in the early 1990s, the Fed temporarily relaxed, causing the real interest rate to dip to close to 0%. Then, in 2001, the Fed acted to reduce the real interest rate again, in response to a slowdown in aggregate economic activity. As there appeared to be no threat of serious inflation and economic activity had not picked up significantly, the real interest rate continued to fall through late 2003. Then, when the economy was growing at a high rate, and there was a greater threat from inflation, the real interest rate increased, through 2006. In 2008, the Fed aggressively reduced the real interest rate in response to the financial crisis and the developing recession. In Chapters 12–14, we study some theories of the business cycle that explain how the central bank can influence the real interest rate in the short run. While the rate of money growth may affect real interest rates in the long run, monetary policy is aimed not at setting the long-run real interest rate but at determining long-run inflation while staying in tune with the short-run effects of monetary policy.

Business Cycles in the United States

As was mentioned above, individual business cycle events may have many causes, and the causes that are important in one business cycle event may be very unimportant in others. For example, a particular recession might be attributed to monetary policy actions, while another recession may have been caused primarily by a downturn in aggregate productivity.

As above, we define business cycles to be the deviations from trend in aggregate economic activity. In Figure 1.13, we show the percentage deviations from trend in real GDP for the period 1947–2015. Recessions in the figure are negative deviations from trend, and the significant recent recessions in the United States were those of 1974–1975, 1981–1982, 1990–1991, 2001, and 2008–2009. What were the causes of these recessions?

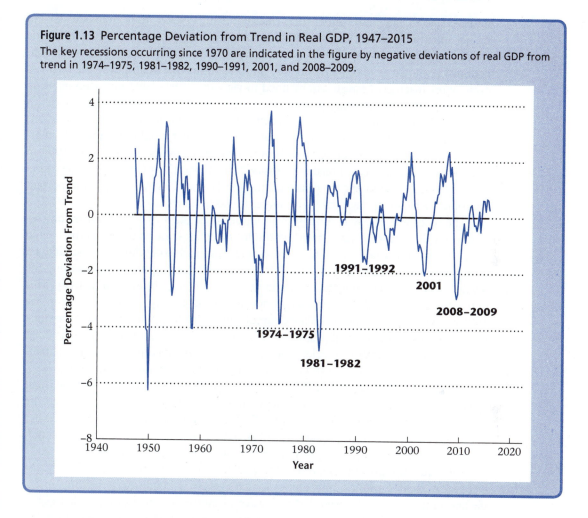

Figure 1.13 Percentage Deviation from Trend in Real GDP, 1947–2015

The key recessions occurring since 1970 are indicated in the figure by negative deviations of real GDP from trend in 1974–1975, 1981–1982, 1990–1991, 2001, and 2008–2009.

Before the 1974–1975 recession, there was a particularly sharp rise in the price of energy on world markets, caused by a restriction of oil output by the Organization of Petroleum Exporting Countries (OPEC). In Chapters 4, 5, and 11, we explain how an increase in the price of energy acts to reduce productivity and leads to a decrease in aggregate output, which occurred in 1974–1975 as we see in Figure 1.13. Other features of the 1974–1975 recession, including a reduction in measured productivity, a fall in employment, and a decrease in consumption and investment expenditures, are all consistent with this recession having been caused by the increase in the price of energy.

The recession of 1981–1982, like the recession of 1974–1975, was preceded by a large increase in the price of energy, which in this case occurred in 1979–1980. For this second recession, the energy price increase perhaps happened too soon before the recession to have been its principal cause. As well, other evidence seems to point to monetary policy as the primary cause of the 1981–1982 recession. Inflation had become relatively high in the 1970s in the United States, and by the early 1980s the Federal

Reserve System (the Fed), under then-chairman Paul Volcker, took dramatic steps to reduce inflation by restricting growth in the supply of money. This produced the side effect of a recession. While there is much controversy among macroeconomists concerning the short-run effects of monetary policy, and the role of money in the business cycle, most macroeconomists are inclined to view the 1981–1982 recession as being caused primarily by monetary policy.

The 1991–1992 recession was mild compared to the previous two major recessions (the negative deviation from trend in Figure 1.13 is smaller), and it was the only interruption in sustained economic growth over a roughly 19-year period from 1982 to 2001 in the United States. For this recession, it is difficult to pinpoint a single cause. Possibly an increase in energy prices during the Persian Gulf War was an important contributing factor, though that price increase was temporary.

The recession of 2001, though even milder than the 1991–1992 recession (see Figure 1.13), appears to have been the result of a collapse in optimism in the United States. During the 1990s, there was a boom in investment expenditures—spending on new plants, equipment, and housing—fed in part by great optimism concerning the revolution in information technology and its implications for future productivity. This optimism was also reflected in a large increase in the average price of stocks in the 1990s. In about 2000, optimism faded rapidly, investment expenditures and the stock market crashed, and the result was the recession of 2001. Also contributing to the 2001 recession were the terrorist attacks of September 2001, which directly disrupted financial activity in New York City and caused travelers to fear air travel and tourism.

The period after the 1981–1982 recession until 2008 is sometimes called the Great Moderation, as aggregate economic fluctuations became less volatile, relative to the 1947–1982 period. However, the 2008–2009 recession was anything but moderate, with the deviation from trend close to −3%. The causes of the 2008–2009 recession are rooted in the financial crisis originating in the United States, which began in 2007 and subsequently spread to the rest of the world. Regulatory failures in the U.S. financial system created profit opportunities for excessively risky mortgage lending, and a decline in the price of housing led to a wave of mortgage foreclosures and stress in financial markets. This recent recession illustrates the importance of financial market factors for aggregate economic activity.

Credit Markets and the Financial Crisis

The financial crisis and subsequent severe recession in 2008–2009 were essentially unanticipated events among professional macroeconomists. Though these events have caused macroeconomists to revise their thinking concerning the importance of credit markets, banking, and financial relationships for aggregate economic activity, this should not challenge our confidence in the use of mainstream macroeconomic theory to make sense of empirical observations and guide economic policy.

Issues related to the financial crisis and the recent recession are discussed in Chapters 6, 10–14, and 18, in particular. A critical aspect of economic theory that is very helpful in understanding the recent crisis is how credit market "frictions" or "imperfections" act to amplify shocks to the economy. Two imperfections that are analyzed, beginning in Chapter 10, are asymmetric information and limited commitment.

Asymmetric information refers to a situation where the economic actors on one side of a market have more information than the economic actors on the other side of the market. For example, financial institutions that extend loans in the credit market may have less information about the creditworthiness of would-be borrowers than do the borrowers themselves. In these circumstances, even borrowers who are very unlikely to default on a loan may be forced to pay a high interest rate on the loan, as lending institutions are unable to differentiate good borrowers from bad borrowers. Then, interest rates will include a default premium, and this default premium tends to rise as lending institutions become increasingly pessimistic about the average creditworthiness of borrowers. Good borrowers suffer due to the asymmetric information problem.

One way to measure the size of the default premium in credit markets is to look at the difference between the long-term interest rate on relatively safe long-term corporate debt, and the interest rate on somewhat risky corporate debt. Figure 1.14 shows the difference (the interest rate "spread") between AAA-rated (safe) corporate bonds and BAA-rated (somewhat risky) corporate bonds for the period 1919–2015. First, note that there was a very large spike in this spread during the Great Depression in the 1930s, and that each of the recessions since 1970 is associated with an increase in the spread (see Figure 1.14). Further, the size of the spread in the 2008–2009 recession was the largest observed since the Great Depression. This points to a large increase in the perceived average risk of default in credit markets. As we will show in Chapters 10 and 11, increases in perceived credit risk due to asymmetric information in consumer and corporate credit markets leads to decreases in aggregate consumption and investment expenditures, just as was observed in 2008–2009.

The second credit market imperfection, limited commitment, refers to a borrower's lack of incentive to repay in the credit market. In general, lending institutions attempt to solve this incentive problem by requiring that a borrower post collateral when taking out a loan. For example, in taking out an auto loan, a borrower posts his or her car as collateral, and a borrower's house serves as collateral for a mortgage loan. Under collateralized lending, in the event that the borrower does not repay his or her debt, the lender can seize the collateral. For a consumer, then, the value of assets held that are collateralizable, which consists mostly of housing in the U.S. economy, can matter for how much the consumer can borrow. For example, if the value of my house increases, this increases my ability to borrow in the form of a home equity loan, and I can use such a loan to finance consumption expenditures. For the economy as a whole, a decline in the price of housing can result in a significant drop in aggregate consumption, if a large fraction of consumers is constrained in their ability to borrow by available collateral.

In Figure 1.15, we show the relative price of housing, captured here by the average price of houses in the United States divided by the consumer price index. This is a measure of the purchasing power of the housing stock, or the value of the aggregate stock of housing as collateral. Note in particular the drop in the relative price of housing of about 40% from its peak in 2006 to the end of 2012. This not only caused problems in the mortgage market, in that some mortgage borrowers then had the incentive to default on their mortgages, but it also caused a decrease in consumption expenditures, because of the decrease in collateralizable wealth.

Figure 1.14 Interest Rate Spread

The figure shows the gap between interest rates on AAA-rated (safe) and BAA-rated (somewhat risky) corporate debt. Increases are observed during recessions, and the largest increase since the Great Depression occurred during the financial crisis in 2008–2009.

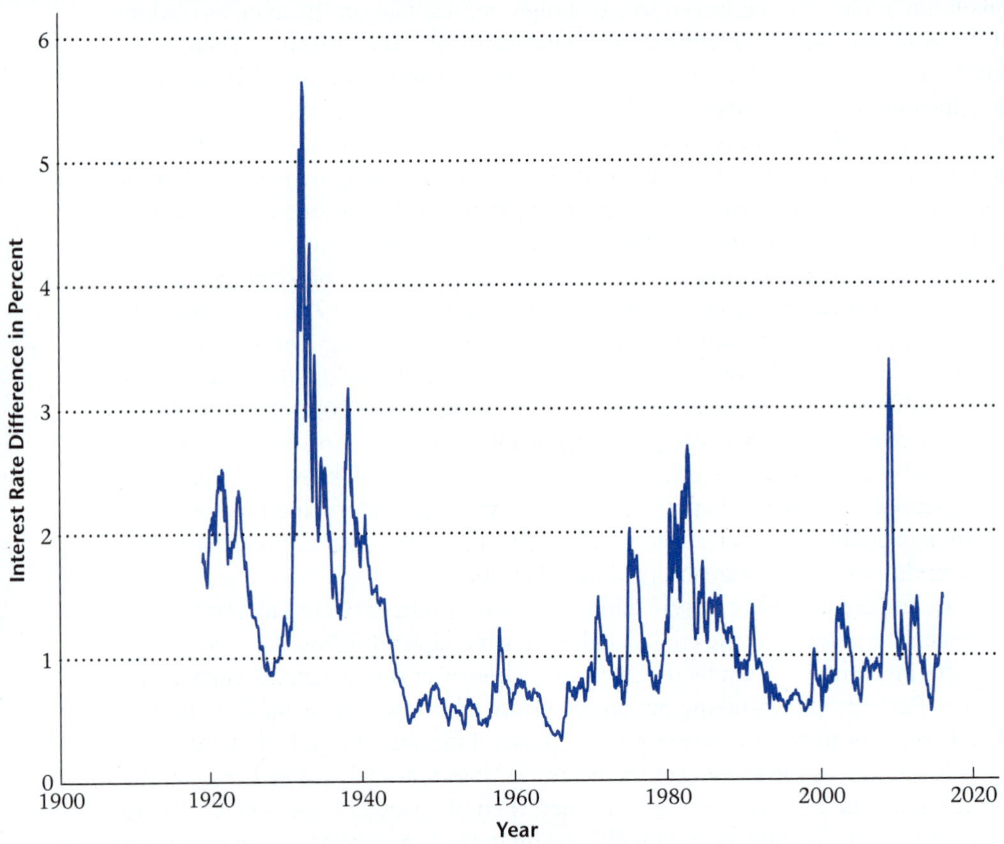

The Current Account Surplus

As the technology for transporting goods and information across countries has advanced and government-imposed impediments to trade have been reduced in the post–World War II period, the United States has become a more open economy. That is, trade in goods and in assets between the United States and the rest of the world has increased. The change in the flow of goods and services between the United States and the rest of the world is shown in Figure 1.16, where we plot U.S. exports (the black line) and imports (the colored line) as percentages of GDP from 1947 to 2015. U.S. exports increased from about 5% of GDP in 1947 to more than 13% of GDP in 2015, while imports increased from somewhat more than 3% in 1947 to about 16% in 2015. As mentioned previously, more trade has a positive effect on general economic welfare, as

Figure 1.15 Relative Price of Housing

The figure shows a drop of about 40% in the relative price of housing from the peak in 2006 to the end of 2012. This represents a drop in the value of collateralizable wealth, which caused a decrease in consumption expenditures.

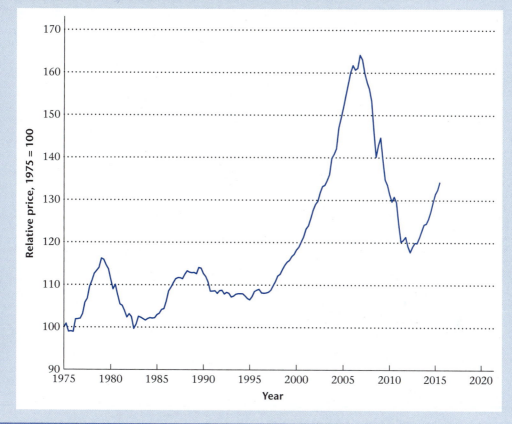

it allows countries to specialize in production and exploit their comparative advantages. However, more trade could also expose a given country to the transmission of business cycle fluctuations from abroad, though this need not necessarily be the case. An interesting feature of the data in Figure 1.16 is the dramatic decrease in both imports and exports, as percentages of GDP, during the 2008–2009 recession.

While the level of trade with the outside world is important in terms of aggregate economic activity and how it fluctuates, the balance of trade also plays an important role in macroeconomic activity and macroeconomic policymaking. One measure of the balance of trade is the **current account surplus**, which is **net exports** of goods and services (exports minus imports) plus **net factor payments** (net income from abroad). In Figure 1.17 we have graphed the current account surplus for the period 1960–2015. In the figure the current account surplus was positive for most of the period 1960–1985, and it has been negative for most of the period 1985–2015.

Figure 1.16 Exports and Imports of Goods and Services as Percentages of GDP

The increase in imports and exports after World War II reflects a general increase in world trade. However, note that trade with the rest of the world decreased significantly during the 2008–2009 recession.

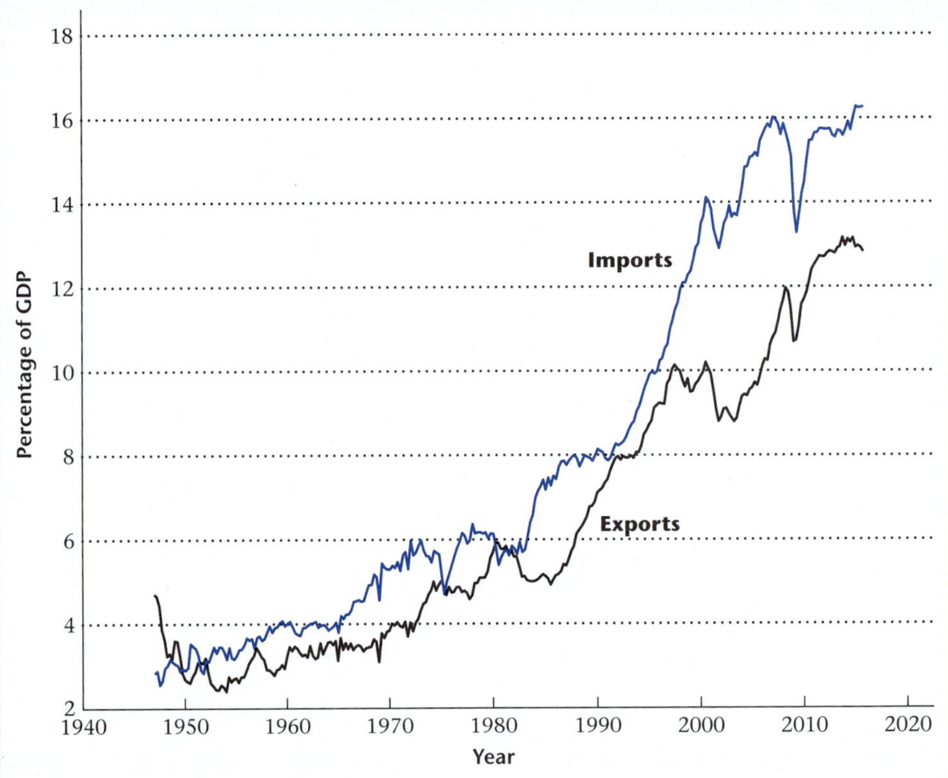

Why is the current account surplus important? When the current account surplus in the United States is negative, there is a **current account deficit**, and the quantity of goods and services purchased abroad by domestic residents is larger than the quantity of domestic goods and services purchased by foreigners. To finance this current account deficit, residents of the United States and/or the U.S. government must be borrowing abroad. Is it a bad idea for a country to run a current account deficit? This need not be the case, for two reasons. First, just as it may make sense for an individual to borrow so as to smooth his or her flow of consumption over time, it may also be beneficial for a country to borrow in the short run by running a current account deficit so as to smooth aggregate consumption over time. Second, persistent current account deficits may make sense if the associated foreign borrowing is used to finance additions to the nation's productive capacity that will allow for higher future living standards.

What accounts for movements over time in the current account surplus? One important influence on the current account surplus is government spending. When the government increases its spending, holding taxes constant, this will increase the government

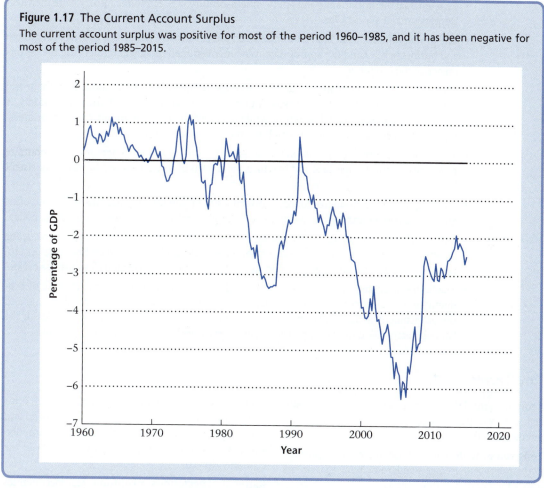

Figure 1.17 The Current Account Surplus

The current account surplus was positive for most of the period 1960–1985, and it has been negative for most of the period 1985–2015.

deficit, which needs to be financed by increased government borrowing. Other important influences on the current account surplus are increases in domestic income, which tend to increase imports, and increases in foreign income, which tend to increase exports.

We will study international trade, the determinants of the current account surplus, and other issues associated with international business cycles and international financial relations in Chapters 16 and 17.

Chapter Summary

- Modern macroeconomics analyzes issues associated with long-run growth and business cycles, using models that are built up from microeconomic principles.
- During the twentieth century, the United States experienced long-run sustained growth in per capita gross national product; we also observed that gross national product exhibits business cycle fluctuations about a smooth long-run trend.

- Two unusual but important events in twentieth-century U.S. economic history were the Great Depression and World War II.

- The primary questions of interest to macroeconomists involve the causes of long-run growth and business cycles and the appropriate role for government policy in influencing the performance of the economy.

- Macroeconomists rely mainly on abstract models to draw conclusions about how the world works, because it is usually very costly or impossible to experiment with the real economy. A good macroeconomic model is simple, while retaining all of the features essential for addressing the macroeconomic issue for which the model was intended.

- The models we construct and use in this book are ones in which consumers and firms optimize given the constraints they face and in which the actions of consumers and firms are consistent in equilibrium.

- Building models from microeconomic principles is important, because this will more often give us the correct answers to questions regarding the effects of changes in economic policy.

- There is relatively little disagreement among macroeconomists concerning approaches to modeling growth, but there are contentious issues in business cycle modeling, between Keynesian macroeconomists and those who argue for non-Keynesian alternative explanations for business cycles.

- The issues discussed in this chapter, to be addressed later in the book, are: the role of productivity in the economy; unemployment and vacancies; taxes, government spending, and the government deficit; inflation and money growth; interest rates; business cycles in the United States; credit markets and the financial crisis; and the current account surplus.

Key Terms

Economic model A description of consumers and firms, their objectives and constraints, and how they interact. (p. 3)

Long-run growth The increase in a nation's productive capacity and average standard of living that occurs over a long period of time. (p. 3)

Business cycles Short-run ups and downs, or booms and recessions, in aggregate economic activity. (p. 3)

Gross domestic product The quantity of goods and services produced within a country's borders during some specified period of time. (p. 3)

Trend The smooth growth path around which an economic variable cycles. (p. 7)

Models Artificial devices that can replicate the behavior of real systems. (p. 9)

Optimize The process by which economic agents (firms and consumers) do the best they can given the constraints they face. (p. 10)

Equilibrium The situation in an economy when the actions of all the consumers and firms are consistent. (p. 10)

Competitive equilibrium Equilibrium in which firms and households are assumed to be price-takers, and market prices are such that the quantity supplied equals the quantity demanded in each market in the economy. (p. 10)

Rational expectations revolution Macroeconomics movement that occurred in the 1970s, introducing more microeconomics into macroeconomics. (p. 12)

Lucas critique The idea that macroeconomic policy analysis can be done in a sensible way only if microeconomic behavior is taken seriously. (p. 12)

Endogenous growth models Models that describe the economic mechanism determining the rate of economic growth. (p. 12)

Keynesian Describes macroeconomists who are followers of J. M. Keynes and who see an active role for government in smoothing business cycles. (p. 12)

Non-Keynesian Describes macroeconomists who pursue business cycle analysis that does not derive from the work of J. M. Keynes. (p. 12)

Real business cycle theory Initiated by Finn Kydland and Edward Prescott, this theory implies that business cycles are caused primarily by shocks to technology and that the government should play a passive role over the business cycle. (p. 12)

Coordination failures A modern incarnation of Keynesian business cycle theory positing that business cycles are caused by self-fulfilling waves of optimism and pessimism, which may be countered with government policy. (p. 13)

New Keynesian economics A modern version of Keynesian business cycle theory in which prices and/or wages are sticky. (p. 13)

Inflation The rate of change in the average level of prices over time. (p. 15)

Federal Reserve System (Fed) The central bank of the United States. (p. 15)

Phillips curve A positive relationship between the deviation of aggregate output from trend and the inflation rate. (p. 16)

Average labor productivity The quantity of aggregate output produced per worker. (p. 16)

Beveridge curve A negative relationship between the unemployment rate and the vacancy rate. (p. 18)

Crowding out The process by which government spending reduces private sector expenditures on investment and consumption. (p. 20)

Government surplus The difference between taxes and government spending. (p. 21)

Government saving Identical to the government surplus. (p. 21)

Government deficit The negative of the government surplus. (p. 21)

Ricardian equivalence theorem Theory asserting that a change in taxation by the government has no effect. (p. 22)

Nominal interest rate The interest rate in money terms. (p.23)

Real interest rate Approximately equal to the nominal interest rate minus the expected rate of inflation. (p. 24)

Current account surplus Exports minus imports plus net factor payments to domestic residents from abroad. (p. 31)

Net exports Exports of goods and services minus imports of goods and services. (p. 31)

Net factor payments These are the payments received by domestic factors of production from abroad minus the payments to foreign factors of production from domestic sources. (p. 31)

Current account deficit Situation in which the current account surplus is negative. (p. 32)

Questions for Review

1.1 What are the primary defining characteristics of macroeconomics?

1.2 What makes macroeconomics different from microeconomics? What do they have in common?

1.3 How much richer was the average American in 2014 than in 1900?

1.4 What are two striking business cycle events in the United States during the last 112 years?

1.5 List six fundamental macroeconomic questions.

1.6 In a graph of the natural logarithm of an economic time series, what does the slope of the graph represent?

1.7 What is the difference between the trend and the business cycle component of an economic time series?

1.8 Explain why experimentation is difficult in macroeconomics.

1.9 Why should a macroeconomic model be simple?

1.10 Should a macroeconomic model be an exact description of the world? Explain why or why not.

1.11 What are the five elements that make up the basic structure of a macroeconomic model?

1.12 Why can macroeconomic models be useful? How do we determine whether or not they are useful?

1.13 Explain why a macroeconomic model should be built from microeconomic principles.

1.14 What are the two key threads in modern business cycle theory?

1.15 Why was productivity growth low from 2010–2015?

1.16 Why might the vacancy rate rise without a commensurate reduction in the unemployment rate?

1.17 What is the principal effect of an increase in government spending?

1.18 Why might a decrease in taxes have no effect?

1.19 What is the cause of inflation in the long run?

1.20 Explain the difference between the nominal interest rate and the real interest rate.

1.21 When did the five most recent recessions occur in the United States?

1.22 What role did credit market imperfections play in the recent financial crisis?

1.23 Is it a bad idea for a country to run a current account deficit? Why or why not?

Problems

1. **LO 3** Consider the following data on real GDP per capita in the United States:

Year	U.S. Real GDP Per Capita (2009 dollars)
1950	$14,432
1960	$17,335
1970	$23,236
1980	$28,472
1990	$36,005
2000	$44,503
2010	$47,790
2011	$48,186
2012	$48,884
2013	$49,247
2014	$50,051

(a) Calculate the percentage growth rates in real GDP per capita in each of the years 2011 through 2014, from the previous year.

(b) Now, instead of calculating the annual percentage growth rates in the years 2011 through 2014 directly, use as an approximation $100 \times (\ln y_t - \ln y_{t-1})$, where y_t is real per capita GDP in year t. How close does this approximation come to the actual growth rates you calculated in part (a)?

(c) Repeat parts (a) and (b), but now calculate the percentage rates of growth in real per capita GDP from 1950 to 1960, from 1960 to 1970, from 1970 to 1980, from 1980 to 1990, from 1990 to 2000, and from 2000 to 2010. In this case, how large an error do you make by approximating the growth rate by the change in the natural log? Why is there a difference here relative to parts (a) and (b)?

2. **LO 3** Suppose that you had the special power to travel in time and to carry out any experiment you wanted on the economy. If you could turn back the clock to the time of the Great Depression, what experiment would you like to run on the U.S. economy? Why?

3. **LO 3** Give an example of a model that is used in some area other than economics, other than the roadmap example explained in this chapter. What is unrealistic about this model? How well does the model perform its intended function?

4. **LO 7** In Figure 1.6, does unemployment change more rapidly when it is increasing, or when it is decreasing? Speculate on why this regularity might be observed in the data.

5. **LO 7** Use Figures 1.8 and 1.9 to determine why the total government deficit was large during the 2008–2009 recession. Was the deficit large because taxes fell, because spending rose, or both?

6. **LO 7** What difference do you notice between the variability in the inflation rate before and after 1985? Provide an explanation for this phenomenon.

7. **LO 7** From Figures 1.11 and 1.12, determine and discuss how fluctuations in the nominal interest rate and inflation have contributed to fluctuations in the real interest rate from 2000 to 2015.

8. **LO 7** In Figure 1.13, discuss the severity of the 2008–2009 recession relative to previous recessions.

9. **LO 7** Determine how increases in the interest rate spread in Figure 1.14 match with recessions in Figure 1.13. Does an increase in the interest rate spread always occur when there is a recession? Does a recession always occur when there is an increase in the interest rate spread? Comment.

10. **LO 7** In Figure 1.15, there were two periods prior to 2006–2012 when the relative price of housing declined. Examine some of the other data figures in this chapter and determine what other events these housing price declines coincide with. Compare these events to what was going on during the period 2006–2012. Discuss.

Working with the Data

Answer these questions using the Federal Reserve Bank of St. Louis's FRED database, accessible at http://research.stlouisfed.org/fred2/

1. Graph gross domestic product (GDP) and gross national product (GNP) in 2009 dollars for 1947 and thereafter. Is there much difference in these two measures of aggregate economic activity for the United States?

2. Total government expenditures consist of expenditures by the federal government and by state and local governments. Calculate and graph the ratio of federal government expenditures to total government expenditures. Has the federal government become larger or smaller relative to state and local governments over time?

3. Produce a graph of the inflation rate and the money growth rate, as measured by the growth rate in M1. Use 12-month percentage changes to measure rates of increase in each case. Discuss what you see in the graph. Does this indicate a clear connnection between money growth and inflation?

Chapter 2

Measurement

Learning Objectives

After studying Chapter 2, students will be able to:

2.1 Construct measures of gross domestic product using the product approach, the expenditure approach, and the income approach.

2.2 State the importance of each expenditure component of GDP, and the issues associated with measuring each.

2.3 Construct real and nominal GDP, and price indices, from data on quantities and prices in different years.

2.4 State the key difficulties in measuring GDP and the price level.

2.5 State the accounting relationships among savings and income in the private and public sectors, and explain the importance of these relationships for wealth accumulation.

2.6 Construct the key labor market measures from the household survey data.

Good economists need good measurement, and good theory. It is also true that good theory requires good measurement, and good measurement requires good theory. Measurements of the performance of the economy motivate macroeconomists to build simple models that can organize our thinking about how the economy works. For example, surveys of consumer prices done every year can tell us something about how prices change over time and, coupled with observations on other economic variables, can help us develop theories that explain why prices change over time. Meanwhile, economic theory can better inform us about the most efficient ways to carry out economic measurement. For example, theories of consumer behavior can tell us something about the appropriate way to use the prices of consumer goods to derive a price index that is a good measure of the price level.

Our goal in this chapter is to understand the basic issues concerning how key macroeconomic variables are measured. These key macroeconomic variables play important roles in the economic models that we construct and study in the remainder of this book. In particular, in the rest of this chapter we examine the measurement of GDP and its components, and the measurement of prices, savings, wealth, capital, and labor market variables.

Measuring GDP: The National Income and Product Accounts

LO 2.1 Construct measures of gross domestic product using the product approach, the expenditure approach, and the income approach.

The chief aim of national income accounting is to obtain a measure of the total quantity of goods and services produced for the market in a given country over a given period of time. For many issues in macroeconomics (though by no means for all), the measure of aggregate economic activity we are interested in is **gross domestic product (GDP)**, which is the dollar value of final output produced during a given period of time within the borders of the United States. GDP is published on a quarterly basis as part of the **National Income and Product Accounts (NIPA)**, two sources for which are the Bureau of Economic Analysis website (http://www.bea.gov/national/index.htm#gdp) and the FRED database (https://research.stlouisfed.org/fred2/).

There are three approaches to measuring GDP, each of which is incorporated in some way in NIPA. All three approaches give exactly the same measure of GDP, provided there are no errors of measurement in using any of these approaches. The three approaches are the **product approach**, the **expenditure approach**, and the **income approach**. We discuss each in turn, using an example.

In our running example, we consider a simple fictional economy that captures the essentials of national income accounting. This is an island economy where there is a coconut producer, a restaurant, consumers, and a government. The coconut producer owns all of the coconut trees on the island, harvests the coconuts that grow on the trees, and in the current year produces 10 million coconuts, which are sold for $2.00 each, yielding total revenue of $20 million. The coconut producer pays wages of $5 million to its workers (who are some of the consumers in this economy), $0.5 million in interest on a loan to some consumers, and $1.5 million in taxes to the government. The relevant data for the coconut producer are shown in Table 2.1.

Table 2.1 Coconut Producer	
Total Revenue	$20 million
Wages	$5 million
Interest on Loan	$0.5 million
Taxes	$1.5 million

Of the 10 million coconuts produced, 6 million go to the restaurant, which specializes in innovative ways of serving coconuts—for example "shredded coconut in its own milk," "coconut soup," and "coconut in the half-shell." The remaining 4 million coconuts are bought by the consumers. Again, all coconuts are $2 each. Coconuts serve two roles in this economy. First, a coconut is an **intermediate good**, a good that is produced and then used as an input to another production process—here, the production of restaurant food. Second, it is a final consumption good, in that coconuts are purchased by consumers. The restaurant sells $30 million in restaurant meals during the year (this is a rather large restaurant). The total cost of coconuts for the restaurant is $12 million, and the restaurant pays its workers $4 million in wages and the government $3 million in taxes. Data for the restaurant are provided in Table 2.2.

Next, we need to calculate after-tax profits for each of the producers (the coconut producer and the restaurant). After-tax profits in this example are simply

$$\text{After-Tax Profits} = \text{Total Revenue} - \text{Wages} - \text{Interest}$$
$$-\text{Cost of Intermediate Inputs} - \text{Taxes}.$$

Therefore, from Tables 2.1 and 2.2 above, we calculate after-tax profits in Table 2.3.

The government's role in this economy is to provide protection from attacks from other islands. In the past, foreign invaders have destroyed coconut trees and made off with coconuts. The government collects taxes to provide national defense. That is, it uses all of its tax revenue to pay wages to the army. Total taxes collected are $5.5 million ($4.5 million from producers and $1 million from consumers), and so the data for the government are as shown in Table 2.4.

Table 2.2   Restaurant

Total Revenue	$30 million
Cost of Coconuts	$12 million
Wages	$4 million
Taxes	$3 million

Table 2.3   After-Tax Profits

Coconut Producer	$13 million
Restaurant	$11 million

Table 2.4   Government

Tax Revenue	$5.5 million
Wages	$5.5 million

Consumers work for the producers and for the government, earning total wages of $14.5 million. They receive $0.5 million in interest from the coconut producer, pay $1 million in taxes to the government, and receive after-tax profits of $24 million from the producers, because some of the consumers own the coconut firm and the restaurant. Data for the consumers are shown in Table 2.5.

Now, given the above-mentioned data for this simple economy, we examine how GDP would be calculated using the three different national income accounting approaches.

The Product Approach to Measuring GDP

The product approach to NIPA is also called the **value-added** approach. This is because the main principle in the product approach is that GDP is calculated as the sum of value added to goods and services across all productive units in the economy. To calculate GDP using the product approach, we add the value of all goods and services produced in the economy and then subtract the value of all intermediate goods used in production to obtain total value added. If we did not subtract the value of intermediate goods used in production, then we would be double-counting. In our example, we do not want to count the value of the coconuts used in the production of restaurant services as part of GDP.

In the example, the coconut producer does not use any intermediate goods in production, so value added in producing coconuts, which is the coconut producer's total revenue, is $20 million. For the restaurant, however, value added is total revenue minus the value of the coconuts used in production; thus, total value added for the restaurant is $18 million. For government production, we have a problem, because the national defense services provided by the government are not sold at market prices. Standard practice here is to value national defense services at the cost of the inputs to production. Here, the only input to production was labor, so the total value added for the government is $5.5 million. Total value added, or GDP, therefore, is $43.5 million. The GDP calculation using the product approach is summarized in Table 2.6.

Table 2.5 Consumers

Wage Income	$14.5 million
Interest Income	$0.5 million
Taxes	$1 million
Profits Distributed from Producers	$24 million

Table 2.6 GDP Using the Product Approach

Value added – coconuts	$20 million
Value added – restaurant food	$18 million
Value added – government	$5.5 million
GDP	$43.5 million

The Expenditure Approach

In the expenditure approach, we calculate GDP as *total spending on all final goods and services production in the economy*. Note again that we do not count spending on intermediate goods. In the NIPA, total expenditure is calculated as

$$\text{Total expenditure} = C + I + G + NX,$$

where C denotes expenditures on consumption, I is investment expenditure, G is government expenditure, and NX is net exports—that is, total exports of U.S. goods and services minus total imports into the United States. We add exports because this includes goods and services produced within the United States. Imports are subtracted because, in general, each of C, I, and G includes some goods and services that were produced abroad, and we do not want to include these in U.S. GDP.

In our example, there is no investment, no exports, and no imports, so that $I = NX = 0$. Consumers spend $8 million on coconuts and $30 million at the restaurant, so that $C = \$38$ million. For government expenditures, again we count the $5.5 million in wages spent by the government as if national defense services had been purchased as a final good at $5.5 million, and so $G = \$5.5$ million. Therefore, calculating GDP using the expenditure approach, we get

$$GDP = C + I + G + NX = \$43.5 \text{ million.}$$

The GDP calculation using the expenditure approach is shown in Table 2.7. Note that we obtain the same answer calculating GDP this way as using the product approach, as we should.

The Income Approach

To calculate GDP using the income approach, we *add up all income received by economic agents contributing to production*. Income includes the profits made by firms. In the NIPA, income includes compensation of employees (wages, salaries, and benefits), proprietors' income (self-employed firm owners), rental income, corporate profits, net interest, indirect business taxes (sales and excise taxes paid by businesses), and depreciation (consumption of fixed capital). Depreciation represents the value of productive capital (plant and equipment) that wears out during the period we are considering. Depreciation is taken out when we calculate profits, and so it needs to be added in again when we compute GDP.

Table 2.7   GDP Using the Expenditure Approach

Consumption	$38 million
Investment	0
Government Expenditures	$5.5 million
Net Exports	0
GDP	$43.5 million

Table 2.8 GDP Using the Income Approach	
Wage Income	$14.5 million
After-Tax Profits	$24 million
Interest Income	$0.5 million
Taxes	$4.5 million
GDP	$43.5 million

In the example, we need to include the wage income of consumers, $14.5 million, as a component of GDP. In addition, we need to count the profits of producers. If we do this on an after-tax basis, total profits for the two producers are $24 million. Next, we add the interest income of consumers (this is net interest), which is $0.5 million. Finally, we need to add the taxes paid by producers to the government, which are essentially government income. This amount is $4.5 million. Total GDP is then $43.5 million, which of course is the same answer that we obtained for the other two approaches. The calculation of GDP using the income approach is summarized in Table 2.8.

Why do the product approach, the expenditure approach, and the income approach yield the same GDP measure? This is because the total quantity of output, or value added, in the economy is ultimately sold, thus showing up as expenditure, and what is spent on all output produced is income, in some form or other, for someone in the economy. If we let Y denote total GDP in the economy, then Y is total aggregate output, and it is also aggregate income. Further, it is also true as an identity that aggregate income equals aggregate expenditure, or

$$Y = C + I + G + NX.$$

This relationship is sometimes referred to as the **income–expenditure identity**, as the quantity on the left-hand side of the identity is aggregate income, and that on the right-hand side is the sum of the components of aggregate expenditure.

An Example with Inventory Investment

One component of investment expenditures is inventory investment, which consists of any goods that are produced during the current period but are not consumed. Stocks of inventories consist of inventories of finished goods (e.g., automobiles that are stored on the lot), goods in process (e.g., automobiles still on the assembly line), and raw materials.

Suppose in our running example that everything is identical to the above, except that the coconut producer produces 13 million coconuts instead of 10 million, and that the extra 3 million coconuts are not sold but are stored as inventory. In terms of the value-added approach, GDP is the total value of coconuts produced, which is now $26 million, plus the value of restaurant food produced, $30 million, minus the value of intermediate goods used up in the production of restaurant food, $12 million, plus value added by the government, $5.5 million, for total GDP of $49.5 million. Note that we value the coconut inventory at the market price of coconuts in the example.

In practice, this need not be the case; sometimes the book value of inventories carried by firms is not the same as market value, though sound economics says it should be.

Now, for the expenditure approach, $C = \$38$ million, $NX = 0$, and $G = \$5.5$ million as before, but now $I = \$6$ million, so GDP $= C + I + G + NX = \$49.5$ million. It may seem odd that the inventory investment of $6 million is counted as expenditure, because this does not appear to be expenditure on a final good or service. The convention, however, is to treat the inventory investment here as if the coconut producer bought $6 million in coconuts from itself.

Finally, in terms of the income approach, wage income to consumers is $14.5 million, interest income to consumers is $0.5 million, taxes are $4.5 million, as before, and total profits after taxes for the two producers are now $30 million, for total GDP of $49.5 million. Here, we add the $6 million in inventories to the coconut producer's profits, because this is an addition to the firm's assets.

An Example with International Trade

To show what can happen when international trade in goods comes into the picture, we take our original example and alter it slightly. Suppose that the restaurant imports 2 million coconuts from other islands at $2 each, in addition to the coconuts purchased from the domestic coconut producer, and that all of these coconuts are used in the restaurant. The restaurant still sells $30 million in restaurant food to domestic consumers.

Here, following the value-added approach, the value added by the domestic coconut producer is $20 million as before. For the restaurant, value added is the value of food produced, $30 million, minus the value of intermediate inputs, which is $16 million, including the cost of imported coconuts. As before, total value added for the government is $5.5 million. Therefore, GDP is total value added for the two producers and the government, or $39.5 million.

Next, using the expenditure approach, consumption of coconuts by consumers is $8 million and restaurant service consumption is $30 million, so that $C = \$38$ million. Government expenditures are the same as in the initial example, with $G = \$5.5$ million, and we have $I = 0$. Total exports are 0, while imports (of coconuts) are $4 million, so that net exports are $NX = -\$4$ million. We then have GDP $= C + I + G + NX = \$39.5$ million.

Finally, following the income approach, the wage income of consumers is $14.5 million, interest income of consumers is $0.5 million, and taxes are $4.5 million, as in the initial example. The after-tax profits of the coconut producer are $13 million, also as before. The change here is in the after-tax profits of the restaurant, which are reduced by $4 million, the value of the imported coconuts, so that after-tax restaurant profits are $7 million. Total GDP is then $39.5 million.

Gross National Product

Before 1991, **gross national product (GNP)** was used in the United States as the official measure of aggregate production. In line with international practice, however, the official measure became GDP in December of 1991. In practice, there is little difference between GDP and GNP in the United States, but in principle the difference could matter significantly. GNP measures the value of output produced by domestic factors of production, whether or not the production takes place (as is the case for GDP) inside U.S. borders. For example, if a Nike plant in Southeast Asia is owned and managed by American residents, then the incomes accruing to U.S. factors of production include the managerial income and profits of this plant, and this is included in U.S. GNP, but not in U.S. GDP. Similarly, if a Honda plant in Ohio has Japanese owners, the profits of the plant would not be included in GNP, as these profits are not income for American residents, but the profits would be included in GDP.

Gross national product is the sum of GDP and net factor payments (NFP) from abroad to domestic residents or

$$GNP = GDP + NFP,$$

where *NFP* denotes net factor payments from abroad. For 2014, GDP for the United States was $17,348.1 billion, and GNP was $17,611.2 billion, so NFP was $263.1 billion. Thus, for this typical year, the difference between GDP and GNP for the United States was 1.74% of GDP, which is small. For some countries, however, there is a significant difference between GDP and GNP, particularly for those countries where a large fraction of national productive capacity is foreign-owned, in which case *NFP* is significant.

What Does GDP Leave Out?

GDP is intended simply as a measure of the quantity of output produced and exchanged in the economy as a whole. Sometimes GDP, or GDP per person, however, is used as a measure of aggregate economic welfare. There are at least two problems with this approach. The first is that aggregate GDP does not take into account how income is distributed across the individuals in the population. At the extreme, if one person in the economy has all the income and the rest of the people have no income, the average level of economic welfare in the economy would be very low. Second, GDP leaves out all nonmarket activity, with work in the home being an example. If people eat restaurant meals rather than eating at home, then GDP rises, because there are now more services produced in the market than before. People should be better off as a result, because they had the option of eating at home but chose to go out. However, the increase in GDP exaggerates the increase in economic welfare, as GDP does not measure the value added when food is cooked at home.

GDP may be an inaccurate measure of welfare, but there are also some problems with GDP as a measure of aggregate output, and two of these problems are the following. First, economic activities in the so-called **underground economy** are, by definition, not counted in GDP. The underground economy includes any unreported economic activity. A high-profile example of underground activity is trade in illegal drugs; a low-profile example is the exchange of baby-sitting services for cash. Economic activity goes underground so as to avoid legal penalties and taxation, and underground activity often involves cash transactions. The size of the underground economy may indeed be significant in the United States, as evidenced by the fact that the quantity of U.S. currency held per U.S. resident was approximately $4,390 in February 2016.[1] Clearly, most

---

[1]*Source:* U.S. Department of Commerce and Board of Governors of the Federal Reserve System.

individuals engaged in standard market transactions do not hold this much currency. This large quantity of currency in circulation can in part be explained by the large amount of U.S. currency held outside the country, but it still reflects the fact that the underground economy matters for the measurement of GDP in the United States.

A second problem in measuring GDP, which we encountered in our example, involves how government expenditures are counted. Most of what the government produces is not sold at market prices. For example, how are we to value roads, bridges, and national defense services? The solution in the NIPA, as in our example, is to value government expenditures at cost, that is, the payments to all of the factors of production that went into producing the good or service. In some cases this could overvalue what is produced; for example, if the government produced something that nobody wanted, such as a bridge to nowhere. In other cases, government production could be undervalued; for example, we may be willing to pay much more for national defense than what it costs in terms of wages, salaries, materials, and so forth.

The Components of Aggregate Expenditure

LO 2.2 State the importance of each expenditure component of GDP, and the issues associated with measuring each.

Typically, particularly in constructing economic models to understand how the economy works, we are interested mainly in the expenditure side of the NIPA. Here, we consider each of the expenditure components in more detail. Table 2.9 gives the GDP components for 2015.

Consumption   Consumption expenditures are the largest expenditure component of GDP, accounting for 68.4% of GDP in 2015 (see Table 2.9). **Consumption** is expenditure on consumer goods and services during the current period, and the components of consumption are durable goods, nondurable goods, and services. Durable goods include items like new automobiles, appliances, and furniture. Nondurables include food and clothing. Services are nontangible items like haircuts and hotel stays. Clearly, the division between durables and nondurables is somewhat imprecise because, for example, shoes (a nondurable) could be viewed as being as durable as washing machines (a durable). Further, some items included in consumption are clearly not consumed within the period. For example, if the period is one year, an automobile may provide services to the buyer for ten years or more, and is, therefore, not a consumption good but might economically be more appropriately considered an investment expenditure when it is bought. The purchase of a used car or other used durable good is not included in GDP, but the services provided (e.g., by a dealer) in selling a used car would be included.

Investment   In Table 2.9, investment expenditures were 16.8% of GDP in 2015. **Investment** is expenditure on goods that are produced during the current period, but are not consumed during the current period. There are two types of investment: fixed investment and inventory investment. **Fixed investment** is production of capital, such as plant, equipment, and housing, and **inventory investment** consists of goods that are essentially

Table 2.9 Gross Domestic Product for 2015

Component of GDP	$Billions	% of GDP
GDP	17,937.8	100.0
Consumption	12,267.9	68.4
Durables	1,328.8	7.4
Nondurables	2,649.8	14.8
Services	8,289.3	46.2
Investment	3,017.8	16.8
Fixed Investment	2,911.3	16.2
Nonresidential	2,302.4	12.8
Residential	608.9	3.4
Inventory Investment	106.5	0.6
Net Exports	531.9	3.0
Exports	2,253.0	12.6
Imports	2,784.9	15.5
Government Expenditures	3,184.0	17.8
Federal Defense	740.9	4.1
Federal Nondefense	483.9	2.7
State and Local	1,959.3	10.9

put into storage. The components of fixed investment are nonresidential investment and residential investment. Nonresidential investment adds to the plant, equipment, and software that make up the capital stock for producing goods and services. Residential investment—housing—is also productive, in that it produces housing services.

Though investment is a much smaller fraction of GDP than is consumption, investment plays a very important role in business cycles. Investment is much more variable than GDP or consumption, and some components of investment also tend to lead the business cycle. For example, an upward or downward blip in housing investment tends to precede an upward or downward blip in GDP. We study this phenomenon further in Chapter 3.

Net Exports As exports were less than imports in 2015, the United States ran a trade deficit in goods and services with the rest of the world—that is, **net exports** were negative (see Table 2.9). Exports were 12.6% of GDP in 2011 while imports were 15.5% of GDP. Trade with the rest of the world in goods and services, therefore, is quite important to the U.S. economy, as we noted in Chapter 1.

Government Expenditures **Government expenditures**, which consist of expenditures by federal, state, and local governments on final goods and services, were 17.8% of GDP in 2015, as seen in Table 2.9. The main components of government expenditures are federal defense spending (4.1% of GDP in 2015), federal nondefense spending (2.7% of GDP in 2015), and state and local spending (10.9% of GDP in 2015). The NIPA also make the important distinction between government consumption and government gross investment, just as we distinguish between private consumption and private investment. An important point is that the government spending included in the NIPA is only the expenditures on final goods and services. This does not include **transfers**, which are very important in the government budget. These outlays essentially transfer purchasing power from one group of economic agents to another, and they include such items as Social Security payments and unemployment insurance payments. Transfers are not included in GDP, as they are simply money transfers from one group of people to another, or income redistribution rather than income creation.

Nominal and Real GDP and Price Indices

LO 2.3 Construct real and nominal GDP, and price indices, from data on quantities and prices in different years.

While the components of GDP for any specific time period give us the total dollar value of goods and services produced in the economy during that period, for many purposes we would like to make comparisons between GDP data in different time periods. This might tell us something about growth in the productive capacity of the economy over time and about growth in our standard of living. A problem, however, is that the average level of prices changes over time, so that generally part of the increase in GDP that we observe is the result of inflation. In this section, we show how to adjust for this effect of inflation on the growth in GDP and, in so doing, arrive at a measure of the price level and the inflation rate.

A **price index** is a weighted average of the prices of a set of the goods and services produced in the economy over a period of time. If the price index includes prices of all goods and services, then that price index is a measure of the general **price level**, or the average level of prices across goods and services. We use price indices to measure the **inflation rate**, which is the rate of change in the price level from one period of time to another. If we can measure the inflation rate, we can also determine how much of a change in GDP from one period to another is purely **nominal** and how much is **real**. A nominal change in GDP is a change in GDP that occurred only because the price level changed, whereas a real change in GDP is an increase in the actual quantity of goods and services (including, for example, the numbers of apples and oranges sold during a period of time), which is what ultimately matters for consumers.

Real GDP

To see how real GDP is calculated in the NIPA, it helps to consider an example. Imagine an economy in which the only goods produced are apples and oranges. In year 1, 50 apples and 100 oranges are produced, and the prices of apples and oranges are $1.00 and $0.80, respectively. In year 2, 80 apples and 120 oranges are produced, and the prices of apples and oranges are $1.25 and $1.60, respectively. These data are displayed in Table 2.10. For convenience in expressing the formulas for real GDP

Table 2.10 Data for Real GDP Example

	Apples	**Oranges**
Quantity in Year 1	$Q_1^a = 50$	$Q_1^o = 100$
Price in Year 1	$P_1^a = \$1.00$	$P_1^o = \$0.80$
Quantity in Year 2	$Q_2^a = 80$	$Q_2^o = 120$
Price in Year 2	$P_2^a = \$1.25$	$P_2^o = \$1.60$

calculations, we let the quantities of apples and oranges, respectively, in year 1 be denoted by Q_1^a and Q_1^o with respective prices denoted by P_1^a and P_1^o. Quantities and prices in year 2 are represented similarly (see Table 2.10).

The calculation of nominal GDP in each year is straightforward here, as there are no intermediate goods. Year 1 nominal GDP is

$$GDP_1 = P_1^a Q_1^a + P_1^o Q_1^o = (\$1.00 \times 50) + (\$0.80 \times 100) = \$130.$$

Similarly, year 2 nominal GDP is

$$GDP_2 = P_2^a Q_2^a + P_2^o Q_2^o = (\$1.25 \times 80) + (\$1.60 \times 120) = \$292,$$

so the percentage increase in nominal GDP from year 1 to year 2 is equal to

$$\left(\frac{GDP_2}{GDP_1} - 1\right) \times 100\% = \left(\frac{292}{130} - 1\right) \times 100\% = 125\%.$$

That is, nominal GDP more than doubled from year 1 to year 2.

The question is, how much of this increase in nominal GDP is accounted for by inflation, and how much by an increase in the real quantity of aggregate output produced? Until 1996, the practice in the U.S. NIPA was first to choose a base year and then to calculate real GDP using these base year prices. That is, rather than multiplying the quantities produced in a given year by current year prices (which is what we do when calculating nominal GDP), we multiply by base year prices to obtain real GDP. In the example, suppose that we use year 1 as the base year, and let $RGDP_1^1$ and $RGDP_2^1$ denote real GDP in years 1 and 2, respectively, calculated using year 1 as the base year. Then, real GDP in year 1 is the same as nominal GDP for that year, because year 1 is the base year, so we have

$$RGDP_1^1 = GDP_1 = \$130.$$

Now, for year 2 real GDP, we use year 2 quantities and year 1 prices to obtain

$$RGDP_2^1 = P_1^a Q_2^a + P_1^o Q_2^o = (\$1.00 \times 80) + (\$0.80 \times 120) = \$176.$$

Therefore, the ratio of real GDP in year 2 to real GDP in year 1, using year 1 as the base year is

$$g_1 = \frac{RGDP_2^1}{RGDP_1^1} = \frac{176}{130} = 1.354,$$

so the percentage increase in real GDP using this approach is $(1.354 - 1) \times 100\% = 35.4\%$. Alternatively, suppose that we use year 2 as the base year and let $RGDP_1^2$ and $RGDP_2^2$ denote real GDP in years 1 and 2, respectively, calculated using this approach. Then, year 2 real GDP is the same as year 2 nominal GDP, that is

$$RGDP_2^2 = GDP_2 = \$292.$$

Year 1 GDP, using year 1 quantities and year 2 prices, is

$$RGDP_1^2 = P_2^a Q_1^a + P_2^o Q_1^o = (\$1.25 \times 50) + (\$1.60 \times 100) = \$222.50.$$

Then, the ratio of real GDP in year 2 to real GDP in year 1, using year 2 as the base year, is

$$g_2 = \frac{RGDP_2^2}{RGDP_1^2} = \frac{292}{222.5} = 1.312,$$

and the percentage increase in real GDP from year 1 to year 2 is $(1.312 - 1) \times 100\% = 31.2\%$.

A key message from the example is that the choice of the base year matters for the calculation of GDP. If year 1 is used as the base year, then the increase in real GDP is 35.4%, and if year 2 is the base year, real GDP is calculated to increase by 31.2%. The reason the choice of the base year matters in the example, and in reality, is that the relative prices of goods change over time. That is, the relative price of apples to oranges is $\frac{\$1.00}{\$0.80} = 1.25$ in year 1, and this relative price is $\frac{\$1.25}{\$1.60} = 0.78$ in year 2. Therefore, apples became cheaper relative to oranges from year 1 to year 2. If relative prices had remained the same between year 1 and year 2, then the choice of the base year would not matter. In calculating real GDP, the problem of changing relative prices would not be too great in calculating GDP close to the base year (say, 2011 or 2010 relative to a base year in 2009), because relative prices would typically not change much over a short period of time. Over many years, however, the problem could be severe, for example, in calculating real GDP in 2011 relative to a base year in 1982. The solution to this problem, adopted in the NIPA, is to use a **chain-weighting** scheme for calculating real GDP.

With the chain-weighting approach, a "Fisher index" is used, and the approach is essentially like using a rolling base period. The chain-weighted ratio of real GDP in year 2 to real GDP in year 1 is

$$g_c = \sqrt{g_1 \times g_2} = \sqrt{1.354 \times 1.312} = 1.333,$$

so that the chain-weighted ratio of real GDP in the two years is a geometric average of the ratios calculated using each of years 1 and 2 as base years.[2] In the example, we calculate the percentage growth rate in real GDP from year 1 to year 2 using the chain-weighting method to be $(1.333 - 1) \times 100\% = 33.3\%$. The growth rate in this case

---

[2]For more detail on the calculation of real GDP using the chain-weighting method, see *A Guide to the NIPA's*, available from the Bureau of Economic Analysis at http://www.bea.doc.gov/bea/an/nipaguid.htm.

falls between the growth rates we calculated using the other two approaches, which is of course what we should get given that chain-weighting effectively averages (geometrically) the growth rates calculated using years 1 and 2 as base years.

Once we have the chain-weighted ratio of real GDP in one year relative to another (g_c in this case), we can calculate real GDP in terms of the dollars of any year we choose. For example, in our example, if we want real GDP in year 1 dollars, then real GDP in year 1 is the same as nominal GDP or $GDP_1 = \$130$, and real GDP in year 2 is equal to $GDP_1 \times g_c = \$130 \times 1.333 = \$173.29$. Alternatively, if we want real GDP in year 2 dollars, then real GDP in year 2 is $GDP_2 = \$292$, and real GDP in year 1 is $\frac{GDP_2}{g_c} = \frac{\$292}{1.333} = \$219.05$.

In practice, the growth rates in real GDP in adjacent years are calculated just as we have done it here, and then real GDP is "chained" together from one year to the next. Chain-weighting should in principle give a more accurate measure of the year-to-year, or quarter-to-quarter, changes in real GDP. In Figure 2.1 we show nominal GDP and real GDP, calculated using the chain-weighting approach, for the United States over the period 1947–2015. Real GDP is measured here in 2009 dollars, so that real GDP is equal to nominal GDP in 2009. Because the inflation rate was generally positive over the period 1947–2015, and was particularly high in the 1970s, real GDP grows in Figure 2.1 at a lower rate than does nominal GDP.

Measures of the Price Level

There are two commonly used measures of the price level. The first is the **implicit GDP price deflator**, and the second is the **consumer price index (CPI)**. The implicit GDP price deflator is measured as

$$\text{Implicit GDP price deflator} = \frac{\text{Nominal GDP}}{\text{Real GDP}} \times 100.$$

Here, multiplying by 100 just normalizes the price deflator to 100 in the year we are choosing nominal GDP to be equal to real GDP. For the example above, the price deflator we calculate would depend on whether we use year 1 or year 2 as a base year, or compute chain-weighted real GDP. We give the results in Table 2.11, and arbitrarily choose chain-weighted real GDP to be in year 1 dollars. Note in Table 2.11 that the answers we get for the percentage rate of inflation between year 1 and year 2 depend critically on how we measure real GDP.

The alternative measure of the price level, the CPI, is not as broadly based as the implicit GDP price deflator, because it includes only goods and services that are purchased by consumers. Further, the CPI is a fixed-weight price index, which takes the quantities in some base year as being the typical goods bought by the average consumer during that base year, and then uses those quantities as weights to calculate the index in each year. Thus, the CPI in the current year would be

$$\text{Current year CPI} = \frac{\text{Cost of base year quantities at current prices}}{\text{Cost of base year quantities at base year prices}} \times 100.$$

Figure 2.1 Nominal GDP (black line) and Chain-Weighted Real GDP (colored line) for the Period 1947–2015

Note that the two time series cross in 2009 because real GDP is measured in year 2009 dollars. The growth rate in real GDP is smaller than the growth rate for nominal GDP because of positive inflation over this period.

Source: Data from U.S. Department of Commerce, Bureau of Economic Analysis, © Stephen D. Williamson.

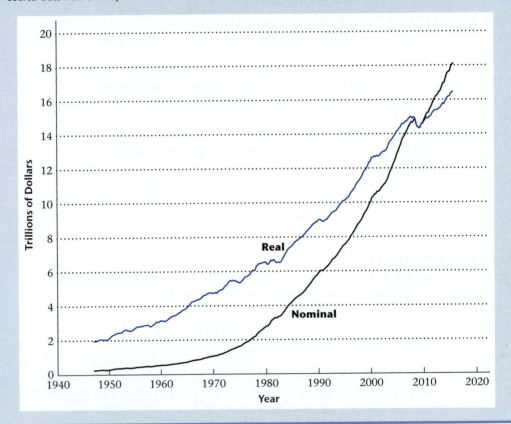

Table 2.11 Implicit GDP Price Deflators, Example

	Year 1	Year 2	%Increase
Year 1 = base year	100	165.9	65.9
Year 2 = base year	58.4	100	71.2
Chain-weighting	100	168.5	68.5

In the example, if we take year 1 as the base year, then the year 1 (base year) CPI is 100, and the year 2 CPI is $\frac{222.5}{130} \times 100 = 171.2$, so that the percentage increase in the CPI from year 1 to year 2 is 71.2%.

In practice, there can be substantial differences between the inflation rates calculated using the implicit GDP price deflator and those calculated using the CPI. Figure 2.2 shows the GDP deflator inflation rate (the black line) and CPI inflation rate (the blue line), calculated quarter by quarter, for the United States over the period 1948–2015. The two measures of the inflation rate track each other broadly, but the CPI inflation rate tends to be more volatile than the GDP deflator inflation rate. At times, there can be large differences between the two measures. For example, in late 1979, the CPI inflation rate exceeded 14%, while the GDP deflator inflation rate was about a bit more than 10%. These differences in inflation rate measures could matter greatly for contracts (e.g., labor contracts) that are indexed to the inflation rate or for the guidance of monetary policy, where close attention is paid to inflation performance.

Figure 2.2 shows the differences we can observe in measured inflation rates, depending on whether we use the CPI or the implicit GDP price deflator as a measure of the price level. As well, over long periods of time there can be very large differences in the rates of inflation calculated using the two alternative price level measures. To see this, in Figure 2.3 we show the CPI and GDP price deflator in levels for the period

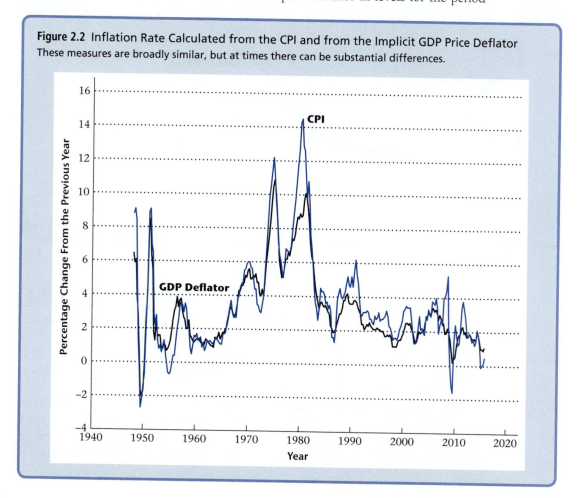

Figure 2.2 Inflation Rate Calculated from the CPI and from the Implicit GDP Price Deflator
These measures are broadly similar, but at times there can be substantial differences.

Figure 2.3 The Price Level as Measured by the CPI and the Implicit GDP Price Deflator, 1947–2015
In the figure, each price level measure is set to 100 in the first quarter of 1947. The CPI increases by a factor of 10.97 over the whole period, while the implicit GDP price deflator increases by a factor of 8.77.
Source: Data from The U.S. Department of Commerce and the Bureau of Labor Statistics, © Stephen D. Williamson.

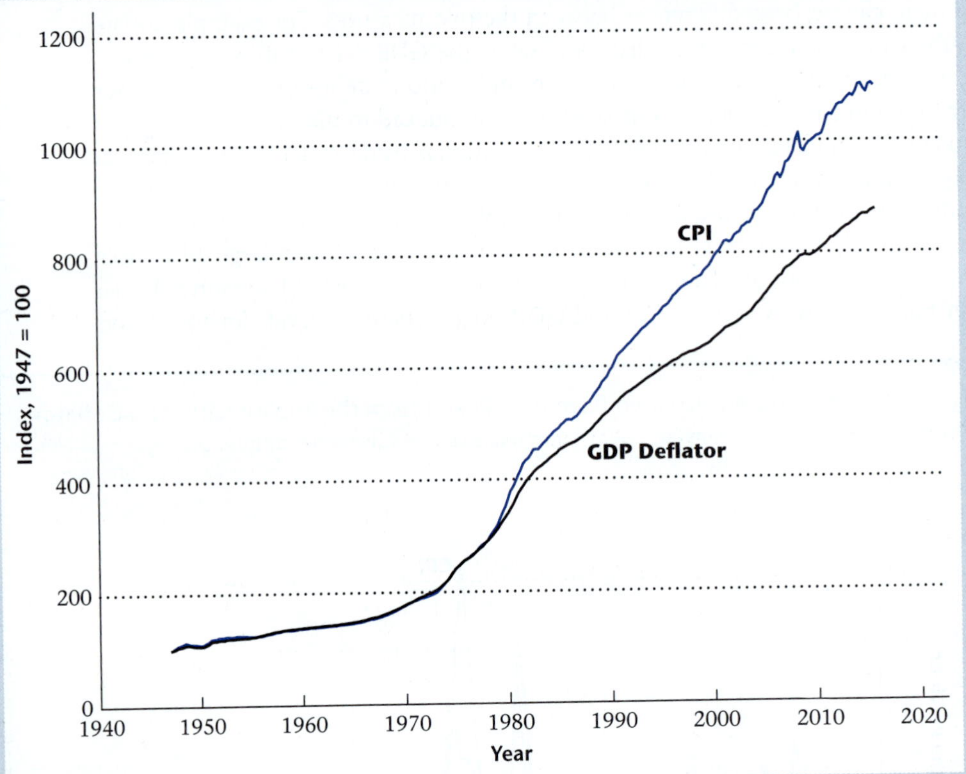

1947–2015, normalizing by setting each measure equal to 100 in the first quarter of 1947. What the picture tells us is that, if we accept the CPI as a good measure of the price level, then the cost of living increased by a factor of 10.97 over 69 years. However, the GDP price deflator indicates an increase in the cost of living by a factor of only 8.77. Put another way, the average annual inflation rate between 1947 and 2015 was 3.55% as measured by the CPI, and 3.21% as measured by the implicit GDP price deflator. These differences reflect a well-known upward bias in the CPI measure of inflation.

The GDP price deflator tends to yield a better measure of the inflation rate than does the CPI. However, in some cases there are alternatives to either the GDP price deflator or the CPI, which serve the purpose better. For example, if we are interested only in measuring the cost of living for consumers living in the United States, then it may be preferable to use the implicit consumption deflator rather than the implicit GDP price deflator as a measure of the price level. The implicit consumption deflator is a price index including only the goods and services that are included in consumption expenditures. The GDP price deflator includes the prices of investment goods, exports, and goods and services sold to the government, none of which would matter directly for consumers. However, if we are looking for a price index reflecting the price of aggregate output produced in the United States, then the GDP price deflator is the appropriate measure.

Problems with Measuring Real GDP and the Price Level

LO 2.4 State the key difficulties in measuring GDP and the price level.

As we saw above, particularly in how the implicit GDP price deflator is derived, the measurement of real GDP and the measurement of the price level are intimately related. If a particular measure of real GDP underestimates growth in real GDP, then the rate of inflation is overestimated. In practice, there are three important problems with measuring real GDP and the price level.

The first problem was mentioned above, which is that relative prices change over time. We showed how chain-weighting corrects for this problem in the measurement of real GDP and, therefore, corrects for the bias that relative price changes would introduce in the measurement of inflation using the implicit GDP price deflator. Changes in relative prices can also introduce severe bias in how the CPI measures inflation. When there is a relative price change, consumers typically purchase less of the goods that have become more expensive and more of those that have become relatively cheap. In the previous example, apples became cheaper relative to oranges in year 2, and the ratio of apples consumed to oranges consumed increased. In computing the CPI, the implicit assumption is that consumers do not change their buying habits when relative price changes occur, which is clearly false. As a result, goods that become relatively more expensive receive a higher weight than they should in the CPI, and, therefore, the CPI-based measure of the rate of inflation is biased upward. This is a serious policy issue because some federal transfer payments, including Social Security, are indexed to the CPI, and, therefore, an upward bias in CPI inflation would also commit the federal government to higher transfer payments, which in turn would increase the size of the federal government budget deficit. Also, federal income tax brackets are geared to CPI inflation. Upward bias in CPI inflation causes tax revenues to fall, increasing the government deficit. Rather than the rate of increase in the CPI, a more accurate measure of the rate of inflation in consumer goods is the implicit consumption price deflator, which is the price deflator associated with chain-weighted real consumption expenditures.

A second problem in measuring real GDP is changes in the quality of goods over time. Consider the case of 2015 vintage cars versus 1950 vintage cars. Clearly, the price of a new car in 2015 was much higher than the price of a new car in 1950, but the 2015 car is very different from the 1950 car. In 2015, most cars sold in the United States had computerized devices to monitor engine performance, automatic transmissions, power

MACROECONOMICS IN ACTION

Comparing Real GDP Across Countries and the Penn Effect

Just as it is useful to obtain a measure of real GDP for a given country so that we can study the growth of output over time in that country, it is also important to be able to make comparisons between real GDPs, or GDPs per person, in different countries. For example, if we can compare real GDP across all countries in the world, we can potentially learn the reasons for differences in the standard of living across countries. This is one of the issues that will concern us when we study economic growth, particularly in Chapter 8.

Coming up with comparable measures of GDP is potentially a daunting task. First, though international organizations have worked to standardize the NIPA across countries, there can still be significant differences in how key data are collected in different countries. For example, poor countries may have limited resources available to devote to data collection. However, even if the prices and quantities of final goods and services were measured without error in all countries, there would still be a problem in making international real GDP comparisons. This is because the prices of identical goods sold in different countries are typically significantly different, even after we express prices in units of the same currency.

To understand the measurement problem, suppose that P denotes the price of goods and services in the United States (in U.S. dollars), and P^* is the price of goods and services in Mexico (in Mexican pesos). Also, suppose that e is the exchange rate of U.S. dollars for Mexican pesos, that is, e is the price of a peso in dollars. Then, eP^* would be the cost of Mexican goods and

services for an American, or the price in dollars of Mexican goods and services. If we observed that $P = eP^*$, then we would say that we observed the *law of one price* or *purchasing power parity*, in that prices of goods and services would be the same in the United States and Mexico, correcting for exchange rates. In fact, what we tend to observe is that $P > eP^*$ for the United States and Mexico; that is, goods and services prices in U.S. dollars tend to be higher in the U.S. than in Mexico. This difference is particularly large for services, such as auto repairs, which are difficult to trade across international borders.

The *Penn effect* refers to the regularity in data on prices and exchange rates across countries, that prices tend to be higher, correcting for currency exchange rates, in high-income countries than in low-income countries. The problem is that, if we made real GDP comparisons across countries by just expressing all prices in the same currencies, then we would exaggerate the differences in income between rich and poor countries. For example, for the United States and Mexico, if the same quantity of a given good were produced in each country, we would tend to measure this as a smaller contribution to real GDP in Mexico than in the United States if we expressed the quantity produced in terms of its value in U.S. dollars.

An approach to correcting for the Penn effect is to make international real GDP comparisons based on purchasing power parity. For example, for the United States and Mexico, if P is the U.S. price level (in U.S. dollars), and P^* is the Mexican price level (in Mexican pesos), then to compare GDP in the United States with GDP in Mexico, we would multiply nominal quantities for Mexico by P/P^* rather than by e. This is the approach taken in the *Penn World Tables*, a comprehensive set of international data developed by Alan Heston, Robert Summers, and Bettina Aten at the University of Pennsylvania.[3] We will make

use of the Penn World Tables when we study economic growth in Chapters 7 and 8.

---

[3]Alan Heston, Robert Summers, and Bettina Aten, Penn World Table Version 6.2, Center for International Comparisons of Production, Income, and Prices at the University of Pennsylvania, September 2006.

windows, air bags, seat belts, and various features to connect with portable electronic devices, none of which were standard equipment (or in some cases even invented) in 1950. In a sense, the 2015 car is "more car," because its quality is higher; therefore, some of the increase in price from 1950 to 2015 simply represents the fact that the buyer is receiving more in exchange for his or her money. To the extent that NIPA does not compensate for changes in quality over time, growth in real GDP is biased downward and inflation is biased upward.

A third problem is how measured GDP takes account of new goods. For example, personal computers and cell phones were introduced in the 1990s, and they did not exist in the NIPA before then. Further, in the last 20 years, cell phones have been integrated with what are essentially hand-held portable computers ("smartphones"). Clearly, we cannot make a straightforward calculation of real GDP growth from the 1980s to the 2010s, as there were no prices existing for smartphones in the 1980s. If the NIPA does not correctly take account of the fact that the new smartphones introduced (initially at very high prices) were a huge quality advance over phone booths, personal desktop computers, and face-to-face communication, then this could bias downward the measure of real GDP growth and bias upward the measure of the inflation rate.

MACROECONOMICS IN ACTION

House Prices and GDP Measurement

A key feature of the financial market crisis that began in the United States in 2008, and spread worldwide, was the dramatic fall in the price of housing in the United States. Figure 2.4 shows the relative price of housing in the United States, measured as the Case-Shiller 20-city house price index, divided by the consumer price index. This relative price is normalized to be equal to 100 in 2000. From 2000 to 2006, there was an extremely large increase in the relative price of

housing—about 70% over six years. This rapid increase in the relative price of housing can be attributed to the high demand for housing generated by innovations in the mortgage market. During this period, there was a dramatic increase in the quantity of mortgage loans made in the so-called "subprime" mortgage market. Subprime mortgages are mortgage loans granted to typically low-income borrowers with a higher-than-average risk of default. Some of these subprime

(Continued)

Figure 2.4 The Relative Price of Housing in the United States

The figure shows the relative price of housing, measured as the price of housing in dollars divided by the consumer price index. Of particular note is the sharp decline beginning in 2006.

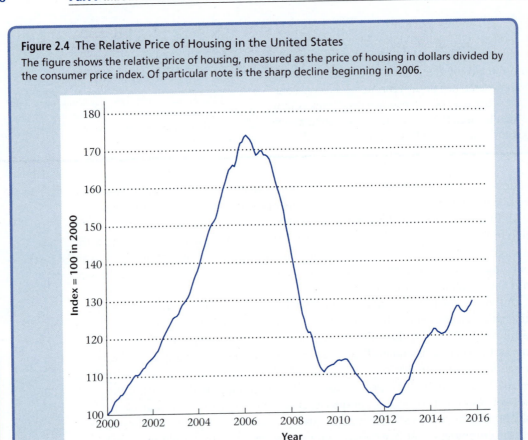

mortgages were made with little screening of borrowers, and with very generous terms (at least in the short run), including low interest rates and low down payments.

An unforseen development was the dramatic decrease in the relative price of housing beginning in 2006. In the figure, from the peak in the relative price of housing until early 2012, the relative price of housing fell about 40%. Exactly why the price of housing decreased over this latter period in the figure is a subject of some debate among economists. Some economists argue that the rapid increase in the price of housing up to 2006 was an asset price "bubble." According to proponents of what we could call the *bubble view*, leading up to 2006

the price of housing became detached from its fundamental economic determinants—incomes, the prices of other goods and services, interest rates, construction costs, scarcity of land—and was propelled by speculation that prices would continue to increase. According to the bubble view, bubbles inevitably pop, which is consistent with the large decrease in house prices beginning in 2006. Alternatively, according to the *fundamental view*, market prices of assets can always be explained (maybe through some hard thinking and research) by factors affecting supply and demand, in this case the supply and demand for housing. A potential explanation for the 2006–2012 decrease in the price of housing is that housing market participants came to realize that much of the subprime mortgage lending that had occurred was to borrowers that could really not afford to live in the houses that they had acquired. Subprime borrowers began to default on their loans and vacate their houses, and new subprime lending was cut off. All this served to reduce the demand for housing and lower the price of houses.

Whether the bubble view or the fundamental view is correct, there is a case to be made that the price of housing in 2015 more correctly reflects the value of housing to residents of the United States than did the price of housing at the peak of the housing boom in 2006. What implications does this have for the measurement of GDP? In 2006, real GDP was 14,613.8 billion (2009) dollars, while real residential construction was

806.6 billion (2009) dollars.[4] Thus, residential construction accounted for about 5.5% of GDP. When residential construction is measured, the output of new housing is measured at the prices at which the houses sell. Thus, if the relative price of housing had been 40% lower in 2006, residential construction would have been 40% lower, or 484.0 billion (2009) dollars instead of 806.6 billion (2009) dollars. This amounts to a reduction in real GDP of 2.2%, which is a significant quantity. Potentially, this is a mismeasurement in GDP comparable to the reduction in real GDP experienced in a moderate recession.

---

[4]*Source:* Department of Commerce, Bureau of Economic Analysis.

Savings, Wealth, and Capital

LO 2.5 State the accounting relationships among savings and income in the private and public sectors, and explain the importance of these relationships for wealth accumulation.

While the components of GDP in the NIPA measure aggregate activity that takes place within the current period, another key aspect of the economy that is of interest to macroeconomists is aggregate productive capacity, and how aggregate savings adds to this productive capacity. In this section we explore, by way of several accounting identities, the relationships among savings, wealth, and capital.

An important distinction in economics is between **flows** and **stocks**. A flow is a rate per unit time, while a stock is the quantity in existence of some object at a point in time. In the NIPA, GDP, consumption, investment, government spending, and net exports are all flows. For example, GDP is measured in dollars spent per period. In contrast, the quantity of housing in existence in the United States at the end of a given year is a stock. In the following, we see that national saving is a flow, while the nation's wealth is a stock. In this case, national saving is the flow that is added to the stock of the nation's wealth in each year. A classic analogy is the example of water flowing into a bathtub, where the quantity of water coming out of the faucet per minute is a flow, while the quantity of water in the bathtub at any point in time is a stock.

Savings can mean very different things, depending on whether we are referring to the private (nongovernment) sector, the government, or the nation as a whole. For the private sector, to determine savings we first need to start with what the private sector has available to spend, which is **private disposable income**, denoted Y^d. We have

$$Y^d = Y + NFP + TR + INT - T,$$

where Y is GDP, NFP is net factor payments from abroad to U.S. residents, TR is transfers from the government to the private sector, INT is interest on the government debt, and T is taxes. Recall that GNP is $Y + NFP$. What the private sector saves is simply what it has available to spend minus what it consumes, and so letting S^p denote **private sector saving**, we have

$$S^p = Y^d - C = Y + NFP + TR + INT - T - C.$$

What the government has available to spend is its tax revenue, T, minus TR, minus INT, and what it consumes is government expenditures, G. Thus, **government saving** S^g is given by

$$S^g = T - TR - INT - G.$$

Government saving is simply the **government surplus**, and the government surplus is the negative of the **government deficit**, denoted D, or

$$D = -S^g = -T + TR + INT + G,$$

which is just government outlays minus government receipts. If we add private saving and government saving, we obtain **national saving**,

$$S = S^p + S^g = Y + NFP - C - G,$$

which is GNP minus private consumption, minus government consumption. Because the income–expenditure identity gives $Y = C + I + G + NX$, we can substitute for Y in the previous equation to obtain

$$S = Y + NFP - C - G$$
$$= C + I + G + NX + NFP - C - G$$
$$= I + NX + NFP.$$

Thus, national saving must equal investment plus net exports plus net factor payments from abroad. The quantity $NX + NFP$ is the **current account surplus** with the rest of the world, which we denote CA; thus, we have

$$S = I + CA.$$

The current account surplus is a measure of the balance of trade in goods with the rest of the world. The above identity reflects the fact that any domestic savings not absorbed by domestic investment must be shipped outside the country in the form of goods and services.

As a flow, national saving represents additions to the nation's wealth. Because $S = I + CA$, wealth is accumulated in two ways. First, wealth is accumulated through investment, I, which is additions to the nation's **capital stock**. The capital stock is the quantity of plants, equipment, housing, and inventories in existence in an economy at a point in time. Second, wealth is accumulated through current account surpluses, CA, because a current account surplus implies that U.S. residents are accumulating claims on foreigners. The current account surplus, CA, represents increases in claims on foreigners because if goods are flowing from the United States to other countries, then these goods must be paid for with a transfer of wealth from outside the United States to U.S. residents. The current account surplus is then a flow, while the quantity of claims on foreigners in existence in the United States is a stock.

Labor Market Measurement

LO 2.6 Construct the key labor market measures from the household survey data.

The labor market variables we focus on here are those measured in the monthly house-hold survey, carried out by the Bureau of Labor Statistics. In this survey, people are divided into three groups: the **employed**—those who worked part-time or full-time during the past week; the **unemployed**—those who were not employed during the past week but actively searched for work at some time during the last four weeks; and **not in the labor force**—those who are neither employed or unemployed. Thus, the labor force is the employed plus the unemployed.

Of key interest in analyzing the results of the household survey are the **unemployment rate**, measured as

$$\text{Unemployment rate} = \frac{\text{Number unemployed}}{\text{Labor force}},$$

the **participation rate**, measured as

$$\text{Participation rate} = \frac{\text{Labor force}}{\text{Total working=age population}},$$

and the **employment/population ratio**, measured as

$$\text{Employment/Population ratio} = \frac{\text{Total employment}}{\text{Total working=age population}}.$$

The unemployment rate is a useful economic measure for at least two reasons. First, it helps determine the level of **labor market tightness**, which captures the degree of difficulty firms face in hiring workers, and the ease with which would-be workers can find a job. Labor market tightness falls as the unemployment rate increases, everything else held constant, as a higher unemployment rate tends to make it easier for a firm to recruit workers, and reflects greater difficulty for a would-be worker in finding a job.[5] Second, the unemployment rate can be used as an indirect measure of economic welfare. While GDP per capita is a reasonable measure of aggregate economic welfare for a nation, the unemployment rate gives us some information on the distribution of income across the population. In spite of the existence of unemployment insurance programs in many countries, unemployment is not perfectly insured, and so income tends to be low for the unemployed. A higher unemployment rate then tends to be associated with greater dispersion in incomes across the population—there is a higher concentration of poor people.

The unemployment rate may have some weakness as a measure of labor market tightness because it does not adjust for how intensively the unemployed are searching for work. When the unemployment rate is high, the unemployed might not search very

---

[5]Another measure of labor market tightness is the number of unemployed divided by the number of job vacancies, where vacancies are the number of job openings in the economy that firms are trying to fill. Unfortunately, the measures that exist of vacanies in the U.S. economy are notoriously poor, at least going back more than a few years from the present.

hard for work—for example, each worker might spend one or two hours per day trying to find work. When the unemployment rate is low, however, the unemployed might all be searching very hard—for example, they might each search eight or ten hours per day. If this were the case, then the unemployment rate would be a biased measure of labor market tightness, since it could actually be harder for a firm to hire a worker in a recession, and easier for a firm to hire a worker during a boom in economic activity, than what the unemployment rate reflects on its own. Though there are more people looking for work in a recession, each of the unemployed might be searching little, and so it could be more difficult to hire a worker, if a firm wants one.

MACROECONOMICS IN ACTION

Alternative Measures of the Unemployment Rate

Figure 2.5 displays three alternative measures of the unemployment rate published by the Bureau of Labor Statistics (BLS). In the figure, U3 is the standard measure of the unemployment rate—the number of working-age people who are actively searching for work as a percentage of the total labor force. The time series U4 adds the number of discouraged workers to both the number of unemployed, and to the labor. A discouraged worker in the Current Population Survey (CPS) carried out monthly by the BLS is a working-age person who is neither employed nor unemployed, but is available to work, looked for work sometime during the previous 12 months, and has a job-market-related reason for not searching for work. Finally, the time series U5 adds marginally attached working-age persons to both the number of unemployed and the labor force to calculate the unemployment rate. The marginally attached are working-age persons who are neither employed nor unemployed, available to work, and looked for work sometime during the previous 12 months. All discouraged workers are marginally attached, but a person could be marginally attached and not discouraged. For example, a person would be classified as discouraged if he or she had been searching

for work, but had stopped searching because of a lack of appropriate job openings. However, a person who is not searching, available to work, and putting zero effort into job search for no apparent reason, would be classified as marginally attached but not discouraged.

Figure 2.5 shows that the three alternative unemployment rate measures—U3, U4, and U5—move together closely over time. Thus, each measure captures changes in labor market conditions in much the same way. An interesting feauture of Figure 2.5 is that the gaps between U3 and U4, and between U3 and U5, rose after the beginning of the most recent recession in late 2007. For example, the measures of U3, U4, and U5 in January 2000 were 4.0%, 4.2%, and 4.8%, respectively. In April 2012, these measures were 8.1%, 8.7%, and 9.5%, respectively. Thus, in January 2000, discouraged workers accounted for 0.2 percentage points in U4, and marginally attached workers accounted for 0.8 percentage points in U5. However, in April 2012, these numbers had increased to 0.6 percentage points and 1.4 percentage points, respectively. Thus, discouraged and marginally attached workers became much more important during the recession that ran from late 2007 to mid-2009.

Figure 2.5 Alternative Measures of the Unemployment Rate

In the figure, U3 denotes the conventional unemployment rate, U4 includes discouraged workers, and U5 includes all marginally attached workers. The differences between U4 and U3, and between U5 and U3, increase during the last recession, which began at the end of 2007.

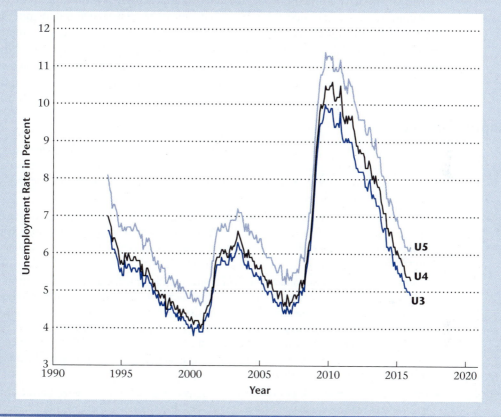

The unemployment rate may also be biased in terms of how it reflects economic welfare. In particular, the standard measure of the unemployment rate does not include the **marginally attached**—would-be workers who are not actively searching, but who would accept a job if offered one. During times of high unemployment, the marginally attached might be a large group. The Bureau of Labor Statistics in fact collects data on the marginally attached, among other groups of people who are members of the labor force but who are not counted in conventional measures of unemployment. The box "Macroeconomics in Action: Alternative Measures of the Unemployment Rate" contains a discussion of how alternative measures of unemployment can correct for some potential measurement problems, and how the alternative unemployment meaures can be used.

Partly because of problems in interpreting what movements in the unemployment rate mean, macroeconomists often focus attention on the level and growth rate of employment when they analyze the implications of labor market activity. Empirically, sometimes we have a greater interest in the behavior of the participation rate or the employment/population ratio than in the unemployment rate. Theoretically, many of the models we analyze in this book do not explain the behavior of unemployment, but we analyze the unemployment rate and its determinants in detail in Chapter 6.

So far, we have learned how aggregate economic activity is measured in the NIPA, how nominal GDP can be decomposed to obtain measures of real GDP and the price level, what the relationships are among savings, wealth, and capital, and what the key measurement issues in the labor market are. Before we begin our study of macroeconomic theory in Chapter 4, in Chapter 3 we deal with business cycle measurement, deriving a set of key business cycle facts that focus our theoretical discussion in the following chapters.

Chapter Summary

- Gross domestic product (GDP) is measured in the National Income and Product Accounts (NIPA) of the United States. GDP can be measured via the product approach, the expenditure approach, or the income approach, which each yield the same quantity of GDP in a given period if there is no measurement error.

- GDP must be used carefully as a measure of aggregate welfare, because it leaves out home production. Further, there are problems with GDP as a measure of aggregate output, because of the existence of the underground economy and because government output is difficult to measure.

- It is useful to take account of how much of nominal GDP growth is accounted for by inflation and how much is growth in real GDP. Two approaches to measuring real GDP are choosing a base year and chain-weighting. The latter is the current method used in the NIPA. Chain-weighting corrects for the bias that arises in real GDP calculations when a base year is used and there are changes in relative prices over time. Problems with real GDP measurement arise because it is difficult to account for changes in the quality of goods over time and because new goods are introduced and others become obsolete.

- Private saving is private disposable income minus consumption, while government saving is government receipts minus government spending and transfers. The government surplus is equal to government saving. National saving is the sum of private and government saving and is equal to investment expenditures plus the current account surplus. National saving is just the accumulation of national wealth, which comes in the form of additions to the capital stock (investment) and additions to domestic claims on foreigners (the current account surplus).

- The labor market variables we focus on are those measured in the household survey of the Bureau of Labor Statistics. The working-age population consists of the employed, the unemployed (those searching for work), and those not in the labor force. Three key labor market variables are the unemployment rate, the participation rate, and the employment/population ratio. The unemployment rate is sometimes used as a measure of labor market tightness, but care must be taken in how the unemployment rate is interpreted in this respect.

Key Terms

Gross domestic product (GDP) The dollar value of final output produced during a given period of time within a country's borders. (p. 39)

National Income and Product Accounts (NIPA) The official U.S. accounts of aggregate economic activity, which include GDP measurements. (p. 39)

Product approach The approach to GDP measurement that determines GDP as the sum of value added to goods and services in production across all productive units in the economy. (p. 39)

Expenditure approach The approach to GDP measurement that determines GDP as total spending on all final goods and services production in the economy. (p. 39)

Income approach The approach to GDP measurement that determines GDP as the sum of all incomes received by economic agents contributing to production. (p. 39)

Intermediate good A good that is produced and then used as an input in another production process. (p. 40)

Value added The value of goods produced minus the value of intermediate goods used in production. (p. 41)

Income–expenditure identity $Y = C + I + G + NX$, where Y is aggregate income (output), C is consumption expenditures, I is investment expenditures, G is government expenditures, and NX is net exports. (p. 43)

Gross national product (GNP) $GNP = GDP$ plus net factor payments to U.S. residents from abroad. (p. 44)

Underground economy All unreported economic activity. (p. 45)

Consumption Goods and services produced and consumed during the current period. (p. 46)

Investment Goods produced in the current period but not consumed in the current period. (p. 46)

Fixed investment Investment in plant, equipment, and housing. (p. 46)

Inventory investment Goods produced in the current period that are set aside for future periods. (p. 46)

Net exports Expenditures on domestically produced goods and services by foreigners (exports) minus expenditures on foreign-produced goods and services by domestic residents (imports). (p. 47)

Government expenditures Expenditures by federal, state, and local governments on final goods and services. (p. 47)

Transfers Government outlays that are transfers of purchasing power from one group of private economic agents to another. (p. 48)

Price index A weighted average of prices of some set of goods produced in the economy during a particular period. (p. 48)

Price level The average level of prices across all goods and services in the economy. (p. 48)

Inflation rate The rate of change in the price level from one period to another. (p. 48)

Nominal change The change in the dollar value of a good, service, or asset. (p. 48)

Real change The change in the quantity of a good, service, or asset. (p. 48)

Chain-weighting An approach to calculating real GDP that uses a rolling base year. (p. 50)

Implicit GDP price deflator Nominal GDP divided by real GDP, all multiplied by 100. (p. 51)

Consumer price index (CPI) Expenditures on base year quantities at current year prices divided by total expenditures on base year quantities at base year prices, all multiplied by 100. (p. 51)

Flow A rate per unit time. (p. 59)

Stock Quantity in existence of some object at a point in time. (p. 59)

Private disposable income GDP plus net factor payments, plus transfers from the government, plus interest on the government debt, minus taxes. (p. 59)

Private sector saving Private disposable income minus consumption expenditures. (p. 60)

Government saving Taxes minus transfers, minus interest on the government debt, minus government expenditures. (p. 60)

Government surplus Identical to government saving. (p. 60)

Government deficit The negative of the government surplus. (p. 60)

National saving Private sector saving plus government saving. (p. 60)

Current account surplus Net exports plus net factor payments from abroad. (p. 60)

Capital stock The quantity of plant, equipment, housing, and inventories in existence in an economy at a point in time. (p. 60)

Employed In the Bureau of Labor Statistics household survey, those who worked part-time or full-time during the past week. (p. 61)

Unemployed In the Bureau of Labor Statistics household survey, those who were not employed during the past week but actively searched for work at some time during the last four weeks. (p. 61)

Not in the labor force In the Bureau of Labor Statistics household survey, those who are neither employed nor unemployed. (p. 61)

Unemployment rate The number of unemployed divided by the number in the labor force. (p. 61)

Participation rate The number in the labor force divided by the working-age population. (p. 61)

Employment/population ratio The ratio of total employment to total working-age population. (p. 61)

Labor market tightness Reflects the degree of difficulty firms face in hiring workers, and the ease with which a would-be worker can find a job. (p. 61)

Marginally attached People of working age who are neither employed nor unemployed, but are available to work and have searched for work in the previous 12 months. (p. 63)

Questions for Review

2.1 What are the three approaches to measuring GDP?

2.2 Explain the concept of value added.

2.3 Why is the income–expenditure identity important?

2.4 What is the difference between GDP and GNP?

2.5 Is GDP a good measure of economic welfare? Why or why not?

2.6 What are two difficulties in the measurement of aggregate output using GDP?

2.7 What is the largest expenditure component of GDP?

2.8 What is investment?

2.9 Is national defense a large fraction of government spending?

2.10 Why does the base year matter in calculating real GDP?

2.11 Explain what chain-weighting is.

2.12 Explain three problems in the measurement of real GDP.

2.13 What are the differences and similarities among private sector saving, government saving, and national saving?

2.14 What are the two ways in which national wealth is accumulated?

2.15 Give two reasons that the unemployment rate may not measure correctly what we want it to measure.

Problems

1. **LO 1** Assume an economy where there are two producers: a wheat producer and a bread producer. In a given year, the wheat producer grows 30 million bushels of wheat of which 25 million bushels are sold to the bread producer at $3 per bushel, and 5 million bushels are stored by the wheat producer to use as seed for next year's crop. The bread producer produces and sells 100 million loaves of bread to consumers for $3.50 per loaf. Determine GDP in this economy during this year using the product and expenditure approaches.

2. **LO 1** Assume an economy with a coal producer, a steel producer, and some consumers (there is no government). In a given year, the coal producer produces 15 million tons of coal and sells it for $5 per ton. The coal producer pays $50 million in wages to consumers. The steel producer uses 25 million tons of coal as an input into steel production, all purchased at $5 per ton. Of this, 15

million tons of coal come from the domestic coal producer and 10 million tons are imported. The steel producer produces 10 million tons of steel and sells it for $20 per ton. Domestic consumers buy 8 million tons of steel, and 2 million tons are exported. The steel producer pays consumers $40 million in wages. All profits made by domestic producers are distributed to domestic consumers.

(a) Determine GDP using (i) the product approach, (ii) the expenditure approach, and (iii) the income approach.
(b) Determine the current account surplus.
(c) What is GNP in this economy? Determine GNP and GDP in the case where the coal producer is owned by foreigners, so that the profits of the domestic coal producer go to foreigners and are not distributed to domestic consumers.

3. **LO 1** Assume an economy with two firms. Firm A produces wheat and firm B produces bread. In a given year, firm A produces 50,000 bushels of wheat, sells 20,000 bushels to firm B at $3 per bushel, exports 25,000 bushels at $3 per bushel, and stores 5,000 bushels as inventory. Firm A pays $50,000 in wages to consumers. Firm B produces 50,000 loaves of bread, and sells all of it to domestic consumers at $2 per loaf. Firm B pays consumers $20,000 in wages. In addition to the 50,000 loaves of bread consumers buy from firm B, consumers import and consume 15,000 loaves of bread, and they pay $1 per loaf for this imported bread. Calculate gross domestic product for the year using (a) the product approach, (b) the expenditure approach, and (c) the income approach.

4. **LO 3** In year 1 and year 2, there are two products produced in a given economy, computers and bread. Suppose that there are no intermediate goods. In year 1, 20 computers are produced and sold at $1,000 each, and in year 2, 25 computers are sold at $1,500 each. In year 1, 10,000 loaves of bread are sold for $1.00 each, and in year 2, 12,000 loaves of bread are sold for $1.10 each.

(a) Calculate nominal GDP in each year.
(b) Calculate real GDP in each year, and the

percentage increase in real GDP from year 1 to year 2 using year 1 as the base year. Next, do the same calculations using the chain-weighting method.
(c) Calculate the implicit GDP price deflator and the percentage inflation rate from year 1 to year 2 using year 1 as the base year. Next, do the same calculations using the chain-weighting method.
(d) Suppose that computers in year 2 are twice as productive as computers in year 1. That is, computers are of higher quality in year 2 in the sense that one computer in year 2 is equivalent to two computers in year 1. How does this change your calculations in parts (a) to (c)? Explain any differences.

5. **LO 3** Assume an economy in which only broccoli and cauliflower are produced. In year 1, 500 million pounds of broccoli are produced and consumed and its price is $0.50 per pound, while 300 million pounds of cauliflower are produced and consumed and its price is $0.80 per pound. In year 2, 400 million pounds of broccoli are produced and consumed and its price is $0.60 per pound, while 350 million pounds of cauliflower are produced and its price is $0.85 per pound.

(a) Using year 1 as the base year, calculate the GDP price deflator in years 1 and 2, and calculate the rate of inflation between years 1 and 2 from the GDP price deflator.
(b) Using year 1 as the base year, calculate the CPI in years 1 and 2, and calculate the CPI rate of inflation. Explain any differences in your results between parts (a) and (b).

6. **LO 1,5** Consider an economy with a corn producer, some consumers, and a government. In a given year, the corn producer grows 30 million bushels of corn and the market price for corn is $5 per bushel. Of the 30 million bushels produced, 20 million are sold to consumers, 5 million are stored in inventory, and 5 million are sold to the government to feed the army. The corn producer pays $60 million in wages to consumers and $20 million in taxes to the government. Consumers pay $10 million in taxes to the government, receive $10 million in interest on

the government debt, and receive $5 million in Social Security payments from the government. The profits of the corn producer are distributed to consumers.

(a) Calculate GDP using (i) the product approach, (ii) the expenditure approach, and (iii) the income approach.
(b) Calculate private disposable income, private sector saving, government saving, national saving, and the government deficit. Is the government budget in deficit or surplus?

7. **LO 4** In some countries, price controls exist on some goods, which set maximum prices at which these goods can be sold. Indeed, the United States experienced a period of wage and price controls when the Nixon administration introduced wage and price controls in 1971. Sometimes the existence of price controls leads to the growth of black markets, where goods are exchanged at prices above the legal maximums. Carefully explain how price controls present a problem for measuring GDP and for measuring the price level and inflation.

8. **LO 4** In this chapter, we learned that the quantity of U.S. currency outstanding per U.S. resident was $4,390 in February 2016. Suppose that we were to try to use this number to estimate the amount of output produced in the underground economy in the United States during 2016. Discuss how we would use this information on the quantity of currency in circulation, and what additional information you would want to have to come up with a good estimate. In your answer, you will need to consider how underground transactions might take place by other means in the United States than through the use of U.S. currency, and how some of U.S. currency is not being used for underground transactions in the United States.

9. **LO 4** Part of gross domestic product consists of production in the so-called FIRE sector (finance, insurance, and real estate). Value added is notoriously difficult to measure in the FIRE sector, as it is hard to determine exactly what the inputs and outputs are. For example, banks are included in the FIRE sector, and we know that they contribute to our well-being by making borrowing and lending more efficient and by providing transac-

tions services. However, as most of the inputs and outputs associated with a bank are not actual physical quantities, it is much more difficult to measure value added in banking than in the production of apples, for example. During the decade 2000–2010, there were several high-profile financial scandals—incidents of individuals and institutions in the financial sector implicated in white-collar crime. Discuss the implications that such criminal financial activity has for the measurement of GDP.

10. **LO 4** In the United States, a large fraction of transactions among banks takes place over Fedwire, which is an electronic payments system operated by the Federal Reserve System.[6] In December 2015, the volume of funds transfers on Fedwire was about $72 trillion, which was more than four times annual GDP in 2015. Do these statistics indicate that there might be some large measurement error in the official U.S. national income accounts, or is this entirely consistent with official GDP numbers being accurate measures of aggregate economic activity? Explain, and discuss your answer.

11. **LO 5** Consider the identity

$$S^P - I = CA + D,$$

where S^P is private sector saving, I is investment, CA is the current account surplus, and D is the government deficit.

(a) Show that the above identity holds.
(b) Explain what the above identity means.

12. **LO 5** Let K_t denote the quantity of capital a country has at the beginning of period t. Also, suppose that capital depreciates at a constant rate d, so that dK_t of the capital stock wears out during period t. If investment during period t is denoted by I_t, and the country does not trade with the rest of the world (the current account surplus is always zero), then we can say that the quantity of capital at the beginning of period $t + 1$ is given by

$$K_{t+1} = (1 - d)K_t + I_t.$$

---

[6]See http://www.federalreserve.gov/paymentsystems/coreprinciples/default.htm

13. Suppose at the beginning of year 0 that this country has 80 units of capital. Investment expenditures are 10 units in each of years 0, 1, 2, 3, 4, . . . , 10. The capital stock depreciates by 10% per year.

    (a) Calculate the quantity of capital at the beginning of years 0, 1, 2, 3, 4, . . . , 10.
    (b) Repeat part (a), except assume now that the country begins year 0 with 100 units of capital. Explain what happens now, and discuss your results in parts (a) and (b).

14. **LO 5** Suppose that the government deficit is 10, interest on the government debt is 5, taxes are 40, government expenditures are 30, consumption expenditures are 80, net factor payments are 10, the current account surplus is −5, and national saving is 20. Calculate the following (not necessarily in the order given):

    (a) Private disposable income
    (b) Transfers from the government to the private sector
    (c) Gross national product
    (d) Gross domestic product
    (e) The government surplus
    (f) Net exports
    (g) Investment expenditures

15. **LO 6** Suppose that the unemployment rate is 5%, the total working-age population is 100 million, and the number of unemployed is 2.5 million. Determine (i) the participation rate; (ii) the labor force; (iii) the number of employed workers; and (iv) the employment/population ratio.

Working with the Data

Answer these questions using the Federal Reserve Bank of St. Louis's FRED database, accessible at http://research.stlouisfed.org/fred2/

1. Calculate consumption of durables, consumption of nondurables, and consumption of services as percentages of total consumption, and plot these time series. Comment on the changes that have taken place over time in the consumption of services relative to durables and nondurables.

2. There exists a debate among monetary policymakers as to the appropriate inflation measure that should be used to guide policies. Four alternatives are the consumer price index, the consumer price index excluding food and energy prices, the personal consumption expenditures chain-type price index (monthly), and the personal consumption expenditures chain-type price index excluding food and energy prices. Calculate 12-month percentage rates of increase in each of these measures from 2000 up to the present, compare, and discuss.

3. The unemployment rate measures only the fraction of the labor force searching for work. Sometimes economists are interested in the length of time that the unemployed have been out of work. One convenient summary measure is the median duration of unemployment. Plot this variable, and comment on how it has evolved over time, particularly during the last recession.

Chapter 3

Business Cycle Measurement

Learning Objectives

After studying Chapter 3, students will be able to:

3.1 State the key regularities in GDP fluctuations.

3.2 Explain the importance of comovement among economic time series.

3.3 State the key properties of comovements among the components of GDP.

3.4 Discuss why comovements between the price level and real GDP and between the inflation rate and real GDP are important to our understanding of business cycles.

3.5 State the key comovements among labor market variables and real GDP.

3.6 Explain the importance of seasonal adjustment.

3.7 State the key business cycle facts.

Before we go on to build models of aggregate economic activity that can explain why business cycles exist and what, if anything, should be done about them, we must understand the key features that we observe in economic data that define a business cycle. In this chapter, we move beyond the study of the measurement of gross domestic product (GDP), the price level, savings, and wealth, which we covered in Chapter 2, to an examination of the regularities in the relationships among aggregate economic variables as they fluctuate over time.

We show that business cycles are quite irregular, in that the changes in real GDP are unpredictable; macroeconomic forecasters often have difficulty predicting the timing of a business cycle upturn or downturn. Business cycles are quite regular, however, in terms of comovements, which is to say that macroeconomic variables move together in highly predictable ways. We focus separately on the components of real GDP, the price level and inflation, and labor market variables.

This chapter describes a set of key business cycle facts concerning comovements in U.S. macroeconomic data. In Chapters 4, 5, 11, and 12, we use these facts to show how our models can make sense of what we observe in the data. Then, in Chapters 13 and 14, we use the key business cycle facts to help us evaluate alternative theories of the business cycle.

Regularities in GDP Fluctuations

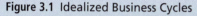

LO 3.1 State the key regularities in GDP fluctuations.

The primary defining feature of **business cycles** is that they are *fluctuations about trend in real GDP*. Recall from Chapter 1 that we represent the trend in real GDP with a smooth curve that closely fits actual real GDP, with the trend representing that part of real GDP that can be explained by long-run growth factors. What is left over, the deviations from trend, we take to represent business cycle activity.

In Figure 3.1 we show idealized business cycle activity in real GDP, with fluctuations about a long-run trend. In the figure, real GDP is represented by the black line,

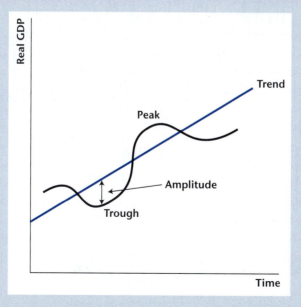

Figure 3.1 Idealized Business Cycles
The black curve is an idealized path for real GDP over time, while the colored line is the growth trend in real GDP. Real GDP cycles around the trend over time, with the maximum negative deviation from trend being a trough and the maximum positive deviation from trend being a peak. The amplitude is the size of the maximum deviation from trend, and the frequency is the number of peaks that occur within a year's time.

while the trend is represented by the colored line. There are **peaks** and **troughs** in real GDP, a peak being a relatively large positive deviation from trend, and a trough a relatively large negative deviation from trend. Peaks and troughs in the deviations from trend in real GDP are referred to as **turning points**. In a manner analogous to wave motion in the physical sciences, we can think of the maximum deviation from trend in Figure 3.1 as the **amplitude** of the business cycle, and the number of peaks in real GDP that occur per year as the **frequency** of the business cycle.

Next, in Figure 3.2 we show the actual percentage deviations from trend in real GDP for the United States over the period 1947–2015. A series of positive deviations from trend culminating in a peak represents a **boom**, whereas a series of negative deviations from trend culminating in a trough represents a **recession**. In Figure 3.2, we have marked five important recessions, occurring in 1973–1975, 1981–1982, 1990–1991, 2001, and 2008–2009. The first two of these recessions were quite

Figure 3.2 Percentage Deviations from Trend in Real GDP from 1947 to 2015

Of particular note are the five most recent recessions: in 1974–1975, 1981–1982, 1990–1991, 2001, and 2008–2009.

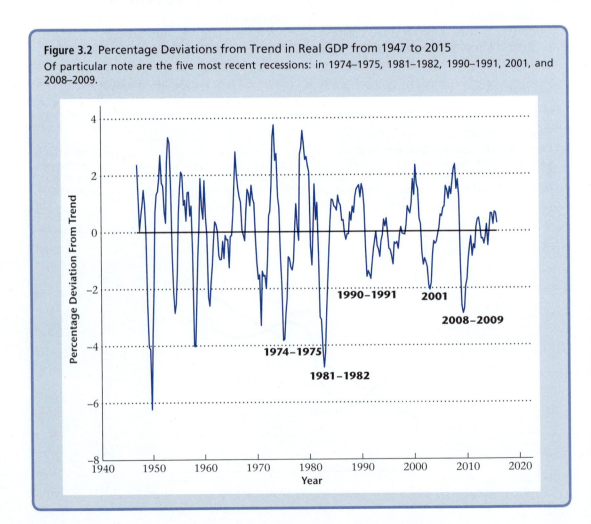

significant, with a deviation from trend in real GDP of 4% or more, whereas the middle two were relatively mild, with deviations from trend in the neighborhood of 2%. The most recent recession, in 2008–2009 was, measured by the percentage deviation from trend, relatively severe, but not as severe as the 1974–1974 or 1981–1982 recessions.[1]

An examination of Figure 3.2 indicates a striking regularity, which is that the deviations from trend in real GDP are **persistent**. That is, when real GDP is above trend, it tends to stay above trend, and when it is below trend, it tends to stay below trend. This feature is quite important in terms of economic forecasting over the short run; persistence implies that we can fairly confidently predict that if real GDP is currently below (above) trend, then it will be below (above) trend several months from now. Other than being persistent, however, the deviations from trend in real GDP are actually quite irregular. There are three other features to note in Figure 3.2:

1. The time series of deviations from trend in real GDP is quite choppy.
2. There is no regularity in the amplitude of fluctuations in real GDP about trend. Some of the peaks and troughs represent large deviations from trend, whereas other peaks and troughs represent small deviations from trend.
3. There is no regularity in the frequency of fluctuations in real GDP about trend. The length of time between peaks and troughs in real GDP varies considerably.

Though deviations from trend in real GDP are persistent, which makes short-term forecasting relatively easy, the above three features imply that longer-term forecasting is difficult. The choppiness of fluctuations in real GDP makes these fluctuations hard to predict, while the lack of regularity in the amplitude and frequency of fluctuations implies that it is difficult to predict the severity and length of recessions and booms. Therefore, predicting future fluctuations in real GDP by looking only at past real GDP is much like attempting to forecast the weather by looking out the window. If it is sunny today, it is likely that it will be sunny tomorrow (weather is persistent), but the fact that it is sunny today may give us very little information on whether it will be sunny one week from today.

Comovement

LO 3.2 Explain the importance of comovement among economic time series.

While real GDP fluctuates in irregular patterns, macroeconomic variables fluctuate together in patterns that exhibit strong regularities. We refer to these patterns in fluctuations as **comovement**. Robert Lucas once remarked that "with respect to

---

[1]The 2008–2009 recession was unusual in that the recovery—the period after the recession was over—was a period of relatively low growth in real GDP, particularly for a recovery period.

MACROECONOMICS IN ACTION

Economic Forecasting and the Financial Crisis

As was discussed in Chapter 1, each macroeconomic model is designed with a particular purpose in mind. First, we might want a model that will help us understand a particular economic phenomenon. For example, we might want to understand why economies grow over time. Second, we might be interested in making predictions about the effects of economic policies, such as the effects on real GDP and employment of a particular government tax proposal. For these types of problems—understanding economic phenomena and predicting the effects of economic policy—it is important to work with structural models. By "structural," we mean models that are built from basic microeconomic principles, and for which private behavioral relationships do not change when policymakers change their behavior. A structural model is said to be immune to the "Lucas critique."[2]

Predicting the effects of economic policies is quite different from macroeconomic forecasting, which involves predicting the course of future economic variables based on what we are observing today. Some economists have argued that economic theory is not a necessary input in a forecasting exercise. Christopher Sims, the winner (with Thomas Sargent) of the 2011 Nobel Prize in Economics is famous in part for inventing vector autoregression methodology, an atheoretical statistical approach to capturing the dynamics in economic time series.[3] This approach was used in the Bayesian vector autoregression (BVAR) models developed at the Federal Reserve Bank

of Minneapolis in the 1970s and 1980s. These BVAR models were used successfully in forecasting. Economic theory is not an input in setting up or running a BVAR model. All that is required is a knowledge of statistics and computation. A BVAR model captures the detail that we see in Figure 3.2 and more; part of what the BVAR will do is to forecast real GDP based on the historical behavior of real GDP—its persistence and variability for example. The BVAR will also take account of the historical relationships between real GDP and other economic variables in producing a forecast.

If we take the ideas of Christopher Sims seriously, the value of macroeconomic knowledge is not in producing forecasts, but in understanding macroeconomic phenomena and guiding macroeconomic policies. That is perhaps at odds with the views of lay people concerning what economists do. Just as meteorologists are expected to do a good job of predicting the weather, macroeconomists are expected to do a good job of predicting important macroeconomic events. Indeed, macroeconomists suffered some criticism after the global financial crisis for not warning of the crisis in advance. Is that criticism justified?

Sometimes economic theory tells us that forecasting is in fact futile. For example, basic theory tells us that the changes in stock prices from one day to the next cannot be forecast. If we knew that the price of a stock would be higher tomorrow than today, then we would buy that stock. As a result, today's market price for the stock would tend to rise (because of the increase in the demand for it), to the point where the

---

[2] See R. Lucas, 1976. "Econometric Policy Evalauation: A Critique," *Carnegie-Rochester Conference Volume on Public Policy* 1, 19–46.

[3] See C. Sims, 1980. "Macroeconomics and Reality," *Econometrica* 48, 1–48.

price of the stock today is the same as the price tomorrow. Similarly, the widely held view that a stock's price will be lower tomorrow than today will tend to force today's stock price down. What we should observe is that, at any point in time, the price of a given stock is the best forecast available of its price tomorrow. Economic theory thus tells us that the changes in stock prices from day to day cannot be forecast. This is sometimes called the "efficient markets hypothesis."

A similar idea applies to financial crises. A financial crisis involves severe turmoil in credit markets. Interest rates and stock prices can move by large amounts, and there is a dramatic reduction in credit market activity. If anyone could predict such an event, they could profit handsomely from that information. Just as with the efficient markets hypothesis, a widely held belief that a financial crisis will happen tomorrow should make it happen today. For example, if people expect a financial crisis to push down the price of stocks by 20%, then the price of stocks should drop by 20% today.

In economic models of financial crises, the fictitious people living in the model know that a financial crisis can happen, but they cannot predict it. As well, it can be the case that the policymakers living in the model cannot predict the financial crisis, and are not able to prevent it.[4] Further, we can have an excellent model of a financial crisis, but an economist equipped with that model will not be able to predict a financial crisis. The economist may, however, be able to use the financial crisis model to design regulations that will prevent a financial crisis from happening, or perhaps mitigate its effects.

The conclusion is that the ability to forecast future events is not a litmus test for macroeconomics. Macroeconomics can be useful in many ways that have nothing to do with forecasting.

---

[4] See, for example, H. Ennis and T. Keister, 2010. "Banking Panics and Policy Responses," *Journal of Monetary Economics* 57, 404–419.

qualitative behavior of comovements among [economic time] series, business cycles are all alike."[5]

Macroeconomic variables are measured as **time series**; for example, real GDP is measured in a series of quarterly observations over time. When we examine comovements in macroeconomic time series, typically we look at these time series two at a time, and a good starting point is to plot the data. Suppose, for example, that we have two macroeconomic time series and we would like to study their comovement. We first transform these two time series by removing trends, and we let x and y denote the percentage deviations from trend in the two time series. One way to plot x and y is in time series form, as in Figure 3.3. What we want to look for first in the time series plot is a pattern of **positive correlation** or **negative correlation** in x and y. In Figure 3.3(a), there is positive correlation between x and y : x is high when y is high, and x is low when y is low. That is, one economic time series tends to be above (below) trend when the other economic time series is above (below) trend. In Figure 3.3(b) x and y are negatively correlated: x is high (low) when y is low (high).

---

[5] From Understanding Business Cycles by Robert E. Lucas, Jr., © 1981 MIT Press.

Figure 3.3 Time Series Plots of x and y

(a) Two time series that are positively correlated. When x is high (low), y tends to be high (low) as well.
(b) Two time series that are negatively correlated. In this case, when x is high (low), y tends to be low (high).

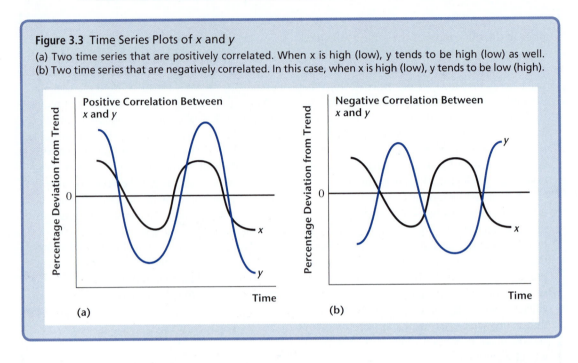

(a)

(b)

Another way to plot the data is as a **scatter plot**, with x on the horizontal axis and y on the vertical axis. In Figure 3.4, each point in the scatter plot is an observation on x and y for a particular time period. Here, whether x and y are positively or negatively correlated is determined by the slope of a straight line that best fits the points in the scatter plot. Figure 3.4(a) shows a positive correlation between x and y, Figure 3.4(b) shows a negative correlation, and Figure 3.4(c) shows a zero correlation. For example, if we had data on aggregate consumption and aggregate income over time, and constructed a scatter plot of consumption (on the y axis) against income (on the x axis), we would observe a positive correlation; a positively sloped straight line would provide a good fit to the points in the scatter plot.

Macroeconomists are often primarily interested in how an individual macroeconomic variable comoves with real GDP. An economic variable is said to be **procyclical** if its deviations from trend are positively correlated with the deviations from trend in real GDP, **countercyclical** if its deviations from trend are negatively correlated with the deviations from trend in real GDP, and **acyclical** if it is neither procyclical nor countercyclical. As an example of comovement between two macroeconomic time series, we consider real GDP and real imports for the United States over the period 1947–2015. In Figure 3.5, we plot the percentage deviations from trend in real GDP (the colored line) and real imports (the black line) in time series form. There is a distinct pattern of positive correlation in Figure 3.5; when GDP is high (low) relative to trend, imports tend to be high (low) relative to trend. This positive correlation also shows up in the scatter plot in Figure 3.6, where we show a graph of observations of percentage deviations from trend in imports versus percentage deviations from trend in GDP. Note that a straight line fit to the points in Figure 3.6 would have a positive slope.

Figure 3.4 Correlations Between Variables y and x

(a) A scatter plot of two variables, x and y, that are positively correlated. (b) x and y are negatively correlated. (c) x and y are uncorrelated.

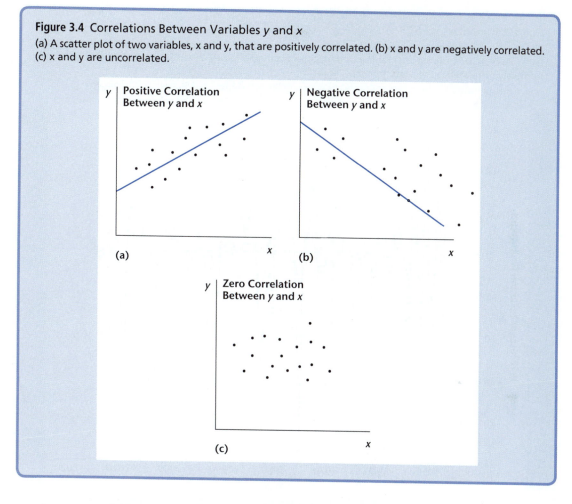

A measure of the degree of correlation between two variables is the **correlation coefficient**. The correlation coefficient between two variables, x and y, takes on values between -1 and 1. If the correlation coefficient is 1, then x and y are **perfectly positively correlated** and a scatter plot of observations on x and y falls on a positively sloped straight line. If the correlation coefficient is -1, then x and y are **perfectly negatively correlated** and a scatter plot would consist of points on a negatively sloped straight line. If the correlation coefficient is 0, then x and y are uncorrelated. In the example above, the percentage deviations from trend in real GDP and real imports have a correlation coefficient of 0.71, indicating positive correlation.

An important element of comovement is the leading and lagging relationships that exist in macroeconomic data. If a macroeconomic variable tends to aid in predicting the future path of real GDP, we say that it is a **leading variable**, whereas if real GDP helps to predict the future path of a particular macroeconomic variable, then that variable is said to be a **lagging variable**. In Figure 3.7 we show idealized time series plots of the percentage deviations from trend in real GDP and two variables, x and y.

Figure 3.5 Imports and GDP

The figure, as an example, shows the time series of percentage deviations from trend in real imports (black line) and real GDP (colored line) for the United States for the period 1947–2015. Imports and GDP are clearly positively correlated, so imports are procyclical.

Source: Data from U.S. Department of Commerce, Bureau of Economic Analysis, © Stephen D. Williamson.

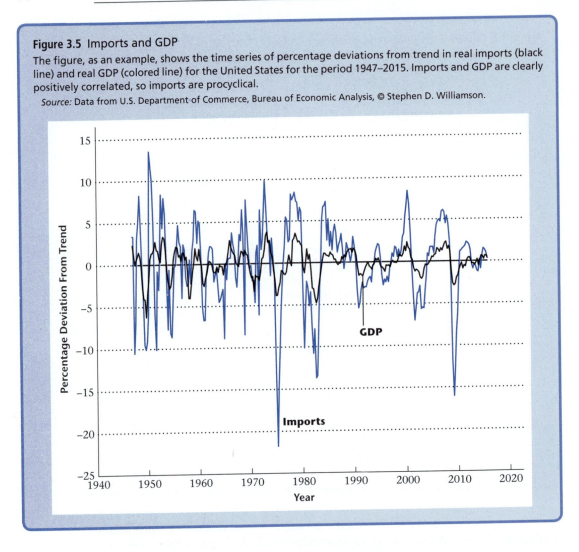

In Figure 3.7(a), variable *x* is a leading variable, whereas variable *y* is a lagging variable in Figure 3.7(b). A **coincident variable** is one which neither leads nor lags real GDP.

A knowledge of the regularities in leading relationships among economic variables can be very useful in macroeconomic forecasting and policymaking. Typically, macroeconomic variables that efficiently summarize available information about future macroeconomic activity are potentially useful in predicting the future path of real GDP. For example, the stock market is a candidate as a useful leading economic variable. Finance theory tells us that stock market prices summarize information about the future profitability of firms in the economy, so movements in stock market prices potentially are important signals about future movements in real GDP. However, the stock market is notoriously volatile—stock market prices can move by large amounts on a given day, for no reason that appears related to any useful new information. Paul Samuelson, a

Figure 3.6 Scatter Plot of Imports and GDP

The figure shows the same data as in Figure 3.5 but in a scatter plot rather than in time series form. Here, we again observe the positive correlation between imports and GDP, as a positively sloped straight line would best fit the scatter plot. Again, imports are procyclical.

Source: Data from U.S. Department of Commerce, Bureau of Economic Analysis, © Stephen D. Williamson.

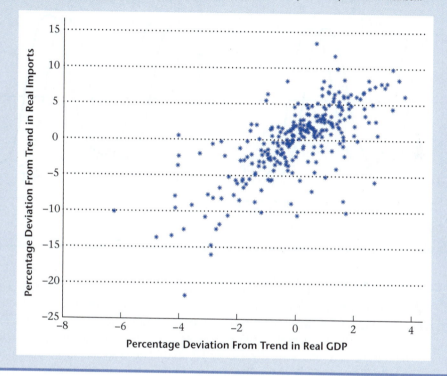

Nobel-prize-winning economist, is famously quoted as saying that "the stock market has forecast nine out of the last five recessions."

Another key leading macroeconomic variable is the number of housing starts in the United States, which is measured on a monthly basis. A housing start occurs when the construction project is started for a private dwelling. This dwelling could be a single detached house, or a unit in a multihousehold building. A housing start therefore represents a commitment to a quantity of residential investment that will take place over the next few months (or possibly a couple of years, for a large apartment building, for example). To undertake such a commitment, the builder should have some confidence that economic conditions will be sufficiently good that the dwelling can be sold quickly once the project is completed. Thus, housing starts will increase and decrease with information that causes economic decision-makers to become more optimistic or pessimistic, respectively, about the future. Residential investment is not a large fraction of GDP, accounting for only 3.4% of GDP in 2014, but it is highly volatile, and it is the highly volatile components of GDP that will contribute most to the decline in GDP

Figure 3.7 Leading and Lagging Variables

In (a), x is a leading variable, as its peaks and troughs tend to precede those of real GDP. In (b), y is a lagging variable, as the peaks and troughs in real GDP tend to lead those in y.

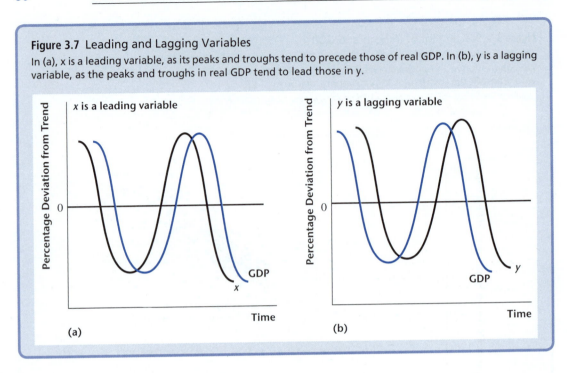

during a recession. Indeed, there is wide agreement that the 2008–2009 recession was triggered by problems in the housing sector and mortgage market.

In Figure 3.8, we show the percentage deviations from trend in real GDP and in housing starts for the period 1959–2015. In the figure, the percentage deviations from trend in housing starts are divided by 10, so that one can see the comovements more clearly. Thus, a 4% deviation from trend in housing starts in the figure represents a 40% deviation from trend in actual housing starts. The figure shows a clear leading relationship between housing starts and GDP. Note in particular that turning points in housing starts tend to lead turning points in real GDP. An additional interesting feature is what it tells us about the recent collapse in the housing market. Housing starts fell from a peak of about 30% above trend in 2006 (about 2.8% in the figure) to about 40% below trend (4.5% in the figure) in 2009. Such a drop is not unprecedented, as we see in the figure, but nevertheless very large.

A final important feature of comovements among economic variables is the key regularities in the variability of economic variables over the business cycle. As we will see, some macroeconomic variables are highly volatile, while others behave in a very smooth way relative to trend. These patterns in variability are an important part of business cycle behavior that we would like to understand. A measure of cyclical variability is the **standard deviation** of the percentage deviations from trend. For example, in Figure 3.5, imports are much more variable than GDP. The standard deviation of the percentage deviations from trend in imports is more than twice that for GDP.

Next we examine some key macroeconomic variables, and we evaluate for each whether they are (1) procyclical or countercyclical, (2) leading or lagging, and (3) more

Figure 3.8 Percentage Deviations in Real GDP (colored line) and Housing Starts (black line), for 1959–2015.

Percentage deviations in housing starts are divided by 10 so we can see the comovement better. Housing starts clearly lead real GDP (note the timing of turning points in particular).

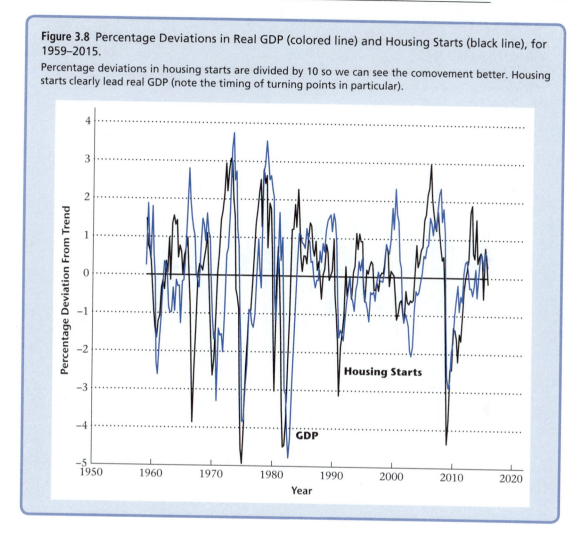

or less variable relative to real GDP. These facts then make up the set of important business cycle regularities that we explain using macroeconomic theory.

The Components of GDP

LO 3.3 State the key properties of comovements among the components of GDP.

In Figure 3.9, we show the percentage deviations from trend in real aggregate consumption (the black line) and real GDP (the colored line). Clearly, the deviations from trend in consumption and in GDP are highly positively correlated, in that consumption tends to be above (below) trend when GDP is above (below) trend; these two time series move very closely together. The correlation coefficient between the percentage deviation from

Figure 3.9 Percentage Deviations from Trend in Real Consumption (black line) and Real GDP (colored line) 1947–2015

From the figure, we can observe that consumption is procyclical, coincident, and less variable than GDP.

Source: Data from U.S. Department of Commerce, Bureau of Economic Analysis, © Stephen D. Williamson.

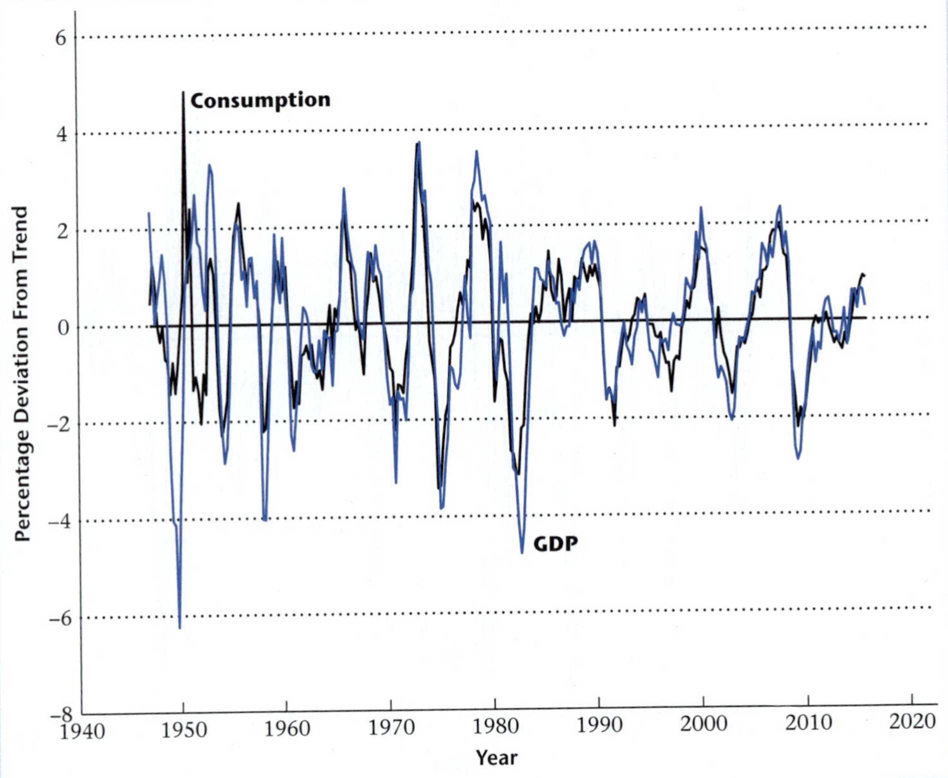

trend in real consumption and the percentage deviation from trend in real GDP is 0.77, which is greater than zero, so consumption is procyclical. There appears to be no discernible lead–lag relationship between real consumption and real GDP in Figure 3.9—the turning points in consumption do not appear to lead or lag the turning points in real GDP. Consumption, therefore, is a coincident variable.

From Figure 3.9, note that consumption is less variable than GDP, in that the deviations from trend in consumption tend to be smaller than those in GDP. In Chapter 8 we study the theory of consumption decisions over time, and this theory explains why consumption tends to be smoother than GDP. For the data displayed in Figure 3.9, the standard deviation of the percentage deviations in real consumption is 77% of that for real GDP. This is a more precise measure of what our eyes tell us about Figure 3.9, which is that consumption is smoother than GDP.

Figure 3.10 Percentage Deviations from Trend in Real Investment (black line) and Real GDP (colored line)

We can observe from the figure that investment is procyclical, coincident, and more variable than GDP.

Source: Data from U.S. Department of Commerce, Bureau of Economic Analysis, © Stephen D. Williamson.

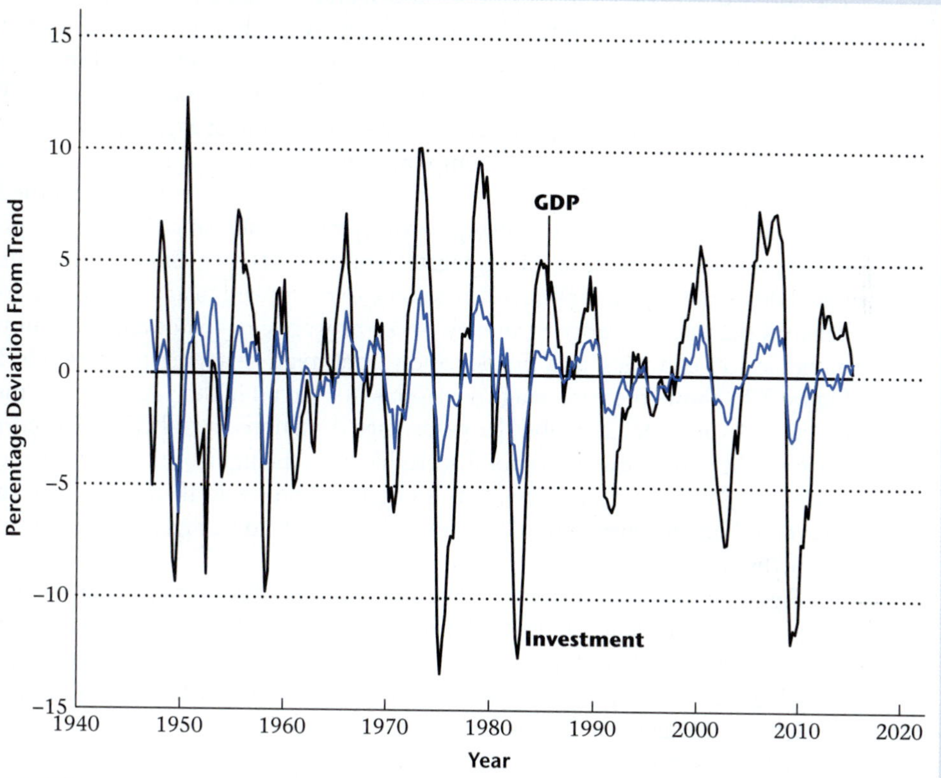

The percentage deviations from trend in real investment (the black line) and real GDP (the colored line) are plotted in Figure 3.10. As with consumption, investment is procyclical, because it tends to be above (below) trend when GDP is above (below) trend. The correlation coefficient between the percentage deviations from trend in investment and those in GDP is 0.80. There is no tendency for investment to lead or lag GDP from Figure 3.10, and so investment is a coincident variable. However, some components of investment, in particular residential investment and inventory investment, tend to lead the business cycle. In contrast to consumption, investment is much more volatile than is GDP. This is indicated in Figure 3.10, where the deviations from trend in investment tend to be much larger than those for GDP. The standard deviation of the percentage deviations from trend in investment is 301% of what it is for GDP. Given that some components of investment lead GDP and that it is highly volatile, investment can play a very important role over the business cycle.

The Price Level and Inflation

LO 3.4 Discuss why comovements between the price level and real GDP and between the inflation rate and real GDP are important to our understanding of business cycles.

The correlation between money prices and aggregate economic activity has long been of interest to macroeconomists. In the 1950s, A. W. Phillips observed that there was a negative relationship between the rate of change in money wages and the unemployment rate in the United Kingdom, a relationship that came to be known as the **Phillips curve**.[6] If we take the unemployment rate to be a measure of aggregate economic activity (as we see in Chapter 6, the unemployment rate is a strongly countercyclical variable; when real GDP is above trend, the unemployment rate is low), then the Phillips curve captures a positive relationship between the rate of change in a money price (the money wage) and the level of aggregate economic activity. Since Phillips made his initial observation, "Phillips curve" has come to be applied to any positive relationship between the rate of change in money prices or wages, or the deviation from trend in money prices or wages, and the deviation from trend in aggregate economic activity. Figure 3.11 shows the percentage deviations from trend in the price level, as measured by the GDP price deflator, and the percentage deviations in real GDP. The correlation between the two time series is not discernible from the figure, but the correlation coefficient is −0.17. Thus the correlation is negative, and weak. If anything, this indicates a **reverse Phillips curve**, in that the price level tends to be high (low) when real GDP is low (high) relative to trend.

Figure 3.12 shows deviations from trend in the inflation rate, as measured by the 12-month rate of change in the GDP price deflator, and the percentage deviations from trend in real GDP. As in Figure 3.11, it may be hard to discern a correlation by examining Figure 3.12, but the correlation coefficient is 0.30, so the inflation rate tends to be high (low) when real GDP is high (low). This thus conforms to conventional views on the Phillips curve.

Figures 3.11 and 3.12 help to illustrate a key feature of observed Phillips curve relationships. Sometimes the Phillips curve relationship is hard to find in the data, and it may exist for some measures of prices and real economic activity and not for others. Further, as we will show in Chapter 15, any Phillips curve relationship tends to be unstable over time, which creates problems if policymakers attempt to use the Phillips curve to help guide policy.

As well, correlations that we observe in the data may change when government policy changes. This is the idea behind the Lucas critique, which was discussed in Chapter 1. For example, if the central bank attempts to control the inflation rate, this will in general affect the correlation between inflation and real economic activity. Indeed, if the central bank seeks to target the rate of inflation at 2% per year and is completely successful, then the correlation between the inflation rate and real GDP will be zero. We will expand on these ideas in Chapter 15.

---

[6] See A. Phillips, 1958. "The Relationship Between Unemployment and the Rate of Change of Money Wages in the United Kingdom, 1861–1957," *Econometrica* 25, 283–299.

Figure 3.11 Percentage Deviations from Trend in the Price Level (the Implicit GDP Price Deflator) and Real GDP

A correlation is difficult to discern in the figure, but the measured correlation coefficient is −0.17. There is a reverse Phillips curve.

Source: Data from U.S. Department of Commerce, Bureau of Economic Analysis, © Stephen D. Williamson.

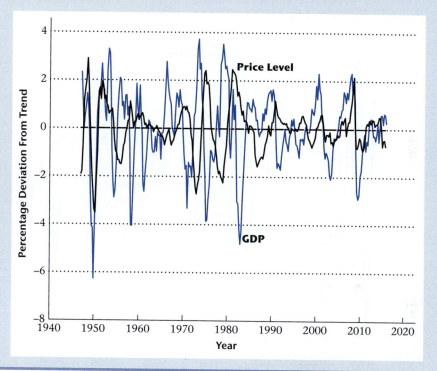

Labor Market Variables

LO 3.5 State the key comovements among labor market variables and real GDP.

The last business cycle regularities we examine are those in labor markets, relating to the variables we determine in the business cycle models in Chapters 11–14. First, in Figure 3.13, we show percentage deviations from trend in employment (black line) and in real GDP (colored line) for the period 1948–2015. Clearly, the deviations from trend in employment closely track those in real GDP, and so employment is a procyclical variable. The correlation coefficient for the data in Figure 3.13 is 0.78. In terms of lead–lag relationships, we can observe a tendency in Figure 3.13 for turning points in employment to lag turning points in GDP, and so employment is a lagging variable. Employment is less variable than GDP, with the standard deviation of the percentage deviation from trend for employment being 65% of that for real GDP in Figure 3.13.

In the macroeconomic models we analyze, a key variable is the market **real wage**, which is the purchasing power of the wage earned per hour worked. This is measured

Figure 3.12 The Inflation Rate and GDP

This figure shows the percentage deviations from trend in real GDP, and the deviations from trend in the inflation rate. The correlation coefficient is 0.30, which conforms to a conventional Phillips curve correlation.

Source: Data from U.S. Department of Commerce, Bureau of Economic Analysis, © Stephen D. Williamson.

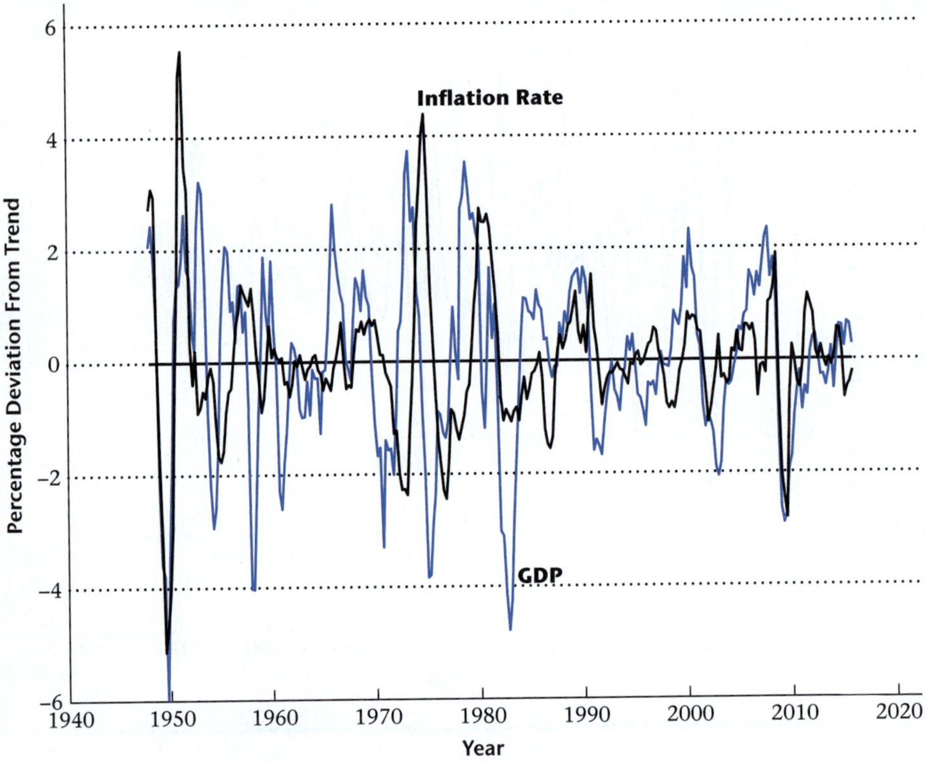

from the data as the average money wage for all workers, divided by the price level. The cyclical behavior of the real wage proves to be crucial in helping us discriminate among different theories of the business cycle in Chapters 13 and 14. The weight of empirical evidence indicates that the real wage is procyclical.[7] We do not show data on the aggregate real wage, as it is difficult to measure the relationship between real wages and real GDP by examining aggregate data. The key problem is that the composition of the labor force tends to change over the business cycle, which tends to bias the correlation between the real wage and real GDP. There is no strong evidence on whether the real wage is a leading or a lagging variable.

---

[7] See G. Solon, R. Barsky, and J. Parker, February 1994, "Measuring the Cyclicality of Real Wages: How Important Is Composition Bias?" *Quarterly Journal of Economics* 109, 1–25.

Figure 3.13 Percentage Deviations from Trend in Employment (black line) and Real GDP (colored line)

Employment is procyclical, it is a lagging variable, and it is less variable than real GDP.

Source: Data from U.S. Department of Commerce, Bureau of Economic Analysis, and Bureau of Labor Statistics, © Stephen D. Williamson.

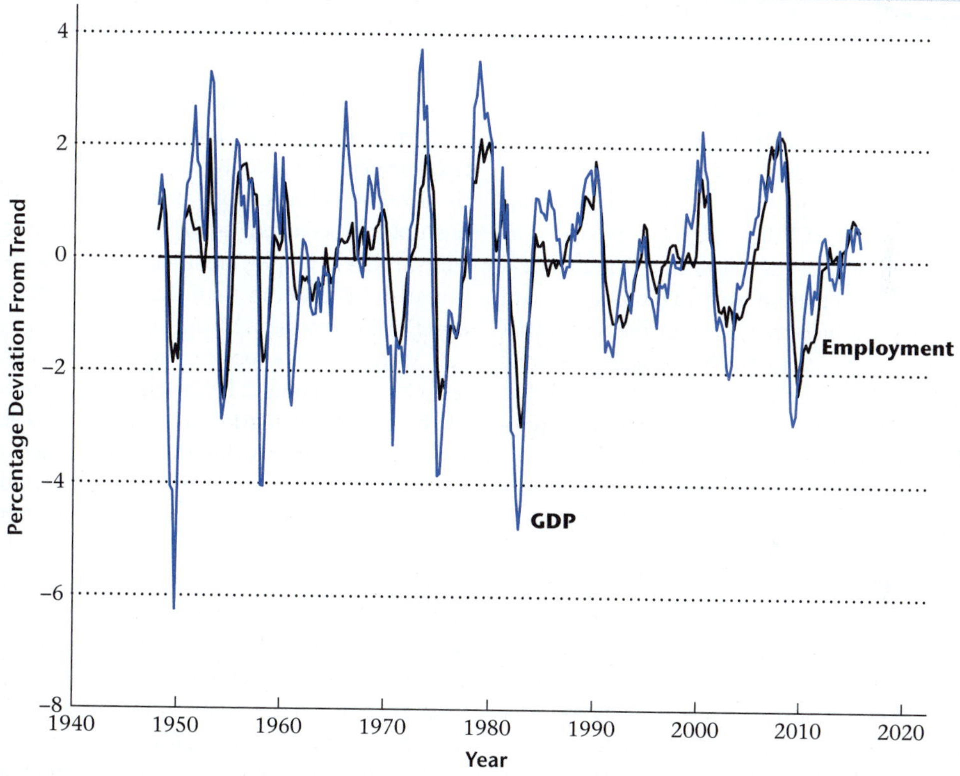

Productivity plays a key role in the economy, as was mentioned in Chapter 1, and in later chapters productivity is an important element in our study of business cycles and economic growth. One measure of productivity is **average labor productivity**, $\frac{Y}{N}$, where y is aggregate output and N is total labor input. For our purposes y is GDP and N is total employment, so we are measuring average labor productivity as output per worker. In Figure 3.15 we show the percentage deviations from trend in real GDP (colored line) and average labor productivity (black line). From the figure, average labor productivity is clearly a procyclical variable. The correlation coefficient for percentage deviations from trend in real GDP and average labor productivity is 0.77. Average labor productivity is less volatile than GDP; the standard deviation of the percentage deviations from trend in average labor productivity is 63% of that for real GDP. Further, there is no apparent tendency for average labor productivity to lead or lag real GDP in Figure 3.15, so average labor productivity is a coincident variable. In Chapters 13 and 14,

MACROECONOMICS IN ACTION

Jobless Recoveries

A feature of employment in the United States that we cannot see clearly in Figure 3.13 is the phenomenon of "jobless recoveries." As we observe in Figure 3.13, employment is procyclical, and it tends to lag real GDP. If we define a "recovery" as the period immediately following a trough in real GDP, the typical pattern we would observe would in fact be a jobless recovery, in the sense that employment tends to reach a trough after real GDP does. However, a jobless recovery, as it has come to be understood, is more than that. Typically, a jobless recovery can be defined to occur when there is an abnormally long period before employment returns to trend after the trough in real GDP.

In Figure 3.14, we show the natural logarithm of aggregate employment over the period 1970–2015, so as to reveal the growth trends in the data. Figure 3.14 shows a different employment measure from what is used in Figure 3.13, in that Figure 3.14 employment is measured at the establishment level (an establishment is an individual productive unit, such as a manufacturing plant), while Figure 3.13 employment is measured at the household level. Establishment-level employment has less measurement error than household-level employment, but is less broad-based.

In Figure 3.14, after the troughs in employment following the 1974–1975 and 1981–1982 recessions, employment follows a typical pattern. After the troughs that occur in 1975 and 1983, employment grows at a higher rate than average trend growth, and returns to trend within two or three years. This pattern occurs in prior recessions as well. However, after each of the three most recent recessions, employment either takes a very long time to return to trend, as after the 1991–1992 recession, or the return to trend has not yet occurred, as for the last two recessions. Indeed, employment was far below trend in early 2012, more than four years after the onset of the recession in late 2007.

Why are we experiencing jobless recoveries? One reason might be the changing structure of the U.S. labor market. David Autor,[8] a professor at MIT, argues that the United States has experienced a marked decline in the fraction of workers possessing middle-level skills, such as clerical and secretarial skills. As a result, skills have become "polarized," with the labor market populated mainly by workers with very high skills, and those with very low skills. Some of the polarization has been the result of technological change, particularly changes in computational and information technologies. A change in the skill composition of the labor force can change the dynamics of business cycles, particularly if employment losses in recessions are primarily in low-skill occupations. Also, a recession could hasten the evolution of the skill composition in the labor market, with middle-skill workers losing their jobs during recessions and either leaving the labor force or embarking on a long period of retraining.

---

[8] See D. Autor, 2010. *The Polarization of Job Opportunities in the U.S. Labor Market*, The Hamilton Project, Center for American Progress.

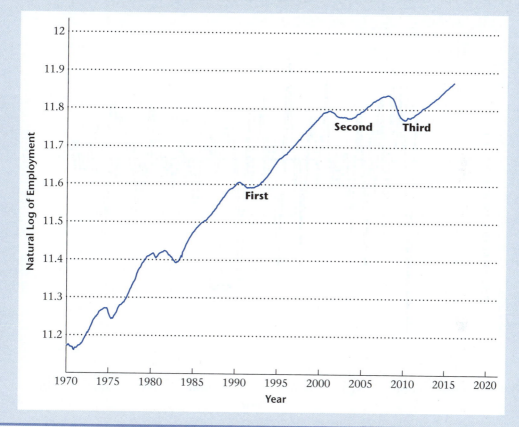

Figure 3.14 Jobless Recoveries

A jobless recovery occurs when employment takes an abnormally long time to return to trend after the trough in real GDP occurs. Jobless recoveries occur in Figure 3.14 after the last three recessions, which occurred in 1991–1992, 2001, and 2008–2009.

the predictions of different business cycle theories for the comovements between average labor productivity and real GDP are important in helping us to evaluate and compare these theories.

Seasonal Adjustment

LO 3.6 Explain the importance of seasonal adjustment.

The economic data we are studying in this chapter, and most data that is used in macroeconomic research and in formulating macroeconomic policy, is **seasonally adjusted**. That is, in most macroeconomic time series, there exists a predictable seasonal component. For example, GDP tends to be low during the summer months when workers are

Figure 3.15 Percentage Deviations from Trend in Average Labor Productivity (black line) and Real GDP (colored line) for 1948–2015

Average labor productivity is procyclical and coincident, and it is less variable than is real GDP.

Source: Data from U.S. Department of Commerce, Bureau of Economic Analysis, and Bureau of Labor Statistics, © Stephen D. Williamson.

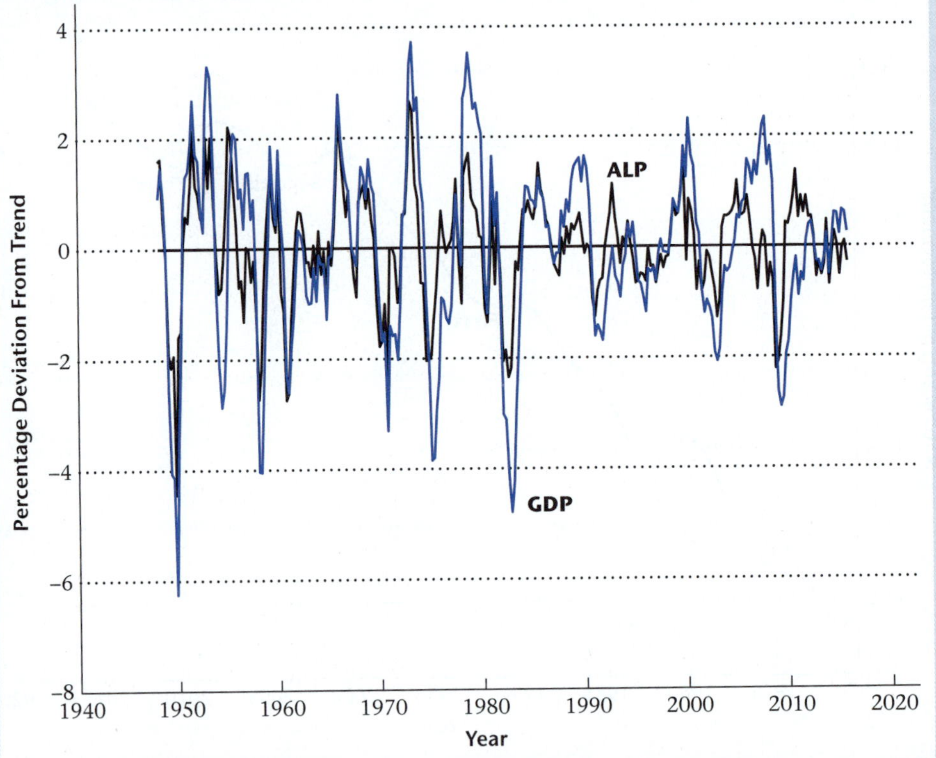

on vacation; investment expenditure tends to be low in the winter months when building roads, bridges, and some types of structures is more difficult; and the unemployment rate tends to be low during the December holiday season, when the quantity of retail transactions is high.

There are various methods for seasonally adjusting data, but the basic idea is to observe historical seasonal patterns and then take out the extra amount that we tend to see on average during a particular week, month, or quarter, simply because of the time of year. Figure 3.16 shows the results of seasonal adjustment for the unemployment rate, which is measured monthly. The seasonally unadjusted unemployment rate tends to be low (as previously mentioned) during December, and also in April, and typically peaks in January and July. This seasonal pattern is in part due to demand factors, like the holiday season. As well, supply factors are important. For example,

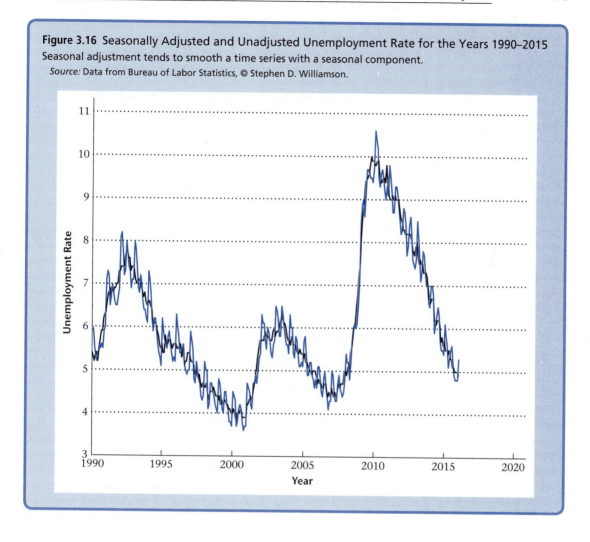

Figure 3.16 Seasonally Adjusted and Unadjusted Unemployment Rate for the Years 1990–2015
Seasonal adjustment tends to smooth a time series with a seasonal component.
Source: Data from Bureau of Labor Statistics, © Stephen D. Williamson.

construction and agricultural activity rise in the warm weather, and students are not in school during the summer months. For the unemployment rate, seasonal factors are quite important—the unemployment rate sometimes moves as much as a percentage point over the year solely due to seasonal factors.

Working with seasonally adjusted data can often be the appropriate thing to do, but one has to be careful that the process of seasonal adjustment is not masking important phenomena that might interest us. For example, there may be economic factors that cause the nature of seasonality to change over time. For example, technological developments may make it less costly to do road construction in the winter, and thus reduce the seasonal fluctuations we see in investment expenditure. If we confine our attention to only seasonally adjusted data, we might not be aware that this process was occurring.

MACROECONOMICS IN ACTION
The Great Moderation and the 2008–2009 Recession

After the 1981–1982 recession, there was a long period, until 2008, sometimes called the Great Moderation, which featured relatively mild fluctuations in real GDP and a relatively low and stable rate of inflation. Here, we will focus exclusively on the first feature, which we can see in Figure 3.2. From 1947 until the end of the 1981–1982 recession, deviations from trend in real GDP in Figure 3.2 were as much or more than ± 4%, but after 1982 and before 2008, deviations from trend were typically no more than ± 2% An instructive view of the Great Moderation, written while it was underway, is in a speech by Ben Bernanke, the current Chair of the Board of Governors of the Federal Reserve System, delivered in 2004 when he was a governor on the board.[9] Bernanke takes note of the Great Moderation, and lists three possible reasons for it. First, there may have been structural changes in the economy that made it more resilient over this period and less susceptible to external shocks. Second, economic policy may have been better, in countering the effects of these external shocks. Third, we may just have been lucky, in the sense that there were fewer shocks to the economy, and these shocks were smaller.

In his speech, Bernanke argues that the Great Moderation was not just good luck, but could be attributed in good part to wiser monetary policy. He also suggests, in part, that structural changes including "the increased depth and sophistication of financial markets . . ."[10] made the economy more resilient. However, our experience in the financial crisis, beginning in 2008, and in the 2008–2009 recession, was anything but moderate. Financial markets once thought to be deep and sophisticated are now considered deeply flawed, in part due to poor regulation. If monetary policymakers were so good at reducing fluctuations in aggregate GDP in the Great Moderation, why could they not prevent or substantially reduce the large economic downturn in 2008–2009?

The Great Moderation episode provides a good lesson for economic policy. With the benefit of hindsight, monetary policymakers, including Ben Bernanke, were too complacent, and too inclined to attribute good economic performance to their own skill. From the point of view of 2015, the Great Moderation now seems most likely to be the product of good luck.

[9]See http://www.federalreserve.gov/BOARDDOCS/SPEECHES/2004/20040220/default.htm.

[10]Remarks by Governor Ben S. Bernanke At the meetings of the Eastern Economic Association, Washington, DC February 20, 2004, Federal Reserve.

Comovement Summary

LO 3.7 State the key business cycle facts.

To summarize the business cycle facts discussed above, we present Tables 3.1 and 3.2. These two tables, particularly Table 3.1, prove very useful, particularly when we discuss the predictions of different theories of the business cycle in Chapters 13 and 14. A first test of the usefulness of macroeconomic theories is their ability to match what we see in macroeconomic data.

Table 3.1   Correlation Coefficients and Variability of Percentage
Deviations from Trend

	Correlation Coefficient	Standard Deviation (% of S.D. of GDP)
Consumption	0.77	77
Investment	0.80	301
Employment	0.78	65
Average Labor Productivity	0.77	63

Table 3.2   Summary of Business Cycle Facts

	Cyclicality	Lead/Lag	Variation Relative to GDP
Consumption	Procyclical	Coincident	Smaller
Investment	Procyclical	Coincident	Larger
Employment	Procyclical	Lagging	Smaller
Real Wage	Procyclical	?	?
Average Labor Productivity	Procyclical	Coincident	Smaller

We have concluded our study of measurement issues, in that we now know the basics of national income accounting, basic macroeconomic accounting identities, price measurement, labor market facts, and business cycle facts. In the next chapters, we proceed to build useful macroeconomic models, starting with some basic microeconomic principles concerning the behavior of consumers and firms.

Chapter Summary

- The key business cycle facts relate to the deviations of important macroeconomic variables from their trends and the comovements in these deviations from trend.
- The most important business cycle fact is that real GDP fluctuates about trend in an irregular fashion. Though deviations from trend in real GDP are persistent, there is no observed regularity in the amplitude or frequency of fluctuations in real GDP about trend.
- Business cycles are similar mainly in terms of the comovements among macroeconomic time series. Comovement can be discerned by plotting the percentage deviations from trend in two economic variables in a time series or in a scatter plot or by calculating the correlation coefficient between the percentage deviations from trend.

- We are interested principally in how a particular variable moves about trend relative to real GDP (whether it is procyclical, countercyclical, or acyclical), whether it is a leading, lagging, or coincident variable (relative to real GDP), and how variable it is relative to real GDP.
- Consumption is procyclical, coincident, and less variable than real GDP.
- Investment is procyclical, coincident, and more variable than real GDP.
- Percentage deviations from trend in the price level are negatively correlated with percentage deviations from trend in real GDP—a reverse Phillips curve.
- Deviations from trend in the inflation rate are positively correlated with percentage deviations from trend in real GDP. This is a conventional Phillips curve correlation.
- In the labor market, employment is procyclical, lagging, and less variable than real GDP. The real wage, too, is procyclical. There is, however, no consensus among macroeconomists on whether the real wage is a leading or lagging variable. Average labor productivity is procyclical, coincident, and less variable than real GDP.
- Many macroeconomic time series used in economic analysis are seasonally adjusted. Seasonal adjustment takes out the predictable seasonal component, for example the effect of extra spending over the December holiday season on the money supply.

Key Terms

Business cycles Fluctuations about trend in real GDP. (p. 71)

Peak A relatively large positive deviation from trend in real GDP. (p. 72)

Trough A relatively large negative deviation from trend in real GDP. (p. 72)

Turning points Peaks and troughs in real GDP. (p. 72)

Amplitude The maximum deviation from trend in an economic time series. (p. 72)

Frequency The number of peaks in an economic time series that occur per year. (p. 72)

Boom A series of positive deviations from trend in real GDP, culminating in a peak. (p. 72)

Recession A series of negative deviations from trend in real GDP, culminating in a trough. (p. 72)

Persistent Describes an economic time series that tends to stay above (below) trend when it has been above (below) trend during the recent past. (p. 73)

Comovement How aggregate economic variables move together over the business cycle. (p. 73)

Time series Sequential measurements of an economic variable over time. (p. 75)

Positive correlation Relationship between two economic time series when a straight line fit to a scatter plot of the two variables has a positive slope. (p. 75)

Negative correlation Relationship between two economic time series when a straight line fit to a scatter plot of the two variables has a negative slope. (p. 75)

Scatter plot A plot of two variables, x and y, with x measured on the horizontal axis and y measured on the vertical axis. (p. 76)

Procyclical Describes an economic variable that tends to be above (below) trend when real GDP is above (below) trend. (p. 76)

Countercyclical Describes an economic variable that tends to be below (above) trend when real GDP is above (below) trend. (p. 76)

Acyclical Describes an economic variable that is neither procyclical nor countercyclical. (p. 76)

Correlation coefficient A measure of the degree of correlation between two variables. (p. 77)

Perfectly positively correlated Describes two variables that have a correlation coefficient of 1. (p. 77)

Perfectly negatively correlated Describes two variables that have a correlation coefficient of -1. (p. 77)

Leading variable An economic variable that helps to predict future real GDP. (p. 77)

Lagging variable An economic variable that past real GDP helps to predict. (p. 77)

Coincident variable An economic variable that neither leads nor lags real GDP. (p. 78)

Standard deviation A measure of variability. The cyclical variability in an economic time series can be measured by the standard deviation of the percentage deviations from trend. (p. 80)

Phillips curve A positive correlation between a money price or the rate of change in a money price and a measure of aggregate economic activity. (p. 84)

Reverse Phillips curve A negative correlation between a money price or the rate of change in a

money price and a measure of aggregate economic activity. (p. 84)

Real wage The purchasing power of the wage earned per hour worked. (p. 85)

Average labor productivity Equal to Y/N where y is aggregate output and N is total labor input. (p. 87)

Seasonal adjustment The statistical process of removing the predictable seasonal component from an economic time series. (p. 89)

Questions for Review

3.1 What is the primary defining feature of business cycles?

3.2 Besides persistence, what are three important features of the deviations from trend in GDP?

3.3 Explain why forecasting GDP over the long term is difficult.

3.4 Why are the comovements in aggregate economic variables important?

3.5 What did Robert Lucas say about the comovements among economic variables?

3.6 How can we discern positive and negative correlation in a time series plot? In a scatter plot?

3.7 Give a noneconomic example of two variables that are positively correlated and an example of two variables that are negatively correlated.

3.8 Why is the index of leading economic indicators useful for forecasting GDP?

3.9 What are the three features of comovement that macroeconomists are interested in?

3.10 Describe the key business cycle regularities in consumption and investment expenditures.

3.11 What are the key business cycle regularities with respect to the price level and inflation?

3.12 Does a Phillips curve relationship exist in the data set that was studied in this chapter?

3.13 What are the key business cycle regularities in the labor market?

Problems

1. **LO 4** In Figure 3.12, what do you observe during the 1970s? Explain the significance of this.

2. **LO 2,5** Average labor productivity tends to be a coincident variable. Examine Figure 3.15 carefully. During the 1991–1992, 2001, and 2008–2009 recessions, how do you observe average labor productivity behaving relative to GDP? Comment on this, and explain what this has to do with the Macroeconomics in Action box on jobless recoveries.

3. **LO 3** Consumption of durables is more variable relative to trend than is consumption of nondurables, and consumption of nondurables is more variable relative to trend than is consumption of

services. Speculate on why we observe these phenomena, and relate this to the key business cycle facts in Tables 3.1 and 3.2.

4. **LO 4** In Figure 3.11, after the 1981–1982 recession, does the price level appear to be procyclical, countercyclical, or acyclical? Why is this important?

5. **LO 4** The Great Moderation in part refers to the moderate variability in real GDP that occurred after the 1981–1982 recession and before the 2008–2009 recession. In Figure 3.12, what do you observe about the behavior of the deviations from trend in the inflation rate over the period 1947–2015? Relate this to the Great Moderation experience, and discuss.

Working with the Data

Answer these questions using the Federal Reserve Bank of St. Louis's FRED database, accessible at http://research.stlouisfed.org/fred2/

1. Calculate the 12-month percentage increase in the consumer price index (CPI), and plot this, along with the unemployment rate. Do you observe a positive correlation, a negative correlation, or a correlation that is essentially zero? Can you find a Phillips curve relation or a reverse Phillips curve?

2. Some economists have thought that the money supply plays an important role in economic activity. Calculate and plot the 12-month growth rates in M1 (a measure of the money supply) and 12-month growth rates in real GDP.
   (a) Are growth in real GDP and in the money supply positively correlated or negatively correlated?
   (b) Does one time series lead the other, or are they coincident?

3. Calculate the percentage rates of increase in real GDP, consumption of durables, consumption of nondurables, and consumption of services, and plot these.
   (a) What do you notice in these plots compared to the information in Figures 3.9 and 3.10?
   (b) Provide an explanation for your observations in part (a).

4. Calculate and graph the ratio of (i) real residential investment to real GDP; (ii) real nonresidential investment to real GDP; and (iii) real inventory investment to real GDP.
   (a) Which of the components of investment shows the most (least) variability, in terms of its contribution to the variability in real GDP?
   (b) Provide possible explanations for the patterns you detected in part (a).

Basic Macroeconomic Models: A One-Period Model and Models of Search and Unemployment

The goal of Part II is to construct working models of the macroeconomy that can be used to analyze some key macroeconomic issues. The basic building blocks in these models are the microeconomic behavior of consumers and firms. We start, in Chapter 4, by analyzing the behavior of a representative consumer and a representative firm, with each making decisions over one period. The representative consumer's fundamental choice in this environment concerns how to allocate time between work and leisure, making himself or herself as well off as possible while obeying his or her budget constraint. The representative firm chooses how much labor it should hire so as to maximize profits. In Chapter 5, we build consumer behavior and firm behavior into a one-period macroeconomic model, in which there is a government that can spend and tax. This model is then used to show that, under ideal conditions, free market outcomes can be socially efficient; that government spending crowds out private consumption while increasing aggregate output; and that increases in productivity increase welfare, consumption, and aggregate output. In Chapter 6, we deal with two different types of models, designed to capture some of the key aspects of labor market behavior. These search models explain the determinants of unemployment, labor market vacancies, and labor market participation. These models are used to understand the effects of shocks to the economy on the unemployment rate, among other variables.

Chapter 4

Consumer and Firm Behavior: The Work–Leisure Decision and Profit Maximization

Learning Objectives

After studying Chapter 4, students will be able to:

4.1 List the properties of the representative consumer's preferences, and explain why it is useful to assume these properties.

4.2 Construct the representative consumer's budget constraint.

4.3 Show how the consumer optimizes given his or her budget constraint to determine labor supply and consumption.

4.4 Determine the effects of changes in the representative consumer's environment on his or her choices.

4.5 List the properties of the production function, and explain why it is useful to assume these properties.

4.6 Show how the representative firm optimizes given its production technology to determine labor demand and output.

4.7 Determine the effects of changes in the representative firm's environment on its labor demand and output choices.

Chapters 2 and 3 focused on how we measure variables of macroeconomic interest. We now turn to the construction and analysis of a particular macroeconomic model. Recall that, in Chapter 1, we described how a macroeconomic model is built from a description of consumers and their preferences over goods and of firms and the technology available to produce goods from available resources. In this chapter, we focus on the behavior of consumers and firms in a simple model environment with only one time period. One-period decision making for consumers and firms limits the kinds of macroeconomic issues we can address with the resulting model. This simplification, however, makes it easier to understand the basic microeconomic principles of consumer and firm optimization on which we build in the rest of this book. Given that there is only one time period, consumers and firms make **static**, as opposed to **dynamic**, decisions. Dynamic decision making involves planning over more than one period, as, for example, when individuals make decisions concerning how much to spend today and how much to save for the future. Dynamic decisions are analyzed in Parts III and IV.

With regard to consumer behavior, we focus on how a consumer makes choices concerning the trade-off between consuming and working. For the consumer, consuming more goods comes at a cost: the consumer must work harder and will enjoy less leisure time. Primarily, we are interested in how a consumer's work–leisure choice is affected by his or her preferences and by the constraints he or she faces. For example, we want to know how a change in the market wage rate and in the consumer's nonwage income affects his or her choices concerning how much to work, how much to consume, and how much leisure time to take. For the firm, we focus on how the available technology for producing goods and the market environment influence the firm's decision concerning how much labor to hire during the period.

As we discussed in Chapter 1, a fundamental principle that we adhere to here is that consumers and firms optimize. That is, a consumer wishes to make himself or herself as well off as possible given the constraints he or she faces. Likewise, a firm acts to maximize profits, given market prices and the available technology. The optimization principle is a very powerful and useful tool in economics, and it helps in sharpening the predictions of economic models. Given optimizing behavior by consumers and firms, we can analyze how these economic agents respond to changes in the environment in which they live. For example, we show how consumers and firms change the quantity of labor supplied and the quantity of labor demanded, respectively, in response to a change in the market wage rate, and how consumers respond to a change in taxes. The knowledge we build up in this chapter concerning these optimal responses is critical in the next chapter, where we study what happens in the economy as a whole when there is an important shock to the system, for example, a large increase in government spending or a major new invention.

The Representative Consumer

To begin, we consider the behavior of a single representative consumer, who acts as a stand-in for all of the consumers in the economy. We show how to represent a consumer's preferences over the available goods in the economy and how to represent the consumer's budget constraint, which tells us what goods are feasible for the consumer to purchase given market prices. We then put preferences together with the budget constraint to determine how the consumer behaves given market prices, and how he or she responds to a change in nonwage income and to a change in the market wage rate.

The Representative Consumer's Preferences

LO 4.1 List the properties of the representative consumer's preferences, and explain why it is useful to assume these properties.

It proves simplest to analyze consumer choice and is just right for the issues we want to address in this chapter and the next, to suppose that there are two goods that consumers desire. The first is a physical good, which we can think of as an aggregation of all consumer goods in the economy, or measured aggregate consumption. We call this the **consumption good**. The second good is **leisure**, which is any time spent not working in the market. In terms of our definition, therefore, leisure could include recreational activities, sleep, and work at home (cooking, yardwork, housecleaning).

For macroeconomic purposes, it proves convenient to suppose that all consumers in the economy are identical. In reality, of course, consumers are not identical, but for many macroeconomic issues diversity among consumers is not essential to addressing the economics of the problem at hand, and considering it only clouds our thinking. Identical consumers, in general, behave in identical ways, and so we need only analyze the behavior of one of these consumers. Further, if all consumers are identical, the economy behaves as if there were only one consumer, and it is, therefore, convenient to write down the model as having only a single **representative consumer**. We must recognize, however, that the representative consumer in our macroeconomic model plays the role of a stand-in for all consumers in the economy.

A key step in determining how the representative consumer makes choices is to show how we can capture the preferences of the representative consumer over leisure and consumption goods by a **utility function**, written as

$$U(C, l),$$

where U is the utility function, C is the quantity of consumption, and l is the quantity of leisure. We refer to a particular combination of consumption and leisure—for example, (C_1, l_1), where C_1 is a particular consumption quantity and l_1 is a particular quantity of leisure—as a **consumption bundle**. The utility function represents how the consumer ranks different consumption bundles. That is, suppose that there are two different consumption bundles, representing different quantities of consumption and leisure, denoted (C_1, l_1) and (C_2, l_2). We say that (C_1, l_1) is strictly preferred by the consumer to (C_2, l_2) if

$$U(C_1, l_1) > U(C_2, l_2);$$

(C_2, l_2) is strictly preferred to (C_1, l_1) if

$$U(C_1, l_1) < U(C_2, l_2);$$

and the consumer is indifferent between the two consumption bundles if

$$U(C_1, l_1) = U(C_2, l_2).$$

It is useful to think of $U(C, l)$ as giving the level of happiness, or utility, that the consumer receives from consuming the bundle (C, l). The actual level of utility, however, is irrelevant; all that matters for the consumer is what the level of utility is from a given consumption bundle *relative* to another one.

To use our representation of the consumer's preferences for analyzing macroeconomic issues, we must make some assumptions concerning the form that preferences take. These assumptions are useful for making the analysis work, and they are also consistent with how consumers actually behave. We assume that the representative consumer's preferences have three properties: more is preferred to less; the consumer likes diversity in his or her consumption bundle; and consumption and leisure are normal goods. We discuss each of these in turn.

1. *More is always preferred to less.*   A consumer always prefers a consumption bundle that contains more consumption, more leisure, or both. This may appear unnatural, because it seems that we can get too much of a good thing. For example, consuming too much of one good may sometimes make one worse off, as when we overeat. In terms of general consumption goods, however, the average consumer in the United States today consumes far more than the average consumer 200 years ago would have dreamed possible, and it certainly seems that the average consumer today in the United States would like to consume more if it were feasible. Indeed, even the extremely wealthy appear to desire more than they have.

2. *The consumer likes diversity in his or her consumption bundle.*   To see that this is a natural property of consumer preferences, consider a consumer who, instead of consuming consumption goods and leisure, is making a decision about where to eat lunch during the week. Lynn can go to one of two restaurants to eat lunch, one of which serves only hamburgers, while the other serves only tuna sandwiches. One choice open to Lynn is to eat a hamburger for lunch on each day of the week, and another choice is to eat tuna sandwiches all week. Suppose that Lynn is indifferent between these two choices. If she has a preference for diversity, Lynn would prefer to alternate between restaurants during the week rather than eat at one place every day. In the case of our representative consumer, who is choosing among consumption bundles with different combinations of consumption goods and leisure, a preference for diversity means that, if the consumer is indifferent between two consumption bundles, then some mixture of the two consumption bundles is preferable to either one. At the extreme, suppose that the consumer is indifferent between a consumption bundle that has six units of consumption and no leisure and another bundle that has no consumption goods and eight units of leisure. Then, a preference for diversity implies that the consumer would prefer a third consumption bundle, consisting of half of each of the other bundles, to having either of the other consumption bundles. This preferable third consumption bundle would have three units of consumption goods and four units of leisure.

3. *Consumption and leisure are normal goods.*   A good is **normal** for a consumer if the quantity of the good that he or she purchases increases when income increases. For example, meals at high-quality restaurants are a normal good for most people; if our income increases, we tend to eat out more in good places.

In contrast, a good is **inferior** for a consumer if he or she purchases less of that good when income increases. An example of an inferior good is food from Bob Evans; most people would tend to eat less at Bob Evans as their income increases. In our model, then, given that consumption and leisure are normal goods, the representative consumer purchases more consumption goods and increases his or her leisure time when income increases. This seems intuitively appealing; if, for example, you received a windfall increase in your income, perhaps through an inheritance, you would probably want to consume more goods as well as taking more vacation time (leisure). In practice, the behavior of consumers is consistent with consumption and leisure being normal goods.

While we postpone discussion of property (3) of the representative consumer's preferences until we have more machinery to analyze how the consumer behaves, our next step is to show how we represent properties (1) and (2) graphically. It is helpful to consider the representative consumer's preferences using a graphical representation of the utility function, called the **indifference map**. The indifference map is a family of **indifference curves**.

> **Definition 1**   An **indifference curve** connects a set of points, with these points representing consumption bundles among which the consumer is indifferent.

Figure 4.1 shows two indifference curves. In the figure, I_1 is an indifference curve, and two points on the indifference curve are (C_1, l_1) (point B) and (C_2, l_2) (point D). Because these two consumption bundles lie on the same indifference curve, we must have $U(C_1, l_1) = U(C_2, l_2)$. That is, being indifferent implies that the consumer receives the same level of happiness from each consumption bundle. Another indifference curve is I_2. Because indifference curve I_2 lies above indifference curve I_1, and we know more is preferred to less, consumption bundles on I_2 are strictly preferred to consumption bundles on I_1. For example, consider point A which represents a consumption bundle with the same quantity of leisure as at point B but with a higher quantity of the consumption good. Because more is preferred to less, A is strictly preferred to B.

An indifference curve has two key properties:

1. An indifference curve slopes downward.
2. An indifference curve is convex, that is bowed-in toward the origin.

Because the indifference map is just the graphical representation of preferences, it should not be surprising that the properties of the indifference curve are related to the properties of preferences, (1) and (2), described above. In fact, property (1) of an indifference curve follows from property (1) of preferences (more is always preferred to less),

Figure 4.1 Indifference Curves

The figure shows two indifference curves for the consumer. Each indifference curve represents a set of consumption bundles among which the consumer is indifferent. Higher indifference curves represent higher welfare for the consumer.

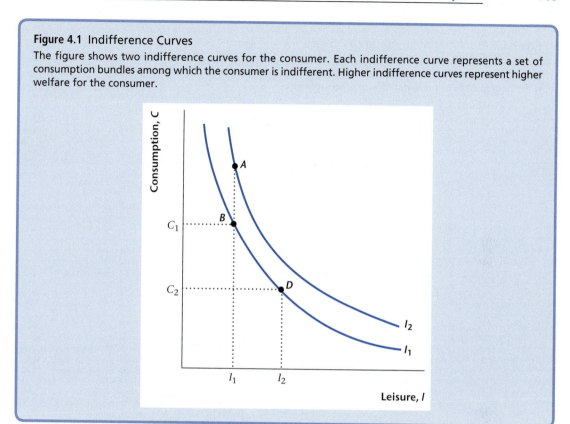

and property (2) of an indifference curve follows from property (2) of preferences (the consumer likes diversity in his or her consumption bundle).

To see why the fact that indifference curves slope downward follows from the assumption that more is preferred to less, consider Figure 4.2. At point A consumption is C_1 and leisure is l_1. Suppose that we now consider holding the quantity of leisure constant for the consumer at l_1 and reduce the consumer's quantity of consumption to C_2, so that the consumer now has the consumption bundle represented by point D. Because more is preferred to less, point D must be on a lower indifference curve (indifference curve I_2) than is point A (on indifference curve I_1). Now we can ask how much leisure we would have to add to l_1, holding consumption constant at C_2, to obtain a consumption bundle B such that the consumer is indifferent between A and B. Point B must lie below and to the right of point A because, if we are taking consumption goods away from the consumer, we need to give him or her more leisure. Thus, the indifference curve I_1 is downward-sloping because more is preferred to less.

To understand why the convexity of the indifference curve follows from the preference of the representative consumer for diversity, we introduce the following concept.

Figure 4.2 Properties of Indifference Curves

Indifference curves are downward-sloping because more is preferred to less. A preference for diversity implies that indifference curves are convex (bowed-in toward the origin). The slope of an indifference curve is the negative of the marginal rate of substitution.

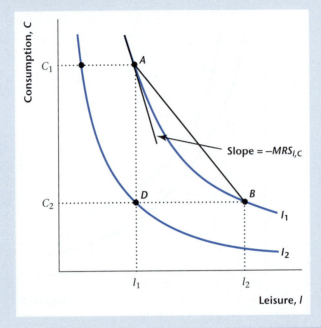

Definition 2   *The marginal rate of substitution of leisure for consumption, denoted $MRS_{l,C}$ is the rate at which the consumer is just willing to substitute leisure for consumption goods.*

We have

$$MRS_{l,C} = -[\text{the slope of the indifference curve passing through } (C, l)].$$

To see why the marginal rate of substitution is minus the slope of the indifference curve, consider consumption bundles A and B in Figure 4.2. There, the rate at which the consumer is willing to substitute leisure for consumption in moving from A to B is the ratio $\frac{C_1 - C_2}{l_2 - l_1}$, or minus the slope of the line segment AB. Minus the slope of AB tells us how much consumption we need to take away for each unit of leisure added as we move from A to B, with the consumer being just indifferent between A and B. If we imagine choosing a point like point B on the indifference curve I_1 below point A but closer and closer to A, then as the distance between that point and A becomes small, the rate at which the consumer is willing to substitute leisure for consumption between A and the chosen point is the marginal rate of substitution, which is minus the slope of the indifference curve at point *A* (or minus the slope of a tangent to the indifference curve at *A*).

Suppose, for example, that Krystyna can choose how many weeks of vacation to take each year, and that she currently works 50 weeks in a year and takes 2 weeks of vacation, so that her leisure time is 2 weeks. To keep things simple, suppose Krystyna consumes only coconuts, so that we can measure her consumption in coconuts. Currently, she eats 500 coconuts per year. If Krystyna were to take one more week of vacation per year, she would be just as happy as she is now if she were to give up 50 coconuts per year. This implies that Krystyna's marginal rate of substitution of leisure for consumption, given her current consumption bundle of 500 coconuts of consumption and 2 weeks of leisure, is 50 coconuts per week.

Stating that an indifference curve is convex [property (2) of the indifference curve] is identical to stating that the marginal rate of substitution is diminishing. That is, note that the indifference curve in Figure 4.2 becomes flatter as we move down the indifference curve from left to right; that is, as the consumer receives more leisure and less of the consumption good. Thus, minus the slope of the indifference curve becomes smaller as leisure increases and consumption decreases. In other words, the marginal rate of substitution is diminishing. This is because, as we increase the quantity of leisure and reduce the quantity of consumption, the consumer needs to be compensated more and more in terms of leisure time to give up another unit of consumption. The consumer requires this extra compensation because of a preference for diversity.

To give a concrete example of a preference for diversity in terms of a consumption–leisure choice, suppose that Allen sleeps 8 hours in every 24-hour period. He therefore has 112 hours per week to split between work and leisure. Consider two situations. In the first, Allen takes 10 hours of leisure per week and works 102 hours, and in the second he takes 102 hours of leisure per week and works 10 hours. In the first circumstance, Allen is willing to give up much more consumption expenditure in exchange for one extra hour of leisure than in the second case.

The Representative Consumer's Budget Constraint

LO 4.2 Construct the representative consumer's budget constraint.

Now that we know something about the representative consumer's preferences, we must also specify his or her constraints and objectives to predict what he or she will do. We assume that the representative consumer behaves competitively. Here, **competitive behavior** means that the consumer is a price-taker; that is, he or she treats market prices as being given and acts as if his or her actions have no effect on those prices. This is certainly an accurate description of reality if the consumer is small relative to the market, but of course this is not literally true if there is only one consumer. Recall, however, that the single representative consumer is a stand-in for all the consumers in the economy. Even though it is obvious that real economies do not have only one consumer, a real economy can still behave as if there were a single representative consumer.

An important assumption that we make at this stage is that there is no money in this economy. That is, there is no government-supplied currency to be used in exchange, and no banks through which people can conduct transactions, for example, through transactions accounts that can be used in conjunction with debit cards and checks. For some macroeconomic issues, the complication of introducing money does not add anything to our analysis and is best left out. Later, however, in Chapters 12–14, we begin to analyze the role that money plays in the macroeconomy, so that we can address issues such as the effects of inflation and the conduct of monetary policy.

An economy without monetary exchange is a **barter** economy. In a barter economy, all trade involves exchanges of goods for goods. There are only two goods here: consumption goods and time. When time is used at home, we call it leisure time, and when time is exchanged in the market, we call it work—more explicitly, labor time. Any trades in this economy must involve exchanges of labor time for consumption goods, or vice versa. The consumer is assumed to have h hours of time available, which can be allocated between leisure time, l, and time spent working (or labor supply), denoted by N^s. The **time constraint** for the consumer is then

$$l + N^s = h, \tag{4-1}$$

which states that leisure time plus time spent working must sum to total time available.

The Consumer's Real Disposable Income

Having specified how the representative consumer allocates time between work and leisure, we can describe the consumer's real disposable income, which is wage income plus dividend income minus taxes.

Labor time is sold by the consumer in the labor market at a price w in terms of consumption goods. That is, one unit of labor time exchanges for w units of consumption goods. Therefore, w is the **real wage**, or the wage rate of the consumer in units of purchasing power. Throughout, the consumption good plays the role of **numeraire**, or the good in which all prices and quantities are denominated. In actual economies, money is the numeraire, but in our barter economy model, the choice of numeraire is arbitrary. We choose the consumption good as numeraire, as this is a common convention.

If the consumer works N^s hours, then his or her real wage income is wN^s, which is expressed in units of the consumption good. The second source of income for the consumer is profits distributed as dividends from firms. We let π be the quantity of profits, in real terms, that the consumer receives. In our model, firms have to be owned by someone, and this someone must be the representative consumer. Any profits earned by firms, therefore, must be distributed to the representative consumer as income, which we can think of as dividends. We refer to π as real **dividend income**.

Finally, the consumer pays taxes to the government. We assume that the real quantity of taxes is a lump-sum amount T. A **lump-sum tax** is a tax that does not depend in any way on the actions of the economic agent who is being taxed. In practice, no taxes are lump sum; for example, the quantity of sales taxes we pay depends on the quantity of taxable goods that we buy, and our income taxes depend on how much we work. Taxes that are not lump sum have important effects on the effective prices that consumers face in the market. For example, an increase in the sales tax on gasoline increases the effective price of gasoline for consumers relative to other goods. This change in the effective relative price of gasoline in turn affects the demand for gasoline and for other goods. These distorting effects of taxation are important, but we confine attention to lump-sum taxation for now, as this is simpler, from a modeling perspective.

Real wage income plus real dividend income minus taxes is the consumer's real disposable income, and this is what the consumer has available to spend on consumption goods.

The Budget Constraint

Now that we know how the representative consumer can allocate time between work and leisure and what his or her real disposable income is, we can derive the consumer's budget constraint algebraically and show it graphically.

We can view the representative consumer as receiving his or her real disposable income and spending it in the market for consumption goods. What actually happens, however, is that the consumer receives income and pays taxes in terms of consumption goods, and then he or she decides how much to consume out of this disposable income. Because this is a one-period economy, which implies that the consumer has no motive to save, and because the consumer prefers more to less, all disposable income is consumed, so that we have

$$C = wN^s + \pi - T, \tag{4-2}$$

or total real consumption equals real disposable income. Equation (4-2) is the consumer's **budget constraint**. Now, substituting for N^s in Equation (4-2) using Equation (4-1), we get

$$C = w(h - l) + \pi - T. \tag{4-3}$$

The interpretation of Equation (4-3) is that the right-hand side is real disposable income, while the left-hand side is expenditure on consumption goods, so that total market expenditure is equal to disposable income.

Alternatively, if we add wl to both sides of Equation (4-3), we get

$$C + wl = wh + \pi - T. \tag{4-4}$$

An interpretation of Equation (4-4) is that the right-hand side is the implicit quantity of real disposable income the consumer has, and the left-hand side is implicit expenditure on the two goods, consumption and leisure. On the right-hand side of Equation (4-4), because the consumer has h units of time, with each unit of time valued in real terms according to the market real wage w, and $\pi - T$ is real dividend income minus taxes, the total quantity of implicit real disposable income is $wh + \pi - T$. On the left-hand side of Equation (4-4), C is what is spent on consumption goods, while wl is what is implicitly "spent" on leisure. That is, W is the market price of leisure time, because each unit of leisure is forgone labor, and labor time is priced at the real wage w. Thus, $C + wl$ is implicit real expenditure on consumption goods and leisure.

To graph the consumer's budget constraint, it is convenient to write Equation (4-4) in slope–intercept form, with C as the dependent variable, to get

$$C = -wl + wh + \pi - T, \tag{4-5}$$

so that the slope of the budget constraint is $-w$, and the vertical intercept is $wh + \pi - T$. In Figure 4.3 we graph the budget constraint, Equation (4-5), as the line AB. Here, we have drawn the budget constraint for the case where $T > \pi$, so that dividend income minus taxes, $\pi - T$, is negative. Further, by setting $C = 0$ in Equation (4-5) and solving for l, we can get the horizontal intercept, $h + \dfrac{\pi - T}{w}$. The vertical intercept is the maximum quantity of consumption attainable for the consumer, which is what is achieved if the consumer works h hours and consumes no leisure. The horizontal intercept is the maximum number of hours of leisure that the consumer can take and still be able to pay the lump-sum tax.

Figure 4.4 shows what the consumer's budget constraint looks like in the case where $T < \pi$, in which case dividend income minus taxes, $\pi - T$, is positive. Here, the budget constraint is somewhat unusual, as it is kinked; the slope of the budget constraint is $-w$ over its upper portion, and the constraint is vertical over its lower portion. There is a kink in the budget constraint because the consumer cannot consume more than h hours of leisure. Thus, at point B we have $l = h$, which implies that the number of hours worked by the consumer is zero. Points along BD all involve the consumer working zero hours and consuming some amount $C \leq \pi - T$—that is, the consumer

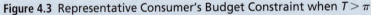

Figure 4.3 Representative Consumer's Budget Constraint when $T > \pi$

The figure shows the consumer's budget constraint for the case in which taxes are greater than the consumer's dividend income. The slope of the budget constraint is $-w$, and the constraint shifts with the quantity of nonwage real disposable income, $\pi - T$. All points in the shaded area and on the budget constraint can be purchased by the consumer.

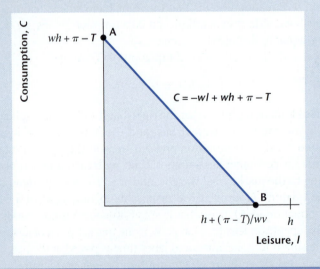

Figure 4.4 Representative Consumer's Budget Constraint when $T < \pi$

The figure shows the consumer's budget constraint when taxes are less than dividend income. This implies that the budget constraint is kinked. The examples we study always deal with this case, rather than the one in which taxes are greater than dividend income. Consumption bundles in the shaded region and on the budget constraint are feasible for the consumer; all other consumption bundles are not feasible.

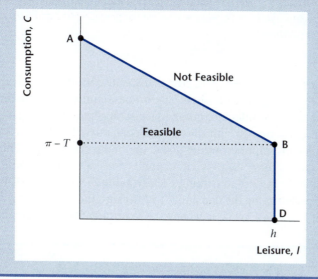

always has the option of throwing away some of his or her dividend income. Even though the consumer does not work at point B we have $C = \pi - T > 0$, as dividend income exceeds taxes. In what follows, we always consider the case where $\pi - T > 0$, as this is the more complicated case (because of the kink in the consumer's budget constraint), and because ultimately it does not make any difference for our analysis whether we look only at the case $\pi - T > 0$ or $\pi - T < 0$.

The representative consumer's budget constraint tells us what consumption bundles are feasible for him or her to consume given the market real wage, dividend income, and taxes. In Figure 4.4, consumption bundles in the shaded region inside and on the budget constraint are feasible; all other consumption bundles are infeasible.

Consumer Optimization

LO 4.3 Show how the consumer optimizes given his or her budget constraint to determine labor supply and consumption.

We have now described the representative consumer's preferences over consumption and leisure, and determined the budget constraint that tells us what combinations of consumption and leisure are feasible. Our next step is to put preferences together with the budget constraint so as to analyze how the representative consumer behaves.

To determine what choice of consumption and leisure the consumer makes, we assume that the consumer is **rational**. Rationality in this context means that the representative consumer knows his or her own preferences and budget constraint and can evaluate which feasible consumption bundle is best for him or her. Basically, we are assuming that the consumer can make an informed optimization decision.

> **Definition 3** *The optimal consumption bundle is the point representing a consumption–leisure pair that is on the highest possible indifference curve and is on or inside the consumer's budget constraint.*

Consider Figure 4.5, and note that we are considering only the case where $T < \pi$, because ignoring the case where $T > \pi$ does not matter. We want to demonstrate why point H, where indifference curve I_1 is just tangent to the budget constraint ABD, is the optimal consumption bundle for the consumer. First, the consumer would never choose a consumption bundle inside the budget constraint. This is because the consumer prefers more to less. For example, consider a point like J in Figure 4.5, which lies inside the budget constraint. Clearly, point F, which is on the budget constraint, is strictly preferred by the consumer to J because the consumer gets more consumption at point F than at J, while receiving the same quantity of leisure. Further, the consumer

Figure 4.5 Consumer Optimization
The consumption bundle represented by point H, where an indifference curve is tangent to the budget constraint, is the optimal consumption bundle for the consumer. Points inside the budget constraint, such as J, cannot be optimal (more is preferred to less), and points such as E and F, where an indifference curve cuts the budget constraint, also cannot be optimal.

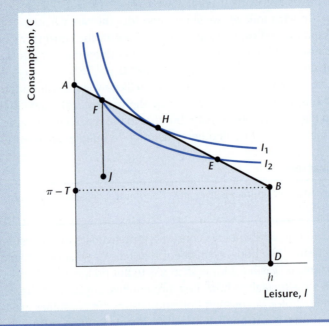

would not choose any points along BD other than B; B is preferred to any point on BD because more consumption goods are preferred to less consumption goods.

In considering the consumer's optimization problem, given our reasoning thus far we can restrict attention solely to points on the line segment AB in Figure 4.5. Which of these points does the consumer choose? Given the assumptions we have made about the representative consumer's preferences, we are guaranteed that there is a single consumption bundle on AB that is optimal for the consumer: the point at which an indifference curve is tangent to AB. Why is this the best the consumer can do? Again, consider Figure 4.5. At a point like F minus the slope of the indifference curve passing through F, or $MRS_{l,C}$, is greater than minus the slope of the budget constraint at F, which is equal to w. Alternatively, at F the rate at which the consumer is willing to trade leisure for consumption is greater than the rate at which the consumer can trade leisure for consumption in the market, or $MRS_{l,C} > w$. The consumer would be better off, therefore, if he or she sacrificed consumption for more leisure by moving from point F in the direction of H. In so doing, the consumer moves to successively higher indifference curves, which is another indication that he or she is becoming better off. Similarly, at point E in Figure 4.5, the indifference curve is flatter than the budget constraint, so that $MRS_{l,C} < w$. Thus, moving from point E toward point H implies that the consumer substitutes consumption for leisure and moves to higher indifference curves, becoming better off as a result. At point H, where an indifference curve is just tangent to the budget constraint, the rate at which the consumer is willing to trade leisure for consumption is equal to the rate at which leisure trades for consumption in the market, and, thus, the consumer is at his or her optimum. In other words, when the representative consumer is optimizing, we have

$$MRS_{l,C} = w, \qquad (4\text{-}6)$$

or the marginal rate of substitution of leisure for consumption is equal to the real wage. In Equation (4-6), this optimizing, or marginal, condition takes the following form: Marginal rate of substitution of leisure for consumption equals the **relative price** of leisure in terms of consumption goods. In general, the relative price of a good x in terms of a good y is the number of units of y that trade for a unit of x. It is generally true that consumer optimization in competitive markets implies that the consumer sets the marginal rate of substitution of any good x for any other good y equal to the relative price of x in terms of y. We use this fact in later chapters.

Given the way we have drawn the budget constraint in Figure 4.5, there seems no obvious reason that the highest indifference curve could not be reached at point B, in which case the consumer would choose to consume all of his or her time as leisure, as in Figure 4.6. However, this could not happen when we take account of the interaction of consumers and firms—it would imply that the representative consumer would not work, in which case nothing would be produced, and, therefore, the consumer would not have anything to consume. The assumption that the consumer always wishes to consume some of both goods (the consumption good and leisure) prevents the consumer from choosing either point A or point B in Figure 4.5.

The assumption that the representative consumer behaves optimally subject to his or her constraints is very powerful in giving us predictions about what the consumer

Figure 4.6 The Representative Consumer Chooses Not to Work
The consumer's optimal consumption bundle is at the kink in the budget constraint, at *B*, so that the consumer does not work or $l = h$. This is a situation that cannot happen, taking into account consistency between the actions of the consumer and of firms.

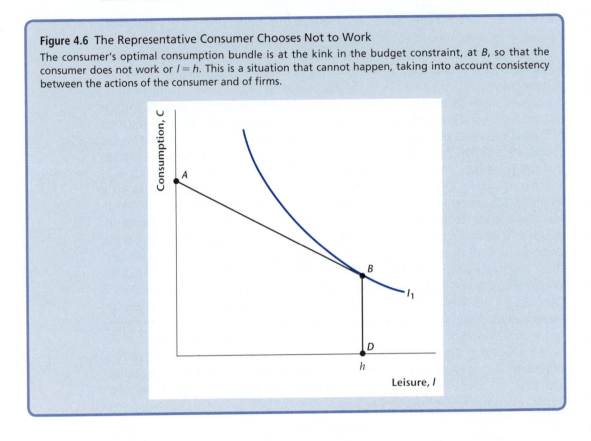

does when his or her budget constraint changes, or when his or her preferences change. Is it plausible to assume that a consumer makes optimizing decisions? In our own lives, we can generally think of many occasions on which we did not make optimal decisions. For example, suppose Jennifer is self-employed and can choose how much vacation to take every year. Suppose that, for ten years, Jennifer takes two weeks of vacation every summer. One year, by chance, she takes three weeks of vacation and finds that she is much happier than before. We might imagine this happening not because Jennifer's preferences or budget constraint changed, but because she does not really know her own preferences without experimenting with different consumption–leisure combinations. This would violate the assumption of rationality that we have made for the representative consumer, who always knows exactly what his or her preferences are. The defense for using optimizing behavior for consumers as a fundamental principle in our models is that mistakes by consumers are not likely to persist for a long time. Eventually, people learn how to behave optimally. Also, what is important, particularly in terms of macroeconomic models, is that people on average behave optimally, not that each individual in the economy always does so. Further, if we were to abandon optimization behavior, there would be many possible alternatives, and it would be extremely difficult to get our models to make any predictions at all. While there is typically only one way to behave optimally, there are many ways in which individuals can be stupid!

How Does the Representative Consumer Respond to a Change in Real Dividends or Taxes?

LO 4.4 Determine the effects of changes in the representative consumer's environment on his or her choices.

Recall from Chapter 1 that a macroeconomic model, once constructed, can be used to conduct "experiments," somewhat like the experiments conducted by a chemist or a physicist using a laboratory apparatus. Now that we have shown how the representative consumer makes choices about consumption and leisure, we are interested as economists in how the consumer responds to changes in the economic environment he or she faces. We carry out two experiments on the representative consumer. The first is to change his or her real dividend income minus taxes, $\pi - T$, and the second is to change the market real wage w that he or she faces. In each case, we are interested in how these experiments affect the quantities of consumption and leisure chosen by the representative consumer.

We first look at a change in real dividend income minus taxes, or $\pi - T$, which is the component of real disposable income that does not depend on the real wage w. In changing $\pi - T$, we hold w constant. A change in $\pi - T$ could be caused either by a change in π or a change in T, or both. For example, an increase in π could be caused by an increase in the productivity of firms, which in turn results in an increase in the dividends that are paid to the consumer. Similarly, if T decreases, this represents a tax cut for the consumer, and disposable income increases. In any case, we think of the increase in $\pi - T$ as producing a **pure income effect** on the consumer's choices, because prices remain the same (w remains constant) while disposable income increases.

For the case where $\pi > T$, we consider an increase in $\pi - T$ (recall that the $\pi < T$ case is not fundamentally different). In Figure 4.7, suppose that initially $\pi = \pi_1$ and $T = T_1$, and then there are changes in π and T so that $\pi = \pi_2$ and $T = T_2$ with $\pi_2 - T_2 > \pi_1 - T_1$. Recall that the vertical intercept of the budget constraint is $wh + \pi - T$, so that initially the budget constraint of the consumer is ABD and, with the increase in $\pi - T$, the constraint shifts out to FJD. FJ is parallel to AB, because the real wage has not changed, leaving the slope of the budget constraint ($-w$) identical to what it was initially. Now suppose that initially the consumer chooses point H, where the highest indifference curve I_1 is reached on the initial budget constraint, and we have $l = l_1$ and $C = C_1$. When $\pi - T$ increases, which consumption bundle does the consumer choose? We have the consumer choosing point K, where the indifference curve I_2 is tangent to the new budget constraint. At point K, we have $l = l_2$ and $C = C_2$, so that consumption and leisure are both higher. Why would this necessarily be the case? Indeed, we could draw indifference curves that are consistent with more being preferred to less and a preference for diversity, and have the consumer choose either less consumption or less leisure when income increases. Recall, however, that we assumed earlier in this chapter that consumption and leisure are normal goods. This means that, if we hold the real wage constant, then an increase in income implies that the representative consumer chooses more consumption and more leisure, as is the case in Figure 4.7.

Figure 4.7 An Increase in $\pi - T$ for the Consumer

Initially the consumer chooses H, and when $\pi - T$ rises, this shifts the budget constraint out in a parallel fashion (the real wage, which determines the slope of the budget constraint, stays constant). Consumption and leisure both increase, as both are normal goods.

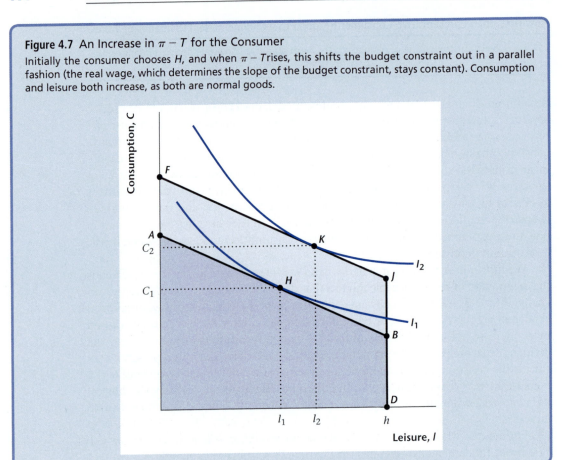

To see why it is natural to assume that consumption and leisure are both normal goods, consider a consumer, Gillian, who receives a windfall increase in her income from winning a lottery. It seems likely that, as a result, Gillian spends more on consumption goods and takes more vacation time, thus working less and increasing leisure time. This would happen only if Gillian's preferences have the property that consumption and leisure are normal goods.

The assumption that consumption and leisure are both normal implies that higher nonwage disposable income increases consumption and reduces labor supply. Thus, for example, given lower real taxes, consumers spend more and work less. The increase in income is given in Figure 4.7 by the distance AF, but the increase in consumption, $C_2 - C_1$, is less than AF. This is because, though nonwage income increases, wage income falls because the consumer is working less. The reduction in income from the decrease in wage income does not completely offset the increase in nonwage income, as consumption has to increase because it is a normal good.

The Representative Consumer and Changes in the Real Wage: Income and Substitution Effects

LO 4.4 Determine the effects of changes in the representative consumer's environment on his or her choices.

The second experiment we conduct is to change the real wage faced by the representative consumer, holding everything else constant. In studying how consumer behavior changes when the market real wage changes, we care about how the consumer's quantity of consumption is affected, but we are perhaps most concerned with what happens to leisure and labor supply. In elementary economics, we typically treat supply curves as being upward-sloping, in that the quantity of a good supplied increases with the market price of the good, holding everything else constant. Labor supply, however, is different. Although it is straightforward to show that the quantity of consumption goods chosen by the consumer increases when the real wage increases, labor supply, N^s, may rise or fall when the real wage rises. Part of this section focuses on why this is the case.

In considering how the behavior of the consumer changes in response to a change in the real wage w, we hold constant real dividends π and real taxes T. We do the experiment in this way to remove the pure income effect on consumer behavior that we studied in the previous subsection. Consider Figure 4.8, where initially the budget constraint is ABD, and an increase in the real wage w causes the budget constraint to shift out to EBD. Here, EB is steeper than AB because the real wage has increased, but the kink in the budget constraint remains fixed at B as nonwage disposable income, $\pi - T$, is unchanged. Initially, the consumer chooses point F, where indifference curve I_1 is tangent to the initial budget constraint. Here, $l = l_1$ and $C = C_1$. When the real wage increases, the consumer might choose a point like H, where indifference curve I_2 is tangent to the new budget constraint. As Figure 4.8 is drawn, leisure remains unchanged at l_1, and consumption increases from C_1 to C_2. What we want to show is that, given that consumption and leisure are normal goods, consumption must increase but leisure may increase or decrease in response to an increase in the real wage. To understand why this is the case, we need to introduce the concepts of *income effect* and *substitution effect*.

The effects of an increase in the real wage on the consumer's optimal choice of consumption and leisure can be broken down into an income effect and a substitution effect as follows. First, given the new higher real wage, suppose that we take away dividend income from the consumer or increase taxes until he or she chooses a consumption bundle O that is on the initial indifference curve I_1. Thus, given the increase in the real wage, we have taken real disposable income away from the consumer so that he or she is just indifferent between the consumption bundle chosen (point O) and the initial consumption bundle (F). It is as if the consumer now faces the budget constraint JKD. The movement from F to O is a pure **substitution effect** in that it just captures the movement along the indifference curve in response to the increase in the real wage. The real wage increases, so that leisure has become more expensive relative to consumption goods, and the consumer substitutes away from the good that has become more expensive (leisure) to the one that has become relatively cheaper (consumption).

Figure 4.8 Increase in the Real Wage Rate—Income and Substitution Effects

An increase in the real wage shifts the budget constraint from *ABD* to *EBD*. The kink in the constraint remains fixed, and the budget constraint becomes steeper. Consumption must increase, but leisure may rise or fall, because of opposing substitution and income effects. The substitution effect is the movement from *F* to *O*; the income effect is the movement from *O* to *H*.

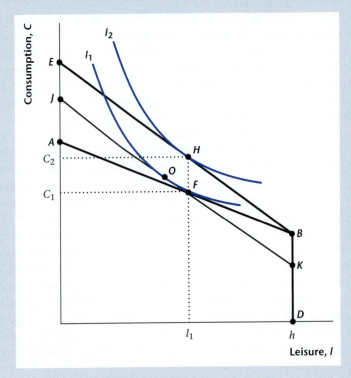

Therefore, the substitution effect of the real wage increase is for consumption to increase and for leisure to decrease, and so the substitution effect is for labor supply, $N^s = h = l$, to increase.

Now, the movement from O to H is then a pure **income effect**, as the real wage stays the same as the budget constraint shifts out from *JKD* to *EBD*, and nonwage income increases. Because both goods are normal, consumption increases and leisure increases in moving from O to H. Thus, when the real wage increases, the consumer can consume more consumption goods and more leisure, because the budget constraint has shifted out. On net, then, consumption must increase, because the substitution and income effects both act to increase consumption. There are opposing substitution and income effects on leisure, however, so that it is ultimately unclear whether leisure rises or falls. Therefore, an increase in the real wage could lead to an increase or a decrease in labor supply N^s.

To understand the intuition behind this result, assume Alex is working 40 hours per week and earning $15.00 per hour, so that his weekly wage income is $600.00.

Now suppose that Alex's wage rate increases to $20.00 per hour and that he is free to set his hours of work. On the one hand, because his wage rate is now higher, the cost of taking leisure has increased, and Alex may choose to work more (the substitution effect). On the other hand, he could now work 30 hours per week, still receive $600.00 in wage income per week, and enjoy 10 more hours of free time (the income effect), so that Alex may choose to reduce his hours of work.

While some of the analysis we do, particularly in Chapter 5, involves work with indifference curves, it is sometimes useful to summarize consumer behavior with supply and demand relationships. In Chapter 9 and in later chapters, it often proves useful to work at the level of supply and demand curves in different markets. Then, an important relationship is the **labor supply curve**, which tells us how much labor the representative consumer wishes to supply given any real wage. To construct the labor supply curve, one could imagine presenting the representative consumer with different real wage rates and asking what quantity of labor the consumer would choose to supply at each wage rate. That is, suppose $l(w)$ is a function that tells us how much leisure the consumer wishes to consume, given the real wage w. Then, the labor supply curve is given by

$$N^s(w) = h - l(w).$$

Now, because the effect of a wage increase on the consumer's leisure choice is ambiguous, we do not know whether labor supply is increasing or decreasing in the real wage. Assuming that the substitution effect is larger than the income effect of a change in the real wage, labor supply increases with an increase in the real wage, and the labor supply schedule is upward-sloping as in Figure 4.9. Furthermore, we know that, because the quantity of leisure increases when nonwage disposable income increases, an increase in nonwage disposable income shifts the labor supply curve to the left, that is, from N^s to N_1^s as shown in Figure 4.10. In analysis where we work with supply and demand relationships, we typically assume that the substitution effect of an increase in the real wage dominates the income effect, so that the labor supply curve is upward-sloping, as in Figure 4.9.

An Example: Consumption and Leisure Are Perfect Complements

An example of consumer optimization that we can work out in a straightforward way, both algebraically and graphically, is the case in which the representative consumer's preferences have the **perfect complements** property. Goods are perfect complements for the consumer if he or she always wishes to consume these goods in fixed proportions. In practice, there are many cases of goods that are perfect complements. For example, right shoes are almost always consumed one-to-one with left shoes, in that a right shoe is typically not much good without the left shoe. Also, cars and tires are usually consumed in fixed proportions of one to four (ignoring the spare tire, of course).

If consumption and leisure are perfect complements, then the consumer always wishes to have $\dfrac{C}{l}$ equal to some constant, or

$$C = al, \tag{4-7}$$

Figure 4.9 Labor Supply Curve

The labor supply curve tells us how much labor the consumer wishes to supply for each possible value for the real wage. Here, the labor supply curve is upward-sloping, which implies that the substitution effect of an increase in the real wage is larger than the income effect for the consumer.

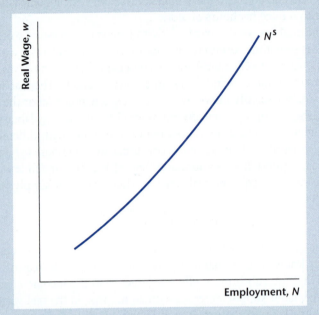

Figure 4.10 Effect of an Increase in Dividend Income or a Decrease in Taxes

The labor supply curve shifts to the left when dividend income increases or taxes fall, as a result of a positive income effect on leisure for the consumer.

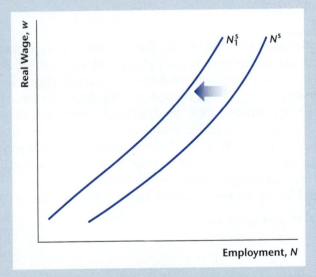

where $a > 0$ is a constant. With perfect complements, the indifference curves of the consumer are L-shaped, as in Figure 4.11, with the right angles of the indifference curves falling along the line $C = al$. At a point such as E on indifference curve I_2, adding more consumption while holding leisure constant simply makes the consumer indifferent, as does adding more leisure while holding consumption constant. The consumer can be better off only if he or she receives more of both goods. Note that perfect complements preferences do not satisfy all the properties for preferences that we assumed in general. More is not always preferred to less, as the consumer is not better off with more of one good unless he or she has more of the other good as well. However, the consumer does have a preference for diversity, but of a very dramatic sort. That is, as we move downward along the indifference curve, the slope does not become flatter in a smooth way but goes instantly from vertical to horizontal.

The optimal consumption bundle for the consumer is always along the line $C = al$, as in Figure 4.11, where the budget constraint is ABD and the consumer optimizes by choosing a point that is on the budget constraint and on the highest indifference curve, which is point F. Algebraically, the quantities of consumption and leisure must solve Equation (4-7) and must also satisfy the budget constraint

$$C = w(h - l) + \pi - T. \tag{4-8}$$

Figure 4.11 Perfect Complements

When consumption and leisure are perfect complements for the consumer, indifference curves are L-shaped with right angles along the line $C = al$, where a is a constant. The budget constraint is ABD, and the optimal consumption bundle is always on the line $C = al$.

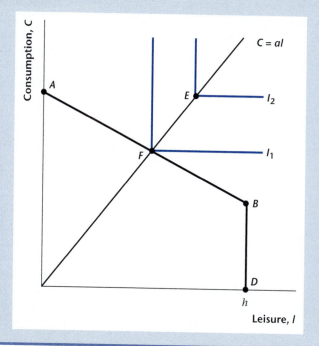

MACROECONOMICS IN ACTION
How Elastic Is Labor Supply?

It is tempting to view poverty as an easy problem to solve. If one assumed that real GDP was essentially fixed, then it might make sense to redistribute income from the lucky rich to the unlucky poor so that we could be collectively better off. Government income redistribution—through the tax system and the provision of goods and services such as parks and health care—might be seen as poverty insurance. We might then argue that since the private sector has failed to provide this insurance against poverty, the government should step in to fill the void.

An important means for redistributing income in the United States and other countries is through the taxation of labor. In particular, federal and state income taxes are progressive, in that income taxes represent a smaller fraction of income for the typical poor person than for the typical rich person. This contrasts with sales taxes, which tend to be regressive—the typical poor person pays a larger fraction of his or her income to the government in the form of sales taxes than does a typical rich person.

It is well understood, though, that income taxation has incentive effects. In our simple model of consumer behavior, an easy way to study the effects of income taxation on a consumer is to assume that the consumer's wage income is taxed at a constant rate, t. Then, supposing that the lump-sum tax is zero, or $T = 0$, the consumer would pay total taxes of $tw(h - l)$, and the consumer's budget constraint would be

$$C = w(1 - t)(h - l) + \pi.$$

Then, if we wanted to analyze the effects of a change in the income tax rate t on labor supply, given the market real wage w, this would be the same as analyzing the effects of a change in the real wage, since now $w(1 - t)$ is the effective real wage for the consumer, and an increase in t is equivalent to a decrease in the consumer's effective real wage. From our analysis in this chapter, theory tells us that an increase in the income tax rate t may cause an increase or a decrease in the quantity of labor supplied, depending on the relative strengths of opposing income and substitution effects. For example, an increase in t will reduce labor supply only if the substitution effect is large relative to the income effect. That is, if the substitution effect is relatively large, then there can be a large disincentive effect on hours of work as the result of an increase in the income tax rate.

This disincentive effect might give us pause if we wanted to think of the income tax as a useful means for redistributing income. If the substitution effect is large, so that the elasticity of labor supply with respect to wages is large, then real GDP should not be considered a fixed pie that can be redistributed at will. An attempt to divide up the pie differently by increasing income tax rates for the rich and reducing them for the poor might actually reduce the size of the pie substantially.

Whether the reduction in real GDP from a redistributive tax system is a serious problem turns on how large the elasticity of labor supply is. Typically, in studying how individuals adjust hours of work in response to changes in wages, labor economists find the effects to be small. Thus, according to microeconomic evidence, the elasticity of labor supply with respect to wages is small, therefore the disincentive effects from income taxation are small, and redistributing the pie will not reduce the size of the pie by very much.

However, for macroeconomists this is not the end of the story. In a working paper,[1] Michael Keane and Richard Rogerson review the evidence on labor supply elasticities. For macroeconomists, the key idea is that what matters for aggregate economic activity is total labor input, which is determined by three factors: (i) how many hours each individual works; (ii) how many individuals are working; and (iii) the quality of the labor hours supplied.

Microeconomic evidence on labor supply typically focuses on the labor hours supplied by individuals and how this responds to wages. This is the so-called intensive margin—how intensively an individual works. However, as Keane and Rogerson point out, changes in aggregate hours worked over both short and long periods of time are influenced in an important way by choices at the extensive margin; that is, the choices of individuals about whether to work or not. While a higher market income tax rate might have little effect on any individual worker's hours of work, it might induce more people to leave the labor force. For example, some people might choose to care for their children at home rather than working in the market. In fact, if we take into account the extensive margin, the aggregate labor supply elasticity is much higher.

Thus, in our macroeconomic model, it is most useful to think of the representative consumer as a fictitious person who stands in for the average consumer in the economy. Hours of work for this fictitious person should be interpreted as average hours of work in the whole economy. Thus, when aggregate hours of work change in practice, because of changes along the intensive and extensive margins, we should think of this as

changes in the representative consumer's hours of work in our model.

Another dimension on which labor supply can change, as mentioned above, is in terms of the quality of labor hours supplied. This is essentially a long-run effect that occurs through occupational choice. For example, if income tax rates are increased for the rich and reduced for the poor, this reduces the incentive of young people to obtain the education required to perform higher-paying jobs. Fewer people will choose to become engineers, and more will choose to become plumbers. The evidence in Keane and Rogerson's article suggests that this effect is large.

What would the United States look like if we chose to be a much more egalitarian society, by using the income tax to redistribute income from rich to the poor? For a very rich person, the after-tax wage earned for an extra hour of work would be much lower than it is now, and for a very poor person, the after-tax wage at the margin would be much higher. Average hours worked among employed people in this egalitarian society would be somewhat lower than now, but there would be many more people who would choose not to participate in the labor force. As well, over the long run, the average level of skills acquired by the population would be much lower. Real GDP would fall.

Some have argued that there is evidence that higher taxation of labor explains differences between the United States and Europe in labor supply and real GDP per capita.[2] However, if we compare Canada and the United States, Canada has a more progressive tax system than does the United States, but Canada also has higher labor force participation. So, the conclusions we might draw about labor market incentive effects are not evident from a cursory look at the data. Drawing firm conclusions, as is usually the case, requires in-depth economic research.

---

[1] M. Keane and R. Rogerson, 2011. "Reconciling Micro- and Macrolabor Supply Elasticities: A Structural Perspective," NBER working paper 17430.

[2] E. Prescott, 2004. "Why Do Americans Work More Than Europeans?" *Minneapolis Federal Reserve Bank Quarterly Review* 28, No. 1, 2–13.

Now, Equations (4-7) and (4-8) are two equations in the two unknowns, C and l, with a, w, h, π, and T given. We can solve these two equations for the two unknowns by substitution to get

$$l = \frac{wh + \pi - T}{a + w},$$

$$C = \frac{a(wh + \pi - T)}{a + w}.$$

From the above solution, note that leisure and consumption increase with nonwage disposable income $\pi - T$, and we can also show that consumption and leisure both increase when the real wage w increases. With perfect complements there are no substitution effects. Further, if a increases, so that the consumer prefers more consumption relative to leisure, then it is obvious that the consumer chooses more of C and less of l at the optimum.

We use perfect complements preferences in examples in Chapter 8. Another simple example that is dealt with in the problems at the end of this chapter is the case where preferences have the **perfect substitutes** property. In that case, the marginal rate of substitution is constant and the indifference curves are downward-sloping straight lines.

The Representative Firm

LO 4.5 List the properties of the production function, and explain why it is useful to assume these properties.

In our model economy, consumers and firms come together to exchange labor for consumption goods. While the representative consumer supplies labor and demands consumption goods, we turn now to the behavior of firms, which demand labor and supply consumption goods. The choices of the firms are determined by the available technology and by profit maximization. As with consumer behavior, we ultimately focus here on the choices of a single, representative firm.

The firms in this economy own productive capital (plant and equipment), and they hire labor to produce consumption goods. We can describe the production technology available to each firm by a **production function**, which describes the technological possibilities for converting factor inputs into outputs. We can express this relationship in algebraic terms as

$$Y = zF(K, N^d), \tag{4-9}$$

where z is total factor productivity, Y is output of consumption goods, K is the quantity of capital input in the production process, N^d is the quantity of labor input measured as total hours worked by employees of the firm, and F is a function. Because this is a one-period or static (as opposed to dynamic) model, we treat K as being a fixed input to production, and N^d as a variable factor of production. That is, in the short run, firms cannot vary the quantity of plant and equipment (K) they have, but they have flexibility in hiring and laying off workers (N^d). **Total factor productivity**, z, captures the degree of sophistication of the production process. That is, an increase in Z makes both factors of production, K and N^d, more productive, in that, given factor inputs, higher z implies that more output can be produced.

For example, suppose that the above production function represents the technology available to a bakery. The quantity of capital, K, includes the building in which the bakery operates, ovens for baking bread, a computer for doing the bakery accounts, and other miscellaneous equipment. The quantity of labor, N^d, is total hours worked by all the bakery employees, including the manager, the bakers who operate the ovens, and the employees who work selling the bakery's products to customers. The variable z, total factor productivity, can be affected by the techniques used for organizing production. For example, bread could be produced either by having each baker operate an individual oven, using this oven to produce different kinds of bread, or each baker could specialize in making a particular kind of bread and use the oven that happens to be available when an oven is needed. If the latter production method produces more bread per day using the same inputs of capital and labor, then that production process implies a higher value of z than does the first process.

For our analysis, we need to discuss several important properties of the production function. Before doing this, we need the following definition.

> **Definition 4** *The **marginal product** of a factor of production is the additional output that can be produced with one additional unit of that factor input, holding constant the quantities of the other factor inputs.*

In the production function on the right side of Equation (4-9), there are two factor inputs, labor and capital. Figure 4.12 shows a graph of the production function, fixing the quantity of capital at some arbitrary value, K^*, and allowing the labor input, N^d, to vary. Some of the properties of this graph require further explanation. The marginal product of labor, given the quantity of labor N^*, is the slope of the production function at point A; this is because the slope of the production function is the additional output produced from an additional unit of the labor input when the quantity of labor is N^* and the quantity of capital is K^*. We let MP_N denote the marginal product of labor.

Next, in Figure 4.13 we graph the production function again, but this time we fix the quantity of labor at N^* and allow the quantity of capital to vary. In Figure 4.13, the marginal product of capital, denoted MP_K, given the quantity of capital K^*, is the slope of the production function at point A.

The production function has five key properties, which we will discuss in turn.

1. *The production function exhibits constant returns to scale.* **Constant returns to scale** means that, given any constant $x > 0$, the following relationship holds:

$$zF(xK, xN^d) = xzF(K, N^d).$$

Figure 4.12 Production Function, Fixing the Quantity of Capital, and Varying the Quantity of Labor

The marginal product of labor is the slope of the production function at a given point. Note that the marginal product of labor declines with the quantity of labor.

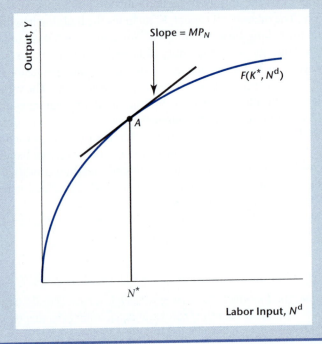

That is, if all factor inputs are changed by a factor x then output changes by the same factor x. For example, if all factor inputs double ($x = 2$), then output also doubles. The alternatives to constant returns to scale in production are **increasing returns to scale** and **decreasing returns to scale**. Increasing returns to scale implies that large firms (firms producing a large quantity of output) are more efficient than small firms, whereas decreasing returns to scale implies that small firms are more efficient than large firms. With constant returns to scale, a small firm is just as efficient as a large firm. Indeed, constant returns to scale means that a very large firm simply replicates how a very small firm produces many times over. Given a constant-returns-to-scale production function, the economy behaves in exactly the same way if there were many small firms producing consumption goods as it would if there were a few large firms, provided that all firms behave competitively (they are price-takers in product and factor markets). Given this, it is most convenient to suppose that there is only one firm in the economy, the **representative firm**. Just as with the representative consumer, it is helpful to think of the representative firm as a convenient stand-in for many firms, which all have the same constant-returns-to-scale production function. In practice, it is clear that in some industries decreasing returns to scale

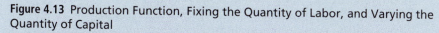

Figure 4.13 Production Function, Fixing the Quantity of Labor, and Varying the Quantity of Capital

The slope of the production function is the marginal product of capital, and the marginal product of capital declines with the quantity of capital.

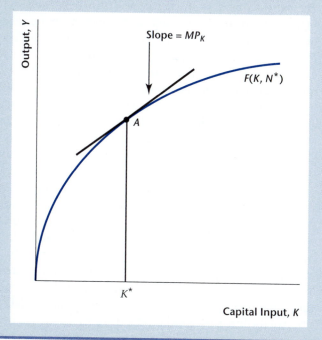

are important. For example, high-quality restaurant food seems to be produced most efficiently on a small scale. Alternatively, increasing returns to scale are important in the automobile industry, where essentially all production occurs in very large-scale firms, such as General Motors (which of course is not as large-scale as it once was). This does not mean, however, that it is harmful to assume that there exists constant returns to scale in production at the aggregate level, as is the case in our model. This is because even the largest firm in the U.S. economy produces a small amount of output relative to U.S. GDP, and the aggregate economy can exhibit constant returns to scale in aggregate production, even if this is not literally true for each firm in the economy.

2. *The production function has the property that output increases when either the capital input or the labor input increases.* In other words, the marginal products of labor and capital are both positive: $MP_N > 0$ and $MP_K > 0$. In Figures 4.12 and 4.13, these properties of the production function are exhibited by the upward slope of the production function. Recall that the slope of the production function in Figure 4.12 is the marginal product of labor and the slope in Figure 4.13 is the marginal product of capital. Positive marginal products are quite natural properties of the production function, as this states simply that more inputs yield

more output. In the bakery example discussed previously, if the bakery hires more workers given the same capital equipment, it will produce more bread, and if it installs more ovens given the same quantity of workers, it will also produce more bread.

3. *The marginal product of labor decreases as the quantity of labor increases.* In Figure 4.12 the declining marginal product of labor is reflected in the concavity of the production function. That is, the slope of the production function in Figure 4.12, which is equal to MP_N, decreases as N^d increases. The following example helps to illustrate why the marginal product of labor should fall as the quantity of labor input increases: Suppose accountants work in an office building that has one photocopy machine, and suppose that they work with pencils and paper but at random intervals need to use the photocopy machine. The first accountant added to the production process, Sara, is very productive—that is, she has a high marginal product—as she can use the photocopy machine whenever she wants. However, when the second accountant, Paul, is added, Sara on occasion wants to use the machine and she gets up from her desk, walks to the machine, and finds that Paul is using it. Thus, some time is wasted that could otherwise be spent working. Paul and Sara produce more than Sara alone, but what Paul adds to production (his marginal product) is lower than the marginal product of Sara. Similarly, adding a third accountant, Julia, makes for even more congestion around the photocopy machine, and Julia's marginal product is lower than Paul's marginal product, which is lower than Sara's. Figure 4.14 shows the representative firm's marginal product of labor schedule. This is a graph of the firm's marginal product, given a fixed quantity of capital, as a function of the labor input. That is, this is the graph of the slope of the production function in Figure 4.12. The marginal product schedule is always positive, and it slopes downward.

4. *The marginal product of capital decreases as the quantity of capital increases.* This property of the production function is very similar to the previous one, and it is illustrated in Figure 4.13 by the decreasing slope, or concavity, of the production function. In terms of the example above, if we suppose that Sara, Paul, and Julia are the accountants working in the office and imagine what happens as we add photocopy machines, we can gain some intuition as to why the decreasing-marginal-product-of-capital property is natural. Adding the first photocopy machine adds a great deal to total output, as Sara, Paul, and Julia now can duplicate documents that formerly had to be copied by hand. With three accountants in the office, however, there is congestion around the machine. This congestion is relieved with the addition of a second machine, so that the second machine increases output, but the marginal product of the second machine is smaller than the marginal product of the first machine, and so on.

5. *The marginal product of labor increases as the quantity of the capital input increases.* To provide some intuition for this property of the production function, return to the example of the accounting firm. Suppose that Sara, Paul, and Julia initially have one photocopy machine to work with. Adding another photocopy

Figure 4.14 Marginal Product of Labor Schedule for the Representative Firm

The marginal product of labor declines as the quantity of labor used in the production process increases.

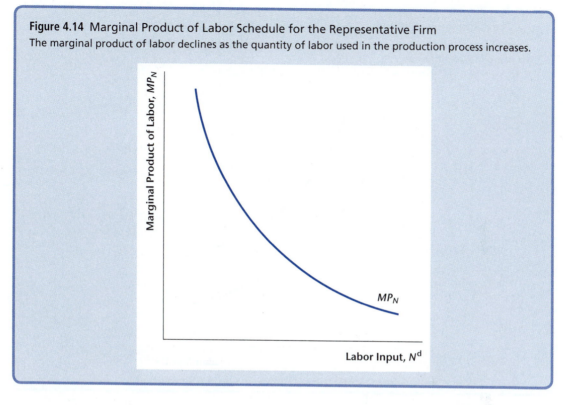

machine amounts to adding capital equipment, and this relieves congestion around the copy machine and makes each of Sara, Paul, and Julia more productive, including Julia, who was the last accountant added to the workforce at the firm. Therefore, adding more capital increases the marginal product of labor, for each quantity of labor. In Figure 4.15 an increase in the quantity of capital from K_1 to K_2 shifts the marginal product of labor schedule to the right, from MP_N^1 to MP_N^2.

The Effect of a Change in Total Factor Productivity on the Production Function

Changes in total factor productivity, z, are critical to our understanding of the causes of economic growth and business cycles, and so we must understand how a change in z alters the production technology. An increase in total factor productivity z has two important effects. First, because more output can be produced given capital and labor inputs when z increases, this shifts the production function up. In Figure 4.16, with the quantity of capital fixed at K^*, there is an upward shift in the production function when z increases from z_1 to z_2. Second, the marginal product of labor increases when z increases. This is reflected in the fact that the slope of the production function when $z = z_2$ in Figure 4.16 is higher than the slope given $Z = z_1$, for any

Figure 4.15 Adding Capital Increases the Marginal Product of Labor

For each quantity of the labor input, the marginal product of labor increases when the quantity of capital used in production increases.

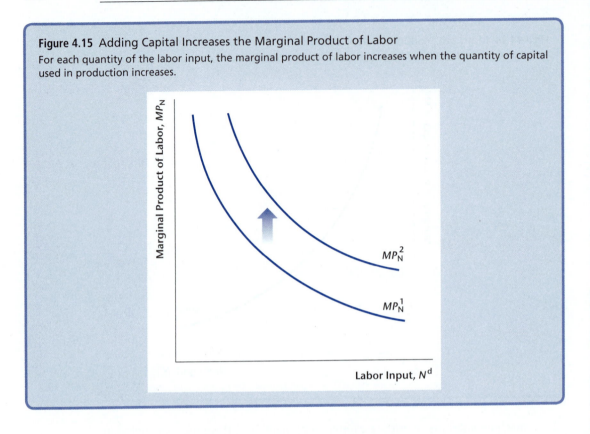

given quantity of the labor input, N^d. In Figure 4.17 the marginal product of labor schedule shifts to the right from MP_N^1 to MP_N^2 when z increases. An increase in z has a similar effect on the marginal product of labor schedule to an increase in the capital stock (see Figure 4.15).

What could cause a change in total factor productivity? In general, an increase in z arises from anything that permits more output to be produced for given inputs. In the macroeconomy, there are many factors that can cause z to increase. One of these factors is technological innovation. The best examples of technological innovations that increase total factor productivity are changes in the organization of production or in management techniques. For example, the assembly line, introduced to automobile manufacturing by Henry Ford (see Macroeconomics in Action: Henry Ford and Total Factor Productivity) brought about a huge increase in the quantity of Model T Fords that could be produced using the same quantities of capital equipment and workers. Some of the most important inventions of the twentieth century—for example, the personal computer—might more appropriately be considered to involve increases in the capital stock rather than increases in z because the new technology is

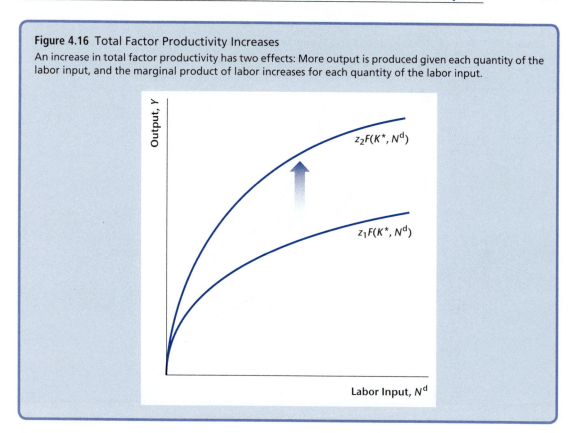

Figure 4.16 Total Factor Productivity Increases

An increase in total factor productivity has two effects: More output is produced given each quantity of the labor input, and the marginal product of labor increases for each quantity of the labor input.

embodied in capital equipment. A second factor that acts to increase z is good weather. Weather is very important for production in the agricultural and construction sectors, in particular. For example, crop yields are higher, given factor inputs, if rainfall is higher (as long as it is not too high), and construction projects proceed more quickly if rainfall is lower. A third factor affecting z is government regulations. For example, if the government imposes regulations requiring that firms install pollution abatement equipment, this may be good for the welfare of the population, but it results in a decrease in z. This happens because pollution abatement equipment increases the quantity of the capital input in the production process but contributes nothing to measured output. Finally, an increase in the relative price of energy is often interpreted as a decrease in z. When the relative price of energy increases, firms use less energy in production, and this reduces the productivity of both capital and labor, thus causing a decrease in z. Major increases in the price of energy occurred in the United States in 1973–1974 and in 1979, 1990, 2000, and then in 2002 through 2008. These energy price increases had important macroeconomic consequences, which we study in Chapters 5, 11, and 13.

Figure 4.17 Effect of an Increase in Total Factor Productivity on the Marginal Product of Labor
When total factor productivity increases, the marginal product of labor schedule shifts to the right.

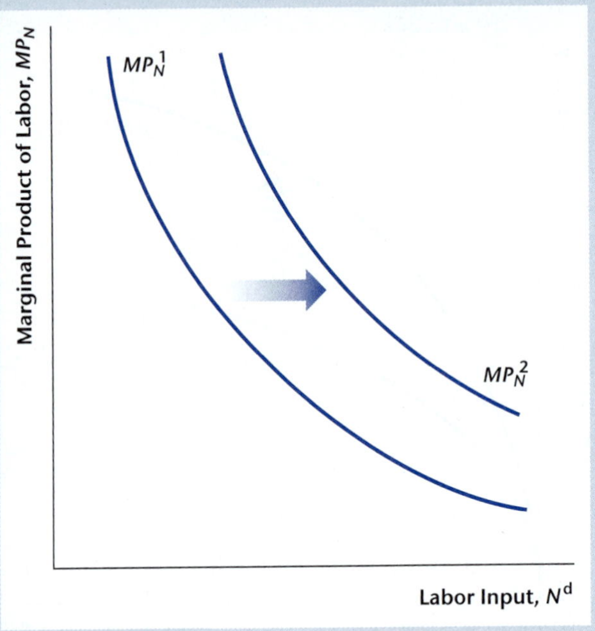

The Profit Maximization Problem of the Representative Firm

LO 4.6 Show how the representative firm optimizes given its production technology to determine labor demand and output.

LO 4.7 Determine the effects of changes in the representative firm's environment on its labor demand and output choices.

Now that we have studied the properties of the representative firm's production technology, we can examine the determinants of the firm's demand for labor. Like the representative consumer, the representative firm behaves competitively, in that it takes as given the real wage, which is the price at which labor trades for consumption goods. The goal of the firm is to maximize its profits, given by $Y - wN^d$, where Y is the total revenue that the firm receives from selling its output, in units of the consumption good, and wN^d is the total real cost of the labor input, or total real variable costs. Then, substituting for Y using the production function $Y = zF(K, N^d)$, the firm's problem is to choose N^d to maximize

$$\pi = zF(K, N^d) - wN^d,$$

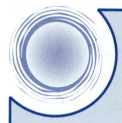

MACROECONOMICS IN ACTION
Henry Ford and
Total Factor Productivity

The Ford Motor Company was founded in 1903 by Henry Ford and a financial backer, but Ford achieved only modest success until the introduction to the market of the Model T Ford in 1908. This car proved to be extremely popular, because it was light, strong, simple, and relatively easy to drive. Given the high demand for Model T cars, Henry Ford decided to increase output, but he did this not by simply replicating his existing production process through the construction of identical plants; rather, he increased total factor productivity, while also augmenting the capital and labor inputs in production. A key element of the total factor productivity increase was the introduction of the assembly line to automobile manufacturing. Henry Ford borrowed this idea from assembly lines used in the Chicago meat-packing industry. However, the general principle at work in the assembly line was known much earlier, for example by Adam Smith, the father of modern economics. In the *Wealth of Nations*, Smith discusses how production was organized in a pin factory, as an illustration of what he called the "division of labor":

> One man draws out the wire, another straightens it, a third cuts it . . . the important business of making a pin is, in this manner, divided into about eighteen distinct operations . . .[3]

Smith was impressed by how the specialization of tasks led to increased productivity in the manufacture of pins. More than a century later, Henry Ford's assembly line replaced an arrangement where automobiles were assembled by teams that each accumulated parts and completed a single automobile in a single location in the plant. Just as in the pin factory, Ford was able to exploit the gains from specialization that the assembly line permitted, where each worker performed only one specialized task, and, therefore, automobiles could be completed at a much higher rate. The increase in total factor productivity at the Ford Motor Company was reflected by the fact that in 1914, 13,000 workers produced 260,720 cars, while in the rest of the U.S. automobile industry 66,350 workers produced 286,770 cars. Thus, output per worker at Ford was almost five times that in the rest of the U.S. auto industry! We do not have measures of the size of the capital stock at Ford and elsewhere in the auto industry, so that there is a slim chance that the higher quantity of output per worker at Ford could have been due simply to higher capital per worker. However, it seems safe to say that total factor productivity at Ford Motor Company increased by a remarkable amount because of the innovations of Henry Ford, and these innovations were quickly imitated in the rest of the auto industry.[4]

[3] From An Enquiry into the Nature and Causes of the Wealth of Nations by Adam Smith, © 1981 Oxford University Press.

[4] See H. Ford, 1926, *My Life and Work*, Doubleday, Page and Co., New York; A. Nevins, 1954, *Ford: The Times, the Man, the Company*, Charles Scribner's and Sons, New York.

THEORY CONFRONTS THE DATA

Total Factor Productivity and the U.S. Aggregate Production Function

So far we have assumed that the production function for the representative firm takes the form $Y = zF(K, N^d)$, where the function F has some very general properties (constant returns to scale, diminishing marginal products, etc.). When macroeconomists work with data to test theories, or when they want to simulate a macroeconomic model on the computer to study some quantitative aspects of a theory, they need to be much more specific about the form the production function takes. A very common production function used in theory and empirical work is the **Cobb–Douglas production function**. This function takes the form

$$Y = zK^a(N^d)^{1-a},$$

where a is a parameter, with $0 < a < 1$. The exponents on K and N^d in the function sum to 1 $(a + 1 - a = 1)$, which reflects constant returns to scale. If there are profit-maximizing, price-taking firms and constant returns to scale, then a Cobb–Douglas production function implies that a will be the share that capital receives of national income (in our model, the profits of firms), and $1 - a$ the share that labor receives (wage income before taxes) in equilibrium. Given this, an empirical estimate of a is the average share of capital in national income, which from the data is about 0.30, or 30%, so a good approximation to the actual U.S. aggregate production function is

$$Y = zK^{0.30}(N^d)^{0.70}. \qquad (4\text{-}10)$$

In Equation (4-10), the quantities Y, K, and N^d can all be measured. For example, Y can be measured as real GDP from the NIPA, K can be measured as the total quantity of capital in existence, built up from expenditures on capital goods in the NIPA, and N^d can be measured as total employment, in the Current Population Survey done by the Bureau of Labor Statistics. But how is total factor productivity z measured? Total factor productivity cannot be measured directly, but it can be measured indirectly, as a residual. That is, from Equation (4-10), if we can measure Y, K, and N^d, then a measure of z is the **Solow residual**, which is calculated as

$$z = \frac{Y}{K^{0.30}(N^d)^{0.70}}. \qquad (4\text{-}11)$$

This measure of total factor productivity is named after Robert Solow.[5] In Figure 4.18, we graph the Solow residual for the United States for the period 1948–2014, calculated using Equation (4-11) and measurements of Y, K, and N^d as described above. Measured total factor productivity grows over time, and it fluctuates about trend. In Chapters 7, 8, and 13, we see how growth and fluctuations in total factor productivity can cause growth and fluctuations in real GDP.

---

[5] See R. Solow, 1957. "Technical Change and the Aggregate Production Function," *Review of Economic Statistics* 39, 312–320.

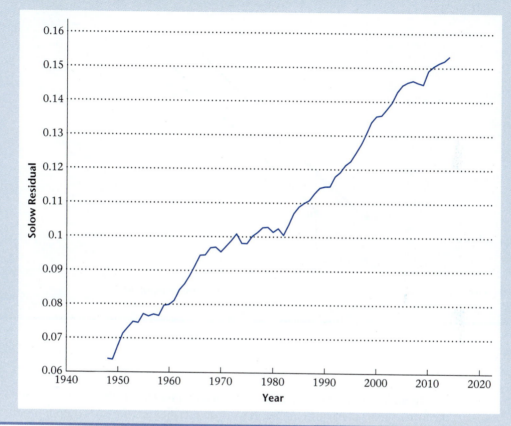

Figure 4.18 The Solow Residual for the United States

The Solow residual is a measure of total factor productivity, and it is calculated here using a Cobb–Douglas production function. Measured total factor productivity has increased over time, and it also fluctuates about trend, as shown for the period 1948–2014.

where K is fixed. Here, π is real profit. In Figure 4.19, we graph the revenue function, $zF(K, N^d)$, and the variable cost function, wN^d. Profit is then the difference between total revenue and total variable cost. Here, to maximize profits, the firm chooses $N^d = N^*$. The maximized quantity of profits, π^*, is the distance AB. For future reference, π^* is the distance ED, where AE is a line drawn parallel to the variable cost function. Thus, AE has slope w. At the profit-maximizing quantity of labor, N^*, the slope of the total revenue function is equal to the slope of the total variable cost function. The slope of the total revenue function, however, is just the slope of the production function, or the marginal product of labor, and the slope of the total variable cost function is the real wage w. Thus, the firm maximizes profits by setting

$$MP_N = w. \tag{4-12}$$

Figure 4.19 Revenue, Variable Costs, and Profit Maximization

$Y = zF(K, N^d)$ is the firm's revenue, while wN^d is the firm's variable cost. Profits are the difference between the former and the latter. The firm maximizes profits at the point where marginal revenue equals marginal cost, or $MP_N = w$. Maximized profits are the distance AB, or the distance ED.

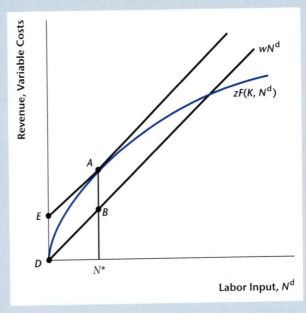

To understand the intuition behind Equation (4-12), note that the contribution to the firm's profits of having employees work an extra hour is the extra output produced minus what the extra input costs—that is, $MP_N - w$. Given a fixed quantity of capital, the marginal product of labor is very high for the first hour worked by employees, and the way we have drawn the production function in Figure 4.12, MP_N is very large for $N^d = 0$, so that $MP_N - w > 0$ for $N^d = 0$, and it is worthwhile for the firm to hire the first unit of labor, as this implies positive profits. As the firm hires more labor, MP_N falls, so that each additional unit of labor is contributing less to revenue, but contributing the same amount, w, to costs. Eventually, at $N^d = N^*$, the firm has hired enough labor so that hiring an additional unit implies $MP_N - w < 0$, which in turn means that hiring an additional unit of labor only causes profits to go down, and this cannot be optimal. Therefore, the profit-maximizing firm chooses its labor input according to Equation (4-12).

In our earlier example of the accounting firm, suppose that there is one photocopy machine at the firm, and output for the firm can be measured in terms of the clients the firm has. Each client pays $20,000 per year to the firm, and the wage rate for an

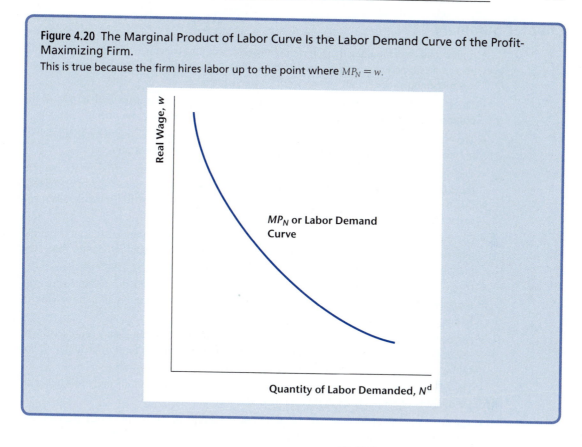

Figure 4.20 The Marginal Product of Labor Curve Is the Labor Demand Curve of the Profit-Maximizing Firm.

This is true because the firm hires labor up to the point where $MP_N = w$.

MP_N or Labor Demand Curve

Real Wage, *w*

Quantity of Labor Demanded, N^d

accountant is \$50,000 per year. Therefore, the real wage is $\dfrac{50{,}000}{20{,}000} = 2.5$ clients. If the firm has 1 accountant, it can handle 5 clients per year, if it has 2 accountants it can handle 9 clients per year, and if it has 3 accountants it can handle 11 clients per year. What is the profit-maximizing number of accountants for the firm to hire? If the firm hires Sara, her marginal product is 5 clients per year, which exceeds the real wage of 2.5 clients, and so it would be worthwhile for the firm to hire Sara. If the firm hires Sara and Paul, then Paul's marginal product is 4 clients per year, which also exceeds the market real wage, and so it would also be worthwhile to hire Paul. If the firm hires Sara, Paul, and Julia, then Julia's marginal product is 2 clients per year, which is less than the market real wage of 2.5 clients. Therefore, it would be optimal in this case for the firm to hire two accountants, Sara and Paul.

Our analysis tells us that the representative firm's marginal product of labor schedule, as shown in Figure 4.20, is the firm's demand curve for labor. This is because the firm maximizes profits for the quantity of labor input that implies $MP_N = w$. Therefore, given a real wage w the marginal product of labor schedule tells us how much labor the firm needs to hire such that $MP_N = w$, and so the marginal product of labor schedule and the firm's demand curve for labor are the same thing.

Chapter Summary

- In this chapter, we studied the behavior of the representative consumer and the representative firm in a one-period, or static, environment. This behavior is the basis for constructing a macroeconomic model that we can work with in Chapter 5.
- The representative consumer stands in for the large number of consumers that exist in the economy as a whole, and the representative firm stands in for a large number of firms.
- The representative consumer's goal is to choose consumption and leisure to make himself or herself as well off as possible while respecting his or her budget constraint.
- The consumer's preferences have the properties that more is always preferred to less and that there is preference for diversity in consumption and leisure. The consumer is a price-taker in that he or she treats the market real wage as given, and his or her real disposable income is real wage income plus real dividend income, minus real taxes.
- Graphically, the representative consumer optimizes by choosing the consumption bundle where an indifference curve is tangent to the budget constraint or, what is the same thing, the marginal rate of substitution of leisure for consumption is equal to the real wage.
- Under the assumption that consumption and leisure are normal goods, an increase in the representative consumer's income leads to an increase in consumption and an increase in leisure, implying that labor supply goes down.
- An increase in the real wage leads to an increase in consumption, but it may cause leisure to rise or fall, because there are opposing income and substitution effects. The consumer's labor supply, therefore, may increase or decrease when the real wage increases.
- The representative firm chooses the quantity of labor to hire so as to maximize profits, with the quantity of capital fixed in this one-period environment.
- The firm's production technology is captured by the production function, which has constant returns to scale, a diminishing marginal product of labor, and a diminishing marginal product of capital. Further, the marginal products of labor and capital are positive, and the marginal product of labor increases with the quantity of capital.
- An increase in total factor productivity increases the quantity of output that can be produced with any quantities of labor and capital, and it increases the marginal product of labor.
- When the firm optimizes, it sets the marginal product of labor equal to the real wage. This implies that the firm's marginal product of labor schedule is its demand curve for labor.

Key Terms

Static decision A decision made by a consumer or firm for only one time period. (p. 99)

Dynamic decision A decision made by a consumer or firm for more than one time period. (p. 99)

Consumption good A single good that represents an aggregation of all consumer goods in the economy. (p. 100)

Leisure Time spent not working in the market. (p. 100)

Representative consumer A stand-in for all consumers in the economy. (p. 100)

Utility function A function that captures a consumer's preferences over goods. (p. 100)

Consumption bundle A given consumption–leisure combination. (p. 100)

Normal good A good for which consumption increases as income increases. (p. 101)

Inferior good A good for which consumption decreases as income increases. (p. 102)

Indifference map A set of indifference curves representing a consumer's preferences over goods; has the same information as the utility function. (p. 102)

Indifference curve A set of points that represents consumption bundles among which a consumer is indifferent. (p. 102)

Marginal rate of substitution Minus the slope of an indifference curve, or the rate at which the consumer is just willing to trade one good for another. (p. 104)

Competitive behavior Actions taken by a consumer or firm if market prices are outside its control. (p. 105)

Barter An exchange of goods for goods. (p. 106)

Time constraint Condition that hours worked plus leisure time sum to total time available to the consumer. (p. 106)

Real wage The wage rate in units of the consumption good. (p. 106)

Numeraire The good in which prices are denominated. (p. 106)

Dividend income Profits of firms that are distributed to the consumer, who owns the firms. (p. 106)

Lump-sum tax A tax that is unaffected by the actions of the consumer or firm being taxed. (p. 106)

Budget constraint Condition that consumption equals wage income plus nonwage income minus taxes. (p. 107)

Rational Describes a consumer who can make an informed optimizing decision. (p. 109)

Optimal consumption bundle The consumption bundle for which the consumer is as well off as possible while satisfying the budget constraint. (p. 110)

Relative price The price of a good in units of another good. (p. 111)

Pure income effect The effect on the consumer's optimal consumption bundle due to a change in real disposable income, holding prices constant. (p. 113)

Substitution effect The effect on the quantity of a good consumed due to a price change, holding the consumer's welfare constant. (p. 115)

Income effect The effect on the quantity of a good consumed due to a price change, as a result of having an effectively different income. (p. 116)

Labor supply curve A relationship describing the quantity of labor supplied for each level of the real wage. (p. 117)

Perfect complements Two goods that are always consumed in fixed proportions. (p. 117)

Perfect substitutes Two goods with a constant marginal rate of substitution between them. (p. 122)

Production function A function describing the technological possibilities for converting factor inputs into output. (p. 122)

Total factor productivity A variable in the production function that makes all factors of production more productive if it increases. (p. 123)

Marginal product The additional output produced when another unit of a factor of production is added to the production process. (p. 123)

Constant returns to scale A property of the production technology whereby if the firm increases all inputs by a factor x this increases output by the same factor x. (p. 123)

Increasing returns to scale A property of the production technology whereby if the firm increases all inputs by a factor x this increases output by more than the factor x. (p. 124)

Decreasing returns to scale A property of the production technology whereby if the firm increases all inputs by a factor x this increases output by less than the factor x. (p. 124)

Representative firm A stand-in for all firms in the economy. (p. 124)

Cobb-Douglas production function A particular mathematical form for the production function that fits U.S. aggregate data well. (p. 132)

Solow residual A measure of total factor productivity obtained as a residual from the production function, given measures of aggregate output, labor input, and capital input. (p. 132)

Questions for Review

All questions refer to the elements of the macroeconomic model developed in this chapter.

4.1 What goods do consumers consume in this model?

4.2 How are a consumer's preferences over goods represented?

4.3 What three properties do the preferences of the representative consumer have? Explain the importance of each.

4.4 What two properties do indifference curves have? How are these properties associated with the properties of the consumer's preferences?

4.5 What is the representative consumer's goal?

4.6 When the consumer chooses his or her optimal consumption bundle while respecting his or her budget constraint, what condition is satisfied?

4.7 How is the representative consumer's behavior affected by an increase in real dividend income?

4.8 How is the representative consumer's behavior affected by an increase in real taxes?

4.9 Why might hours worked by the representative consumer decrease when the real wage increases?

4.10 What is the representative firm's goal?

4.11 Why is the marginal product of labor diminishing?

4.12 What are the effects on the production function of an increase in total factor productivity?

4.13 Explain why the marginal product of labor curve is the firm's labor demand curve.

Problems

1. **LO 1** Using a diagram show that if the consumer prefers more to less, then indifference curves cannot cross.

2. **LO 1, 3** In this chapter, we showed an example in which the consumer has preferences for consumption with the perfect complements property. Suppose, alternatively, that leisure and consumption goods are perfect substitutes. In this case, an indifference curve is described by the equation

    $$i = al + bC,$$

    where a and b are positive constants, and u is the level of utility. That is, a given indifference curve has a particular value for u, with higher indifference curves having higher values for u.

    (a) Show what the consumer's indifference curves look like when consumption and leisure are perfect substitutes, and determine graphically and algebraically what consumption bundle the consumer chooses. Show that the consumption bundle the consumer chooses depends on the relationship between a/b and w, and explain why.

    (b) Do you think it likely that any consumer would treat consumption goods and leisure as perfect substitutes?

    (c) Given perfect substitutes, is more preferred to less? Do preferences satisfy the diminishing marginal rate of substitution property?

3. **LO 1, 3, 4** Consider the consumer choice example in this chapter, where consumption and leisure are perfect complements. Assume that the consumer always desires a consumption bundle where the quantities of consumption and leisure are equal, that is, $a = 1$.

    (a) Suppose that $w = 0.75$, $\pi = 0.8$, and $T = 6$. Determine the consumer's optimal choice of consumption and leisure, and show this in a diagram.

    (b) Now suppose that $w = 1.5$, $\pi = 0.8$, and $T = 6$. Again, determine the consumer's optimal choice of consumption and leisure, and show this in your diagram. Explain how and why the consumer's optimal consumption bundle changes, with reference to income and substitution effects.

4. **LO 4** Suppose that the government imposes a proportional income tax on the representative consumer's wage income. That is, the consumer's wage income is $w(1 - t)(h - l)$ where t is the tax rate. What effect does the income tax have on

consumption and labor supply? Explain your results in terms of income and substitution effects.

5. **LO 4** Suppose, as in the federal income tax code for the United States, that the representative consumer faces a wage income tax with a standard deduction. That is, the representative consumer pays no tax on wage income for the first x units of real wage income, and then pays a proportional tax t on each unit of real wage income greater than x. Therefore, the consumer's budget constraint is given by $C = w(h - l) + \pi$ if $w(h - l) \le x$, or $C = (1 - t)w(h - l) + tx + \pi$ if $w(h - l) \ge x$. Now, suppose that the government reduces the tax deduction x. Using diagrams, determine the effects of this tax change on the consumer, and explain your results in terms of income and substitution effects. Make sure that you consider two cases. In the first case, the consumer does not pay any tax before x is reduced, and in the second case, the consumer pays a positive tax before x is reduced.

6. **LO 4** Typically, older workers reduce their hours of work for a period until they retire. How could we capture such an effect in the consumer model in this chapter? Draw a diagram and illustrate how this works.

7. **LO 2, 4** Suppose that a consumer can earn a higher wage rate for working overtime. That is, for the first q hours the consumer works, he or she receives a real wage rate of w_1, and for hours worked more than q he or she receives w_2, where $w_2 > w_1$. Suppose that the consumer pays no taxes and receives no nonwage income, and he or she is free to choose hours of work.

   (a) Draw the consumer's budget constraint, and show his or her optimal choice of consumption and leisure.
   (b) Show that the consumer would never work q hours, or anything very close to q hours. Explain the intuition behind this.
   (c) Determine what happens if the overtime wage rate w_2 increases. Explain your results in terms of income and substitution effects. You must consider the case of a worker who initially works overtime, and a worker who initially does not work overtime.

8. **LO 4** Show that the consumer is better off with a lump-sum tax rather than a proportional tax on

wage income (as in question 3) given that either tax yields the same revenue for the government. You must use a diagram to show this. (Hint: The consumption bundle the consumer chooses under the proportional tax must be just affordable given the lump-sum tax.)

9. **LO 1, 2, 3, 4** Recall that leisure time in our model of the representative consumer is intended to capture any time spent not working in the market, including production at home such as yard work and caring for children. Suppose that the government were to provide free day care for children and, for the purpose of analyzing the effects of this, assume that this has no effect on the market real wage w, taxes T, and dividend income π. Determine the effects of the day care program on consumption, leisure, and hours worked for the consumer.

10. **LO 2, 4** Suppose that a consumer cannot vary hours of work as he or she chooses. In particular, he or she must choose between working q hours and not working at all, where $q > 0$. Suppose that dividend income is zero, and that the consumer pays a tax T if he or she works, and receives a benefit b when not working, interpreted as an unemployment insurance payment.

    (a) If the wage rate increases, how does this affect the consumer's hours of work? What does this have to say about what we would observe about the behavior of actual consumers when wages change?
    (b) Suppose that the unemployment insurance benefit increases. How will this affect hours of work? Explain the implications of this for unemployment insurance programs.

11. **LO 2, 4** Suppose a two-person household. Person 1 has h_1 units of time available and takes l_1 units of leisure time, and person 2 has h_2 units of time available and takes l_2 units of leisure time. Collectively, the two persons in the household care about their total consumption c, and their total leisure $l = l_1 + l_2$, and they have preferences over their total consumption and total leisure just as specified in this chapter. But person 1 faces a market wage w_1, and person 2 faces a market wage w_2, with $w_1 > w_2$.

    (a) Draw the budget constraint faced by the two-person household. What will the household do, that is, how much does each household member work?

(b) What happens if the market wage of person 2 rises?

(c) Explain your results and interpret.

12. **LO 7** Suppose that the government imposes a producer tax. That is, the firm pays t units of consumption goods to the government for each unit of output it produces. Determine the effect of this tax on the firm's demand for labor.

13. **LO 7** Suppose that the government subsidizes employment. That is, the government pays the firm s units of consumption goods for each unit of labor that the firm hires. Determine the effect of the subsidy on the firm's demand for labor.

14. **LO 5, 7** Suppose that the firm has a minimum quantity of employment, N^*, that is, the firm can produce no output unless the labor input is greater than or equal to N^*. Otherwise, the firm produces output according to the same production function as specified in this chapter. Given these circumstances, determine the effects of an increase in the real wage on the firm's choice of labor input. Construct the firm's demand curve for labor.

15. **LO 6, 7** Supposing that a single consumer works for a firm, the quantity of labor input for the firm, N, is identical to the quantity of hours worked by the consumer, $h - l$. Graph the relationship between output produced, Y on the vertical axis and leisure hours of the consumer, l, on the horizontal axis, which is implied by the production function of the firm. (In Chapter 5, we refer to this relationship as the production possibilities frontier.) What is the slope of the curve you have graphed?

16. **LO 7** In the course of producing its output, a firm causes pollution. The government passes a law that requires the firm to stop polluting, and the firm discovers that it can prevent the pollution by hiring x workers for every worker that is producing output. That is, if the firm hires N workers, then xN workers are required to clean up the pollution caused by the N workers who are actually producing output. Determine the effect of the pollution regulation on the firm's profit-maximizing choice of labor input, and on the firm's labor demand curve.

17. **LO 7** Suppose a firm has a production function given by $Y = zK^{0.3}N^{0.7}$.

(a) If $z = 1$ and $K = 1$, graph the production function. Is the marginal product of labor positive and diminishing?

(b) Now, graph the production function when $z = 1$ and $K = 1$. Explain how the production function changed from part (a).

(c) Next, graph the production function when $z = 1$ and $K = 2$. What happens now?

(d) Given this production function, the marginal product of labor is given by $MP_N = 0.7K^{0.3}N^{-0.3}$. Graph the marginal product of labor for $(z, K) = (1, 1), (2, 1), (1, 2)$, and explain what you get.

Working with the Data

Answer these questions using the Federal Reserve Bank of St. Louis's FRED database, accessible at http://research.stlouisfed.org/fred2/

1. The employment–population ratio, from the Current Population Survey, is a measure that might correspond to the concept of employment, N, in our model.

(a) Plot the employment–population ratio for the years 1980–2016.

(b) Given that the real wage in the United States increased from 1980 to 2016, comment on what you observe in your plot.

(c) How would you tell a story about the income and substitution effects in labor supply decisions that would be consistent with this data? What is our model of consumer behavior in this chapter missing that might explain what is going on in your chart?

(d) Do you think that the ratio of employment to the total population is a good measure of average hours worked per person in the economy? Explain why or why not.

2. Plot the average weekly hours of production and nonsupervisory employees (total private).
   (a) What do you notice about how this time series behaves around recession dates (the shaded areas)?
   (b) In our model, the representative consumer supplies labor time in the market, and this quantity of labor supplied captures total employment in the economy. But in practice, total hours worked by all workers is affected by how much each person works, and by how many people are working. Comment on what you observe in the time series, and how this relates to our model and how we want to interpret it.

Chapter 5

A Closed-Economy One-Period Macroeconomic Model

Learning Objectives

After studying Chapter 5, students will be able to:

5.1 Define and construct a competitive equilibrium for the closed-economy one-period (CEOP) macroeconomic model.

5.2 Show that the competitive equilibrium and the Pareto optimum for the CEOP model are the same thing.

5.3 Analyze and interpret the effects of changes in exogenous variables in the CEOP model.

5.4 Decompose the effects of an increase in total factor productivity in the CEOP model into income and substitution effects.

5.5 Analyze the effects of a distorting labor income tax in the simplified CEOP model.

5.6 Analyze the determinants of the size of government and private consumption.

In Chapter 4, we studied the microeconomic behavior of a representative consumer and a representative firm. In this chapter, our first goal is to take this microeconomic behavior and build it into a working model of the macroeconomy. Then we use this model to illustrate how unconstrained markets can produce economic outcomes that are socially efficient. This social efficiency proves to be useful in how we use our model to analyze some important macroeconomic issues. We show how increases in government spending increase aggregate output and crowd out private consumption expenditures and how increases in productivity lead to increases in aggregate output and the standard of living. Next we will consider a version of the model where the economic outcome in an economy with unconstrained private markets is not socially efficient, because government tax collection distorts private decisions. This allows us to explore how the incentive effects of the income tax matter for aggregate economic activity. Finally, we will consider an alternative—but related—model, in which we can study the optimal size of government.

We start our approach to macroeconomic modeling in this chapter by analyzing how consumers and firms interact in markets in a **closed economy**. This is a model of a single country that has no interaction with the rest of the world—it does not trade with other countries. It is easier to first understand how a closed economy works, and much of the economic intuition we build up for the closed-economy case carries over to an **open economy**, where international trade is allowed. Further, for many economic questions, particularly the ones addressed in this chapter, the answers are not fundamentally different if we allow the economy to be open.

There are three different actors in this economy, the representative consumer who stands in for the many consumers in the economy that sell labor and buy goods, the representative firm that stands in for the many firms in the economy that buy labor and sell goods, and the government. We have already described the behavior of the representative consumer and representative firm in detail in Chapter 4, and we only need to explain what the government does.

Government

The behavior of the government is quite simple in our model. It wishes to purchase a given quantity of consumption goods, G, and finances these purchases by taxing the representative consumer. In practice, governments provide many different goods and services, including roads and bridges, national defense, air traffic control, and education. Which goods and services the government should provide is the subject of much political and economic debate, but economists generally agree that the government has a special role to play in providing **public goods**, such as national defense, which are difficult or impossible for the private sector to provide. National defense is a good example of a public good, because it is difficult or impossible to get individuals to pay for national defense in a private market according to how much national defense services each one receives and how much each individual values national defense.

To keep things as simple as possible, for now we are not specific about the public goods nature of government expenditure. Later in this chapter we will be explicit about public goods, and consider how we should determine the optimal size of the government sector. What we want to capture here, however, is that government spending uses up resources, and we model this by assuming that government spending simply involves taking goods from the private sector. Output is produced in the private sector, and the government purchases an **exogenous** amount G of this output, with the remainder consumed by the representative consumer. An exogenous variable is determined outside the model, while an **endogenous** variable is determined by the model itself. Government spending is exogenous in our model, as we are assuming that government spending is independent of what happens in the rest of the economy. The government must abide by the **government budget constraint**, which we write as

$$G = T,$$

or government purchases equal taxes, in real terms.

Introducing the government in this way allows us to study some basic effects of **fiscal policy**. In general, fiscal policy refers to the government's choices over its expenditures, taxes, transfers, and borrowing. Recall from Chapter 2 that government expenditures are purchases of final goods and services, while transfers are simply reallocations of purchasing power from one set of individuals to another. Because this is a one-period economic environment, the government's choices are very limited, as described by the above government budget constraint. The government cannot borrow to finance government expenditures, because there is no future in which to repay its debt, and the government does not tax more than it spends, as this would imply that the government would foolishly throw goods away. The government budget deficit, which is $G - T$ here, is always zero. Thus, the only elements of fiscal policy we study in this chapter are the setting of government purchases, G, and the macroeconomic effects of changing G. In Chapter 9, we begin to explore what happens when the government can run deficits and surpluses.

Competitive Equilibrium

LO 5.1 Define and construct a competitive equilibrium for the closed-economy one-period (CEOP) macroeconomic model.

Now that we have looked at the behavior of the representative consumer, the representative firm, and the government, what remains in constructing our model is to show how consistency is obtained in the actions of all these economic agents. Once we have done this, we can use this model to make predictions about how the whole economy behaves in response to changes in the economic environment.

Mathematically, a macroeconomic model takes the exogenous variables, which for the purposes of the problem at hand are determined outside the system we are modeling, and determines values for the endogenous variables, as outlined in Figure 5.1. In the model we are working with here, the exogenous variables are G, z, and K—that is, government spending, total factor productivity, and the economy's capital stock, respectively. The endogenous variables are C, N^s, N^d, T, Y, and w—that is, consumption, labor supply, labor demand, taxes, aggregate output, and the market real wage, respectively. Making use of the model is a process of running experiments to determine how changes in the exogenous variables change the endogenous variables. By running these experiments, we hope to understand real-world macroeconomic events and say something about macroeconomic policy. For example, one of the experiments we run on our model in this chapter is to change exogenous government spending and then determine the effects on consumption, employment, aggregate output, and the real wage. This helps us to understand, for example, the events that occurred in the U.S. economy during World War II, when there was a large increase in government spending.

Figure 5.1 A Model Takes Exogenous Variables and Determines Endogenous Variables

Exogenous variables are determined outside a macroeconomic model. Given the exogenous variables, the model determines the endogenous variables. In experiments, we are interested in how the endogenous variables change when there are changes in exogenous variables.

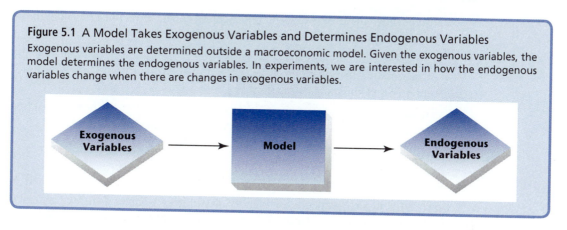

By consistency we mean that, given market prices, demand is equal to supply in each market in the economy. Such a state of affairs is called a **competitive equilibrium**. Here, competitive refers to the fact that all consumers and firms are price-takers, and the economy is in equilibrium when the actions of all consumers and firms are consistent. When demand equals supply in all markets, we say that **markets clear**. In our model economy, there is only one price, which is the real wage w. We can also think of the economy as having only one market, on which labor time is exchanged for consumption goods. In this labor market, the representative consumer supplies labor and the representative firm demands labor. A competitive equilibrium is achieved when, given the exogenous variables G, z, and K, the real wage w is such that, at that wage, *the quantity of labor the consumer wishes to supply is equal to the quantity of labor the firm wishes to hire.* The consumer's supply of labor is in part determined by taxes T and dividend income π. In a competitive equilibrium, T must satisfy the government budget constraint, and π must be equal to the profits generated by the firm.

More formally, a competitive equilibrium is a set of endogenous quantities, C (consumption), N^s (labor supply), N^d (labor demand), T (taxes), and Y (aggregate output), and an endogenous real wage w, such that, given the exogenous variables G (government spending), z (total factor productivity), and K (capital stock), the following are satisfied:

1. The representative consumer chooses C (consumption) and N^s (labor supply) to make himself or herself as well off as possible subject to his or her budget constraint, given w (the real wage), T (taxes), and π (dividend income). That is, the representative consumer optimizes given his or her budget constraint, which is determined by the real wage, taxes, and the profits that the consumer receives from the firm as dividend income.

2. The representative firm chooses N^d (quantity of labor demanded) to maximize profits, with maximized output $Y = zF(K, N^d)$, and maximized profits $\pi = Y - wN^d$. The firm treats z (total factor productivity), K (the capital stock), and w (the real wage) as given. That is, the representative firm optimizes given total factor productivity, its capital stock, and the market real wage. In

equilibrium, the profits that the representative firm earns must be equal to the dividend income that is received by the consumer.

3. The market for labor clears, that is, $N^d = N^s$. The quantity of labor that the representative firm wants to hire is equal to the quantity of labor the representative consumer wants to supply.

4. The government budget constraint is satisfied, that is, $G = T$. The taxes paid by consumers are equal to the exogenous quantity of government spending.

An important property of a competitive equilibrium is that

$$Y = C + G, \tag{5-1}$$

which is the income–expenditure identity. Recall from Chapter 2 that we generally state the income–expenditure identity as $Y = C + I + G + NX$, where I is investment and NX is net exports. In this economy, there is no investment expenditure, as there is only one period, and net exports are zero, as the economy is closed, so that $I = 0$ and $NX = 0$.

To show why the income–expenditure identity holds in equilibrium, we start with the representative consumer's budget constraint,

$$C = wN^s + \pi - T, \tag{5-2}$$

or consumption expenditures equal real wage income plus real dividend income minus taxes. In equilibrium, dividend income is equal to the firm's maximized profits, or $\pi = Y - wN^d$, and the government budget constraint is satisfied, so that $T = G$. If we then substitute in Equation (5-2) for π and T, we get

$$C = wN^s + Y - wN^d - G. \tag{5-3}$$

In equilibrium, labor supply is equal to labor demand, or $N^s = N^d$, which then gives us, substituting for N^s in Equation (5-3) and rearranging, the identity in Equation (5-1).

There are many ways to work with macroeconomic models. Modern macroeconomic researchers sometimes work with an algebraic representation of a model, sometimes with a formulation of a model that can be put on a computer and simulated, and sometimes with a model in graphical form. We use the last approach most often in this book. In doing graphical analysis, sometimes the simplest approach is to work with a model in the form of supply and demand curves, with one supply curve and one demand curve for each market under consideration. As the number of markets in the model increases, this approach becomes most practical, and in Chapters 11–14 and some later chapters, we work mainly with models in the form of supply and demand curves. These supply and demand curves are derived from the microeconomic behavior of consumers and firms, as was the case when we examined labor supply and labor demand curves in Chapter 4, but the underlying microeconomic behavior is not explicit. For our analysis here, however, where exchange takes place between the representative consumer and the representative firm in only one market, it is relatively straightforward to be entirely explicit about microeconomic principles. The approach we follow in this chapter is to study competitive equilibrium in our model by examining the consumer's and the firm's decisions in the same diagram, so that we can determine how aggregate consistency is achieved in competitive equilibrium.

We want to start first with the production technology operated by the representative firm. In a competitive equilibrium, $N^d = N^s = N$—that is, labor demand equals labor supply—and we refer to N as employment. Then, as in Chapter 4, from the production function, output is given by

$$Y = zF(K, N), \tag{5-4}$$

and we graph the production function in Figure 5.2(a), for a given capital stock K. Because the representative consumer has a maximum of h hours to spend working, N can be no larger than h, which implies that the most output that could be produced in this economy is Y^* in Figure 5.2(a).

Another way to graph the production function, which proves very useful for integrating the firm's production behavior with the consumer's behavior, is to use the fact that, in equilibrium, we have $N = h - l$. Substituting for N in the production function Equation (5-4), we get

$$Y = zF(K, h - l), \tag{5-5}$$

which is a relationship between output Y and leisure l, given the exogenous variables z and K. If we graph this relationship, as Figure 5.2(b), with leisure on the horizontal axis and Y on the vertical axis, then we get a mirror image of the production function in Figure 5.2(a). That is, the point $(l, Y) = (h, 0)$ in Figure 5.2(b) corresponds to the point $(N, Y) = (0, 0)$ in Figure 5.2(a). When the consumer takes all of his or her time as leisure, then employment is zero and nothing gets produced. As leisure falls in Figure 5.2(b) from h, employment increases in Figure 5.2(a) from zero, and output increases. In Figure 5.2(b), when $l = 0$, the consumer is using all of his or her time for work and consuming no leisure and the maximum quantity of output, Y^*, is produced. Because the slope of the production function in Figure 5.2(a) is MP_N, the marginal product of labor, the slope of the relationship in Figure 5.2(b) is $-MP_N$, because this relationship is just the mirror image of the production function.

Now, because in equilibrium $C = Y - G$, from the income–expenditure identity, given Equation (5-5) we get

$$C = zF(K, h - l) - G,$$

which is a relationship between C and l, given the exogenous variables z, K, and G. This relationship is graphed in Figure 5.2(c), and it is just the relationship in Figure 5.2(b) shifted down by the amount G, because consumption is output minus government spending in equilibrium. The relationship in Figure 5.2(c) is called a **production possibilities frontier** (PPF), and it describes what the technological possibilities are for the economy as a whole, in terms of the production of consumption goods and leisure. Though leisure is not literally produced, all of the points in the shaded area inside the PPF and on the PPF in Figure 5.2(c) are technologically possible in this economy. The PPF captures the trade-off between leisure and consumption that the available production technology makes available to the representative consumer in the economy. The points on the PPF on AB are not feasible for this economy, as consumption is negative. Only the points on the PPF on DB are feasible, because here enough consumption goods

Figure 5.2 The Production Function and the Production Possibilities Frontier

(a) shows the equilibrium relationship between the quantity of leisure consumed by the representative consumer and aggregate output. The relationship in (b) is the mirror image of the production function in (a). In (c), we show the production possibilities frontier (PPF), which is the technological relationship between C and I, determined by shifting the relationship in (b) down by the amount G. The shaded region in (c) represents consumption bundles that are technologically feasible to produce in this economy.

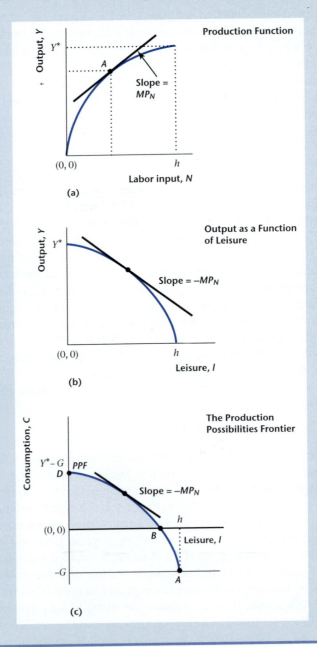

are produced so that the government can take some of these goods and still leave something for private consumption.

As in Figure 5.2(b), the slope of the PPF in Figure 5.2(c) is $-MP_N$. Another name for the negative of the slope of the PPF is the **marginal rate of transformation**. The marginal rate of transformation is the rate at which one good can be converted technologically into another; in this case, the marginal rate of transformation is the rate at which leisure can be converted in the economy into consumption goods through work. We let $MRT_{l,C}$ denote the marginal rate of transformation of leisure into consumption. Then, we have

$$MRT_{l,C} = MP_N = -(\text{the slope of the PPF}).$$

Our next step is to put the PPF together with the consumer's indifference curves, and to show how we can analyze a competitive equilibrium in a single diagram in Figure 5.3. In the figure, the PPF is given by the curve HF. From the relationship between the production function and the PPF in Figure 5.2, and given what we know about the profit-maximizing decision of the firm from Chapter 4, we can determine the production point on the PPF chosen by the firm, given the equilibrium real wage w. That is, the representative firm chooses the labor input to maximize profits in equilibrium by setting $MP_N = w$, and so in equilibrium minus the slope of the PPF must be equal to w, because $MRT_{l,C} = MP_N = w$ in equilibrium. Therefore, if w is an equilibrium real wage rate, we can draw a line AD in Figure 5.3 that has slope $-w$ and that is tangent to the PPF at point J, where $MP_N = w$. Then, the firm chooses labor demand equal to $h - l^*$ and produces $Y^* = zF(K, h - l^*)$, from the production function. Maximized profits for the firm are $\pi^* = zF(K, h - l^*) - w(h - l^*)$ (total revenue minus the cost of hiring labor), or the distance DH in Figure 5.3 (recall this from Chapter 4). Now, DB in Figure 5.3 is equal to $\pi^* - G = \pi^* - T$, from the government budget constraint $G = T$.

An interesting feature of the figure is that ADB in the figure is the budget constraint that the consumer faces in equilibrium, because the slope of AD is $-w$ and the length of DB is the consumer's dividend income minus taxes, where dividend income is the profits that the firm earns and distributes to the consumer. Because J represents the competitive equilibrium production point, where C^* is the quantity of consumption goods produced by the firm and $h - l^*$ is the quantity of labor hired by the firm, it must be the case (as is required for aggregate consistency) that C^* is also the quantity of consumption goods that the representative consumer desires and l^* is the quantity of leisure the consumer desires. This implies that an indifference curve (curve I_1 in Figure 5.3) must be tangent to AD (the budget constraint) at point J in Figure 5.3. Given this, in equilibrium at point J we have $MRS_{l,C} = w$—that is, the marginal rate of substitution of leisure for consumption for the consumer is equal to the real wage. Because $MRT_{l,C} = MP_N = w$ in equilibrium, we have, at point J in Figure 5.3,

$$MRS_{l,C} = MRT_{l,C} = MP_N, \tag{5-6}$$

or the marginal rate of substitution of leisure for consumption is equal to the marginal rate of transformation, which is equal to the marginal product of labor. That is, because the consumer and the firm face the same market real wage in equilibrium, the rate at which the consumer is just willing to trade leisure for consumption is the same

Figure 5.3 Competitive Equilibrium

This figure brings together the representative consumer's preferences and the representative firm's production technology to determine a competitive equilibrium. Point J represents the equilibrium consumption bundle. ADB is the budget constraint faced by the consumer in equilibrium, with the slope of AD equal to minus the real wage and the distance DB equal to dividend income minus taxes.

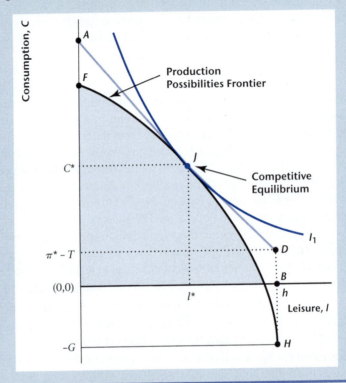

as the rate at which leisure can be converted into consumption goods using the production technology.

The condition expressed in Equation (5-6) is important in the next subsection in establishing the economic efficiency of a competitive equilibrium. The connection between market outcomes and economic efficiency is critical in making the analysis of macroeconomic issues with this model simple.

Optimality

LO 5.2 Show that the competitive equilibrium and the Pareto optimum for the CEOP model are the same thing.

Now that we know what the characteristics of a competitive equilibrium are from Figure 5.3, we can analyze the connection between a competitive equilibrium and economic efficiency. This connection is important for two reasons. First, this illustrates how free markets can produce socially optimal outcomes. Second, it proves to be much easier to analyze a social optimum than a competitive equilibrium in this model, and so our analysis in this section allows us to use our model efficiently.

An important part of economics is analyzing how markets act to arrange production and consumption activities and asking how this arrangement compares with some ideal or efficient arrangement. Typically, the efficiency criterion that economists use in evaluating market outcomes is **Pareto optimality**. (Pareto, a nineteenth-century Italian economist, is famous for, among other things, his application of mathematics to economic analysis and introducing the concept of indifference curves.)

Definition 1 *A competitive equilibrium is **Pareto optimal** if there is no way to rearrange production or to reallocate goods so that someone is made better off without making someone else worse off.*

For this model, we would like to ask whether the competitive equilibrium is Pareto optimal, but our job is relatively easy because there is only one representative consumer, so that we do not have to consider how goods are allocated across people. In our model, we can focus solely on how production is arranged to make the representative consumer as well off as possible. To construct the Pareto optimum here, we introduce the device of a fictitious social planner. This device is commonly used to determine efficiency in economic models. The social planner does not have to deal with markets, and he or she can simply order the representative firm to hire a given quantity of labor and produce a given quantity of consumption goods. The planner also has the power to coerce the consumer into supplying the required amount of labor. Produced consumption goods are taken by the planner, G is given to the government, and the remainder is allocated to the consumer. The social planner is benevolent, and he or she chooses quantities so as to make the representative consumer as well off as possible. In this way, the choices of the social planner tell us what, in the best possible circumstances, could be achieved in our model economy.

The social planner's problem is to choose C and l, given the technology for converting l into C, to make the representative consumer as well off as possible. That is, the social planner chooses a consumption bundle that is on or within the *PPF*, and that is on the highest possible indifference curve for the consumer. In Figure 5.4 the Pareto optimum is located at point B, where an indifference curve is just tangent to the *PPF*—curve *AH*. The social planner's problem is very similar to the representative consumer's problem of making himself or herself as well off as possible given his or her budget constraint. The only difference is that the budget constraint of the consumer is a straight line, while the *PPF* is bowed-out from the origin (i.e., it is concave).

From Figure 5.4, because the slope of the indifference curve is minus the marginal rate of substitution, $-MRS_{l,C}$, and the slope of the *PPF* is minus the marginal rate of

Figure 5.4 Pareto Optimality

The Pareto optimum is the point that a social planner would choose where the representative consumer is as well off as possible given the technology for producing consumption goods using labor as an input. Here the Pareto optimum is *B*, where an indifference curve is tangent to the *PPF*.

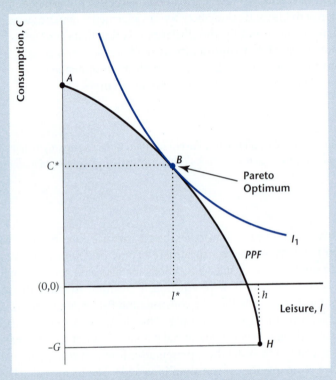

transformation, $-MRT_{l,C}$, or minus the marginal product of labor, $-MP_N$, the Pareto optimum has the property that

$$MRS_{l,C} = MRT_{l,C} = MP_N.$$

This is the same property that a competitive equilibrium has, or Equation (5-6). Comparing Figures 5.3 and 5.4, we easily see that the Pareto optimum and the competitive equilibrium are the same thing, because a competitive equilibrium is the point where an indifference curve is tangent to the *PPF* in Figure 5.3, and the same is true of the Pareto optimum in Figure 5.4. A key result of this chapter is that, for this model, the competitive equilibrium is identical to the Pareto optimum.

There are two fundamental principles in economics that apply here, and these are the following:

Definition 2   *The **first fundamental theorem of welfare economics** states that, under certain conditions, a competitive equilibrium is Pareto optimal.*

> **Definition 3**   *The second fundamental theorem of welfare economics* states that, under certain conditions, a Pareto optimum is a competitive equilibrium.

These two theorems are often referred to as the "first welfare theorem" and the "second welfare theorem." In our model, one can clearly see, from Figures 5.3 and 5.4, that the first and second welfare theorems hold, because there is one competitive equilibrium and one Pareto optimum, and they are clearly the same thing. In other kinds of economic models, however, showing whether or not the first and second welfare theorems hold can be hard work.

The idea behind the first welfare theorem goes back at least as far as Adam Smith's *Wealth of Nations*. Smith argued that an unfettered market economy composed of self-interested consumers and firms could achieve an allocation of resources and goods that was socially efficient, in that an unrestricted market economy would behave as if an "invisible hand" were guiding the actions of individuals toward a state of affairs that was beneficial for all. The model we have constructed here has the property that a competitive equilibrium, or unfettered market outcome, is the same outcome that would be chosen by the invisible hand of the fictitious social planner.

The first welfare theorem is quite remarkable, because it appears to be inconsistent with the training we receive early in life, when we are typically encouraged to have empathy for others and to share our belongings. Most people value generosity and compassion, and so it certainly seems surprising that individuals motivated only by greed and profit maximization could achieve some kind of social utopia. If we consider, however, economies with many consumers instead of a single representative consumer, then a Pareto optimum might have the property that some people are very poor and some are very rich. That is, we may not be able to make the poor better off without making the rich worse off. At the extreme, a state of affairs where one person has all of society's wealth may be Pareto optimal, but few would argue that this is a sensible way to arrange an economy. Pareto optimality is a very narrow concept of social optimality. In some instances, society is interested in equity as well as efficiency, and there may be a trade-off between the two.

Sources of Social Inefficiencies

What could cause a competitive equilibrium to fail to be Pareto optimal? In practice, many factors can result in inefficiency in a market economy.

First, a competitive equilibrium may not be Pareto optimal because of **externalities**. An externality is any activity for which an individual firm or consumer does not take account of all associated costs and benefits; externalities can be positive or negative. For example, pollution is a common example of a negative externality. Suppose that Disgusting Chemical Corporation (DCC) produces and sells chemicals, and in the production process generates a by-product that is released as a gas into the atmosphere. This by-product stinks and is hazardous, and there are people who live close to DCC who are worse off as the result of the air pollution that DCC produces; however, the negative externality that is produced in the form of pollution costs to the neighbors of DCC is not reflected in any way in DCC's profits. DCC, therefore, does not take the pollution externality into account in deciding how much labor to hire and the quantity of chemicals to produce. As a result, DCC tends to produce more of these pollution-causing chemicals than is socially optimal. The key problem is that there is not a market on which pollution (or the rights to pollute) is traded. If such a market existed, then private markets would not fail to produce a socially optimal outcome. This is because the people who bear the costs of pollution could sell the rights to pollute to DCC, and there would then be a cost to DCC for polluting, which DCC would take into account in making production decisions. In practice, there do not exist markets in pollution rights for all types of pollution that exist, though there have been some experiments with such markets. Typically, governments take other kinds of approaches to try to correct the negative externalities generated by pollution, such as regulation and taxation.

A positive externality is a benefit that other people receive for which an individual is not compensated. For example, suppose that DCC has an attractive head office designed by a high-profile architect in a major city. This building yields a benefit to people who can walk by the building on a public street and admire the fine architecture. These people do not compensate the firm for this positive externality, as it would be very costly or impossible to set up a fee structure for the public viewing of the building. As a result, DCC tends to underinvest in its head office. Likely, the building that DCC would construct would be less attractive than if the firm took account of the positive externality. Positive externalities, therefore, lead to social inefficiencies, just as negative externalities do, and the root cause of an externality is a market failure; it is too costly or impossible to set up a market to buy and sell the benefits or costs associated with the externality.

A second reason that a competitive equilibrium may not be Pareto optimal is that there are **distorting taxes**. In Chapter 4 we discussed the difference between a lump-sum tax, which does not depend on the actions of the person being taxed, and a distorting tax, which does. An example of a distorting tax in our model would be if government purchases were financed by a proportional wage income tax rather than by a lump-sum tax. That is, for each unit of real wage income earned, the representative consumer pays t units of consumption goods to the government, so that t is the tax rate. Then, wage income is $w(1-t)(h-l)$, and the effective wage for the consumer is $w(1-t)$. Then, when the consumer optimizes, he or she sets $MRS_{l,C} = w(1-t)$, while the firm optimizes by setting $MP_N = w$. Therefore, in a competitive equilibrium

$$MRS_{l,C} < MP_N = MRT_{l,C},$$

so that the tax drives a "wedge" between the marginal rate of substitution and the marginal product of labor. Equation (5-6), therefore, does not hold, as required for a Pareto optimum, so that the competitive equilibrium is not Pareto optimal and the first welfare theorem does not hold. In a competitive equilibrium, a proportional wage income tax tends to discourage work (so long as the substitution effect of a change in the wage is larger than the income effect), and there tends to be too much leisure consumed relative to consumption goods. We will explore the aggregate effects of distorting taxes on labor income later in this chapter. In practice, all taxes, including sales taxes, income taxes, and property taxes, cause distortions. Lump-sum taxes are, in fact, infeasible to implement in practice,[1] though this does not mean that having lump-sum taxes in our model is nonsense. The assumption of lump-sum taxation in our model is a convenient simplification, in that for most of the macroeconomic issues we address with this model, the effects of more realistic distorting taxation are unimportant.

A third reason market economies do not achieve efficiency is that firms may not be price-takers. If a firm is large relative to the market, then we say it has monopoly power (monopoly power need not imply only one firm in an industry), and it can use its monopoly power to act strategically to restrict output, raise prices, and increase profits. Monopoly power tends to lead to underproduction relative to what is socially optimal. There are many examples of monopoly power in the United States. For example, local cable television markets are dominated by a few producers, as is automobile manufacturing.

Because there are good reasons to believe that the three inefficiencies discussed above—externalities, tax distortions, and monopoly power—are important in modern economies, two questions arise. First, why should we analyze an economy that is efficient in the sense that a competitive equilibrium for this economy is Pareto optimal? The reason is that in studying most macroeconomic issues, an economic model with inefficiencies behaves much like an economic model without inefficiencies. However, actually modeling all of these inefficiencies would add clutter to our model and make it more difficult to work with, and it is often best to leave out these extraneous details. The equivalence of the competitive equilibrium and the Pareto optimum in our model proves to be quite powerful in terms of analyzing a competitive equilibrium. This is because determining the competitive equilibrium need only involve solving the social planner's problem and not the more complicated problem of determining prices and quantities in a competitive equilibrium.

A second question that arises concerning real-world social inefficiencies is whether Adam Smith was completely off track in emphasizing the tendency of unrestricted markets to produce socially efficient outcomes. Though there are many market failures in the world that justify government intervention to correct the problem, the tendency of unregulated markets to produce efficient outcomes is a powerful one.

How to Use the Model

The key to using our model is the equivalence between the competitive equilibrium and the Pareto optimum. We need only draw a picture as in Figure 5.5, where we are essentially considering the solution to the social planner's problem. Here, the *PPF* is curve *AH*, and the competitive equilibrium (or Pareto optimum) is at point *B*, where

---

[1]This is because any lump-sum tax is large enough that some people cannot pay it. Therefore, some people must be exempt from the tax; but, if this is so, then people will alter their behavior so as to be exempt from the tax, and as a result the tax will distort private decisions.

Figure 5.5 Using the Second Welfare Theorem to Determine a Competitive Equilibrium

Because the competitive equilibrium and the Pareto optimum are the same thing, we can analyze a competitive equilibrium by working out the Pareto optimum, which is point B in the figure. At the Pareto optimum, an indifference curve is tangent to the *PPF*, and the equilibrium real wage is equal to minus the slope of the *PPF* and minus the slope of the indifference curve at B.

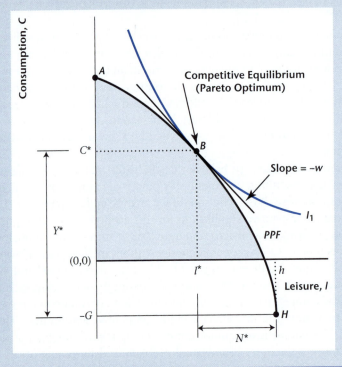

an indifference curve, I_1, is tangent to the *PPF*. The equilibrium quantity of consumption is then C^*, and the equilibrium quantity of leisure is l^*. The quantity of employment is $N^* = h - l^*$, as shown in Figure 5.5, and the quantity of output is $Y^* = C^* + G$, as also shown in the figure. The real wage w is determined by minus the slope of the *PPF*, or minus the slope of the indifference curve I_1 at point B. The real wage is determined in this way because we know that, in equilibrium, the firm optimizes by setting the marginal product of labor equal to the real wage, and the consumer optimizes by setting the marginal rate of substitution equal to the real wage.

What we are primarily interested in now is how a change in an exogenous variable affects the key endogenous variables C, Y, N, and w. The exogenous variables G, z, and K, which are government spending, total factor productivity, and the capital stock, respectively, all alter the endogenous variables by shifting the *PPF* in particular ways. We examine these effects and their interpretation in the next sections.

Figure 5.5 illustrates a key concept of this chapter in the clearest possible way. What is produced and consumed in the economy is determined entirely by the interaction of consumer preferences with the technology available to firms. Though economic activity involves a complicated array of transactions among many economic actors, fundamentally aggregate economic activity boils down to the preferences of consumers, as captured by the representative consumer's indifference curves, and the technology of firms, as captured by the *PPF*. Both consumer preferences and the firm's technology are important for determining aggregate output, aggregate consumption, employment, and the real wage. A change either in indifference curves or the *PPF* affects what is produced and consumed.

Working with the Model: The Effects of a Change in Government Purchases

LO 5.3 Analyze and interpret the effects of changes in exogenous variables in the CEOP model.

Recall from Chapter 1 that working with a macroeconomic model involves carrying out experiments. The first experiment we conduct here is to change government spending G, and ask what this does to aggregate output, consumption, employment, and the real wage. In Figure 5.6, an increase in G from G_1 to G_2 shifts the *PPF* from PPF_1 to PPF_2, where the shift down is by the same amount, $G_2 - G_1$, for each quantity of leisure, l. This shift leaves the slope of the *PPF* constant for each l. The effect of shifting the *PPF* downward by a constant amount is very similar to shifting the budget constraint for the consumer through a reduction in his or her nonwage disposable income, as we did in Chapter 4. Indeed, because $G = T$, an increase in government spending must necessarily increase taxes by the same amount, which reduces the consumer's disposable income. It should not be surprising, then, that the effects of an increase in government spending essentially involve a negative income effect on consumption and leisure.

In Figure 5.6 the initial equilibrium is at point A, where indifference curve I_1 is tangent to PPF_1, the initial *PPF*. Here, equilibrium consumption is C_1, while the equilibrium quantity of leisure is l_1, and so equilibrium employment is $N_1 = h - l_1$. The initial equilibrium real wage is minus the slope of the indifference curve (or minus the slope of PPF_1) at point A. Now, when government spending increases, the *PPF* shifts to PPF_2, and the equilibrium point is at B, where consumption and leisure are both lower, at C_2 and l_2, respectively. Why do consumption and leisure decrease? This is because consumption and leisure are normal goods.[2] Given the normal goods assumption, a negative income effect from the downward shift in the *PPF* must reduce consumption and leisure. Because leisure falls, employment, which is $N_2 = h - l_2$, must rise. Further, because employment increases, the quantity of output must rise. We know this because the quantity of capital is fixed in the experiment, whereas employment has increased. With the same quantity of one factor of production (capital), and more of the other (labor), and total factor productivity held constant, output must increase.

---

[2]Alert readers will notice that the definition of what a normal good is needs to be altered here from how we defined it in Chapter 1, because we are dealing with a shift in the nonlinear *PPF* rather than a shift in a linear budget constraint. The spirit of the approach remains the same, however. For more details, see the Mathematical Appendix.

Figure 5.6 Equilibrium Effects of an Increase in Government Spending

An increase in government spending shifts the *PPF* down by the amount of the increase in *G*. There are negative income effects on consumption and leisure, so that both *C* and *l* fall, and employment rises, while output (equal to $C + G$) increases.

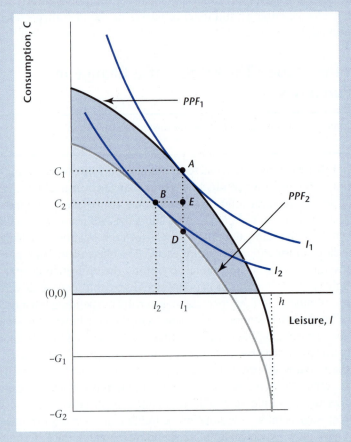

The income–expenditure identity tells us that $Y = C + G$; therefore, $C = Y - G$, and so

$$\Delta C = \Delta Y - \Delta G,$$

where Δ denotes "the change in." Thus, because $\Delta Y > 0$, we have $\Delta C > -\Delta G$, so that private consumption is **crowded out** by government purchases, but it is not completely crowded out as a result of the increase in output. In Figure 5.6, ΔG is the distance AD, and ΔC is minus the distance AE. A larger government, reflected in increased government spending, results in more output being produced, because there is a negative income effect on leisure and, therefore, a positive effect on labor supply. However, a larger government reduces private consumption, through a negative income effect produced by the higher taxes required to finance higher government spending. As the representative consumer pays higher taxes, his or her disposable income falls, and in equilibrium he or she spends less on consumption goods, and works harder to support a larger government.

What happens to the real wage when G increases? In Figure 5.6, the slope of PPF_2 is identical to the slope of PPF_1 for each quantity of leisure, l. Therefore, because the PPF becomes steeper as l increases (the marginal product of labor increases as employment decreases), PPF_2 at point B is less steep than is PPF_1 at point A. Thus, because minus the slope of the PPF at the equilibrium point is equal to the equilibrium real wage, the real wage falls as a result of the increase in government spending. The real wage must fall, as we know that equilibrium employment rises, and the representative firm would hire more labor only in response to a reduction in the market real wage.

Now, a question we might like to ask is whether or not fluctuations in government spending are a likely cause of business cycles. Recall that in Chapter 3 we developed a set of key business cycle facts. If fluctuations in government spending are important in causing business cycles, then it should be the case that our model can replicate these key business cycle facts in response to a change in G. The model predicts that, when government spending increases, aggregate output and employment increase, and consumption and the real wage decrease. One of our key business cycle facts is that employment is procyclical. This fact is consistent with government spending shocks causing business cycles, because employment always moves in the same direction as aggregate output in response to a change in G. Additional business cycle facts are that consumption and the real wage are procyclical, but the model predicts that consumption and the real wage are countercyclical in response to government spending shocks. This is because, when G changes, consumption and the real wage always move in the direction opposite to the resulting change in Y. Therefore, government spending shocks do not appear to be a good candidate as a cause of business cycles. Whatever the primary cause of business cycles, it is unlikely to be the fact that governments change their spending plans from time to time. This does not mean, however, that large changes in government spending have not on occasion given rise to large macroeconomic effects, as we show in the following "Theory Confronts the Data" box.

Working with the Model: A Change in Total Factor Productivity

LO 5.4 Decompose the effects of an increase in total factor productivity in the CEOP model into income and substitution effects.

An increase in total factor productivity involves a better technology for converting factor inputs into aggregate output. As we see in this section, increases in total factor productivity increase consumption and aggregate output, but there is an ambiguous effect on employment. This ambiguity is the result of opposing income and substitution effects on labor supply. While an increase in government spending essentially produces only an income effect on consumer behavior, an increase in total factor productivity generates both an income effect and a substitution effect.

THEORY CONFRONTS THE DATA

Government Spending in World War II

Wars typically involve huge increases in government expenditure, and they therefore represent interesting "natural experiments" that we can examine as an informal empirical test of the predictions of our model. An interesting example involves the effects of increased government spending in the United States during World War II. Shortly after the beginning of U.S. involvement in World War II in late 1941, aggregate output was channeled from private consumption to military uses, and there was a sharp increase in total real GDP. Figure 5.7 shows the natural logarithms of real GDP, real consumption

expenditures, and real government expenditures for the period 1929–2014. Of particular note is the extremely large increase in government expenditures that occurred during World War II, which clearly swamps the small fluctuations in G about trend that happened before and after World War II. Clearly, GDP also increases above trend in the figure during World War II, and consumption dips somewhat below trend. Thus, these observations on the behavior of consumption and output during World War II are consistent with our model, in that private consumption is crowded out somewhat and output increases.

Suppose that total factor productivity z increases. As mentioned previously, the interpretation of an increase in z is as a technological innovation (a new invention or an advance in management techniques), a spell of good weather, a relaxation in government regulations, or a decrease in the price of energy. The interpretation of the increase in z and the resulting effects depend on what we take one period in the model to represent relative to time in the real world. One period could be many years—in which case, we interpret the results from the model as capturing what happens over the long run—or one period could be a month, a quarter, or a year—in which case, we are studying short-run effects. After we examine what the model tells us, we provide interpretations in terms of the **short-run** and **long-run** economic implications. In general, the short run in macroeconomics typically refers to effects that occur within a year's time, whereas the long run refers to effects occurring beyond a year's time. However, what is taken to be the boundary between the short run and the long run can vary considerably in different contexts.

The effect of an increase in z is to shift the production function up, as in Figure 5.8. An increase in z not only permits more output to be produced given the quantity of labor input, but it also increases the marginal product of labor for each quantity of labor input; that is, the slope of the production function increases for each N. In Figure 5.8, z increases from z_1 to z_2. We can show exactly the same shift in the production function as a shift outward in the *PPF* in Figure 5.9 from *AB* to *AD*. Here, more consumption is attainable given the better technology, for any quantity of leisure consumed. Further, the trade-off between consumption and leisure has improved, in that the new *PPF* is

Figure 5.7 GDP, Consumption, and Government Expenditures

During World War II, an increase in government spending was associated with an increase in aggregate output and a slight decrease in consumption, as is consistent with our model.

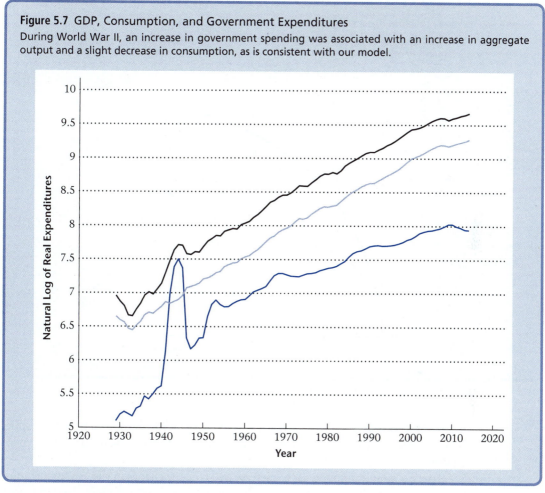

steeper for any given quantity of leisure. That is, because MP_N increases and the slope of the PPF is $-MP_N$, the PPF is steeper when z increases.

Figure 5.9 allows us to determine all the equilibrium effects of an increase in z. Here, indifference curve I_1 is tangent to the initial PPF at point F. After the shift in the PPF, the economy is at a point such as H, where there is a tangency between the new PPF and indifference curve I_2. What must be the case is that consumption increases in moving from F to H, in this case increasing from C_1 to C_2. Leisure, however, may increase or decrease, and here we have shown the case where it remains the same at l_1. Because $Y = C + G$ in equilibrium and because G remains constant and C increases, there is an increase in aggregate output, and because $N = h - l$, employment is unchanged (but employment could have increased or decreased). The equilibrium real wage is minus the slope of the PPF at point H (i.e., $w = MP_N$). When we separate the income and substitution effects of the increase in z, in the next stage of our analysis, we show that the real wage must increase in equilibrium. In Figure 5.9, the PPF clearly

Figure 5.8 Increase in Total Factor Productivity

An increase in total factor productivity shifts the production function up and increases the marginal product of labor for each quantity of the labor input.

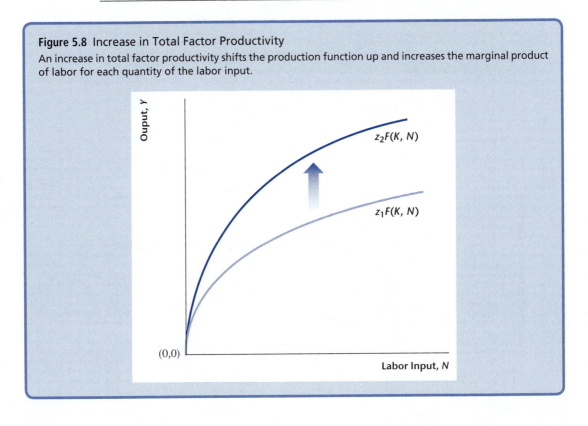

is steeper at H than at F, so that the real wage is higher in equilibrium, but we show how this must be true in general, even when the quantities of leisure and employment change.

To see why consumption has to increase and why the change in leisure is ambiguous, we separate the shift in the PPF into an income effect and a substitution effect. In Figure 5.10, PPF_1 is the original PPF, and it shifts to PPF_2 when z increases from z_1 to z_2. The initial equilibrium is at point A, and the final equilibrium is at point B after z increases. The equation for PPF_2 is given by

$$C = z_2 F(K, h - l) - G.$$

Now consider constructing an artificial PPF, called PPF_3, which is obtained by shifting PPF_2 downward by a constant amount. That is, the equation for PPF_3 is given by

$$C = z_2 F(K, h - l) - G - C_0.$$

Here C_0 is a constant that is large enough so that PPF_3 is just tangent to the initial indifference curve I_1. What we are doing here is taking consumption (i.e., "income") away from the representative consumer to obtain the pure substitution effect of an increase in z. In Figure 5.10 the substitution effect is then the movement from A to D, and the income effect is the movement from D to B. Much the same as when we

Figure 5.9 Competitive Equilibrium Effects of an Increase in Total Factor Productivity

An increase in total factor productivity shifts the *PPF* from *AB* to *AD*. The competitive equilibrium changes from *F* to *H* as a result. Output and consumption increase, the real wage increases, and leisure may rise or fall. Because employment is $N = h - l$, employment may rise or fall.

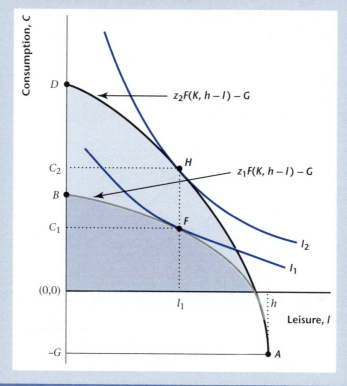

considered income and substitution effects for a consumer facing an increase in his or her wage rate, here the substitution effect is for consumption to increase and leisure to decrease, so that hours worked increase. Also, the income effect is for both consumption and leisure to increase. As before, consumption must increase as both goods are normal, but leisure may increase or decrease because of opposing income and substitution effects.

Why must the real wage increase in moving from *A* to *B*, even if the quantities of leisure and employment rise or fall? First, the substitution effect involves an increase in $MRS_{l,C}$ (the indifference curve gets steeper) in moving along the indifference curve from *A* to *D*. Second, because PPF_2 is just PPF_3 shifted up by a fixed amount, the slope of PPF_2 is the same as the slope of PPF_3 for each quantity of leisure. As the quantity of leisure is higher at point *B* than at point *D*, the *PPF* is steeper at *B* than at *D*, and so $MRS_{l,C}$ also increases in moving from *D* to *B*. Thus, the real wage, which is equal to the marginal rate of substitution in equilibrium, must be higher in equilibrium when *z* is higher.

Figure 5.10 Income and Substitution Effects of an Increase in Total Factor Productivity

Here, the effects of an increase in total factor productivity are separated into substitution and income effects. The increase in total factor productivity involves a shift from PPF_1 to PPF_2. The curve PPF_3 is an artificial PPF, and it is PPF_2 with the income effect of the increase in z taken out. The substitution effect is the movement from A to D, and the income effect is the movement from D to B.

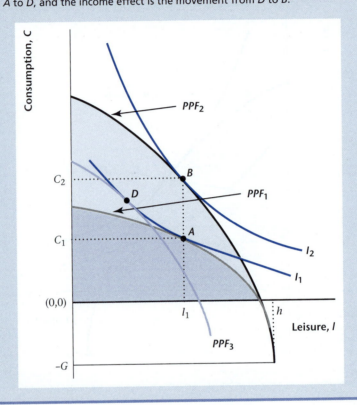

The increase in total factor productivity causes an increase in the marginal productivity of labor, which increases the demand for labor by firms, driving up the real wage. Workers now have more income given the number of hours worked, and they spend the increased income on consumption goods. Because there are offsetting income and substitution effects on the quantity of labor supplied, however, hours worked may increase or decrease. An important feature of the increase in total factor productivity is that the welfare of the representative consumer must increase. That is, the representative consumer must consume on a higher indifference curve when z increases. Therefore, increases in total factor productivity unambiguously increase the aggregate standard of living.

Interpretation of the Model's Predictions

Figure 5.9 tells a story about the long-term economic effects of long-run improvements in technology, such as those that have occurred in the United States since World

War II. There have been many important technological innovations since World War II, particularly in electronics and information technology. Also, some key observations from post–World War II U.S. data are that aggregate output has increased steadily, consumption has increased, the real wage has increased, and hours worked per employed person has remained roughly constant. Figure 5.9 matches these observations in that it predicts that a technological advance leads to increased output, increased consumption, a higher real wage, and ambiguous effects on hours worked. Thus, if income and substitution effects roughly cancel over the long run, then the model is consistent with the fact that hours worked per person have remained roughly constant over the post–World War II period in the United States. There may have been many other factors in addition to technological change affecting output, consumption, the real wage, and hours worked over this period in U.S. history. Our model, however, tells us that empirical observations for this period are consistent with technological innovations having been an important contributing factor to changes in these key macroeconomic variables.

A second interpretation of Figure 5.9 is in terms of short-run aggregate fluctuations in macroeconomic variables. Could fluctuations in total factor productivity be an important cause of business cycles? Recall from Chapter 3 that three key business cycle facts are that consumption is procyclical, employment is procyclical, and the real wage is procyclical. From Figure 5.9, our model predicts that, in response to an increase in z, aggregate output increases, consumption increases, employment may increase or decrease, and the real wage increases. Therefore, the model is consistent with procyclical consumption and real wages, as consumption and the real wage always move in the same direction as output when z changes. Employment, however, may be procyclical or countercyclical, depending on the strength of opposing income and substitution effects. For the model to be consistent with the data requires that the substitution effect dominate the income effect, so that the consumer wants to increase labor supply in response to an increase in the market real wage. Thus, it is certainly possible that total factor productivity shocks could be a primary cause of business cycles, but to be consistent with the data requires that workers increase and decrease labor supply in response to increases and decreases in total factor productivity over the business cycle.

Some macroeconomists, the advocates of **real business cycle theory**, view total factor productivity shocks as the most important cause of business cycles. This view may seem to be contradicted by the long-run evidence that the income and substitution effects on labor supply of real wage increases appear to roughly cancel in the post–World War II period. Real business cycle theorists, however, argue that much of the short-run variation in labor supply is the result of **intertemporal substitution of labor**, which is the substitution of labor over time in response to real wage movements. For example, a worker may choose to work harder in the present if he or she views his or her wage as being temporarily high, while planning to take more vacation in the future. The worker basically "makes hay while the sun shines." In this way, even though income and substitution effects may cancel in the long run, in the short run the substitution effect of an increase in the real wage could outweigh the income effect. We explore intertemporal substitution further in Chapters Chapters 9–14.

THEORY CONFRONTS THE DATA

Total Factor Productivity and Real GDP

Shocks to total factor productivity appear to play a key role in business cycles. As evidence of this, Figure 5.11 shows the percentage deviations from trend in real GDP and in the Solow residual for the period 1948–2010. Recall from Chapter 4 that the Solow residual is a measure of total factor productivity, calculated as the quantity of real output that cannot be accounted for by capital and labor inputs. Clearly, the figure shows that the Solow residual and real GDP move together closely. This observation is part of the motivation for real business cycle theory, which we shall study in detail in Chapter 13. Real business cycle theorists argue that shocks to

total factor productivity are the primary source of business cycles, and that seems hard to deny given Figure 5.11, if we accept that the Solow residual is a good measure of total factor productivity (there are some doubts about this, as we discuss in Chapter 13). Our data fit the predictions of our model closely. In particular, the fluctuations in real GDP and the Solow residual in Figure 5.11 are tracked closely by fluctuations about trend in consumption and employment (see Chapter 3), as the theory predicts (so long as the substitution effect on labor supply of an increase in total factor productivity outweighs the income effect).

Figure 5.11 Deviations from Trend in GDP and the Solow Residual

Deviations from trend in the Solow residual closely track deviations from trend in real GDP, as is consistent with real business cycle theory.

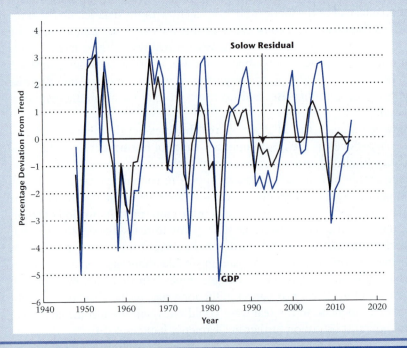

MACROECONOMICS IN ACTION

Government Expenditures and the American Recovery and Reinvestment Act of 2009

The American Recovery and Reinvestment Act (ARRA) was signed into law by President Obama on February 17, 2009[3]. This act of Congress was motivated by the belief that the government has an obligation to pursue economic policies that will increase aggregate economic activity when real GDP falls below trend, as occurred in 2008–2009 (see Figure 3.2). Keynesian macroeconomics, which we will study and evaluate in Chapters 13 and 14, provides the foundation for the belief that the government has an important role to play in smoothing business cycles.

The ARRA authorized a total of $787 billion in changes in items in the budget of the U.S. government. Since $787 billion represents 5.5% of annual GDP for 2008 in the United States, this appears to be a very large number. However, to understand the implications of the ARRA for the aggregate economy, we need to determine the economic importance of the different items included in the Act. First, about $288 billion of the $787 billion consisted of tax cuts for individuals and corporations. Next, about $209 billion was accounted for by government transfers. Neither of these two items is part of G, government spending, as we have represented it in our one-period model. A tax cut is just a reduction in government revenue or receipts, and recall from Chapter 2 that a government transfer (e.g., for unemployment insurance) is

not part of GDP, since it is not expenditure on a final good or service, and is therefore not included in G. This leaves about $290 billion in government expenditures on goods and services in the ARRA. If this were all spent in one year (which it was not—the extra expenditure authorized continued into 2010 and 2011), then this would account for a 10.1% increase in government expenditures over annual government expenditures in 2008, or an amount equal to 2.0% of 2008 GDP. Thus, even if we take out the parts of the ARRA that are not included in measured GDP, the increase in expenditure is large.

Next, to get a perspective on government expenditures authorized in the ARRA, consider Figure 5.12, where we show government expenditures as a percentage of GDP for 1947–2015. An interesting feature of the figure is that government expenditures as a fraction of GDP have been falling on trend since the mid-1950s. Another interesting feature is that this quantity held roughly steady at about 22% during the Republican administrations of Ronald Reagan and George H. W. Bush, from 1980 to 1992, but declined during the Democratic Clinton administration from 1992 to 2000. Government spending fell to less than 19% of GDP at the beginning of the 2008–2009 recession, but had risen to more than 20% by the end of 2009. One might have expected a larger increase in government spending as a percentage of GDP from the ARRA, particularly as GDP fell during the

---

[3] See http://en.wikipedia.org/wiki/Recovery_bill

(Continued)

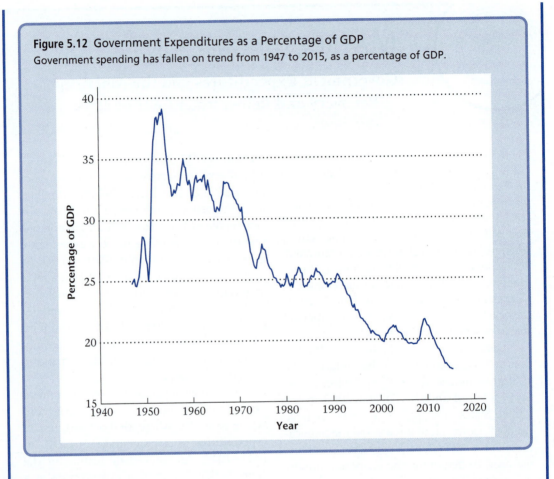

Figure 5.12 Government Expenditures as a Percentage of GDP

Government spending has fallen on trend from 1947 to 2015, as a percentage of GDP.

recession, but state and local expenditures declined during the recession, partly offsetting the effects of higher federal spending. Thus, the net effect of the level of spending authorized in the ARRA does not seem to be a big deal.

To understand the broader spending implications of the ARRA, in Figure 5.13 we show total government outlays as a percentage of GDP for 1947–2015. Government outlays include government expenditures on goods and services as well as transfers and interest on the government debt (recall the discussion from Chapter 2). While Figure 5.12 appears to indicate a declining role for government in the

economy since World War II, Figure 5.13 indicates an increasing role. The difference is due to growth in transfers. While all levels of government are spending less on goods and services as a fraction of GDP, government transfer programs have grown enormously. These transfer programs include Social Security and Medicare (at the federal level), and Medicaid and unemployment insurance (at the state level). Thus, in terms of the total budget of all levels of government, the additional spending on goods and services and government transfers in the ARRA adds a large amount to an already large quantity of total government outlays. Note that, in Figure 5.12,

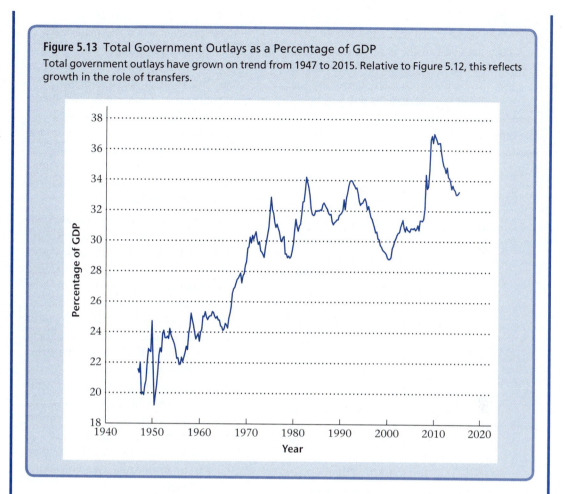

Figure 5.13 Total Government Outlays as a Percentage of GDP

Total government outlays have grown on trend from 1947 to 2015. Relative to Figure 5.12, this reflects growth in the role of transfers.

total government outlays, at about 37% of GDP in the first quarter of 2012, is at its highest level over the whole period since 1947.

The taxation and transfer items in the ARRA have implications for the government budget deficit and for deficit financing, which we will explore in later chapters. For now we will focus on what an additional 2% of GDP in spending by the government on goods and services might mean for aggregate economic activity, using our one-period model as a vehicle for organizing our thinking.

First, in the context of our one-period model, what could cause GDP to fall, as it did in 2008–2009? One possibility is that there was a decline in total factor productivity, which would cause the *PPF* to shift inward. In response to such a shock to the economy the government could engineer an increase in *G*, government spending on goods, which would act to increase real GDP, increase employment, and reduce consumption, as in Figure 5.6. However, our model certainly does not tell us that this government policy response makes

(Continued)

any sense, as the initial reduction in real GDP was just the result of the economy's optimal response to bad circumstances. Increasing G to offset the reduction in GDP caused by the negative shock to productivity will just serve to reduce leisure and consumption, and make the representative consumer worse off. Is our model missing something here? Consider some alternatives:

1. In the one-period model as we have constructed it, government spending is a deadweight loss to the economy. That is, when the government spends in the model, it buys goods and throws them away. Some types of government expenditures work exactly like this in practice. For example, military expenditure, while it protects us, economically is a pure loss of resources for the economy as a whole. However, some types of government spending act to make the economy more productive. For example, government spending on roads and bridges effectively increases the nation's capital stock, and shifts out the *PPF*. Indeed, it is straightforward to extend the one-period model to the analysis of productive government spending, as you are asked to do in the end-of-chapter problems. In the ARRA, much of the spending increases might be classified as productive government spending, including $90.9 billion of spending on education, $80.9 billion on infrastructure, $61.3 billion on energy projects, and $8.9 billion on science. Why spend this money now? One argument is that a recession is an ideal time for productive government expenditures, such as bridge and road improvements, that will have to be done anyway. Why not undertake these projects when the materials and labor can be had at a low price? On the negative side, some of these projects may have been ill-considered, and introduced in a hasty way, and therefore not likely to be productive at all. We can also extend our model to take account of public goods, such as national parks, which yield consumption value to consumers. We do this later in this chapter.

2. Prominent supporters of the ARRA, for example the Nobel-prize-winning economist Paul Krugman, who writes in the *New York Times*, typically use Keynesian arguments to argue in favor of the spending program. Keynesian thought, which we will address in Chapters 13 and 14, holds that there are short-run inefficiencies in the economy, which imply that the economy may not operate at the Pareto optimum. Government "stimulus"—short-run increases in government expenditure—can, according to Keynesians, push the economy toward the Pareto optimum, thus correcting the inefficiency.

3. The one-period model does not account for financial factors, which appear to be at the heart of the causes of the 2008–2009 recession. This is certainly a valid criticism. How can we make recommendations about government policy in a model that does not incorporate features that appear to be important for the problem at hand? The counterargument is that we need to start somewhere. The one-period model gives us some insight into how the economy works, and a solid base on which to build.

A Distorting Tax on Wage Income, Tax Rate Changes, and the Laffer Curve

LO 5.5 Analyze the effects of a distorting labor income tax in the simplified CEOP model.

We are now ready to consider a version of the model in which there is a distorting tax. As was discussed earlier in this chapter, distorting taxes imply in general that a competitive equilibrium is not Pareto optimal, and so we will not be able to use the same approach to analyzing the model as previously. The distorting tax we will consider is a proportional tax on wage income. This will capture, in a simple way, some features of income taxation in the United States and other countries, and will allow us to discuss some fiscal policy issues, including the incentive effects of income taxation. We will show that, surprisingly, it is possible for tax revenue collected by the government to increase when the income tax rate goes down, a feature illustrated in what has come to be known as the "Laffer curve." The form that the Laffer curve takes in the U.S. economy is of key importance for the effects of tax rate changes on labor supply and on tax revenue for the government.

A Simplified One-Period Model with Proportional Income Taxation

To keep the analysis simple and transparent for the purpose at hand, assume that output is produced only with labor as an input, with production by the representative firm according to the relationship

$$Y = zN^d, \tag{5-7}$$

with Y denoting aggregate output, N^d the firm's labor input, and z total factor productivity. Here, with labor the only factor of production, we have continued to assume that there is constant returns to scale in production, so that increasing N^d by a factor x increases output Y by the same factor x.

Now, in a competitive equilibrium, since labor demand equals labor supply, or $N^d = h - l$ and consumption plus government spending equals output, or $C + G = Y$, therefore from Equation (5-7) we can write the *PPF* as

$$C = z(h - l) - G, \tag{5-8}$$

and we have graphed the *PPF* as *AB* in Figure 5.14. Note that the *PPF* is now linear. At point A, the representative consumer takes zero units of leisure and consumes the maximum amount of consumption possible, $zh - G$, while at point B the consumer consumes zero and works $\frac{G}{z}$ units of time (with $l = h - \frac{G}{z}$) so as to supply the government with G units of goods.

To purchase G units of goods, the government imposes a proportional tax on the consumer's wage income. Assume that this is the only tax in this economy. In particular, there are no lump-sum taxes, or $T = 0$. Letting t denote the tax rate, the consumer will pay $tw(1 - l)$ in taxes to the government, so that we can write the consumer's budget constraint as

$$C = w(1 - t)(h - l) + \pi, \tag{5-9}$$

Figure 5.14 The Production Possibilities Frontier in the Simplified Model

The production possibilities frontier is linear. The maximum quantity of consumption (when the quantity of leisure is zero) is $zh - G$.

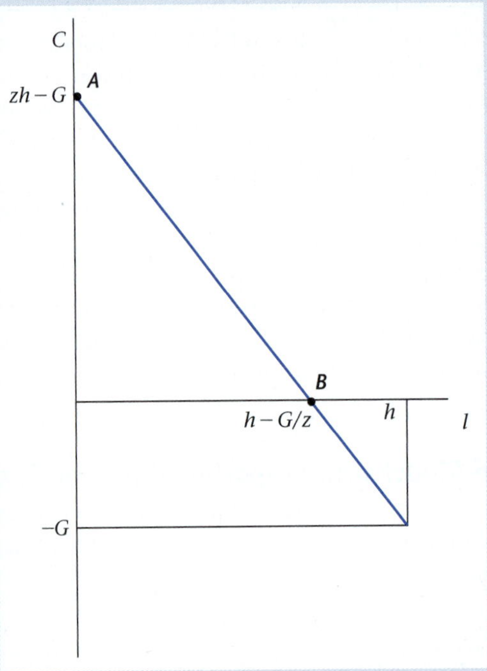

or consumption is equal to after-tax wage income plus dividend income. Note that $w(1 - t)$ is the effective wage rate for the consumer, or the after-tax real wage.

Next, consider the profit maximization problem for the representative firm. Profits for the firm are given by

$$\pi = Y - wN^d = (z - w)N^d, \tag{5-10}$$

from Equation (5-7). The firm chooses N^d to make π as large as possible, given z and w. Here, $z - w$ is the profit that the firm makes for each unit of labor input, and this is the same no matter how much labor the firm hires. Thus, if $z > w$, then the firm earns positive profits for each unit of labor hired, and it would want to hire an infinite quantity of labor. If $z < w$, then profits are negative for any quantity of labor hired, so the firm would hire no labor. However, if $z = w$, then profits are zero for the firm no matter what it does, so the firm is indifferent concerning how much labor to hire. As a result, the firm's demand curve for labor, denoted by $N^d(w)$, is infinitely elastic at the wage $w = z$, as shown in Figure 5.15.

Therefore, in equilibrium, no matter what the supply curve for labor $N^s(w)$ is (as determined by the representative consumer's behavior), the equilibrium wage must be

Figure 5.15 The Labor Demand Curve in the Simplified Model

Since productivity is constant at z, the representative firm's demand curve for labor is infinitely elastic at $w = z$.

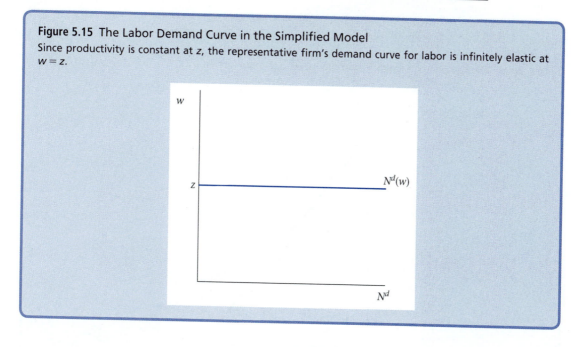

$w = z$. This simplifies our work dramatically. Further, since $w = z$ in equilibrium, therefore from Equation (5-10) the firm must earn zero profits in equilibrium, or $\pi = 0$, so dividend income for the representative consumer must also be zero in equilibrium. Therefore, setting $w = z$ and $\pi = 0$ in Equation (5-9), in equilibrium the consumer's budget constraint in equilibrium is

$$C = z(1 - t)(h - l). \qquad (5\text{-}11)$$

In equilibrium, the consumer chooses consumption C and leisure l to satisfy his or her budget constraint (Equation (5-11)), and markets clear, which is summarized by Equation (5-8). Note that Equations (5-8) and (5-11) in turn imply that the government's budget constraint is satisfied, since if we substitute for C in Equation (5-8) using Equation (5-11), we get $G = zt(h - l)$, or total government spending equals total tax revenue. We can depict a competitive equilibrium as in Figure 5.16. Here, AB is the PPF, or the combinations of C and l that satisfy Equation (5-8). As well, the budget constraint faced by the consumer in equilibrium is DF, or the combinations of C and l that satisfy Equation (5-11). In equilibrium, the tax rate t adjusts so that the point on DF that the consumer chooses is at point H, where DF intersects AB, which is what is required for market clearing. Therefore, in equilibrium, an indifference curve is tangent to DF at point H. This indifference curve necessarily cuts the PPF as shown, since AB is steeper than DF ($z > z(1 - t)$).

One conclusion is that the Pareto optimum, at E, is different from the competitive equilibrium, at H. That is, because the income tax distorts private decisions, the competitive equilibrium is not socially efficient. The welfare loss due to the distorting tax

Figure 5.16 Competitive Equilibrium in the Simplified Model with a Proportional Tax on Labor Income

The competitive equilibrium is point *H*, and the Pareto optimum is point *E*.

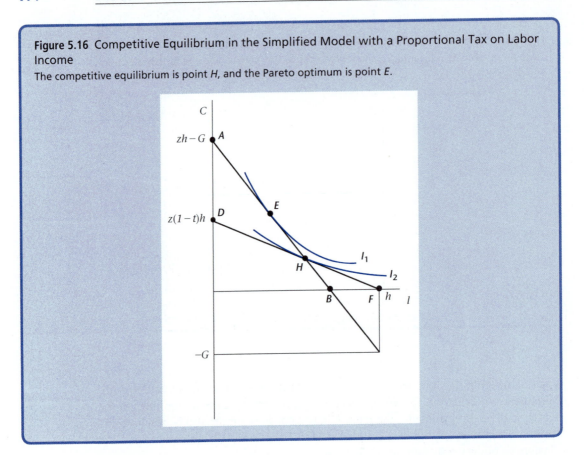

can be measured by how much better off the consumer is at point *E* than at point *H* (note that *H* is on a lower indifference curve than *E*). A second conclusion is that consumption and output must be higher and leisure lower at point *E* than at point *H*. This is due to the fact that indifference curves cannot cross, a property of indifference curves illustrated in a problem in Chapter 4. That is, the distorting income tax gives consumers a disincentive to work, and tends to lower aggregate consumption and aggregate output. Of course, if the government needs to collect taxes, and all taxes distort private decisions, it is necessary to put up with these negative incentive effects of income taxation. But a good tax system will account for these disincentive effects, in a way that collects tax revenue efficiently.

Income Tax Revenue and the Laffer Curve   To get another perspective on a competitive equilibrium with an income tax, we will take the following approach. First, we can ask how much income tax revenue the government could generate for each tax rate *t*, taking into account the quantity of labor that the consumer will want to supply at each of those tax rates. Then, we can determine the equilibrium tax rate (or tax rates) that will finance government expenditures *G*. This approach will be informative about the potential effects of changing the tax rate.

To start, we know that in equilibrium the consumer faces his or her budget constraint Equation (5-11), and chooses C and l to satisfy Equation (5-11) given the tax rate t, and the equilibrium real wage $w = z$. If we ask what quantity of leisure the consumer would choose given each tax rate t, we can derive a function $l(t)$, which describes the quantity of leisure the consumer chooses if the after-tax real wage is $z(1 - t)$, taking z as given. This would then tell us that the tax revenue that the government can collect if the income tax rate is t is

$$REV = tz[h - l(t)], \qquad (5\text{-}12)$$

where REV is total revenue from the income tax. In Equation (5-12), t is the tax rate, and $z[h - l(t)]$ is the **tax base**, which is the value of the quantity traded in the market of the object being taxed, which in this case is the quantity of labor, valued in terms of consumption goods by multiplying by the real wage rate z. It is important to recognize in Equation (5-12) that total tax revenue depends not only on the tax rate, but also on the size of the tax base, which in turn depends on the tax rate. If the tax base does not change when t increases, then tax revenue will increase when the tax rate increases. However, it is possible for tax revenue to go *down* when t increases. This would occur if $l(t)$ increases sufficiently when t increases, that a declining tax base offsets the effect of an increase in the tax rate on REV in Equation (5-12) so that REV falls when t increases. For this to occur, the substitution effect of a change in the after-tax real wage would have to be large relative to the income effect. That is, since an increase in t implies a decrease in the equilibrium real wage $z(1 - t)$, for REV to decline when t increases there would have to be a large decrease in the quantity of labor supplied, $h - l(t)$, or in other words a large disincentive to work due to a higher income tax rate.

In Figure 5.17, we show a typical graph for Equation (5-12), where we plot total tax revenue against the tax rate, taking into account the effects of the consumer's choice concerning the quantity of labor supplied in response to the tax rate. The curve AB in the figure is called a **Laffer curve**. The Laffer curve gets its name from the economist Arthur Laffer, and "Laffer curve" typically denotes any curve that shows the quantity of tax revenue generated by the government as a function of a tax rate. Theoretically, we cannot say a lot about the shape of the curve between the points A and B in Figure 5.17. In practice, the shape of the curve between A and B depends on the details of labor supply behavior for all possible after-tax real wage rates. However, points A and B will always be on the curve, since if the tax rate t is zero, then tax revenue must be zero ($t = 0$ implies $REV = 0$ in Equation (5-12)), which gives us point A, and the consumer will not work and the tax base is zero if $t = 1$ ($t = 1$ implies $l(1) = h$ and $REV = 0$ in Equation (5-12)), which gives us point B. In the figure, there is a maximum amount of tax revenue that the government can generate. That is, if the tax rate is t^*, then the maximum tax revenue REV^* accrues to the government.

Now, given the quantity of government spending G, in our model the government will have to choose the tax rate t to generate enough revenue to finance this quantity of spending, or from Equation (5-12), in equilibrium,

$$G = tz[h - l(t)],$$

Figure 5.17 A Laffer Curve

The Laffer curve is the relationship between income tax revenue and the income tax rate. Tax revenue must be zero when $t = 0$ (the tax rate is zero) and $t = 1$ (because no one will work if all income is taxed away). The government can maximize tax revenue by setting $t = t^*$. If the government wishes to finance government spending equal to G, it can set a tax rate of t_1 (on the good side of the Laffer curve) or t_2 (on the bad side of the Laffer curve).

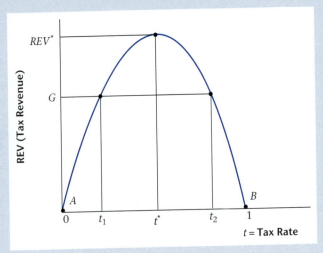

which is another version of the government's budget constraint. In Figure 5.17, note first that if $G > REV^*$, then it is impossible for the government to collect enough tax revenue to finance its spending. However, if $G < REV^*$ (the case we want to consider), then given the quantity of government spending G, there are two possible equilibrium tax rates. What is true in general is that there will be *at least* two tax rates that can generate enough tax revenue to finance any quantity of government expenditure $G < REV^*$. We have shown a simple Laffer curve, where if $G < REV^*$ in the figure, then there are two possible equilibrium tax rates, shown here as t_1 and t_2, where $t_2 > t_1$. It is possible that the Laffer curve could have a more complicated shape, with the potential for *more* than two equilibrium tax rates.

Now, given that there are two equilibrium tax rates, t_1 and t_2, for any quantity of government expenditure G, consider what a competitive equilibrium will look like in the context of the diagram we used earlier in this section. In Figure 5.18, the competitive equilibrium with the low tax rate t_1 is given by point F, while the one with the high tax rate t_2 is given by point H. Recall that a competitive equilibrium will always lie on the PPF given by curve AB, and on the budget constraint faced by the consumer in equilibrium. When the tax rate is t_2, the consumer's budget constraint is less steep, and lies below the budget constraint in the equilibrium where the tax rate is t_1. Therefore, we can say that the quantity of consumption, C, is higher, the quantity of labor supplied, $h - l$, is higher, leisure l is lower, and aggregate output ($Y = C + G$) is higher in the low-tax-rate equilibrium than in the high-tax-rate equilibrium. Further, since

Figure 5.18 There Can Be Two Competitive Equilibria

Given government spending equal to G, as in Figure 5.15, there are two equilibrium tax rates. The low-tax-rate (high-tax-rate) equilibrium is at point $F(H)$. In the low-tax-rate equilibrium consumption and output are higher, and leisure is lower, than in the high-tax-rate equilibrium.

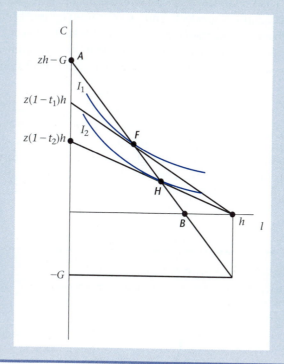

point F must be on a higher indifference curve than point H, the consumer is better off in the equilibrium with a low tax rate than in the one with a higher tax rate.

A sensible government would never choose the high tax rate t_2 since it could collect the same quantity of tax revenue with the low tax rate t_1 and make the representative consumer better off.

A Model of Public Goods: How Large Should the Government Be?

LO 5.6 Analyze the determinants of the size of government and private consumption.

To this point in this chapter, we have considered only one type of government spending in our model. When the government purchases goods, G, consumers receive no benefit from these goods. We have assumed thus far that goods confiscated by the government through taxation are simply thrown away. While this approach allows us to focus on the resource costs of government activity, and may capture the essence of some types of government spending—defense expenditures, for example—much of government spending has other effects that we should model.

It will help to simplify. Assume that there is no production, and that the economy consists only of a representative consumer and the government. The representative consumer has no choice about how to use his or her time, and simply receives an exogenous quantity of goods, Y. Thus, GDP is fixed by assumption, so that we can focus on the problem of how resources should be allocated between the government and the private sector. As we assumed in our basic model, the government can tax the consumer lump-sum, with T denoting the total tax, so the consumer's budget constraint is

$$C + T = Y. \tag{5-13}$$

The government takes the goods it collects as taxes, and transforms those private consumption goods into public goods using its technology. Assume that one unit of consumption goods acquired through taxation can be transformed by the government into q units of public goods. These public goods represent public parks, public transportation, health services, and other goods and services that governments typically

Figure 5.19 The Optimal Choice of Government Spending
At point A the equilibrium is Pareto optimal if the government chooses $G = G^*$. Points B and D represent suboptimal choices for the government.

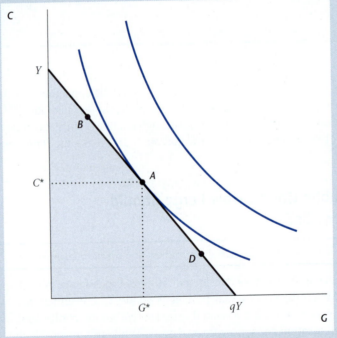

provide. We then have $G = qT$, so substituting for T in Equation (5-13) and rearranging, we get the PPF for this economy,

$$C = Y - \frac{G}{q}. \tag{5-14}$$

In Equation (5-14), q represents the efficiency of the government relative to the private sector. The larger is q, the smaller is the drain in resources, at the margin, from converting private goods into public goods. In Figure 5.19, we show the PPF for this economy (Equation 5-14) along with indifference curves representing the preferences of the representative consumer over private and public goods—C and G, respectively. Preferences over private and public goods have the same properties as did the consumer's preferences over consumption and leisure in Chapter 4.

If the government were behaving optimally, it would choose the quantity of government spending to be G^*, as in Figure 5.19, which would imply taxes $T = \frac{G^*}{q}$ and quantity of private consumption C^*. The competitive equilibrium for this economy would then be at point A in Figure 5.19, where an indifference curve for the representative consumer is tangent to the PPF, which is Pareto optimal. However, there is nothing to prevent the government from choosing a quantity of government spending that is too small, for example at point B in Figure 5.19, or a quantity that is too large, for example at point D.

Note that what is happening in Figure 5.3 is quite different from Figure 5.19. In Figure 5.3, individual private sector economic agents respond optimally to market prices, markets clear, and the resulting equilibrium happens to be Pareto optimal. However, in Figure 5.19, for the government to arrive at a Pareto optimum requires that it be able to figure out the representative consumer's preferences and to understand its own technology for converting private goods into public goods. The private sector is able to solve a very complicated resource allocation problem, through the decisions of many economic agents responding to their own circumstances and information. It is much more difficult for the government to solve its problem of determining the optimal quantity of G, since the government must collect a lot of detailed information in order to make an informed decision.

In Figure 5.19, what are the factors determining G^*, the optimal quantity of government spending? Clearly, this decision depends on total GDP, Y, q, the relative efficiency of the government and the private sector, and the consumer's preferences over private and public goods. To gain some perspective on this, we will consider how the government's decision is altered by changes in Y and q, respectively.

First, in Figure 5.20, we consider what happens when GDP increases from Y_1 to Y_2. The production possibilities frontier shifts out from PPF_1 to PPF_2 and the slope of the PPF remains unchanged, since that is determined by q. Assuming, as we did in our basic model in this chapter, that private goods and public goods are both normal, the equilibrium point will shift from A to B, and the government will choose to increase spending. Thus, with a higher level of GDP, there is a positive income effect on both private and public goods, and the government will choose to spend more on public goods, as that is what the public wants. Whether public goods increase as a fraction of GDP depends on whether public goods are luxury goods or not. If public goods are luxury

Figure 5.20 The Effects of an Increase in GDP

Y increases, shifting out the *PPF*. Assuming normal goods, government spending increases.

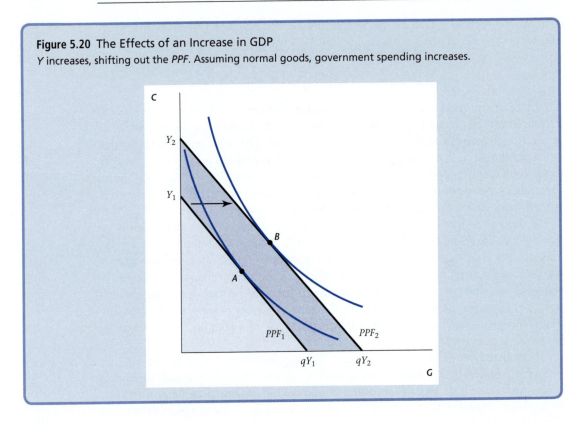

goods, for example if private sector economic agents wish to spend a larger fraction of their income supporting public parks as their income increases, then the size of the government as a percentage of GDP will grow as GDP increases. It seems likely that public goods are luxury goods, as in fact government spending tends to account for a larger fraction of GDP as countries develop. However, there could be other factors that contribute to this. For example, as countries develop they acquire better technologies for collecting taxes, making it less costly to support government activity. This would be reflected in q rather than Y.

Second, Figure 5.21 shows the effects of an increase in q, the efficiency with which the government can convert private goods into public goods, from q_1 to q_2. In this case the *PPF* shifts to the right from PPF_1 to PPF_2 and the *PPF* becomes more flat. As we know from our analysis in this chapter and in Chapter 4, there will be income and substitution effects in the government's choice of the optimal quantity of spending. In the figure, the equilibrium point moves from A to B. In separating the income and substitution effects, the line tangent to indifference curve I_1 at point D has the same slope as PPF_2, the movement from A to D is the substitution effect, and the movement

Figure 5.21 The Effects of an Increase in Government Efficiency

q increases, shifting out the *PPF*, and making the slope of the *PPF* flatter. Government spending, if chosen optimally by the government, will increase, but private spending may increase (if the substitution effect is small) or decrease (if the substitution effect is large).

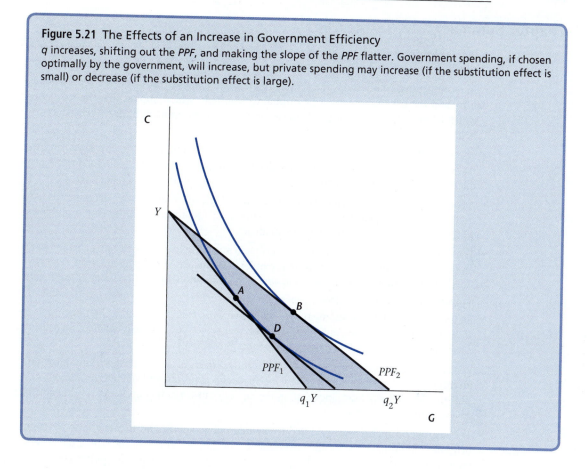

from *D* to *B* is the income effect. The income effect increases both *C* and *G*, and the substitution effect reduces *C* and increases *G*, since it is now cheaper for the government to produce *G*, in terms of private goods foregone. Thus, *G* increases but *C* may increase or decrease.

Thus, if the government becomes more efficient relative to the private sector, then the government should expand, but this need not imply that the private sector contracts. Note that the government could be quite inefficient—*q* could be quite small—but it could still be the case that the government would want to provide some public goods. This could occur, for example, if public goods and private goods are poor substitutes (there is much curvature in the indifference curves).

Now that we have gained some knowledge from a one-period model concerning how the macroeconomy functions, we can move on to consider unemployment in Chapter 6, and the causes and consequences of economic growth in Part III.

Chapter Summary

- In this chapter, we took the consumer behavior and firm behavior developed in Chapter 4, added government behavior, and constructed a complete one-period macroeconomic model.

- In a competitive equilibrium, the actions of the representative consumer, the representative firm, and the government must be mutually consistent, which implies that the market on which labor is exchanged for goods must clear, and the government budget constraint must hold.

- In a competitive equilibrium, aggregate output, consumption, employment, taxes, and the real wage (the endogenous variables) are determined given the capital stock, total factor productivity, and government spending (the exogenous variables).

- A competitive equilibrium can be represented in a single diagram, and this diagram was used to illustrate the equivalence between the competitive equilibrium and the Pareto optimum, which is an economically efficient state of affairs.

- The model shows how an increase in government spending has a pure negative income effect on the representative consumer, so that employment increases and consumption decreases. Government spending thus crowds out private consumption, but not completely, as there is an increase in aggregate output.

- An increase in total factor productivity, which may arise from improved technology, leads to an increase in output, consumption, and the real wage, but employment may increase or decrease due to opposing income and substitution effects.

- With a distorting tax on wage income, the incentive effects of tax rate changes have important incentive effects on labor supply. These incentive effects produce a Laffer curve, and it is possible that for high tax rates, increases in the tax rate cause a reduction in tax revenue for the government.

- The one-period model was modified to include public goods, and to show how we might determine an optimal size for the government. The model shows that the size of the government increases with GDP, through a pure income effect on the demand for public goods. The size of the government also increases as public goods provision becomes more efficient.

Key Terms

Closed economy An economy that does not trade with the rest of the world. (p. 143)

Open economy An economy that engages in trade with the rest of the world. (p. 143)

Public Goods Goods that are difficult or impossible for the private sector to provide, for example, national defense. (p. 143)

Exogenous variable A variable determined outside the model. (p. 143)

Endogenous variable A variable that the model determines. (p. 143)

Government budget constraint An equation describing the sources and uses of government revenues. (p. 144)

Fiscal policy The government's choices over government expenditures, taxes, transfers, and government borrowing. (p. 144)

Competitive equilibrium A state of the economy where prices and quantities are such that the behavior of price-taking consumers and firms is consistent. (p. 145)

Market clearing When supply equals demand in a particular market or markets. (p. 145)

Production possibilities frontier The boundary of a set that describes what consumption bundles are technologically feasible to produce. (p. 147)

Marginal rate of transformation Minus the slope of the *PPF*, or the rate at which one good in the economy can be technologically exchanged for another. (p. 149)

Pareto optimality A state of the economy that cannot be improved on by making one consumer better off without making another worse off. (p. 151)

First fundamental theorem of welfare economics (or first welfare theorem) Result stating that, under certain conditions, a competitive equilibrium is Pareto optimal. (p. 152)

Second fundamental theorem of welfare economics (or second welfare theorem) Result stating that, under certain conditions, a Pareto optimum is a competitive equilibrium. (p. 153)

Externality The effect an action taken by an economic agent has on another economic agent or agents, where the agent performing the action does not take into account this effect on others. (p. 153)

Distorting tax A tax, such as an income tax, that creates a difference between the effective prices faced by buyers and sellers of some good. (p. 154)

Crowding out The displacement of private expenditures by government purchases. (p. 158)

Short run Typically describes macroeconomic effects that occur within a year's time. (p. 160)

Long run Typically describes macroeconomic effects that occur beyond a year's time. (p. 160)

Real business cycle theory A theory postulating that the primary cause of aggregate fluctuations is fluctuations in total factor productivity. (p. 165)

Intertemporal substitution of labor The substitution of labor over time by a worker in response to movements in real wages. (p. 165)

Tax base The quantity that is subject to a particular tax. For example, the tax base for the tax on labor income is the quantity of labor supplied. (p. 175)

Laffer curve The relationship between the tax revenue collected by the government and the tax rate. (p. 175)

Questions for Review

5.1 Why is it useful to study a closed-economy model?

5.2 What is the role of the government in the one-period, closed-economy model?

5.3 Can the government run a deficit in the one-period model? Why or why not?

5.4 What are the endogenous variables in the model?

5.5 What are the exogenous variables in the model?

5.6 What are the four conditions that a competitive equilibrium must satisfy for this model?

5.7 What is the economic significance of the slope of the production possibilities frontier?

5.8 Why is the competitive equilibrium in this model Pareto optimal?

5.9 Explain the difference between the first and second welfare theorems. Why is each useful?

5.10 Give three reasons that an equilibrium might not be Pareto optimal.

5.11 What are the effects of an increase in government purchases?

5.12 Why does government spending crowd out government purchases?

5.13 What are the equilibrium effects of an increase in total factor productivity?

5.14 Explain why employment may rise or fall in response to an increase in total factor productivity.

5.15 Why does a distorting tax on labor income lead to an inefficient economic outcome?

5.16 How are the incentive effects of income taxation important for the Laffer curve?

5.17 Explain what happens when the economy is on the bad side of the Laffer curve and the income tax rate falls.

5.18 What are the two determinants of the optimal quantity of public goods?

5.19 What happens to public goods provision and private consumption when GDP increases, and when the opportunity cost of public goods provision becomes larger?

Problems

1. **LO 3** Suppose that the government decides to reduce taxes. In the model used in this chapter, determine the effects this has on aggregate output, consumption, employment, and the real wage, and explain your results.

2. **LO 3** Suppose that there is a natural disaster that destroys part of the nation's capital stock.
   (a) Determine the effects on aggregate output, consumption, employment, and the real wage, with reference to income and substitution effects, and explain your results.
   (b) Do you think that changes in the capital stock are a likely cause of business cycles? Explain with reference to your answer to part (a) and the key business cycle facts described in Chapter 3.

3. **LO 3** Suppose that total factor productivity, z, affects the productivity of government production just as it affects private production. That is, suppose that when the government collects taxes, it acquires goods that are then turned into government-produced goods according to $G = zT$ so that z units of government goods are produced for each unit of taxes collected. With the government setting G, an increase in z implies that smaller quantity of taxes are required to finance the given quantity of government purchases G. Under these circumstances, using a diagram determine the effects of an increase in z on output, consumption, employment, and the real wage, treating G as given. Explain your results.

4. **LO 3** Suppose that the representative consumer's preferences change, in that his or her marginal rate of substitution of leisure for consumption increases for any quantities of consumption and leisure.
   (a) Explain what this change in preferences means in more intuitive language.
   (b) What effects does this have on the equilibrium real wage, hours worked, output, and consumption?

   (c) Do you think that preference shifts like this might explain why economies experience recessions (periods when output is low)? Explain why or why not, with reference to the key business cycle facts in Chapter 3.

5. **LO 3** Suppose that government spending makes private firms more productive; for example, government spending on roads and bridges lowers the cost of transportation. This means that there are now two effects of government spending, the first being the effects discussed in this chapter of an increase in G and the second being similar to the effects of an increase in the nation's capital stock K.
   (a) Show that an increase in government spending that is productive in this fashion could increase welfare for the representative consumer.
   (b) Show that the equilibrium effects on consumption and hours worked for an increase in government spending of this type are ambiguous but that output increases. You must consider income and substitution effects to show this.

6. **LO 3** In the one-period model, education can be represented as time spent by the representative consumer that is neither leisure time nor time applied to producing output. What the economy gains in the future is that the representative consumer then has more time available, as measured in terms of effective units of labor time (adjusted for skill level, or what economists call human capital).
   (a) Using the one-period model, show what effects additional education has in the present on consumption, leisure, employment, aggregate output, and the real wage.
   (b) Similarly, show the effects the additional education that people acquire today will have in the future on consumption, leisure, employment, aggregate output, and the real wage.

(c) What does your analysis in parts (a) and (b) have to say about the trade-offs society makes between the present and the future in investing in education?

7. **LO 3** Suppose that, in the basic one-period model, there is no government spending and no taxes. Production by the representative firm produces pollution in proportion to the amount of output produced. Given any consumption bundle (a consumption–leisure pair), the consumer is worse off the more pollution there is.
   (a) In a diagram, show the competitive equilibrium and the Pareto optimum. Show that the competitive equilibrium is not Pareto optimal, and explain why. Is more or less output produced in the competitive equilibrium than at the Pareto optimum? Explain.
   (b) Now, suppose that the government imposes a proportional tax t on the output of the firm, and rebates the proceeds of the tax in a lump-sum fashion, as a transfer TR to the representative consumer. Show that the tax can be set in such a way that the competitive equilibrium is Pareto optimal. Explain your results.

8. **LO 5** In the simplified model with proportional taxation there can be two equilibria, one with a high tax rate and one with a low tax rate. Now, suppose that government spending increases. Determine the effects of an increase in G on consumption, leisure, labor supply, real output, and the tax rate in a high-tax-rate equilibrium and in a low-tax-rate equilibrium. How do your results differ? Explain why.

9. **LO 5** Suppose that the substitution effect of an increase in the real wage is always larger than the income effect for the representative consumer. Also assume that the economy is always in the low-tax-rate equilibrium on the good side of the Laffer curve. Determine the effects of an increase in total factor productivity, z, on the Laffer curve, on the equilibrium tax rate, and on consumption, leisure, the quantity of labor supplied, and output.

10. **LO 6** Consider the model of public goods in the last section of this chapter.
    (a) Suppose that preferences over private consumption C and public goods G are such that

these two goods are perfect substitutes; that is, the marginal rate of substitution of public goods for private goods is a constant $b > 0$. Determine the optimal quantity of public goods that the government should provide, and interpret your results. Make sure you show all of the relevant cases. What happens when b changes, or when q changes?
    (b) Repeat part (a), except with perfect complements preferences; that is, for the case where the representative consumer always wishes to consume private consumption goods and public goods in fixed proportions, or $C = aG$, with $a > 0$.

11. **LO 6** Extend the model of public goods, in the last section of this chapter, as follows. Suppose that output is produced, as in the simplified model with proportional taxation, only with labor, and that $z = 1$. Here, however, there is lump-sum taxation, and the PPF is given by $Y = h - l - G$. Now the consumer has preferences over three goods: private goods C, public goods G, and leisure l. Assume that C and l are perfect complements for the consumer; that is, the consumer always wants to consume C and l in fixed proportions, with $C = dl$, and $d > 0$.
    (a) Suppose, just as in part (a) of problem 10, that public goods and private goods are perfect substitutes. Determine the effects of an increase in G on consumption and labor supply, and explain your results.
    (b) Alternatively, assume, just as in part (b) of problem 10, that public goods and private goods are perfect complements. Again, determine the effects of an increase in G on consumption and labor supply, and explain your results.

12. **LO 6** Change the model of public goods in the following fashion. Suppose that T units of goods acquired as taxes from the private sector produces $T^{1/2}/a$ units of public goods, where $a > 0$. Determine the production possibilities frontier (PPF), and illustrate it in a diagram. Show in your diagram what happens to consumption of private and public goods if a increases, and discuss your results.

Working with the Data

Answer these questions using the Federal Reserve Bank of St. Louis's FRED database, accessible at http://research.stlouisfed.org/fred2/

1. Plot the 12-month percentage growth rates in real GDP and in total real government purchases from 1948 to 2015. Calculate these growth rates from quarterly data.
   (a) Does there appear to be any relationship between the growth rates in GDP and in government purchases?
   (b) What does your answer to part (a) tell you about the role in business cycles of fluctuations in government purchases?

2. Plot the 12-month percentage growth rates in total real government expenditures and in real government expenditures from 1948 to 2015. Calculate these growth rates from quarterly data. Do you think your plot shows any evidence that government spending crowds out private consumption? Why or why not?

Chapter 6

Search and Unemployment

Learning Objectives

After studying Chapter 6, students will be able to:

6.1 List the key labor market facts concerning the unemployment rate, the participation rate, and the employment/population ratio.

6.2 Describe the Beveridge curve, and explain its importance.

6.3 In the one-sided search model, explain how the reservation wage is determined.

6.4 Show how the one-sided search model determines the unemployment rate.

6.5 Use the one-sided search model to determine the effects of changes in the labor market on the reservation wage and the unemployment rate.

6.6 Construct an equilibrium in the two-sided search model.

6.7 Use the two-sided search model to explain how shocks to the labor market change labor force participation, unemployment, vacancies, aggregate output, and labor market tightness.

In Chapters 4 and 5, we developed a one-period competitive equilibrium macroeconomic model to provide a basic understanding of the factors determining aggregate output and the allocation of time between leisure and market work. In this chapter, our goal is to build on those basic ideas, by taking account of labor market frictions. In macroeconomics there are several types of frictions that take us beyond basic competitive equilibrium models, and allow us to understand and explain more about how the macroeconomy works. One such friction is "search." In general, it takes time for an individual who wants to work to find a suitable job with a firm that wishes to hire him or her. Similarly, it takes time for a firm to fill a vacancy. Search is required on both sides of the labor market; there are always would-be workers searching for jobs, and firms searching for workers to fill vacancies.

Every month, the Bureau of Labor Statistics measures the number of unemployed—people of working age who are not employed, but are actively searching for work. It is important to understand what determines unemployment. In particular, we are interested in how government policy affects search behavior, and whether the unemployment rate might be inefficiently high or low.

Our first goal in this chapter will be to examine the behavior of the unemployment rate in the United States. As well, we will study the behavior of three other key labor market variables: the vacancy rate, the participation rate, and the employment/population ratio. We will show how the unemployment rate, the vacancy rate, the participation rate, and the employment/population ratio move over the business cycle, and discuss some of the determinants of these three variables.

We will study two different search models of unemployment in this chapter: a one-sided search model, and a two-sided search model. In a one-sided search model, we focus on the behavior of an unemployed person searching for work, who receives job offers and must decide, on receiving an offer, whether to accept the offer or continue searching. This is one-sided, in the sense that we consider only the supply side of the labor market—the behavior of firms is left out. This allows us to focus our attention on a subset of the key determinants of unemployment. In the two-sided search model, we incorporate the behavior of firms (the demand side of the labor market), and also consider the labor force participation decisions of would-be workers. The analysis of the two-sided search model complements what can be learned from a one-sided search model, and expands our understanding of how the labor market works.

The two-sided search model of unemployment is based on the work of Peter Diamond, Dale Mortensen, and Christopher Pissarides, for which they received the Nobel Prize in Economics in 2010. Both search models are quite different from our one-period model constructed in Chapters 4 and 5. Though the search models we will construct are built up from the optimizing behavior of consumers and firms, search models require that we construct an equilibrium in a different way than in the competitive equilibrium model of Chapter 5. In a search process with labor market frictions we cannot think in terms of prices moving to clear markets in which there are many participants.

Labor Market Facts

Before studying a search model of unemployment, we will explore the empirical behavior of the unemployment rate, the participation rate, the employment/population ratio, and the vacancy rate in the United States. This will give us a set of labor market facts that will serve as the backdrop for the search models we work with in this chapter. We want to use our models to explain these facts, and to help us sort out what is causing particular features of the data.

The Unemployment Rate, Participation Rate, and Employment/Population Ratio

LO 6.1 List the key labor market facts concerning the unemployment rate, the participation rate, and the employment/population ratio.

Recall from Chapter 2 that if N is the working-age population, Q is the labor force (employed plus unemployed), and U is the number of unemployed, then the unemployment rate and participation rate are defined by

$$\text{unemployment rate} = \frac{U}{Q},$$

$$\text{participation rate} = \frac{Q}{N}.$$

As well, we will be interested in the behavior of the employment/population ratio, defined by

$$\text{employment/population ratio} = \frac{Q - U}{N}.$$

Figure 6.1 shows a plot of the unemployment rate for the United States for the years 1948–2016. The unemployment rate is a countercyclical variable: high during

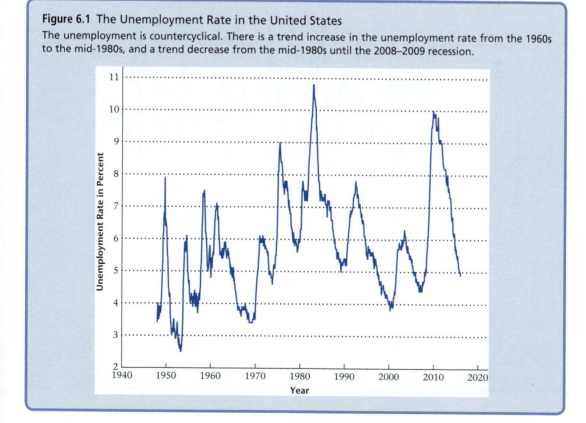

Figure 6.1 The Unemployment Rate in the United States

The unemployment is countercyclical. There is a trend increase in the unemployment rate from the 1960s to the mid-1980s, and a trend decrease from the mid-1980s until the 2008–2009 recession.

recessions and low during booms. In particular, note in the figure that the unemployment rate spiked during the recessions of 1973–1975, 1981–1982, 1991–1992, and
2008–2009, and decreased during the periods between recessions. The cyclical behavior
of the unemployment rate can be seen even more clearly in Figure 6.2, which displays
the percentage deviations from trend in real GDP and the deviations from trend in the
unemployment rate. In the figure, it is clear that the unemployment rate tends to be
above (below) trend when real GDP is below (above) trend; that is, the unemployment
rate is strongly countercyclical.

In addition to the cyclical behavior of the unemployment rate, there also appear to
be longer-run movements in the unemployment rate in Figure 6.1. For example, from
the late 1960s until the mid-1980s there was a trend increase in the unemployment

Figure 6.2 Deviations from Trend in the Unemployment Rate and Real GDP
The unemployment rate is clearly countercyclical, in that the deviation from trend in the unemployment
rate tends to be positive (negative) when the percentage deviation from trend in real GDP is negative
(positive).

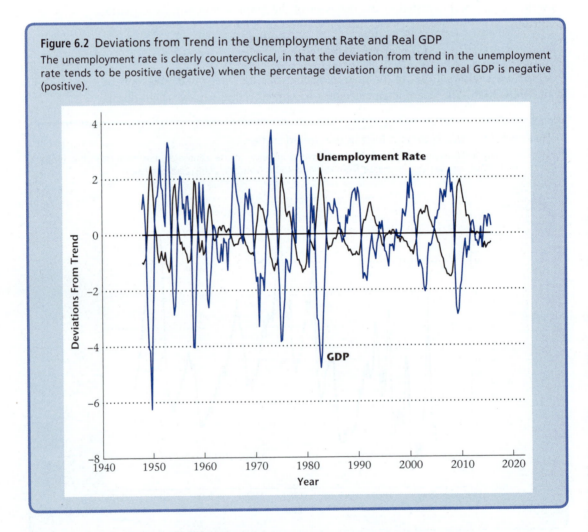

rate, and there was a trend decrease from the mid-1980s until the recession of 2008–2009. We would like to understand the reasons for both the cyclical behavior and the long-run behavior of the unemployment rate.

The labor force participation rate is shown in Figure 6.3. In the figure, note that the participation rate increased from about 59% in the late 1940s to more than 67% in 2000. The large decline beginning in 2000, to about 63% in 2016, is quite striking. Figure 6.4 shows how the behavior of men and women has contributed to aggregate labor force participation. As the labor force participation rate of men has declined steadily since 1948, the increase in aggregate labor force participation that occurred before 2000 was due entirely to the behavior of women. Since 2000, the participation rate of women has declined, but not by as much as that for men.

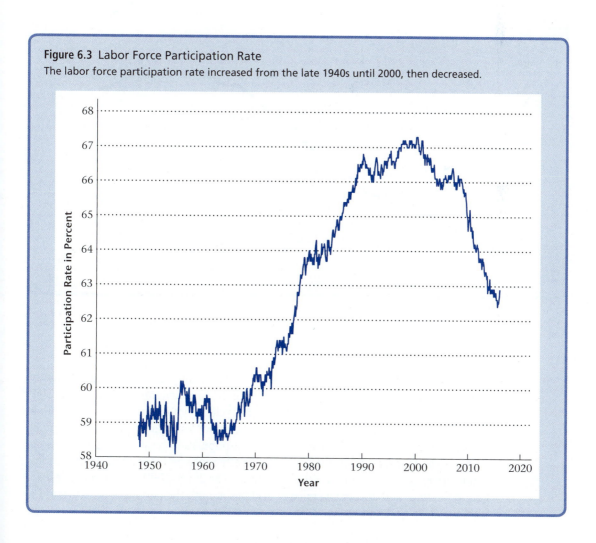

Figure 6.3 Labor Force Participation Rate

The labor force participation rate increased from the late 1940s until 2000, then decreased.

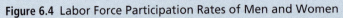

Figure 6.4 Labor Force Participation Rates of Men and Women

The increase in the total labor force participation rate, seen in Figure 6.5, that occurred from the late 1940s until 2000, was due entirely to the increased labor force participation of women, since the labor force participation rate of men has been declining since 1948.

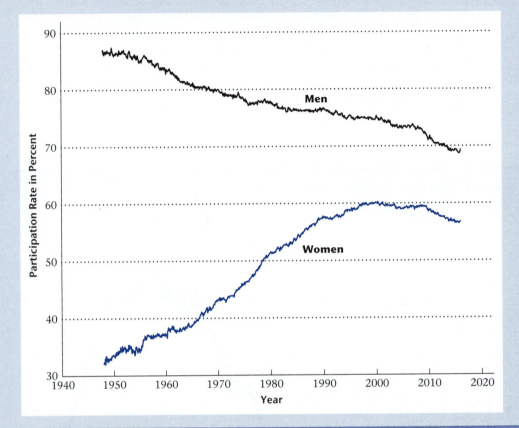

Figure 6.5 illustrates the cyclical behavior of the aggregate participation rate by showing the percentage deviations from trend in the participation rate and in real GDP. In the figure, the participation rate is clearly procyclical, but it is much less volatile than is real GDP. Further, as is clear in Figure 6.6, the labor force participation rate is much less cyclically variable than is the employment/population ratio. During a recession, workers who lose their jobs tend to search for other jobs and remain in the labor force as unemployed, rather than leave the labor force. The 2008–2009 recession is an exception to the rule, in that there were large declines in both the participation rate and the employment/population ratio.

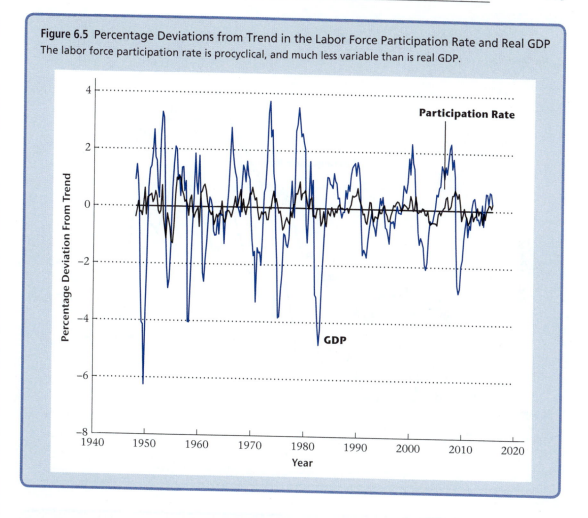

Figure 6.5 Percentage Deviations from Trend in the Labor Force Participation Rate and Real GDP
The labor force participation rate is procyclical, and much less variable than is real GDP.

The Vacancy Rate and the Beveridge Curve

LO 6.2 Describe the Beveridge curve, and explain its importance.

At any point in time, firms recruit new workers by advertising job vacancies they wish to fill. If we let A denote the number of vacancies in the economy as a whole, the vacancy rate is defined by

$$\text{vacancy rate} = \frac{A}{A + Q - U},$$

which is the ratio of the number of vacancies to vacancies plus the number employed. Since December 2000, the vacancy rate has been measured as part of the **Job Openings and Labor Turnover Survey (JOLTS)** conducted by the Bureau of Labor Statistics.

Figure 6.6 Labor Force Participation Rate and Employment/Population Ratio
The labor force participation rate is much less cyclically volatile than is the employment/population ratio.

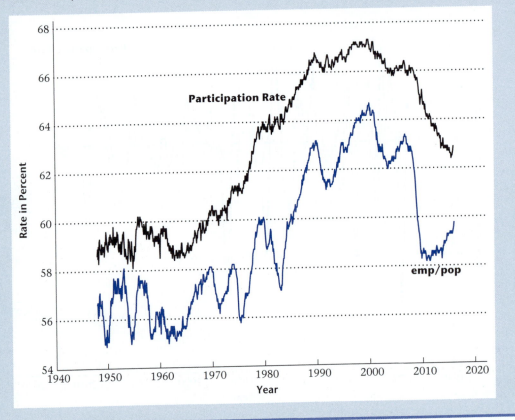

MACROECONOMICS IN ACTION

Unemployment and Employment in the United States and Europe

Economists who study labor markets have long been interested in the differences between the United States and Europe in labor market outcomes. There has been much interest, for example, in explaining why, since the 1970s, unemployment rates have increased in European countries relative to the United States.

Most research has focussed on how labor market rigidities in Europe, including generous unemployment insurance, high minimum wages, high taxes, and tough restrictions on the hiring and firing of employees, act to increase European unemployment. The United States is generally characterized as being a country with a small amount of labor market rigidity, and so the question for many researchers has been only whether the greater rigidity in Europe can generate the observed quantitative difference in unemployment rates between Europe and the United States.

Richard Rogerson, in an article in the *Journal of the European Economic Association,*[1] comes up with a different characterization of European labor market problems that suggests some new directions for economic research. Rogerson examines the behavior of the employment/population ratios in Europe and the United States, as well as unemployment rates in the two places. For Europe, he focuses on three countries: France, Germany, and Italy. Rogerson documents an increase in the gap between the European unemployment rate and the unemployment rate in the United States of about 6% between the 1970s and 2000, just as other authors have found. However, in terms of the employment/population ratio, Rogerson finds a relative deterioration in Europe that begins much earlier. He finds that a gap opened in the 1950s, and that the size of this gap increased by about 18% between the 1950s and 2000. That is, the trend increase in the employment/population ratio that we observe in Figure 6.6 for the United States did not occur in Europe. This is perhaps a more startling finding than the relative deterioration in Europe in terms of unemployment rates, since it indicates a fundamental difference in

growth in labor inputs in the United States and Europe.

What might explain this difference in labor market outcomes? Rogerson explores the labor market data further, but rather than seeking an explanation in terms of labor market rigidities, he studies the sectoral composition of output in Europe and the United States. Just as in the United States, Europe has experienced a sectoral shift from manufacturing to services since the 1950s. However, the nature of the sectoral shift was different in Europe. In the United States there was much more growth in the service sector than was the case in Europe. Thus, one explanation for the difference in labor market outcomes is the following. In both Europe and the United States, unemployment increased because of a sectoral shift from manufacturing to services, as workers were displaced from manufacturing jobs and experienced a spell of unemployment in transitioning to employment in the service sector. However, in Europe this generated more long-term unemployment because the service sector was not growing to the extent it was in the United States, so that service sector growth could not absorb all of the workers who were displaced from manufacturing jobs. As well, it is possible that labor market rigidities in Europe exacerbated the transition, as protections for unemployed workers discouraged displaced workers from acquiring the new skills required for service-sector employment. In any event, these are only conjectures, which need to be carefully investigated in future research.

---

[1]R. Rogerson, 2004. " Two Views on the Deterioration of European Labor Market Outcomes," *Journal of the European Economic Association* 2, 447–455.

In Figure 6.7, we plot the vacancy rate and the unemployment rate. Due to data availability, we can only show short time series, for the period 2000–2015, but this shows clearly that the unemployment rate and the vacancy rate are negatively correlated, and that the vacancy rate is a procyclical variable. In particular, the vacancy rate decreased after the onset of the 2001 recession, and the 2008–2009 recession.

Figure 6.7 The Vacancy Rate and the Unemployment Rate

The vacancy rate and the unemployment rate are negatively correlated, and the vacancy rate is procyclical.

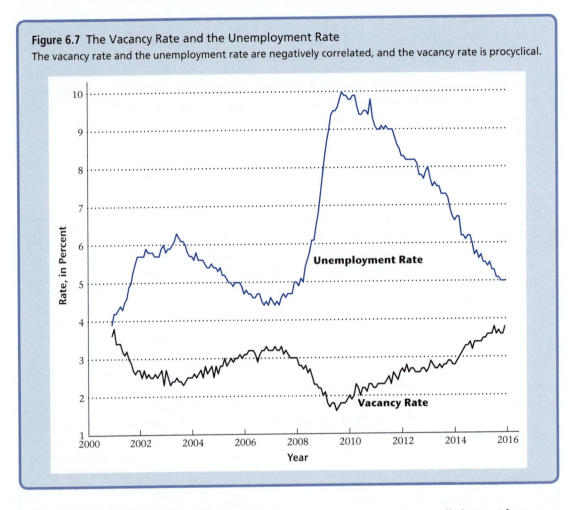

An interesting regularity that we observe in the data is the so-called **Beveridge curve**, which is a downward-sloping curve reflecting the observed relationship between the unemployment rate and the vacancy rate. Figure 6.8 shows the observed Beveridge curve relationship for the period 2000–2015. In the figure, it is useful to date the observations to show the shift in the curve that occurred at the end of the 2008–2009 recession. The dots in the figure denote the observations for December 2000 through December 2007, and the solid line connects observations from December 2007 through December 2015. Until about December 2009, the observations appear to fall on a stable downward-sloping curve, but the last set of observations appears to lie on a curve that has shifted to the right. We would like to use our model to explain what gives rise to the Beveridge curve relationship, and what could have caused the curve to shift at the end of the last recession.

A One–Sided Search Model of Unemployment

The first search model that we will study in this chapter is a "one-sided model." In this model, we focus on the behavior of an unemployed worker, who searches for work,

Figure 6.8 The Beveridge Curve

The points in the scatter plot are observations on the unemployment rate and the vacancy rate for December 2000 through December 2007, and those points exhibit a clear Beveridge curve relation—a downward-sloping curve. A solid line joins observations from December 2007 through December 2015. The Beveridge curve appears to have shifted in about December 2009.

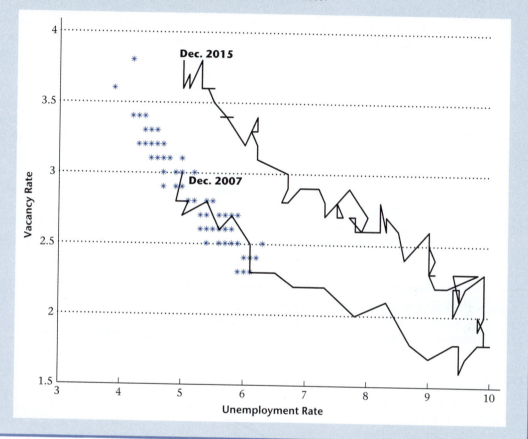

receives job offers that pay particular wages, and must decide when to accept a job and stop searching. This model is convenient for highlighting some key ways in which labor markets work, and it will leave out some other important details—for example, the behavior of firms who are hiring workers and the choices of individuals to be in or out of the labor force—that we will include in our next model.

An important goal in this basic model is to capture the nature of unemployment as a different economic activity from leisure, in that it involves active search. The first search models were developed in the late 1960s,[2] and they have since been refined and put into wide use in labor economics and macroeconomics. This model will allow us to think about the factors that motivate the search behavior of unemployed workers, and it will permit us to analyze some of the determinants of the unemployment rate.

---

[2]See J. McCall, 1970, "Economics of Information and Job Search," *Quarterly Journal of Economics* 84, 113–126.

The Welfare of Employed and Unemployed Workers

For simplicity, the workers in our model will all be in the labor force; that is, they will be either employed or unemployed, with U denoting the fraction of workers who are unemployed, and $1 - U$ the fraction who are employed. The jobs of the employed differ according to the wages that they are paid, where w will denote the real wage associated with a particular job. Let $V_e(w)$ denote the value of being employed. This is the welfare of a worker who is employed and earning a real wage, w, and it takes into account the worker's preferences and all possible future events, including the chances of the worker being separated from his or her job, and what will happen to the worker in such an event. We will let s denote the **separation rate**; that is, s is the fraction of workers who will become randomly separated from their jobs every period. This is a simple way to capture job separations that occur in practice because of firings and quits arising from poor matches between workers and firms. We depict the function $V_e(w)$ in Figure 6.9. Note that $V_e(w)$ increases with w, as the worker is better off with higher-paying jobs, and $V_e(w)$ is concave because the worker experiences diminishing marginal utility from higher-paying jobs. That is, the increase in welfare for the worker from an extra unit of real wage income becomes smaller as real wage income increases, reflected in the declining slope of $V_e(w)$.

The function $V_e(w)$ shifts down if the separation rate s increases. Given an increase in the separation rate, there is a greater chance of an employed worker losing his or her

Figure 6.9 The Welfare of an Employed Worker

The worker's welfare is increasing in the real wage, w, that he or she earns on the job, and the function is concave because the marginal benefit from a higher real wage declines as the real wage increases.

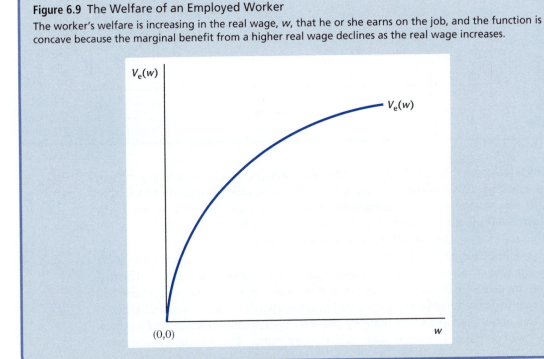

job and becoming unemployed. This makes employment less attractive, and the welfare from being employed at any wage must fall.

Now, we want to consider the welfare of an unemployed worker, which we denote by V_u. The key determinant of V_u is the size of the unemployment insurance (UI) benefit that an unemployed worker receives. For simplicity, we will assume that the UI benefit is a constant real amount, b, that does not depend on the wage the unemployed worker earned when he or she was employed. Another important determinant of V_u is the frequency with which the unemployed worker receives job offers, and we will denote this frequency by p. That is, each period a fraction, p, of all the unemployed workers will receive job offers. Two important facts are the following:

- V_u increases when b increases. An increase in the UI benefit increases an unemployed worker's welfare.
- V_u increases when p increases. With a higher p the chances are better for the unemployed worker of receiving a job offer he or she will take, and this will increase welfare.

The Reservation Wage

LO 6.3 In the one-sided search model, explain how the reservation wage is determined.

Now that we know how a worker's welfare is determined when employed and unemployed, we can work out how the unemployed worker will make choices. When an unemployed worker receives a job offer, it will be a job offer at a particular wage, w. The key decision for the unemployed worker on receiving a job offer is whether to take the offer or continue searching for work. If a low-wage job is turned down, there is some possibility of receiving a higher-wage offer in the future, but the worker must bear a period of unemployment and uncertainty before such an offer is received. Therefore, if a bad job is turned down, this involves a trade-off between the short-run losses from unemployment and the uncertain long-run benefits from a good job. Clearly, some wage offer will be sufficiently high that the unemployed worker will accept it, and he or she would also accept any wage offer that was higher than this amount. We call this the **reservation wage** and denote it by w^*.

When a wage offer, w, is received, this implies a level of welfare for the job, $V_e(w)$. The unemployed worker will accept the job if the welfare from taking it is higher than the welfare of being unemployed, and will decline it otherwise. That is, the worker will accept the job if $V_e(w) \geq V_u$ and will turn it down if $V_e(w) < Vu$. In Figure 6.10 we have $V_e(w) \geq V_u$ if $w \geq w^*$ and $V_e(w) < V_u$ if $w < w^*$, and so w^* is the reservation wage that determines acceptance or rejection of job offers.

The reservation wage will change if there are shifts in either $V_e(w)$ or V_u. For example, suppose that the unemployment benefit increases. This causes an increase in V_u from V_u^1 to V_u^2 in Figure 6.11. As a result, the reservation wage increases from w_1^* to w_2^*. Therefore, with an increase in the unemployment benefit, there is a smaller cost to turning down a job to hold out for a higher wage offer, and an unemployed worker will then become more picky concerning the jobs that he or she will take.

Figure 6.10 The Reservation Wage

The reservation wage, w^*, is determined by the intersection of the $V_e(w)$ curve (the welfare from employment) and the V_u curve (the welfare from unemployment).

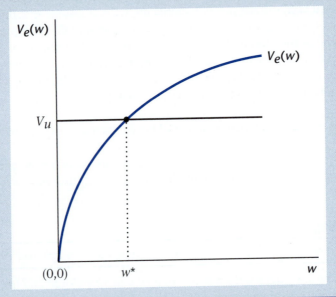

Figure 6.11 An Increase in the Unemployment Insurance Benefit, b

The increase in benefits increases the welfare from unemployment from V_u^1 to V_u^2. The reservation wage then increases from w_1^* to w_2^*

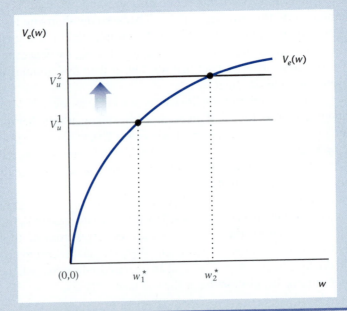

The Determination of the Unemployment Rate

LO 6.4 Show how the one-sided search model determines the unemployment rate.

Having shown how an unemployed worker chooses his or her reservation wage, we can complete our search model of unemployment and show how it determines the long-run rate of unemployment. In the model, there will be flows between the pool of employed workers and the pool of unemployed workers each period. Some employed workers will be separated from their jobs and become unemployed, while some unemployed workers will receive job offers that are sufficiently attractive to accept. If U is the unemployment rate—that is, the fraction of the labor force that is unemployed—then given that the separation rate is s, the flow of workers from employment to unemployment will be $s(1 - U)$. Now, let $H(w)$ denote the fraction of unemployed workers receiving a wage offer whose offer is greater than w, where $H(w)$ is depicted in Figure 6.12. Note that $H(w)$ is decreasing in w. Now, if unemployed workers choose a reservation wage, w^*, then, given that a fraction, p, of the unemployed receive a job offer and that a fraction, $H(w^*)$, of those receiving an offer are offered a wage greater than w^*, the portion of the unemployed who will be employed next period will be the fraction who receive a wage offer at or above their reservation wage. Therefore, the flow of workers from unemployment to employment will be $UpH(w^*)$.

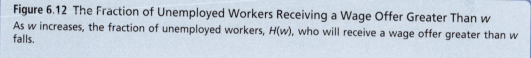

Figure 6.12 The Fraction of Unemployed Workers Receiving a Wage Offer Greater Than w

As w increases, the fraction of unemployed workers, $H(w)$, who will receive a wage offer greater than w falls.

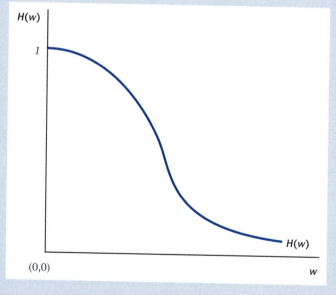

In a long-run equilibrium, the flow of workers from employment to unemployment must be equal to the flow of workers from unemployment to employment, and so we must have

$$s(1 - U) = UpH(w^*). \qquad (6\text{-}1)$$

This equation determines the unemployment rate, U, given s, p, and the reservation wage, w^*. In Figure 6.13 we depict the left-hand and right-hand sides of Equation (6-1), with the intersection of these two curves determining the long-run equilibrium unemployment rate, denoted by U^*.

Figure 6.14 shows how the reservation wage and the unemployment rate are determined in equilibrium. In Figure 6.14(a), the reservation wage w^* is determined by the intersection of the V_u and $V_e(w)$ curves, while Figure 6.14(b) determines the unemployment rate given the reservation wage, w^*.

Now that we have a complete model that determines the reservation wage and the long-run unemployment rate, we can use this model to analyze the effects on these two variables of changes in the economic environment.

Figure 6.13 The Determination of the Unemployment Rate, U^*, in the One-Sided Search Model
In the figure, $s(1 - U)$ is the flow of workers from employment to unemployment, and $UpH(w^*)$ is the flow of workers from unemployment to employment. The long-run unemployment rate, U^*, is determined by the intersection of the two lines.

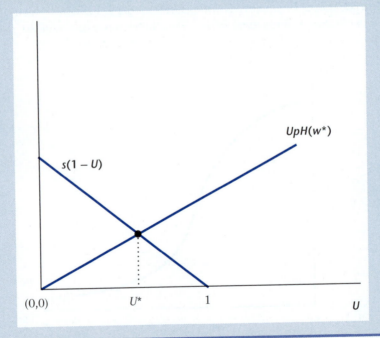

Figure 6.14 The Determination of the Reservation Wage and the Unemployment Rate in the One-Sided Search Model

The reservation wage, w^*, is determined in panel (a) by the intersection of the curves $V_e(w)$ and V_u. Then, given the reservation wage, the long-run unemployment rate is determined in panel (b).

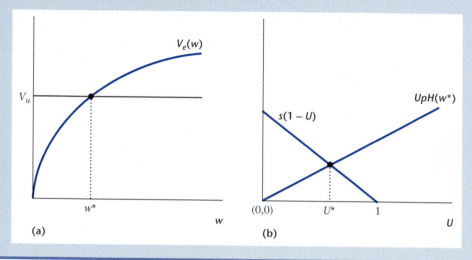

An Increase in Unemployment Insurance Benefits

LO 6.5 Use the one-sided search model to determine the effects of changes in the labor market on the reservation wage and the unemployment rate.

The first experiment we will carry out is to look at the effects of a change in UI benefits. In Figure 6.15(a), an increase in benefits, b, increases the welfare of the unemployed, V_u, from V_u^1 to V_u^2. The effect of this is to increase the reservation wage from w_1^* to w_2^*. This then implies that the fraction of unemployed workers receiving an acceptable wage offer is smaller. That is, since $H(w)$ is decreasing in w, we have $H(w_2^*) < H(w_1^*)$. In Figure 6.15(b), this implies that the line $Up\,H(w_1^*)$ shifts down to $Up\,H(w_2^*)$. As a result, the unemployment rate increases from U_1 to U_2 in the long run.

   The intuition behind this result is that more generous UI benefits imply that unemployed workers can afford to be more picky about the jobs they accept. On average, then, spells of unemployment will tend to be longer, and the long-run unemployment rate must increase. Relatively higher unemployment insurance benefits in part explain higher average unemployment rates in Europe and Canada than in the United States.

An Increase in the Job Offer Rate

LO 6.5 Use the one-sided search model to determine the effects of changes in the labor market on the efficiency wage and the unemployment rate.

A second experiment is to look at the effects of an increase in the job offer rate, p, on the reservation wage and the long-run unemployment rate. Suppose the job offer rate, p,

Figure 6.15 An Increase in the Unemployment Insurance Benefit, *b*

The rise in UI benefit increases the value of unemployment from V_u^1 to V_u^2 in panel (a), causing the reservation wage to increase. This decreases the flow of workers from unemployment to employment in panel (b), and the unemployment rate rises in the long run.

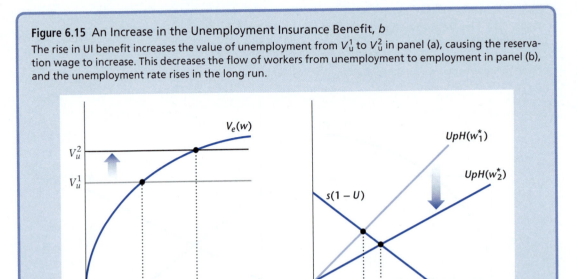

(a)   (b)

increases. Such a change would result from an increase in the efficiency with which firms and unemployed workers are matched. This could occur for two reasons. First, there might be technological change, such as better information technology, which could increase the likelihood of matches between unemployed workers and firms with vacancies. For example, the Internet greatly increases an unemployed worker's ability to find work at low cost. Second, p could increase because of government intervention. In many countries, the government plays an active role in finding work for unemployed workers, through government-run employment centers and the like.

In Figure 6.16 we show the long-run equilibrium effects of an increase in p. Here, when p increases, this raises the welfare of the unemployed from V_u^1 to V_u^2 in Figure 6.16(a). As a result, the reservation wage increases from w_1^* to w_2^*, since unemployed workers can now afford to be more picky, as they will not have to wait as long for another wage offer if the current offer is turned down. In Figure 6.16(b), there are two effects on the flow of workers from unemployment to employment. The direct effect is that an increase in p from p_1 to p_2 increases the flow of workers from unemployment to employment, since job offers are now received at a higher rate. This shifts the line $UpH(w^*)$ up. The indirect effect is that the reservation wage rises, reducing $H(w^*)$, the fraction of workers receiving a job offer who accept the offer. On net, it is not clear whether $UpH(w^*)$ will rise or fall, but in Figure 6.16 we show it increasing from $Up_1H(w_1^*)$ to $Up_2H(w_2^*)$, which implies that the unemployment rate falls in

Figure 6.16 An Increase in the Job Offer Rate, p

When p increases, this increases the welfare of the unemployed, who are now more likely to find work, and the reservation wage increases from w_1^* to w_2^* in panel (a). In panel (b), there are two effects on $UpH(w^*)$, in that p has increased, which increases the flow of workers from unemployment to employment, but w^* has increased, which reduces this flow. It is not clear how the unemployment rate is affected, but we show it decreasing in the figure.

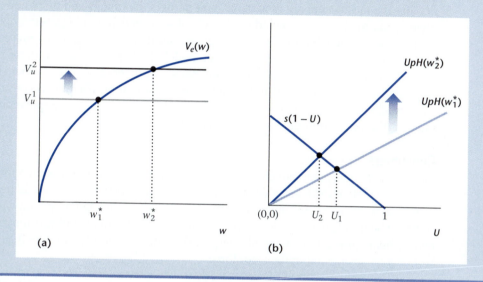

(a)

(b)

long-run equilibrium from U_1 to U_2. However, if the indirect effect is greater than the direct effect, the unemployment rate will rise.

The implications of this for government policy are important. If the government uses resources to find work for unemployed workers, then this may be counterproductive if its goal is to decrease the unemployment rate. It may be the case that unemployed workers simply become more picky about acceptable jobs, causing the unemployment rate to rise. Also, workers may or may not be better off as a result. The welfare of the unemployed is affected positively, because unemployed workers have better choices, and the employed will in general be working at higher-paying jobs, but there is a cost of the government's unemployment program that will ultimately have to be financed through taxation, and this will reduce the welfare of those taxed. The net effect on economic welfare is therefore uncertain.

A Two–Sided Model of Search and Unemployment

The early search models, developed by economists in the late 1960s, and closely related to our one-sided search model, have been refined and put into wide use in labor economics and macroeconomics. The model we will work with in this section is a simplified version of a framework constructed by Dale Mortensen and Christopher Pissarides,[3] who shared the 2010 Nobel Prize in Economics with Peter Diamond for their work in search economics.

The search model we will construct and work with is two-sided in that we will take account of both sides of the labor market—the supply side, as in the one-sided model, and the demand side. This allows us to give a broader picture of how the labor market fits into the macroeconomy as a whole, and permits the understanding of additional phenomena and decisions, including the role of firms in determining unemployment, choices concerning labor market participation, and the effects of labor market factors on aggregate economic activity. As in the model of Chapters 4 and 5, there is one period, but in this search model there are many consumers and firms, rather than a single representative consumer and a single representative firm. There are N consumers, who are all potential workers, so we can think of N as the working-age population. The number of firms is endogenous, to be determined by the model.

Consumers

Each of the N consumers can choose to work outside the market or to search for market work. Think of work outside the market as home production, which could be child care, yard work, or household chores, for example. Let Q denote the quantity of consumers who decide to search for work, so that $N - Q$ is the number of consumers who choose home production. We will interpret Q as the labor force, and $N - Q$ as those working-age people not in the labor force.

Let $P(Q)$ define a supply curve for workers who choose to search for market work. Thus, $P(Q)$ represents the expected payoff to searching for market work that would induce Q consumers to search. The supply curve $P(Q)$ is depicted in Figure 6.17. In the figure, the supply curve is upward-sloping because the value of home production is different for different consumers. Therefore, if the expected payoff from searching is higher, this induces more consumers to forego home production to search for market work.

Firms

In order to produce, a firm must post a vacancy in order to (hopefully) match with a worker. Recruiting workers is costly, in that we assume it costs the firm k (in units of consumption goods) to post a vacancy. Firms that do not post a vacancy are inactive and cannot produce. Let A denote the number of active firms, which is the number that choose to post vacancies.

Matching

At the beginning of the period, there will be Q consumers searching for work and A firms posting vacancies. We want to capture, in a simple way, the idea that matching workers with firms is a time-consuming and costly process. In general, firms are very different from each other in the kinds of jobs they offer, and workers have very

---

[3]D. Mortensen and C. Pissarides 1994. "Job Creation and Job Destruction in the Theory of Unemployment," *Review of Economic Studies* 61, 397–416.

Figure 6.17 The Supply Curve of Consumers Searching for Work

The curve $P(Q)$ defines the expected payoff required to induce Q consumers to search for work. The supply curve is upward sloping because different consumers have different payoffs to working in the home.

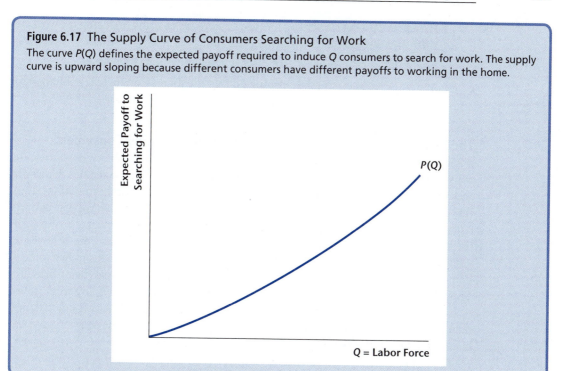

different characteristics. This makes the process of matching firms with workers difficult. In standard models of labor search, difficulties in matching are captured by a **matching function**. Letting M denote the number of successful matches between workers and firms, M is determined by

$$M = em(Q, A). \tag{6-2}$$

In Equation (6-2), the matching function on the right-hand side of the equation is much like a production function that "produces" matches between workers and firms as "output," given "inputs" of searching consumers and firms. The variable e denotes **matching efficiency**, and plays much the same role as does total factor productivity in the production function we studied in Chapter 4. With higher e, more matches occur given the numbers of consumers and firms searching. Matching efficiency, e, can increase in practice due to better information, for example more efficient search technologies such as Internet advertising, or because the skills that consumers have are better-matched to the skills that firms want.

The function m has properties that are very similar to the function F described in Chapter 4 in the context of production. In particular,

1. The function m has constant returns to scale. Recall that this means that

$$em(xQ, xA) = xem(Q, A) \tag{6-3}$$

for any $x > 0$. For the matching function, constant returns to scale implies that a large economy is no more efficient at producing matches between workers and firms than a small economy, and vice versa.

2. If there are no consumers searching for work or no firms searching for workers, then there are no matches, or $m(0, A) = m(Q, 0) = 0$.

3. The number of matches M increases when either Q or A increases.

4. Marginal products are diminishing, in that the increase in matches obtained for a one-unit increase in Q decreases as Q increases, and similarly for A.

The Supply Side of the Labor Market: Optimization by Consumers

If a consumer chooses to search for work, he or she may find a job, in which case the consumer would be counted as employed by the Bureau of Labor Statistics. However, the consumer may not find work even if he or she chooses to search. In that instance, the consumer would be counted as unemployed, since he or she has been actively engaged in search, but is not employed. If the consumer finds work, he or she earns the real wage w, and we will assume that, if unemployed, the consumer receives an unemployment insurance (UI) benefit b. Thus, the consumer knows his or her value of home production, the wage if he or she finds work, and the unemployment benefit if he or she is unemployed. The consumer also knows the chances of finding work, given by the matching function. If there are Q consumers searching and M successful matches, then for an individual consumer, the probability of finding work is M/Q or from the matching function Equation (6-2),

$$p_c = \frac{em(Q, A)}{Q}, \tag{6-4}$$

where p_c is the probability of finding work for a consumer. Then, given the constant-returns-to-scale property of the matching function, setting $x = 1/Q$ in Equation (6-3), and defining $j \equiv A/Q$, from Equation (6-4) we get

$$p_c = em\left(1, \frac{A}{Q}\right) = em(1, j). \tag{6-5}$$

Therefore, from Equation (6-5), the probability of finding work for a consumer depends only on the ratio $j = A/Q$, which is the ratio of firms searching for workers relative to consumers searching for work. This ratio is a measure of **labor market tightness**. Since Equation (6-5) gives the probability of finding work for a consumer, the probability of being unemployed if a consumer chooses to search for work is then

$$1 - p_c = 1 - em(1, j) \tag{6-6}$$

Recall that $P(Q)$ defines the supply curve for the number of consumers choosing to search for work, Q. In equilibrium, $P(Q)$ must be equal to the expected payoff a consumer receives from searching, so

$$P(Q) = p_c w + (1 - p_c)b = b + em(1, j)(w - b) \tag{6-7}$$

In Equation (6-7), the expression after the first equality is the expected payoff the consumer obtains from searching for work—the probability of finding a job multiplied by the market wage, plus the probability of being unemployed multiplied by the unemployment insurance benefit—and the expression after the second equality is obtained by substituting for p_c using Equation (6-5).

Figure 6.18 is an illustration of Equation (6-7). In the figure, the "market price" for searching workers, or the expected payoff to searching for work on the vertical axis, is determined by the market wage w, the UI benefit b, and market tightness j. Then, given this market price, the supply curve for searching workers determines the quantity of searching workers Q. In Chapters 4 and 5, a worker in a competitive equilibrium model observes the market wage and then decides how much labor to sell on the market at that wage. However, in the two-sided search model, a would-be worker takes into account not just the market wage, but his or her chances of finding work and the UI benefit if his or her job search fails.

The Demand Side of the Labor Market: Optimization by Firms

Firms that choose to bear the cost k of posting a vacancy have a probability $p_f = M/A$ of finding a worker, since the ratio of total matches to the number of firms searching

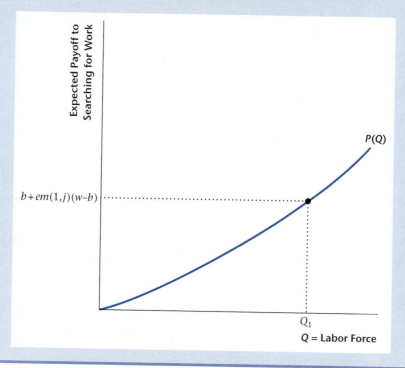

Figure 6.18 The Supply Side of the Labor Market

The market wage, the UI benefit, and labor market tightness determine the expected payoff to searching for work for a consumer. Then, given this expected payoff, the supply curve for searching consumers determines the labor force.

determines the chances of achieving a successful match. Then, from the matching function Equation (6-1), we obtain

$$p_f = \frac{em(Q, A)}{A} = em\left(\frac{Q}{A}, 1\right) = em\left(\frac{1}{j}, 1\right), \tag{6-8}$$

where the second equality follows from Equation (6-3), the constant-returns-to-scale property of the matching function.

Given a successful match with a worker, the firm and worker produce output z, so the profit the firm receives from the match is $z - w$, or output minus the wage paid to the worker. Firms will enter the labor market, posting vacancies, until the expected net payoff from doing so is zero, or $p_f(z - w) - k = 0$. Given Equation (6-8), we can write this equation as

$$em\left(\frac{1}{j}, 1\right) = \frac{k}{z - w}, \tag{6-9}$$

which determines labor market tightness j, given the wage w, productivity z, and the cost of posting a vacancy k. We depict this in Figure 6.19, where, given $k/(z - w)$, labor market tightness is j_1.

Figure 6.19 The Demand Side of the Labor Market

Firms post vacancies up to the point where the probability for a firm of matching with a worker is equal to the ratio of the cost of posting a vacancy to the profit the firm receives from a successful match.

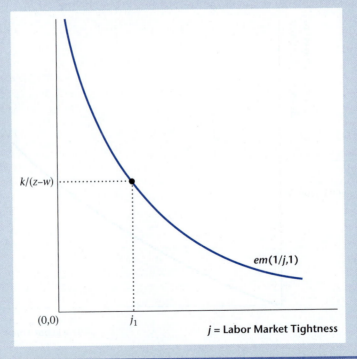

Equilibrium

LO 6.6 Construct an equilibrium in the two-sided search model.

When a firm is matched with a worker, together they can produce output z. In this model, z is both total factor productivity and average labor productivity, since we can think of this as a model with no capital where one firm and one worker produce z units of output. The firm and worker need to come to an agreement concerning the wage w that the worker is to receive. In economic theory, there is a large body of work that addresses how economic agents bargain, with one particularly famous contribution made by John Nash, who developed what is now known as **Nash bargaining theory**.[4]

In the Nash bargaining solution, two individuals strike a bargain that depends on what each person faces as an alternative if the two cannot agree, and on the relative bargaining power of the two people. Critical to the solution in the case of the firm and the worker in our setup is the notion of surplus: the surplus the worker receives as a result of the bargain; the surplus the firm receives; and the total surplus available to the firm and the worker, which is what they collectively stand to gain from coming to an agreement. In this case, the worker will receive a surplus of $w - b$, which is the wage the worker receives minus the employment insurance benefit, where b represents the alternative for the worker if he or she cannot come to an agreement with the firm. The firm's surplus is $z - w$, which is the profit the firm makes. Then, if we add the worker's surplus and the firm's surplus, we obtain total surplus, which is $z - b$.

Nash bargaining theory in this circumstance dictates that the firm and the worker will each receive a constant share of the total surplus. Let a denote the worker's share of total surplus, where $0 < a < 1$. Here a represents the bargaining power of the worker. Then, the worker and firm agree to a contract such that the worker's surplus is a fraction a of total surplus, or

$$w - b = a(z - b), \tag{6-10}$$

so if we solve Equation (6-10) for the wage, we obtain

$$w = az + (1 - a)b. \tag{6-11}$$

Then, the last step to determine an equilibrium solution is to substitute for w in Equations (6-7) and (6-9) using Equation (6-11), obtaining

$$P(Q) = b + em(1, j)a(z - b), \tag{6-12}$$

and

$$em\left(\frac{1}{j}, 1\right) = \frac{k}{(1 - a)(z - b)}, \tag{6-13}$$

and then Equations (6-12) and (6-13) solve for the endogenous variables j and Q. We depict the two Equations (6-12) and (6-13) in Figure 6.20. In panel (b) of the

---

[4]See J. Nash, 1950. "The Bargaining Problem," *Econometrica* 18, 155–162.

Figure 6.20 Equilibrium in the Two-Sided Search Model

In panel (b), the ratio of the cost of posting a vacancy to the firm's surplus from a successful match determines labor market tightness. Then, in panel (a), labor market tightness determines the size of the labor force.

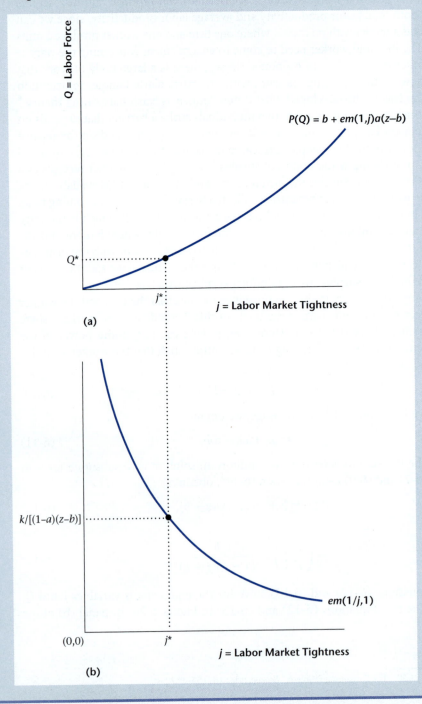

figure, we depict Equation (6-13), which determines labor market tightness j. The smaller is the cost of posting a vacancy, k, relative to the firm's share of total surplus $(1 - a)(z - b)$, the greater will be the inducement for firms to post vacancies and enter the labor market, which will make j larger. In panel (a) of the figure, Equation (6-10) describes an upward-sloping relationship between Q and j, which is the relationship defined by Equation (6-12). If labor market tightness j is higher, then the chances of finding a job are greater for consumers, more of them will decide to search for work, and therefore Q will be higher. For example, in Figure 6.18 higher j increases the expected payoff to searching for work, and then a higher supply of searching workers, Q, is forthcoming. In Figure 6.20, given labor market tightness j^* determined in panel (b); in panel (a) we determine the quantity of consumers who choose to search, Q^*.

Once we have determined j and Q, we can work backward to determine all other variables of interest. First, the number of consumers who do not search for work is $N - Q$, and these are the people who would be counted as not in the labor force. Second, since Q is the number of people in the labor force, the unemployment rate is

$$U = \frac{Q(1 - p_c)}{Q} = 1 - em(1, j), \qquad (6\text{-}14)$$

using Equation (6-6). Similarly, the vacancy rate is the number of vacancies that go unfilled, relative to the number of jobs that were originally posted, so the vacancy rate is

$$v = \frac{A(1 - p_f)}{A} = 1 - em\left(\frac{1}{j}, 1\right) \qquad (6\text{-}15)$$

Finally, the quantity of aggregate output in this economy is $Y = Mz$, which is the number of matches multiplied by the output produced in each match. From Equation (6-2), and using the constant-returns-to-scale property of the matching function, we can express aggregate output as

$$Y = em(Q, A)z = Qem(1, j)z. \qquad (6\text{-}16)$$

In Equation (6-16), aggregate output is then increasing in Q and increasing in j. Thus, if there is a larger labor force or a tighter labor market, aggregate output will be higher.

Working with the Two-Sided Search Model

LO 6.7 Use the two-sided search model to explain how shocks to the labor market change labor force participation, unemployment, vacancies, aggregate output, and labor market tightness.

Our next goal is to take the two-sided search model that was constructed in the previous section, and put it to work. We want to use the model to gain an understanding of how the labor market works, and to explain some of the features of the data discussed at the beginning of this chapter. As with the model in Chapter 5, what we can learn from the model comes from examining how the endogenous variables in the model change when an exogenous variable changes. We will look at three different experiments: an increase in the UI benefit, an increase in productivity, and a decrease in matching efficiency.

An Increase in the UI Benefit

If the UI benefit b increases, this has the effect of reducing the total surplus from a match between a worker and a firm, $z - b$, and increasing the wage, w, from Equation (6-11). In Figure 6.21, initial labor market tightness is j_1 and initially there are Q_1 consumers in the labor force. With the reduction in total surplus, in panel (b) of the figure, $k/[(1 - a)(z - b)]$ increases, and this causes labor market tightness to fall to j_2 in equilibrium, since posting vacancies has now become less attractive for firms. In panel (a), the increase in b and decrease in total surplus causes the curve to shift up, as the expected payoff to searching for work increases. Then, in equilibrium the labor force Q could rise or fall, though it is shown decreasing in the figure, to Q_2. Because labor market tightness has decreased, this makes job market search less attractive for consumers, and this tends to reduce the size of the labor force. However, the increase in the employment insurance benefit b acts to make labor search more attractive, which tends to increase Q. With two effects working in different directions, the net effect on the labor force is ambiguous. However, from Equations (6-14) and (6-15), it is clear that the unemployment rate must rise and the vacancy rate must fall, because of the reduction in labor market tightness, which acts to reduce the probability of finding a job for a consumer, and increase the probability of a successful match for a firm posting a vacancy.

In terms of aggregate output, from Equation (6-16), the effect is ambiguous. Lower labor market tightness j acts to reduce output, but Q may rise or fall, so in principle there could be a decrease or an increase in aggregate output. Our intuition might tell us that better social insurance, provided through UI, should reduce real GDP, since people will be less inclined to work. However, the model tells us that it is possible that more generous UI could have the effect of drawing more people into the labor force and therefore increasing aggregate output.

These results in the model are broadly consistent with observations on average unemployment rates across different countries. In particular, the unemployment rates in Canada and Western Europe have tended historically to be higher than the unemployment rate in the United States. This is consistent with our model, in that UI is more generous in Canada and Western Europe than in the United States. In general, higher UI benefits act to encourage job search and to increase unemployment.

An Increase in Productivity

Next we consider what happens when productivity, z, increases. In Figure 6.22, panel (b), this acts to reduce $k/[(1 - a)(z - b)]$ and so labor market tightness increases in equilibrium from j_1 to j_2. This occurs because higher productivity increases the total surplus available from a match between a firm and a worker, and firms then find it

Figure 6.21 An Increase in the UI Benefit, *b*

An increase in *b* reduces the surplus the firm receives from a match, which reduces labor market tightness in (b). Then, in (a), the increase in *b* shifts the curve up. The labor force could increase or decrease.

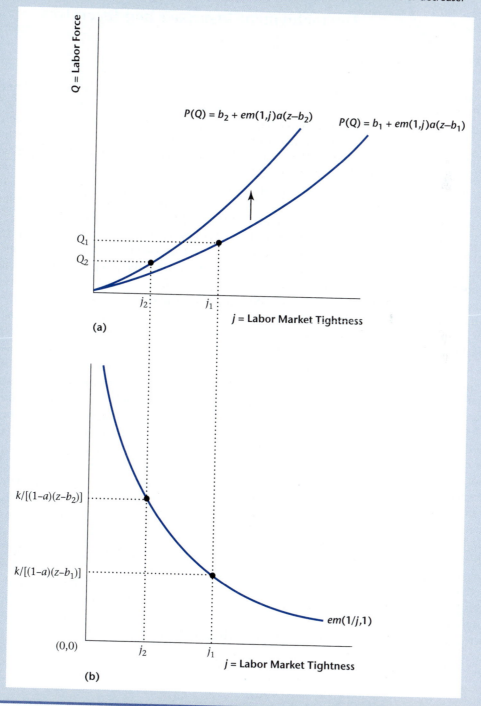

MACROECONOMICS IN ACTION

Unemployment Insurance and Incentives

The two-sided search model illustrates one effect of UI, which is that higher UI benefits tend to increase the market wage and reduce the surplus that the firm receives from a match with a worker, thus reducing vacancies. This makes it more difficult for would-be workers to find jobs, which increases the unemployment rate. There are also other effects of UI that we have not included in the two-sided search model. A second effect is captured in the one-sided search model—higher UI payments can make the unemployed more choosy about the types of jobs they will accept. This will increase the average duration of unemployment for a typical unemployed worker, and the unemployment rate. A third effect, not included in either search model that we have considered in this chapter, has to do with the influence of UI on on-the-job performance. For those employed, effort is required to retain a job. If an employer feels that a worker does not meet some threshold level of effort, then the worker could be fired. Of course, it is difficult for the employer to observe a worker's effort level perfectly, so, in general, some errors might be made by the employer in that workers with good levels of effort might at times be fired and some workers with poor levels of effort might be retained. However, in general, if a worker increases his or her effort level on the job, the chance of being fired is reduced. With higher UI benefits, though, the cost of being fired from a job is lower, and workers, therefore, exert less effort on the job and stand a greater chance of losing their jobs. Higher UI benefits, therefore, act to increase the rate of transition from employment to unemployment through this effect, and this increases the unemployment rate. A fourth effect of UI is its influence on the effort that the unemployed put into searching for work. Just as the unemployed become more choosy concerning the job offers they take with higher UI benefits, they also tend to search less intensively, because higher UI benefits decrease the cost of being unemployed.

A key feature of the latter three effects of UI on behavior—the effect on job acceptances, the effect on on-the-job effort, and the effect on search effort—is that all of these effects are imperfectly observable. That is, there are moral hazard problems associated with UI, just as there are moral hazard problems for other forms of insurance (including deposit insurance, which will be discussed in Chapter 17). It is difficult for the provider of UI to observe whether the unemployed are turning down good job offers, whether workers are being fired because their effort is too low, or whether long spells of unemployment are the result of low search effort. Indeed, the fact that UI is provided by the government in the United States may indicate that the moral hazard problems associated with UI are so severe that UI would not be provided by a private insurer in the absence of government provision.

UI systems need to be designed with moral hazard problems in mind, and the UI system in the United States certainly has features that, at least partially, correct for moral hazard. For example, the level of benefits does not imply full insurance, in that the replacement rate (the ratio of benefits when unemployed to wages when employed) is about 0.5, and benefits are limited in duration for individuals, typically extending for only about six months of unemployment. An optimal UI system achieves an optimal trade off between the benefits of insurance and the costs of moral hazard. If there is too much insurance (for example, if the unemployed receive benefits equal to their wages on the job forever), then workers and the unemployed have poor incentives; but, if there is too little insurance, unemployment is too painful.

What would an optimal unemployment insurance system look like, and how close does the UI system in the United States come to such an optimal system? Several articles in the economics literature have attempted to address these questions. An approach that is useful in this context is a dynamic contracting model, which allows us to think about economic problems in a dynamic framework where information is not perfect, as is the case with unemployment insurance. An early article by S. Shavell and L. Weiss[5] shows that the optimal unemployment insurance benefit decreases over time. That is, in contrast to the UI system in the United States, where benefits are constant for six months of unemployment and then go to zero, optimally benefits should decrease over time continuously and extend indefinitely. The optimal benefit schedule looks like this because the longer a person has been unemployed, the more likely it is that they are not looking very hard for a job, and so a person should be penalized with lower benefits the longer they have been unemployed. However, a person may have been unemployed for a long time simply because he or she was unlucky, so it does not make sense to reduce benefits to zero for the long-term unemployed.

Another paper by Cheng Wang and Stephen Williamson[6] broadens the approach of Shavell and Weiss. Wang and Williamson show that an optimal unemployment insurance system should be more individual-specific, while having the Shavell–Weiss feature that UI benefits decline with the duration of unemployment. That is, the level of benefits for an unemployed person should depend not only on the length of time since the person became unemployed and the wage when employed but also on the whole history of employment and unemployment for that person. Such an optimal system would be implemented by having each U.S. citizen hold an account with the UI authority that would be credited during periods of employment and debited during periods of unemployment when the individual is drawing UI benefits. The level of the current UI benefit allowed would depend on the balance in the account at that time. While such a system looks far different from the UI system currently in place in the United States, the discouraging news is that the welfare gain from moving to an optimal system would be small. Wang and Williamson's estimate is that a welfare increase equivalent to about 1% of GDP, at most, would result from switching from the current UI system in the United States to an optimal system.

[5]S. Shavell and L. Weiss, 1979. "The Optimal Payment of Unemployment Insurance Benefits Over Time," *Journal of Political Economy* 87, 1347–1362.

[6]C. Wang and S. Williamson, 2002. "Moral Hazard, Optimal Unemployment Insurance, and Experience Rating," *Journal of Monetary Economics* 49, 1337–1371.

Figure 6.22 An Increase in Productivity, z

An increase in productivity acts to increase the surplus from a match for both workers and firms. In panel (b), labor market tightness increases, and the curve shifts up in panel (a), so that the labor force must increase.

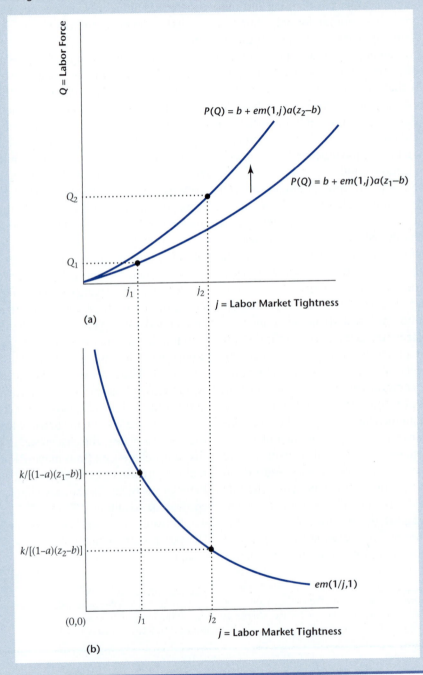

more attractive to post vacancies. Then, in panel (b) of Figure 6.22, higher z shifts up the curve, and so the labor force increases from Q_1 to Q_2, since consumers find it more attractive to enter the labor force, both because wages are higher and because the chances of finding a job are greater. From Equations (6-14) and (6-15), since labor market tightness has risen, the unemployment rate falls and the vacancy rate rises. Further, from Equation (6-16), since Q and j both increase, there is an increase in aggregate output.

These predictions are consistent with both long-run observations and the comovements in labor market variables over the business cycle. In terms of matching long-run observations, first, in Figure 4.18 in Chapter 4, we observe an increase over time in productivity in the United States, and in Figure 6.3, we see that this coincides with an increase in the labor force participation rate over most of the sample. However, we still have something left to explain, as the labor force participation rate falls from 2000 to 2015, over a period of time when productivity was rising. Second, Figure 1.1 in Chapter 1 documents a trend increase in output over time in the United States, which is explained in the model as arising from a productivity increase. Third, in Figure 6.6 we observe, between 1960 and 2000, a trend increase in the employment/population ratio, which is consistent with the observed trend increase in productivity over that period, and the predictions of the model. We will have to work harder, however, to explain the decrease in the employment/population ratio that occurs from 2000 to 2010.

In terms of cyclical behavior, start with the comovement between aggregate productivity observed in Figure 5.11 in Chapter 5, which shows that the percentage deviations from trend in productivity and real GDP are highly positively correlated. Our model tells us that this is consistent with productivity shocks playing an important role in business cycles, as productivity causes output to increase in the model. Further, an increase in productivity in the model also produces an increase in employment (employment is procyclical), an increase in the labor force participation rate (labor force participation is procyclical), an increase in the vacancy rate (the vacancy rate is procyclical), and a decrease in the unemployment rate (the unemployment rate is countercyclical). All of these predictions of the model are consistent with the data. It is important to note that the increase in the vacancy rate and the decrease in the unemployment rate in response to a productivity increase will imply that productivity shocks will produce a downward-sloping Beveridge curve, as observed in the data in Figure 6.8.

The match between empirical observation and the predictions of the model for this experiment gives us some reasons to think that productivity may be an important driving force, both for long-run growth and for business cycles. We will study the role of productivity in economic growth in Chapters 7 and 8, and will examine some further implications of productivity shocks for business cycles in Chapters 13 and 14.

Decrease in Matching Efficiency

The factor e in the matching function represents matching efficiency, which is the ease with which firms and workers can get together. Matching efficiency can increase through better information technologies that speed up the matching of jobs with particular skill requirements with workers who have particular skills. More importantly, particularly for short-run phenomena, matching efficiency can decrease when the degree of mismatch between the skills firms need and the skills consumers possess increases. This can occur, for example, when there is a **sectoral shock** to the economy. A sectoral shock could be any shock to consumers' preferences or to production technologies that causes factors of production to migrate across sectors of the economy. A sector could be defined by the type of product produced, or by geography. Examples of changes in the U.S. economy resulting from sectoral shocks are the long-run shift in production in the United States from manufacturing to services, and the shift in automobile production from the north to the south. Sectoral shocks produce mismatch in the labor market, either because the skills of workers leaving a declining sector do not match the skills required in a growing sector (e.g., textile workers do not have the skills required to work in financial services), or because unemployed workers and vacancies are located in different geographical areas (e.g., unemployed auto workers in Michigan find it costly to move to Alabama to fill job vacancies).

In Figure 6.23, we show the effects of a decrease in matching efficiency. In panel (b) of the figure, the decrease in e acts to shift the curve to the left, so that labor market tightness falls from j_1 to j_2. Essentially, because firms find it more difficult to find the right workers, entry of firms into the labor market decreases, and the labor market becomes less tight. In panel (a) of the figure, the curve shifts to the left, and so Q must fall from Q_1 to Q_2. Thus, fewer consumers choose to search for work (the labor force contracts) because the chances of finding work are lower, and the chances of finding work are lower for two reasons. First, lower matching efficiency reduces the probability of a match and, second, there are fewer firms searching.

From Equation (6-14), the unemployment rate must rise when e falls, since j and e have fallen. With respect to vacancies there are two effects working in different directions. In Equation (6-15), the decrease in labor market tightness acts to increase vacancies, but the decrease in e decreases vacancies. However, from Equation (6-13), we know that the right-hand side does not change when e changes, so the left-hand side remains unchanged as well, so from Equation (6-15) the vacancy rate must remain constant. Therefore, since Q falls and $j = A/Q$ also falls, A must fall as well. As a result, from Equation (6-16) aggregate output must go down, since e, Q, and j have all fallen.

Thus, a decrease in the efficiency of matching, for example because of an increase in the mismatch of skills with jobs in the labor market, results in a smaller labor force, fewer job postings, a higher unemployment rate, lower aggregate output, and no change in the vacancy rate. All of these predictions are consistent with observations from the 2008–2009 recession, and the recovery from the recession. In particular, a decrease in matching efficiency can cause the shift to the right in the Beveridge curve that we observe after late 2009 in Figure 6.8, in that lower e causes the unemployment rate to increase with no effect on the vacancy rate.

Figure 6.23 A Decrease in Matching Efficiency, *e*

This acts to shift the curves down in panels (a) and (b). Labor market tightness and the labor force must both decrease.

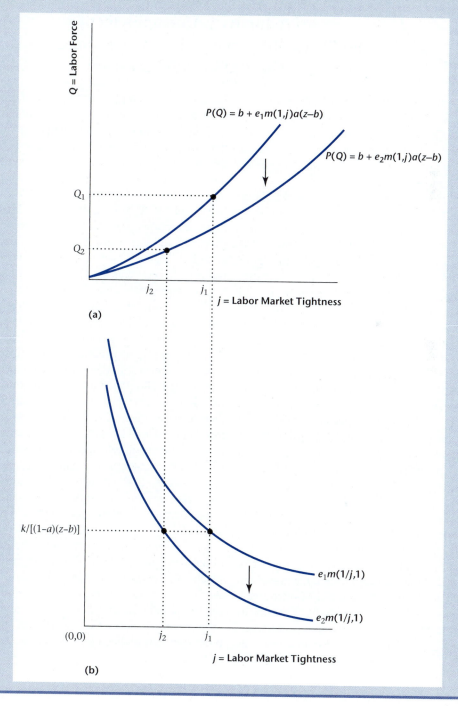

THEORY CONFRONTS THE DATA

Productivity, Unemployment, and Real GDP in the United States and Canada: The 2008–2009 Recession

During the 2008–2009 recession, the Canadian and U.S. economies behaved quite differently, particularly with regard to labor market activity. Our goal in this feature is to use the two-sided search model constructed in this chapter to make sense of the data from this episode.

In Figures 6.24 through 6.26 we show, respectively, data on productivity, the unemployment rate, and real GDP in Canada and the United States, from the first quarter of 2008 through the third quarter of 2015. In Figure 6.24, the measure of productivity we are using is average labor productivity (real GDP divided by total employment), which corresponds well to the concept of productivity in the two-sided search model. Productivity measures in the figure have been normalized to 100 in the first quarter of 2008. Figure 6.24 shows that, while productivity initially declined during the 2008–2009 recession in both countries, increases in productivity began as the two economies recovered. However, the recovery in productivity growth in Canada was much more sluggish than in the United States, and a gap between U.S. and Canadian productivity persists into 2015.

Next, in Figure 6.25 we show unemployment rates for Canada and the United States for the same period of time. The unemployment rate in Canada has tended historically to be higher than in the United States. Indeed, at the beginning of 2008, the unemployment rate was about 6% in Canada and about 5% in the United States. However, during the 2008–2009 recession the unemployment rate increased by a much larger amount in the United States than in Canada. By late 2015, the unemployment rates had returned to historical norms, with the unemployment rate in Canada about two percentage points higher than in the United States. Finally, in Figure 6.26, the paths for real GDP are depicted, again from the first quarter of 2008 to the third quarter of 2015, with real GDP normalized to 100 in the first quarter of 2008 for both countries. This last figure shows that the recent recession was both deeper and longer in the United States than in Canada, with a stronger recovery in Canada. A positive gap between real GDP in Canada and the United States persists into 2015.

What could explain these observations? Some aspects of the data seem puzzling. For example, the two-sided search model tells us that an increase in productivity will increase aggregate output and reduce the unemployment rate. But this should tell us that, given the good productivity performance in the United States relative to Canada, real GDP should have grown more in the United States than in Canada and the unemployment rate should have performed better in the United States than in Canada during the 2008–2009 recession. However, real GDP grew less in the United States, and the unemployment rate increased more. What is going on?

A potential explanation is that the degree of mismatch in the U.S. labor market increased much more in the United States than in Canada during the 2008–2009 recession. This mismatch can be traced in the United States to the dramatic drop in construction activity, which was felt disproportionately in different geographical regions.

Thus, there was a key sectoral shift during the 2008–2009 recession from construction to other sectors, and the increases in unemployment were much higher in some areas of the United States than in others. In contrast, Canada experienced only a moderate decline in construction during the 2008–2009 recession, and housing construction in particular recovered strongly relative to the United States.

Thus, the two-sided search model could potentially explain the data in Figures 6.24–6.26, if we take account of the increase in labor market mismatch that occurred in the United States. In spite of the good performance in productivity in the United States relative to Canada, unemployment was relatively high and real GDP growth relatively low during the period in question, potentially because of labor market mismatch.

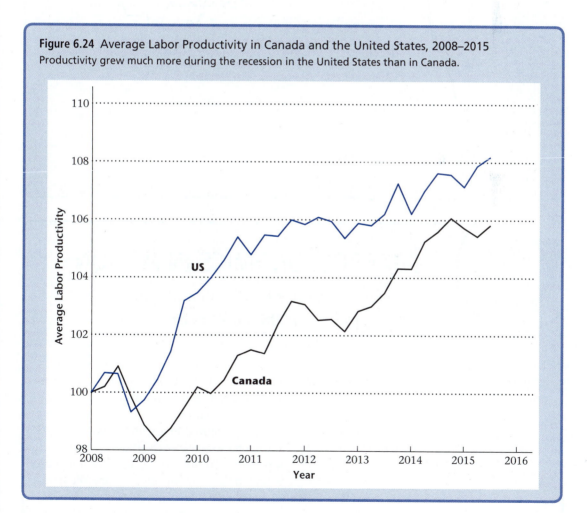

Figure 6.24 Average Labor Productivity in Canada and the United States, 2008–2015
Productivity grew much more during the recession in the United States than in Canada.

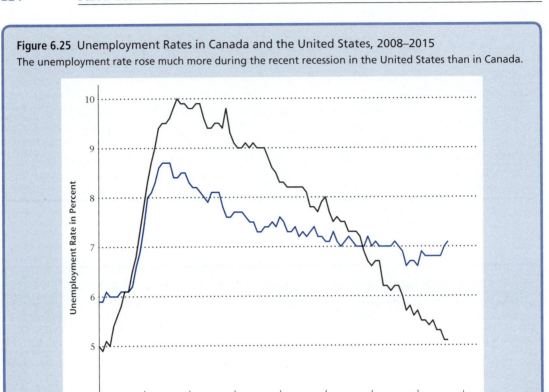

Figure 6.25 Unemployment Rates in Canada and the United States, 2008–2015

The unemployment rate rose much more during the recent recession in the United States than in Canada.

MACROECONOMICS IN ACTION

The Natural Rate of Unemployment and the 2008–2009 Recession

The "natural rate of unemployment" is a term originally coined by Milton Friedman, who defined it as

" . . . the level that would be ground out by the Walrasian system of general equilibrium equations, provided there is imbedded in them the actual structural characteristics of the labor and commodity markets . . . "[7]

[7]From The Role of Monetary Policy by Milton Friedman, © 1968 American Economic Review.

Friedman did not have modern search theory at hand to put some formal structure on what he meant, but it appears that Friedman's notion of a natural rate of unemployment could be captured in a search model, related to the one we have been studying. Friedman appeared to think that there were long-run factors in the economy determining the natural rate of unemployment, such as the generosity of unemployment insurance, the tax system, and demographic factors. Further, he argued that there could be short-run departures from the natural rate because of temporary shocks to the economy, such as changes in monetary policy or productivity shocks.

The natural rate of unemployment is closely related to the concept of an "output gap," which plays a central role in New Keynesian economics. The output gap has a specific theoretical meaning in a New Keynesian model, in that it is the difference between potential aggregate output and actual aggregate output, where potential aggregate output is the equilibrium level of output that would arise if prices and wages were not sticky.

The language involving natural rates of unemployment and output gaps typically suggests that there is something wrong with a departure from the natural rate of unemployment or the existence of a positive output gap. Keynesian economists, for example, believe that if the unemployment rate is above the natural rate, then there are idle resources that could be utilized through policy intervention to "stimulate" the economy.

Suppose that we accept the Keynesian view that the unemployment rate fluctuates around some long-run natural rate, and that fluctuations around this natural rate are due to the existence of sticky wages and prices. What problems could result? The first is the practical problem of measuring the natural rate of unemployment. Clearly we should not measure the natural rate as some historical average unemployment rate. Over some periods of time this would lead to significant policy errors. For example, from Figure 6.1, if the natural rate of unemployment in 1985 were measured as the average unemployment rate over the previous 20 years, policymakers over the next 15 years until 2000 would have thought that labor markets were too tight, and would have been attempting to introduce more slack into the economy. This would have been inappropriate, as there was a downward trend in the unemployment rate from 1985 to 2000.

Clearly then, one would have to be more sophisticated about measuring the natural unemployment rate, for instance by taking into account the relationship between the natural rate and the long-run factors determining it. Ultimately however, in using this approach the policymaker must take a stand on how the natural rate of unemployment should be measured. This is perhaps too much to ask.

Modern search theory, as it has been applied in macroeconomics, typically dispenses with the notion of a natural rate of unemployment as, once one has a good model that can determine the unemployment rate at any point in time, the concept of a natural rate is useless. A good search model can tell us a great deal about the determinants of the unemployment rate, and can be useful for telling us what policy measures are appropriate in what contexts.

In the context of the 2008–2009 recession, a widespread view (particularly among Keynesians) appeared to be that, because aggregate GDP fell so quickly, and the unemployment rose so quickly (see Figure 6.1) in 2008 and 2009, the level of GDP and the unemployment rate that existed in late 2007 could and should be achieved two years later. Further, a common view was that the unemployment rate of late 2007 could be achieved in short order through a sufficiently large program of government spending increases, tax cuts, and accommodative monetary policy. However, the key problem was that there was nothing that could be done immediately to make world financial markets work in the same way that they did in late 2007, and even if this could be done, it is not clear that it should have been. Belief in natural unemployment rates and output gaps can lead us to think that we can achieve something that is essentially impossible or ill-advised. While the concept of a natural rate of unemployment might have been useful for Milton Friedman in 1968, economic science has advanced to the point where we it seems we can do better.

Figure 6.26 Real GDP in Canada and the United States, 2008–2015

The recession was shallower and shorter in Canada than in the United States, and percentage real GDP growth was higher in Canada than in the United States over the sample period.

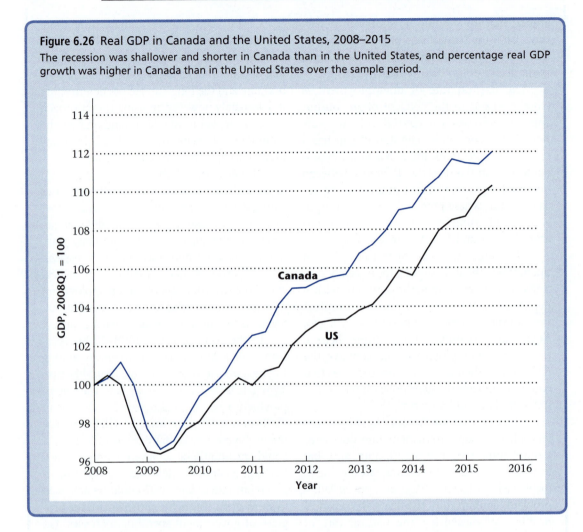

Chapter Summary

- The key determinants of the unemployment rate are aggregate economic activity, demographics, government intervention, and sectoral shifts.

- The participation rate is affected by demographics and by the different labor market behavior of men and women.

- The unemployment rate is a countercyclical variable, whereas the participation rate is procyclical.

- The employment/population ratio is more cyclically variable than is the participation rate.

- The Beveridge curve is a downward-sloping relationship between the unemployment rate and the vacancy rate. A Beveridge curve relation can be observed in the data, though the Beveridge curve appears to shift at the end of 2009.

- In the two-sided search model, firms pay a cost to post a vacancy, and consumers must decide whether to work at home or to search for market work.

- In the two-sided search model, when a worker is matched with a firm, they bargain over the wage, which is determined by the outside opportunities of the worker and the firm, and by relative bargaining power.

- The two-sided search model determines labor market tightness (the ratio of firms searching to consumers searching for work), labor force, market wage, vacancy rate, unemployment rate, and real GDP.

- An increase in the UI benefit acts to reduce the surplus of a firm in a match, which acts to reduce labor market tightness, increase the unemployment rate, and reduce the vacancy rate. The size of the labor force may rise or fall, as may aggregate output.

- In the two-sided search model, an increase in productivity acts to increase the surplus of both workers and firms in matches, and this increases labor market tightness and the size of the labor force. The unemployment rate falls, the vacancy rate rises, and aggregate output rises.

- A decrease in matching efficiency reduces labor market tightness and the size of the labor force. The unemployment rate increases, the vacancy rate does not change, and aggregate output falls. Changes in matching efficiency are a potential explanation for the recent behavior of unemployment and vacancies in the United States.

Key Terms

Job Openings and Labor Turnover Survey (JOLTS) A survey conducted monthly by the Bureau of Labor Statistics, that includes measurement of the vacancy rate. (p. 193)

Beveridge curve A negative relationship observed between the vacancy rate and the unemployment rate. (p. 196)

Separation rate The rate at which employed workers become separated from their jobs. (p. 198)

Reservation wage The wage such that an unemployed worker will accept any job offering this wage or more. (p. 199)

Matching function In the two-sided search model, a function that determines the number of successful matches between workers and firms, given the number of firms posting vacancies and the number of consumers searching for work. (p. 207)

Matching efficiency A measure of the rate at which a given number of individuals search for work and firms searching for workers create matches. (p. 207)

Labor market tightness The ratio of firms posting vacancies to consumers searching for work. (p. 208)

Nash bargaining theory Developed by John Nash. A simple theory that determines the terms of exchange between two parties from their relative bargaining power, and the surplus each party stands to gain from exchange. (p. 211)

Sectoral shock Any shock to consumers' preferences or to production technologies that causes factors of production to migrate across sectors of the economy. (p. 220)

Questions for Review

6.1 What are the short-run regularities in the behavior of the unemployment rate?

6.2 What are the long-run regularities in the behavior of the unemployment rate?

6.3 How has the labor force participation rate behaved over time? Do women and men behave similarly with respect to labor force participation?

6.4 Is the participation rate procyclical or countercyclical?

6.5 How does the employment/population ratio behave relative to the participation rate?

6.6 How does the vacancy rate behave relative to the unemployment rate, and how does this matter for the Beveridge curve?

6.7 What causes shifts in the welfare of the employed in the one-sided search model?

6.8 What causes shifts in the welfare of the unemployed in the one-sided search model?

6.9 What determines the reservation wage in the one-sided search model?

6.10 How does an increase in the UI benefit affect the reservation wage in the one-sided search model, and why?

6.11 How does an increase in the tax on wage income affect the reservation wage in the one-sided search model, and why?

6.12 How will an increase in the UI benefit affect the long-run unemployment rate in the one-sided search model, and why?

6.13 How will an increase in the job offer rate affect the reservation wage and the long-run unemployment rate in the one-sided search model? What implications does this have for government policy?

6.14 In the two-sided search model, what determines a consumer's decision to search for work?

6.15 In the two-sided search model, what determines a firm's decision to post a vacancy?

6.16 What are total surplus, worker surplus, and firm surplus in the two-sided search model?

6.17 In the two-sided search model, when a worker and firm are matched, what determines the wage paid to the worker?

6.18 In the two-sided search model, what are the effects of an increase in the UI benefit?

6.19 In the two-sided search model, what are the effects of an increase in productivity?

6.20 In the two-sided search model, what are the effects of a decrease in matching efficiency?

6.21 What explains the observed Beveridge relation from 2000 to 2012?

Problems

1. **LO 5** Determine the effects of an increase in the separation rate, s, on the reservation wage and on the long-run unemployment rate in the one-sided search model of unemployment. Explain your results.

2. **LO 5** Suppose there is an increase in total factor productivity, which implies that all firms offer higher wages. In the one-sided search model of unemployment, determine the effects of this on the reservation wage and on the long-run unemployment rate. Explain your results.

3. **LO 5** Suppose that the government makes it more difficult to qualify for unemployment insurance, for example, by increasing the duration of employment required before collecting UI benefits during an unemployment spell. Determine the effects of this change in government policy on the reservation wage and the long-run unemployment rate in the one-sided search model of unemployment.

4. **LO 6, 7** What does the two-sided search model predict would be the effects of laborsaving devices in the home, for example dishwashers, washing machines, and vacuum cleaners? Use diagrams to show the effects on the unemployment rate, the vacancy rate, the labor force, the number of firms, aggregate output, and labor market tightness, and discuss your results.

5. **LO 6, 7** Suppose the government's goal is to reduce the unemployment rate. Some legislators propose that the government should give a subsidy s to any firm that hires a worker. Some other legislators argue that it would be more effective to simply pay consumers to stay home rather than

searching for work; that is, anyone who chooses not to participate in the labor force should receive a payment q. Which policy is more effective in achieving the government's goal? Explain using the two-sided search model, with the aid of diagrams. [In your answer, do not concern yourself with how the subsidies from the government are financed.]

6. LO 6, 7 Suppose that there is technological change that reduces the cost of recruiting for firms. Using the two-sided search model, determine the effects on the unemployment rate, the vacancy rate, the labor force, the number of firms, aggregate output, and labor market tightness. Use diagrams, and explain your results.

7. LO 6, 7 Adapt the two-sided search model to include government activity as follows. Suppose that the government can operate firms, subject to the same constraints as private firms. In particular, the government must incur a cost k to post a vacancy. Supposing that the government oper-

ates G firms, then the number of matches in the economy as a whole is $M = em(Q, A + G)$, where A is the number of private firms that choose to post vacancies. Assume that the government pays the same wages as do private sector firms. Determine the effects of G on the unemployment rate, the vacancy rate, the labor force, the number of private firms, the total number of firms (private and government-run), aggregate output, and labor market tightness. Explain your results.

8. LO 6, 7 Suppose that all social programs simultaneously become more generous. In particular suppose that there is an increase in UI benefits, and also an increase in welfare benefits, which are represented in the two-sided search model as payments to everyone who is not in the labor force. What will be the effects on the unemployment rate, the vacancy rate, the labor force, the number of firms, the aggregate output, and the labor market tightness? Explain your results

Working with the Data

Answer these questions using the Federal Reserve Bank of St. Louis's FRED database, accessible at http://research.stlouisfed.org/fred2/

1. There are alternative measures of the unemployment rate that include the "marginally attached" and " discouraged workers." Plot these special unemployment rates relative to the standard measure of the unemployment rate, and comment on the differences that you see.

2. Plot the separation rate (total nonfarm). How does the separation rate behave during recessions? What does this tell you about the source of decreases in employment during recessions?

3. Plot employment as measured in the current population survey, and as measured in the establishment survey. How are these measures different, and how do they behave differently?

PART III

Economic Growth

In this part, we study the primary facts of economic growth and the key macroeconomic models that economists have used to understand these facts. In Chapter 7, we first examine the Malthusian model of economic growth, in which population growth increases with the standard of living. Any improvement in the technology for producing goods leads to more population growth, and in the long run there is no improvement in the standard of living. The Malthusian model does a good job of explaining economic growth in the world prior to the Industrial Revolution in the nineteenth century, but it cannot explain growth experience after 1800. What Malthus did not envision was the role of capital accumulation in economic growth. Capital accumulation plays an important role in the Solow model of economic growth, which is the preeminent framework used in modern economic growth theory. The Solow growth model predicts that long-run improvements in the standard of living are generated by technological progress, that countries with high (low) savings rates tend to have high (low) levels of per capita income, and that countries with high (low) rates of population growth tend to have low (high) levels of per capita income. The Solow growth model gives much more optimistic implications than does the Malthusian model concerning the prospects for improvements in the standard of living. Finally, in Chapter 7 we study growth accounting, an approach to attributing economic growth to growth in factors of production and in productivity.

In Chapter 8, we first study the predictions of the Solow growth model for convergence in standards of living across countries. In the data, there is a tendency for convergence in per capita incomes among the richest countries in the world, but apparently no tendency for convergence among all countries. The Solow model is consistent with this if we allow for differences in the adoption of technology across countries, or differences in the efficiency with which factors of production are allocated across firms in individual economies. Next in Chapter 8, we examine an endogenous growth model, which allows us to analyze the determinants of the rate of economic growth. This endogenous growth model has the property that differences in standards of living persist across countries, and that education is an important factor in determining the rate of economic growth.

Chapter 7

Economic Growth: Malthus and Solow

Learning Objectives

After studying Chapter 7, students will be able to:

7.1 List the seven key economic growth facts, and explain their importance.

7.2 Construct the steady state in the Malthusian model, and analyze the effects of changes in exogenous factors on population, per capita consumption, and land per worker.

7.3 Explain the usefulness of the Malthusian model.

7.4 Construct the competitive equilibrium in the Solow growth model.

7.5 Use the Solow growth model to analyze the effects of changes in exogenous factors on income per worker, capital per worker, and the economy's growth rate.

7.6 List the facts about growth in real GDP, employment, the capital stock, and total factor productivity in the United States over the period 1950–2014.

7.7 Determine the Solow residual and growth rates in real GDP, capital stock, employment, and the Solow residual from data on real GDP, capital stock, and employment.

The two primary phenomena that macroeconomists study are business cycles and economic growth. Though much macroeconomic research focuses on business cycles, the study of economic growth has also received a good deal of attention, especially since the late 1980s. Robert Lucas[1] has argued that the potential social gains from a greater understanding of business cycles are dwarfed by the gains from understanding growth. This is because, even if (most optimistically) business cycles could be completely eliminated, the worst events we would be able to avoid would be reductions of real GDP

---

[1]See R. Lucas, 1987, *Models of Business Cycles,* Basil Blackwell, Oxford, UK.

below trend on the order of 5%, based on post–World War II U.S. data. However, if changes in economic policy could cause the growth rate of real GDP to increase by 1% per year for 100 years, then GDP would be 2.7 times higher after 100 years than it would otherwise have been.

The effects of economic growth have been phenomenal. Per capita U.S. income in 2014 was $50,051,[2] but before the Industrial Revolution in the early nineteenth century, per capita U.S. income was only several hundred 2014 dollars. In fact, before 1800 the standard of living differed little over time and across countries. Since the Industrial Revolution, however, economic growth has not been uniform across countries, and there are currently wide disparities in standards of living among the countries of the world. In 2009, income per capita in Mexico was 29.7% of what it was in the United States, in Egypt it was 12.9% of that in the United States, and in Burundi it was about 1.0% of the U.S. figure. Currently, there also exist large differences in rates of growth across countries. Between 1960 and 2009, while real income per capita was growing at an average rate of 1.89% in the United States, the comparable figure for Madagascar was −0.24%, for Zimbabwe it was −1.40%, for Singapore it was 4.69%, and for Taiwan it was 5.41%.[3]

In this chapter we first discuss some basic economic growth facts, and this provides a useful context in which to organize our thinking using some standard models of growth. The first model we study formalizes the ideas of Thomas Malthus, who wrote in the late eighteenth century. This Malthusian model has the property that any improvement in the technology for producing goods leads to increased population growth, so that in the long run there is no improvement in the standard of living. The population is sufficiently high that there is no increase in per capita consumption and per capita output. Consistent with the conclusions of Malthus, the model predicts that the only means for improving the standard of living is population control.

The Malthusian model yields quite pessimistic predictions concerning the prospects for long-run growth in per capita incomes. Of course, the predictions of Malthus were wrong, as he did not foresee the Industrial Revolution. After the Industrial Revolution, economic growth was in part driven by growth in the stock of capital over time and was not limited by fixed factors of production (such as land), as in the Malthusian model.

Next we study the Solow growth model, which is the most widely used model of economic growth, developed by Robert Solow in the 1950s.[4] The Solow growth model makes important predictions concerning the effects of savings rates, population growth, and changes in total factor productivity on a nation's standard of living and growth rate of GDP. We show that these predictions match economic data quite well.

A key implication of the Solow growth model is that a country's standard of living cannot continue to improve in the long run in the absence of continuing increases in

---

[2]Bureau of Economic Analysis, Department of Commerce.

[3]The income per capita statistics come from A. Heston, R. Summers, and B. Aten, *Penn World Table Version 7.0*, Center for International Comparisons at the University of Pennsylvania (CICUP), May 2011, available at pwt.sas.upenn.edu.

[4]See R. Solow, 1956. "A Contribution to the Theory of Economic Growth," *Quarterly Journal of Economics 70*, 65–94.

total factor productivity. In the short run, the standard of living can improve if a country's residents save and invest more, thus accumulating more capital. However, the Solow growth model tells us that building more productive capacity will not improve long-run living standards unless the production technology becomes more efficient. The Solow model therefore implies more optimistic prospects for long-run improvement in the standard of living than is the case for the Malthusian model, but only to a point. The Solow model tells us that improvements in knowledge and technical ability are necessary to sustain growth.

The Solow growth model is an **exogenous growth model**, in that growth is caused in the model by forces that are not explained by the model itself. To gain a deeper understanding of economic growth, it is useful to examine the economic factors that cause growth, and this is done in **endogenous growth models**, one of which we examine in Chapter 8.

Finally, in this chapter we study growth accounting, which is an approach to attributing the growth in GDP to growth in factor inputs and in total factor productivity. Growth accounting can highlight interesting features of the data, such as the long-term trends in productivity growth and growth in factors of production, and how each contributes to growth in total real GDP.

Economic Growth Facts

LO 7.1 List the seven key economic growth facts, and explain their importance.

Before proceeding to construct and analyze models of economic growth, we summarize the key empirical regularities relating to growth within and across countries. This gives us a framework for evaluating our models and helps in organizing our thinking about growth. The important growth facts are the following:

1. *Before the Industrial Revolution in about 1800, standards of living differed little over time and across countries.* There appeared to have been essentially no improvement in standards of living for a long period of time prior to 1800. Though population and aggregate income grew, with growth sometimes interrupted by disease and wars, population growth kept up with growth in aggregate income, so that there was little change in per capita real income. Living standards did not vary much across the countries of the world. In particular, Western Europe and Asia had similar standards of living.

2. *Since the Industrial Revolution, per capita income growth has been sustained in the richest countries. In the United States, average annual growth in per capita income has been about 2% since 1900.* The Industrial Revolution began about 1800 in the United Kingdom, and the United States eventually surpassed the United Kingdom as the world industrial leader. Figure 7.1 shows the natural logarithm of per capita income in the United States for the years 1900–2014. Recall from Chapter 1 that the slope of the natural log of a time series is approximately equal to the growth rate. What is remarkable about the figure is that a straight line would be a fairly good fit to the natural log of per capita income in the United

Figure 7.1 Natural Logarithm of Real Per Capita GDP

Except for the Great Depression and World War II, real per capita GDP in the United States has grown roughly at 2% per year since 1900.

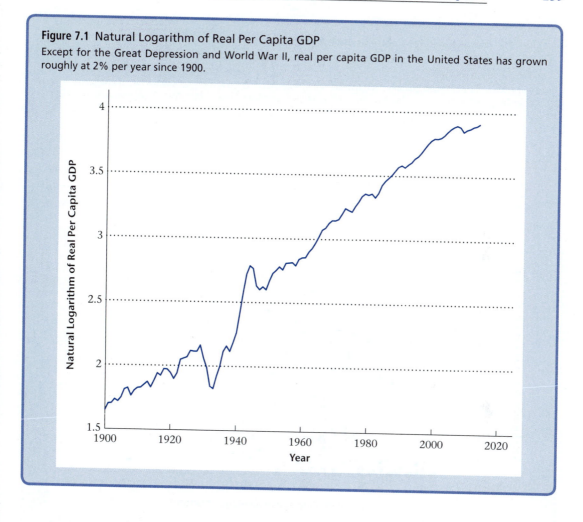

States over this period of 114 years. In other words, average per capita income growth in the United States has not strayed far from an average growth rate of about 2% per year for the whole period, except for major interruptions like the Great Depression (1929–1939) and World War II (1941–1945) and the variability introduced by business cycles.

3. *There is a positive correlation between the rate of investment and output per worker across countries.* In Figure 7.2 we show a scatter plot of output per worker (as a percentage of output per worker in the United States) versus the rate of investment (as a percentage of aggregate output) in the countries of the world in 2007. A straight line fit to these points would have a positive slope, so the two variables are positively correlated, though the correlation is low. Thus, countries in which a relatively large (small) fraction of output is channeled into investment tend to have a relatively high (low) standard of living. This fact is particularly important in checking the predictions of the Solow growth model against the data.

Figure 7.2 Real Income Per Capita vs. Investment Rate

The figure shows a positive correlation across the countries of the world, between the output per capita and the investment rate.

Source: Alan Heston, Robert Summers and Bettina Aten, *Penn World Table Version 7.0,* Center for International Comparisons of Production, Income and Prices at the University of Pennsylvania, May 2011. Reprinted with permission.

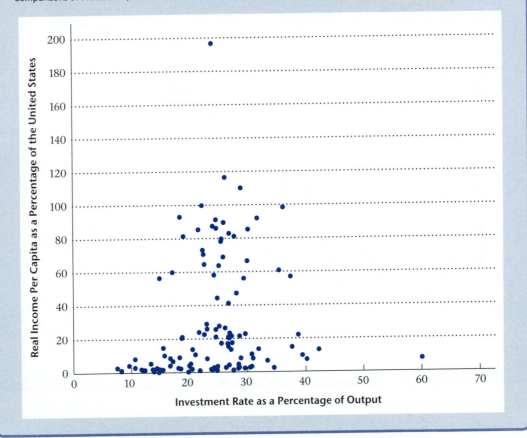

4. *There is a negative correlation between the population growth rate and output per worker across countries.* Figure 7.3 shows a scatter plot of real income per capita (as a percentage of real income per capita in the United States) in 2007 versus the average annual population growth rate for 1960–2007 for the countries of the world. Here, a straight line fit to the points in the figure would have a negative slope, so the two variables are negatively correlated. Countries with high (low) population growth rates tend to have low (high) standards of living. As with the previous fact, this one is important in matching the predictions of the Solow growth model with the data.

5. *Differences in per capita incomes increased dramatically among countries of the world between 1800 and 1950, with the gap widening between the countries of Western Europe, the United States, Canada, Australia, and New Zealand, as a group, and the*

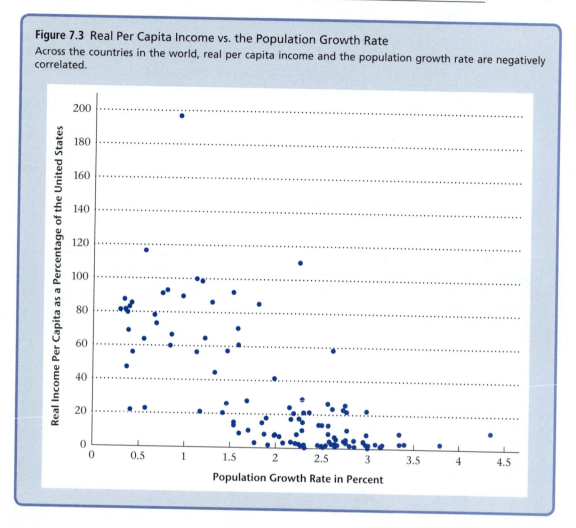

Figure 7.3 Real Per Capita Income vs. the Population Growth Rate

Across the countries in the world, real per capita income and the population growth rate are negatively correlated.

rest of the world. A question that interests us in this chapter and the next is whether standards of living are converging across countries of the world. The Industrial Revolution spread in the early nineteenth century from the United Kingdom to Western Europe and the United States, then to the new countries of Canada, Australia, and New Zealand. The countries of Africa, Asia, and South America were mainly left behind, with some Asian (and to some extent South American) countries closing the gap with the rich countries later in the twentieth century. Between 1800 and 1950, there was a divergence between living standards in the richest and poorest countries of the world.[5]

6. *There is essentially no correlation across countries between the level of output per capita in 1960 and the average rate of growth in output per capita for the years 1960–2007.* Standards of living would be converging across countries if real

[5]See S. Parente and E. Prescott, 2000. *Barriers to Riches,* MIT Press, Cambridge, MA.

income (output) per capita were converging to a common value. For this to happen, it would have to be the case that poor countries (those with low levels of real income per capita) are growing at a higher rate than are rich countries (those with high levels of real income per capita). Thus, if convergence in real incomes per capita is occurring, we should observe a negative correlation between the growth rate in real per capita income and the level of real per capita income across countries. Figure 7.4 shows data for 1960–2007, the period for which good data exists for most of the countries in the world. The figure shows the average rate of growth in output per worker for the period 1960–2007, versus the level of real per capita income (as a percentage of real per capita income in the United States) in 1960 for a set of 99 countries. There is essentially no correlation shown in the figure, which indicates that, for all countries of the world, convergence is not detectable for this period.

Figure 7.4 Growth Rate in Per Capita Income vs. Level of Per Capita Income
There is no correlation between the two variables in the figure, indicating no tendency for convergence in per capita incomes in the world over the period 1960–2007. There is much greater divergence in growth experience for the poor countries of the world than for the rich ones.

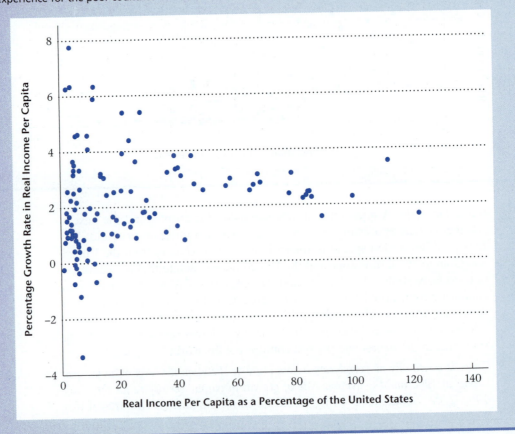

7. *Richer countries are much more alike in terms of rates of growth of real per capita income than are poor countries.* In Figure 7.4, we observe that there is a much wider vertical scatter in the points on the left-hand part of the scatter plot than on the right-hand side. That is, the variability in real income growth rates is much smaller for rich countries than for poor countries.

In this chapter and Chapter 8, we use growth facts 1 to 7 to motivate the structure of our models and as checks on the predictions of those models.

The Malthusian Model of Economic Growth

In 1798, Thomas Malthus, a political economist in England, wrote the highly influential "An Essay on the Principle of Population."[6] Malthus did not construct a formal economic model of the type that we would use in modern economic arguments, but his ideas are clearly stated and coherent and can be easily translated into a structure that is easy to understand.

Malthus argued that any advances in the technology for producing food would inevitably lead to further population growth, with the higher population ultimately reducing the average person to the subsistence level of consumption they had before the advance in technology. The population and level of aggregate consumption could grow over time, but in the long run there would be no increase in the standard of living unless there were some limits on population growth. Malthusian theory is, therefore, very pessimistic about the prospects for increases in the standard of living, with collective intervention in the form of forced family planning required to bring about gains in per capita income.

The following model formalizes Malthusian theory. The model is a dynamic one with many periods, though for most of the analysis we confine attention to what happens in the current period and the future period (the period following the current period). We start with an aggregate production function that specifies how current aggregate output, Y, is produced using current inputs of land, L, and current labor, N; that is,

$$Y = zF(L, N), \tag{7-1}$$

where z is total factor productivity, and F is a function having the same properties, including constant returns to scale, that we specified in Chapter 4, except here land replaces capital in the production function. It helps to think of Y as being food, which is perishable from period to period. In this economy there is no investment (and, therefore, no saving—recall from Chapter 2 that savings equals investment in a closed economy) as we assume there is no way to store food from one period to the next and no technology for converting food into capital. For simplicity, there is assumed to be no government spending. Land, L, is in fixed supply. That is, as was the case in Western

---

[6]See T. Malthus, 1798. " An Essay on the Principle of Population," St. Paul's Church-Yard, London, available at http://129.237.201.53/books/malthus/population/malthus.pdf.

Europe in 1798, essentially all of the land that could potentially be used for agriculture is under cultivation. Assume that each person in this economy is willing to work at any wage and has one unit of labor to supply (a normalization), so that N in Equation (7-1) is both the population and the labor input.

If we let N' denote the population next period, then

$$N' = N + \text{Births} - \text{Deaths},$$

or

$$N' = N + N(\text{birth rate} - \text{death rate}), \qquad (7\text{-}2)$$

where the birth rate is the ratio of births to population, and the death rate is the ratio of deaths to population. Now, particularly before the Industrial Revolution, it is natural that the birth rate would be an increasing function of consumption per capita, $\frac{C}{N}$, which is a measure of nutrition, with C denoting aggregate consumption. As consumption per person rises, and nutrition improves, people will have more children by choice, as they are then better able to provide for them, and better nutrition also increases fertility. Similarly, the death rate is a decreasing function of $\frac{C}{N}$, because better nutrition decreases infant mortality, and generally makes the population more healthy, thus increasing the average life span. This implies that we can write Equation (7-2) (after dividing both sides by N) as

$$\frac{N'}{N} = g\left(\frac{C}{N}\right), \qquad (7\text{-}3)$$

where g is an increasing function. Note that $\frac{N'}{N}$ in Equation (7-3) is one plus the population growth rate. We show the relationship described by Equation (7-3) in Figure 7.5.

In equilibrium, all goods produced are consumed, so $C = Y$, which is the income–expenditure identity for this economy (because $I = G = NX = 0$ here; see Chapter 2). Therefore, substituting C for Y in Equation (7-3), in equilibrium we have

$$C = zF(L, N). \qquad (7\text{-}4)$$

We can then use Equation (7-4) to substitute for C in Equation (7-3) to get

$$\frac{N'}{N} = g\left(\frac{zF(L, N)}{N}\right). \qquad (7\text{-}5)$$

Now, recall from Chapter 4 that the constant-returns-to-scale property of the production function implies that

$$xzF(L, N) = zF(xL, xN)$$

for any $x > 0$, so if $x = \frac{1}{N}$ in the above equation, then

$$\frac{zF(L, N)}{N} = zF\left(\frac{L}{N}, 1\right).$$

As a result, we can rewrite Equation (7-5), after multiplying each side by N, as

$$N' = g\left[zF\left(\frac{L}{N}, 1\right)\right]N. \qquad (7\text{-}6)$$

Figure 7.5 Population Growth Depends on Consumption per Worker in the Malthusian Model

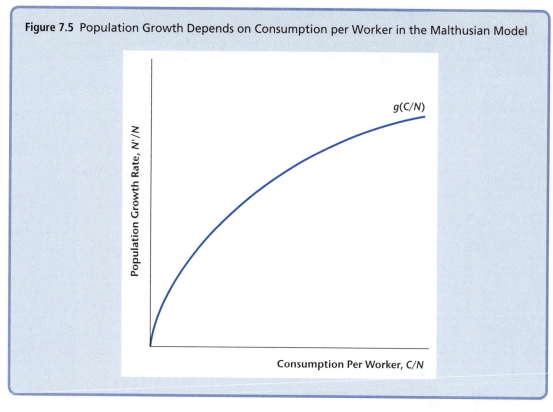

Equation (7-6) tells us how the population evolves over time in equilibrium, as it gives the future population as a function of the current population. We assume that the relationship described in Equation (7-6) can be depicted as in Figure 7.6.[7] In the figure N^* is a rest point or **steady state** for the population, determined by the point where the curve intersects the 45° line. If the current population is N^* then the future population is N^*, and the population is N^* forever after. In the figure, if $N < N^*$ then $N' > N$ and the population increases, whereas if $N > N^*$ then $N' < N$ and the population decreases. Thus, whatever the population is currently, it eventually comes to rest at N^* in the long run. In other words, the steady state N^* is the long-run equilibrium for the population.

The reason that population converges to a steady state is the following. Suppose, on the one hand, that the population is currently below its steady state value. Then there will be a relatively large quantity of consumption per worker, and this will imply that the population growth rate is relatively large and positive, and the population will increase. On the other hand, suppose that the population is above its steady state value. Then there will be a small quantity of consumption per worker, and the population growth rate will be relatively low and negative, so that the population will decrease.

---

[7]For example, if $F(L, N) \mathrm{D} L^{\alpha}N^{1-\alpha}$ and $g\left(\frac{C}{N}\right) \mathrm{D} \left(\frac{C}{N}\right)^{\gamma}$, with $0 < \alpha < 1$ and $0 < \gamma < 1$, we get these properties.

Figure 7.6 Determination of the Population in the Steady State

In the figure, N^* is the steady state population, determined by the intersection of the curve and the 45° line. If $N > N^*$ then $N' < N$ and the population falls over time, and if $N < N^*$ then $N' > N$ and the population rises over time.

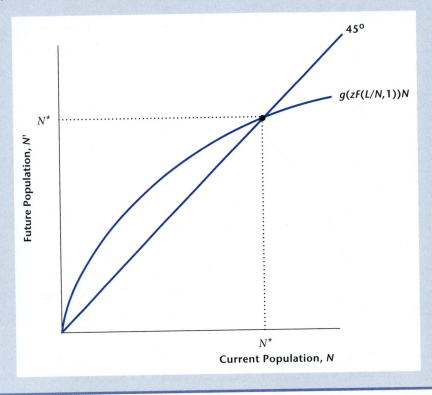

Because the quantity of land is fixed, when the population converges to the long-run equilibrium N^*, aggregate consumption (equal to aggregate output here) converges, from Equation (7-4), to

$$C^* = zF(L, N^*).$$

Analysis of the Steady State in the Malthusian Model

LO 7.2 Construct the steady state in the Malthusian model, and analyze the effects of changes in exogenous factors on population, per capita consumption, and land per worker.

Because the Malthusian economy converges to a long-run steady state equilibrium with constant population and constant aggregate consumption, it is useful to analyze this steady state to determine what features of the environment affect steady state variables. In this subsection, we show how this type of analysis is done.

Given that the production function F has the constant returns to scale property, if we divide the left-hand and right-hand sides of Equation (7-1) by N and rearrange, we get

$$\frac{Y}{N} = zF\left(\frac{L}{N}, 1\right).$$

Then letting lowercase letters denote per-worker quantities, that is, $y \equiv \frac{Y}{N}$ (output per worker), $l \equiv \frac{L}{N}$ (land per worker), and $c \equiv \frac{C}{N}$ (consumption per worker), we have

$$y = zf(l), \tag{7-7}$$

where $zf(l)$ is the **per-worker production function**, which describes the quantity of output per worker y that can be produced for each quantity of land per worker l, with the function f defined by $f(l) \equiv F(l, 1)$. The per-worker production function is displayed in Figure 7.7. Then, as $c = y$ in equilibrium, from Equation (7-7) we have

$$c = zf(l). \tag{7-8}$$

We can also rewrite Equation (7-3) as

$$\frac{N'}{N} = g(c). \tag{7-9}$$

Now, we can display Equations (7-8) and (7-9) in Figure 7.8. In the steady state, $N' = N = N^*$, so $\frac{N'}{N} = 1$, and in panel (b) of the figure this determines c^*, the steady

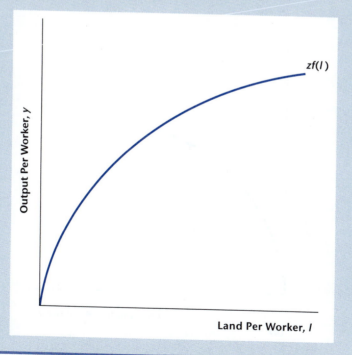

Figure 7.7 The Per-Worker Production Function

This describes the relationship between output per worker and land per worker in the Malthusian model, assuming constant returns to scale.

Figure 7.8 Determination of the Steady State in the Malthusian Model

In panel (b), steady state consumption per worker c^* is determined as the level of consumption per worker that implies no population growth. Given c^*, the quantity of land per worker in the steady state l^* is determined from the per-worker production function in panel (a).

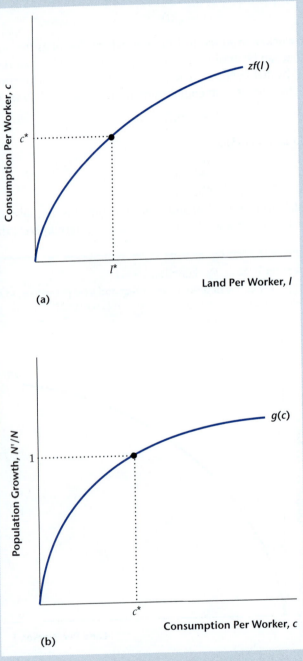

state quantity of consumption per worker. Then, in panel (a) of the figure, c^* determines the steady state quantity of land per worker, l^*. Because the quantity of land is fixed at L, we can determine the steady state population as $N^* = \frac{L}{l^*}$. In the model, we can take the standard of living as being given by steady state consumption per worker, c^*. Therefore, the long-run standard of living is determined entirely by the function g, which captures the effect of the standard of living on population growth. The key property of the model is that nothing in panel (a) of Figure 7.8 affects c^*, so that improvements in the production technology or increases in the quantity of land have no effect on the long-run standard of living.

The Effects of an Increase in z on the Steady State

We now consider an experiment in which total factor productivity increases, which we can interpret as an improvement in agricultural techniques. That is, suppose that the economy is initially in a steady state, with a given level of total factor productivity z_1, which then increases permanently to z_2. The steady state effects are shown in Figure 7.9. In panel (a) of the figure, the per-worker production function shifts up from $z_1 f(l)$ to $z_2 f(l)$. This has no effect on steady state consumption per worker c^*, which is determined in panel (b) of the figure. In the new steady state, in panel (a) the quantity of land per worker falls from l_1^* to l_2^*. This implies that the steady state population increases from $N_1^* = \frac{L}{l_1^*}$ to $N_2^* = \frac{L}{l_2^*}$.

The economy does not move to the new steady state instantaneously, as it takes time for the population and consumption to adjust. Figure 7.10 shows how the adjustment takes place in terms of the paths of consumption per worker and population. The economy is in a steady state before time T, at which time there is an increase in total factor productivity. Initially, the effect of this is to increase output, consumption, and consumption per worker, as there is no effect on the current population at time T. However, because consumption per worker has increased, there is an increase in population growth. As the population grows after period T, in panel (a) of the figure, consumption per worker falls (given the fixed quantity of land), until consumption per worker converges to c^*, its initial level, and the population converges to its new higher level N_2^*.

This then gives the pessimistic Malthusian result that improvements in the technology for producing food do not improve the standard of living in the long run. A better technology generates better nutrition and more population growth, and the extra population ultimately consumes all of the extra food produced, so that each person is no better off than before the technological improvement.

Population Control

How can society be better off in a Malthusian world? The prescription Malthus proposed was state-mandated population control. If the government were to institute something like the " one child only" policy introduced in China, this would have the effect of reducing the rate of population growth for each level of consumption per worker. In panel (b) of Figure 7.11, the function $g_1(c)$ shifts down to $g_2(c)$ as the result of the population control policy. In the steady state, consumption per worker increases from c_1^* to c_2^* in panel (b) of the figure, and this implies that the quantity of land per worker rises in the steady state in panel (a) from l_1^* to l_2^*. Because the quantity

Figure 7.9 The Effect of an Increase in z in the Malthusian Model

When z increases, land per worker decreases in the steady state (so the population increases) and consumption per worker remains the same.

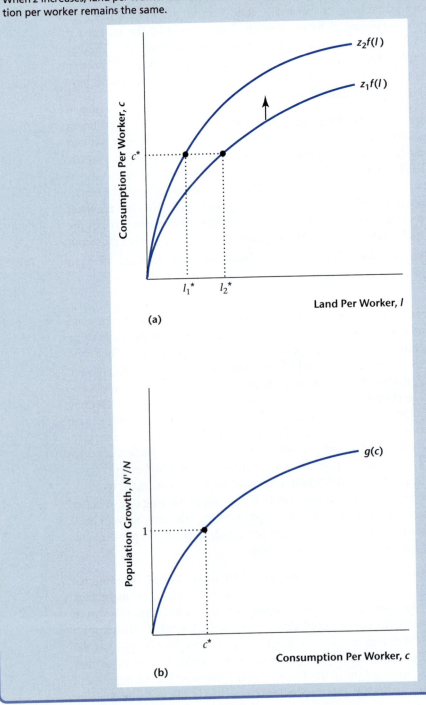

Figure 7.10 Adjustment to the Steady State in the Malthusian Model When z Increases

In the figure, z increases at time T, which causes consumption per worker to increase and then decline to its steady state value over time, with the population increasing over time to its steady state value.

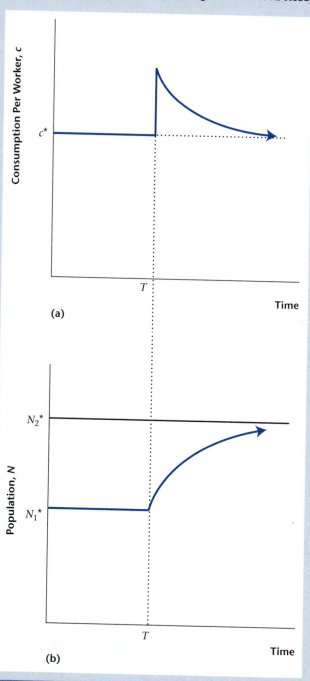

(a)

(b)

Figure 7.11 Population Control in the Malthusian Model

In the figure, population control policy shifts the function $g_1(c)$ to $g_2(c)$. In the steady state, consumption per worker increases and land per worker decreases (the population falls).

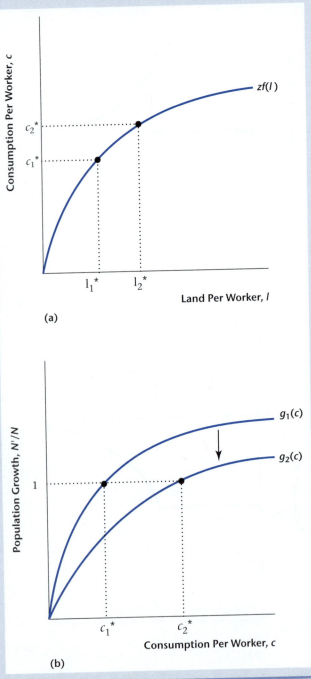

(a)

(b)

of land is fixed, the population falls in the steady state from $N_1^* = \frac{L}{l_1^*}$ to $N_2^* = \frac{L}{l_2^*}$. Here, a reduction in the size of the population increases output per worker and consumption per worker, and everyone is better off in the long run.

How Useful Is the Malthusian Model of Economic Growth?

LO 7.3 Explain the usefulness of the Malthusian model.

Given what was known in 1798, when Malthus wrote his essay, the Malthusian model could be judged to be quite successful. Our first economic growth fact, discussed at the beginning of this chapter, was that before the Industrial Revolution in about 1800, standards of living differed little over time and across countries. The Malthusian model predicts this, if population growth depends in the same way on consumption per worker across countries. Before the Industrial Revolution, production in the world was mainly agricultural; the population grew over time, as did aggregate production, but there appeared to have been no significant improvements in the average standard of living. This is all consistent with the Malthusian model.

As is well-known from the perspective of the early twenty-first century however, Malthus was far too pessimistic. There was sustained growth in standards of living in the richest countries of the world after 1800 without any significant government population control in place in the countries with the strongest performance. As well, the richest countries of the world have experienced a large drop in birth rates. Currently, in spite of advances in health care that have increased life expectancy dramatically in the richer countries, population in most of these richer countries would be declining without immigration. Thus, Malthus was ultimately wrong, both concerning the ability of economies to produce long-run improvements in the standard of living and the effect of the standard of living on population growth.

Why was Malthus wrong? First, he did not allow for the effect of increases in the capital stock on production. In contrast to land, which is limited in supply, there is no limit to the size of the capital stock, and having more capital implies that there is more productive capacity to produce additional capital. In other words, capital can reproduce itself. The Solow growth model, which we develop later in this chapter, allows us to explore the role of capital accumulation in growth.

Second, Malthus did not account for all of the effects of economic forces on population growth. While it is clear that a higher standard of living reduces death rates through better nutrition and health care, there has also proved to be a reduction in birth rates. As the economy develops, there are better opportunities for working outside the home. In terms of family decisions, the opportunity cost of raising a large family becomes large in the face of high market wages, and more time is spent working in the market rather than raising children at home.

The Solow Model: Exogenous Growth

The Solow growth model is very simple, yet it makes sharp predictions concerning the sources of economic growth, what causes living standards to increase over time, what happens to the level and growth rate of aggregate income when the savings rate or the population growth rate rises, and what we should observe happening to relative living standards across countries over time. This model is much more optimistic about the prospects for long-run improvements in the standard of living than is the Malthusian model. Sustained increases in the standard of living can occur in the model, but sustained technological advances are necessary for this. As well, the Solow model does a good job of explaining the economic growth facts discussed early in this chapter.

In constructing this model, we begin with a description of the consumers who live in the model environment and of the production technology. As with the Malthusian model we treat dynamics seriously here. We study how this economy evolves over time in a competitive equilibrium, and a good part of our analysis concerns the steady state of the model, which we know, from our analysis of the Malthusian model, is the long-run equilibrium or rest point.

Consumers

As in the Malthusian model, there are many periods, but we will analyze the economy in terms of the "current" and the "future" periods. In contrast to the Malthusian model, we suppose that the population grows exogenously. That is, there is a growing population of consumers, with N denoting the population in the current period. As in the Malthusian model, N also is the labor force or employment (there is no unemployment). The population grows over time, with

$$N' = (1 + n)N, \qquad (7\text{-}10)$$

where N' is the population in the future period and $n > -1$. Here, n is the rate of growth in the population, which is assumed to be constant over time. We are allowing for the possibility that $n < 0$, in which case the population would be shrinking over time.

In each period, a given consumer has one unit of time available, and we assume that consumers do not value leisure, so that they supply their one unit of time as labor in each period. In this model, the population is identical to the labor force, because we have assumed that all members of the population work and there is no unemployment. We then refer to N as the number of workers or the labor force and to n as the growth rate in the labor force.

Consumers collectively receive all current real output Y as income (through wage income and dividend income from firms), because there is no government sector and no taxes. In contrast to all of the models we have considered to this point, consumers here face a decision concerning how much of their current income to consume and how much to save. For simplicity, we assume that consumers consume a constant fraction of income in each period; that is,

$$C = (1 - s)Y, \qquad (7\text{-}11)$$

where C is current consumption. For consumers, $C + S = Y$, where S is aggregate savings, so from Equation (7-11) we have $S = sY$ and s is then the aggregate savings rate. In Chapters 9 and 10 we discuss in more depth how consumers make their consumption–savings decisions.

The Representative Firm

Output is produced by a representative firm, according to the production function

$$Y = zF(K, N), \qquad (7\text{-}12)$$

where Y is current output, z is current total factor productivity, K is the current capital stock, and N is the current labor input. The production function F has all of the properties that we studied in Chapter 4. As in the Malthusian model, constant returns to scale implies that dividing both sides of Equation (7-12) by N and rearranging, we get

$$\frac{Y}{N} = zF\left(\frac{K}{N}, 1\right). \qquad (7\text{-}13)$$

In Equation (7-13), $\frac{Y}{N}$ is output per worker (synomous here with real income per capita), and $\frac{K}{N}$ is capital per worker, and so the equation tells us that if the production function has constant returns to scale, then output per worker [on the left-hand side of Equation (7-13)] depends only on the quantity of capital per worker [on the right-hand side of Equation (7-13)]. For simplicity, as in the Malthusian model we can rewrite Equation (7-13) as

$$y = zf(k),$$

where y is output per worker, k is capital per worker, and $f(k)$ is the per-worker production function, which is defined by $f(k) \equiv F(k, 1)$. We use lowercase letters in what follows to refer to per-worker quantities. The per-worker production function is graphed in Figure 7.12. A key property of the per-worker production function is that its slope is the marginal product of capital, MP_K. This is because adding one unit to k, the quantity of capital per worker, increases y, output per worker, by the marginal product of capital, because $f(k) = F(k, 1)$. As the slope of the per-worker production function is MP_K, and because MP_K is diminishing with K, the per-worker production function in the figure is concave—that is, its slope decreases as k increases.

We suppose that some of the capital stock wears out through use each period. That is, there is depreciation, and we assume that the depreciation rate is a constant d, where $0 < d < 1$. Then, the capital stock changes over time according to

$$K' = (1 - d)K + I, \qquad (7\text{-}14)$$

where K' is the future capital stock, K is the current capital stock, and I is the investment.

Competitive Equilibrium

LO 7.4 Construct the competitive equilibrium in the Solow growth model.

Now that we have described the behavior of consumers and firms in the Solow growth model, we can put this behavior together and determine how consistency is achieved in a competitive equilibrium. In this economy, there are two markets in the current period. In the first market, current consumption goods are traded for current labor; in

Figure 7.12 The Per-Worker Production Function

This function is the relationship between aggregate output per worker and capital per worker determined by the constant-returns-to-scale production function. The slope of the per-worker production function is the marginal product of capital, MP_K.

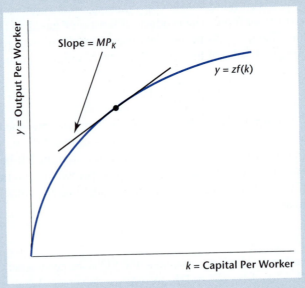

the second market, current consumption goods are traded for capital. That is, capital is the asset in this model, and consumers save by accumulating it. The labor market and the capital market must clear in each period. In the labor market, the quantity of labor is always determined by the inelastic supply of labor, which is N. That is, because the supply of labor is N no matter what the real wage, the real wage adjusts in the current period so that the representative firm wishes to hire N workers. Letting S denote the aggregate quantity of saving in the current period, the capital market is in equilibrium in the current period if $S = I$; that is, if what consumers wish to save equals the quantity of investment. However, because $S = Y - C$ in this economy—that is, national savings is aggregate income minus consumption as there is no government—we can write the equilibrium condition as

$$Y = C + I, \tag{7-15}$$

or current output is equal to aggregate consumption plus aggregate investment. From Equation (7-14) we have that $I = K' - (1 - d)K$, and so using this and Equation (7-11) to substitute for C and I in Equation (7-15), we get

$$Y = (1 - s)Y + K' - (1 - d)K,$$

or, rearranging terms and simplifying,

$$K' = sY + (1 - d)K; \tag{7-16}$$

that is, the capital stock in the future period is the quantity of aggregate savings in the current period ($S = Y - C = sY$) plus the capital stock left over from the current period that has not depreciated. If we now substitute for Y in Equation (7-16) using the production function from Equation (7-12), we get

$$K' = szF(K, N) + (1 - d)K. \tag{7-17}$$

Equation (7-17) states that the stock of capital in the future period is equal to the quantity of savings in the current period (identical to the quantity of investment) plus the quantity of current capital that remains in the future after depreciation.

It is convenient to express Equation (7-17) in per-worker terms, by dividing each term on the right-hand and left-hand sides of the equation by N, the number of workers, to get

$$\frac{K'}{N} = sz\frac{F(K, N)}{N} + (1 - d)\frac{K}{N},$$

and then multiplying the left-hand side by $1 = \frac{N'}{N'}$, which gives

$$\frac{K'}{N}\frac{N'}{N'} = sz\frac{F(K, N)}{N} + (1 - d)\frac{K}{N}.$$

We can rewrite the above equation as

$$k'(1 + n) = szf(k) + (1 - d)k. \tag{7-18}$$

In Equation (7-18), $k' = \frac{K'}{N'}$ is the future quantity of capital per worker, $\frac{N'}{N} = 1 + n$ from Equation (7-10), and the first term on the right-hand side of Equation (7-18) comes from the fact that $\frac{F(K, N)}{N} = F(\frac{K}{N}, 1)$ because the production function has constant returns to scale, and $F(\frac{K}{N}, 1) = f(k)$ by definition. We can then divide the right-hand and left-hand sides of Equation (7-18) by $1 + n$ to obtain

$$k' = \frac{szf(k)}{1 + n} + \frac{(1 - d)k}{1 + n}. \tag{7-19}$$

Equation (7-19) is a key equation that summarizes most of what we need to know about competitive equilibrium in the Solow growth model, and we use this equation to derive the important implications of the model. This equation determines the future stock of capital per worker, k' on the left-hand side of the equation, as a function of the current stock of capital per worker, k, on the right-hand side.

In Figure 7.13 we graph the relationship given by Equation (7-19). In the figure, the curve has a decreasing slope because of the decreasing slope of the per-worker production function $f(k)$ in Figure 7.12. In the figure, the 45° line is the line along which $k' = k$, and the point at which the 45° line intersects the curve given by Equation (7-19) is the steady state. Once the economy reaches the steady state, where current capital per worker $k = k^*$, then future capital per worker $k' = k^*$, and the economy has k^* units of capital per worker forever after. If the current stock of capital per worker, k, is less than the steady state value, so that $k < k^*$, then from the figure $k' > k$, and the capital stock per worker increases from the current period to the future period.

Figure 7.13 Determination of the Steady State Quantity of Capital per Worker
The colored curve is the relationship between current capital per worker, k, and future capital per worker, k', determined in a competitive equilibrium in the Solow growth model. The steady state quantity of capital per worker is k^*, given by the intersection of the 45° line (the black line) with the colored curve.

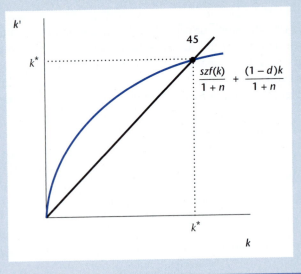

In this situation, current investment is sufficiently large, relative to depreciation and growth in the labor force, that the per-worker quantity of capital increases. However, if $k > k^*$, then we have $k' < k$, and the capital stock per worker decreases from the current period to the future period. In this situation, investment is sufficiently small that it cannot keep up with depreciation and labor force growth, and the per-worker quantity of capital declines from the current period to the future period. Therefore, if the quantity of capital per worker is smaller than its steady state value, it increases until it reaches the steady state, and if the quantity of capital per worker is larger than its steady state value, it decreases until it reaches the steady state.

Because the Solow growth model predicts that the quantity of capital per worker converges to a constant, k^*, in the long run, it also predicts that the quantity of output per worker converges to a constant, which is $y^* = zf(k^*)$ from the per-worker production function. The Solow model then tells us that if the savings rate s, the labor force growth rate n, and total factor productivity z are constant, then real income per worker cannot grow in the long run. Thus, since real income per worker is also real income per capita in the model, we can take y as a measure of the standard of living. The model then concludes that there can be no long-run betterment in living standards under these circumstances. Why does this happen? The reason is that the marginal product of capital is diminishing. Output per worker can grow only as long as capital per worker continues to grow. However, the marginal return to investment, which is determined by the marginal product of capital, declines as the per-worker capital stock grows. In other words, as the capital stock per worker grows, it takes more and more investment per worker in the current period to produce one unit of additional capital per worker for the future period. Therefore, as the economy grows, new investment ultimately only just keeps up with depreciation and the growth of the labor force, and growth in per-worker output ceases.

In the long run, when the economy converges to the steady state quantity of capital per worker, k^*, all real aggregate quantities grow at the rate n, which is the growth rate in the labor force. The aggregate quantity of capital in the steady state is $K = k^*N$, and because k^* is a constant and N grows at the rate n, K must also grow at the rate n. Similarly, aggregate real output is $Y = y^*N = zf(k^*)N$, and so Y also grows at the rate n. Further, the quantity of investment is equal to savings, so that investment in the steady state is $I = sY = szf(k^*)N$, and because $szf(k^*)$ is a constant, I also grows at the rate n in the steady state. As well, aggregate consumption is $C = (1 - s)zf(k^*)N$, so that consumption also grows at the rate n in the steady state. In the long run, therefore, if the savings rate, the labor force growth rate, and total factor productivity are constant, then growth rates in aggregate quantities are determined by the growth rate in the labor force. This is one sense in which the Solow growth model is an exogenous growth model. In the long run, the Solow model tells us that growth in key macroeconomic aggregates is determined by exogenous labor force growth when the savings rate, the labor force growth rate, and total factor productivity are constant.

Analysis of the Steady State

LO 7.5 Use the Solow growth model to analyze the effects of changes in exogenous factors on income per worker, capital per worker, and the economy's growth rate.

In this section, we put the Solow growth model to work. We perform some experiments with the model, analyzing how the steady state or long-run equilibrium is affected by changes in the savings rate, the population growth rate, and total factor productivity. We then show how the response of the model to these experiments is consistent with what we see in the data.

To analyze the steady state, we start with Equation (7-19), which determines the future capital stock per worker, k' given the current capital stock per worker, k. In the steady state, we have $k = k' = k^*$, and so substituting k^* in Equation (7-19) for k and k' we get

$$k^* = \frac{szf(k^*)}{1+n} + \frac{(1-d)k^*}{1+n},$$

multiplying both sides of this equation by $1 + n$ and rearranging, we get

$$szf(k^*) = (n + d)k^*. \tag{7-20}$$

Equation (7-20) solves for the steady state capital stock per worker, k^*. It is this equation we wish to analyze to determine the effects of changes in the savings rate s, in the population growth rate n, and in total factor productivity z on the steady state quantity of capital per worker, k^*.

We graph the left-hand and right-hand sides of Equation (7-20) in Figure 7.14, where the intersection of the two curves determines the steady state quantity of capital

Figure 7.14 Determination of the Steady State Quantity of Capital per Worker

The steady state quantity of capital, k_1^*, is determined by the intersection of the curve $szf(k^*)$ with the line $(n + d)k^*$.

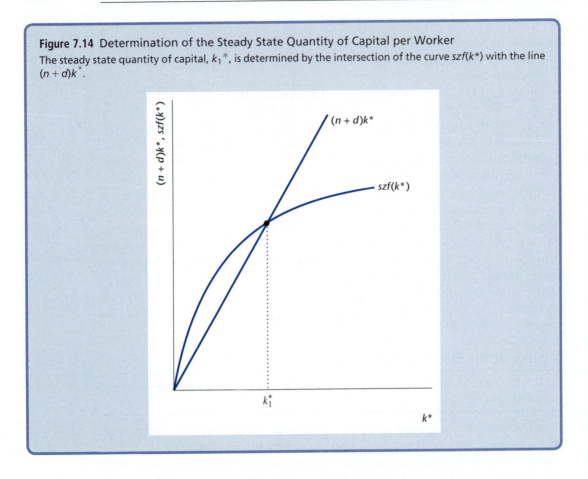

per worker, which we denote by k_1^* in the figure. The curve $szf(k^*)$ is the per-worker production function multiplied by the savings rate s, and so this function inherits the properties of the per-worker production function in Figure 7.12. The curve $(n + d)k^*$ in Figure 7.14 is a straight line with slope $n + d$.

The Steady State Effects of an Increase in the Savings Rate A key experiment to consider in the Solow growth model is a change in the savings rate s. We can interpret a change in s as occurring due to a change in the preferences of consumers. For example, if consumers care more about the future, they save more, and s increases. A change in s could also be brought about through government policy, for example, if the government were to subsidize savings (though in Chapter 9, we show that this has opposing income and substitution effects on savings). With regard to government policy, we need to be careful about interpreting our results, because to be completely rigorous we should build a description of government behavior into the model.

In Figure 7.15, we show the effect of an increase in the savings rate, from s_1 to s_2, on the steady state quantity of capital per worker. The increase in s shifts the curve $szf(k^*)$ up, and k^* increases from k_1^* to k_2^*. Therefore, in the new steady state, the

Figure 7.15 Effect of an Increase in the Savings Rate on the Steady State Quantity of Capital per Worker

An increase in the savings rate shifts the curve $szf(k^*)$ up, resulting in an increase in the quantity of capital per worker from k_1^* to k_2^*.

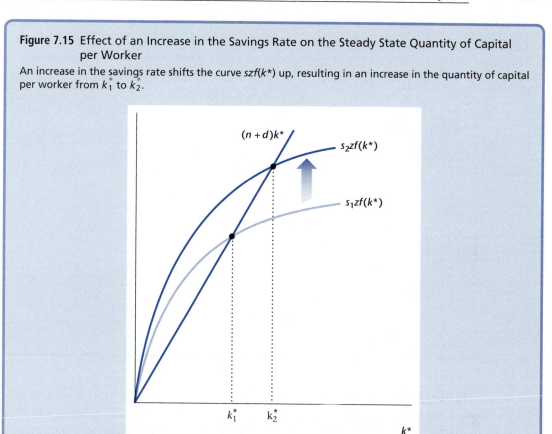

quantity of capital per worker is higher, which implies that output per worker is also levels of capital per worker and output per worker are higher in the new steady state, the increase in the savings rate has no effect on the growth rates of aggregate variables. Before and after the increase in the savings rate, the aggregate capital stock K, aggregate output Y, aggregate investment I, and aggregate consumption C grow at the rate of growth in the labor force, n. This is perhaps surprising, as we might think that a country that invests and saves more, thus accumulating capital at a higher rate, would grow faster.

Though the growth rates of aggregate variables are unaffected by the increase in the savings rate in the steady state, it may take some time for the adjustment from one steady state to another to take place. In Figure 7.16, we show the path that the natural logarithm of output follows when there is an increase in the savings rate, with time measured along the horizontal axis. Before time T, aggregate output is growing at the constant rate n (recall that if the growth rate is constant, then the time path of the natural logarithm is a straight line), and then the savings rate increases at time T. Aggregate output then adjusts to its higher growth path after period T, but in the transition

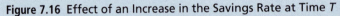

Figure 7.16 Effect of an Increase in the Savings Rate at Time *T*

The figure shows the natural logarithm of aggregate output. Before time *T*, the economy is in a steady state. At time *T*, the savings rate increases, and output then converges in the long run to a new higher steady state growth path.

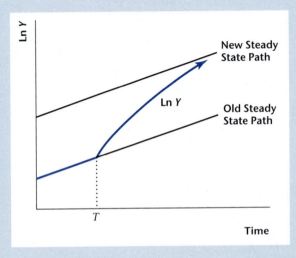

to the new growth path, the rate of growth in Y is higher than n. The temporarily high growth rate in transition results from a higher rate of capital accumulation when the savings rate increases, which translates into a higher growth rate in aggregate output. As capital is accumulated at a higher rate, however, the marginal product of capital diminishes, and growth slows down, ultimately converging to the steady state growth rate n.

Consumption per Worker and Golden Rule Capital Accumulation   We know from Chapter 2 that GDP, or GDP per person, is often used as a measure of aggregate welfare. However, what consumers ultimately care about is their lifetime consumption. In this model, given our focus on steady states, an aggregate welfare measure we might want to consider is the steady state level of consumption per worker. In this subsection, we show how to determine steady state consumption per worker from a diagram similar to Figure 7.15. Next we show that there is a given quantity of capital per worker that maximizes consumption per worker in the steady state. This implies that an increase in the savings rate could cause a decrease in steady state consumption per worker, even though an increase in the savings rate always increases output per worker.

Consumption per worker in the steady state is $c = (1 - s)zf(k^*)$, which is the difference between steady state income per worker, $y^* = zf(k^*)$, and steady state savings per worker, which is $szf(k^*)$. If we add the per-worker production function to Figure 7.15, as we have done in Figure 7.17, then the steady state quantity of capital per worker in the figure is k_1^*, and steady state consumption per worker is the distance AB, which is the difference between output per worker and savings per worker.

Figure 7.17 Steady State Consumption per Worker

Consumption per worker in the steady state is shown as the distance *AB*, given the steady state quantity of capital per worker, $k_1{}^*$.

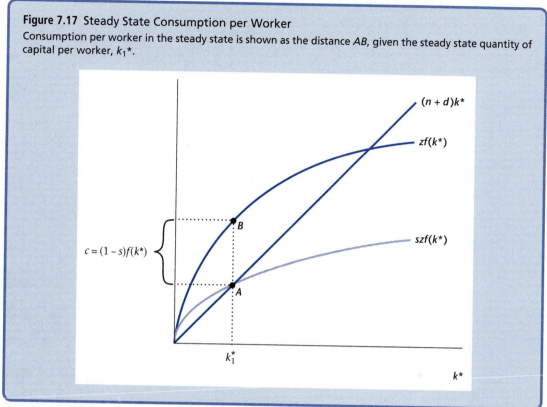

Consumption per worker in the steady state is also the difference between output per worker, $y^* = zf(k^*)$, and $(n + d)k^*$.

The consumption per worker in the steady state is given by

$$c^* = zf(k^*) - (n + d)k^*.$$

We show in Figure 7.18 how to construct consumption per worker in the steady state, c^*, as a function of capital per worker in the steady state, k^*, as shown in Figure 7.18(b). There is a quantity of capital per worker for which consumption per worker is maximized, which we denote by k_{gr}^* in the figure. If the steady state quantity of capital is k_{gr}^*, then maximum consumption per worker is c^{**}. Here, k_{gr}^* is called the **golden rule quantity of capital per worker**. The golden rule has the property, from Figure 7.18(a), that the slope of the per-worker production function where $k^* = k_{gr}^*$ is equal to the slope of the function $(n + d)k^*$. That is, because the slope of the per-worker production function is the marginal product of capital, MP_K, at the golden rule steady state we have

$$MP_K = n + d.$$

Therefore, when capital is accumulated at a rate that maximizes consumption per worker in the steady state, the marginal product of capital equals the population growth rate plus the depreciation rate.

Figure 7.18 The Golden Rule Quantity of Capital per Worker

This quantity, which maximizes consumption per worker in the steady state, is k^*_{gr}, and the maximized quantity of consumption per worker is c^{**}. The golden rule savings rate sgr achieves the golden rule quantity of capital per worker in a competitive equilibrium steady state.

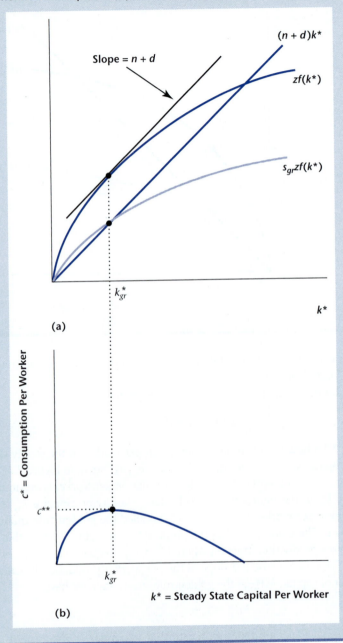

How can the golden rule be achieved in the steady state? In Figure 7.18(a), we show that if the savings rate is s_{gr}, then the curve $s_{gr}zf(k^*)$ intersects the line $(n + d)k^*$, where $k^* = k_{gr}^*$. Thus, s_{gr} is the **golden rule savings rate**. If savings takes place at the golden rule savings rate, then in the steady state the current population consumes and saves the appropriate amount so that, in each succeeding period, the population can continue to consume this maximum amount per person. The golden rule is a biblical reference, which comes from the dictum that we should treat others as we would like ourselves to be treated.

From Figure 7.18(b), if the steady state capital stock per worker is less than k_{gr}^*, then an increase in the savings rate s increases the steady state capital stock per worker and increases consumption per worker. However, if $k^* > k_{gr}^*$, then an increase in the savings rate increases k^* and causes a decrease in consumption per worker.

Suppose that we calculated the golden rule savings rate for the United States and found that the actual U.S. savings rate was different from the golden rule rate. For example, suppose we found that the actual savings rate was lower than the golden rule savings rate. Would this necessarily imply that the government should implement a change in policy that would increase the savings rate? The answer is no, for two reasons. First, any increase in the savings rate would come at a cost in current consumption. It would take time to build up a higher stock of capital to support higher consumption per worker in the new steady state, and the current generation may be unwilling to bear this short-term cost. Second, in practice, savings behavior is the result of optimizing decisions by individual consumers. In general, we should presume that private market outcomes achieve the correct trade-off between current consumption and savings, unless we have good reasons to believe that there exists some market failure that the government can efficiently correct.

The Steady State Effects of an Increase in Labor Force Growth   The next experiment we carry out with the Solow model is to ask what happens in the long run if the labor force growth rate increases. As labor is a factor of production, it is clear that higher labor force growth ultimately causes aggregate output to grow at a higher rate. But what is the effect on output per worker in the steady state? With aggregate output growing at a higher rate, there is a larger and larger " income pie" to split up, but with more and more workers to share this pie. As we show, the Solow growth model predicts that capital per worker and output per worker will decrease in the steady state when the labor force growth rate increases, but aggregate output will grow at a higher rate, which is the new rate of labor force growth.

In Figure 7.19 we show the steady state effects of an increase in the labor force growth rate, from n_1 to n_2. Initially, the quantity of capital per worker is k_1^*, determined by the intersection of the curves $szf(k^*)$ and $(n_1 + d)k^*$. When the population growth rate increases, this results in a decrease in the quantity of capital per worker from k_1^* to k_2^*. Because capital per worker falls, output per worker also falls, from the per-worker production function. That is, output per worker falls from $zf(k_1^*)$ to $zf(k_2^*)$. The reason for this result is that when the labor force grows at a higher rate, the current labor force faces a tougher task in building capital for next period's consumers, who are a

Figure 7.19 Steady State Effects of an Increase in the Labor Force Growth Rate

An increase in the labor force growth rate from n_1 to n_2 causes a decrease in the steady state quantity of capital per worker.

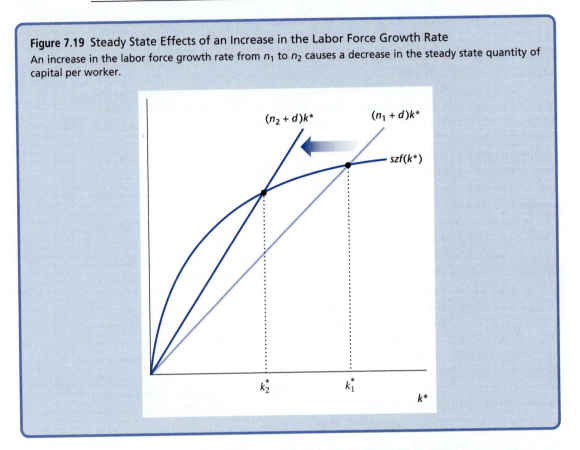

proportionately larger group. Thus, output per worker and capital per worker are ultimately lower in the steady state.

We have already determined that aggregate output, aggregate consumption, and aggregate investment grow at the labor force growth rate n in the steady state. Therefore, when the labor force growth rate increases, growth in all of these variables must also increase. This is an example that shows that higher growth in aggregate income need not be associated, in the long run, with higher income per worker.

The Steady State Effects of an Increase in Total Factor Productivity If we take real income per worker to be a measure of the standard of living in a country, what we have shown thus far is that, in the Solow model, an increase in the savings rate or a decrease in the labor force growth rate can increase the standard of living in the long run. However, increases in the savings rate and reductions in the labor force growth rate cannot bring about an ever-increasing standard of living in a country. This is because the savings rate must always be below 1 (no country would have a savings rate equal to 1, as this would imply zero consumption), and the labor force growth rate cannot fall indefinitely. The Solow model predicts that a country's standard of living can continue to increase in the long run only if there are continuing increases in total factor productivity, as we show here.

THEORY CONFRONTS THE DATA

The Solow Growth Model, Investment Rates, and Population Growth

Now that we know something about the predictions that the Solow growth model makes, we can evaluate the model by matching its predictions with the data. It has only been relatively recently that economists have had access to comprehensive national income accounts data for essentially all countries in the world. The Penn World Tables, which are the work of Alan Heston, Robert Summers, and Bettina Aten at the University of Pennsylvania,[8] allow for comparisons of GDP, among other macroeconomic variables, across countries. Making these comparisons is a complicated measurement exercise, as GDP in different countries at a given point in time is measured in different currencies, and simply making adjustments using foreign exchange rates does not give the right answers. A limitation of the Penn World Tables is that they only extend back to 1950. A few decades of data may not tell us all we need to know, in terms of matching the long-run predictions of the Solow growth model. Can the steady state be achieved within a few decades? As we will see, however, two of the predictions of the Solow model appear to match the data in the Penn World Tables quite well.

Two key predictions of the Solow growth model are first, in the long run, an increase in the savings rate causes an increase in the quantity of income per worker; second, an increase in

the labor force growth rate causes a decrease in the quantity of income per worker. We examine in turn the fit of each of these predictions with the data.

The savings rate in the Solow growth model is the ratio of investment expenditures to GDP, and since the population is identical to the labor force in the model, income per worker is the same thing as income per capita. The Solow model thus predicts that, if we look at data from a set of countries in the world, we should see a positive correlation between GDP per capita and the ratio of investment to GDP. This is the correlation that we discussed in the Economic Growth Facts section earlier in this chapter. In Figure 7.2 we observe that a positively sloped line would provide the best fit for the points in the figure, so that the investment rate and income per worker are positively correlated across the countries of the world. Clearly, as the Solow model predicts, countries with high (low) ratios of investment to GDP also have high (low) quantities of income per worker.

Next, the Solow model predicts that, in data for a set of countries, we should observe the labor force growth rate to be negatively correlated with real income per capita. The prediction from the Solow growth model is that the population growth rate and the level of income per worker should be negatively correlated, which is the fourth economic growth fact we discussed early in this chapter. In Figure 7.3, we observe a negative correlation between the population growth rate and income per worker across countries, as the Solow model predicts.

---

[8] The real income per capita statistics come from A. Heston, R. Summers, and B. Aten, *Penn World Table Version 7.0,* Center for International Comparisons at the University of Pennsylvania (CICUP), May 2011, available at pwt.econ.upenn.edu.

In Figure 7.20 we show the effect of increases in total factor productivity. First, an increase in total factor productivity from z_1 to z_2 results in an increase in capital per worker from k_1^* to k_2^* and an increase in output per worker as a result. A further increase in total factor productivity to z_3 causes an additional increase in capital per worker to k_3^* and an additional increase in output per worker. These increases in capital per worker and output per worker can continue indefinitely, as long as the increases in total factor productivity continue.

This is a key insight that comes from the Solow growth model. An increase in a country's propensity to save or a decrease in the labor force growth rate imply one-time increases in a country's standard of living, but there can be unbounded growth in the standard of living only if total factor productivity continues to grow. The source of continual long-run betterment in a country's standard of living, therefore, can only be the process of devising better methods for putting factor inputs together to produce output, thus generating increases in total factor productivity.

In contrast to the Malthusian model, where the gains from technological advance are dissipated by a higher population, the Solow model gives a more optimistic outlook for increases in the standard of living over time. If we accept the Solow model, it tells us that the steady increase in per capita income that occurred since 1900 in the United States (see Figure 7.1) was caused by sustained increases in total factor productivity over a period of

Figure 7.20 Increases in Total Factor Productivity in the Solow Growth Model
Increases in total factor productivity from z_1 to z_2 and from z_2 to z_3 cause increases in the quantity of capital per worker from k_1^* to k_2^* and from k_2^* to k_3^*. Thus, increases in total factor productivity lead to increases in output per worker.

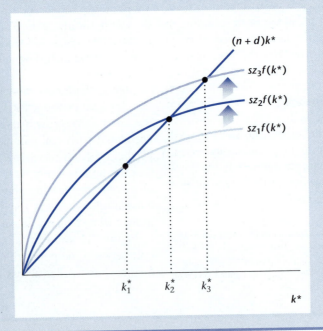

MACROECONOMICS IN ACTION
Resource Misallocation and Total Factor Productivity

Much macroeconomic research on the sources of total factor productivity growth and on explanations for the differences in total factor productivity across countries focuses on the determinants of productivity for an individual firm. This is the approach we take in using the Solow growth model to help us understand economic growth, in that output in the Solow growth model is produced by a representative firm, and aggregate total factor productivity is the same as total factor productivity for this representative firm.

While there is much we can learn about the relationship between productivity and economic growth by studying how an individual firm behaves, macroeconomists have recently begun to recognize the important role played by the allocation of capital and labor across different firms in an economy in determining aggregate productivity. To understand how the allocation of factors of production across firms can affect aggregate total factor productivity, first consider how factors of production would be allocated in a perfect world with no inefficiencies. In such a world, we know that market forces will tend to reallocate labor and capital from less productive firms to more productive firms. In a particular industry, for example the automobile industry, manufacturers with low total factor productivity will earn lower profits than those manufacturers with high productivity, and the low-productivity firms will tend to go out of business while the high-productivity firms grow. Across industries, labor and capital will tend to flow to those industries where productivity is highest, because in those industries the wages and the returns to capital will tend to be higher. This is the process that led to the growth of the information

technology sector in the United States while the manufacturing sector was shrinking in relative terms.

Now, in the imperfect world that we live in, an economy may have distortions that prevent market forces from efficiently allocating capital and labor. First, government taxes and subsidies can distort the returns to capital and labor across firms. For example, the federal government subsidizes ethanol production. This subsidy acts to increase the relative price of corn, which in turn makes it more profitable to allocate land to corn production rather than soybean production, for example. The ethanol subsidy makes it more profitable to use corn in the production of ethanol than as cattle feed. Thus, the ethanol subsidy acts to change the pattern of production in the economy relative to what it would otherwise be. In some cases, taxes and subsidies can correct externalities (see Chapter 5), and thus increase economic efficiency. However, the ethanol subsidy, while perhaps well-intentioned, appears to act on net as a source of inefficiency.

Second, labor and capital could be misallocated across firms because of political corruption. For example, if a government contract is allocated to the firm that will give government officials the largest bribe rather than to the firm that is most efficient, this can cause a misallocation of factors of production across firms.

Third, there can be inefficiencies in the allocation of credit across firms in an industry or across industries. We can think of these inefficiencies as altering the returns to capital in different firms or industries. For example, it is sometimes argued that monopoly power in the Japanese banking industry leads to inefficiencies

(Continued)

in credit allocation, in that lending decisions by banks can be determined more by personal relationships between a borrower and a banker than by profitability.

If distortions in an economy act to allocate labor and capital away from firms where total factor productivity is highest, then this will reduce aggregate productivity below what it would be in a world without distortions. Some recent research indicates that these distortions could be very important in practice, and that differences in distortions could be a key determinant of differences in productivity and per capita income across countries. Research by Diego Restuccia and Richard Rogerson[9] considers hypothetical tax and subsidy distortions and shows that the resulting

misallocation in factors of production across firms could reduce aggregate productivity by 30%–50%. Related work by Chang-Tai Hsieh and Peter Klenow[10] takes a very different approach but arrives at similar conclusions. Hsieh and Klenow analyze microeconomic data on manufacturing in China and India and determine that if distortions were reduced to the level that exists in the United States, then total factor productivity in manufacturing would rise by 30%–50% in China and 40%–60% in India. These magnitudes are substantial and indicate that efforts in developing countries (and in rich countries as well) to root out inefficient taxes and subsidies, corruption, and monopoly power could have very large effects on standards of living.

[9]D. Restuccia and R. Rogerson, 2008. " Policy Distortions and Aggregate Productivity with Heterogeneous Establishments," *Review of Economic Dynamics* 11, 707–720.

[10]C. Hsieh and P. Klenow, 2009, " Misallocation and Manufacturing TFP in China and India," *Quarterly Journal of Economics* 124, 1403–1448.

MACROECONOMICS IN ACTION
Recent Trends in Economic Growth in the United States

Figure 7.1 shows sustained growth in real GDP per capita in the United States, extending back to the turn of the twentieth century. The Solow growth model, if subjected to constant growth in total factor productivity (TFP), will indeed exhibit constant growth in real GDP per capita in the long run. Thus, Figure 7.1 seems consistent with the idea that the growth process in the United States is driven by TFP growth, just as it is in the Solow growth model.

But why should TFP grow at roughly a constant rate over the long run? TFP growth in the Solow growth model is exogenous. While exogenous TFP growth at a constant rate over a long

period of time fits the U.S. per capita real GDP time series reasonably well, the economic growth theory we have described thus far in this book will not tell us why TFP should grow at a constant rate. Thus, who is to say that the sustained growth we have seen in the United States in the past will continue into the future?

Figure 7.21 shows the natural logarithm of real GDP, over the period 1947–2015, along with a linear trend fit to the data. The trend, which is the best fit to the real GDP time series, indicates that the average growth rate in real GDP over this period was 3.21%. As can be seen from Figure 7.21, real GDP was above trend

Figure 7.21 Real GDP and Linear Trend

The figure shows the natural logarithm of real GDP, and a linear trend that best fits the data. Real GDP grew on average at a rate of 3.21% from 1947 to 2015, but average growth was lower from 1947 to 1965 and after the 2008–2009 recession. As of 2015, real GDP shows no sign of returning to the 1947–2007 trend.

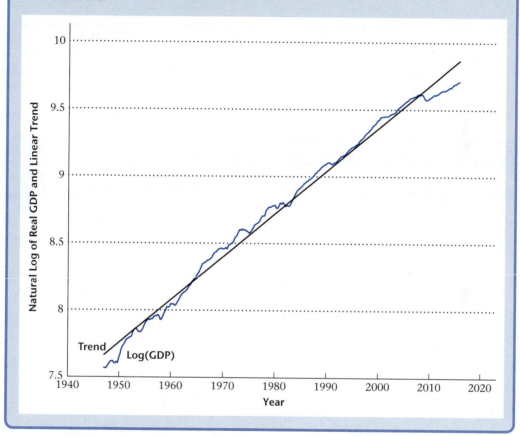

more often than not during the period 1960–2000, but mostly below trend from 1947 to 1965 and after 2008.

Further, even though the last recession in 2008–2009 is now long over, real GDP would have to be growing faster than 3.24% in order to return to the linear trend, and that has not happened. Real GDP has shown no tendency to make up for lost growth and return to the post–1947 trend.

There are at least two possiblities. One is that there are particular reasons why the recovery from the recent recession should be more prolonged than for a typical recession. For example, a book by Carmen Reinhart and Kenneth Rogoff[11] examines evidence from eight centuries of financial crises, and the authors argue that financial crises are typically followed by a long period of macroeconomic adjustment.

---

[11]C. Reinhart and K. Rogoff, 2009. *This Time Is Different: Eight Centuries of Financial Folly*, Princeton University Press, Princeton, NJ.

(Continued)

That idea certainly deserves attention, though the economic mechanism driving the prolonged downturn following a financial crisis is not well understood. Further, even six years after the 2008–2009 recession is over, and the effects of the financial crisis have had time to wear off, the growth rate in real GDP is not increasing.

A second possibility is that what we see in Figure 7.21 is a downward adjustment after the 2008–2009 recession to a lower growth path. To see this more clearly, consider only the path of real GDP from the end of the 2008–2009

recession, in the second quarter of 2009, as shown in Figure 7.22. In the figure, the trend line that fits the time series shows an average growth rate of 2.04%, more than a percentage point below the average growth rate of 3.21% for the whole period 1947–2015. As well, note that growth has been quite smooth since the 2008–2009 recession, with only small deviations from the 2.04% growth trend. Compare this actual experience to the higher trend growth path, which is the 3.21% path that fits the time series for the period 1947–2015.

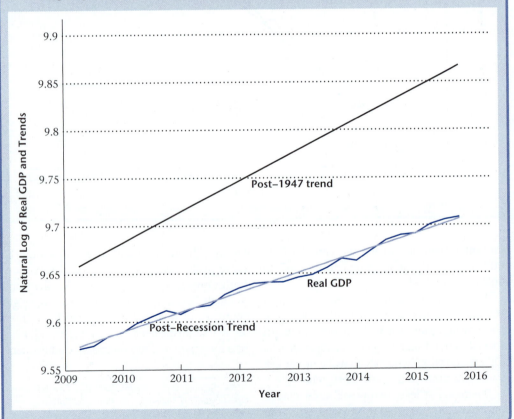

Figure 7.22 Real GDP after the 2008–2009 recession, and Trends
Trend growth from the second quarter of 2009 to the end of 2015 was 2.04%, more than one percentage point lower than the post–1947 trend. The figure shows the post–1947 trend, which represents both a higher growth rate and a higher level of real GDP.

> Thus, since the 2008–2009 recession, there has not only been a reduction in the rate of growth in real GDP of more than a percentage point, but a downward level adjustment in real GDP, that was not "made-up" after the recession ended. The reasons for this abrupt change in growth experience are as yet poorly understood, but it could be the result of basic structural changes occurring in the U.S. economy. There may be important long-term changes that have occurred in U.S. labor markets, or the United States may have lost its edge as a world technological leader. Untangling these issues will most certainly be an active topic of macroeconomic research.

114 years. If technological advances can be sustained for such a long period, there appears to be no reason why these advances cannot occur indefinitely into the future.

Growth Accounting

If aggregate real output is to grow over time, it is necessary for a factor or factors of production to be increasing over time, or for there to be increases in total factor productivity. Typically, growing economies are experiencing growth in factors of production and in total factor productivity. A useful exercise is to measure how much of the growth in aggregate output over a given period of time is accounted for by growth in each of the inputs to production and by increases in total factor productivity. This exercise is called **growth accounting**, and it can be helpful in developing theories of economic growth and for discriminating among different theories. Growth accounting was introduced in the 1950s by Robert Solow, who also developed the growth model we have just studied in the previous section.[12]

Growth accounting starts by considering the aggregate production function from the Solow growth model,

$$Y = zF(K, N),$$

where Y is aggregate output, z is total factor productivity, F is the production function, K is the capital input, and N is the labor input. To use the aggregate production function in conjunction with data on output and factor inputs, we need a specific form for the function F. The widely used Cobb–Douglas production function, discussed in Chapter 4, provides a good fit to U.S. aggregate data, and it is also a good analytical tool for growth accounting. For the production function to be Cobb–Douglas, the function F takes the form

$$F(K, N) = K^a N^{1-a}, \tag{7-21}$$

where a is a number between 0 and 1. Recall from Chapter 4 that, in a competitive equilibrium, a is the fraction of national income that goes to the capital input, and $1 - a$ is the fraction that goes to the labor input. In postwar U.S. data, the labor share in

---

[12]See R. Solow, 1957. "Technical Change and the Aggregate Production Function," *Review of Economic Statistics* 39, 312–320.

national income has been roughly constant at 70%, so we can set $a = 0.3$, and our production function is then

$$Y = zK^{0.3}N^{0.7}. \tag{7-22}$$

If we have measures of aggregate output, the capital input, and the labor input, denoted $\hat{Y}$, $\hat{K}$, and $\hat{N}$, respectively, then total factor productivity z can be measured as a residual, as discussed in Chapter 4. The Solow residual, denoted $\hat{z}$, is measured from the production function, Equation (7-22), as

$$\hat{z} = \frac{\hat{Y}}{\hat{K}^{0.3}\hat{N}^{0.7}}. \tag{7-23}$$

The Solow residual is of course named after Robert Solow. This measure of total factor productivity is a residual, because it is the output that remains to be accounted for after we measure the direct contribution of the capital and labor inputs to output, as discussed in Chapter 4. Total factor productivity has many interpretations, as we studied in Chapters 4 and 5, and so does the Solow residual. Increases in measured total factor productivity could be the result of new inventions, good weather, new management techniques, favorable changes in government regulations, decreases in the relative price of energy, a better allocation of resources across productive units in the economy, or any other factor that causes more aggregate output to be produced given the same quantities of aggregate factor inputs.

Solow Residuals and Long-Run Productivity Growth

LO 7.6 List the facts about growth in real GDP, employment, the capital stock, and total factor productivity in the United States over the period 1950–2014.

A first exercise we work through is to calculate and graph Solow residuals from post–World War II U.S. data and then explain what is interesting in the resulting figure. Using GDP for $\hat{Y}$, measured aggregate output, total employment for $\hat{N}$, and a measure of the capital stock for $\hat{K}$, we calculated the Solow residual $\hat{z}$ using Equation (7-23) and plotted its natural logarithm in Figure 7.23, for the period 1948–2014. Since the slope of the graph in Figure 7.23 gives us a measure of productivity growth, we can see in the figure that productivity growth was high in the 1950s and 1960s, low in the 1970s, high in the 1980s and 1990s, and somewhat lower beginning in the early 2000s. In Table 7.1, we show the average percentage growth in the Solow residual from 1950 to 1960, 1960 to 1970, 1970 to 1980, 1980 to 1990, 1990 to 2000, 2000 to 2009, and for the period 2009–2014, after the last recession ends. Of particular note in Table 7.1 is that productivity growth has not been particularly low since the last recession, at 1.1%, which is higher than the productivity growth rate during the 1970s, though not as large as during some other decades. In the previous "Macroeconomics in Action" box ("Recent Trends . . . ") we noted a marked decline in 2009–2015 growth in real GDP from average experience over the period 1947–2015. So, clearly, this low growth rate in GDP was not driven by low growth in measured total factor productivity.

In this chapter, we used the Solow growth model to show that growth in total factor productivity is a principal driver of long-run standards of living and real GDP growth.

Figure 7.23 Natural Log of the Solow Residual, 1948–2014

The Solow residual is a measure of total factor productivity.

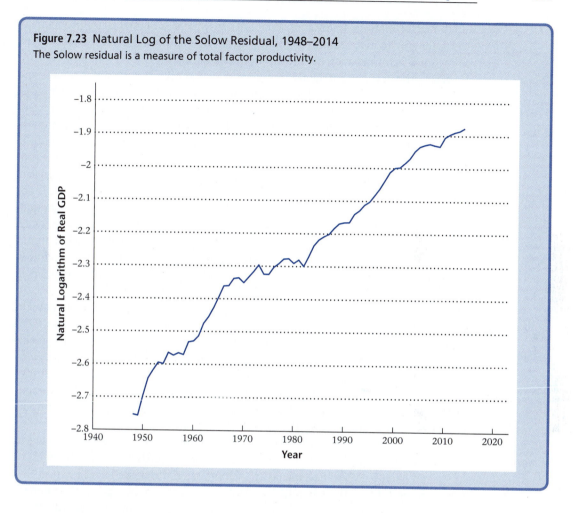

Table 7.1 Average Annual Growth Rates in the Solow Residual

Years	Average Annual Growth Rate
1950–1960	1.7
1960–1970	1.8
1970–1980	0.6
1980–1990	1.3
1990–2000	1.7
2000–2009	0.7
2009–2014	1.11

But, though economists know a lot about the consequences of total factor productivity growth for growth in aggregate economic activity, we know less about the factors determining total factor productivity growth in the long run.

What problems present themselves when, as economists, we attempt to understand the factors that are driving productivity growth, and use that understanding to forecast future productivity growth? First, as with many economic phenomena, measurement is difficult. In Chapter 2, we discussed the difficulties in measuring real GDP growth, relating to changes in the types and quality of goods and services over time, and the underground economy. If we use the Solow residual as a measure of total factor productivity, we not only have to worry about the possible mismeasurement of aggregate output (real GDP), but the mismeasurement of the inputs - labor and capital. For example, it is not hard to count the number of workers who are employed in producing GDP, but it is hard to measure differences in their skills and hours worked, which we need to know to properly determine an aggregate measure of the labor input. Similarly, capital is some aggregate measure of a diverse set of machines and buildings. It may be even harder to aggregate all of these different types of capital into a single aggregate measure than it is to come up with a measure of aggregate GDP.

The second difficulty relates to forecasting future total factor productivity growth. For example we know, with the benefit of hindsight, that the personal computer revolution was a key element in productivity growth in the 1980s and 1990s, starting with the introduction of the PC in the early 1980s, which helped to fuel the internet revolution of the 1990s, along with smartphone communication technology in the 2000s. But, for most mortals, it would have been hard to imagine how what we knew about mainframe computers in the 1960s would translate into the revolution in the computing and information technology that actually transpired.

The uncertainty we face concerning future technological progress is reflected in polar positions among economists. For example, Robert Gordon[13] argues that most of our great technological achievements are behind us, and that we should expect low growth in the future. Alternatively, Joel Mokyr[14] is much more optimistic, taking a historical perspective on the role of technological change in economic growth. What should we conclude about the prospects for growth in productivity in the future? Perhaps we just have to wait and see.

A Growth Accounting Exercise

LO 7.7 Determine the Solow residual and growth rates in real GDP, capital stock, employment, and the Solow residual from data on real GDP, capital stock, and employment.

Now that we know how the Solow residual is constructed and what some of its empirical properties are, we can do a full growth accounting exercise. By way of an example, we show here how we can use the Cobb–Douglas production function Equation (7-22)

---

[13]See R. J. Gordon, 2016. *The Rise and Fall of American Growth: The U.S. Standard of Living Since the Civil War,* Princeton University Press.

[14]See J. Mokyr, 2015. "Secular Stagnation: Not In Your Life," http://pratclif.com/2015/secular-stagnation_files/vox-moekr.pdf)

Table 7.2 Measured GDP, Capital Stock, Employment, and Solow Residual

Year	$\hat{Y}$ (billions of 2009 dollars)	$\hat{K}$ (billions of 2009 dollars)	$\hat{N}$ (millions)	$\hat{z}$
1950	2184.0	8004.2	58.9	8.50
1960	3108.7	11509.0	65.8	10.04
1970	4722.0	16819.7	78.7	12.00
1980	6450.4	22629.8	99.3	12.74
1990	8955.0	29286.6	118.8	14.44
2000	12682.2	37283.6	136.9	17.06
2010	14418.7	44944.9	139.9	18.24
2014	15961.7	47109.5	146.3	19.30

and observations on GDP, the capital stock, and employment to obtain measures of the contributions to growth in real output of growth in the capital stock, in employment, and in total factor productivity.

To do growth accounting, we use Equation (7-23) to calculate the Solow residual $\hat{z}$. In Table 7.2 we show data on real GDP, the capital stock, and employment at ten-year intervals from 1950 to 2000, and then for 2000–2009, and 2009–2014, as 2009 marks the end of the 2008–2009 recession. This is the data we use to carry out our growth accounting exercise. The Solow residual $\hat{z}$ in the table was calculated using Equation (7-23).

Taking the data from Table 7.2, we calculate the average annual growth rates for measured output, capital, employment, and the Solow residual for the periods 1950–1960, 1960–1970, 1970–1980, 1980–1990, 1990–2000, 2000–2009, and 2009–2014. If X_n is the value of a variable in year n, and X_m is the value of that variable in year m, where $n > m$, then the average annual growth rate in X between year m and year n, denoted by g_{mn}, is given by

$$g_{mn} = \left(\frac{X_n}{X_m}\right)^{\frac{1}{n-m}} - 1.$$

For example, in Table 7.2, GDP in 1950 is 2184.0 billion 2005 dollars, or $Y_{1950} = 2184.0$. Further, $Y_{1960} = 3108.7$ from Table 7.2. Then, we have $n - m = 10$, and the average annual growth rate in GDP from 1950 to 1960 in Table 7.3 is $\left(\frac{3108.7}{2184.0}\right)^{\frac{1}{10}} - 1 = 0.0359$, or 3.59%.

Table 7.3 shows that average annual growth in real GDP was very high during the 1960s, and somewhat lower in the 1950s, 1970s, 1980s, and 1990s. The very high growth in the 1960s came from all sources, as growth in capital was very high, growth in employment was somewhat high, and growth in total factor productivity (as measured by growth in $\hat{z}$) was high. Note that in spite of the productivity slowdown in the 1970s, output grew at a reasonably high rate, due to high growth in factors of production. During the 1970s, capital was accumulated at a high rate. Further, employment

Table 7.3 Average Annual Growth Rates

Years	$\hat{Y}$	$\hat{K}$	$\hat{N}$	$\hat{z}$
1950–1960	3.6	3.7	1.1	1.7
1960–1970	4.3	3.9	1.8	1.8
1970–1980	3.2	3.0	2.4	0.6
1980–1990	3.3	2.6	1.8	1.3
1990–2000	3.5	2.4	1.4	1.7
2000–2009	1.4	2.1	0.2	0.7
2009–2014	2.1	0.9	0.9	1.1

MACROECONOMICS IN ACTION

Development Accounting

The growth accounting approach taken in this section is framed in terms of the structure of the Solow growth model. Aggregate output is produced using inputs of labor and capital, and we can proceed to use aggregate data to disentangle the contributions of labor, capital, and TFP to economic growth.

Once we go deeper into studying the economic growth process, we need to take a broader view of the determinants of economic growth, as is done to some extent in Chapter 8. One useful approach is to specify the aggregate production function as

$$Y = zF(hN, K),$$

where h is the quantity of human capital per worker, and N is the number of workers. Human capital is a measure of the stock of skills and education a person possesses, and so hN is the total labor input to aggregate production, which increases with the skills and education that have been acquired by the average person.

Thus, we can attribute growth in real GDP in a particular country to growth in aggregate human capital, growth in physical capital, K, and growth in TFP. As well, we could consider making comparisons across countries, whereby we explain how much of the differences in incomes across countries can be explained by three factors: differences in human capital, differences in physical capital, and differences in TFP.

Work by Chang-Tai Hsieh and Peter Klenow[15] provides a nice summary of published economic research on development accounting. Hsieh and Klenow frame the question by discussing how, in terms of economic theory and empirical evidence, economists have attributed differences in incomes across countries to fundamental differences in geography, climate, luck, institutions, culture, government policies, rule of

---

[15]C. Hsieh and P. Klenow, 2010. "Development Accounting," *American Economic Journal: Macroeconomics* 2, 207–223.

law, and corruption. These fundamentals in turn feed into differences in human capital, physical capital, and TFP, which in turn determine differences in incomes across countries.

Hsieh and Klenow tell us that the conclusions of economic research in development are that differences in incomes across countries can be attributed as follows: 10%–30% to differences in human capital, about 20% to differences in physical capital, and 50%–70% to differences in TFP. This is consistent with our results from analyzing the Solow growth model, which predicts that sustained growth in per capita incomes is driven by sustained growth in TFP. If we look at a set of countries, the Solow model tells us that differences in TFP should explain much of the differences in per capita incomes across countries, which is what we actually see.

Human capital differences across countries, though less important than TFP differences, are still an important contributor to differences in incomes across countries. As well, it is possible that human capital differences also contribute to differences in incomes by affecting differences in TFP. High human capital countries with highly educated workforces may be very good at research and development, which drives TFP growth. This process is not captured in the Solow growth model, but is the subject of much ongoing macroeconomic research.

What determines human capital accumulation in a particular country? Government policy may be important, for example the funding of public education, the tax treatment of private education, and subsidies for on-the-job training. As well, how efficiently a society uses the innate abilities of a population can be important. Work by Chang-Tai Hsieh, Erik Hurst, Charles Jones, and Peter Klenow[16] sheds some light on this topic.

Think of an economy as solving a large problem of allocating people with different kinds of innate ability to different occupations. Some people have a comparative advantage in medicine, and those people should be doctors; some have a comparative advantage in accounting, and those people should be accountants. But society may not be very good at solving that problem. There may be inequality in educational opportunities or discrimination that prevents visible minorities from gaining entry to high-skilled occupations. The treatment of women in the workplace may distort female occupational choices.

Hsieh, Hurst, Jones, and Klenow observe that in the United States in 1960 the fraction of doctors, lawyers, and managers, respectively, who were white men was 94%, 96%, and 86%. By 2008, those numbers had changed to 63%, 61%, and 57%, respectively. To these authors, those observations suggest that it is possible that society might have come up with a better allocation of talent in 2008 than what it had in 1960, and they set out to measure the economic consequences. In their paper, Hsieh, Hurst, Jones, and Klenow argue that 17%–20% of growth in real GDP over the period 1960–2008 can be attributed to a better allocation of raw talent among occupations in the United States. They do not attempt to explain exactly which factors explain this; for example, they cannot tell us whether affirmative action programs were an important contributor to this better allocation. However, these numbers are striking, and indicate that removing barriers to efficient occupational choice can improve society's average economic well-being substantially.

---

[16]C. Hsieh, E. Hurst, C. Jones, and P. Klenow, 2011. "The Allocation of Talent and U.S. Economic Growth," working paper, Stanford University, available at http://klenow.com/HHJK.pdf.

growth was unusually high, in part because of rapid increases in the female labor force participation rate. While growth in capital and employment declined in the 1980s and 1990s, there was a pickup in total factor productivity growth. This increase in total factor productivity growth was the driving force behind the high growth rate in aggregate output in the 1990s. Growth during the period 2000–2009 was particularly low, in part because of cyclical factors; that is, 2009 marks the end of the last recession, when real GDP was temporarily low. However, the average growth in employment, at 0.2% over this nine-year period, is very low, even accounting for the effects of the recession. Then, growth in the period 2009–2014, which is a recovery phase from the recession, would have seen unusually high growth in real GDP, but output growth was in fact unusually low, at only 2.1%. Note that productivity growth, while somewhat soft from 2009–2014, was not as low as during the 1970s, or the period 2000–2009. The major contributor to low growth from 2009–2014 was low growth in factor inputs—both labor and capital.

In the next chapter, we study the persistence in disparities in standards of living across countries of the world and how the Solow growth model addresses these facts. As well, we introduce an endogenous growth model, which is used to discuss convergence in incomes across countries and the role of education in growth, among other issues.

Chapter Summary

- We discussed seven economic growth facts. These were:
  1. Before the Industrial Revolution in about 1800, standards of living differed little over time and across countries.
  2. Since the Industrial Revolution, per capita income growth has been sustained in the richest countries. In the United States, average annual growth in per capita income has been about 2% since 1900.
  3. There is a positive correlation between the rate of investment and output per capita across countries.
  4. There is a negative correlation between the population growth rate and output per capita across countries.
  5. Differences in per capita incomes increased dramatically among countries of the world between 1800 and 1950, with the gap widening between the countries of Western Europe, the United States, Canada, Australia, and New Zealand, as a group, and the rest of the world.
  6. There is essentially no correlation across countries between the level of output per worker in 1960 and the average rate of growth in output per worker for the years 1960–2007.
  7. Richer countries are much more alike in terms of rates of growth of real per capita income than are poor countries.
- The first model was the Malthusian growth model, in which population growth depends positively on consumption per worker, and output is produced from the labor input and a fixed quantity of land.
- The Malthusian model predicts that an increase in total factor productivity has no effect on consumption per worker in the long run, but the population increases. The standard of living can only increase in the long run if population growth is reduced, perhaps by governmental population control.
- The Solow growth model is a model of exogenous growth in that, in the long-run steady state of this model, growth in aggregate output, aggregate consumption, and aggregate investment is explained by exogenous growth in the labor force.
- In the Solow growth model, output per worker converges in the long run to a steady state level, in the absence of a change in total factor productivity. The model predicts that output

per worker increases in the long run when the savings rate increases or when the population growth rate decreases. Both of these predictions are consistent with the data.

- An increase in the savings rate could cause consumption per worker to increase or decrease in the Solow growth model. The golden rule savings rate maximizes consumption per worker in the steady state. The Solow growth model also predicts that a country's standard of living, as measured by income per worker, cannot increase in the long run unless there is ever-increasing total factor productivity.

- Growth accounting is an approach to measuring the contributions to growth in aggregate output from growth in the capital stock, in employment, and in total factor productivity. The latter is measured by the Solow residual.

Key Terms

Exogenous growth model A model in which growth is not caused by forces determined by the model. (p. 234)

Endogenous growth model A model in which growth is caused by forces determined by the model. (p. 234)

Steady state A long-run equilibrium or rest point. The Malthusian model and Solow model both have the property that the economy converges to a single steady state. (p. 241)

Per-worker production function In the Malthusian model, $y = zf(l)$, where y is output per worker, z is total factor productivity, l is the quantity of land per worker, and f is a function. This describes the relationship between output per worker and land per worker, given constant returns to scale. In the Solow growth model, the per-worker production function is

$y = zf(k)$, where y is output per worker, z is total factor productivity, k is the quantity of capital per worker, and f is a function. The per-worker production function in this case describes the relationship between output per worker and capital per worker, given constant returns to scale. (p. 243)

Golden rule quantity of capital per worker The quantity of capital per worker that maximizes consumption per worker in the steady state. (p. 259)

Golden rule savings rate The savings rate that implies consumption per worker is maximized in the steady state of a competitive equilibrium. (p. 261)

Growth accounting Uses the production function and data on aggregate output, the capital input, and the labor input, to measure the contributions of growth in capital, the labor force, and total factor productivity to growth in aggregate output. (p. 269)

Questions for Review

7.1 What is the difference between exogenous growth and endogenous growth?

7.2 What are the seven economic growth facts?

7.3 What is the effect of an increase in total factor productivity on steady state population and consumption per worker in the Malthusian model?

7.4 What can increase the standard of living in the Malthusian model?

7.5 Was Malthus right? Why or why not?

7.6 What are the characteristics of a steady state in the Solow growth model?

7.7 In the Solow growth model, what are the steady state effects of an increase in the savings rate, of an increase in the population growth rate, and of an increase in total factor productivity?

7.8 Explain what determines the golden rule quantity of capital per worker and the golden rule savings rate.

7.9 In what sense does the Solow growth model give optimistic conclusions about the prospects for improvement in the standard of living, relative to the Malthusian model?

7.10 Why is a Cobb–Douglas production function useful for analyzing economic growth?

7.11 What is the parameter a in the production function in Equation (7-21)?

7.12 What does the Solow residual measure, and what are its empirical properties?

Problems

1. **LO 2** In the Malthusian model, suppose that the quantity of land increases. Using diagrams, determine what effects this has in the long-run steady state and explain your results.

2. **LO 2** In the Malthusian model, suppose that there is a technological advance that reduces death rates. Using diagrams, determine the effects of this in the long-run steady state and explain your results.

3. **LO 5** In the Solow growth model, suppose that the marginal product of capital increases for each quantity of the capital input, given the labor input.
   (a) Show the effects of this on the aggregate production function.
   (b) Using a diagram, determine the effects on the quantity of capital per worker and on output per worker in the steady state.
   (c) Explain your results.

4. **LO 5** Suppose that the depreciation rate increases. In the Solow growth model, determine the effects of this on the quantity of capital per worker and on output per worker in the steady state. Explain the economic intuition behind your results.

5. **LO 5** Suppose that the economy is initially in a steady state and that some of the nation's capital stock is destroyed because of a natural disaster or a war.
   (a) Determine the long-run effects of this on the quantity of capital per worker and on output per worker.
   (b) In the short run, does aggregate output grow at a rate higher or lower than the growth rate of the labor force?
   (c) After World War II, growth in real GDP in Germany and Japan was very high. How do your results in parts (a) and (b) shed light on this historical experience?

6. **LO 5** If total factor productivity decreases, determine using diagrams how this affects the golden rule quantity of capital per worker and the golden rule savings rate. Explain your results.

7. **LO 5** Modify the Solow growth model by including government spending as follows. The government purchases G units of consumption goods in the current period, where $G = gN$ and g is a positive constant. The government finances its purchases through lump-sum taxes on consumers, where T denotes total taxes, and the government budget is balanced each period, so that $G = T$. Consumers consume a constant fraction of disposable income—that is, $C = (1 - s)(Y - T)$, where s is the savings rate, with $0 < s < 1$.
   (a) Derive equations similar to Equations (7-18), (7-19), and (7-20), and show in a diagram how the quantity of capital per worker, k^*, is determined.
   (b) Show that there can be two steady states, one with high k^* and the other with low k^*.
   (c) Ignore the steady state with low k^* (it can be shown that this steady state is "unstable"). Determine the effects of an increase in g on capital per worker and on output per worker in the steady state. What are the effects on the growth rates of aggregate output, aggregate consumption, and aggregate investment?
   (d) Explain your results.

8. **LO 5** Determine the effects of a decrease in the population growth rate on the golden rule quantity of capital per worker and on the golden rule savings rate. Explain your results.

9. **LO 5** Consider a numerical example using the Solow growth model. Suppose that $F(K, N) = K^{0.5}N^{0.5}$, with $d = 0.1$, $s = 0.2$, $n = 0.01$, and $z = 1$, and take a period to be a year.
   (a) Determine capital per worker, income per capita, and consumption per capita in the steady state.
   (b) Now, suppose that the economy is initially in the steady state that you calculated in part (a). Then, s increases to 0.4.
      i. Determine capital per worker, income per capita, and consumption per capita

in each of the 10 years following the increase in the savings rate.

ii. Determine capital per worker, income per capita, and consumption per capita in the new steady state.

iii. Discuss your results; in particular, comment on the speed of adjustment to the new steady state after the change in the savings rate, and the paths followed by capital per worker, income per capita, and consumption per capita.

10. **LO 5** Suppose that we modify the Solow growth model by allowing long-run technological progress. That is, suppose that $z = 1$ for convenience, and that there is labor-augmenting technological progress, with a production function

$$Y = F(K, bN),$$

where b denotes the number of units of " human capital" per worker, and bN is "efficiency units" of labor. Letting b' denote future human capital per worker, assume that $b' = (1 + f)b$, where f is the growth rate in human capital.

(a) Show that the long-run equilibrium has the property that $k^{**} = \frac{K}{bN}$ is a constant. At what rate does aggregate output, aggregate consumption, aggregate investment, and per capita income grow in this steady state? Explain.

(b) What is the effect of an increase in f on the growth in per capita income? Discuss relative to how the standard Solow growth model behaves.

11. **LO 5** Alter the Solow growth model so that the production technology is given by $Y = zK$, where Y is output, K is capital, and z is total factor productivity. Thus, output is produced only with capital.

(a) Show that it is possible for income per person to grow indefinitely.

(b) Also show that an increase in the savings rate increases the growth rate in per capita income.

(c) From parts (a) and (b), what are the differences between this model and the basic Solow growth model? Account for these differences and discuss.

12. **LO 5** Consider a numerical example. In the Solow model, assume that $n = 0$, $s = 0.2$, $d = 0.1$,

and $F(K, N) = K^{0.3}N^{0.7}$. Suppose that initially, in period $t = 0$, $z = 1$ and the economy is in a steady state.

(a) Determine consumption, investment, savings, and aggregate output in the initial steady state.

(b) Suppose that at $t = 1$, total factor productivity falls to $z = 0.9$ and then returns to $z = 1$ for periods $t = 2, 3, 4, \ldots$. Calculate consumption, investment, savings, and aggregate output for each period $t = 1, 2, 3, 4, \ldots$.

(c) Repeat part (b) for the case where, at $t = 1$, total factor productivity falls to $z = 0.9$ and then stays there forever.

(d) Discuss your results in parts (a)–(c).

13. **LO 7** Consider the following data:

Year	$\hat{Y}$ (billions of 2009 dollars)	$\hat{K}$ (billions of 2009 dollars)	$\hat{N}$ (millions)
2002	12908.9	39132.6	136.5
2003	13271.1	40043.2	137.7
2004	13773.5	41021.7	139.2
2005	14234.2	41988.9	141.7
2006	14613.8	43045.5	144.4
2007	14873.7	43972.7	146.1
2008	14830.4	44659.0	145.4
2009	14418.7	44944.9	139.9
2010	14783.8	45243.8	139.1
2011	15020.6	45610.0	139.9
2012	15354.6	46059.1	142.5
2013	15583.3	46557.0	143.9
2014	15961.7	47109.5	146.3

(a) Calculate the Solow residual for each year from 2002 to 2014.

(b) Calculate percentage rates of growth in output, capital, employment, and total factor productivity for the years 2002 to 2014. In each year, what contributes the most to growth in aggregate output? What contributes the least? Are there any surprises here? If so, explain.

Working with the Data

Answer these questions using the Federal Reserve Bank of St. Louis's FRED database, accessible at http://research.stlouisfed.org/fred2/

1. Construct time series plots of real GDP, the ratio of consumption to GDP, and the ratio of investment to GDP. In these plots, does what you see conform to the predictions of the Solow growth model? Explain why or why not.

2. In the current population survey (CPS), there are measures of the total working-age population, the labor force, and total employment. Plot these time series in one chart. In the Solow growth model, the population, the labor force, and total employment are exactly the same thing. Do you think that following this modeling approach might miss important elements of labor market behavior? If so, what?

3. The Solow growth model predicts that in the steady state, output per worker grows at the rate of growth in total factor productivity (TFP). Use the ratio of real GDP to total employment (from the current population survey) as a measure of output per worker, and plot this. At what rate does this measure of output per worker grow, on average? What does this tell us about TFP growth?

Chapter 8

Income Disparity Among Countries and Endogenous Growth

Learning Objectives

After studying Chapter 8, students will be able to:

8.1 Show how the Solow model is used to derive predictions about convergence in incomes per capita across countries.

8.2 Construct an equilibrium in the endogenous growth model.

8.3 Use the endogenous growth model to show the effects of economic policy on growth.

8.4 Show the implications of the endogenous growth model for the convergence in incomes per capita across countries.

This chapter extends the material in Chapter 7 to some additional issues related to the predictions of the Solow growth model and to the study of endogenous growth theory. Here, we are particularly interested in learning more about the reasons for the large income disparities that continue to exist among the countries of the world.

The Solow growth model makes strong predictions concerning the ability of poor countries to catch up with rich countries. In particular, in the Solow model, per capita income converges among countries that are initially rich and poor but otherwise identical. The model tells us that countries that are initially poor in terms of per capita income grow at a faster rate than countries that are initially rich. In the context of the Solow growth model, the richest countries of the world look roughly as if they have converged. That is, among the countries that were relatively rich in 1960, subsequent average annual growth rates of per capita income did not differ that much. However, among the poorer countries of the world, per capita income does not appear to be converging, and the poorest countries of the world seem to be falling behind the richest ones, rather than catching up. Therefore, if we suppose that all countries are identical, particularly with regard to the technology they have access to, then the Solow model is not entirely consistent with the way in which the distribution of income is evolving in the world.

However, what if different countries do not have access to the same technology? This can arise if groups that might lose from technological change in particular countries have the power to prevent new technologies from being adopted. For example, if the legal structure in a country gives power to labor unions, then these unions might prevent firms from introducing technologies that make the skills of union members obsolete. As well, political barriers to international trade (tariffs, import quotas, and subsidies) shield firms from international competition and block the incentives to develop new technologies. Then, if different countries have different barriers to technology adoption, this can explain the differences in standards of living across countries, in a manner consistent with the Solow growth model.

We might also observe different aggregate technological capacities across countries if there are differences in the efficiency with which factors of production are allocated across firms in different economies. For example, in sub-Saharan Africa, political corruption and poor financial arrangements may increase profit opportunities for firms that are politically well-connected or happen to know the right bankers, but do not actually possess efficient technologies for producing goods. Rich countries need not be immune from these types of problems. For example, recent work on income and wealth inequality within countries by Thomas Piketty[1] among others, makes the case that, in the United States and other countries, inequality in wealth has increased, and that this tends to breed corruption.

An alternative set of models that can explain persistent differences in standards of living across countries is the set of endogenous growth models. In this chapter, we consider a simple model of endogenous growth, and we show how some of the predictions of this model differ from those of the Solow growth model. The endogenous growth model we study shows how the accumulation of skills and education is important to economic growth. We use the model to evaluate how economic policy might affect the quantity of resources allocated to skills and education and how this affects growth.

In contrast to the Solow growth model, the endogenous growth model we study does not predict convergence in levels of per capita income across countries when countries are identical except for being initially rich and initially poor. In fact, the endogenous growth model predicts that differences in per capita income persist forever. The model indicates some of the factors that can be important in explaining the continuing disparities in living standards between the richest and poorest countries of the world.

Convergence

LO 8.1 Show how the Solow model is used to derive predictions about convergence in incomes per capita across countries.

In Chapter 7, we discussed large disparities that exist in levels of per capita income and in growth rates of per capita income across the countries of the world. While these statistics tell us something about the wide variation in standards of living and in growth

---

[1]See T. Piketty, 2014. *Capital in the Twenty-First Century*, Cambridge, MA: Harvard University Press.

experience in the world, we would also like to know whether these disparities are increasing or decreasing over time and why. Is there a tendency for poor countries to catch up with rich countries with respect to standards of living? If the poor countries are not catching up, why is this so, and what could the poor countries do about it?

The Solow growth model makes strong predictions about the ability of poor countries to catch up with rich ones. For example, suppose two countries are identical with respect to total factor productivities (they share the same technology), labor force growth rates, and savings rates. However, the rich country initially has a higher level of capital per worker than does the poor country. Given the per-worker production function, the rich country also has a higher quantity of output per worker than the poor country. The Solow growth model predicts that both countries will converge to the same level of capital per worker and output per worker. Ultimately, the poor country will catch up with the rich country with regard to living standards.

In Figure 8.1, we show the relationship between current capital per worker, k, and future capital per worker, k', from the Solow growth model. The poor country initially has quantity k_p of capital per worker, while the rich country initially has quantity k_r of capital per worker. Capital per worker and output per worker grow in both countries, but in the long run, both countries have k^* units of capital per worker and the same quantity of output per worker. In Figure 8.2 we show the paths followed over time by real income per worker in the rich country and the poor country. The initial gap between the rich and poor countries narrows over time and disappears in the long run.

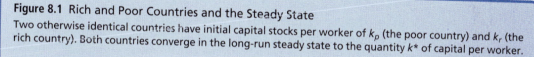

Figure 8.1 Rich and Poor Countries and the Steady State

Two otherwise identical countries have initial capital stocks per worker of k_p (the poor country) and k_r (the rich country). Both countries converge in the long-run steady state to the quantity k^* of capital per worker.

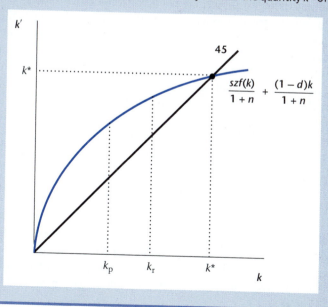

Figure 8.2 Convergence in Income per Worker Across Countries in the Solow Growth Model
Two otherwise identical countries, one with lower income per worker (the poor country) than the other (the rich country), both converge in the long-run steady state to the same level of income per worker, y_1^*.

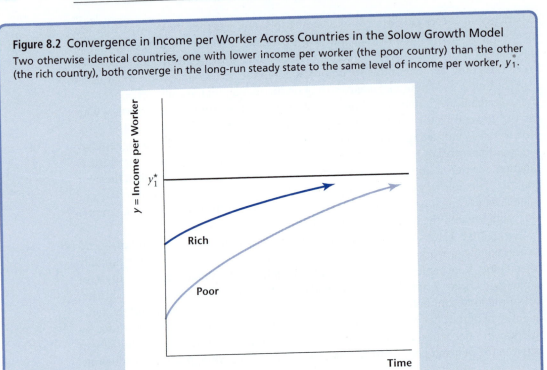

Both the countries in the above example also have identical growth rates of aggregate output (equal to their identical labor force growth rates) in the long run. Recall that the Solow growth model predicts that aggregate output will grow at the rate of labor force growth in the long run, and so if the rich and poor countries have the same labor force growth rate, their long-run growth rates in aggregate output will be identical. Supposing that the rich and poor countries also have the same initial labor force levels, the growth paths of aggregate output, as predicted by the Solow growth model, will be the same in the long run. In Figure 8.3, the black line denotes the long-run growth path of the natural logarithm of aggregate output in the rich and poor countries. As predicted by the Solow growth model, if aggregate output is initially lower in the poor country, its growth rate in aggregate output will be larger than that for the rich country, and this will cause the level of aggregate output in the poor country to catch up to the level in the rich country. In the long run, growth in aggregate output in the rich and poor countries converges to the same rate.

Therefore, given no differences among countries in terms of access to technology, the Solow model is quite optimistic about the prospects for countries of the world that are currently poor. Under these conditions the model predicts that, left alone, the countries of the world will converge to similar standards of living, with some differences across countries explained by differences in savings rates and population growth rates.

Figure 8.3 Convergence in Aggregate Output Across Countries in the Solow Growth Model
The initially rich country and the initially poor country converge in the long run to the same long-run growth path, where aggregate output grows at a constant rate.

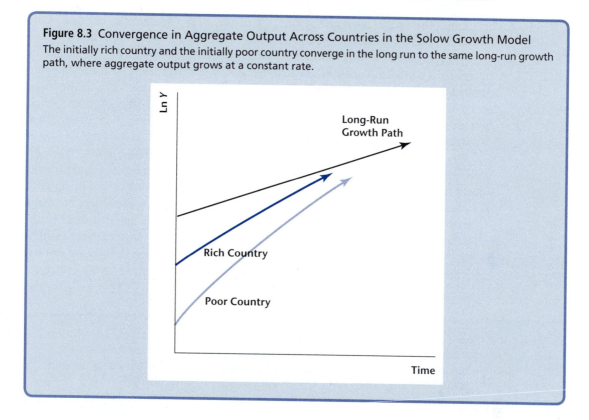

However, there are several good reasons why different countries will not have access to the same technology, and as a result total factor productivity differs across countries. First, it could take time for workers and managers to learn to use a new technology. In Chapter 7, we discussed how the productivity slowdown that occurred in the United States from the late 1960s into the 1980s could be explained as a learning period over which new information technology was absorbed. Such a process is called **learning by doing**. Just as learning by doing plays a role in the adoption of a technology that is new in the world, it can be important in how technologies spread from country to country. In general, we should expect a learning period for the technologies that are used in rich countries to spread to poorer countries. As a result, learning by doing could cause total factor productivity differences among countries to persist.

Second, productivity differences can persist across countries because of barriers to the adoption of new technology.[2] Such barriers could be the result of union power which, while it protects the interests of existing workers in firms, can prevent the reorganization of production or the introduction of new types of capital equipment. As well, barriers to technology adoption could be the result of trade restrictions or government subsidies that protect domestic industries. A protected industry will be less inclined to invest in research and development that makes it more competitive in world markets.

---

[2] See S. Parente and E. Prescott, 2000. *Barriers to Riches*, Cambridge, MA: MIT Press.

Third, the level of aggregate technology can differ across countries because of the efficiency with which factors of production are allocated across firms in the economy. For example, political corruption can result in advantages for inefficient firms, for instance if a politician's relatives are awarded government contracts, or if subsidies are granted to industries in exchange for bribes. As well, the less developed is the financial sector of the economy, the less ill-equipped is the economy to allocate resources to their best uses. For example, in an economy with poor financial markets, an innovative new firm may find it difficult to borrow to start up.

To the extent that learning by doing, barriers to the adoption of new technology, and inefficiencies in the allocation of factors of production differ across countries, this causes total factor productivity to differ, and convergence in standards of living does not occur. To see how this works, consider Figure 8.4. Suppose that there are three different countries, which we call poor, middle income, and rich, and that these countries have levels of total factor productivity z_p, z_m, and z_r, respectively, where $z_p < z_m < z_r$. We also suppose that these countries have identical population growth rates and identical savings rates. Then in Figure 8.4, in the steady state the poor,

Figure 8.4 Differences in Total Factor Productivity Can Explain Disparity in Income per Worker Across Countries

If countries have different levels of total factor productivity due to differing barriers to technology adoption, then capital per worker and income per worker differ across countries in the steady state.

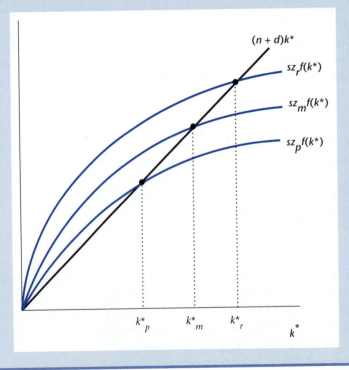

THEORY CONFRONTS THE DATA

Is Income Per Worker Converging in the World?

If income per worker were converging among countries of the world, we would observe over time that the dispersion in income per worker was falling. As well, if we observed the countries of the world at a given point in time, we would see that income per worker was growing at a higher rate in poor countries than in rich countries. That is, we should see a negative correlation between the rate of growth in income per worker and the level of income per worker across countries.

In this section, we look at the evidence for convergence in the world economy. From fact (6) in the Economic Growth Facts section in Chapter 7 recall that, when we look at all countries in the world, there is essentially no correlation between the level of output per worker in 1960 and the average growth rate of output per worker between 1960 and 2007. Fact (7) is that richer countries are much more alike in terms of rates of growth of real per capita income than are poor countries. Therefore, between 1960 and 2007 there appeared to be no convergence among all the countries in the world. However, there is evidence for convergence among the richest countries of the world for the same period, since these countries behave roughly like a group of countries that has achieved convergence, in that their growth rates of per capita income do not differ much (at least relative to what we see for poor countries).

The following story makes these observations on convergence from the data consistent with the predictions of the Solow growth model. First, we can think of the richest countries of the world in 1960 (the Western European countries, the United States, Canada, Australia, and New Zealand) as having access to roughly the same technology. The Solow growth model then tells us that we should expect convergence in standards of living among these countries, with some minor differences accounted for by differences in population growth and savings rates. Second, the tendency for differences in standards of living to persist among the poor countries of the world can be explained in the Solow model by different levels of total factor productivity in those countries brought about by differing barriers to technology adoption, and differing degrees of inefficiency in the allocation of factors of production among firms in the economy.

To support the idea that persistent disparity in per capita income across countries could be caused by barriers to technology adoption, we need additional evidence for the existence of such barriers and evidence that the barriers differ significantly among countries. In their book, *Barriers to Riches,* Stephen Parente and Edward Prescott provide considerable evidence of both types in examining experience in particular industries and countries.[3] They argue that evidence of resistance to the adoption of new technology can be found in the textiles industry and in the mining industry in the United States. Further, if we look at particular industries and measure productivities in those industries across countries, the evidence supports the idea that barriers to technology adoption are important for explaining productivity differences.

A key feature of the data that supports the idea that there are barriers preventing poor countries from adopting the technologies used by the richest countries of the world is that growth

---

[3]See S. Parente and E. Prescott, 2000. *Barriers to Riches,* Cambridge, MA: MIT Press.

(Continued)

miracles have not occurred for the very rich. In the United States, as we observed in Chapter 7 the growth rate of per capita income has not strayed far from 2% per annum since 1900. The important growth miracles after World War II occurred in Japan, South Korea, Taiwan, Singapore, and Hong Kong. At the time when growth took off in these countries, they were all well behind the standard of living in the United States. The growth miracles in these countries are consistent with barriers to technology adoption being removed, which then allowed per capita income to quickly approach that of the United States.

Some economists have studied the extent of the effect of the misallocation of factors of production across firms in explaining cross-country differences in standards of living. For example, Chang-Tai Hsieh and Peter Klenow estimate that if capital and labor were allocated as efficiently across firms in China and India as in the United States, then total factor productivity would by 30%–50% higher in China, and 40%–60% higher in India.[4] This evidence suggests that the elimination of government corruption, inefficiencies in the financial sector, and inefficient taxes and subsidies, could go a long way toward making the countries of the world look more alike in terms of their standards of living.

---

[4]C. Hsieh and P. Klenow, 2009. " Misallocation and Manufacturing TFP in China and India," *Quarterly Journal of Economics* 124, 1403–1448.

MACROECONOMICS IN ACTION

Measuring Economic Welfare: Per Capita Income, Income Distribution, Leisure, and Longevity

In this chapter, we have focused attention on a particular measure of a nation's economic well-being, per capita real GDP. As was discussed in Chapter 2, per capita GDP is a good measure of market economic activity, which is indeed highly positively correlated with aggregate economic welfare. However, per capita real GDP misses several dimensions of economic activity and economic welfare that are important for assessing a country's economic health, and for making comparisons across countries.

What does per capita real GDP miss as a measure of aggregate economic welfare? First, this measure takes no account of how income is distributed across the population. At the extreme, society is not well-off if one person has all the income and the rest of the population has nothing. Everything else held constant, in a society we might prefer a more egalitarian distribution of income. The issue of income and wealth distribution has become more pressing in recent years. For reasons having to do with the demand for high-skilled workers, changes in technology, and import competition from less-developed countries, the wage gap between high-skilled and low-skilled workers has grown in the United States. This has tended to increase the dispersion in income across households in developed countries. As well, there has been a growing public concern, particularly following the financial crisis, that people working in the upper echelons of the financial industry and receiving top incomes were somehow undeserving of their rewards. Such concerns are legitimate, as some of those high financial incomes were the result of government bailouts (redistribution of income by the government from the poor to the rich), corruption, and possibly fraud.

A second drawback to real GDP per capita as a measure of economic welfare is that it does not account for leisure. A country may be well-off in part because its inhabitants spend all of their time working, and little time enjoying the fruits of their labor. Third, the health of the population matters, something that we can measure by longevity. Finally, a country may have high income but low consumption, if it invests a lot, or is indebted to the residents of other countries. We would rather account for economic welfare by measuring consumption instead of income.

Research by Charles Jones and Peter Klenow[5] is aimed at deriving a single number for a given country that can capture all of the above factors, and that is a measure of economic welfare that can be compared across countries. The welfare measure is derived from a choice-theoretic framework, and yields a number in units of consumption for the average person.

The Jones–Klenow results are very interesting. In one sense, their research is assuring in that it shows that real GDP per capita is useful as a rough guide in making welfare comparisons across countries. Jones and Klenow find that the correlation between their welfare measure and real GDP per capita across countries is 0.95. However, the Jones–Klenow measure shrinks the difference between Western European countries and the United States. For example, in 2000, France had per capita real income that was 70% of what it was in the United States, but by the Jones–Klenow welfare measure, residents of France were 94% as well off as residents of the United States. This shrinkage is due to the fact that the French are more egalitarian, they take more leisure, and they live longer than Americans.

---

[5]C. Jones and P. Klenow, 2011. "Beyond GDP? Welfare Across Countries and Time," working paper, Stanford University, available at http://klenow.com/Jones_Klenow.pdf.

---

middle income, and rich countries have levels of capital per worker of k_p^*, k_m^*, and k_r^*, respectively, so that output per worker in the steady state is ranked according to poor, middle income, and rich, in ascending order. In the steady state, standards of living are permanently different in the three countries, but aggregate output grows at the same rate. Thus, the Solow model can explain disparities across countries in per capita income, if there are factors that cause aggregate total factor productivity to differ across countries.

If the large disparity in per capita incomes across countries of the world is in part due to differences in total factor productivity, what can poor countries do to catch up with the rich countries? First, governments can promote greater competition among firms. If monopoly power is not protected by governments, then firms have to develop and implement new technologies to remain competitive, so that productivity will be higher. Second, governments can promote free trade. Just as with greater domestic competition, greater competition among countries promotes innovation and the adoption of the best technologies. Third, governments should privatize production where there is no good economic case for government ownership. Government ownership where it is unnecessary often leads to protection of employment at the expense of efficiency, and this tends to lower total factor productivity. Fourth, governments can act to mitigate political corruption.

Endogenous Growth: A Model of Human Capital Accumulation

Perhaps the primary deficiency of the Solow growth model is that it does not explain a key observation, which is growth itself. The Solow model relies on increases in total factor productivity coming from outside the model to generate long-run increases in per capita output, and this seems unsatisfactory, as we would like to understand the economic forces behind increases in total factor productivity. Total factor productivity growth involves research and development by firms, education, and training on the job, and all of these activities are responsive to the economic environment. We might like an economic growth model to answer the following questions: How does total factor productivity growth respond to the quantity of public funds spent on public education? How is total factor productivity growth affected by subsidies to research and development? Does it make sense to have the government intervene to promote economic growth? While the Solow growth model cannot answer these questions, a model of endogenous growth, where growth rates are explained by the model, potentially can.

The endogenous growth model that we work with here is a simplification of a model developed by Robert Lucas.[6] Another important earlier contributor to research on endogenous growth was Paul Romer.[7] In the model, the representative consumer allocates his or her time between supplying labor to produce output and accumulating **human capital**, where human capital is the accumulated stock of skills and education that a worker has at a point in time. The higher the human capital that workers have, the more they can produce, and the more new human capital they can produce. Thus, a higher level of human capital means that the economy can grow at a faster rate.

If we think in terms of real-world economies, at any given time some of the working-age population is employed and producing goods and services, some are in school, and some are unemployed or not in the labor force. There is a social opportunity cost associated with people of working age who are in school, as these people could otherwise be producing goods and services. By acquiring schooling, however, people accumulate skills (human capital), and a more highly skilled labor force in the future permits more future output to be produced. Also, a more highly skilled population can better pass on skills to others, and so human capital accumulation is more efficient if the level of human capital is higher.

Human capital accumulation, therefore, is an investment, just like investment in plant and equipment, as there are associated current costs and future benefits. However, there are good reasons to think that physical investment is fundamentally different from human capital investment, in addition to the obvious difference that physical investment is embodied in machines and buildings, and human capital investment is embodied in people. Recall that in the Solow growth model there are diminishing marginal returns to the accumulation of physical capital, because adding more capital to a fixed labor force should eventually yield lower increases in output at the margin. Human capital

---

[6] R. Lucas, 1988. " On the Mechanics of Economic Development," *Journal of Monetary Economics* 22, July, 3–42.

[7] See P. Romer, 1986. " Increasing Returns and Long-Run Growth," *Journal of Political Economy* 94, 500–521.

accumulation differs in that there appears to be no limit to human knowledge or to how productive individuals can become given increases in knowledge and skills. Paul Romer has argued that a key feature of knowledge is **nonrivalry**.[8] That is, a particular person's acquisition of knowledge does not reduce the ability of someone else to acquire the same knowledge. Most goods are rivalrous; for example, my consumption of hotel services limits the ability of others to benefit from hotel services, as only a fixed number of hotel rooms is available in a given city at a given time. Physical capital accumulation also involves rivalry, as the acquisition of plant and equipment by a firm uses up resources that could be used by other firms to acquire plant and equipment. Diminishing marginal returns to human capital investment seems unnatural. The lack of diminishing returns to human capital investment leads to unbounded growth in the model we study here, even though there are no exogenous forces propelling economic growth.

The Representative Consumer

Our endogenous growth model has a representative consumer, who starts the current period with H^s units of human capital. In each period, the consumer has one unit of time (as in the Malthusian model and the Solow model, the fact that there is one unit of time is simply a normalization), which can be allocated between work and accumulating human capital. For simplicity, we assume the consumer does not use time for leisure. Let u denote the fraction of time devoted to working in each period, so that the number of **efficiency units of labor** devoted to work is uH^s. That is, the number of units of labor that the consumer effectively supplies is the number of units of time spent working multiplied by the consumer's quantity of human capital. The consumer's quantity of human capital is the measure of the productivity of the consumer's time when he or she is working. For each efficiency unit of labor supplied, the consumer receives the current real wage w. For simplicity, we assume the consumer cannot save, and so the consumer's budget constraint in the current period is

$$C = wuH^s, \tag{8-1}$$

or consumption is equal to total labor earnings.

Though the consumer cannot save, he or she can trade-off current consumption for future consumption by accumulating human capital. Because u units of time are used for work, the remainder, $1 - u$, is used for human capital accumulation. The technology for accumulating human capital is given by

$$H^{s'} = b(1 - u)H^s; \tag{8-2}$$

that is, the stock of human capital in the future period, denoted by $H^{s'}$, varies in proportion to the number of current efficiency units of labor devoted to human capital accumulation, which is $(1 - u)H^s$. Here, b is a parameter that captures the efficiency of the human capital accumulation technology, with $b > 0$. Thus, Equation (8-2) represents the idea that accumulating skills and education is easier, the more skills and education an individual (or society) has.

---

[8]See P. Romer, 1990. "Endogenous Technological Change," *Journal of Political Economy* 98, S71–S102.

The Representative Firm

For simplicity there is no physical capital in this model, and the representative firm produces output using only efficiency units of labor. The production function is given by

$$Y = zuH^d, \tag{8-3}$$

where Y is current output, $z > 0$ is the marginal product of efficiency units of labor, and uH^d is the current input of efficiency units of labor into production. That is, uH^d is the demand for efficiency units of labor by the representative firm. The production function in Equation (8-3) has constant returns to scale, because there is only one input into production, efficiency units of labor, and increasing the quantity of efficiency units of labor increases output in the same proportion. For example, increasing efficiency units of labor uH^d by 1% increases current output by 1%.

The representative firm hires the quantity of efficiency units of labor, uH^d, that maximizes current profits, where profits are

$$\pi = Y - wuH^d,$$

which is the quantity of output produced minus the wages paid to workers. Substituting for Y from Equation (8-3), we get

$$\pi = zuH^d - wuH^d = (z - w)uH^d. \tag{8-4}$$

If $z - w < 0$, then in Equation (8-4) profits are negative if the firm hires a positive quantity of efficiency units of labor, so that the firm maximizes profits by setting $uH^d = 0$. If $z - w > 0$, then profits are $z - w$ for each efficiency unit hired, so that the firm wants to hire an infinite quantity of workers to maximize profits. If $z = w$, then the firm's profits are zero for any quantity of workers hired, so that the firm is indifferent about the quantity of efficiency units of labor hired. We conclude that the firm's demand curve for efficiency units of labor is infinitely elastic at $w = z$. In Figure 8.5 we show the firm's demand curve for efficiency units of labor, which is just a special case of the demand curve being identical to the marginal product schedule for efficiency units of labor. Here, the marginal product of efficiency units of labor is a constant, z. Thus, no matter what the supply curve for efficiency units of labor, the intersection between demand and supply always occurs, as in Figure 8.5, at a real wage of $w = z$. In other words, the equilibrium real wage per efficiency unit of labor is always $w = z$. This then implies that the real wage per hour of work is $wH^d = zH^d$, and so the real wage as we would measure it empirically changes in proportion to the quantity of human capital of the representative consumer.

Competitive Equilibrium

LO 8.2 Construct an equilibrium in the endogenous growth model.

Working out the competitive equilibrium is quite straightforward. There is only one market each period, on which consumption goods are traded for efficiency units of labor, and we know already that this market always clears at a real wage of $w = z$.

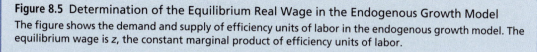

Figure 8.5 Determination of the Equilibrium Real Wage in the Endogenous Growth Model
The figure shows the demand and supply of efficiency units of labor in the endogenous growth model. The equilibrium wage is z, the constant marginal product of efficiency units of labor.

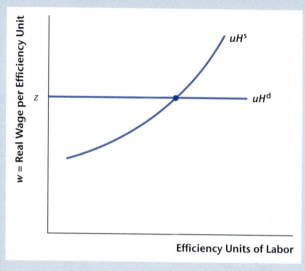

Market clearing gives $uH^s = uH^d$ (the supply of efficiency units of labor is equal to the demand), and so $H^s = H^d = H$. Therefore, substituting in Equations (8-1) and (8-2) for w and H^s, we get

$$C = zuH, \tag{8-5}$$

and

$$H' = b(1 - u)H. \tag{8-6}$$

Therefore, Equation (8-6) determines future human capital H' given current human capital H, and we show this relationship in Figure 8.6. The slope of the colored line in the figure is $b(1 - u)$, and if $b(1 - u) > 1$, then we have $H' > H$, so that future human capital is always greater than current human capital, and, therefore, human capital grows over time without bound. From Equation (8-6), the growth rate of human capital is

$$\frac{H'}{H} - 1 = b(1 - u) - 1, \tag{8-7}$$

which is a constant. What is important here is that the growth rate of human capital increases if b increases or if u decreases. Recall that b determines the efficiency of the human capital accumulation technology, which could be interpreted as the efficiency of the educational sector. Thus, the model predicts that countries with more efficient education systems should experience higher rates of growth in human capital. If u decreases, then more time is devoted to human capital accumulation and less to

Figure 8.6 Human Capital Accumulation in the Endogenous Growth Model

The colored line shows the quantity of future human capital H' as a function of current human capital H. As drawn $H' > H$ for any H, so human capital continues to increase forever.

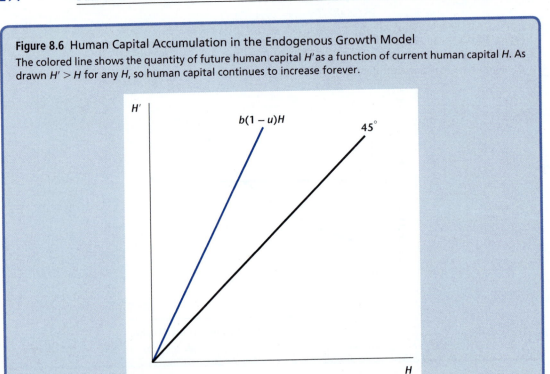

producing output in each period. As seems natural, this causes the growth rate in human capital to increase.

Now, Equation (8-5) will also hold in the future period, so that $C' = zuH'$ where C' is future consumption, and, therefore, from Equation (8-5) we can determine the growth rate of consumption, which is

$$\frac{C'}{C} - 1 = \frac{zuH'}{zuH} - 1 = \frac{H'}{H} - 1 = b(1 - u) - 1;$$

that is, the growth rate of consumption is identical to the growth rate of human capital. Further, from Equations (8-3) and (8-5), $C = Y$, which we also know must hold in equilibrium, given the income–expenditure identity from Chapter 2 (our model has no investment, no government, and no net exports). Therefore, human capital, consumption, and output all grow at the same rate, $b(1 - u) - 1$, in equilibrium.

This model economy does not grow because of any exogenous forces. There is no population growth (there is a single representative consumer), and the production technology does not change over time (b and z remain fixed). Growth occurs, therefore, because of endogenous forces, with the growth rate determined by b and u. The key element in the model that leads to unbounded growth is the fact that the production function, given by Equation (8-3), does not exhibit decreasing returns to scale in human capital. That is, the production function has constant returns to scale in human capital, because output increases in proportion to human capital, given u. For example, if human capital increases by 10%, then, holding u constant, output increases by 10%. In the Solow growth model, growth is limited because of the decreasing marginal product of physical capital, but here the marginal product of human capital does not decrease as the quantity of human capital used in production increases. The marginal product of human capital does not fall as human capital increases, because knowledge and skills are nonrivalrous; additional education and skills do not reduce the extra output that can be achieved through the acquisition of more education and skills.

Economic Policy and Growth

LO 8.3 Use the endogenous growth model to show the effects of economic policy on growth.

Our endogenous growth model suggests that government policies can affect the growth rates of aggregate output and consumption. Because the common growth rate of human capital, consumption, and output depends on b and u, it is useful to think about how government policy might affect b and u. As b is the efficiency of the human capital accumulation technology, b could be affected by government policies that make the educational system more efficient. For example, this might be accomplished through the implementation of better incentives for performance in the school system, or possibly by changing the mix of public and private education. Exactly what policies the government would have to pursue to increase b we cannot say here without being much more specific in modeling the education system. However, it certainly seems feasible for governments to affect the efficiency of education, and politicians seem to believe this, too.

Government policy could also change the rate of economic growth by changing u. For example, this could be done through taxes or subsidies to education. If the government subsidizes education, then such a policy would make human capital accumulation more desirable relative to current production, and so u would decrease and the growth rate of output and consumption would increase.

Suppose that the government had the power to decrease u or to increase b, thus increasing the growth rate of consumption and output. Would this be a good idea or not? To answer this question, we would have to ask how the representative consumer's welfare would change as a result. Clearly, a decrease in u increases the growth rate of consumption, which is $b(1 - u) - 1$, but there is also a second effect, in that the level of consumption goes down. That is, current consumption is $C = zuH$, and so in the very first period if u decreases, then C must also fall, because initial human capital H is given. Recall from Chapter 1 that if we graph the natural logarithm of a variable against time, then the slope of the graph is approximately the growth rate. Because consumption grows at the constant rate $b(1 - u) - 1$ in equilibrium, if we graph the natural log of consumption against time, this is a straight line. The slope of the graph of consumption increases as u decreases and the growth rate of consumption increases, and the vertical intercept of the graph decreases as u decreases, as this reduces consumption in the very first period. There is, therefore, a trade-off for the representative consumer when u decreases: Consumption is sacrificed early on, but consumption grows at a higher rate, so that consumption ultimately is higher than it was with a higher level of u.

Thus, the path for consumption shifts as in Figure 8.7. In the figure, consumption is lower after the change in u until period T, and after period T, consumption is higher than it would otherwise have been.

It is not clear that the consumer would prefer the new consumption path with the higher growth rate of consumption, even though consumption is higher in the long run. There is a cost to higher growth, which is that consumption in the near term must be forgone. Which consumption path the consumer prefers depends on how patient he or she is. Preferences could be such that the consumer is very impatient, in which case he or she would tend to prefer the initial consumption path with a low growth rate of consumption. Alternatively, the consumer might be very patient, tending to prefer the new consumption path with a high growth rate of consumption. The conclusion is that, even if the government could engineer a higher rate of growth by causing u to fall—say through education subsidies—this may not be desirable because of the near-term costs involved.

We could do a similar analysis for the case in which the government causes the growth rate of consumption to increase through an increase in b, the parameter governing the efficiency of human capital accumulation. In this case, the model is not explicit about the near-term costs of increasing the growth rate of consumption by increasing

Figure 8.7 Effect of a Decrease in u on the Consumption Path in the Endogenous Growth Model
The figure shows the effect of a decrease in u, which increases the fraction of time spent accumulating human capital each period. The growth path for consumption (consumption is equal to income) pivots; thus, there is a short-run decrease in consumption, but consumption is higher in the long run.

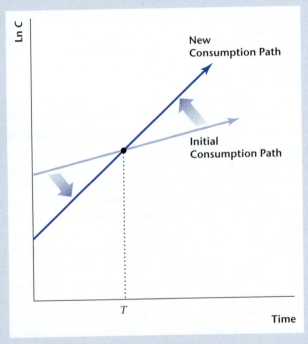

b. That is, current consumption is given by $C = zuH$, and so consumption in the very first period does not depend on *b*. However, if the government were to increase *b* through education policy, for example, this would entail some real resource costs. Suppose that the government chose to make public education more efficient by increasing monitoring of teacher and student performance. Clearly, there would be a cost to this monitoring in terms of labor time. We might represent this cost in our model as a reduction in the level of consumption, as labor is diverted from goods production to government monitoring activities. Therefore, *b* would increase, which would increase the growth rate of consumption, but as in the case in which we examined the effects of a decrease in *u*, there would be a decrease in consumption in the very first period. Thus, the relationship between the new consumption path after the increase in *b* and the initial consumption path would be just as in Figure 8.7. As in the case where *u* falls, it is not clear whether the representative consumer is better off when the growth rate of consumption is higher, because there are short-term costs in terms of lost consumption.

Convergence in the Endogenous Growth Model

LO 8.4 Show the implications of the endogenous growth model for the convergence in incomes per capita across countries.

In the Solow growth model, with exogenous growth, countries that are in all respects identical, except for their initial quantities of capital per worker, have in the long run the same level and growth rate of income per worker. We showed in the previous section that this prediction of the Solow growth model is consistent with data on the evolution of per capita income in the richest countries of the world but not with data for poorer countries. To explain disparities among the poor countries, and disparities between the rich and poor, with the Solow model, we must appeal to significant differences among countries in something exogenous in the Solow growth model, which could be total factor productivity.

In the endogenous growth model we have constructed here, convergence does not occur even if countries are identical in all respects except that there are differences in the initial level of human capital. To see this, note first that in the endogenous growth model, consumption is equal to income, and there is only one consumer, so that per capita income is identical to aggregate income. Accordingly, current consumption is given by $C = zuH$, and consumption grows at a constant rate $b(1 - u) - 1$, so that the natural log of consumption graphed against time is a straight line, as we showed in Figure 8.7. Now, suppose that we consider two countries that have the same technology and allocate labor in the same way between goods production and human capital accumulation. That is, *b*, *z*, and *u* are the same in the two countries. However, suppose that these countries differ according to their initial human capital levels. The rich country has a high level of initial human capital, denoted H_r, and the poor country has a low level of human capital, denoted H_p, which implies that consumption in the rich country is initially $C = zuH_r$, which is greater than initial consumption in the poor country, $C = zuH_p$. Now, because *b* and *u* are identical in the two countries, $b(1 - u) - 1$, the growth rate of consumption, is also identical for the rich and poor countries. Therefore, the growth paths of consumption for the rich country and the poor country are as in

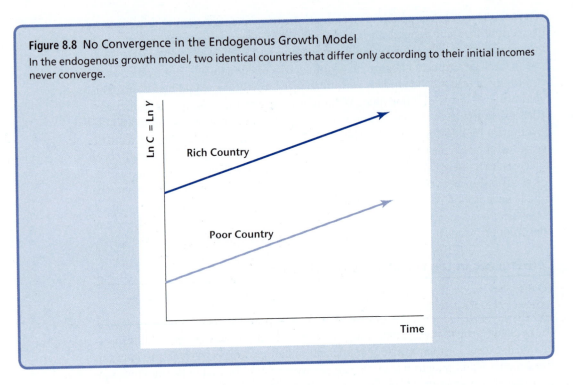

Figure 8.8 No Convergence in the Endogenous Growth Model
In the endogenous growth model, two identical countries that differ only according to their initial incomes never converge.

Figure 8.8. That is, initial differences in income and consumption across rich and poor countries persist forever, and there is no convergence.

How do we reconcile the predictions of the endogenous growth model concerning convergence with the facts? The model appears consistent with the fact that there are persistent differences in per capita income among poorer countries and persistent differences in per capita income between the poorer countries of the world and the richer countries. However, the model appears inconsistent with the fact that per capita incomes seem to have converged among the richer nations of the world. Perhaps an explanation for this is that in regions of the world where labor and capital are mobile, and where skills are more easily transferred, there are important **human capital externalities**, as discussed by Robert Lucas.[9] A human capital externality exists when contact with others with high levels of human capital increases our human capital or makes us more productive. Human capital externalities can explain the existence of cities and the specialized activities that take place there. Why, for example, would people specializing in financial activities want to bear the congestion and pollution of New York City unless there were significant positive externalities involved in working there? In highly developed regions of the world where there are greater opportunities, through business contacts and education in other countries and regions, for taking advantage of human capital externalities, large differences in the levels of human capital across regions

---

[9] R. Lucas, 1988. " On the Mechanics of Economic Development," *Journal of Monetary Economics* 22, July, 3–42.

MACROECONOMICS IN ACTION

Education and Growth

In cross-country economic data, economists have observed that there is a positive correlation between the level of education of a country's population (as measured for example by average years of schooling across the population) and the rate of growth in real GDP[10]. Mark Bils and Peter Klenow estimate that in terms of average educational attainment of a country in 1960, one more year of schooling on average is associated with 0.30 more percentage points in average annual growth in GDP per capita from 1960 to 1990[11]. One might be tempted to conclude, given this observation, that a more highly educated population *causes* the economic growth rate to rise. Then, some might argue that, since economic growth is a good thing, it would be a good idea for the government to take steps to increase schooling and boost growth. However, this argument would be sloppy economics.

A correlation observed in economic data need not reflect causation, just as correlations observed in other kinds of scientific data need not tell us what causes what. For example, one could conclude from observing a positive correlation in the incidence of lung cancer and smoking across the population that lung cancer causes people to smoke. There are at least two other possible explanations for the lung cancer/smoking correlation. One is that there is some third factor that is correlated with both the incidence of lung cancer and with smoking, and that

is actually the root explanation for the correlation. For example, it could be that poor people tend to have lung cancer, and poor people tend to smoke, and that there is something about being poor (bad living conditions, for example) that causes lung cancer. A second alternative explanation—the one backed by a large body of scientific evidence—is that smoking causes lung cancer.

Now, in terms of the correlation between average educational attainment and economic growth, we have an analogous empirical problem to the one of interpreting the correlation between lung cancer and smoking. That is, the correlation between education and growth could mean that (i) higher education causes the growth rate of GDP to be higher; (ii) some third factor causes educational attainment and the growth rate of GDP to be positively correlated; or (iii) higher economic growth causes more education. In fact, all of (i)–(iii) could be at work, and as economists we are interested in how each of (i)–(iii) contributes to the correlation, in part because this will be informative about the potential effects of government policies toward education. This is the type of exercise carried out by Mark Bils and Peter Klenow in an article in the *American Economic Review.*[12]

What are the particular economic mechanisms at work in cases (i)–(iii) above? For (i), the model of endogenous growth we studied in the previous section of this chapter provides some insight into how more education can cause the economic growth rate to be higher. In the model,

---

[10]See, for example, R. Barro, 1990. " Economic Growth in a Cross Section of Countries," *Quarterly Journal of Economics* 106, 407–443.

[11]M. Bils and P. Klenow, 2000. " Does Schooling Cause Growth?" *American Economic Review* 90, 1160–1183.

[12]M. Bils and P. Klenow, 2000. " Does Schooling Cause Growth?" *American Economic Review* 90, 1160–1183.

(Continued)

if the average individual in society devotes more time to accumulating human capital, which we can interpret as education, then aggregate output will grow at a higher rate. For (ii), how might factors other than education and economic growth cause educational attainment and the economic growth rate to move together? As Bils and Klenow argue, in countries with sound legal systems that adequately enforce property rights, educational attainment is high because people know that investing in education will have large future payoffs. In such societies, the growth rate of GDP is also high, in part because the enforcement of property rights leads to greater innovation, research, and development. Thus, we will see a positive correlation across countries between education and growth, but not because

of a direct causal relationship between the two. Finally, for (iii), educational attainment could be high because people anticipate high future economic growth. A high rate of future economic growth will imply a high rate of return to education, since a high rate of growth should increase the gap between the wages of high-skill and low-skill workers.

Bils and Klenow essentially find that causation running from education to growth accounts for only about 30% of the relationship between education and growth. This suggests that if we are interested in government policies that promote growth, then perhaps improvements in patent policy or in the role of government in research and development are more important than improvements in education policy.

cannot persist, and there is convergence in income per worker. However, less developed countries interact to a low degree with highly developed countries, and people with high levels of human capital tend to move to the highly developed countries from the less developed countries (the " brain drain"). Thus, differences in human capital can persist across very rich and very poor countries.

We have now completed our study of economic growth in this part. In Part IV, we move on to a detailed examination of savings behavior and government deficits, and we begin building a model that is the basis for our study of business cycles.

Chapter Summary

- If all countries are identical, except for initial differences in capital per worker, the Solow growth model predicts that there will be convergence among countries. That is, in the long run, all countries will have the same level of income per worker, and aggregate income will be growing at the same rate in all countries.

- In the data, there is evidence for convergence among the richest countries of the world, but convergence does not appear to be occurring among all countries or among the poorest countries.

- The Solow growth model is consistent with the data if total factor productivity differs across countries. Productivity differences can result from learning by doing, barriers to technology adoption, and inefficiencies within countries in the allocation of factors of production.

- We constructed an endogenous growth model with human capital accumulation. This model has the property that, even with no increases in total factor productivity and no population growth, there can be unlimited growth in aggregate output and aggregate consumption, fueled by growth in the stock of human capital (i.e., skills and education).

- In the endogenous growth model, the rate of growth of output and consumption is determined by the efficiency of human capital accumulation and the allocation of labor time between goods production and human capital accumulation.

- If the government could introduce policies that altered the efficiency of human capital accumulation or the allocation of labor time, it could alter the rate of economic growth in the endogenous growth model.

- Increasing the rate of economic growth may or may not improve economic welfare, because an increase in the growth rate of aggregate consumption is always associated with lower consumption in the short run.

- In the endogenous growth model, per capita incomes do not converge across rich and poor countries, even if countries are identical except for initial levels of human capital.

Key Terms

Learning by doing The process by which total factor productivity increases over time with the use of a new technology. (p. 285)

Human capital The accumulated stock of skills and education that a worker has at a point in time. (p. 290)

Nonrivalry A feature of knowledge, in that acquisition of knowledge does not reduce the ability of others to acquire it. (p. 291)

Efficiency units of labor The effective number of units of labor input after adjusting for the quantity of human capital possessed by workers. (p. 291)

Human capital externalities Effects that exist if the human capital of others affects one's productivity. (p. 298)

Questions For Review

8.1 If countries are initially identical, except with respect to levels of capital per worker, what does the Solow model predict will happen to these countries in the long run? Is this consistent with the data?

8.2 How is the Solow model consistent with evidence on convergence across countries?

8.3 What are three sources of differences in productivity across countries?

8.4 How can a country overcome low productivity?

8.5 What causes economic growth in the endogenous growth model?

8.6 Why is knowledge nonrivalrous?

8.7 What two factors affect the growth rate of income and consumption in the endogenous growth model?

8.8 If the government could increase the rate of growth of consumption, should it? Why or why not?

8.9 Is there convergence in the levels and rates of growth of per capita income in the endogenous growth model? Why or why not?

Problems

1. **LO 1** Could differences across countries in population growth account for the persistence in income disparity across countries? Use the Solow growth model to address this question and discuss.

2. **LO 1** In the Solow growth model, suppose that the per-worker production function is given by $y = zk^{.3}$, with $s = 0.25$, $d = 0.1$, and $n = 0.02$.
   (a) Suppose that in country A, $z = 1$. Calculate per capita income and capital per worker.

(b) Suppose that in country B, $z = 2$. Calculate per capita income and capital per worker.

(c) As measured by GDP per capita, how much richer is country B than country A? What does this tell us about the potential for differences in total factor productivity to explain differences in standards of living across countries?

3. **LO 1** Suppose that there are two countries with different levels of total factor productivity, and that these differences exist because of barriers to technology adoption in the low-productivity country. Also suppose that these two countries do not trade with each other. Now, suppose that residents of each country were free to live in either country. What would happen, and what conclusions do you draw from this?

4. **LO 1** Suppose, in the Solow growth model, that learning by doing is captured as a cost of installing new capital. In particular, suppose that for each unit of investment, r units of goods are used up as a cost to firms.

(a) Determine how r affects the steady state quantity of capital per worker, and per capita income.

(b) Now suppose that r differs across countries. How will these countries differ in the long run? Discuss.

5. **LO 1** Suppose there are two countries, A and B, and each is a Solow growth model economy. In each country, a fraction a of the population is rich, and a fraction $1-a$ is poor. Suppose that rich people save a fraction s_r of their income, and poor people save a fraction s_p of their income, no matter what country they live in. In country A, suppose that rich people as a group receive a fraction x_A of total income, while in country B rich people as a group receive x_B fraction of total income. Assume that $x_A > x_B$.

(a) In a steady state, how does country A differ from country B?

(b) How does income per person of the rich and poor compare across countries?

(c) If you were a poor person, where would you rather live, in country A or country B? What if you are rich?

(d) Explain your results.

6. **LO 2** Suppose that z, the marginal product of efficiency units of labor, increases in the endogenous growth model. What effects does this have on the rates of growth and the levels of human capital, consumption, and output? Explain your results.

7. **LO 3** Introduce government activity in the endogenous growth model as follows. In addition to working u units of time in producing goods, the representative consumer works v units of time for the government and produces gvH goods for government use in the current period, where $g > 0$. The consumer now spends $1 - u - v$ units of time each period accumulating human capital.

(a) Suppose that v increases with u decreasing by an equal amount. Determine the effects on the level and the rate of growth of consumption. Draw a diagram showing the initial path followed by the natural logarithm of consumption and the corresponding path after v increases.

(b) Suppose that v increases with u held constant. Determine the effects on the level and the rate of growth of consumption. Draw a diagram showing the initial path followed by the natural logarithm of consumption and the corresponding path after v increases.

(c) Explain your results and any differences between parts (a) and (b).

8. **LO 3** Suppose that the government makes a one-time investment in new public school buildings, which results in a one-time reduction in consumption. The new public school buildings increase the efficiency with which human capital is accumulated. Determine the effects of this on the paths of aggregate consumption and aggregate output over time. Is it clear that this investment in new schools is a good idea? Explain.

9. **LO 3** Reinterpret the endogenous growth model in this chapter as follows. Suppose that there are two groups of people in a country, the low-skilled workers and the high-skilled workers. The low-skilled workers have less human capital per person initially than do the high-skilled workers. In the economy as a whole, output is produced

using efficiency units of labor, and total factor productivity is z, just as in the endogenous growth model in this chapter. Each individual in this economy accumulates human capital on their own, and each has one unit of time to split between human capital accumulation and work. However, now $b = b_h$ for the high-skilled, $b = b_l$ for the low-skilled, $u = u_h$ for the high-skilled, and $u = u_l$ for the low-skilled. In the United States, there has been an increase in the gap between the wages of high-skilled workers and low-skilled workers, that has occurred over the last 30 years or so. Determine how this model can explain this observation, and discuss.

10. **LO 4** Suppose there are two countries. In the rich country, the representative consumer has H_r units of human capital, and total factor productivity is z_r. In the poor country, the representative consumer has H_p units of human capital, and total factor productivity is z_p. Assume that b and u are the same in both countries, $H_r > H_p$, and $z_r > z_p$.

(a) How do the levels of per capita income, the growth rates of per capita income, and real wages compare between the rich and poor countries?

(b) If consumers could choose their country of residence, where would they want to live?

(c) If each country could determine immigration policy, what should they do to maximize the welfare of the current residents?

(d) What is the immigration policy that maximizes the welfare of the citizens of both countries?

(e) Explain your results. Do you think this is a good model for analyzing the effects of immigration? Why or why not?

11. **LO 2** In the endogenous growth model, suppose that there are three possible uses of time. Let u denote the fraction of time spent working, s the fraction of time spent neither working nor accumulating human capital (call this *unemployment*), and $1 - u - s$ the fraction of time spent accumulating human capital. Assume that $z = 1$ and $b = 4.2$. Also assume that the economy begins period 1 with 100 units of human capital.

(a) Suppose that for periods 1, 2, 3, . . . , 10, $u = .7$ and $s = 0.05$. Calculate aggregate consumption, output, and the quantity of human capital in each of these periods.

(b) Suppose that, in period 11, $u = 0.6$ and $s = 0.15$. Then, in periods 12, 13, 14, . . . , $u = 0.7$ and $s = 0.05$. Calculate aggregate consumption, output, and the quantity of human capital in periods 11, 12, 13, . . . , 20.

(c) Suppose alternatively that in period 11, $u = 0.6$ and $s = 0.05$. Again, calculate aggregate consumption, output, and the quantity of human capital in periods 11, 12, 13, . . . , 20.

(d) Now suppose that in period 11, $u = 0.6$ and $s = 0.10$. Calculate aggregate consumption, output, and the quantity of human capital in periods 11, 12, 13, . . . , 20.

(e) What do you conclude from your results in parts (a)–(d)? Discuss.

Working with the Data

To answer these questions, use the Penn World Table data available at http://datacentre2.chass.utoronto.ca/pwt62/[13]

1. Calculate the standard deviation of income per worker for the countries of the world for 1960 and 2007. Does this indicate that convergence is occurring or not? For the same years, calculate the standard deviation of income per worker for the poor countries (less than 20% of income per worker in the United States in 1960) and for the rich countries (greater than 20% of income per worker in the United States in 1960). What does this tell you about convergence among the rich and the poor?

[13]Penn World Table Version 6.2, Center for International Comparisons of Production, Income and Prices by Alan Heston, Robert Summers and Bettina Aten at the University of Pennsylvania, September 2006, Computing in the Humanities and Social Sciences, Faculty of Arts & Science, University of Toronto.

2. Suppose that we divide the countries of the world into three groups: low income per worker in 1960 (less than 33% of income per worker in the United States), middle income per worker in 1960 (between 33% and 67% of income per worker in the United States), and high income per worker in 1960 (greater than 67% of income per worker in the United States).

(a) Calculate average income per worker for the low income, middle income, and high income countries, respectively, for 1960 and 2007, and calculate the rates of growth of average income for the low, middle, and high income countries between 1960 and 2007.

(b) Do the statistics you calculated in part (a) indicate any tendency for convergence among these three groups of countries?

PART IV

Savings, Investment, and Government Deficits

In this part, we explore further the macroeconomics of intertemporal decisions and dynamic issues. We start in Chapter 9 by considering the consumption–savings decisions of consumers, building on our knowledge of consumer behavior from Chapter 4. We then study the Ricardian equivalence theorem, which states that, under certain conditions, a change in the timing of taxes by the government has no effects on real macroeconomic variables or on the welfare of consumers. A key implication of the Ricardian equivalence theorem is that a cut in taxes by the government is not a free lunch.

The Ricardian equivalence theorem provides a foundation on which to build our understanding of some key credit market " frictions," which matter a great deal for macroeconomic policy. We explore the issues related to these key frictions in Chapter 10. The first frictions relate to credit market imperfections—asymmetric information and limited commitment—that cause the interest rates at which credit market participants borrow to exceed the rates at which they lend, and result in situations where borrowers are required to post collateral to get loans. Credit market imperfections played an important role in the global financial crisis of 2008–2009, and we will explore this in Chapter 10. Another credit market friction relates to the fact that people live only for finite periods of time, which potentially provides a role for social security programs. Pay-as-you-go and fully funded social security systems are studied in the latter sections of Chapter 10.

In Chapter 11, we use what was learned about the microeconomics of consumption–savings behavior in Chapters 9 and 10, along with an analysis of the intertemporal labor supply behavior of consumers and the investment decisions of firms, to construct a complete intertemporal macroeconomic model. This model is the basis for most of what we do in the rest of this book. The model is used in Chapter 11 to show the effects of macroeconomic shocks on output, employment, consumption, investment, the real wage, and the real interest rate. As well, we focus on the effects of expectations about the future on current events.

Chapter 9

A Two-Period Model: The Consumption–Savings Decision and Credit Markets

Learning Objectives

After studying Chapter 9, students will be able to:

9.1 Construct a consumer's lifetime budget constraint and preferences in the two-period model, and solve his or her optimization problem.

9.2 Show how the consumer responds to changes in his or her current income, future income, and the market real interest rate.

9.3 Construct the government's present-value budget constraint.

9.4 Show how a competitive equilibrium is constructed in the two-period model.

9.5 Explain the Ricardian equivalence theorem.

9.6 Discuss how the Ricardian equivalence theorem helps us understand the burden of the government debt.

This chapter focuses on **intertemporal decisions** and the implications of intertemporal decision making for how government deficits affect macroeconomic activity. Intertemporal decisions involve economic trade-offs across periods of time. In Chapters 7 and 8, we studied the Solow growth model, where consumers made arbitrary intertemporal decisions about consumption and savings, consuming a constant fraction of income. In this chapter, we analyze these decisions at a deeper level, studying the microeconomic behavior of a consumer who must make a dynamic **consumption–savings decision**. In doing so, we apply what we learned in Chapter 4 concerning how a consumer optimizes subject to his or her budget constraint. We then study a model with many consumers and with a government that need not balance its budget and can issue debt to finance a government budget deficit. An important implication of this model is that the **Ricardian equivalence theorem** holds. This theorem states that there are conditions under which the size of the government's deficit is irrelevant, in that it does not affect any macroeconomic variables of importance or the economic welfare of any individual.

The consumption–savings decision involves intertemporal choice, as this is fundamentally a decision involving a trade-off between current and future consumption. Similarly, the government's decision concerning the financing of government expenditures is an intertemporal choice, involving a trade-off between current and future taxes. If the government decreases taxes in the present, it must borrow from the private sector to do so, which implies that future taxes must increase to pay off the higher government debt. Essentially, the government's financing decision is a decision about the quantity of government saving or the size of the government deficit, making it closely related to the consumption–savings decisions of private consumers.

To study the consumption–savings decisions of consumers and the government's intertemporal choices, we work in this chapter with a **two-period model**, which is the simplest framework for understanding intertemporal choice and dynamic issues. We treat the first period in the model as the current period and the second period as the future period. In intertemporal choice, a key variable of interest is the **real interest rate**, which in the model is the interest rate at which consumers and the government can borrow and lend. The real interest rate determines the relative price of consumption in the future in terms of consumption in the present. With respect to consumer choice, we are interested in how savings and consumption in the present and in the future are affected by changes in the market real interest rate and in the consumer's present and future incomes. With respect to the effects of real interest rate changes, income and substitution effects are important, and we can apply here what was learned in Chapters 4 and 5 about how to isolate income and substitution effects in a consumer's choice problem.

An important principle in the response of consumption to changes in income is **consumption smoothing**. That is, there are natural forces that cause consumers to wish to have a smooth consumption path over time, as opposed to a choppy one. Consumption-smoothing behavior is implied by particular properties of indifference curves that we have already studied in Chapter 4. Consumption-smoothing behavior also has important implications for how consumers respond in the aggregate to changes in government policies or other features of their external environment that affect their income streams.

While it remains true here, as in the one-period model studied in Chapter 5, that an increase in government spending has real effects on macroeconomic activity, the Ricardian equivalence theorem establishes conditions under which the timing of taxation does not matter for aggregate economic activity. David Ricardo, for whom the Ricardian equivalence theorem is named, is best known for his work in the early nineteenth century on the theory of comparative advantage and international trade. Ricardian equivalence runs counter to much of public debate, which attaches importance to the size of the government deficit. We explain why Ricardian equivalence is important in economic analysis and why the Ricardian equivalence theorem is a useful starting point for thinking about how the burden of the government debt is shared.

A key implication of the Ricardian equivalence theorem is that a tax cut is not a free lunch. A tax cut may not matter at all, or it may involve a redistribution of wealth within the current population or across generations.

Some interesting issues arise due to " frictions" in credit markets that cause departures from Ricardian equivalence. These frictions are important in analyzing the effects of financial crises, and in understanding how social security systems work. These issues will be addressed in Chapter 10.

To maintain simplicity and to retain focus on the important ideas in this chapter, our two-period model leaves out production and investment. In Chapter 11, we reintroduce production and add investment decisions by firms so that we can understand more completely the aggregate determination of output, employment, consumption, investment, the real wage rate, and the interest rate.

A Two-Period Model of the Economy

A consumer's consumption–savings decision is fundamentally a decision involving a trade-off between current and future consumption. By saving, a consumer gives up consumption in exchange for assets in the present to consume more in the future. Alternatively, a consumer can dissave by borrowing in the present to gain more current consumption, thus sacrificing future consumption when the loan is repaid. Borrowing (or dissaving) is thus negative savings.

A consumer's consumption–savings decision is a dynamic decision, in that it has implications over more than one period of time, as opposed to the consumer's static work–leisure decision considered in Chapters 4 and 5. We model the consumer's dynamic problem here in the simplest possible way, namely, in a two-period model. In this model, we denote the first period as the current period and the second period as the future period. For some economic problems, assuming that decision making by consumers takes place over two periods is obviously unrealistic. For example, if a period is a quarter, and because the working life of a typical individual is about 200 quarters, then a 200-period model might seem more appropriate. However, the results we consider in this chapter all generalize to more elaborate models with many periods or an infinite number of periods. The reason for studying models with two periods is that they are simple to analyze, while capturing the essentials of dynamic decision making by consumers and firms.

Consumers

There are no difficulties, in terms of what we want to accomplish with this model, in supposing that there are many different consumers rather than a single representative consumer. Therefore, we assume that there are N consumers, and we can think of N being a large number. We assume that each consumer lives for two periods, the current period and the future period. We further suppose that consumers do not make a work–leisure decision in either period but simply receive exogenous income. Assuming that incomes are exogenous allows us to focus attention on what we are interested in here, which is the consumer's consumption–savings decision. Let y be a consumer's real income in the current period, and y' be real income in the future period. Throughout, we use lowercase letters to refer to variables at the individual level and uppercase letters for aggregate variables. Primes denote variables in the future period (for example, y' denotes the consumer's future income). Each consumer pays lump-sum taxes t in the current period and t' in the future period. Suppose that incomes can be different for different consumers, but that all consumers pay the same taxes. If we let a consumer's savings in the current period be s, then the consumer's budget constraint in the current period is

$$c + s = y - t, \tag{9-1}$$

where c is current-period consumption. Here, Equation (9-1) states that consumption plus savings in the current period must equal disposable income in the current period. We assume that the consumer starts the current period with no assets. This does not matter in any important way for our analysis.

In Equation (9-1), if $s > 0$, then the consumer is a lender on the credit market, and if $s < 0$, the consumer is a borrower. We suppose that the financial asset that is traded in the credit market is a bond. In the model, bonds can be issued by consumers as well as by the government. If a consumer lends, he or she buys bonds; if he or she borrows, there is a sale of bonds. There are two important assumptions here. The first is that all bonds are indistinguishable, because consumers never default on their debts, so that there is no risk associated with holding a bond. In practice, different credit instruments are associated with different levels of risk. Interest-bearing securities issued by the U.S. government are essentially riskless, while corporate bonds may be risky if investors feel that the corporate issuer might default, and a loan made by a bank to a consumer may also be quite risky. The second important assumption is that bonds are traded directly in the credit market. In practice, much of the economy's credit activity is channeled through financial intermediaries, an example of which is a commercial bank. For example, when a consumer borrows to purchase a car, the loan is usually taken out at a commercial bank or other depository institution; a consumer typically does not borrow directly from the ultimate lender (in the case of a commercial bank, the ultimate lenders include the depositors at the bank). For the problems we address with this model, we simplify matters considerably, without any key loss in the insights we get, to assume away credit risk and financial institutions like commercial banks. Credit risk and financial intermediation are discussed in detail in Chapters 10 and 17.

In our model, one bond issued in the current period is a promise to pay $1 + r$ units of the consumption good in the future period, so that the real interest rate on each bond is r. Because this implies that one unit of current consumption can be exchanged in the credit market for $1 + r$ units of the future consumption good, the relative price of future consumption in terms of current consumption is $\frac{1}{1+r}$. Recall from Chapter 1 that in practice the real interest rate is approximately the nominal interest rate (the interest rate in money terms) minus the inflation rate. We study the relationship between real and nominal interest rates in Chapter 12.

A key assumption here is that the real rate of interest at which a consumer can lend is the same as the real rate of interest at which a consumer can borrow. In practice, consumers typically borrow at higher rates of interest than they can lend at. For example, the interest rates on consumer loans are usually several percentage points higher than the interest rates on bank deposits, reflecting the costs for the bank of taking deposits and making loans. The assumption that borrowing and lending rates of interest are the same matters for some of what we do here, and we ultimately show what difference this makes to our analysis.

In the future period, the consumer has disposable income $y' - t'$ and receives the interest and principal on his or her savings, which totals $(1 + r)s$. Because the future period is the final period, the consumer chooses to finish this period with no assets, consuming all disposable income and the interest and principal on savings (we assume there are no bequests to descendants). We then have

$$c' = y' - t' + (1 + r)s, \qquad (9\text{-}2)$$

where c' is consumption in the future period. In Equation (9-2), if $s < 0$, the consumer pays the interest and principal on his or her loan (retires the bonds he or she issued in the current period) and then consumes what remains of his or her future-period disposable income.

The consumer chooses current consumption and future consumption, c and c', respectively, and savings s to make himself or herself as well off as possible while satisfying the budget constraints, Equations (9-1) and (9-2).

The Consumer's Lifetime Budget Constraint

LO 9.1 Construct a consumer's lifetime budget constraint and preferences in the two-period model, and solve his or her optimization problem.

We can work with diagrams similar to those used in Chapter 4 to analyze the consumer's work–leisure decision, if we take the two budget constraints expressed in Equations (9-1) and (9-2) and write them as a single lifetime budget constraint. To do this, we first use Equation (9-2) to solve for s to get

$$s = \frac{c' - y' + t'}{1 + r}. \qquad (9\text{-}3)$$

Then, substitute for s from Equation (9-3) in Equation (9-1) to get

$$c + \frac{c' - y' + t'}{1 + r} = y - t,$$

or rearranging,

$$c + \frac{c'}{1 + r} = y + \frac{y'}{1 + r} - t - \frac{t'}{1 + r}. \qquad (9\text{-}4)$$

Equation (9-4) is the consumer's **lifetime budget constraint**, and it states that the **present value** of lifetime consumption $c + \frac{c'}{1+r}$ equals the present value of lifetime income $y + \frac{y'}{1+r}$ minus the present value of lifetime taxes $t + \frac{t'}{1+r}$. The present value here is the value in terms of period 1 consumption goods. That is, $\frac{1}{1+r}$ is the relative price of future consumption goods in terms of current consumption goods, because a consumer can give up 1 unit of current consumption goods and obtain $1 + r$ units of future consumption goods by saving for one period. The problem of the consumer is now simplified, in that he or she chooses c and c' to make himself or herself as well off as possible, while satisfying the budget constraint Equation (9-4) and given r, y, y', t, and t'. Once we have determined what the consumer's optimal consumption is in the current and future periods, we can determine savings, s, from the current-period budget constraint Equation (9-1).

For a numerical example to illustrate present values, suppose that current income is $y = 110$ while future income is $y' = 120$. Taxes in the current period are $t = 20$, and taxes in the future period are $t' = 10$. Also suppose that the real interest rate is 10%, so that $r = 0.1$. In this example, the relative price of future consumption goods in terms of current consumption goods is $\frac{1}{1+r} = 0.909$. Here, when we discount future income and future taxes to obtain these quantities in units of current consumption goods, we multiply by the discount factor 0.909. The fact that the discount factor is less than 1 indicates that having a given amount of income in the future is worth less to the consumer than having the same amount of income in the current period. The present discounted value of lifetime income is

$$y + \frac{y'}{1+r} = 110 + (120 \times 0.909) = 219.1,$$

and the present value of lifetime taxes is

$$t + \frac{t'}{1+r} = 20 + (10 \times 0.909) = 29.1.$$

Then, in this example, we can write the consumer's lifetime budget constraint from Equation (9-4) as

$$c + 0.909c' = 190.$$

We label the present value of lifetime disposable income, the quantity on the right-hand side of Equation (9-4), as **lifetime wealth**, we, because this is the quantity of resources that the consumer has available to spend on consumption, in present-value terms, over his or her lifetime. We then have

$$we = y + \frac{y'}{1+r} - t - \frac{t'}{1+r}, \tag{9-5}$$

and we can rewrite Equation (9-4) as

$$c + \frac{c'}{1+r} = we. \tag{9-6}$$

In Figure 9.1 we graph the consumer's lifetime budget constraint as expressed in Equation (9-6). Writing this equation in slope–intercept form, we have

$$c' = -(1 + r)c + we(1 + r). \tag{9-7}$$

Therefore, in Equation (9-7) and in Figure 9.1, the vertical intercept, $we(1 + r)$, is what could be consumed in the future period if the consumer saved all of his or her current-period disposable income and consumed lifetime wealth (after earning the

Figure 9.1 Consumer's Lifetime Budget Constraint

The lifetime budget constraint defines the quantities of current and future consumption the consumer can acquire, given current and future income and taxes, through borrowing and lending on the credit market. To the northwest of the endowment point E, the consumer is a lender with positive savings; to the southeast of E, he or she is a borrower with negative savings.

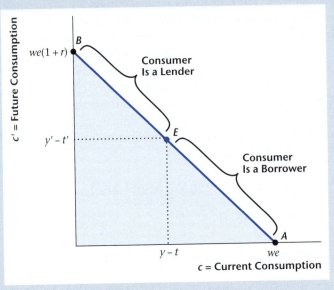

real interest rate r on savings) in the future period. The horizontal intercept in Equation (9-7) and Figure 9.1, we, is what could be consumed if the consumer borrowed the maximum amount possible against future-period disposable income and consumed all of lifetime wealth in the current period. The slope of the lifetime budget constraint is $-(1+r)$, which is determined by the real interest rate. Point E in Figure 9.1 is the **endowment point**, which is the consumption bundle the consumer gets if he or she simply consumes disposable income in the current period and in the future period—that is, $c = y - t$ and $c' = y' - t'$—with zero savings in the current period. You can verify by substituting $c = y - t$ and $c' = y' - t'$ in Equation (9-4) that the endowment point satisfies the lifetime budget constraint. Any point along BE in Figure 9.1 implies that $s \geq 0$, so that the consumer is a lender, because $c \leq y - t$. Also, a consumption bundle along AE in Figure 9.1 implies that the consumer is a borrower with $s \leq 0$.

Any point on or inside AB in the shaded area in Figure 9.1 represents a feasible consumption bundle; that is, a combination of current-period and future-period consumptions that satisfies the consumer's lifetime budget constraint. As may be clear by now, the way we approach the consumer's problem here is very similar to our analysis of the consumer's work–leisure decision in Chapter 4. Once we describe the consumer's preferences and add indifference curves to the budget constraint as depicted in Figure 9.1, we can determine the consumer's optimal consumption bundle.

The Consumer's Preferences

LO 9.1 Construct a consumer's lifetime budget constraint and preferences in the two-period model, and solve his or her optimization problem.

As with the consumer's work–leisure decision in Chapter 4, the consumption bundle that is chosen by the consumer, which here is a combination of current-period and future-period consumptions, is determined jointly by the consumer's budget constraint and his or her preferences. Just as in Chapter 4, we assume that preferences have three properties, which are the following:

1. More is always preferred to less. Here, this means that more current consumption or more future consumption always makes the consumer better off.
2. The consumer likes diversity in his or her consumption bundle. Here, a preference for diversity has a specific meaning in terms of the consumer's desire to smooth consumption over time. Namely, the consumer has a dislike for having large differences in consumption between the current period and the future period. Note that this does not mean that the consumer would always choose to have equal consumption in the current and future periods.
3. Current consumption and future consumption are normal goods. This implies that if there is a parallel shift to the right in the consumer's budget constraint, then current consumption and future consumption both increase. This is related to the consumer's desire to smooth consumption over time. If there is a parallel shift to the right in the consumer's budget constraint, this is because lifetime wealth *we* has increased. Given the consumer's desire to smooth consumption over time, any increase in lifetime wealth implies that the consumer chooses more consumption in the present and in the future.

As in Chapter 4, we represent preferences with an indifference map, which is a family of indifference curves. A typical indifference map is shown in Figure 9.2, where the marginal rate of substitution of consumption in the current period for consumption in the future period, or $MRS_{c,c'}$, is minus the slope of an indifference curve. For example, $MRS_{c,c'}$ at point A in Figure 9.2 is minus the slope of a tangent to the indifference curve at point A. Recall that a preference for diversity, or diminishing marginal rate of substitution, is captured by the convexity in an indifference curve, which here also represents a consumer's desire to smooth consumption over time. On indifference curve I_1, at point A the consumer has a large quantity of current consumption and a small quantity of future consumption, and he or she needs to be given a large quantity of current consumption to willingly give up a small quantity of future consumption (minus the slope of the indifference curve at A is small). Conversely, at point B the consumer has a small quantity of current consumption and a large quantity of future consumption, and he or she needs to be given a large quantity of future consumption

Figure 9.2 A Consumer's Indifference Curves

The figure shows the indifference map of a consumer. Indifference curves are convex and downward-sloping. Minus the slope of an indifference curve is the marginal rate of substitution of current consumption for future consumption.

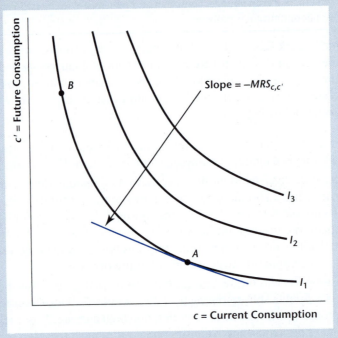

to give up a small quantity of current consumption (minus the slope of the indifference curve is large). Thus, the consumer does not like large differences in consumption between the two periods.

As an example to show why consumption smoothing is a natural property for preferences to have, suppose that Sara is a consumer living on a desert island, and that she eats only coconuts. Suppose that coconuts can be stored for two weeks without spoiling, and that Sara has 20 coconuts to last for this week (the current period) and next week (the future period). One option that Sara has is to eat 5 coconuts this week and 15 coconuts next week. Suppose that Sara is just indifferent between this first consumption bundle and a second bundle that involves eating 17 coconuts this week and 3 coconuts next week. However, eating only 5 coconuts in the first week or only 3 coconuts in the second week leaves Sara rather hungry. She would, in fact, prefer to eat 11 coconuts in the first week and 9 coconuts in the second week, rather than either of the other two consumption bundles. This third consumption bundle combines half of the first consumption bundle with half of the second consumption bundle. That is, $\frac{5 + 17}{2} = 11$ and $\frac{15 + 3}{2} = 9$. Sara's preferences reflect a desire for

---

Table 9.1   Sara's Desire for Consumption Smoothing

	Week 1 Coconuts	Week 2 Coconuts	Total Consumption
Bundle 1	5	15	20
Bundle 2	17	3	20
Preferred Bundle	11	9	20

---

consumption smoothing or a preference for diversity in her consumption bundle, that seems natural. In Table 9.1 we show the consumption bundles amongst which Sara chooses.

Consumer Optimization

LO 9.1 Construct a consumer's lifetime budget constraint and preferences in the two-period model, and solve his or her optimization problem.

As with the work–leisure decision we considered in Chapter 4, the consumer's optimal consumption bundle here is determined by where an indifference curve is tangent to the budget constraint. In Figure 9.3, we show the optimal consumption choice for a consumer who decides to be a lender. The endowment point is at E, while the consumer chooses the consumption bundle at point A, where $(c, c') = (c^*, c'^*)$. At point A, it is then the case that

$$MRS_{c,c'} = 1 + r; \tag{9-8}$$

that is, the marginal rate of substitution of current consumption for future consumption (minus the slope of the indifference curve) is equal to the relative price of current consumption in terms of future consumption ($1 + r$, which is minus the slope of the consumer's lifetime budget constraint). Recall from Chapter 4 that Equation (9-8) is a particular case of a standard marginal condition that is implied by consumer optimization (at the optimum, the marginal rate of substitution of good 1 for good 2 is equal to the relative price of good 1 in terms of good 2). Here, the consumer optimizes by choosing the consumption bundle on his or her lifetime budget constraint where the rate at which he or she is willing to trade off current consumption for future consumption is the same as the rate at which he or she can trade current consumption for future consumption in the market (by saving). At point A in Figure 9.3, the quantity of savings is $s = y - t - c^*$, or the distance BD. Similarly, Figure 9.4 shows the case of a consumer who chooses to be a borrower. That is, the endowment point is E and the consumer chooses point A, where $(c, c') = (c^*, c'^*)$. Here, the quantity the consumer borrows in the first period is $-s = c^* - y + t$, or the distance DB.

In the next stage in our analysis, we consider some experiments that tell us how the consumer responds to changes in current income, future income, and interest rates.

Figure 9.3 A Consumer Who Is a Lender

The optimal consumption bundle for the consumer is at point *A*, where the marginal rate of substitution (minus the slope of an indifference curve) is equal to $1 + r$ (minus the slope of the lifetime budget constraint). The consumer is a lender, as the consumption bundle chosen implies positive savings, with *E* being the endowment point.

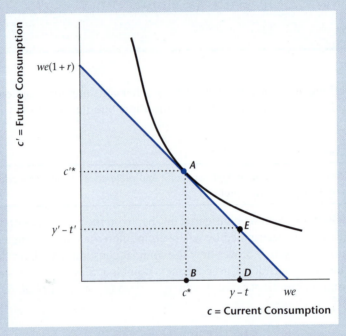

An Increase in Current-Period Income

LO 9.2 Show how the consumer responds to changes in his or her current income, future income, and the market real interest rate.

From Chapter 4, we know that an increase in a consumer's dividend income or a reduction in taxes amounts to a pure income effect, which increases consumption and reduces labor supply. Here, we want to focus on how an increase in the consumer's current income affects intertemporal decisions. In particular, we want to know the effects of an increase in current income on current consumption, future consumption, and savings. As we show, these effects reflect the consumer's desire for consumption smoothing.

Suppose that, holding the interest rate, taxes in the current and future periods, and future income constant, a consumer receives an increase in period 1 income. Asking the consumer's response to this change in income is much like asking how an individual would react to winning a lottery. In Figure 9.5 the initial endowment point is at E_1, and the consumer initially chooses the consumption bundle represented by point *A*. In this figure we have shown the case of a consumer who is initially a lender, but it does

Figure 9.4 A Consumer Who Is a Borrower

The optimal consumption bundle is at point A. Because current consumption exceeds current disposable income, saving is negative, and so the consumer is a borrower.

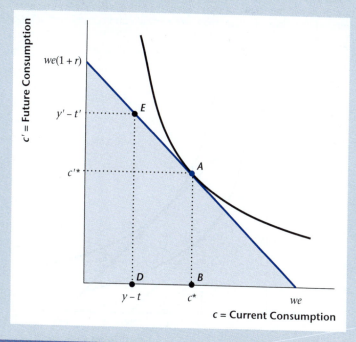

not make a difference for what we want to show if the consumer is a borrower. We suppose that current-period income increases from y_1 to y_2. The result is that lifetime wealth increases from

to

$$we_1 = y_1 + \frac{y'}{1+r} - t - \frac{t'}{1+r}$$

$$we_2 = y_2 + \frac{y'}{1+r} - t - \frac{t'}{1+r},$$

and the change in lifetime wealth is

$$\Delta we = we_2 - we_1 = y_2 - y_1.$$

The effect is that the budget constraint shifts to the right by the amount $y_2 - y_1$, which is the distance $E_1 E_2$, where E_2 is the new endowment point. The slope of the budget constraint remains unchanged, as the real interest rate is the same.

Because current-period consumption and future consumption are normal goods, the consumer now chooses a consumption bundle represented by a point like B, where

Figure 9.5 The Effects of an Increase in Current Income for a Lender

When current income increases, lifetime wealth increases from we_1 to we_2. The lifetime budget constraint shifts out, and the slope of the constraint remains unchanged, because the real interest rate does not change. Initially, the consumer chooses A, and he or she chooses B after current income increases. Current and future consumption both increase (both goods are normal), and current consumption increases by less than the increase in current income.

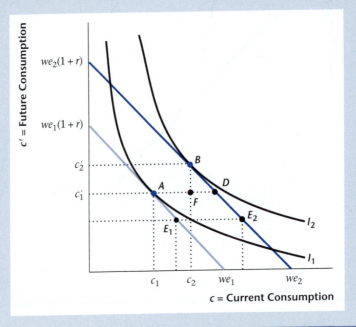

consumption in both periods has risen from the previous values. Current consumption increases from c_1 to c_2, and future consumption increases from c_1' to c_2'. Thus, if current income increases, the consumer wishes to spread this additional income over both periods and not consume it all in the current period. In Figure 9.5 the increase in current income is the distance AD, while the increase in current consumption is the distance AF, which is less than the distance AD. The change in the consumer's savings is given by

$$\Delta s = \Delta y - \Delta t - \Delta c, \tag{9-9}$$

and because $\Delta t = 0$, and $\Delta y > \Delta c > 0$, we have $\Delta s > 0$. Thus, an increase in current income causes an increase in consumption in both periods and an increase in savings.

Our analysis tells us that any one consumer who receives an increase in his or her current income consumes more during the current period but also saves some of the increase in income so as to consume more in the future. This behavior arises because of the consumer's desire to smooth consumption over time. This behavior is intuitively reasonable. For example, consider a consumer, Paul, who is currently 25 years of age and wins $1 million in a lottery. Paul could certainly spend all of his lottery winnings on consumption goods within the current year and save nothing, but it would seem more sensible if he consumed a small part of his winnings in the current year and saved a substantial fraction to consume more for the rest of his life.

If all consumers act to smooth their consumption relative to their income, then aggregate consumption should likewise be smooth relative to aggregate income. Indeed, this prediction of our theory is consistent with what we see in the data. Recall from Chapter 3 that real aggregate consumption is less variable than is real GDP. The difference in variability between aggregate consumption and GDP is even larger if we take account of the fact that some of what is included in aggregate consumption is not consumption in the economic sense. For example, purchases of new automobiles are included in the NIPA as consumption of durables, but the purchase of a car might more appropriately be included in investment, because the car yields a flow of consumption services over its entire lifetime. In the data, expenditures on consumer durables are much more variable than actual consumption, measured as the flow of consumption services that consumers receive from goods. In Figure 9.6 we show the percentage

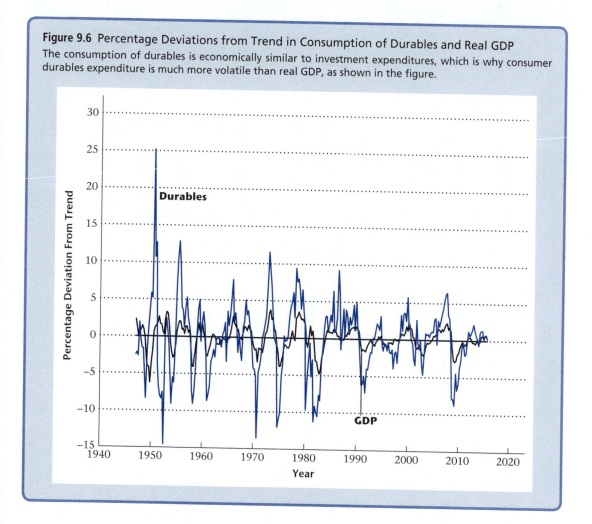

Figure 9.6 Percentage Deviations from Trend in Consumption of Durables and Real GDP
The consumption of durables is economically similar to investment expenditures, which is why consumer durables expenditure is much more volatile than real GDP, as shown in the figure.

deviations from trend in the consumption of durables, and in GDP for the period 1947–2015. Clearly, the consumption of durables is much more variable than aggregate income, and if we compare Figure 9.6 to Figure 3.10 in Chapter 3, it is clear that durables consumption behaves much like aggregate investment. However, Figure 9.7 depicts the percentage deviations from trend in the consumption of nondurables and services and in real GDP. Here, clearly there is much less variability in the consumption of nondurables and services—which comes fairly close to measuring a flow of consumption services—than in real GDP. What we observe in Figure 9.7 accurately reflects the tendency of consumers to smooth consumption over time relative to income.

Though aggregate data on consumption and income are clearly qualitatively consistent with consumption-smoothing behavior on the part of consumers, macroeconomists have been interested in the quantitative match between consumption theory and the

Figure 9.7 Percentage Deviations from Trend in Consumption of Nondurables and Services and Real GDP

The consumption of nondurables and services is fairly close to a pure flow of consumption services, so it is not surprising that consumption of nondurables and services is much smoother than real GDP, reflecting the motive of consumers to smooth consumption relative to income.

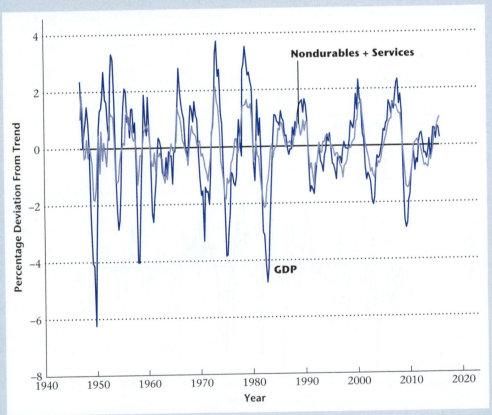

data. The question is whether or not measured consumption is smooth enough relative to measured income to be consistent with theory. Generally, the conclusion from empirical work is that, while the theory points in the right direction, there is some **excess variability** of aggregate consumption relative to aggregate income. That is, while consumption is smoother than income, as the theory predicts, consumption is not quite smooth enough to tightly match the theory.[1] Thus, the theory needs some more work if it is to fit the facts. Two possible explanations for the excess variability in consumption are the following:

1. There are imperfections in the credit market. Our theory assumes that a consumer can smooth consumption by borrowing or lending at the market real interest rate r. In reality, consumers cannot borrow all they would like at the market interest rate, and market loan interest rates are typically higher than the interest rates at which consumers lend. As a result, in reality consumers may have less ability to smooth consumption than they do in the theory. We could complicate the model by introducing credit market imperfections, and this might help to explain the data better. However, this would make the model considerably more complicated. We further discuss credit market imperfections later in this chapter.

2. When all consumers are trying to smooth consumption in the same way simultaneously, this changes market prices. The consumption-smoothing theory we have studied thus far does not take into account the interaction of consumers with each other and with other sectors of the economy. All consumers may wish to smooth consumption over time, but aggregate consumption must fall during a recession because aggregate income is lower then. Similarly, aggregate consumption must rise in a boom. The way that consumers are reconciled to having high consumption when output is high, and low consumption when output is low, is through movements in market prices, including the market interest rate. Shortly, we will study how individual consumers react to changes in the real interest rate.

An Increase in Future Income

LO 9.2 Show how the consumer responds to changes in his or her current income, future income, and the market real interest rate.

While a consumer's response to a change in his or her current income is informative about consumption-smoothing behavior, we are also interested in the effects on consumer behavior of a change in income that is expected to occur in the future. Suppose, for example, that Jennifer is about to finish her college degree in four months, and she lines up a job that starts as soon as she graduates. On landing the job, Jennifer's future income has increased considerably. How would she react to this future increase in income? Clearly, this would imply that she would plan to increase her future consumption, but Jennifer also likes to smooth consumption, so that she should want to have

---

[1] See, for example, O. P. Attanasio, 1999. " Consumption," in *Handbook of Macroeconomics*, J. Taylor and M. Woodford, eds., 741–812, Elsevier.

higher current consumption as well. She can consume more currently by borrowing against her future income and repaying the loan when she starts working.

In Figure 9.8 we show the effects of an increase for the consumer in future income, from y_1' to y_2'. This has an effect similar to the increase in current income on lifetime wealth, with lifetime wealth increasing from we_1 to we_2, and shifting the budget constraint up by the amount $y_2' - y_1'$. Initially, the consumer chooses consumption bundle A, and he or she chooses B after the increase in future income. Both current and future consumptions increase; current consumption increases from c_1 to c_2, and future consumption increases from c_1' to c_2'. The increase in future consumption, which is the distance AF in Figure 9.8, is less than the increase in future income, which is the distance AD. This is because, as with the increase in current income, the consumer wants to smooth consumption over time. Rather than spend all the increase in income in the future, the consumer saves less in the current period so that current consumption can increase. The change in saving is given by Equation (9-9), where $\Delta t = \Delta y = 0$, and because $\Delta c > 0$, we must have $\Delta s < 0$—that is, savings decreases.

In the case of an expected increase in future income, the consumer acts to smooth consumption over time, just as when he or she receives an increase in current income. The difference is that an increase in future income leads to smoothing backward, with the consumer saving less in the current period so that current consumption can

Figure 9.8 An Increase in Future Income
An increase in future income increases lifetime wealth from we_1 to we_2, shifting the lifetime budget constraint to the right and leaving its slope unchanged. The consumer initially chooses point A, and he or she chooses B after the budget constraint shifts. Future consumption increases by less than the increase in future income, saving decreases, and current consumption increases.

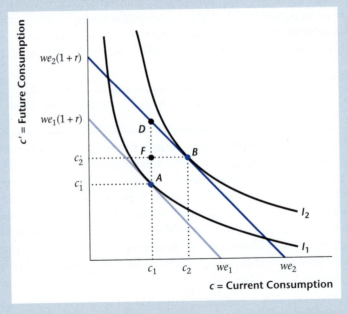

increase, whereas an increase in current income leads to smoothing forward, with the consumer saving more in the current period so that future consumption can increase.

Temporary and Permanent Changes in Income

LO 9.2 Show how the consumer responds to changes in his or her current income, future income, and the market real interest rate.

When a consumer receives a change in his or her current income, it matters a great deal for his or her current consumption–savings choice whether this change in income is temporary or permanent. For example, Allen would respond quite differently to receiving a windfall increase in his income of $1,000, say by winning a lottery, as opposed to receiving a $1,000 yearly salary increase that he expects to continue indefinitely. In the case of the lottery winnings, we might expect that Allen would increase current consumption by only a small amount, saving most of the lottery winnings to increase consumption in the future. If Allen received a permanent increase in his income, as in the second case, we would expect his increase in current consumption to be much larger.

The difference between the effects of temporary and permanent changes in income on consumption was articulated by Milton Friedman in his **permanent income hypothesis**.[2] Friedman argued that a primary determinant of a consumer's current consumption is his or her permanent income, which is closely related to the concept of lifetime wealth in our model. Changes in income that are temporary yield small changes in permanent income (lifetime wealth), which have small effects on current consumption, whereas changes in income that are permanent have large effects on permanent income (lifetime wealth) and current consumption.

In our model, we can show the effects of temporary versus permanent changes in income by examining an increase in income that occurs only in the current period versus an increase in income occurring in the current period and the future period. In Figure 9.9 the budget constraint of the consumer is initially AB, and he or she chooses the consumption bundle represented by point H, on indifference curve I_1. Then, the consumer experiences a temporary increase in income, with current income increasing from y_1 to y_2, so that the budget constraint shifts out to DE. The real interest rate does not change, so that the slope of the budget constraint remains constant. The distance HL is equal to the change in current income, $y_2 - y_1$. Now, the consumer chooses point J on indifference curve I_2, and we know from our previous discussion that the increase in current consumption, $c_2 - c_1$, is less than the increase in current income, $y_2 - y_1$, as saving increases due to consumption-smoothing behavior.

Now, suppose that the increase in income is permanent. We interpret this as an equal increase of $y_2 - y_1$ in both current and future income. That is, initially future income is y_1' and it increases to y_2' with $y_2' - y_1' = y_2 - y_1$. Now, the budget constraint is given by FG in Figure 9.9, where the upward shift in the budget constraint from DE is the distance LM, which is $y_2' - y_1' = y_2 - y_1$. The consumer now chooses point K on indifference curve I_3. At point K, current consumption is c_3. Given that current and

---

[2]See M. Friedman, 1957. *A Theory of the Consumption Function,* Princeton, NJ: Princeton University Press.

Figure 9.9 Temporary Versus Permanent Increases in Income

A temporary increase in income is an increase in current income, with the budget constraint shifting from *AB* to *DE* and the optimal consumption bundle changing from *H* to *J*. When there is a permanent increase in income, current and future incomes both increase, and the budget constraint shifts from *AB* to *FG*, with the optimal consumption bundle changing from *H* to *K*.

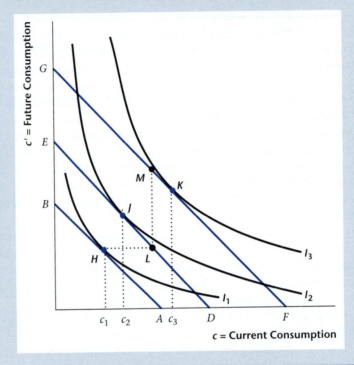

future consumption are normal goods, current consumption increases from point *H* to point *J* and from point *J* to point *K*. Therefore, if income increases permanently, this has a larger effect on current consumption than if income increases only temporarily. If income increases only temporarily, there is an increase in saving, so that consumption does not increase as much as does income. However, if there is a permanent increase in income, then there need not be an increase in saving, and current consumption could increase as much as or more than does income.

Why is it important that consumers respond differently to temporary and permanent changes in their income? Suppose that the government is considering cutting taxes, and this tax cut could be temporary or permanent. For now, ignore how the government will go about financing this tax cut (we consider this later in the chapter). If consumers receive a tax cut that increases lifetime wealth, then this increases aggregate consumption. However, if consumers expect the tax cut to be temporary, the increase in consumption is much smaller than if they expect the tax cut to be permanent.

THEORY CONFRONTS THE DATA

Consumption Smoothing and the Stock Market

Thus far, our theory tells us that, in response to increases in their lifetime wealth, consumers increase consumption, but in such a way that their consumption path is smoothed over time. One way in which consumers' wealth changes is through variation in the prices of stocks traded on organized stock exchanges, such as the New York Stock Exchange or NASDAQ.

How should we expect aggregate consumption to respond to a change in stock prices? On the one hand, publicly traded stock is not a large fraction of national wealth. That is, a large fraction of national wealth includes the housing stock and the capital of privately held companies, which are not traded on the stock market. Therefore, even if there is a large change in stock prices, this need not represent a large change in national wealth. On the other hand, financial theory tells us that when the price of a stock changes we should expect this price change to be permanent.

Financial theory tells us (with some qualifications) that stock prices are **martingales**. A martingale has the property that the best prediction of its value tomorrow is its value today. In the case of a stock price, the best prediction of tomorrow's stock price is today's stock price. The reason that stock prices follow martingales is that, if they did not, then there would be opportunities for investors to make profits.

That is, suppose that a stock price does not follow a martingale, and suppose first that the best forecast is that tomorrow's stock price will be higher than today's stock price. Then, investors would want to buy the stock today so as to make a profit by selling it tomorrow. Ultimately, this would force up the market price of the stock

today, to the point where the price today is what it is expected to be tomorrow. Similarly, if the price of the stock today were greater than what the stock's price was expected to be tomorrow, investors would want to sell the stock today so they could buy it at a cheaper price tomorrow. In this case, investors' actions would force the current stock price down to the point where it was equal to its expected price tomorrow. Because the current price of a stock is the best forecast of its future price, any change in prices is a surprise, and this change in prices is expected to be permanent.

A change in the overall value of the stock market does not represent a change in a large fraction of national wealth, and this would tend to dampen the effect of price movements in the stock market on aggregate consumption. However, the fact that any change in stock prices is expected to be permanent tends to amplify the effects of changes in stock prices, as we know that permanent changes in wealth have larger effects on consumption than do temporary changes in wealth. What do the data tell us? In Figure 9.10 we show a time series plot of the percentage deviations from trend in the Standard and Poor's composite stock price index for the United States, and percentage deviations from trend in real consumption of nondurables and services. The data plotted are quarterly data for the period 1957–2015. Here, note in particular that the stock price index is highly volatile relative to consumption. Deviations from trend in the stock price index of 20%–25% in absolute value occur, while the deviations from trend in consumption are at most about plus or minus 2%. A close examination of Figure 9.10 indicates

(Continued)

that deviations from trend in the stock price index are positively correlated with deviations from trend in consumption. Figure 9.11 shows this more clearly, where we graph the same data as in Figure 9.10, except in a scatter plot. A positively sloped line in Figure 9.11 would provide the best fit to the data in the scatter plot, indicating that the stock price and consumption are positively correlated.

The data indicate that the stock market is potentially an important channel for the effects of changes in wealth on aggregate consumption behavior. The fact that consumption and stock prices move together is consistent with the notion that shocks to the financial system that are reflected in the prices of publicly traded stocks can cause significant movements in aggregate consumption. Though the value of publicly traded stock is not a large part of national wealth, the fact that stock price changes are expected to be permanent potentially contributes to the influence of the stock market on consumption behavior.

Figure 9.10 Stock Price Index and the Consumption of Nondurables and Services

Percentage deviations from trend in stock prices and consumption are positively correlated, though stock prices are much more volatile than consumption.

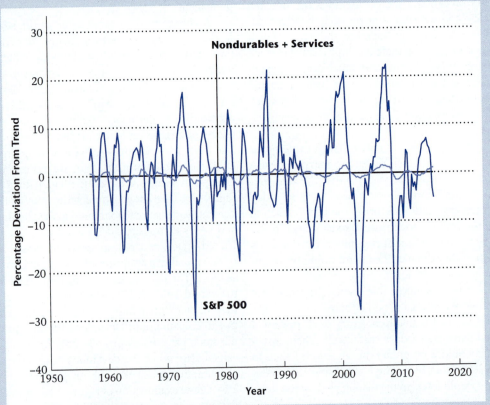

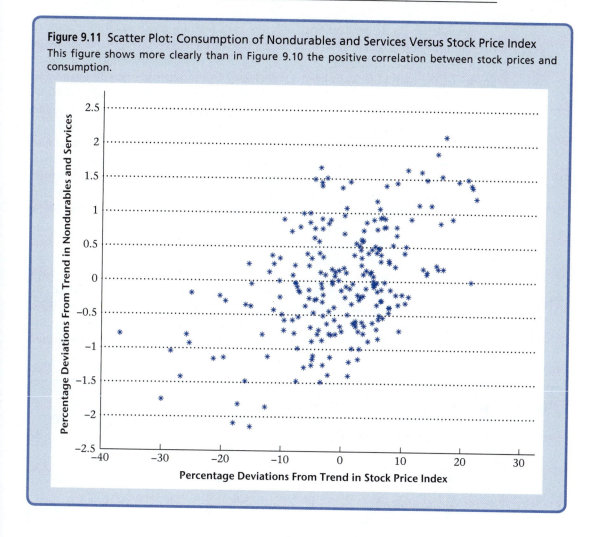

Figure 9.11 Scatter Plot: Consumption of Nondurables and Services Versus Stock Price Index
This figure shows more clearly than in Figure 9.10 the positive correlation between stock prices and consumption.

An Increase in the Real Interest Rate

LO 9.2 Show how the consumer responds to changes in his or her current income, future income, and the market real interest rate.

To this point, we have examined how changes in a consumer's current income and future income affect his or her choices of consumption in the current and future periods. These are changes that shift the consumer's budget constraint but do not change its slope. In this subsection, we study how the consumer responds to a change in the real interest rate, which changes the slope of the budget constraint. Changes in the market real interest rate are ultimately an important part of the mechanism by which shocks to the economy, fiscal policy, and monetary policy affect real activity, as we show in Chapters 11–14. A key channel for interest rate effects on real activity is through aggregate consumption.

Because $\frac{1}{1+r}$ is the relative price of future consumption goods in terms of current consumption goods, a change in the real interest rate effectively changes this intertemporal relative price. In Chapter 4, in the consumer's work–leisure choice problem, a change in the real wage was effectively a change in the relative price of leisure and consumption, and a change in the real wage had income and substitution effects. Here, in our two-period framework, a change in the real interest rate also has income and substitution effects in its influence on consumption in the present and the future.

Suppose that the consumer faces an increase in the real interest rate, with taxes and income held constant in both periods. This makes the budget constraint steeper, because the slope of the budget constraint is $-(1+r)$. Further, under the assumption that the consumer never has to pay a tax larger than his or her income, so that $y' - t' > 0$, an increase in r decreases lifetime wealth we, as shown in Equation (9-5). Also from Equation (9-5), we have

$$we(1+r) = (y-t)(1+r) + y' - t',$$

and because $y > t$, there is an increase in $we(1+r)$ when r increases. Therefore, we know that an increase in r causes the budget constraint to pivot, as in Figure 9.12, where r increases from r_1 to r_2, resulting in a decrease in we from we_1 to we_2. We also know that the budget constraint must pivot around the endowment point E, because

Figure 9.12 An Increase in the Real Interest Rate
An increase in the real interest rate causes the lifetime budget constraint of the consumer to become steeper and to pivot around the endowment point E.

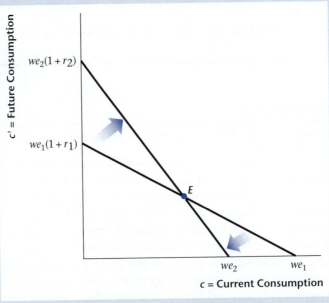

it must always be possible for the consumer to consume his or her disposable income in each period, no matter what the real interest rate is.

A change in r results in a change in the relative price of consumption in the current and future periods; that is, an increase in r causes future consumption to become cheaper relative to current consumption. A higher interest rate implies that the return on savings is higher, so that more future consumption goods can be obtained for a given sacrifice of current consumption goods. As well, for a given loan in the first period, the consumer has to forgo more future consumption goods when the loan is repaid. We can use what we learned about income and substitution effects in Chapter 4 to understand how an increase in the real interest rate affects the consumer's behavior. However, it turns out that the income effects of an increase in the real interest rate work in different directions for lenders and borrowers, which is what we want to show next.

First, consider the case of a lender. In Figure 9.13 consider a consumer who is initially a lender and faces an increase in the market real interest rate from r_1 to r_2. Initially, lifetime wealth is we_1, and this changes to we_2. The budget constraint pivots around the endowment point E. Initially, the consumer chose the consumption bundle A, and we suppose that the consumer chooses B after the increase in the real interest rate. To find the substitution effect of the real interest rate increase, we draw an artificial budget constraint FG, which has the same slope as the new budget constraint, and is just tangent to the initial indifference curve I_1. Thus, we are taking wealth away from the consumer until he or she is as well off as before the increase in r. Then, the movement from A to D is a pure substitution effect, and in moving from A to D future consumption increases and current consumption decreases, as future consumption has become cheaper relative to current consumption. The remaining effect, the movement from D to B, is a pure income effect, which causes both current-period and future-period consumption to increase (recall that we assumed that current and future consumption are normal goods). Therefore, future consumption must increase, as both the income and substitution effects work in the same direction. However, current-period consumption may increase or decrease, as the substitution effect causes current consumption to decrease, and the income effect causes it to increase. If the income effect is larger than the substitution effect, then current consumption increases. The effect on savings depends on the change in current consumption, as we are holding constant current disposable income. Thus, saving may increase or decrease. Saving increases if the substitution effect is larger than the income effect, and saving decreases otherwise. An increase in the real interest rate makes saving more attractive, because the relative price of future consumption is lower (the substitution effect), but it makes saving less attractive as there is a positive income effect on period 1 consumption, which tends to reduce saving.

Consider the following example, which shows the intuition behind the income and substitution effects of a change in the real interest rate. Suppose Christine is currently a lender, whose disposable income in the current year is $40,000. She currently saves 30% of her current income, and she faces a real interest rate of 5%. Her income next year will also be $40,000 (in current year dollars), and so initially she consumes $0.7 \times \$40,000 = \$28,000$ this year, and she consumes $\$40,000 + (1 + 0.05) \times \$12,000 = \$52,600$ next year. Now, suppose that the real interest rate rises to 10%.

Figure 9.13 An Increase in the Real Interest Rate for a Lender

When the real interest rate increases for a lender, the substitution effect is the movement from *A* to *D*, and the income effect is the movement from *D* to *B*. Current consumption and saving may rise or fall, while future consumption increases.

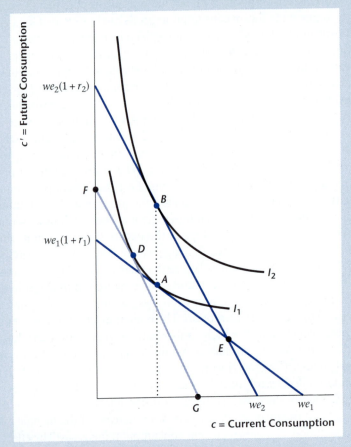

How should Christine respond? If she continues to consume $28,000 in the current year and saves $12,000, then she has future consumption of $53,200, an increase over initial future consumption, reflecting the substitution effect. However, if she consumes the same amount next year, she can now save less in the current year to achieve the same result. That is, she could save $11,454 in the current year, which would imply that she could consume $52,600 next year. Then, she consumes $40,000 − $11,454 = $28,546, which is more than before, reflecting the income effect. What Christine does depends on her own preferences and how strong the relative income and substitution effects are for her as an individual.

Now, consider the effects of an increase in *r* for a borrower. In Figure 9.14, *r* increases from r_1 to r_2, and lifetime wealth changes from we_1 to we_2. The endowment

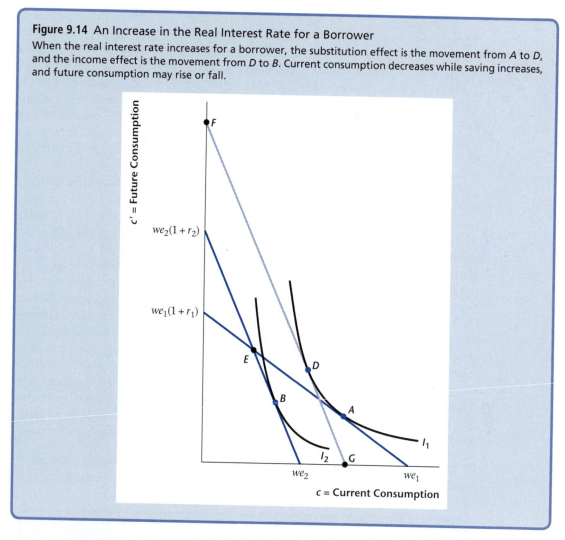

Figure 9.14 An Increase in the Real Interest Rate for a Borrower

When the real interest rate increases for a borrower, the substitution effect is the movement from A to D, and the income effect is the movement from D to B. Current consumption decreases while saving increases, and future consumption may rise or fall.

point is at E, and the consumer initially chooses consumption bundle A; then, he or she chooses B after r increases. Again, we can separate the movement from A to B into substitution and income effects, by drawing an artificial budget constraint FG, which is parallel to the new budget constraint and tangent to the initial indifference curve I_1. Therefore, we are essentially compensating the consumer with extra wealth to make him or her as well off as initially when facing the higher interest rate. Then, the substitution effect is the movement from A to D, and the income effect is the movement from D to B. Here, the substitution effect is for future consumption to rise and current consumption to fall, just as was the case for a lender. However, the income effect in this case is negative for both current consumption and future consumption. As a result, current consumption falls for the borrower, but future consumption may rise or fall, depending on how strong the opposing substitution and income effects are. Savings must rise, as current consumption falls and current disposable income is held constant.

As an example, suppose that Christopher is initially a borrower, whose income in the current year and next year is $40,000 (in current year dollars). Initially, Christopher takes out a loan of $20,000 in the current year, so that he can consume $60,000 in the current year. The real interest rate is 5%, so that the principal and interest on his loan is $21,000, and he consumes $19,000 next year. Now, suppose alternatively that the real interest rate is 10%. If Christopher holds constant his consumption in the future, this must imply that his current consumption goes down, reflecting the negative income effect. That is, if he continues to consume $19,000 next year, given a real interest rate of 10%, he can borrow only $19,091 this year, which implies that his current year consumption is $59,091.

For both lenders and borrowers, there is an **intertemporal substitution effect** of an increase in the real interest rate. That is, a higher real interest rate lowers the relative price of future consumption in terms of current consumption, and this leads to a substitution of future consumption for current consumption and, therefore, to an increase in savings. In much of macroeconomics, we are interested in aggregate effects, but the above analysis tells us that there are potentially confounding income effects in determining the effect of an increase in the real interest rate on aggregate consumption. The population consists of many consumers, some of whom are lenders, and some of whom are borrowers. Though consumption decreases for each borrower when the real interest rate goes up, what happens to the consumption of lenders depends on the strength of opposing income and substitution effects. Though there is a tendency for the negative income effects on the consumption of borrowers to offset the positive income effects on the consumption of lenders, leaving us with only the substitution effects, there is no theoretical guarantee that aggregate consumption will fall when the real interest rate rises.

Tables 9.2 and 9.3 summarize our discussion of the effects of an increase in the real interest rate.

An Example: Perfect Complements   A convenient example to work with is the case in which a consumer has preferences with the perfect complements property. Recall from

Table 9.2   Effects of an Increase in the Real Interest Rate for a Lender

Current consumption	?
Future consumption	Increases
Current savings	?

Table 9.3   Effects of an Increase in the Real Interest Rate for a Borrower

Current consumption	Decreases
Future consumption	?
Current savings	Increases

Chapter 4 that if two goods are perfect complements, they are always consumed in fixed proportions. In the case of current consumption and future consumption, the perfect complements property implies that the consumer always chooses c and c' such that

$$c' = ac, \qquad (9\text{-}10)$$

where a is a positive constant. In Figure 9.15, the consumer's indifference curves, for example I_1 and I_2, are L-shaped with the right angles on the line $c' = ac$. Perfect complementarity is an extreme case of a desire for consumption smoothing, in that the consumer never wants to deviate from having current and future consumption in fixed proportions. The consumer's budget constraint is AB in the figure, which is described by the equation

$$c + \frac{c'}{1 + r} = we, \qquad (9\text{-}11)$$

where

$$we = y - t + \frac{y' - t'}{1 + r}. \qquad (9\text{-}12)$$

In Figure 9.15 the optimal consumption bundle is at a point such as D, which is on the consumer's budget constraint and on the line $c' = ac$. Therefore, we can solve algebraically for current and future consumption c and c', respectively, by solving the

Figure 9.15 Example with Perfect Complements Preferences

The consumer desires current and future consumptions in fixed proportions, with $c' = ac$. With indifference curves representing perfect complementarity between current and future consumption, the optimal consumption bundle is at point D on the lifetime budget constraint AB.

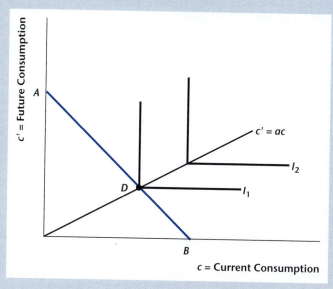

Equations (9-10) and (9-11) for the two variables c and c', given r and we. Using substitution, we get

$$c = \frac{we(1+r)}{1+r+a}, \tag{9-13}$$

$$c' = \frac{awe(1+r)}{1+r+a}, \tag{9-14}$$

or substituting for we in Equations (9-13) and (9-14) using Equation (9-12), we obtain

$$c = \frac{(y-t)(1+r)+y'-t'}{1+r+a}, \tag{9-15}$$

$$c' = a\left[\frac{(y-t)(1+r)+y'-t'}{1+r+a}\right]. \tag{9-16}$$

From Equations (9-15) and (9-16), current and future consumptions increase with current income y and future income y'. The effects of a change in the interest rate r are more complicated, but essentially the effect of an increase in r on c and c' depends only on whether the consumer is a lender or a borrower. This is because there are no substitution effects when preferences have the perfect complements property. We explore this further in the problems at the end of this chapter.

Government

LO 9.3 Construct the government's present-value budget constraint.

Now that we have studied how consumers behave, to complete our description of the model we need only describe what the government does. We can then explore the equilibrium effects of tax policy.

We suppose that the government wishes to purchase G consumption goods in the current period and G' units in the future period, with these quantities of government purchases given exogenously. The aggregate quantity of taxes collected by the government in the current period is T. Recall that there are N consumers who each pay a current tax of t, so that $T = Nt$. Similarly, in the future-period total taxes are equal to T', and we have $T' = Nt'$. The government can borrow in the current period by issuing bonds. Recall that government bonds and private bonds are indistinguishable, with these bonds all bearing the same real interest rate r. Letting B denote the quantity of government bonds issued in the current period, the government's current-period budget constraint is

$$G = T + B, \tag{9-17}$$

that is, government spending is financed through taxes and the issue of bonds. Put another way, the current-period government deficit, $G - T$, is financed by issuing bonds. In the future period, the government's budget constraint is

$$G' + (1+r)B = T'. \tag{9-18}$$

The left-hand side of Equation (9-18) is total government outlays in the future, consisting of future government purchases and the principal and interest on the government bonds issued in the current period. These government outlays are financed through future taxes, the quantity on the right-hand side of Equation (9-18). The government's budget constraints allow for the possibility that $B < 0$. If $B < 0$ this would imply that the government was a lender to the private sector, rather than a borrower from it. In practice, the government engages in direct lending to the private sector, and it issues debt to private economic agents, so that it is a lender and a borrower.

Recall that, when we analyzed a consumer's budget constraint, we took the budget constraints for the current and future periods and collapsed them into a single lifetime budget constraint. Here, we can accomplish something similar, in taking the government's budget constraints expressed in Equations (9-17) and (9-18) and collapsing them into a single **government present-value budget constraint**. We obtain this constraint by first solving Equation (9-18) for B to get

$$B = \frac{T' - G'}{1 + r},$$

and then substituting in Equation (9-17) for B to get

$$G + \frac{G'}{1 + r} = T + \frac{T'}{1 + r}. \tag{9-19}$$

Equation (9-19) is the government present-value budget constraint, and it states that the present value of government purchases must equal the present value of taxes. This is similar to the consumer's lifetime budget constraint, which states that the present value of consumption is equal to the present value of lifetime disposable income. An interpretation of the government present-value budget constraint is that the government must eventually pay off all of its debt by taxing its citizens.

Competitive Equilibrium

LO 9.4 Show how a competitive equilibrium is constructed in the two-period model.

Now that we have described the behavior of the consumers and the government in our model, we can proceed with the final step in putting the model into working order, which is to specify how a competitive equilibrium is achieved.

The market in which the N consumers in this economy and the government interact is the credit market, in which consumers and the government can borrow and lend. In trading in the credit market, consumers and the government are effectively trading future consumption goods for current consumption goods. Recall that the relative price at which future consumption goods trade for current consumption goods is $\frac{1}{1+r}$, which is determined by the real interest rate r.

In a competitive equilibrium for this two-period economy, three conditions must hold:

1. Each consumer chooses first- and second-period consumption and savings optimally given the real interest rate r.

2. The government present-value budget constraint, Equation (9-19), holds.

3. The credit market clears.

The credit market clears when the net quantity that consumers want to lend in the current period is equal to the quantity that the government wishes to borrow. Letting S^p denote the aggregate quantity of private savings—that is, the savings of consumers—the credit market equilibrium condition is

$$S^p = B, \qquad (9\text{-}20)$$

or the aggregate quantity of private savings is equal to the quantity of debt issued by the government in the current period. Equation (9-20) also states that national saving, which is equal to aggregate private saving minus B, is equal to zero in equilibrium. Recall from Chapter 2 that a national income accounts identity states that $S^p + S^g = I + CA$, where S^g is government savings, I is investment, and CA is the current account surplus. Here, $S^g = -B$, $I = 0$ because there is no capital accumulation in this model, and $CA = 0$ because this is a closed economy model. Also recall that $S = S^p + S^g$, where S is national saving.

The equilibrium condition Equation (9-20) implies that

$$Y = C + G, \qquad (9\text{-}21)$$

where Y is aggregate income in the current period (the sum of incomes across all N consumers) and C is aggregate consumption in the current period (the sum of consumptions across all N consumers). Recall from Chapter 2 that Equation (9-21) is the income–expenditure identity for this economy, because there is no investment, and no interaction with the rest of the world (net exports equal zero). To see why Equation (9-21) follows from Equation (9-20), note that

$$S^p = Y - C - T; \qquad (9\text{-}22)$$

that is, aggregate private saving is equal to current-period income minus aggregate current consumption minus aggregate current taxes. Also, from the government's current-period budget constraint, Equation (9-17), we have

$$B = G - T. \qquad (9\text{-}23)$$

Then, substituting in Equation (9-20) for S^p from Equation (9-22) and for B from Equation (9-23), we get

$$Y - C - T = G - T,$$

or rearranging,

$$Y = C + G.$$

This result proves to be useful in the next section, as the economy can be shown to be in a competitive equilibrium if either Equation (9-20) or Equation (9-21) holds.

The Ricardian Equivalence Theorem

LO 9.5 Explain the Ricardian equivalence theorem.

From Chapter 5, recall that an increase in government spending comes at a cost, in that it crowds out private consumption expenditures. However, in Chapter 5, we could not disentangle the effects of taxation from the effects of government spending, because the government was unable to borrow in the model considered there. That is certainly not true here, where we can independently evaluate the effects of changes in government spending and in taxes.

What we want to show here is a key result in macroeconomics, called the Ricardian equivalence theorem. This theorem states that a change in the timing of taxes by the government is neutral. By neutral, we mean that in equilibrium a change in current taxes, exactly offset in present-value terms by an equal and opposite change in future taxes, has no effect on the real interest rate or on the consumption of individual consumers. This is a very strong result, as it says that there is a sense in which government deficits do not matter, which seems to run counter to standard intuition. As we will see, however, this is an important starting point for thinking about why government deficits *do* matter, and a key message that comes from the logic of the Ricardian equivalence theorem is that *a tax cut is not a free lunch.*

To show why the Ricardian equivalence theorem holds in this model, we need only make some straightforward observations about the lifetime budget constraints of consumers and the government's present-value budget constraint. First, because each of the N consumers shares an equal amount of the total tax burden in the current and future periods, with $T = Nt$ and $T' = Nt'$, substituting in the government's present-value budget constraint, Equation (9-19) gives

$$G + \frac{G'}{1+r} = Nt + \frac{Nt'}{1+r},\tag{9-24}$$

and then rearranging we get

$$t + \frac{t'}{1+r} = \frac{1}{N}\left[G + \frac{G'}{1+r}\right],\tag{9-25}$$

which states that the present value of taxes for a single consumer is the consumer's share of the present value of government spending. Next, substitute for the present value of taxes from Equation (9-25) in a consumer's lifetime budget constraint, Equation (9-4) to get

$$c + \frac{c'}{1+r} = y + \frac{y'}{1+r} - \frac{1}{N}\left[G + \frac{G'}{1+r}\right].\tag{9-26}$$

Now, suppose that the economy is in equilibrium for a given real interest rate r. Each consumer chooses current consumption and future consumption c and c', respectively, to make himself or herself as well off as possible subject to the lifetime budget constraint, Equation (9-26) (the present-value government budget constraint) holds, Equation (9-19) holds, and the credit market clears, so current aggregate income is equal to current aggregate consumption plus current government spending, $Y = C + G$.

Next, consider an experiment in which the timing of taxes changes in such a way that the government budget constraint continues to hold at the interest rate r. That is, current taxes change by Δt for each consumer, with future taxes changing by $-\frac{\Delta t}{1+r}$ so that the government budget constraint continues to hold, from Equation (9-24). Then, from Equation (9-26) there is no change in the consumer's lifetime wealth, the right-hand side of Equation (9-26), given r, because y, y', N, G, and G' remain unaffected. Because the consumer's lifetime wealth is unaffected, given r, the consumer makes the same decisions, choosing the same quantities of current and future consumption. This is true for every consumer, so given r, aggregate consumption C is the same. Thus, it is still the case that $Y = C + G$, so the credit market clears. Therefore, with the new timing of taxes and the same real interest rate, each consumer is optimizing, the government's present-value budget constraint holds, and the credit market clears, so r is still the equilibrium real interest rate.

Therefore, we have shown that a change in the timing of taxes has no effect on equilibrium consumption or the real interest rate. Because each consumer faces the same budget constraint before and after the change in the timing of taxes, all consumers are no better or worse off with the change in taxes. We have, thus, demonstrated that the Ricardian equivalence theorem holds in this model.

Though the timing of taxes has no effect on consumption, welfare, or the market real interest rate, there are effects on private saving and government saving. That is, because aggregate private saving is $S^p = Y - T - C$ and government saving is $S^g = T - G$, any change in the timing of taxes that decreases current taxes T increases current private saving and decreases government saving by equal amounts. To give a more concrete example, suppose that there is a cut in current taxes, so that $\Delta t < 0$. Then, the government must issue more debt today to finance the tax cut, and it will have to increase taxes in the future to pay off this higher debt. Consumers anticipate this, and they increase their savings by the amount of the tax cut, because this is how much extra they have to save to pay the higher taxes they will face in the future. In the credit market, there is an increase in savings by consumers, which just matches the increase in borrowing by the government, so there is no effect on borrowing and lending among consumers, and therefore, no effect on the market real interest rate.

Ricardian Equivalence: A Graph

We can show how the Ricardian equivalence theorem works by considering the effects of a current tax cut on an individual consumer. Here, the consumer also faces an increase in taxes in the future, as the government must pay off the current debt issued to finance the tax cut. Suppose that a consumer initially faces taxes t^* and t'^* in the current period and future period, respectively. In Figure 9.16 he or she has an endowment point E_1, and chooses consumption bundle A. Now, suppose there is a tax cut in the current period, so that $\Delta t < 0$. Therefore, the government must borrow $N\Delta t$ more in period 1 to finance the larger current government deficit, and taxes must rise for each consumer by $-\Delta t(1 + r)$ in the future period to pay off the increased government debt. The effect of this on the consumer is that lifetime wealth we remains unchanged, as the present value of taxes has not changed. The budget constraint is unaffected, and the consumer still chooses point A in Figure 9.16. What changes is that the endowment

Figure 9.16 Ricardian Equivalence with a Cut in Current Taxes for a Borrower

A current tax cut with a future increase in taxes leaves the consumer's lifetime budget constraint unchanged, and so the consumer's optimal consumption bundle remains at A. The endowment point shifts from E_1 to E_2, so that there is an increase in saving by the amount of the current tax cut.

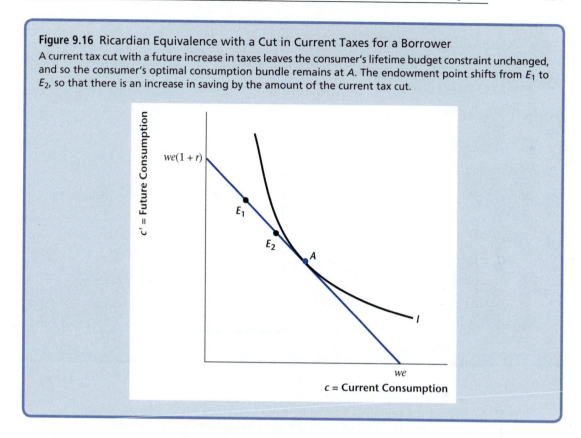

point moves to E_2; that is, the consumer has more disposable income in the current period and less disposable income in the future period due to the tax cut in the current period. Because the consumer buys the same consumption bundle, what he or she does is to save all of the tax cut in the current period to pay the higher taxes that he or she faces in the future period.

Ricardian Equivalence and Credit Market Equilibrium

Finally, we will consider a graph that shows the workings of the credit market under Ricardian equivalence. In Figure 9.17, the curve $S_1^p(r)$ denotes the private supply of credit, which is the total desired saving of private consumers given the market real interest rate r, drawn given a particular timing of taxes between the current and future periods. We have drawn $S_1^p(r)$ as upward-sloping, under the assumption that substitution effects outweigh the income effects of changes in interest rates when we add these effects across all consumers. The government demand for credit is B_1, the exogenous supply of bonds issued by the government in the current period. The equilibrium real interest rate that clears the credit market is r_1.

Now, if the government reduces current taxes by the same amount for each individual, this results in an increase in government bonds issued from B_1 to B_2. This is not the end of the story, as savings behavior changes for each consumer. In fact, total

Figure 9.17 Ricardian Equivalence and Credit Market Equilibrium
With a decrease in current taxes, government debt increases from B_1 to B_2, and the credit supply curve shifts to the right by the same amount. The equilibrium real interest rate is unchanged, and private saving increases by an amount equal to the reduction in government saving.

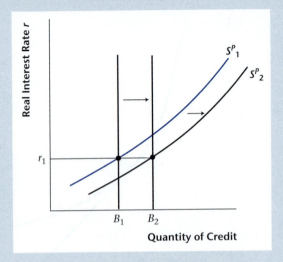

savings, or the supply of credit, increases for each consumer by an amount such that the credit supply curve shifts to the right by an amount $B_2 - B_1$ for each r, to $S_2^p(r)$. Therefore, the equilibrium real interest rate remains unchanged at r_1, and private savings increases by the same amount by which government savings falls.

Previously, when we looked at the effects of an increase in a consumer's current disposable income on current consumption, we determined that, because of the consumer's consumption-smoothing motive, some of the increase in disposable income would be saved. Thus, a temporary increase in disposable income would lead to a less than one-for-one increase in current consumption. In the real world, where individual consumption decisions are made over long horizons, any temporary increase in a consumer's disposable income should lead to a relatively small increase in his or her permanent income, in line with Friedman's permanent income hypothesis. Thus, Friedman's permanent income hypothesis would appear to imply that a temporary change in taxes leads to a very small change in current consumption. The Ricardian equivalence theorem carries this logic one step further by taking into account the implications of a current change in taxes for future taxes. For example, because any current tax cut must be paid for with government borrowing, this government borrowing implies higher future taxes to pay off the government debt. In making their lifetime wealth calculations, consumers recognize that the current tax cut is exactly offset by higher taxes in the future, and they save all of the current tax cut to pay the higher future taxes.

A key message from the Ricardian equivalence theorem is that a tax cut is not a free lunch. While a current tax cut can give all consumers higher current disposable incomes, and this seems like a good thing, consumers must pay for the current tax cut by bearing higher taxes in the future. Under the conditions studied in our model, the costs of a tax cut exactly offset the benefits, and consumers are no better off with the tax cut than without it.

Ricardian Equivalence and the Burden of the Government Debt

LO 9.6 Discuss how the Ricardian equivalence theorem helps us understand the burden of the government debt.

At the individual level, debt represents a liability that reduces an individual's lifetime wealth. The Ricardian equivalence theorem implies that the same logic holds for the government debt, which the theorem tells us represents our future tax liabilities as a nation. The government debt is a burden in that it is something we owe to ourselves; the government must pay off its debt by taxing us in the future. In the model in which we explained the Ricardian equivalence theorem above, the burden of the debt is shared equally among consumers. In practice, however, many issues in fiscal policy revolve around how the burden of the government debt is shared, among the current population and between generations. To discuss these issues, we need to address the role played by four key assumptions in our analysis of the Ricardian equivalence theorem.

1. The first key assumption is that when taxes change, in the experiment we considered above, they change by the same amount for all consumers, both in the present and in the future. For example, when a particular consumer received a tax cut in the current period, this was offset by an equal and opposite (in present-value terms) increase in taxes in the future, so that the present-value tax burden for each individual was unchanged. Now, if some consumers received higher tax cuts than others, then lifetime wealth could change for some consumers, and this would necessarily change their consumption choices and could change the equilibrium real interest rate. In the future, when the higher debt is paid off through higher future taxes, consumers might share unequally in this taxation, so that the burden of the debt might not be distributed equally. The government can redistribute wealth in society through tax policy, and the public debate concerning changes in taxes often focuses on how these tax changes affect consumers at different income levels.

2. A second key assumption in the model is that any debt issued by the government is paid off during the lifetimes of the people alive when the debt was issued. In practice, the government can postpone the taxes required to pay off the debt until long in the future, when the consumers who received the current benefits of a higher government debt are either retired or dead. That is, if the government cuts taxes, then the current old receive higher disposable incomes, but it is the current young who will have to pay off the government debt in the future through higher taxes. In this sense, the government debt can be a burden on the young, and it can involve an intergenerational redistribution of wealth. In some instances, intergenerational wealth redistribution can improve matters for everyone, as with some social security programs. We explore this issue in the Chapter 10.

3. A third assumption made above was that taxes are lump sum. In practice, as mentioned in Chapters 4 and 5, all taxes cause distortions, in that they change the effective relative prices of goods faced by consumers in the market. These distortions represent welfare losses from taxation. That is, if the government collects $1 million in taxes, the welfare cost to the economy is something greater than $1 million, because of the distortions caused by taxation. The study of optimal taxation in public finance involves examining how large these welfare costs are for different kinds of taxes. For example, it could be that the welfare cost of income taxation at the margin is higher than the welfare cost of sales taxes at the margin. If the government taxes optimally, it minimizes the welfare cost of taxation, given the quantity of tax revenue it needs to generate. One of the trade-offs made by the government in setting taxes optimally is the trade-off between current taxation and future taxation. The government debt represents a burden, in that the future taxes required to pay off the debt will cause distortions. Some work on optimal taxation by Robert Barro,[3] among others, shows that the government should act to smooth tax rates over time, so as to achieve the optimal trade-off between current and future taxation.

4. A fourth key assumption made above is that there is a **perfect credit market**, in the sense that consumers can borrow and lend as much as they please, subject to their lifetime budget constraints, and they can borrow and lend at the same interest rate. In practice, consumers face constraints on how much they can borrow; for example, credit cards have borrowing limits, and sometimes consumers cannot borrow without collateral (as with mortgages and auto loans).[4] Consumers also typically borrow at higher interest rates than they can lend at. For example, the gap between the interest rate on a typical bank loan and the interest rate on a typical bank deposit can be 6 percentage points per annum or more. Further, the government borrows at lower interest rates than does the typical consumer. While all consumers need not be affected by **credit market imperfections**, to the extent that some consumers are credit-constrained, these credit-constrained consumers could be affected beneficially by a tax cut, even if there is an offsetting tax liability for these consumers in the future. In this sense, the government debt may not be a burden for some segments of the population; it may in fact increase welfare for these groups. We explore this idea further in Chapter 10.

The Ricardian equivalence theorem captures a key reality: Current changes in taxes have consequences for future taxes. However, there are many complications associated with real-world tax policy that essentially involve shifts in the distribution of taxation across the population and in the distribution of the burden of the government debt. These complications are left out of our analysis of the Ricardian equivalence theorem.

---

[3]See R. Barro, 1979. " On the Determination of the Public Debt," *Journal of Political Economy* 87, 940–971.

[4]Collateral is the security that a borrower puts up when the loan is made. If the borrower defaults on the loan, then the collateral is seized by the lender. With a mortgage loan, the collateral is the house purchased with the mortgage loan, and with an auto loan, the collateral is the car that was purchased.

For some macroeconomic issues, the distributional effects of tax policy are irrelevant, but for other issues they matter a great deal. For example, if you were a macroeconomist working for a political party, how a particular tax policy affected the wealth of different consumers in different ways might be the key to your party's success, and you would want to pay close attention to this. As well, as you will see in Chapter 10, so-called "pay-as-you-go" social security systems work because of the intergenerational redistributional effects of tax policy, and credit market imperfections that cause Ricardian equivalence to fail are key to understanding the recent financial crisis.

MACROECONOMICS IN ACTION
Default on Government Debt

A useful measure of a country's indebtedness is the ratio of government debt outstanding to total annual GDP. For the United States, this measure is shown in Figure 9.18. The figure shows that the ratio of federal government debt to GDP for the United States grew from about 63% at the end of 2007 to about 109% at the end of 2015. Is this a troubling sign?

Government debt can indeed reach levels that are unsustainable. A key element in the model constructed in this chapter is the government's present-value budget constraint, which was constructed under the assumption that the government will always pay its bills. But in the real world, a government faces uncertainty, and may find itself in circumstances in which paying its bills is not feasible—the government cannot meet the interest payments on its debt. It is also possible that default by the government is the preferable course of action, even though paying its bills may be feasible.

Most of our experience with sovereign default—the default of governments on their debts—relates to countries that have a large amount of external debt. That is, most countries default in circumstances in which a large amount of government debt is held by foreigners. Then, the trade-off that the government faces is that domestic residents can gain in the present through default, since the government does not have to levy the taxes required to pay off the external debt. Those holding the debt—foreigners—lose when default occurs. But domestic residents will lose in the future, as those in other countries will be reluctant to lend to the domestic government in the future. Borrowing abroad is useful for a government because, just as for a single consumer, smoothing aggregate consumption by borrowing from foreigners is welfare improving. If international credit is cut off, this is detrimental to the welfare of domestic residents.

Two important facts concerning typical sovereign defaults are (i) they typically occur after severe recessions, and (ii) they are preceded by large run-ups in the interest rates on the government's debt. That is, a recession impairs the ability of the government to finance the interest payments on its debt, financial market participants see this happening, and those financial market participants will then only hold the government's debt if it bears a default premium, reflected in a higher interest rate.

In recent history, two important cases of sovereign default were the Argentinian default

(Continued)

in 2001, and the Greek default in 2012. Both of these defaults were associated with severe recessions and with large increases in interest rates on the government debt of the countries in question. While Argentinian debt at the time of its default was close to 170% of GDP—much higher than the debt-to-GDP ratio in the United States at the end of 2015—Greece had a debt-to-GDP ratio of 109% in 2011 just before its default, which is in the ballpark of the current federal debt level for the United States.

But, some countries can have very high debt levels without defaulting, or any observable signal that default is likely. For example, in 2013, the debt-to-GDP ratio in Japan was 238%, but there were no signals then, nor are there any now, of an impending Japanese sovereign default.

So, what is going on? Economists typically use models designed to think about private credit market default to understand why governments default. One such model was constructed by Timothy Kehoe and David Levine.[5] In Kehoe and Levine's model, a borrower chooses to repay his or her debts because defaulting implies that he or she will not have access to credit in the future. The borrower weighs the short-term benefit from not paying his or her debts, against the long-term cost of credit market exclusion. Such a theory goes only so far in explaining sovereign default, in part because the temptation to default in the Kehoe-Levine model is highest in good times. But we know that sovereign default tends to occur in bad times.

Cristina Arellano modifies the Kehoe–Levine approach in constructing a model that can better explain the observed behavior of governments in credit markets. In Arellano's model, the benefit from defaulting is larger in bad times, and so this is when default tends to occur, as we observe.

But, what if we think in terms of the closed-economy model we worked with in this chapter? In such a model—or in the real world if a government does not borrow from other countries—the government debt is something we owe to ourselves. So how can we use what economists know about sovereign debt to think about domestically held government debt, and the government's incentives to default?

One approach would be to think in terms of the distributional consequences of default. If the government chose to default on its debt, the benefits would be distributed across the population in a way that depends on the reduction in taxes this would entail for different people. And, the costs would depend on who is holding the government debt. Under a progressive tax system, the rich pay a higher fraction of income in taxes, so if the government defaults and tax reductions are made in proportion to a person's current taxes, then the rich benefit more from default than the poor. In the United States,[6] the very poor may have little or nothing in the way of financial assets, not even a transactions account at a bank. In the general population, only about 10% of the population holds bonds directly, though a much larger fraction of the population holds government debt indirectly through mutual funds, pension fund accounts, and bank accounts. Roughly, we can say that the poor hold proportionately less government debt than middle-income people, and that middle-income people hold proportionately more government debt than the rich, who hold proportionately more risky assets such as stocks. Thus, we would expect the costs of government default to be borne more by middle-income people.

So, in general, if the government defaults, the winners will tend to be the rich and (somewhat) the poor, and middle-income people will tend to be the losers. Thus, whether or not the government chooses to default will depend on the relative political leverage of these different groups, and on how the state of the world (boom or recession for example) affects the marginal costs and benefits for different groups.

[5]T. Kehoe and D. Levine, 1993. "Debt-Constrained Asset Markets," *Review of Economic Studies* 60, 865–888.

[6]See *Federal Reserve Bulletin*, "Changes in U.S. Family Finances from 2010 to 2013: Evidence from the Survey of Consumer Finances," September 2014.

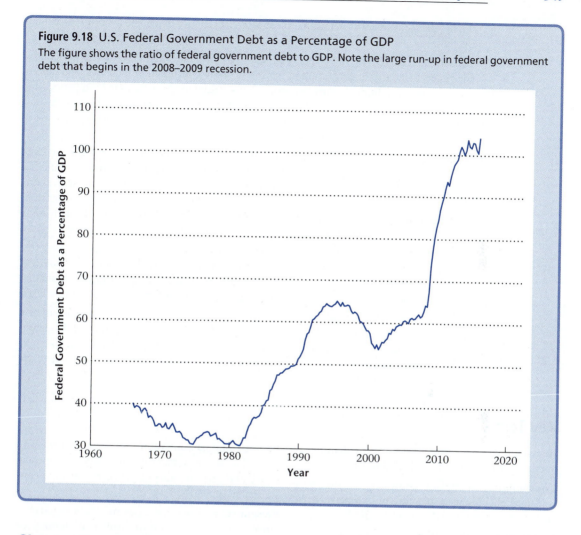

Figure 9.18 U.S. Federal Government Debt as a Percentage of GDP

The figure shows the ratio of federal government debt to GDP. Note the large run-up in federal government debt that begins in the 2008–2009 recession.

Chapter Summary

- A two-period macroeconomic model was constructed to understand the intertemporal consumption–savings decisions of consumers and the effects of fiscal policy choices concerning the timing of taxes and the quantity of government debt.

- In the model, there are many consumers, and each makes decisions over a two-period horizon where a consumer's incomes in the two periods are given, and the consumer pays lump-sum taxes in each period to the government.

- The lifetime budget constraint of the consumer states that the present value of consumption over the consumer's two-period time horizon is equal to the present value of disposable income.

- A consumer's lifetime wealth is his or her present value of disposable income.

- A consumer's preferences have the property that more is preferred to less with regard to current and future consumption, there is a preference for diversity in current and future consumption, and current and future consumption are normal goods. A preference for diversity implies that consumers wish to smooth consumption relative to income over the present and the future.

- Consumption smoothing yields the result that, if income increases in the current period for a consumer, then current consumption increases, future consumption increases, and current saving increases. If future income increases, then consumption increases in both periods and current saving decreases. A permanent increase in income (when current and future income increase) has a larger impact on current consumption than does a temporary increase in income (only current income increases).

- If there is an increase in the real interest rate that a consumer faces, then there are income and substitution effects on consumption. Because an increase in the real interest rate causes a reduction in the price of future consumption in terms of current consumption, the substitution effect is for current consumption to fall, future consumption to rise, and current saving to rise when the real interest rate rises. For a lender (borrower), the income effect of an increase in the real interest rate is positive (negative) for both current and future consumption.

- The Ricardian equivalence theorem states that changes in current taxes by the government that leave the present value of taxes constant have no effect on consumers' consumption choices or on the equilibrium real interest rate. This is because consumers change savings by an amount equal and opposite to the change in current taxes to compensate for the change in future taxes.

- Ricardian equivalence depends critically on the notion that the burden of the government debt is shared equally among the people alive when the debt is issued. The burden of the debt is not shared equally when: (1) there are current distributional effects of changes in taxes; (2) there are intergenerational distribution effects; (3) taxes cause distortions; or (4) there are credit market imperfections.

Key Terms

Intertemporal decisions Decisions involving economic trade-offs across periods of time. (p. 306)

Consumption–savings decision The decision by a consumer about how to split current income between current consumption and savings. (p. 306)

Ricardian equivalence theorem Named for David Ricardo, this theorem states that changes in the stream of taxes faced by consumers that leave the present value of taxes unchanged have no effect on consumption, interest rates, or welfare. (p. 307)

Two-period model An economic model where all decision makers (consumers and firms) have two-period planning horizons, with the two periods typically representing the present and the future. (p. 307)

Real interest rate The rate of return on savings in units of consumption goods. (p. 307)

Consumption smoothing The tendency of consumers to seek a consumption path over time that is smoother than income. (p. 307)

Lifetime budget constraint Condition that the present value of a consumer's lifetime disposable income equals the present value of his or her lifetime consumption. (p. 310)

Present value The value, in terms of money today or current goods, of a future stream of money or goods. (p. 310)

Lifetime wealth The present value of lifetime disposable income for a consumer. (p. 311)

Endowment point The point on a consumer's budget constraint where consumption is equal to disposable income in each period. (p. 312)

Excess variability The observed fact that measured consumption is more variable than theory appears to predict. (p. 321)

Permanent income hypothesis A theory developed by Milton Friedman that implies a consumer's current consumption depends on his or her permanent income. Permanent income is closely related to lifetime wealth in our model. (p. 323)

Martingale An economic variable with the property that the best forecast of its value tomorrow is its value today. Finance theory implies that stock prices are martingales. (p. 325)

Intertemporal substitution effect Substitution by a consumer of a good in one time period for a good in another time period, in response to a change in the relative price of the two goods. The intertemporal substitution effect of an increase in the real interest rate is for current consumption to fall and future consumption to rise. (p. 332)

Government present-value budget constraint Condition that the present value of government purchases is equal to the present value of tax revenues. (p. 335)

Perfect credit market An idealized credit market in which consumers can borrow and lend all they want at the market interest rate, and the interest rate at which consumers lend is equal to the interest rate at which they borrow. (p. 342)

Credit market imperfections Constraints on borrowing, or differences between borrowing and lending rates of interest. (p. 342)

Questions for Review

All questions refer to the macroeconomic model developed in this chapter.

9.1 Why do consumers save?

9.2 How do consumers save in the two-period model?

9.3 What factors are important to a consumer in making his or her consumption–savings decision?

9.4 What is the price of future consumption in terms of current consumption?

9.5 Show how to derive the consumer's lifetime budget constraint from the consumer's current-period and future-period budget constraints.

9.6 What is the slope of a consumer's lifetime budget constraint?

9.7 What are the horizontal and vertical intercepts of a consumer's lifetime budget constraint?

9.8 If a consumer chooses the endowment point, how much does he or she consume in each period, and how much does he or she save?

9.9 What are the three properties of a consumer's preferences?

9.10 How is the consumer's motive to smooth consumption captured by the shape of an indifference curve?

9.11 What are the effects of an increase in current income on consumption in each period, and on savings?

9.12 Give two reasons why consumption is more variable in the data than theory seems to predict.

9.13 What are the effects of an increase in future income on consumption in each period, and on savings?

9.14 What produces a larger increase in a consumer's current consumption, a permanent increase in the consumer's income or a temporary increase?

9.15 What does theory tell us about how the value of stocks held by consumers should be related to consumption behavior? Does the data support this?

9.16 What are the effects of an increase in the real interest rate on consumption in each period, and on savings? How does this depend on income and substitution effects and whether the consumer is a borrower or lender?

9.17 How does the government finance its purchases in the two-period model?

9.18 State the Ricardian equivalence theorem.

9.19 Give four reasons that the burden of the government debt is not shared equally in practice.

Problems

1. **LO 2** A consumer's income in the current period is $y = 100$, and income in the future period is $y' = 120$. He or she pays lump-sum taxes $t = 20$ in the current period and $t' = 10$ in the future period. The real interest rate is 0.1, or 10%, per period.
   (a) Determine the consumer's lifetime wealth.
   (b) Suppose that current and future consumptions are perfect complements for the consumer and that he or she always wants to have equal consumption in the current and future periods. Draw the consumer's indifference curves.
   (c) Determine what the consumer's optimal current-period and future-period consumptions are, and what optimal saving is, and show this in a diagram with the consumer's budget constraint and indifference curves. Is the consumer a lender or a borrower?
   (d) Now suppose that instead of $y = 100$, the consumer has $y = 140$. Again, determine optimal consumption in the current and future periods and optimal saving, and show this in a diagram. Is the consumer a lender or a borrower?
   (e) Explain the differences in your results between parts (c) and (d).

2. **LO 2** An employer offers his or her employee the option of shifting x units of income from next year to this year. That is, the option is to reduce income next year by x units and increase income this year by x units.
   (a) Would the employee take this option (use a diagram)?
   (b) Determine, using a diagram, how this shift in income will affect consumption this year and next year and saving this year. Explain your results.

3. **LO 2** Consider the following effects of an increase in taxes for a consumer.
   (a) The consumer's taxes increase by Δt in the current period. How does this affect current consumption, future consumption, and current saving?
   (b) The consumer's taxes increase permanently, increasing by Δt in the current and future periods. Using a diagram, determine how

this affects current consumption, future consumption, and current saving. Explain the differences between your results here and in part (a).

4. **LO 2** Suppose that the government introduces a tax on interest earnings. That is, borrowers face a real interest rate of r before and after the tax is introduced, but lenders receive an interest rate of $(1 - x)r$ on their savings, where x is the tax rate. Therefore, we are looking at the effects of having x increase from zero to some value greater than zero, with r assumed to remain constant.
   (a) Show the effects of the increase in the tax rate on a consumer's lifetime budget constraint.
   (b) How does the increase in the tax rate affect the optimal choice of consumption (in the current and future periods) and saving for the consumer? Show how income and substitution effects matter for your answer, and show how it matters whether the consumer is initially a borrower or a lender.

5. **LO 2, 5** A consumer receives income y in the current period, income y' in the future period, and pays taxes of t and t' in the current and future periods, respectively. The consumer can borrow and lend at the real interest rate r. This consumer faces a constraint on how much he or she can borrow, much like the credit limit typically placed on a credit card account. That is, the consumer cannot borrow more than x, where $x < we - y + t$, with we denoting lifetime wealth. Use diagrams to determine the effects on the consumer's current consumption, future consumption, and savings of a change in x, and explain your results.

6. **LO 2, 5** A consumer receives income y in the current period, income y' in the future period, and pays taxes of t and t' in the current and future periods, respectively. The consumer can lend at the real interest rate r. The consumer is given two options. First, he or she can borrow at the interest rate r but can only borrow an amount x or less, where $x < we - y + t$. Second, he or she can borrow an unlimited amount at the interest rate r_2, where $r_2 > r$. Use a diagram to determine which option the consumer chooses, and explain your results.

7. **LO 2, 5** Suppose that all consumers are identical, and also assume that the real interest rate r is fixed. Suppose that the government wants to collect a given amount of tax revenue R, in present-value terms. Assume that the government has two options: (i) a proportional tax of s per unit of savings, in that the tax collected per consumer is $s(y - c)$; (ii) a proportional tax u on consumption in the current and future periods, so that the present value of the total tax collected per consumer is $uc + \frac{uc'}{1+r}$. Note that the tax rate s could be positive or negative. For example if consumers borrow, then s would need to be less than zero for the government to collect tax revenue. Show that option (ii) is preferable to option (i) if the government wishes to make consumers as well off as possible, and explain why this is so. [Hint: Show that the consumption bundle that consumers choose under option (i) could have been chosen under option (ii), but was not.]

8. **LO 2, 5** Assume a consumer who has current-period income $y = 200$, future-period income $y' = 150$, current and future taxes $t = 40$ and $t' = 50$, respectively, and faces a market real interest rate of $r = 0.05$, or 5% per period. The consumer would like to consume equal amounts in both periods; that is, he or she would like to set $c = c'$, if possible. However, this consumer is faced with a credit market imperfection, in that he or she cannot borrow at all; that is, $s \geq 0$.
   (a) Show the consumer's lifetime budget constraint and indifference curves in a diagram.
   (b) Calculate his or her optimal current-period and future-period consumption and optimal saving, and show this in your diagram.
   (c) Suppose that everything remains unchanged, except that now $t = 20$ and $t' = 71$. Calculate the effects on current and future consumption and optimal saving, and show this in your diagram.
   (d) Now, suppose alternatively that $y = 100$. Repeat parts (a) to (c), and explain any differences.

9. **LO 5** Assume an economy with 1,000 consumers. Each consumer has income in the current period of 50 units and future income of 60 units and pays a lump-sum tax of 10 units in the current period and 20 units in the future period. The market real interest rate is 8%. Of the 1,000

consumers, 500 consume 60 units in the future, while 500 consume 20 units in the future.
   (a) Determine each consumer's current consumption and current saving.
   (b) Determine aggregate private saving, aggregate consumption in each period, government spending in the current and future periods, the current-period government deficit, and the quantity of debt issued by the government in the current period.
   (c) Suppose that current taxes increase to 15 units for each consumer. Repeat parts (a) and (b) and explain your results.

10. **LO 2** Suppose a consumer who has a marginal rate of substitution of current consumption for future consumption that is a constant, b.
   (a) Determine how this consumer's choice of current consumption, future consumption, and savings depends on the market real interest rate r, and taxes and income in the current and future periods. Show this in diagrams.
   (b) Now, suppose that current taxes rise and future taxes fall, in such a way that the present value of taxes is unaffected. How does this affect consumption in the current and future periods, and savings for the consumer?

11. **LO 5** Suppose that a consumer has income y in the current period, income y' in the future period, and faces proportional taxes on consumption in the current and future periods. There are no lump-sum taxes. That is, if consumption is c in the current period and c' in the future period, the consumer pays a tax sc in the current period, and $s'c'$ in the future period where s is the current-period tax rate on consumption, and s' is the future-period tax rate on consumption. The government wishes to collect total tax revenue in the current and future periods, which has a present value of R. Now, suppose that the government reduces s and increases s', in such a way that it continues to collect the same present value of tax revenue R from the consumer, given the consumer's optimal choices of current-period and future-period consumptions.
   (a) Write down the lifetime budget constraint of the consumer.
   (b) Show that lifetime wealth is the same for the consumer, before and after the change in tax rates.

(c) What effect, if any, does the change in tax rates have on the consumer's choice of current and future consumptions, and on savings? Does Ricardian equivalence hold here? Explain why or why not.

12. **LO 5** Suppose in our two-period model of the economy that the government, instead of borrowing in the current period, runs a government loan program. That is, loans are made to consumers at the market real interest rate r, with the aggregate quantity of loans made in the current period denoted by L. Government loans are financed by lump-sum taxes on consumers in the current period, and we assume that government spending is zero in the current and future periods. In the future period, when the government loans are repaid by consumers, the government rebates this amount as lump-sum transfers (negative taxes) to consumers.

(a) Write down the government's current-period budget constraint and its future-period budget constraint.

(b) Determine the present-value budget constraint of the government.

(c) Write down the lifetime budget constraint of a consumer.

(d) Show that the size of the government loan program (i.e., the quantity L) has no effect on current consumption or future consumption for each individual consumer and that there is no effect on the equilibrium real interest rate. Explain this result.

Working with the Data

Answer these questions using the Federal Reserve Bank of St. Louis's FRED database, accessible at http://research.stlouisfed.org/fred2/

1. Plot the ratio of aggregate consumption to GDP. Comment on the features of your time series plot. What principle of consumption behavior helps to explain what you see?

2. Calculate and plot the percentage change in federal government receipts (adjust for inflation by dividing receipts by the implicit GDP deflator), and the percentage change in real GDP. Does what you see in the chart conform to Ricardian equivalence? Explain why or why not.

3. Plot the percentage change in the relative price of housing, along with the percentage change in real consumption of nondurables and services. Calculate the relative price of housing as the Case and Shiller 20-city home price index divided by the consumer price index. What do you see in the plot? Does the value of housing appear to matter for consumption behavior? If so, why should it? If not, why not?

Chapter 10

Credit Market Imperfections: Credit Frictions, Financial Crises, and Social Security

Learning Objectives

After studying Chapter 10, students will be able to:

10.1 Construct the basic credit market imperfections problem for the consumer, with a kinked budget constraint.

10.2 Adapt the credit markets model to deal with asymmetric information.

10.3 Show how limited commitment makes collateral important in the credit markets model.

10.4 Show how pay-as-you-go social security works, and demonstrate what conditions are required so that it increases economic welfare.

10.5 Show how fully-funded social security programs function, and explain their economic role.

In Chapter 9, we explored the basic elements of consumer behavior in credit markets—how consumers act to smooth consumption over time in response to changes in their incomes and in market interest rates. As well, we studied the aggregate effects of changes in government tax policy. A key theoretical result from Chapter 9 is the Ricardian equivalence theorem, which states that a change in the timing of taxes can have no effects on consumer behavior or interest rates, provided that some special conditions hold. The Ricardian equivalence theorem provides us with a firm foundation for understanding the circumstances under which government tax policy will matter. In particular, as discussed in Chapter 9, the Ricardian equivalence theorem will not hold if the tax burden is not shared equally among consumers, if there is intergenerational redistribution resulting from a change in taxes, if there are tax distortions, or if there are credit market imperfections.

The cases under which Ricardian equivalence does not hold have practical importance in at least two respects. First, credit market imperfections, or " frictions," which cause Ricardian equivalence to fail, are key to understanding some important features of how credit markets work. For example, in practice the interest rates at which consumers and firms can lend are lower than the interest rates at which they can borrow, consumers and firms cannot always borrow up to the quantity they would like at market interest rates, and borrowers are sometimes required to post collateral against a loan. All of these features of actual loan contracts can be understood as arising because of credit market frictions.

In this chapter, we will study two types of credit market frictions: **asymmetric information** and **limited commitment**. Asymmetric information refers to a situation where, in a particular market, some market participant knows more about his or her own characteristics than do other market participants. In the credit market context we examine, asymmetric information exists in that a particular borrower knows more about his or her own creditworthiness than do potential lenders. This credit market friction then leads to differences between the interest rates at which consumers can lend and borrow. The loan interest rate reflects a **default premium** which acts to compensate lenders for the fact that some borrowers will default on their loans. Even good borrowers who will not default must pay the default premium, as lenders are unable to distinguish between good and bad borrowers. Asymmetric information is an important element that we can use to help understand the 2008–2009 financial crisis, and other such financial crises, which are characterized by dramatic increases in **interest rate spreads**. These interest rate spreads are gaps between the interest rates on risky loans and safer loans, or between the rates of interest at which some class of borrowers can lend and borrow. As well, during the financial crisis there was a dramatic decrease in the quantity of lending in some segments of the credit market, which asymmetric information can help explain.

A second credit market friction, limited commitment, refers to situations in which it is impossible for a market participant to commit in advance to some future action. In credit markets, there can be lack of commitment in the sense that a borrower cannot commit to repaying a loan. Given the choice, a rational borrower would choose to default on a loan if there were no penalty for doing so. A typical incentive device used by lenders to prevent this type of strategic default is the posting of collateral. Indeed, most lending in credit markets is collateralized. For example, in consumer credit markets, an individual who takes out a mortgage loan is required to post his or her house as collateral, and when a consumer buys a car with a car loan, the car serves as collateral against the loan. When collateral is posted as part of a credit contract, the borrower gives the lender the right to seize the collateral in the event that the borrower defaults on the loan.

Limited commitment can lead to situations where consumers are constrained in their borrowing by how much wealth they have that can serve as collateral—their **collateralizable wealth**. For a typical consumer, collateralizable wealth is restricted to houses and cars, but could potentially include other assets. If a consumer is collateral-constrained, then a change in the value of collateral will matter for how much they can consume in the present. This effect mattered, for example, during the period leading up to the 2008–2009 financial crisis, when there was a large decrease in the price of housing, which acted to reduce consumer expenditure. From the late 1990s until the peak in housing prices in the United States in 2006, a significant fraction of consumer expenditure was financed by borrowing, through mortgages and home equity loans, using housing as collateral. With the decrease in housing prices in the United States that began in 2006, the value of collateralizable wealth in the U.S. economy fell, and consumer spending also decreased by a large amount, fueling the 2008–2009 recession. We will explore this idea in depth in this chapter.

A second aspect in which the failure of Ricardian equivalence has practical significance, in addition to credit market frictions, relates to the market failure that creates a role for social security programs. Government social security programs typically mandate some level of saving by the working-age population in order to provide for benefits to retirees. It might seem that such programs can only make us worse off, since rational consumers know best how to save for their own retirement. However, government-provided social security can be rationalized by appealing to a credit market failure—the fact that those currently alive cannot write financial contracts with those as yet unborn. In the absence of such contracts, economic outcomes are not efficient. The first welfare theorem (see Chapter 5) does not hold, and there is a role for government in transferring resources across generations—taxing the working-age population to pay benefits to retirees through social security. We explore how social security works, and the effects of alternative types of social security programs, in this chapter. A key policy issue with respect to social security is the "privatization" of social security; that is, the replacement of "pay-as-you-go" systems with " fully funded" programs. We will study this issue in detail.

Credit Market Imperfections and Consumption

LO 10.1 Construct the basic credit market imperfections problem for the consumer, with a kinked budget constraint.

Our first step in the analysis of credit market imperfections is to show how Ricardian equivalence fails with a standard type of credit market friction—a gap between the interest rates at which a consumer can lend and borrow. Here, we will start with the basic credit market model from Chapter 9, where an individual consumer lives for two periods, the current and future period. The consumer receives income y in the current period, y' in the future period, and consumes c and c' in the current and future periods, respectively. The consumer's savings in the current period is denoted by s.

We want to show how a consumer who is credit-constrained can be affected by a change in taxes that would not have any effect on the consumer's choices if there were perfect credit markets. Consider a consumer who lends at a real interest rate r_1 and borrows at a real interest rate r_2, where $r_2 > r_1$. This difference in borrowing and lending rates of interest arises in practice, for example, when borrowing and lending is carried out through banks, and it is costly for banks to sort credit risks. If the bank borrows from lenders (depositors in the bank) at the real interest rate r_1, and it makes loans at the real interest rate r_2, the difference $r_2 - r_1 > 0$ could arise in equilibrium to compensate the bank for the costs of making loans. The difference between borrowing and lending rates of interest leads to a more complicated lifetime budget constraint. As in Chapter 9, the current-period budget constraint of the consumer is given by

$$c + s = y - t.$$

Here, because the consumer faces different interest rates if he or she borrows or lends, the future-period budget constraint is

$$c' = y' - t' + s(1 + r_1),$$

if $s \geq 0$ (the consumer is a lender), and

$$c' = y' - t' + s(1 + r_2),$$

if $s \leq 0$ (the consumer is a borrower). Going through the same mechanics as in Chapter 9 to derive the consumer's lifetime budget constraint, we obtain

$$c + \frac{c'}{1 + r_1} = y + \frac{y'}{1 + r_1} - t - \frac{t'}{1 + r_1} = we_1, \qquad (10\text{-}1)$$

if $c \leq y - t$ (the consumer is a lender), and

$$c + \frac{c'}{1 + r_2} = y + \frac{y'}{1 + r_2} - t - \frac{t'}{1 + r_2} = we_2, \qquad (10\text{-}2)$$

if $c \geq y - t$ (the consumer is a borrower).

We graph the consumer's budget constraint in Figure 10.1, where AB is given by Equation (10-1) and has slope $-(1 + r_1)$, and DF is given by Equation (10-2) and has slope $-(1 + r_2)$. The budget constraint is AEF, where E is the endowment point. Thus, the budget constraint has a kink at the endowment point, because the consumer lends at a lower interest rate than he or she can borrow at.

In a world where there are many different consumers, all having different indifference curves and different incomes, and where each consumer has a kinked budget constraint as in Figure 10.1, there is a significant number of consumers in the population whose optimal consumption bundle is the endowment point. For example, in Figure 10.2 the consumer faces budget constraint AE_1B, and the highest indifference curve on the budget constraint is reached at E_1, the endowment point. For this consumer, at the endowment point, the lending rate is too low to make lending worthwhile, and the borrowing rate is too high to make borrowing worthwhile.

Suppose that in Figure 10.2 the consumer receives a tax cut in the current period; that is, period 1 taxes change by $\Delta t < 0$, with a corresponding change of $-\Delta t(1 + r_1)$ in future taxes. This is the consumer's future tax liability implied by the tax cut, assuming that the interest rate that the government pays on its debt is r_1, the lending rate of interest. Assume that interest rates do not change. The effect of the change in current

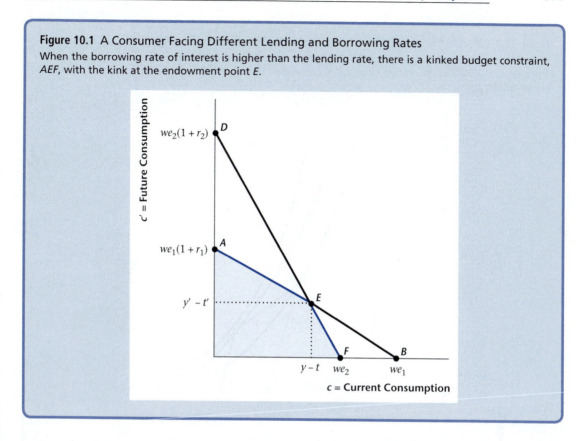

Figure 10.1 A Consumer Facing Different Lending and Borrowing Rates
When the borrowing rate of interest is higher than the lending rate, there is a kinked budget constraint, *AEF*, with the kink at the endowment point *E*.

and future taxes is to shift the endowment point to E_2, and given the way we have drawn the consumer's indifference curves, the consumer now chooses E_2 as his or her optimal consumption bundle on indifference curve I_2. Because he or she chooses the endowment point before and after the tax cut, period 1 consumption increases by the amount of the tax cut, $-\Delta t$. Contrast this with the Ricardian equivalence result in Chapter 9 where the consumer would save the entire tax cut and consumption would be unaffected.

The reason that the consumer's current consumption increases is that the government is effectively making a low interest loan available to him or her through the tax cut scheme. In Figure 10.2, the consumer would like to consume at point G if he or she could borrow at the interest rate r_1. Giving the consumer a tax cut of $-\Delta t$ with a corresponding future tax liability of $-\Delta t(1 + r_1)$ is just like having the government loan the consumer $-\Delta t$ at the interest rate r_1. Because the consumer would take such a loan willingly if it was offered, this tax cut makes the consumer better off.

Therefore, to the extent that credit market imperfections are important in practice, there can be beneficial effects of positive government debt. The government effectively acts like a bank that makes loans at below-market rates. If credit market imperfections matter significantly, then the people that are helped by current tax cuts are those who

Figure 10.2 Effects of a Tax Cut for a Consumer with Different Borrowing and Lending Rates

The consumer receives a current tax cut, with a future increase in taxes, and this shifts the budget constraint from AE_1B to AE_2F. The consumer's optimal consumption bundle shifts from E_1 to E_2, and the consumer consumes the entire tax cut.

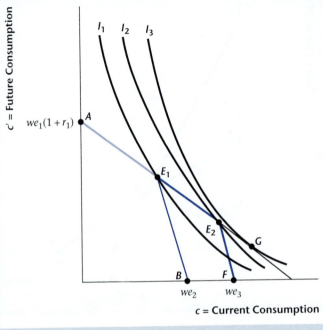

are affected most by credit market imperfections, and this might suggest to us that tax policy could be used in this way to increase general economic welfare. However, tax policy is quite a blunt instrument for relieving perceived problems due to credit market imperfections. A preferable policy might be to target particular groups of people—for example, small businesses, farmers, or homeowners—with direct government credit programs. In fact, there are many such programs in place in the United States, which are administered through government agencies such as the Small Business Administration. In considering government credit policies, though, careful evaluation needs to be done to determine whether direct lending by the government is a good idea in each particular circumstance. There may be good reasons for a particular private market credit imperfection. For example, real loan interest rates may be high in a particular segment of the credit market because the costs of screening and evaluating loans are very high, and the government would face the same high costs. This would then imply that the government has no special advantage in offering credit to these borrowers, and it would be inefficient for the government to get into the business of lending to them.

Credit Market Imperfections, Asymmetric Information, and the Financial Crisis

LO 10.2 Adapt the credit markets model to deal with asymmetric information.

A key feature of credit markets that can give rise to a budget constraint for a consumer like the one depicted in Figure 10.1 is asymmetric information. For our purposes, asymmetric information is particularly interesting because of the role it appears to have played in the recent financial crisis. In particular, the quality of information in credit markets appears to have declined significantly during 2008, with important implications for market interest rates, the quantity of lending, and aggregate economic activity.

Our first goal is to model asymmetric information in a simple and transparent way, using the tools we have already built up. It will be useful to consider an economy that has banks, in addition to the consumers and the government that were in the Chapter 9 two-period credit model. In our model, as in the real world, a bank is a **financial intermediary** that borrows from one set of individuals and lends to another set. We will study financial intermediaries in more depth in Chapter 17. In the model, a bank borrows from its depositors in the current period, and each depositor is an ultimate lender in the economy, with a depositor receiving a real interest rate on their deposits, held with the bank until the future period, equal to r_1. The bank takes all of its deposits in the current period (which in the model are consumption goods), and makes loans to borrowers. The problem for the bank is that some of the borrowers will default on their loans in the future period. To make things simple, suppose that a fraction a of the borrowers in the economy are good borrowers who have positive income in the future period, while a fraction $1 - a$ of borrowers are bad, in that they receive zero income in the future period, and therefore will default on any loan that is extended to them. However, there is asymmetric information in the credit market. Each borrower knows whether he or she is good or bad, but the bank cannot distinguish bad borrowers from the good borrowers who will pay off their loans with certainty. Assume that the bank can observe a consumer's income at the time it is received, so it knows which are good and bad borrowers once the future period arrives.

Now assume, again for simplicity, that all good borrowers are identical. Then, if the bank charges each borrower a real interest rate r_2 on loans, then each good borrower chooses the same loan quantity, which we will denote L. Bad borrowers do not want to reveal that they are bad to the bank, otherwise they will not receive a loan, so each bad borrower mimics the behavior of good borrowers by also choosing the loan quantity L. Now, one of the reasons that banks exist is that large lending institutions are able to minimize risk by diversifying. In this case, the bank diversifies by lending to a large number of borrowers. This assures that as the number of loans gets very large, the fraction of the bank's borrowers defaulting will be a, the fraction of bad borrowers in the population. For example, if I flip a coin n times, the fraction of flips that turn up heads will get very close to $\frac{1}{2}$ as n gets large, just as the fraction of good borrowers the bank faces gets very close to a as the number of borrowers gets large. For each L units of deposits acquired by the bank, for which the bank will have to pay out $L(1 + r_1)$ to depositors in the future period, the average payoff to the bank will be $aL(1 + r_2)$ in the future period, since fraction a of the bank's loans will be made to good borrowers, who will repay the bank $L(1 + r_2)$, and fraction $1 - a$ of the bank loans will be made to bad borrowers, who will repay zero. Thus, the average profit the bank makes on each loan is

$$\pi = aL(1 + r_2) - L(1 + r_1) = L[a(1 + r_2) - (1 + r_1)]. \qquad (10\text{-}3)$$

In equilibrium, each bank must earn zero profits, since negative profits would imply that banks would want to shut down, and positive profits would imply that banks would want to expand indefinitely. Therefore, $\pi = 0$ in equilibrium, which from Equation (10-3) implies that

$$r_2 = \frac{1 + r_1}{a} - 1. \qquad (10\text{-}4)$$

From Equation (10-4), note that when $a = 1$ and there are no bad borrowers, $r_1 = r_2$, and there is no credit market imperfection. This is then just the standard credit model that we studied in Chapter 9. Note also from Equation (10-4) that r_2 increases as a decreases, given r_1, so that the credit market imperfection becomes more severe as the fraction of bad borrowers in the population increases. Each good borrower must pay a default premium on a loan from the bank, which is equal to the difference $r_2 - r_1$. This difference grows as the fraction of good borrowers in the population decreases.

Now, in Figure 10.3, consider what happens to a typical consumer's budget constraint as a decreases, given r_1. Before a decrease in a the budget constraint is AED, where E is the endowment point. When a falls, the budget constraint shifts to AEF. From our previous analysis in Chapter 9, we know that, for a consumer who is a

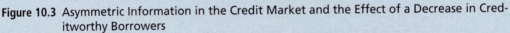

Figure 10.3 Asymmetric Information in the Credit Market and the Effect of a Decrease in Creditworthy Borrowers

Asymmetric information creates a kinked budget constraint AED, with the kink at the endowment point E. A decrease in the fraction of creditworthy borrowers in the population shifts the budget constraint to AEF.

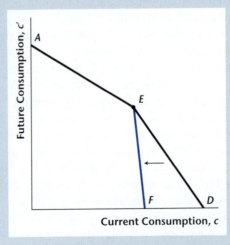

THEORY CONFRONTS THE DATA

Asymmetric Information and Interest Rate Spreads

Our analysis of asymmetric information in the credit market predicts that, in segments of the credit market where default is possible and lenders have difficulty sorting would-be borrowers, increases in the perceived probability of default will cause increases in interest rates, even for borrowers who are objectively creditworthy. In Figure 10.4, we show the difference in the interest rate on corporate debt rated BAA, and the interest rate on AAA corporate debt. In the

Figure 10.4 Interest Rate Spread

The highest spread historically was during the Great Depression, and the spread in general tends to be high during recessions. After the Great Depression, the highest spread was observed during the 2008–2009 recession.

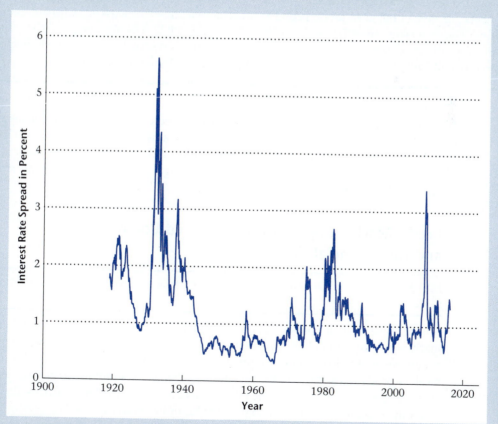

(Continued)

United States, there are three dominant private agencies that rate corporate and government debt: Fitch, Moody's, and Standard and Poor's. Debt rated AAA is the highest grade, judged to be essentially default-free, while BAA is judged to have some risk of default. While the objectivity and abilities of the major credit-rating agencies were called into question in the global financial crisis, for our purposes we will take the difference in the interest rates (the interest rate spread) on BAA debt and AAA debt shown in Figure 10.4 to represent the difference in interest rates in segments of the credit market that are perceived as somewhat risky, and essentially riskless, respectively.

In Figure 10.4, note that the interest rate spread reached its historical high of close to 6% during the Great Depression in the early 1930s, at about the time of the most severe period in the banking crisis of the Great Depression. After World War II, periods when the interest rate spread is high tend to correspond to recessions, in particular the recessions in 1974–1975, 1981–1982, 1990–1991, 2001, and 2008–2009. However, typically the interest rate spread increased toward the end of a recession, when defaults tend to reach their peak. What is unusual about the 2008–2009 recession is not only the size of the interest rate spread, which was larger than at any point since the Great Depression, but also the fact that the interest rate spread was high at the beginning of the recession (GDP declined beginning in the fourth quarter of 2008). This high interest rate spread reflected the fact that a principal cause of the recession was the financial crisis, which created a great deal of uncertainty in credit markets. The degree of asymmetric information increased in some segments of the credit market (including the market for BAA corporate debt), due to the fact that lenders were increasingly uncertain about what firms were at risk and what firms were not. Faced with high interest rates, even good borrowers (who had great difficulty identifying themselves as such) reduced their borrowing.

borrower, that is, who chooses a consumption bundle on ED before the decline in *a*, consumption in the current period and borrowing must decrease when *a* falls. That is, with asymmetric information in the credit market and an increase in the incidence of default among borrowers, good borrowers face higher loan interest rates and reduce their borrowing and consumption as a result.

Credit Market Imperfections, Limited Commitment, and the Financial Crisis

LO 10.3 Show how limited commitment makes collateral important in the credit markets model.

Another type of credit market imperfection that is important to how real-world credit markets function, and played an important role in the recent financial crisis, is limited commitment. Any loan contract represents an intertemporal exchange—the borrower receives goods and services in the present in exchange for a promise to give the lender claims to goods and services in the future. However, when the future arrives, the borrower may find it advantageous not to keep his or her promise.

Lenders are not stupid, of course, and will therefore set up a loan contract in a way that gives the borrower the incentive to pay off the loan as promised. One incentive device used widely by lenders is the requirement that a borrower post **collateral**. In general, collateral is an asset owned by the borrower that the lender has a right to seize if the borrower defaults on the loan (does not meet the promised payment). Most people are familiar with the role played by collateral in automobile loans and mortgage loans. For a typical auto loan, the auto itself serves as collateral, while an individual's house is the collateral for his or her mortgage loan. Collateral is also used in short-term lending among large financial institutions. For example, a **repurchase agreement** is a short-term loan for which a safe asset, such as government-issued debt, serves as collateral.

For macroeconomic activity, the use of collateral in loan contracts can potentially be very important. For example, mortgages are used by homeowners not only to finance the purchase of homes but also to finance consumption. If the extent to which home-owners can borrow is constrained by the value of houses, and the price of houses falls, then this will cause a decline in the quantity of lending in the economy as a whole, and a drop in current aggregate consumption.

To see how this works, consider an individual consumer exactly like the typical consumer we studied in Chapter 9, who also owns a quantity of an asset, denoted by H, which can be sold in the future period at the price p per unit, so that the value of the asset in the future is pH. To make this example concrete, think of H as the size of the consumer's house, and p as the price of housing per unit. Assume that the house is illiquid, which means that it is difficult to sell quickly. We will represent this by sup-posing that the consumer cannot sell the house in the current period. The consumer's lifetime wealth is then

$$we = y - t + \frac{y' - t' + pH}{1 + r}, \tag{10-5}$$

which is the same expression as the one for lifetime wealth of a consumer in Chapter 9, except that we add the quantity $\frac{pH}{1+r}$ to lifetime wealth. This quantity is the future value of the house, discounted to give its value in units of current consumption. The con-sumer's lifetime budget constraint, as in Chapter 9, is

$$c + \frac{c'}{1 + r} = we, \tag{10-6}$$

but now our definition of we is different.

In our model, the lenders in the credit market know that there is a limited commit-ment problem. For simplicity, assume that the lender has no recourse if a borrower defaults on a loan. In particular, assume the law does not allow the lender to confiscate any or all of the consumer's future income y' if default occurs. This implies that, without collateral, the borrower will always default and, knowing this, rational lenders would not want to offer the borrower a loan. However, the consumer can borrow if he or she posts his or her house as collateral. Lenders will then be willing to lend an amount to the con-sumer that will imply a loan payment in the future no larger than the value of the col-lateral, as otherwise the consumer would default on the loan. That is, given that s is the consumer's saving in the current period, with $-s$ the quantity of borrowing in the current period, the amount borrowed by the consumer must satisfy the collateral constraint

$$-s(1 + r) \le pH, \tag{10-7}$$

as $-s(1 + r)$ is the loan payment for the consumer in the future period, and pH the value of the collateral in the future period. Then, since $s = y - t - c$ for the consumer, we can substitute for s in the collateral constraint Equation (10-7) and rearrange to obtain

$$c \leq y - t + \frac{pH}{1 + r}. \tag{10-8}$$

The collateral constraint, rewritten in the form of Equation (10-8), states that current period consumption can be no greater than current disposable income plus the amount that can be borrowed by the consumer by pledging the future value of the house as collateral.

Now, the consumer's problem is to make himself or herself as well off as possible, given his or her lifetime budget constraint, Equation (10-6), and also given the collateral constraint, Equation (10-8), where lifetime wealth we is given by Equation (10-5). As long as the value of collateral in the future, pH, is small enough, the collateral constraint implies that the budget constraint is kinked, as in Figure 10.5, where the budget constraint is initially ABD. In the figure, the endowment point is E, and if the consumer chose point B, at the kink in the budget constraint, then he or she would have a binding collateral constraint, borrowing up to the full amount that lenders will permit, and consuming future disposable income in the future period, with $c' = y' - t'$.

Figure 10.5 Limited Commitment with a Collateral Constraint
The consumer can borrow only with collateralizable wealth as security against the loan. As a result, the budget constraint is kinked. Initially, the budget constraint is ABD and it shifts to FGH with a decrease in the price of collateral. For a constrained borrower, this causes no change in future consumption, but current consumption drops by the same amount as the decrease in the value of collateral if the borrower is collateral-constrained.

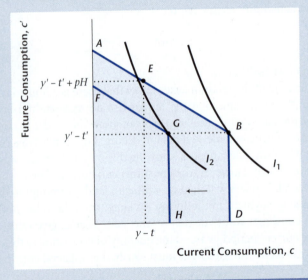

Next, suppose that the price of houses, p, declines, with everything else held constant. This reduces the quantity of the consumer's collateralizable wealth—the quantity of wealth that the consumer can borrow against—and also reduces lifetime wealth we. As a result, in Figure 10.5, the budget constraint shifts from ABD to FGH. Note that the slope of AB is the same as the slope of FG, since the interest rate r has not changed, and that the point G is directly to the left of point B, since future disposable income $y' - t'$ is also unchanged.

If the collateral constraint, Equation (10-8), does not bind for the consumer, either before or after the decrease in p, then the consumer is affected in exactly the same way as in our analysis of the effects of a change in future income in Chapter 9. An unconstrained consumer will initially choose a point somewhere between A and B (but not including B) before the decrease in p, and will choose a point between F and G (but not including G) after the decrease in p. The unconstrained consumer can smooth the effects of the decrease in wealth resulting from the fall in p, by reducing consumption in both the current and future periods.

However, suppose that the consumer's collateral constraint binds, both before and after the decrease in p. Then, as in Figure 10.5, the consumer chooses to consume at point B initially, on indifference curve I_1. When p falls, the budget constraint shifts to FGH, and the consumer chooses point G, on indifference curve I_2. A constrained consumer cannot smooth the effects of the decrease in his or her wealth. For any consumer, a decrease in wealth must be absorbed in a reduction in consumption, either in the present or in the future. However, in this case, since the collateral constraint binds, all of the reduction of consumption occurs in the current period. In the figure, future consumption at points B and G is the same, but current consumption c falls by the reduction in lifetime wealth; that is, by the change in the present value of collateralizable wealth. To see this another way, if the collateral constraint Equation (10-8) binds, it holds as an equality, so that

$$c = y - t + \frac{pH}{1+r},$$

and if $y - t$ remains unchanged, then any reduction in the present value of collateralizable wealth, $\frac{pH}{1+r}$, is reflected in a one-for-one reduction in current consumption, c.

The permanent income hypothesis tells us that, in a world with perfect credit markets, the motive of consumers to smooth consumption over time acts to lessen the impact of changes in wealth on consumer expenditure in the aggregate. Here, our analysis tells us that if credit market imperfections arising from limited commitment matter in an important way for a significant fraction of the population, then changes in the value of collateralizable wealth (principally housing, for the consumer sector) can matter a great deal for aggregate consumption.

Social Security Programs

Social security programs are government-provided means for saving for retirement. As such they are programs that help individuals smooth their consumption over their lifetimes. But if credit markets work well, then why do we need the government to

THEORY CONFRONTS THE DATA

The Housing Market, Collateral, and Consumption

Figure 10.6 shows the relative price of housing in the United States, as measured by the Case–Shiller 20-city home price index, divided by the consumer price index, normalized to equal 100 in January 2000. A remarkable feature of the figure is the large increase in the relative price of housing to the peak in 2006. In particular, the purchasing power of the average house in the United States increased by almost 80% between 2000 and 2006. The U.S. housing stock then lost most of this accumulated value from 2006 to 2012.

In Figure 10.7, we show the percentage deviations from trend in aggregate consumption. Note in Figure 10.6 that the relative price

Figure 10.6 The Relative Price of Housing in the United States

The figure shows the relative price of housing, measured as the Case–Shiller price index divided by the consumer price index, scaled to equal 100 in 2000. Of particular note is the very rapid increase from 2000 to 2006, and the rapid decline from 2006 to 2012.

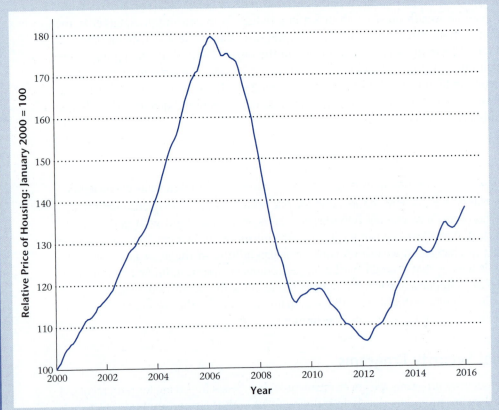

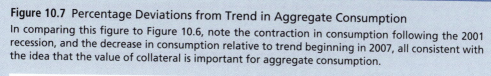

Figure 10.7 Percentage Deviations from Trend in Aggregate Consumption

In comparing this figure to Figure 10.6, note the contraction in consumption following the 2001 recession, and the decrease in consumption relative to trend beginning in 2007, all consistent with the idea that the value of collateral is important for aggregate consumption.

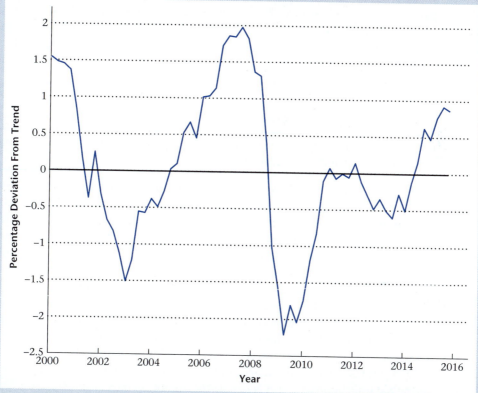

of housing continues to increase through the 2001 recession, when consumption declines below trend and does not begin recovering until 2003. The 2001 recession was relatively mild, as was the decline in consumption, in part because the value of housing as collateral continued to increase through the recession. Consumers were then able to continue to finance their consumption by borrowing against the value accumulated in their houses. Once the relative price of housing starts to decrease in 2006, this coincides with a subsequent decrease in consumption relative to trend, and the rapid decrease in consumption below trend in 2008–2009. What we see in Figures 10.6 and 10.7 is consistent with the idea that the value of collateral in credit markets contributes in an important way to the behavior of aggregate consumption expenditures.

provide us with consumption-smoothing services? As macroeconomists, if we want to provide a rationale for social security, we must be able to find some type of credit market failure that the government can correct. One purpose of this section is to explore this idea, and to examine how social security systems work in practice.

There are essentially two types of programs: **pay-as-you-go** and **fully funded social security**, though in practice social security could be some mix of the two. With pay-as-you-go social security, the program simply involves transfers between the young and the old, while fully funded social security is a government-sponsored savings program where the savings of the young are used to purchase assets, and the old receive the payoffs on the assets that were acquired when they were young. We discuss the two types of social security program in turn.

Pay-As-You-Go Social Security

LO 10.4 Show how pay-as-you-go social security works, and demonstrate what conditions are required so that it increases economic welfare.

In the United States, social security operates as a pay-as-you-go system, in that taxes on the young are used to finance social security transfers to the old. While public discussion may make it appear that the system is in fact fully funded, as the difference between social security tax revenue and social security benefits is used to purchase interest-bearing federal government securities, this is merely an accounting convention and is unimportant for the economic consequences of U.S. social security.

To see the implications of pay-as-you-go social security for the distribution of wealth over time and across consumers, we use the basic credit market model of Chapter 9, but modify it to accommodate intergenerational redistribution of income by the government. Assume for simplicity that social security has no effect on the market real interest rate r, which we suppose is constant for all time. Each consumer lives for two periods, youth and old age, and so in any period there is a young generation and an old generation alive. Let N denote the number of old consumers currently alive, and N' the number of young consumers currently alive. Assume that

$$N' = (1 + n)N, \tag{10-9}$$

so that the population is growing at the rate n, just as in the Solow growth model used in Chapters 7 and 8, though here people are finite-lived. A given consumer receives income y when young and income y' when old, and we allow (as in Chapter 9) for the fact that incomes can differ across consumers. For simplicity, assume that government spending is zero in all periods.

Now, suppose that no social security program exists before some date T, and that before date T the taxes on the young and old are zero in each period. Then, pay-as-you-go social security is established at date T and continues forever after. Here, for simplicity we suppose that the social security program guarantees each old-age consumer in periods T and later a benefit of b units of consumption goods. Then, the tax for each old consumer in periods T and after is $t' = -b$. The benefits for old consumers must be financed by taxes on the young, and we assume that each young consumer is taxed an equal amount, t. Then, because total social security benefits equal total taxes on the young, we have

$$Nb = N't, \tag{10-10}$$

and so, using Equation (10-9) to substitute for N' in Equation (10-11), we can solve for t, obtaining

$$t = \frac{b}{1+n}. \tag{10-11}$$

How do consumers benefit from social security? Clearly, the consumers who are old when the program is introduced in period T gain, as these consumers receive the social security benefit but do not have to suffer any increase in taxes when they are young. In Figure 10.8, the lifetime budget constraint of a consumer who is old in period T is AB if there is no social security program, where the slope of AB is $-(1+r)$ and the endowment point with no social security is E_1, determined by disposable income of y when young and y' when old. With the social security program, this consumer receives disposable income y when young and $y' + b$ when old and has an endowment point

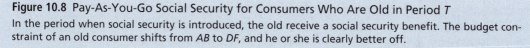

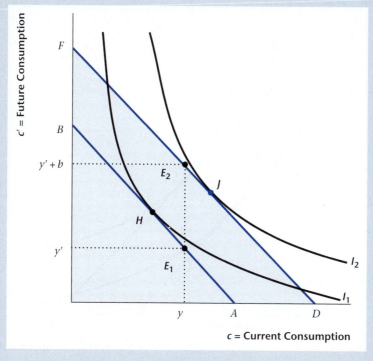

Figure 10.8 Pay-As-You-Go Social Security for Consumers Who Are Old in Period T

In the period when social security is introduced, the old receive a social security benefit. The budget constraint of an old consumer shifts from AB to DF, and he or she is clearly better off.

given by E_2 on the budget constraint DF (with slope $-(1 + r)$) in the figure. The optimal consumption bundle shifts from H to J, and the consumer is clearly better off because his or her budget constraint has shifted out and he or she is able to choose a consumption bundle on a higher indifference curve.

What happens to consumers born in periods T and later? For these consumers, in Figure 10.9, the budget constraint would be AB without social security, with an endowment point at E_1 and the budget constraint having slope $-(1 + r)$. With social security, disposable income when young is $y - t = y - \frac{b}{1+n}$ from Equation (10-11) and disposable income when old is $y' + b$, and the endowment point shifts to E_2 in the figure on the budget constraint DF. Because the market real interest rate has not changed, the slope of DF is $-(1 + r)$. The slope of E_1E_2 is $-(1 + n)$, so in the figure we have shown the case where $n > r$. In this case, the budget constraint shifts out for this consumer, with the optimal consumption bundle shifting from H to J, and the consumer is better off. However, the budget constraint would shift in, and the consumer would be worse off if $n < r$.

That is, the consumer's lifetime wealth is given by

$$we = y - \frac{b}{1+n} + \frac{y'+b}{1+r} = y + \frac{y'}{1+r} + \frac{b(n-r)}{(1+r)(1+n)}.$$

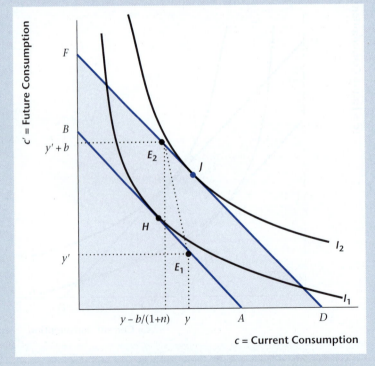

Figure 10.9 Pay-As-You-Go Social Security for Consumers Born in Period T and Later
If $n > r$, the budget constraint shifts out from AB to DF, and the consumer is better off.

Whether the consumer is better off or worse off with the social security program is determined by whether *we* increases or decreases, or by whether $n > r$ or $n < r$.

Therefore, social security makes everyone better off here only if the population growth rate is greater than the real interest rate. Otherwise, the old in the initial period are made better off at the expense of the current young and each future generation. The reason why social security can potentially improve welfare is that there is a kind of private market failure here that the government can exploit. That is, there is no way for people to trade with those who are not born yet, and the young and old alive in a given period cannot trade, as the young would like to exchange current consumption goods for future consumption goods, and the old would like to exchange current consumption goods for past consumption goods. The government is able to use its power to tax to bring about intergenerational transfers that may yield a Pareto improvement, whereby welfare increases for all consumers in the present and the future.

For pay-as-you-go social security to improve welfare for the consumer currently alive and those in future generations requires that the "rate of return" of the social security system be sufficiently high. This rate of return increases with the population growth rate n, as the population growth rate determines how large a tax burden there is for the young generation in paying social security benefits to the old. The smaller is this tax burden for each young person, the higher is the ratio of the social security benefit in old age to the tax paid to support social security when young, and this ratio is effectively the rate of return of the social security system. If n is larger than r, then the rate of return of the social security system is higher than the rate of return in the private credit market, and this is why social security increases welfare for everyone in this circumstance.

The issue of whether social security can bring about a Pareto improvement for consumers in all generations relates directly to contemporary issues facing the U.S. social security system. Currently, the social security taxes paid by the working population are more than sufficient to finance payments of social security benefits to the old. This will change, however, as the baby boom generation retires, a process which has begun, and will continue to about 2030. As this large cohort retires, if social security benefits are to remain at their current levels, then this will require either a larger social security tax for the young or more immigration to increase the size of the working population that can pay the tax. Otherwise, benefits will have to be reduced. If we suppose that immigration will not change, then some group will have to lose. That is, if benefits remain at current levels, then the working population that pays the higher social security tax, roughly until 2030, will receive a low return on social security. If benefits are reduced, then the baby boom generation will receive a low return on social security. The former is a more likely outcome, as the baby boom generation has a great deal of political power due to its size.

Fully Funded Social Security

LO 10.5 Show how fully-funded social security programs function, and explain their economic role.

To analyze fully funded social security, we can use the same apparatus as for the pay-as-you-go case. Again, suppose that government spending is zero forever, and in this case we assume for simplicity that taxes are zero as well.

In the absence of social security a consumer's lifetime budget constraint is given by AB in Figure 10.10, where the slope of AB is $-(1 + r)$. The consumer's endowment is given by point E, and we suppose that this consumer optimizes by choosing point D, where saving is positive. Fully funded social security is a program whereby the government invests the proceeds from social security taxes in the private credit market, with social security benefits determined by the payoff the government receives in the private credit market. Alternatively, the government could allow the consumer to choose in which assets to invest his or her social security savings. Here, this makes no difference, as there is a single real rate of return, r, available on the credit market.

In any event, fully funded social security is effectively a forced savings program, and it matters only if the amount of social security saving is a binding constraint on consumers. That is, fully funded social security makes a difference only if the social security system mandates a higher level of saving than the consumer would choose in the absence of the program. Such a case is illustrated in Figure 10.9, where the amount of social security saving required by the government is $y - c_1$, so that the consumer receives the consumption bundle F. Clearly, the consumer is worse off than he or she was at point D in the absence of the program. At best, fully funded social security is ineffective, if the amount of social security saving is not binding, or if

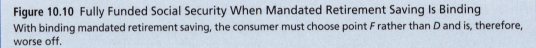

Figure 10.10 Fully Funded Social Security When Mandated Retirement Saving Is Binding

With binding mandated retirement saving, the consumer must choose point F rather than D and is, therefore, worse off.

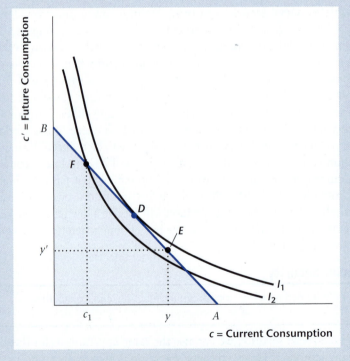

consumers can undo forced savings by borrowing against their future social security benefits when young. If fully funded social security is a binding constraint on at least some people in the population, then it can only make things worse for optimizing consumers. Proposals to "privatize" social security in the United States by allowing consumers to invest their social security savings in private assets are essentially proposals to move toward a fully funded rather than pay-as-you-go social security. Such proposals may in fact be welfare-improving for all generations, but this depends critically on how the transition to a fully funded social security system is financed by the federal government.

What if the population growth rate is sufficiently low that pay-as-you-go social security is dominated by savings in the private market? Is there any rationale for establishing a social security system so as to force consumers to save for their retirement? The answer is yes, as social security may be a device that solves a commitment problem for the government. This commitment problem takes the following form. In a perfect world, the government could announce to the public that no one will receive assistance from the government in retirement. In such a world, the public believes this announcement, all individuals save for their retirement, and consumption is optimally smoothed for everyone over their lifetimes. The problem is that the public understands that the government cannot commit to such a policy. If people are old and destitute, the government will feel obliged to provide assistance for them. Since people then anticipate that they will receive some minimal standard of living on government assistance in retirement in any event, the poor in particular will not save for retirement. It may be preferable, given the government's commitment problem, to establish a government-mandated universal social security program, thus inducing something closer to an optimal amount of saving for retirement.

Suppose that we accept the argument that a social security system is a convenient device to get around the government's inability to commit. Which system is best, pay-as-you-go or fully funded? An argument in favor of the pay-as-you-go system currently in place in the United States is the following. Fully funded programs encounter two problems. First, they potentially allow public pension funds to be run inefficiently because of political interference. This problem occurs if the government manages the public pension fund rather than letting retirees manage their own retirement accounts. The existence of such a large quantity of assets in a public pension fund, seemingly at public disposal, often provides a tempting target for lawmakers and lobbyists. For example, in Canada, the Canada Pension Plan is a mixed fully funded and pay-as-you-go system, and has been the target of groups that advocate socially responsible investing. The theory behind socially responsible investing is that it is possible to change the behavior of firms or to reduce their activities by directing investments away from them. For example, tobacco companies are a typical target of socially responsible investing, for obvious reasons. While socially responsible investing may be well-intentioned, it may at best be ineffective, and at worst have the effect of constraining the management of public pension funds in ways that reduce benefits to retirees. A pay-as-you-go system avoids the issue entirely. With pay-as-you-go, the government is not put in the position of deciding which investments are morally appropriate and which are not, and political activity can be focused in ways that are potentially much more productive.

MACROECONOMICS IN ACTION

Social Security and Incentives

What determines when an individual retires? In analyzing retirement decisions, economists find it useful to think in terms of decisions by an individual over his or her whole lifetime, incorporating related decisions concerning education and skill acquisition, consumption, savings, leisure time, and fertility. As well, the structure of social security systems can play a very important role.

In the simple model we laid out in this chapter, retirement benefits are received as a lump sum in old age. Modeling social security in this way gives us some insight into how social security programs work, in a straightforward way. But actual social security programs provide for benefits that are not lump sum, and are not even allocated at a fixed annual rate. Typically, benefits depend on the earnings received over a worker's lifetime, and on when the worker retires.

Participants in a research program sponsored by the National Bureau of Economic Research[1] studied social security programs in the United States, Canada, Japan, and a group of European countries. What these economists noticed was that labor force participation rates had dropped among older workers, and they linked this behavior to the structure of social security programs.

Labor force participation could fall for reasons other than changes in social security programs. For example, we know from our analysis of labor supply decisions in Chapter 4 that there is an income effect on the demand for leisure. Further, the nature of many types of work is all-or-nothing—workers must work full-time or not all, though of course there is much part-time work in the economy as well. However, with a significant fraction of the work force effectively constrained to work full-time, workers have to make adjustments in response to market wages on other margins than how much they work in a given day or a given week. One of those margins is age of retirement. Thus, when people become wealthier, they may consume more leisure, not by working fewer hours when employed, but by retiring at an earlier age and taking their leisure in retirement.

Health may also affect retirement. A worker may suffer a dramatic health event that lowers his or her individual productivity and wage rate, bringing on earlier retirement. So, if workers are on average healthier, they will tend to retire later. As well, better health implies a longer lifetime, which implies that people will want to work longer to accumulate more wealth for a longer period of retirement. But better health also means that a person will enjoy his or her leisure time more, which will tend to make him or her retire earlier. So better health on average may increase or decrease retirement age.

The NBER researchers took factors like wealth, income, and health, among other things, into account in analyzing the effects of social security programs on retirement in these different countries. Ultimately they studied the microeconomic behavior of workers, so that they could estimate the quantitative incentive effects of social security, and what would happen if the incentives were changed through social security reform.

What the NBER researchers concluded was that the incentive effects on labor force participation of social security programs are quite large. The key problem is that, for example, a worker in his or her early 60s in many countries will actually be wealthier, in lifetime terms, if he or she retires.

[1]See J. Gruber and D. Wise, 2002. "Social Security Programs and Retirement Around the World: Micro Estimation," National Bureau of Economic Research Working Paper 9407, http://www.nber.org/papers/w9407.

If a 63-year-old worker chooses to work another year, he or she will receive another year's wages, and will not receive social security benefits. But postponing the date at which the worker claims benefits will increase the level of benefits they ultimately receive. Unfortunately, in many countries, the net wealth benefit of working another year, later in life, is negative. The NBER research economists found that this incentive effect mattered a lot for labor force participation in these countries.

Has the labor force participation of older people fallen in the United States? Well, yes and no. In the United States, the total labor force participation rate rose from about 59% in 1948 to a peak of about 67% in 1999, and has since fallen to about 63% in early 2016, as we show in Figure 10.11. But labor force participation of those 55 and over, as depicted in Figure 10.12, shows the reverse pattern, decreasing from 43% in 1948 to a low of 30% in 1992, and then increasing to about 40% in early 2016. This represents the effects of an array of factors, so we cannot conclude from Figures 10.11 and 10.12 that the bad incentive effects of social security are not operative in the United States. Indeed, the NBER researchers found that social security reform would have significant positive incentive effects, even in the United States.

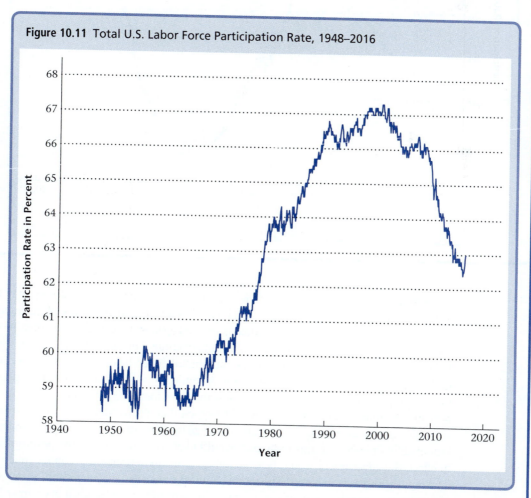

Figure 10.11 Total U.S. Labor Force Participation Rate, 1948–2016

(*Continued*)

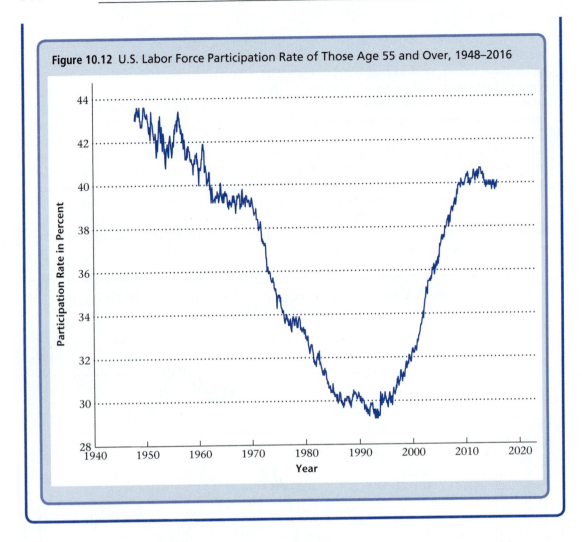

Figure 10.12 U.S. Labor Force Participation Rate of Those Age 55 and Over, 1948–2016

A second problem with fully funded social security programs is that they may be subject to a **moral hazard** problem. Moral hazard is a well-known feature of insurance, and refers to the fact that if an individual is insured against a particular loss, then he or she will take less care to prevent the loss from happening. For example, if a person were fully insured against damages to his or her automobile, then he or she will take less care in driving in parking lots. In the case of a fully funded social security program, suppose that the program allows people to choose how they save for retirement, constraining them only in how much they save. What would happen if an individual chose to invest in a very risky asset, was unlucky, and became destitute in retirement? Given the government's lack of ability to commit, this individual would likely be bailed out by the government. In effect, the government would be called upon to insure retirement accounts, much as it insures the deposits in banks. The moral hazard problem associated with the provision of deposit insurance by the government is well known, and we will study it in Chapter 18.

Just as with banks, if retirement accounts were insured, then the managers of retirement accounts would tend to take on too much risk. They would know that if their highly risky investments pay off, so much the better, but if these assets do not pay off, then they will be bailed out by the government. The moral hazard problem implies that another level of regulation would be needed to make sure that retirement account managers do not take on too much risk. The provision of government insurance for retirement accounts, and the necessary regulation required to solve the moral hazard problem, potentially create enough costs that a pay-as-you-go system would be preferable.

Chapter Summary

- With a credit market imperfection, modeled as a situation where the lending interest rate is less than the borrowing interest rate, Ricardian equivalence does not hold. A current tax cut that just changes the timing of taxes, with no effect on lifetime wealth, will increase current consumption and have no effect on savings.

- One credit market imperfection is asymmetric information, under which lenders cannot perfectly observe the creditworthiness of would-be borrowers. In a credit market with good and bad borrowers, the lending interest rate is less than the borrowing interest rate, reflecting a default premium on the loan interest rate. An increase in the fraction of bad borrowers in the market increases the default premium and reduces the quantity of lending.

- A second credit market imperfection is limited commitment—borrowers have an incentive to default on their debts. Lenders give borrowers the incentive to repay by requiring that borrowers post collateral. However, when borrowers are collateral-constrained, a decrease in the price of collateralizable wealth reduces lending and consumption.

- Social security programs can be rationalized by a credit market failure—the inability of the unborn to trade with those currently alive. There are two types of government-provided social security programs—pay-as-you-go programs and fully funded programs.

- Pay-as-you-go social security, which funds retirement benefits from taxes on the working-age population, increases welfare for everyone if the real interest rate is less than the rate of growth in the population.

- Fully funded social security at best has no effect, and at worst constrains retirement savings in ways that make consumers worse off.

- Even if the population growth rate is low, social security can be justified if we think that the government is unable to commit to providing social assistance to destitute senior citizens. In that event, pay-as-you-go systems may in fact be less costly than fully funded systems.

Key Terms

Asymmetric information Refers to a situation where, in a particular market, some market participant knows more about his or her own characteristics than do other market participants. (p. 352)

Limited commitment Refers to situations in which it is impossible for a market participant to commit in advance to some future action. (p. 352)

Default premium The portion of a loan interest rate that compensates the lender for the possibility that the borrower may default on the loan. (p. 352)

Interest rate spread The gap between interest rates on risky loans and safer loans, or the difference between interest rates at which some class of individuals can lend and borrow. (p. 352)

Collateralizable wealth Assets that can serve as collateral. (p. 352)

Financial intermediary A financial institution that borrows from a large set of ultimate lenders and lends to a large set of ultimate borrowers. Examples are banks, insurance companies, and mutual funds. (p. 357)

Collateral An asset owned by a borrower that, as part of a loan contract, the lender is permitted to seize if the borrower were to default. (p. 361)

Repurchase agreement A short-term loan under which a government security serves as collateral. (p. 361)

Pay-as-you-go social security A social security system where benefits to the old are financed by taxes on the working population. (p. 364)

Fully funded social security A social security system where the social security payments of the working population are invested in assets, and the payoffs on these assets finance the social security benefits of old people. (p. 364)

Moral hazard A situation in which insurance against a potential loss reduces the effort taken by the insured to prevent the loss. (p. 374)

Questions for Review

10.1 What effects do credit market imperfections have on the interest rates faced by lenders and borrowers?

10.2 What are the effects of a tax cut on consumption and savings in the presence of a credit market imperfection? Does Ricardian equivalence hold?

10.3 Does the existence of credit market imperfections imply that there is a useful role for government tax policy?

10.4 What are two sources of credit market imperfections?

10.5 Explain how a default premium can arise, and what would cause it to increase.

10.6 If the default premium increases, what is the effect on the consumption and savings of an individual consumer?

10.7 For a borrower who is collateral-constrained, what happens when the value of collateralizable wealth falls? How does this matter for the financial crisis?

10.8 Under what conditions will a pay-as-you-go social security system improve welfare for those currently alive and for all future generations?

10.9 What are the effects of a fully funded social security system?

10.10 How does the government's ability to commit matter for social security programs?

Problems

1. **LO 2** Suppose that there is a credit market imperfection due to asymmetric information. In the economy, a fraction b of consumers consists of lenders, who each receive an endowment of y units of the consumption good in the current period, and 0 units in the future period. A fraction $(1 - b)a$ of consumers are good borrowers who each receive an endowment of 0 units in the current period and y units in the future period. Finally, a fraction $(1 - b)(1 - a)$ of consumers are bad borrowers who receive 0 units of endowment in the current and future periods. Banks cannot distinguish between good and bad borrowers. The

government sets $G = G' = 0$, and each consumer is asked to pay a lump-sum tax of t in the current period and t' in the future period. The government also cannot distinguish between good and bad borrowers, but as with banks can observe endowments.

(a) Write down the government's budget constraint, making sure to take account of who is able to pay their taxes and who does not.

(b) Suppose that the government decreases t and increases t' in such a way that the government budget constraint holds. Does this have any effect on each consumer's decisions about how much to consume in each period and how much to save? Show with the aid of diagrams.

(c) Does Ricardian equivalence hold in this economy? Explain why or why not.

2. **LO 3** Suppose there is a credit market imperfection due to limited commitment. As in the setup with collateralizable wealth we examined in this chapter, each consumer has a component of wealth that has value pH in the future period, cannot be sold in the current period, and can be pledged as collateral against loans. Suppose also that the government requires each consumer to pay a lump-sum tax t in the current period, and a tax t' in the future period. Also suppose that there is limited commitment with respect to taxation as well. That is, if a consumer refuses to pay his or her taxes, the government can seize the consumer's collateralizable wealth, but cannot confiscate income (the consumer's endowment). Assume that if a consumer fails to pay off his or her debts to private lenders, and also fails to pay his or her taxes, the government has to be paid first from the consumer's collateralizable wealth.

(a) Show how the limited commitment problem puts a limit on how much the government can spend in the current and future periods.

(b) Write down the consumer's collateral constraint, taking into account the limited commitment problem with respect to taxes.

(c) Suppose that the government reduces t and increases t' so that the government budget constraint continues to hold. What will be the effects on an individual consumer's consumption in the present and the future? Does Ricardian equivalence hold in this economy? Explain why or why not.

3. **LO 2, 3** Suppose that there is limited commitment in the credit market, but lenders are uncertain about the value of collateral. Each consumer has a quantity of collateral H, but from the point of view of the lender, there is a probability a that the collateral will be worth p in the future period, and probability $1 - a$ that the collateral will be worthless in the future period. Suppose that all consumers are identical.

(a) Determine the collateral constraint for the consumer, and show the consumer's lifetime budget constraint in a diagram.

(b) How will a decrease in a affect the consumer's consumption and savings in the current period, and consumption in the future period? Explain your results.

4. **LO 2, 3** Suppose a credit market with a good borrowers and $1 - a$ bad borrowers. The good borrowers are all identical, and always repay their loans. Bad borrowers never repay their loans. Banks issue deposits that pay a real interest rate r_1, and make loans to borrowers. Banks cannot tell the difference between a good borrower and a bad one. Each borrower has collateral, which is an asset that is worth A units of future consumption goods in the future period.

(a) Determine the interest rate on loans made by banks.

(b) How will the interest rate change if each borrower has more collateral?

(c) Explain your results, and discuss.

5. **LO 3** Suppose that there are two groups of consumers in the population, constrained and unconstrained, with equal numbers of each. The constrained consumers look like the ones in Figure 10.5, while the unconstrained consumers have so much housing wealth that collateral to support any amount of borrowing they would like to do is not a problem. The government decides that it will tax each of the unconstrained consumers an equal amount in the current period, and distribute this tax revenue equally among the constrained consumers as transfers.

(a) Take the market real interest rate as given, and determine the effects of this redistribution by the government on the total demand for consumption goods in the current period, and in the future period [do not try to work out the equilibrium effects; just determine what the net effect on the demand for consumption goods will be, given the real interest rate].

(b) What do your results tell you about fiscal policy aimed at redistributing income toward those who will tend to spend more of it?

(c) Determine an efficient tax policy. This will be the tax policy that relaxes the limited commitment constraints for consumers.

(d) Discuss your results in parts (a) and (b).

6. **LO 4** Use the social security model developed in this chapter to answer this question. Suppose that

the government establishes a social security program in period T, which provides a social security benefit of b (in terms of consumption goods) for each old person forever. In period T the government finances the benefits to the current old by issuing debt. This debt is then paid off in period $T + 1$ through lump-sum taxes on the young. In periods $T + 1$ and later, lump-sum taxes on the young finance social security payments to the old.

(a) Show, using diagrams, that the young and old alive at time T all benefit from the social security program under any circumstances.

(b) What is the effect of the social security program on consumers born in periods $T + 1$ and later? How does this depend on the real interest rate and the population growth rate?

7. **LO 4** Suppose a pay-as-you-go social security system where social security is funded by a proportional tax on the consumption of the young. That is, the tax collected by the government is sc, where s is the tax rate and c is consumption of the young. Retirement benefits are given out as a fixed amount b to each old consumer. Can social security work to improve welfare for everyone under these conditions? Use diagrams to answer this question.

8. **LO 4** Use the social security model developed in this chapter to answer this question. Suppose that a government pay-as-you-go social security system has been in place for a long time,

providing a social security payment to each old person of b units of consumption. Now, in period T, suppose that the government notices that $r > n$, and decides to eliminate this system. During period T, the government reduces the tax of each young person to zero, but still pays a social security benefit of b to each old person alive in period T. The government issues enough one-period government bonds, D_T, to finance the social security payments in period T. Then, in period $T + 1$, to pay off the principal and interest on the bonds issued in period T, the government taxes the old currently alive, and issues new one-period bonds D_{T+1}. The taxes on the old in period $T + 1$ are just large enough that the quantity of debt per old person stays constant; that is, $D_{T+1} = (1 + n)D_T$. Then, the same thing is done in periods $T + 2, T + 3, \ldots$, so that the government debt per old person stays constant forever.

(a) Are the consumers born in periods T, $T + 1, T + 2, \ldots$ better or worse off than they would have been if the pay-as-you-go social security program had stayed in place? Explain using diagrams.

(b) Suppose that the government follows the same financing scheme as above, but replaces the pay-as-you-go system with a fully funded system in period T. Are consumers better off or worse off than they would have been with pay-as-you-go? Explain using diagrams.

Working with the Data

Answer these questions using the Federal Reserve Bank of St. Louis's FRED database, accessible at http://research.stlouisfed.org/fred2/

1. There are several alternative measures of national housing prices available for the United States. Choose at least three of these measures, and compare and contrast what they tell us about the boom and bust in the housing market that occurred after 2000.

2. Calculate the difference between the interest rate on a three-month certificate of deposit (CD) and the three-month treasury bill rate, and plot this in a time series plot. What do you notice? In particular, are there any regularities associated with recessions, and the most recent (2008–2009) recession? Discuss what these regularities suggest.

3. Plot a credit card loan interest rate, and an automobile loan interest rate, and compare the two. What do you think accounts for the difference between these two rates?

Chapter 11

A Real Intertemporal Model with Investment

Learning Objectives

After studying Chapter 11, students will be able to:

11.1 Explain the decisions made by the representative consumer in the real intertemporal model.

11.2 Explain the decisions made by the representative firm in the real intertemporal model.

11.3 Show how the firm's investment decision is structured, and determine how changes in the environment faced by the firm affect investment.

11.4 Construct the output supply curve.

11.5 Construct the output demand curve.

11.6 Show how a competitive equilibrium is determined in the real intertemporal model.

11.7 Use the real intertemporal model to explain the effects of particular shocks to the economy.

This chapter brings together the microeconomic behavior we have studied in previous chapters, to build a model that can serve as a basis for analyzing how macroeconomic shocks affect the economy, and that can be used for evaluating the role of macroeconomic policy. With regard to consumer behavior, we have examined work–leisure choices in Chapter 4 and intertemporal consumption–savings choices in Chapters 9 and 10. From the production side, in Chapter 4 we studied a firm's production technology and its labor demand decision, and then in Chapter 5 we showed how changes in total factor productivity affect consumption, employment, and output in the economy as a whole. In Chapters 9 and 10, we looked at the effects of choices by the government concerning the financing of government expenditure and the timing of taxes. While the Solow growth model studied in Chapters 7 and 8 included savings and investment, in this chapter we examine in detail how investment decisions are made at the level of the firm. This detail is important for our understanding of how interest rates and credit market conditions affect firms' investment decisions.

In this chapter, we complete a model of the real side of the economy. The real intertemporal model we construct here shows how real aggregate output, real consumption, real investment, employment, the real wage, and the real interest rate are determined in the macroeconomy. To predict nominal variables, we need to add money to the real intertemporal model, which is done in Chapter 12. The intertemporal aspect of the model refers to the fact that both consumers and firms make intertemporal decisions, reflecting trade-offs between the present and the future.

Recall from Chapter 2 that the defining characteristic of investment—expenditure on plants, equipment, and housing—is that it consists of the goods that are produced currently for future use in the production of goods and services. For the economy as a whole, investment represents a trade-off between present and future consumption. Productive capacity that is used for producing investment goods could otherwise be used for producing current consumption goods, but today's investment increases future productive capacity, which means that more consumption goods can be produced in the future. To understand the determinants of investment, we must study the microeconomic investment behavior of a firm, which makes an intertemporal decision regarding investment in the current period. When a firm invests, it forgoes current profits so as to have a higher capital stock in the future, which allows it to earn higher future profits. As we show, a firm invests more the lower its current capital stock, the higher its expected future total factor productivity, and the lower the real interest rate.

The real interest rate is a key determinant of investment as it represents investment's opportunity cost. A higher real interest rate implies that the opportunity cost of investment is larger, at the margin, and so investment falls. Movements in the real interest rate are an important channel through which shocks to the economy affect investment, as we show in this chapter. Further, monetary policy may affect investment through its influence on the real interest rate, as we show in Chapters 13 and 14.

In addition to the effect of the market interest rate, the investment decisions of firms depend on credit market risk, as perceived by lenders. That is, firms may find it more difficult to borrow to finance investment projects if lenders, including banks and other financial institutions, perceive lending in general to be more risky. Perceptions of an increase in the degree of riskiness in lending were an important factor in the global financial crisis. In this chapter, we will show how credit market risk can play a role in investment behavior, by incorporating asymmetric information, a credit market imperfection. The role of asymmetric information in a firm's investment decision will turn out to be very similar to its role in a consumer's consumption–savings decision, as studied in Chapter 10.

A good part of this chapter involves model building, and there are several important steps we must take before we can use this model to address important economic issues. This requires some patience and work, but the payoff arrives in the last part of this chapter and continues through the remainder of this book, where this model is the basis for our study of monetary factors in Chapter 12, business cycles in Chapters 13 and 14, and for other issues in later chapters.

This chapter focuses on the macroeconomic effects on aggregate output, investment, consumption, the real interest rate, and labor market variables of aggregate shocks to government spending, total factor productivity, the nation's capital stock, and credit market risk. Although we studied elements of some of these effects in Chapters 5, 9, and 10, there are new insights in this chapter involving the effects on the interest rate and investment of these shocks, and the effect of the anticipation of future shocks on current macroeconomic activity. For example, including intertemporal factors show how credit markets play a role in the effects of government spending on the economy. As well, we will be able to use the real intertemporal model to analyze aspects of the impact of the financial crisis on aggregate economic activity.

As in Chapters 4 and 5, we work with a model that has a representative consumer, a representative firm, and a government, and, for simplicity, ultimately we specify this model at the level of supply and demand curves. We are able to capture the essential behavior in this model economy by examining the participation of the representative consumer, the representative firm, and the government in two markets: the market for labor in the current period, and the market for goods in the current period. The representative consumer supplies labor in the current labor market and purchases consumption goods in the current goods market, while the representative firm demands labor in the current labor market, supplies goods in the current goods market, and demands investment goods in the current goods market. The government demands goods in the current goods market in terms of government purchases.

The Representative Consumer

LO 11.1 Explain the decisions made by the representative consumer in the real intertemporal model.

The behavior of the representative consumer in this model brings together our knowledge of the consumer's work–leisure choice from Chapter 4 with what we know about intertemporal consumption behavior from Chapter 9. In the model we are constructing here, the representative consumer makes a work–leisure decision in each of the current and future periods, and he or she makes a consumption–savings decision in the current period.

The representative consumer works and consumes in the current period and the future period. He or she has h units of time in each period and divides this time between work and leisure in each period. Let w denote the real wage in the current period, w' the real wage in the future period, and r the real interest rate. The consumer pays lump-sum taxes T to the government in the current period and T' in the future period. His or her goal is to choose current consumption C, future consumption C', leisure time in the current and future periods, l and l', respectively, and savings in the current period, S^p, to make himself or herself as well off as possible, given his or her budget constraints in the current and future periods. The representative consumer is a price-taker who takes w, w', and r as given. Taxes are also given from the consumer's point of view.

In the current period, the representative consumer earns real wage income $w(h - l)$, receives dividend income π from the representative firm, and pays taxes T, so that his or her current-period disposable income is $w(h - l) + \pi - T$, just as in Chapter 4. As in Chapter 9, disposable income in the current period is then split between consumption and savings, and savings takes the form of bonds that earn the one-period real interest rate r. Just as in Chapter 9, savings can be negative, in which case the consumer borrows by issuing bonds. The consumer's current budget constraint is then

$$C + S^p = w(h - l) + \pi - T. \tag{11-1}$$

In the future period, the representative consumer receives real wage income $w'(h - l')$, receives real dividend income π' from the representative firm, pays taxes T' to the government, and receives the principal and interest on savings from the current period, $(1 + r)S^p$. Because the future period is the last period and because the consumer is assumed to make no bequests, all wealth available to the consumer in the future is consumed, so that the consumer's future budget constraint is

$$C' = w'(h - l') + \pi' - T' + (1 + r)S^p. \tag{11-2}$$

Just as in Chapter 9, we can substitute for savings S^p in Equation (11-1) using Equation (11-2) to obtain a lifetime budget constraint for the representative consumer:

$$C + \frac{C'}{1 + r} = w(h - l) + \pi - T + \frac{w'(h - l') + \pi' - T'}{1 + r}. \tag{11-3}$$

This constraint states that the present value of consumption (on the left-hand side of the equation) equals the present value of lifetime disposable income (on the right-hand side of the equation). A difference from the consumer's lifetime budget constraint in Chapter 9 is that the consumer in this model has some choice, through his or her current and future choices of leisure, l and l', over his or her lifetime wealth.

The representative consumer's problem is to choose C, C', l, and l' to make himself or herself as well off as possible while respecting his or her lifetime budget constraint, as given by Equation (11-3). We cannot depict this choice for the consumer conveniently in a graph, as the problem is four-dimensional (choosing current and future consumption and current and future leisure), while a graph is two-dimensional. It is straightforward, however, to describe the consumer's optimizing decision in terms of three marginal conditions we have looked at in Chapters 4 and 9. These are as follows:

1. The consumer makes a work–leisure decision in the current period, so that when he or she optimizes, we have

$$MRS_{l,C} = w; \tag{11-4}$$

that is, the consumer optimizes by choosing current leisure and consumption so that the marginal rate of substitution of leisure for consumption is equal to the real wage in the current period. This is the same marginal condition as in the work–leisure problem for a consumer that we considered in Chapter 4. Recall that, in general, a consumer optimizes by setting the marginal rate of substitution of one good for another equal to the relative price of the two goods. In Equation (11-4), the current real wage w is the relative price of leisure in terms of consumption goods.

2. Similarly, in the future the consumer makes another work–leisure decision, and he or she optimizes by setting

$$MRS_{l',C'} = w'; \qquad (11\text{-}5)$$

that is, at the optimum, the marginal rate of substitution of future leisure for future consumption must be equal to the future real wage.

3. With respect to his or her consumption–savings decision in the current period, as in Chapter 9, the consumer optimizes by setting

$$MRS_{C,C'} = 1 + r; \qquad (11\text{-}6)$$

that is, the marginal rate of substitution of current consumption for future consumption equals the relative price of current consumption in terms of future consumption.

Current Labor Supply

Our ultimate focus is on interaction between the representative consumer and the representative firm in the markets for current labor and current consumption goods, and so we are interested in the determinants of the representative consumer's supply of labor and his or her demand for current consumption goods.

First, we consider the representative consumer's current supply of labor, which is determined by three factors—the current real wage, the real interest rate, and lifetime wealth. These three factors affect current labor supply as listed below.

1. *The current quantity of labor supplied increases when the current real wage increases.* The consumer's marginal condition, Equation (11-4), captures the idea that substitution between current leisure and current consumption is governed by the current real wage rate w. Recall from Chapter 4 that a change in the real wage has opposing income and substitution effects on the quantity of leisure, so that an increase in the real wage could lead to an increase or a decrease in the quantity of leisure, depending on the size of the income effect. Here, we assume that the substitution effect of a change in the real wage is always larger than the income effect, implying that leisure decreases and hours worked increases in response to an increase in the real wage. This might seem inconsistent with the fact, pointed out in Chapter 4, that over the long run, income and substitution effects on labor supply appear to cancel. However, the model we are building here is intended mainly for analyzing short-run phenomena. As we argued in Chapter 4, the canceling of income and substitution effects in the long run can be consistent with the substitution effect dominating in the short run, as we assume here.

2. *The quantity of current labor supplied increases when the real interest rate increases.* The consumer can substitute intertemporally not only by substituting current consumption for future consumption, as we studied in Chapter 9, but also by

substituting current leisure for future leisure. In substituting leisure between the two periods, the representative consumer responds to the current price of leisure relative to the future price of leisure, which is $\frac{w(1 + r)}{w'}$. Here, w is the price of current leisure (labor) in terms of current consumption, w' is the price of future leisure in terms of future consumption, and $1 + r$ is the price of current consumption in terms of future consumption. Therefore, an increase in the real interest rate r, given w and w', results in an increase in the price of current leisure relative to future leisure. Assuming again that the substitution effect is larger than the income effect, the consumer wants to consume less current leisure and more future leisure. An example of how this **intertemporal substitution of leisure** effect works is as follows. Suppose that Paul is self-employed and that the market interest rate rises. Then, Paul faces a higher return on his savings, so that if he works more in the current period and saves the proceeds, in the future he can both consume more and work less. It may be helpful to consider that leisure, like consumption, is a good. When the real interest rate increases, and substitution effects dominate income effects for lenders, current consumption falls (from Chapter 6), just as current leisure decreases when the real interest rate increases and substitution effects dominate.

3. *Current labor supply decreases when lifetime wealth increases.*   From Chapter 4, we know that an increase in current nonwage disposable income results in an increase in the quantity of leisure and a decrease in labor supply for the consumer, as leisure is a normal good. Further, in Chapter 9, we showed how income effects generalize to the intertemporal case where the consumer chooses current and future consumption. An increase in lifetime wealth increases the quantities of current and future consumption chosen by the consumer. Here, when there is an increase in lifetime wealth, there is an increase in current leisure and, thus, a decrease in current labor supply, because current leisure is assumed to be normal. The key wealth effect for our analysis in this chapter is the effect of a change in the present value of taxes for the consumer. Any increase in the present value of taxes implies a decrease in lifetime wealth and an increase in current labor supply.

Given these three factors, we can construct an upward-sloping current labor supply curve as in Figure 11.1. In the figure, the current real wage w is measured along the vertical axis, and current labor supply N is on the horizontal axis. The current labor supply curve is labeled $N^s(r)$ to indicate that labor supply depends on the current real interest rate. If the real interest rate rises, say from r_1 to r_2, then the labor supply curve shifts to the right, as in Figure 11.2, because labor supply increases for any current real wage w. In Figure 11.3, an increase in lifetime wealth shifts the labor supply curve to the left from $N_1^s(r)$ to $N_2^s(r)$. Such an increase in lifetime wealth could be caused by a decrease in the present value of taxes for the consumer. In Figure 11.3 the real interest rate is held constant as we shift the current labor supply curve to the left.

The Current Demand for Consumption Goods
Now that we have dealt with the determinants of the representative consumer's current labor supply, we can turn to his or her demand for current consumption goods. The

Figure 11.1 The Representative Consumer's Current Labor Supply Curve

The current labor supply curve slopes upward, under the assumption that the substitution effect of an increase in the real wage outweighs the income effect.

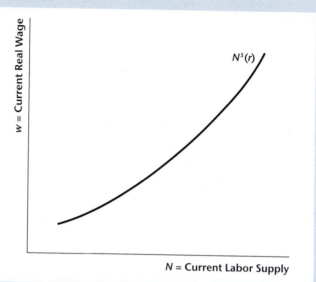

Figure 11.2 An Increase in the Real Interest Rate Shifts the Current Labor Supply Curve to the Right

This is because the representative consumer consumes less leisure in the current period and more leisure in the future when r increases.

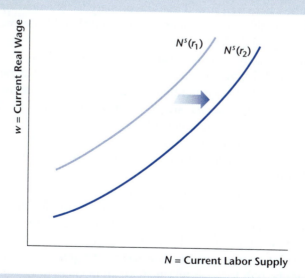

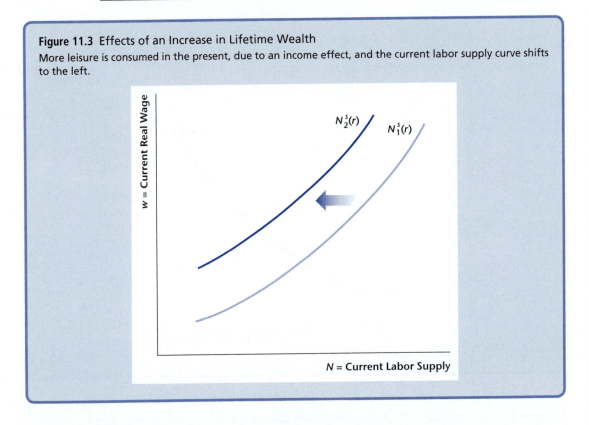

Figure 11.3 Effects of an Increase in Lifetime Wealth
More leisure is consumed in the present, due to an income effect, and the current labor supply curve shifts to the left.

determinants of the demand for current consumption goods were studied in Chapter 9, where we showed that the primary factors affecting current consumption are lifetime wealth and the real interest rate. Further, lifetime wealth is affected by current income, and by the present value of taxes.

Given our analysis of the consumption–savings behavior of consumers in Chapter 9, it proves useful here to construct a demand curve that represents the quantity demanded of current consumption goods by the representative consumer, as a function of current aggregate income, Y, as shown in Figure 11.4. Recall from Chapter 9 that if the real interest rate is held constant and current income increases for the consumer, then current consumption will increase. In Figure 11.4, we graph the quantity of current consumption chosen by the representative consumer, for each level of real income Y, holding constant the real interest rate r. In the figure, the demand for consumption goods is on the vertical axis, and aggregate income is on the horizontal axis. We let $C^d(r)$ denote the demand curve for current consumption goods, indicating the dependence of the demand for consumption on the real interest rate. Recall from Chapter 9 that, if current income increases for the consumer, then consumption and savings both increase, so that the quantity of consumption increases by less than one unit for each unit increase in income. In Figure 11.4, the slope of the curve $C^d(r)$ is the MPC or **marginal propensity to consume**, which is the amount by

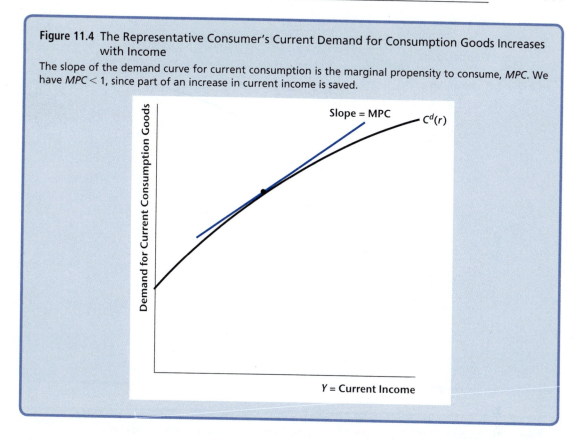

Figure 11.4 The Representative Consumer's Current Demand for Consumption Goods Increases with Income

The slope of the demand curve for current consumption is the marginal propensity to consume, *MPC*. We have *MPC* < 1, since part of an increase in current income is saved.

which current consumption increases when there is a unit increase in aggregate real income Y.

When there is an increase in the real interest rate, assuming again that the substitution effect of this increase dominates the income effect, there will be a decrease in the demand for current consumption goods because of the intertemporal substitution of consumption (recall our analysis from Chapter 9). In Figure 11.5, if the real interest rate increases from r_1 to r_2, the demand curve for current consumption shifts down from $C^d(r_1)$ to $C^d(r_2)$. Also, holding constant r and Y, if there is an increase in lifetime wealth, then, as in Figure 11.6, the demand curve for current consumption shifts up from $C_1^d(r)$ to $C_2^d(r)$. Such an increase in lifetime wealth could be caused by a decrease in the present value of taxes for the consumer, or by an increase in future income.

The demand for current consumption goods is only part of the total demand in the economy for current goods. What remains for us to consider are the demands for current goods coming from firms (the demand for investment goods) and from the government (government purchases). Total demand for current goods will be summarized later in this chapter by the output demand curve, which incorporates the behavior of the representative consumer, the representative firm, and the government.

Figure 11.5 An Increase in the Real Interest Rate from r_1 to r_2 Shifts the Demand for Consumption Goods Down

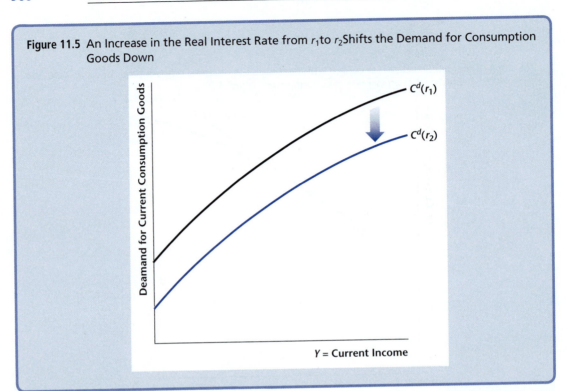

Figure 11.6 An Increase in Lifetime Wealth Shifts the Demand for Consumption Goods Up

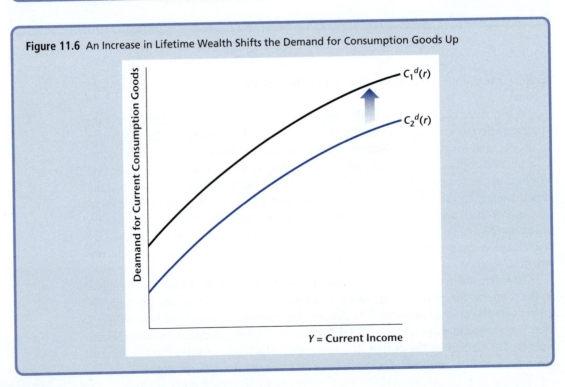

The Representative Firm

LO 11.2 Explain the decisions made by the representative firm in the real intertemporal model.

Now that we have covered the important features of the consumer's current labor supply and current consumption demand decisions, we can turn to the key decisions of the representative firm for the current labor market and the current goods market.

The representative firm, as in Chapter 4, produces goods using inputs of labor and capital. The key differences here are that output is produced in both the current and future periods, and that the firm can invest in the current period by accumulating capital so as to expand the capacity to produce future output. In the current period, the representative firm produces output according to the production function

$$Y = zF(K, N), \tag{11-7}$$

where Y is current output, z is total factor productivity, F is the production function, K is current capital, and N is current labor input. Here, K is the capital with which the firm starts the current period, and this quantity is given. The production function F is identical in all respects to the production function we studied in Chapter 4.

Similarly, in the future period, output is produced according to

$$Y' = z'F(K', N'), \tag{11-8}$$

where Y' is the future output, z' is the future total factor productivity, K' is the future capital stock, and N' is the future labor input.

Recall from Chapter 2 that investment, as measured in the NIPA, is expenditure on plant, equipment, housing, and inventory accumulation. Here, we model investment goods as being produced from output. That is, for simplicity we assume that it requires one unit of consumption goods in the current period to produce one unit of capital. The representative firm invests by acquiring capital in the current period, and the essence of investment is that something must be forgone in the current period to gain something in the future. What is forgone by the firm when it invests is current profits; the firm uses some of the current output it produces to invest in capital, which becomes productive in the future. As in the Solow growth model introduced in Chapter 7, capital depreciates at the rate d when used. Letting I denote the quantity of current investment, the future capital stock is given by

$$K' = (1 - d)K + I. \tag{11-9}$$

That is, the future capital stock is the current capital stock net of depreciation plus the quantity of current investment that has been added in the current period. Further, the quantity of capital left at the end of the future period is $(1 - d)K'$. Because the future period is the last period, it would not be useful for the representative firm to retain this quantity of capital, and so the firm liquidates it. We suppose that the firm can take the quantity $(1 - d)K'$, the capital left at the end of the future period, and convert it one-for-one back into consumption goods, which it can then sell. This is a simple way to model a firm's ability to sell off capital for what it can fetch on the secondhand market. For example, a restaurant that goes out of business can sell its used tables, chairs, and kitchen equipment secondhand in a liquidation sale.

Profits and Current Labor Demand

Now that we know how the firm produces output in the present and the future and how investment can take place, we are ready to determine present and future profits for the firm. The goal of the firm is to maximize the present value of profits over the current and future periods, and this allows us to determine the firm's demand for current labor, as well as the firm's quantity of investment, which we discuss in the next subsection. For the representative firm, current profits in units of the current consumption goods are

$$\pi = Y - wN - I, \tag{11-10}$$

which is current output (or revenue) Y minus wages paid to workers in the current period minus current investment. The firm can produce one unit of capital using one unit of output, so that each unit of investment decreases current profits by one unit. Future profits for the firm are

$$\pi' = Y' - w'N' + (1 - d)K', \tag{11-11}$$

which is future output minus wages paid to workers in the future plus the value of the capital stock net of depreciation at the end of the future period.

Profits earned by the firm in the current and future periods are paid out to the shareholders of the firm as dividend income in each period. There is one shareholder in this economy, the representative consumer, and the firm acts in the interests of this shareholder. This implies that the firm maximizes the present value of the consumer's dividend income, which serves to maximize the lifetime wealth of the consumer. Letting V denote the present value of profits for the firm, the firm maximizes

$$V = \pi + \frac{\pi'}{1 + r} \tag{11-12}$$

by choosing current labor demand N, future labor demand N', and current investment I.

The firm's choice of current labor demand N affects only current profits π in Equation (11-10). As in Chapter 4, the firm hires current labor until the current marginal product of labor equals the current real wage, that is, $MP_N = w$. Also as in Chapter 4, the demand curve for labor in the current period is identical to the marginal product of labor schedule, as the MP_N schedule tells us how much labor the firm needs to hire so that $MP_N = w$. In Figure 11.7 we show the representative firm's demand curve for labor, N^d, with the current real wage w on the vertical axis and the current quantity of labor N on the horizontal axis. Recall from Chapter 4 that the labor demand curve is downward-sloping because the marginal product of labor declines with the quantity of labor employed.

Figure 11.7 The Demand Curve for Current Labor Is the Representative Firm's Marginal Product of Labor Schedule

The curve slopes downward because the marginal product of labor declines as the labor input increases.

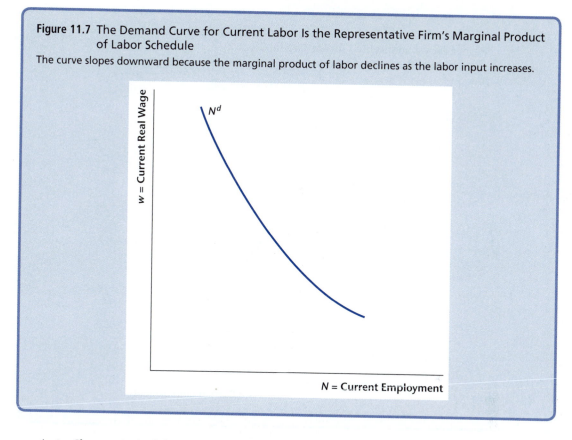

As in Chapter 4, the labor demand curve shifts with changes in total factor productivity z or with changes in the initial capital stock K. A higher current level of total factor productivity z or a higher level of K shifts the labor demand curve to the right, for example, from N_1^d to N_2^d in Figure 11.8.

The firm chooses labor demand in the future period in a similar way to its choice of current-period labor demand. Ignoring this future choice in our analysis allows us to simplify our model in a way that makes the model's predictions clearer while doing no harm.

The Representative Firm's Investment Decision

LO 11.3 Show how the firm's investment decision is structured, and determine how changes in the environment faced by the firm affect investment.

Having dealt with the representative firm's labor demand decision, and given its goal of maximizing the present value of its profits, we can proceed to a central aspect of this chapter, which is analyzing the investment choice of the firm.

A key principle in economic decision making is that the optimal level of an economic activity is chosen so that the marginal benefit of the activity is equal to its

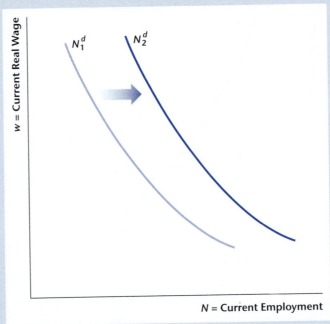

Figure 11.8 The Current Demand Curve for Labor Shifts Due to Changes in Current Total Factor Productivity *z* and in the Current Capital Stock *K*

Here, an increase in *z* or in *K* shifts the curve to the right reflecting the resulting increase in the marginal product of labor.

marginal cost. In this respect, there is nothing different about the choice of investment by the representative firm, which will involve equating the marginal cost of investment with the marginal benefit of investment. We let $MC(I)$ denote the **marginal cost of investment** for the firm, where

$$MC(I) = 1. \tag{11-13}$$

In other words, the marginal cost of investment for the firm is what it gives up, in terms of the present value of profits, V, by investing in one unit of capital in the current period. This marginal cost is 1, as from Equations (11-10) and (11-12), an additional unit of current investment I reduces current profits π by one unit, which reduces the present value of profits V by one unit.

The **marginal benefit from investment**, denoted by $MB(I)$, is what one extra unit of investment in the current period adds to the present value of profits, V. In Equation (11-11), all the benefits from investment come in terms of future profits π', and there are two components to the marginal benefit. First, an additional unit of current investment adds one unit to the future capital stock K'. This implies that the firm will produce more output in the future, and the additional output produced is equal to the firm's future marginal product of capital, MP'_K. Second, each unit of current investment implies that there will be an additional $1 - d$ units of capital remaining at the end of the future period (after depreciation in the future period), which can be liquidated. Thus, one unit of additional investment in the current period implies an additional $MP'_K + 1 - d$ units of future profits π'. In calculating the marginal benefit of investment we have to discount these future profits, and so we then have

$$MB(I) = \frac{MP'_K + 1 - d}{1 + r}. \tag{11-14}$$

The firm invests until the marginal benefit from investment is equal to the marginal cost—in other words, $MB(I) = MC(I)$—or from Equations (11-13) and (11-14),

$$\frac{MP'_K + 1 - d}{1 + r} = 1. \tag{11-15}$$

We can rewrite (11-15) as

$$MP'_K - d = r. \tag{11-16}$$

Equation (11-16) states that the firm invests until the **net marginal product of capital**, $MP'_K - d$, is equal to the real interest rate. The net marginal product of capital, $MP'_K - d$, is the marginal product of capital after taking account of the depreciation of the capital stock. The intuition behind the **optimal investment rule**, Equation (11-16), is that the opportunity cost of investing in more capital is the real rate of interest, which is the rate of return on the alternative asset in this economy. That is, in the model there are two assets: bonds traded on the credit market and capital held by the representative firm. If the firm invests in capital, it is foregoing lending in the credit market, where it can earn a real rate of return of r.

Effectively, the representative consumer holds the capital of the firm indirectly, because the consumer owns the firm and receives its profits as dividend income. From the consumer's point of view, the rate of return that he or she receives between the current and future periods when the firm engages in investment is the net marginal product of capital. As the firm acts in the interests of the consumer, it would not be optimal for the firm to invest beyond the point where the net marginal product of capital is equal to the real interest rate, as in Equation (11-16), because this would imply that the consumer was receiving a lower rate of return on his or her savings than could be obtained by lending in the credit market at the real interest rate r. Thus, the real interest rate represents the opportunity cost of investing for the representative firm.

Another aspect of the firm's investment decision can help clarify the role of the market real interest rate in the firm's optimal choice. Suppose that, given the optimal choice of investment for the firm, $\pi = Y - wN - I < 0$. How is this possible? Such a situation is much like what occurs when a consumer chooses to consume more than his or her income during the current period. That is, the firm borrows the amount $I + wN - Y$ so as to help finance current investment, and must repay the quantity $(1 + r)(I + wN - Y)$. In the future period. It will only be optimal for the firm to borrow up to the point where the net rate of return on investment is equal to the market real interest rate, as borrowing any more would be unprofitable. This is just another sense in which the market real interest rate is the opportunity cost of investment for the firm.

The optimal investment rule, Equation (11-16), determines a negative relationship between the quantity of capital K' that the firm desires in the future period, and the real interest rate. That is, if the market real interest rate, r, increases, then the firm will choose smaller K', so as to increase MP'_K. However, our interest is in showing how the firm determines investment I given the real interest rate r. But from Equation (11-9), we have $K' = (1 - d)K + I$, so effectively there is a negative relationship between I and MP'_K (given K), because one unit of investment yields a one-unit increase in the future capital stock K'. In Figure 11.9, we graph the firm's **optimal investment schedule**, with the interest rate on the vertical axis and the demand for investment goods, I^d, on the horizontal axis. Given Equation (11-16), the optimal investment schedule is the firm's net marginal product of capital, as a function of investment, given the initial quantity of capital K. In the figure, if the real interest rate is r_1 then the firm wishes to invest I_1, and if the real interest rate falls to r_2 then investment increases to I_2. Note the similarity here to the firm's current labor demand decision, as represented, for example, in Figure 11.1. When making its current labor demand decision, the relevant price to consider is the current real wage, and the firm hires labor until the marginal product of labor is equal to the real wage. In making its investment decision, the relevant price is the real interest rate, and the firm acquires capital (invests) until the net marginal product of capital is equal to the real interest rate.

Optimal investment I^d is determined in part by the market real interest rate r, as reflected in the negative slope of the optimal investment schedule in Figure 11.9. Also, the optimal investment schedule shifts due to any factor that changes the future marginal product of capital. Primarily, we are interested in the following two types of shifts in the optimal investment schedule:

1. The optimal investment schedule shifts to the right if future total factor productivity z' increases. From Chapter 4, recall that an increase in total factor productivity increases the marginal product of capital, for each level of the capital stock. Therefore, if total factor productivity is expected to be higher in the future, so that z' increases, this increases the future marginal product of capital, and the firm is more willing to invest during the current period. Higher investment in the current period leads to higher future productive capacity, so that the firm can take advantage of high future total factor productivity.

2. The optimal investment schedule shifts to the left if the current capital stock K is higher. A higher capital stock at the beginning of the current period implies, from Equation (11-9), that for a given level of current investment I, the future capital stock K' will be larger. That is, if K is larger, then there is more of this initial capital left after depreciation in the current period to use in future production. Therefore, higher K implies that the future marginal product of capital, MP'_K, will decrease for each level of investment, and the optimal investment schedule will then shift to the left.

In Figure 11.10 we show a shift to the right in the optimal investment schedule, which could be caused either by an increase in future total factor productivity z', or by

Figure 11.9 Optimal Investment Schedule for the Representative Firm

The optimal investment rule states that the firm invests until $MP_K - d = r$. The future net marginal product schedule $MP_K - d$ is the representative firm's optimal investment schedule, because this describes how much investment is required for the net marginal product of future capital to equal the real interest rate.

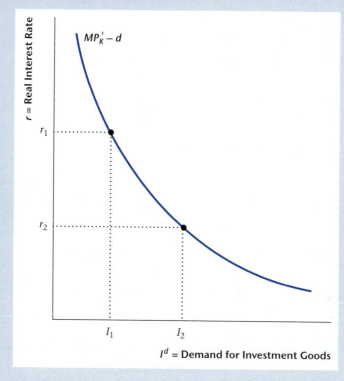

I^d = Demand for Investment Goods

a lower current quantity of capital K. Note that the optimal investment schedule also shifts if the depreciation rate d changes, but we ask the reader to determine the resulting shift in the curve as a problem at the end of this chapter.

This theory of investment can potentially explain why aggregate investment expenditures tend to be more variable over the business cycle than aggregate output or aggregate consumption, features of macroeconomic data that we highlighted in Chapter 3. A key implication of consumer behavior is smoothing; consumers wish to smooth consumption over time relative to their income, and this explains why consumption tends to be less variable than income. However, investment behavior is not about smoothing but about the response of the firm's investment behavior to perceived marginal rates of return to investment. Provided that the real interest rate and anticipated future total factor productivity vary sufficiently over the business cycle, our theory of the business cycle can explain the variability in observed investment expenditures. That is, investment is variable if the real interest rate is variable, causing movements along the optimal investment schedule in Figure 11.10, or if there is variability in anticipated future total factor productivity, causing the optimal investment schedule to shift over time.

Figure 11.10 The Optimal Investment Schedule Shifts to the Right if Current Capital Decreases or Future Total Factor Productivity Is Expected to Increase

This is because either of these changes causes the future marginal product of capital to increase. The figure shows the effect of a decrease in current capital from K_1 to K_2.

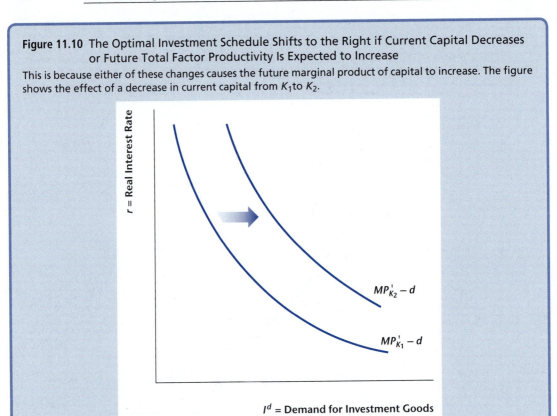

I^d = Demand for Investment Goods

Optimal Investment: A Numerical Example   To make the firm's optimal investment decision more concrete, consider the following numerical example. Christine, a small-scale farmer, has an apple orchard, which has 10 trees in the current period; that is, $K = 10$. For simplicity, suppose that the quantity of labor required to operate the orchard does not depend on the number of trees Christine has, at least for the number of trees that Christine can plant on her land. In the current period, the 10 trees produce 100 bushels of apples; that is, $Y = 100$. Christine can invest in more trees by taking some of the apples, extracting the seeds (which we assume makes the apples useless), and planting them. Very few of the seeds grow, and it takes 1 bushel of apples to yield 1 tree that will be productive in the future period. The first extra tree that Christine grows is on her best land, and, therefore, it will have a high marginal product, bearing a relatively large amount of fruit. The second tree is planted on slightly worse land, and so will have a smaller marginal product, and so on. Each period, some trees die. In fact, at the end of each period, Christine loses 20% of her trees, and so the depreciation rate is $d = 0.2$. At the end of the future period, Christine can liquidate her trees. Because each bushel of apples can produce a tree, it is possible to exchange 1 tree for 1 bushel of apples on the open market, so that the liquidation value of a tree remaining in the future period, after depreciation, is 1 bushel of apples. The real interest rate is 5%, or

Table 11.1 Data for Christine's Orchard

K′ = trees in the future	I	Y′	V	MP′ − d
8	0	95	196.6	—
9	1	98	199.2	2.8
10	2	100	200.9	1.8
11	3	101	201.6	0.8
12	4	101.5	201.8	0.3
13	5	101.65	201.7	−0.35
14	6	101.75	201.6	−0.10
15	7	101.77	201.4	−0.18

$r = 0.05$ in units of apples. Table 11.1 shows the quantity of future output that will be produced when the number of trees Christine has in the future is 8, 9, 10, . . . , 15, as well as the associated level of investment, present discounted value of profits (in units of apples), and the net marginal product of capital (trees) in the future.

From Table 11.1, the present value of profits is maximized when the number of trees in the future is 12 and the quantity of investment is 4 bushels of apples. For each unit of investment from 1 to 4, the net marginal product of capital in the future is greater than the real interest rate, which is 0.05, and the net marginal product of capital is less than 0.05 for each unit of investment above 4. Therefore, it is optimal to invest as long as the net marginal product of future capital is greater than the real interest rate.

Investment with Asymmetric Information and the Financial Crisis

In Chapter 10, we discussed and analyzed the importance of credit market imperfections in consumer credit markets, and some of the implications for the global financial crisis. One feature of credit markets that can give rise to credit market imperfections is asymmetric information—a situation where would-be borrowers in the credit market know more about their creditworthiness than do would-be lenders. The purpose of this section is to show how asymmetric information matters for the investment choices of firms, just as it matters for a consumer's saving behavior, and to explore the importance of this for the financial crisis.

As in Chapter 10, it will help to model borrowing and lending in the credit market as occurring only through banks. Anyone who wishes to lend holds a deposit with a bank that bears the market real interest rate r. Assume that these deposits are completely safe—a bank that takes deposits in the current period is always able to pay the rate of return r to each depositor in the future period. Also suppose that, instead of a single representative firm, there are many firms in the economy. Some of these firms will choose to lend in the current period, and these firms will have positive profits in the current period, with $\pi = Y - wN - I > 0$. There will also be some firms that choose to borrow. Among these borrowing firms, there are good firms, which have negative current profits, or $\pi = Y - wN - I < 0$. There are also bad firms that borrow in the credit market, but have no intention of producing anything in the future. The managers of a bad firm are assumed to simply take the amount borrowed in the credit market and consume it as executive compensation rather than investing in new capital.

Unfortunately, a bank is not able to distinguish between a good firm and a bad firm, and therefore treats all firms wishing to borrow in the same way. This is the asymmetric information problem—each borrowing firm knows whether it is good or bad, but the bank cannot tell the difference. So that the bank can make good on its promise to pay each depositor a rate of return of r on his or her deposits, the bank must charge each borrower a real interest rate on loans that is greater than r. That is, if we let r^l denote the loan interest rate, we will have $r < r^l$, and the difference $r^l - r$ is a default premium, similar to the default premium we analyzed in Chapter 10. By lending to a large number of borrowers, the bank is able to accurately predict the chances of lending to a bad borrower. Then, the default premium charged to good borrowers will compensate the bank for loans made to bad borrowers that will yield nothing for the bank.

For a firm that is a lender, investment is financed out of retained earnings. Such a firm has revenue remaining after paying its wage bill in the current period (the quantity $Y - wN$), uses some of this revenue to finance investment, and lends the remainder $(Y - wN - I)$ to the bank at the real interest rate r. For such a lending firm, the analysis of the firm's investment decision is identical to what we did in the previous subsection, and the firm's optimal investment rule is given by Equation (11-16), with the optimal investment schedule depicted in Figure 11.9.

A good firm that borrows will borrow at the real interest rate

$$r^l = r + x,$$

where x is the default premium, and so the opportunity cost of investment for a good borrowing firm is $r + x$, and the optimal investment schedule for this firm is

$$MP'_K - d = r + x,$$

or

$$MP'_K - d - x = r. \tag{11-17}$$

In Equation (11-17), note that the default premium acts to reduce the net marginal product of capital, given the safe credit market interest rate r. In Figure 11.11, we show the effect on the optimal investment schedule of a good borrowing firm when there is an increase in the default premium. Such an increase in the default premium could occur if banks perceive that bad borrowing firms have become more prevalent. In the figure, the default premium increases from x_1 to x_2. As a result, the optimal investment schedule for the firm shifts down (or to the left), and the firm will choose to invest less at each level of the safe market real interest rate r.

Figure 11.11 The Effect of an Increased Default Premium on a Firm's Optimal Investment Schedule

An increase in the default premium, from x_1 to x_2, shifts the optimal investment schedule down, so that the firm will invest less given any safe real interest rate r.

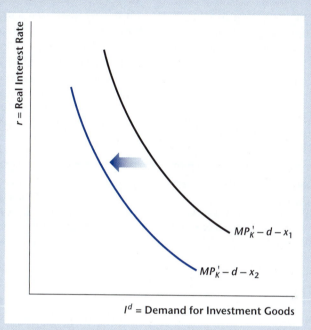

$MP_K' - d - x_1$

$MP_K' - d - x_2$

I^d = Demand for Investment Goods

r = Real Interest Rate

THEORY CONFRONTS THE DATA

Investment and the Interest Rate Spread

Theory tells us that we should observe a negative relationship between the default premium and investment expenditures. If the asymmetric information problem becomes worse in credit markets where firms borrow to finance investment projects, the default premium should increase and we should see a decline in investment expenditures. In Chapter 10, we examined a particular measure of the default premium, the difference between the interest rates on AAA-rated and BAA-rated corporate bonds; that is, the difference

between interest rates on essentially default-free corporate debt, and risky corporate debt.

In Figure 11.12, we show a time series plot of the percentage deviations from trend in aggregate investment expenditures and the deviations from trend in the AAA/BAA interest rate spread. The deviations from trend in the spread are multiplied by 10 to make the comovements more discernible. Note that the two time series are clearly negatively correlated, which is even more apparent in the scatter plot of the same two variables

(Continued)

in Figure 11.13. The calculated correlation coefficient between the two time series in Figures 11.12 and 11.13 is −0.54. Clearly, a negatively sloped straight line would provide the best fit to the scatter plot. In Figure 11.12, note in particular the behavior of the spread and investment expenditures around the recessions in 1974–1975, 1981–1982, 1990–1991, 2001, and 2008–2009.

During the financial crisis leading up to the 2008–2009 recession, an important phenomenon was the increase that occurred in financial market uncertainty. Financial institutions, including banks, became increasingly unsure about which firms were likely to default on loans. This uncertainty was reflected in a sharp increase in the interest rate spread in Figure 11.12. As a result, even healthy firms suffered. In our model, a firm may know that it will be able to repay a loan in the future, but in spite of this it will face a higher default premium in the face of increased credit market uncertainty. For a given safe market interest rate (the interest rate r faced by bank depositors), a given firm will choose to invest and borrow less. In the aggregate, investment expenditures will fall, as reflected in the data in Figures 11.12 and 11.13.

Figure 11.12 Investment and the Interest Rate Spread

The figure shows percentage deviations from trend in investment expenditures and deviations from trend in the spread between interest rates on AAA-rated and BAA-rated corporate debt. There is a clear negative correlation, and the spread tends to be high during recessions, at times when investment is low.

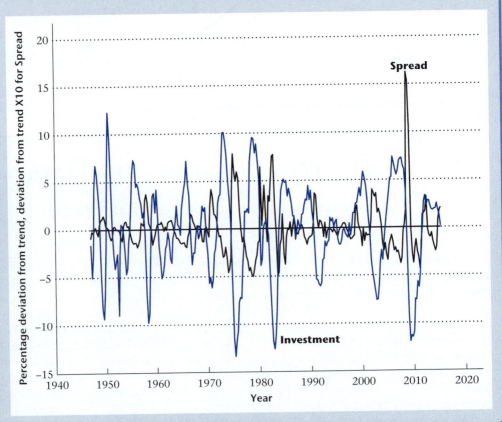

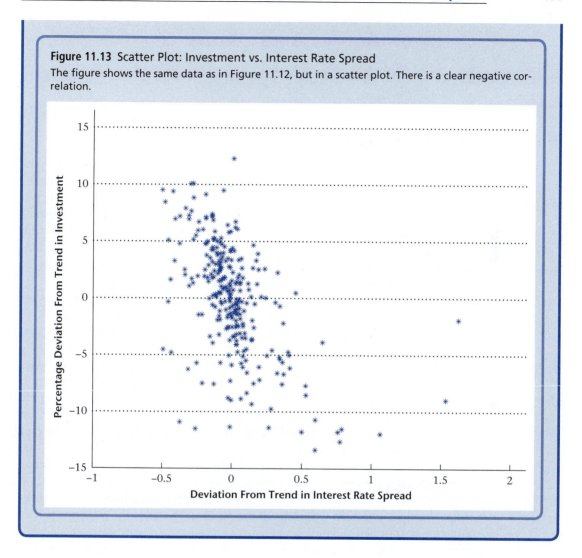

Figure 11.13 Scatter Plot: Investment vs. Interest Rate Spread

The figure shows the same data as in Figure 11.12, but in a scatter plot. There is a clear negative correlation.

Government

We have now shown how the representative consumer and the representative firm behave in the markets for current goods and current labor. We need only to consider government behavior before we show how all these economic agents interact in a competitive equilibrium. Government behavior is identical to what it was in Chapter 9. The government sets government purchases of consumption goods exogenously in each period. The quantity of government purchases in the current period is G, and in the future government purchases are G'. The government finances government purchases in the current period through taxation and by issuing government bonds. Then in the future, the government pays off the interest and principal on its bonds and finances future government spending through future lump-sum taxation. As in Chapter 9, the government must satisfy its present-value budget constraint,

$$G + \frac{G'}{1+r} = T + \frac{T'}{1+r}. \tag{11-18}$$

Competitive Equilibrium

Our analysis thus far has focused on the behavior of the representative consumer, the representative firm, and the government in two markets, the current-period labor market and the current-period goods market. In this real intertemporal model, the representative consumer supplies labor in the current-period labor market, and demands consumption goods in the current-period goods market. The representative firm demands labor in the current period, supplies goods in the current period, and demands investment goods in the current period. Finally, the government demands goods in the current period, in terms of government purchases.

Perceptive readers might wonder why we have neglected the future markets for labor and goods and the market for credit. First, markets in the future are neglected to make our model simple to work with, and this simplification is essentially harmless at this level of analysis. Second, later in this chapter, we show that we have not actually neglected the credit market, as equilibrium in the current-period goods market implies that the credit market clears, just as we showed in the two-period model in Chapter 9.

This section shows how a competitive equilibrium for our model, where supply equals demand in the current-period labor and goods markets, can be expressed in terms of diagrams. We put together the labor supply and labor demand curves to capture how the labor market functions; then, we derive an output supply curve that describes how the supply of goods is related to the real interest rate. Finally, we derive an output demand curve, which describes how the sum of the demand for goods from the representative consumer (consumption goods), the representative firm (investment goods), and the government (government purchases) is related to the real interest rate. Putting the output demand and supply curves together in a diagram with the labor market gives us a working model, which is used to address some key issues in macroeconomics in the following sections and in later chapters.

The Current Labor Market and the Output Supply Curve

LO 11.4 Construct the output supply curve.

First we consider how the market for labor in the current period works. In Figure 11.14(a), we show the labor demand curve for the representative firm and the labor supply curve for the representative consumer, as derived in the previous sections, with the current real wage, w, on the vertical axis and the current quantity of labor, N, on the horizontal axis. Recall from earlier sections in this chapter that the labor supply curve slopes upward, as we are assuming that the substitution effect of an increase in the real wage dominates the income effect, and recall that the position of the labor

Figure 11.14 Determination of Equilibrium in the Labor Market Given the Real Interest Rate r

In (a), the intersection of the current labor supply and demand curves determines the current real wage and current employment, and the production function in (b) then determines aggregate output.

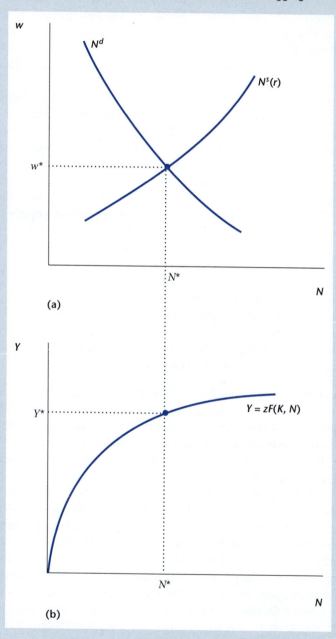

supply curve depends on the real interest rate r. Also, we determined that an increase (decrease) in the real interest rate causes an increase (decrease) in labor supply for each real wage w, and the labor supply curve shifts to the right (left). Given the real interest rate r, the equilibrium real wage in Figure 11.14(a) is w^*, the equilibrium quantity of employment is N^*, and from the production function in Figure 11.14(b), we determine the quantity of aggregate output supplied (given the real interest rate), which is Y^*. Recall from Chapter 4 that the position of the production function is determined by current total factor productivity z and by the current capital stock K. An increase in z or K would shift the production function up.

Our next step is to use the diagrams in Figure 11.14 to derive an output supply curve, which describes how much output is supplied by firms for each possible level for the real interest rate. In Figure 11.15(a), the labor supply curves for two different interest rates, r_1 and r_2, are shown, where $r_1 < r_2$. Thus, with the increase in the real interest rate, the current labor supply curve shifts to the right, the current equilibrium real wage falls from w_1 to w_2, and current employment increases from N_1 to N_2. Further, current output increases from Y_1 to Y_2, in Figure 11.15(b), from the production function. We can then construct a curve, called the **output supply curve**, which is an upward-sloping curve consisting of all combinations of current output and real interest rates, (Y, r), for which the current labor market is in equilibrium. This curve is denoted Y^s in Figure 11.15(c). Two points on the Y^s curve are (Y_1, r_1) and (Y_2, r_2), because at real interest rate r_1 the labor market is in equilibrium when the representative firm produces current output Y_1 and at real interest rate r_2 the labor market is in equilibrium when the representative firm produces current output Y_2. Thus, the output supply curve slopes upward because of the intertemporal substitution effect on labor supply. If the real interest rate is higher, the representative consumer will choose to supply more labor, resulting in an increase in employment and output.

Shifts in the Output Supply Curve   When we work with our real intertemporal model, we need to know how changes in particular exogenous variables shift supply and demand curves. In this subsection, we show how three factors—lifetime wealth, current total factor productivity, and the current capital stock—can shift the output supply curve. The latter two factors have much the same effect, so we deal with these together.

The output supply curve shifts either because of a shift in the current labor supply curve (not arising because of a change in the real interest rate; the output supply curve already takes this into account), because of a shift in the current labor demand curve, or because of a shift in the production function. From our analysis of consumer behavior, we know that a change in lifetime wealth shifts the labor supply curve, whereas a change in either current total factor productivity or the current capital stock shifts the labor demand curve and the production function. We deal with each of these shifts in turn.

Recall from our discussion of the representative consumer's behavior, earlier in this chapter, that a decrease in lifetime wealth reduces the consumer's demand for current leisure, due to an income effect, and so the consumer supplies more labor for any current real wage. Therefore, the labor supply curve shifts to the right. What would cause a reduction in lifetime wealth for the representative consumer? The key factor, from our point of view, is an increase in government spending, either in the present or in

Figure 11.15 Construction of the Output Supply Curve

The output supply curve Y^s is an upward-sloping curve as in (c), consisting of real current output and real interest rate pairs for which the labor market is in equilibrium.

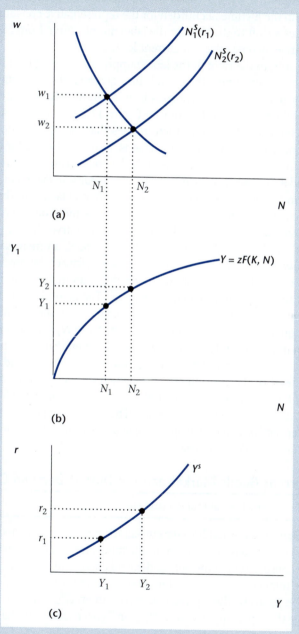

the future. From the present-value government budget constraint, Equation (11-18), any increase in government spending, either in the present or the future (i.e., an increase in G or G') must be reflected in an increase in the present value of taxes for the consumer, $T + \frac{T'}{1+r}$. Therefore, an increase in G, in G', or in both, results in an increase in the lifetime tax burden for the representative consumer. In Figure 11.16(a), this causes a shift to the right in the labor supply curve from $N_1^s(r_1)$ to $N_2^s(r_1)$, as there is a negative income effect on current leisure.

The shift to the right in the labor supply curve in Figure 11.16(a) implies that, for a given real interest rate, the equilibrium quantity of employment in the labor market is higher; that is, employment rises from N_1 to N_2, given a particular real interest rate r_1. From the production function in Figure 11.16(b), output rises from Y_1 to Y_2 given the real interest rate r_1. This then implies that the output supply curve shifts to the right, from Y_1^s to Y_2^s, in 11.16(c). That is, output is higher for each possible value for the real interest rate. The conclusion is that *an increase in G or G' shifts the labor supply curve and the output supply curve to the right, because of the income effect on labor supply*.

From Chapter 4, recall that an increase in total factor productivity or in the capital stock shifts the production function up, because more output can be produced for any level of the labor input, and the labor demand curve shifts to the right, because the marginal product of labor increases. In our model, an increase in current total factor productivity z, or in the current capital stock K, causes the production function to shift up. In Figure 11.17(b) we show the results of an increase in z from z_1 to z_2, but the effect of an increase in K would be identical. The labor demand curve shifts to the right in Figure 11.17(a), from N_1^d to N_2^d. As a result, given the real interest rate r_1, the equilibrium quantity of employment rises from N_1 to N_2. Therefore, from the production function in Figure 11.17(b), as employment is higher and z is higher, output increases from Y_1 to Y_2. The same effects (an increase in employment and output) would happen for any level of the real interest rate, which implies that the output supply curve in Figure 11.17(c) must shift to the right. The results would be identical if there had been an increase in the current capital stock. The conclusion is that *an increase in z or K causes the production function to shift up, the labor demand curve to shift to the right, and the output supply curve to shift to the right*.

The Current Goods Market and the Output Demand Curve

LO 11.5 Construct the output demand curve.

Now that we understand how the current labor market works and how the output supply curve is constructed, we can turn to the functioning of the current-period goods market and the construction of the output demand curve. This then completes our model.

The total current demand for goods Y^d is the sum of the demand for current consumption goods by the representative consumer, $C^d(Y^d, r)$, the demand for investment goods by the representative firm, $I^d(r)$, and government purchases of current goods, G:

$$Y^d = C^d(r) + I^d(r) + G. \tag{11-19}$$

Here, we use the notation $C^d(r)$ and $I^d(r)$ to reflect how the demand for current consumption goods and the demand for investment goods depend negatively on the real interest

Figure 11.16 An Increase in Current or Future Government Spending Shifts the Y^s Curve

This is because the increase in government spending increases the present value of taxes for the representative consumer, and current leisure falls, shifting the labor supply curve to the right in (a) and shifting the output supply curve to the right in (c).

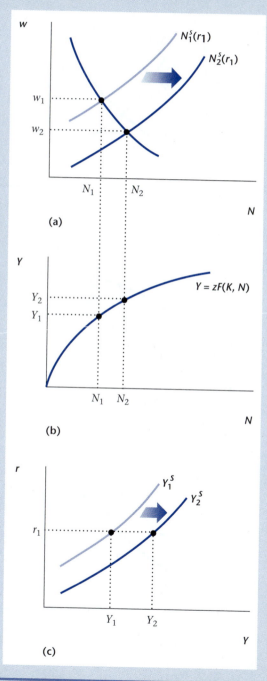

Figure 11.17 An Increase in Current Total Factor Productivity Shifts the Y^s Curve

This is because an increase in z increases the marginal product of current labor, shifting the labor demand curve to the right in (a), and also shifting the production function up in (b). As a result, the output supply curve shifts to the right in (c).

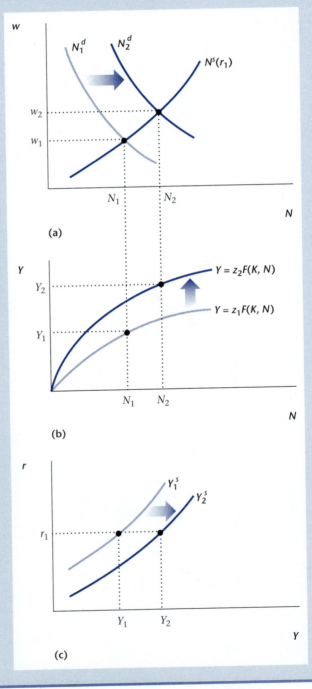

(a)

(b)

(c)

Figure 11.18 The Demand for Current Goods

This is an upward-sloping curve, as the demand for consumption goods increases with current income. The slope of the demand curve for current goods is the marginal propensity to consume (*MPC*).

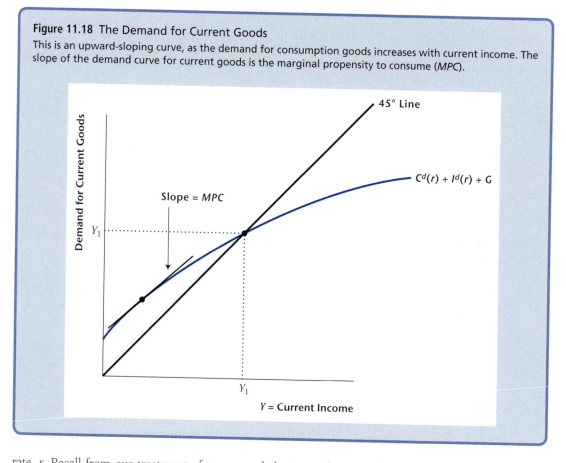

rate, r. Recall from our treatment of consumer behavior earlier in this chapter that the demand for current consumption goods also depends on the lifetime wealth of the representative consumer, one component of which is current income. In Figure 11.18 we show the total demand for goods, the right-hand side of Equation (11-19), as a function of current aggregate income, Y. Since the demands for investment goods and government purchases do not depend on aggregate income, the slope of the curve $C^d(r) + I^d(r) + G$ in the figure is the marginal propensity to consume, MPC. What will be the equilibrium demand for current goods in the market, given the real interest rate, r? This will be determined by the point at which the curve $C^d(r) + I^d(r) + G$ intersects the 45° line, which is where the demand for goods induced by the quantity of income Y (through the dependence of the demand for consumption goods on income) is just equal to Y. Therefore, in Figure 11.18 the demand for current goods is Y_1, which is the quantity of aggregate income that generates a total demand for goods just equal to that quantity of aggregate income.

The next step is to construct the **output demand curve**, which is a negative relationship between current aggregate output and the real interest rate. In Figure 11.19(a), if the real interest rate is r_1, the current demand for goods is $C^d(r_1) + I^d(r_1) + G$. If the real interest rate were r_2 with $r_2 > r_1$, the current demand for goods will fall for each level of aggregate current income Y, as the demand for current consumption goods and

Figure 11.19 Construction of the Output Demand Curve

The output demand curve Y^d in (b) is a downward-sloping one describing the combinations of real output and the real interest rate for which the current goods market is in equilibrium.

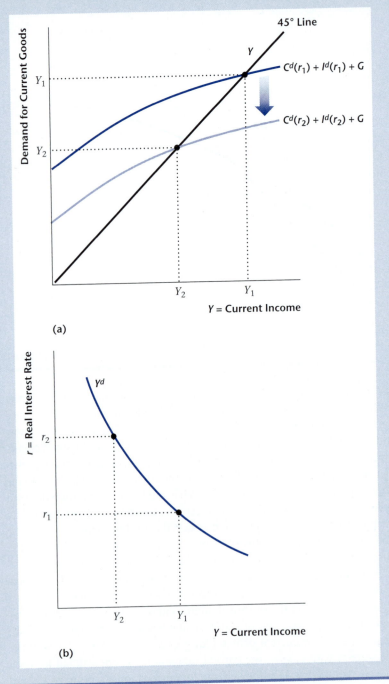

(a)

(b)

for current investment goods will be lower. Thus, the demand for goods will shift down to $C^d(r_2) + I^d(r_2) + G$. As a result, the equilibrium quantity of goods demanded will fall from Y_1 to Y_2. Now, in Figure 11.19(b), we can construct a downward-sloping curve in a diagram with the real interest rate, r, on the vertical axis, and current aggregate income, Y, on the horizontal axis. This curve, Y^d, is the output demand curve, and a point on the curve, (Y, r), represents the level of demand for goods (output), Y, given the real interest rate r. Note that two points on the output demand curve are (Y_1, r_1) and (Y_2, r_2), corresponding to Figure 11.19(a).

Shifts in the Output Demand Curve   Before we put all the elements of our real intertemporal model together—the output demand curve, the output supply curve, the production function, and the current labor supply and demand curves—we need to understand the important factors that shift the output demand curve. The output demand curve shifts as a result of the shift in the demand for current consumption goods, $C^d(r)$, a shift in the demand for investment goods, $I^d(r)$, or because of a change in the current quantity of government purchases G. In Figure 11.20, we show the effects of an increase in the demand for goods coming from an increase in government spending, from G_1 to G_2. In Figure 11.20(a), the demand for current goods shifts up when current government purchases increase from G_1 to G_2. Then, given the real interest rate r_1, the quantity of current goods demanded will increase from Y_1 to Y_2. As a result, in Figure 11.20(b), the output demand curve shifts to the right from Y_1^d to Y_2^d; that is, the quantity of current goods demanded is higher for any real interest rate, including r_1. Other important factors that will shift the Y^d curve to the right, in a manner identical to the results for an increase in G in Figure 11.20 are the following:

- *A decrease in the present value of taxes shifts the Y^d curve to the right.* A decrease in the present value of taxes is caused by a reduction in current taxes, future taxes, or both. When this happens, the lifetime wealth of the representative consumer rises, and therefore the demand for consumption goods, $C^d(r)$, increases, which causes a shift to the right in the output demand curve.
- *An increase in future income Y' shifts the Y^d curve to the right.* If the representative consumer anticipates that his or her future income will be higher, then lifetime wealth increases, resulting in an increase in the demand for current consumption goods, $C^d(r)$.
- *An increase in future total factor productivity z' causes the Y^d curve to shift to the right.* If the representative firm expects total factor productivity to be higher in the future, this increases the firm's demand for goods, so that $I^d(r)$ increases.
- *A decrease in the current capital stock K causes the Y^d curve to shift to the right.* When there is a lower current capital stock, perhaps because of destruction, then the demand for investment goods, $I^d(r)$, increases for each r.

The Complete Real Intertemporal Model

LO 11.6 Show how a competitive equilibrium is determined in the real intertemporal model.

We now have all the building blocks for our real intertemporal model, and so we can put these building blocks together and use the model to address some interesting

Figure 11.20 The Output Demand Curve Shifts to the Right if Current Government Spending Increases

The curve shifts in a similar manner if taxes decrease (in the present or the future), if future income is anticipated to increase, if future total factor productivity is expected to increase, or if the current capital stock declines.

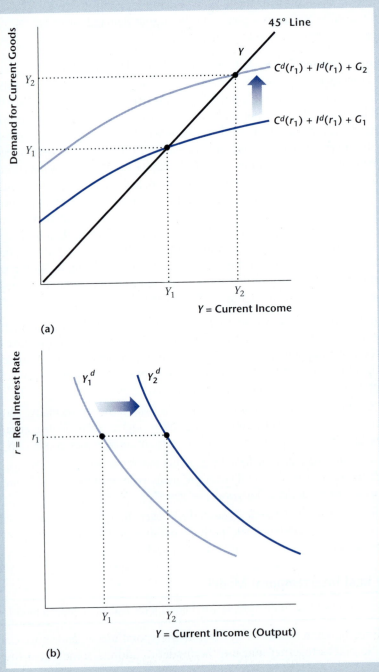

economic issues. Our model is presented in Figure 11.21, where a competitive equilibrium consists of a state of affairs where supply equals demand in the current labor market in panel (a) and in the current goods market in panel (b). In Figure 11.21(a), N^d is the current labor demand curve, while $N^s(r^*)$ is the current labor supply curve, the position of which depends on the equilibrium real interest rate r^*, which is determined in panel (b). The equilibrium real wage is given by w^*, and the equilibrium quantity of employment is N^*, where w^* and N^* are determined by the intersection of the demand and supply curves for current labor. Equilibrium output and the equilibrium real interest rate are Y^* and r^*, respectively, in Figure 11.21(b), and they are determined by the intersection of the output demand curve Y^d with the output supply curve Y^s.

To use the model to help us understand how the macroeconomy works, we perform some experiments. These experiments each involve changing the value of some exogenous variable or variables, and then asking how the solution of the model is different as a result. We then show how we interpret the results of these experiments in terms of real-world macroeconomic events. Our experiments answer the following questions:

1. How does an increase in current government purchases, anticipated to be temporary, affect current macroeconomic variables?

2. What are the effects on current macroeconomic variables of a decrease in the current capital stock, brought about by a natural disaster or a war?

3. How does a temporary increase in total factor productivity affect macroeconomic variables, and how does this fit the key business cycle facts?

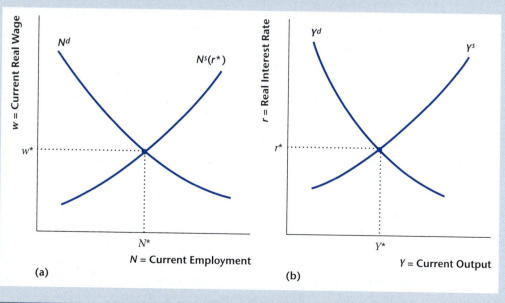

Figure 11.21 The Complete Real Intertemporal Model
(a) The current real wage and current employment are determined by the intersection of the current labor supply and demand curves, given the real interest rate. (b) Current aggregate output and the real interest rate are determined by the intersection of the output supply and demand curves.

4. If total factor productivity is expected to increase in the future, how does this affect current macroeconomic variables?

5. How do credit market frictions affect macroeconomic activity?

6. What are the effects of sectoral shocks on the economy?

The Equilibrium Effects of a Temporary Increase in *G*: Stimulus, the Multiplier, and Crowding Out

LO 11.7 Use the real intertemporal model to explain the effects of particular shocks to the economy.

This may seem like ground we have covered already, as we analyzed the effects of a change in government purchases in the one-period model in Chapter 5. There we learned that there is an income effect of government spending that acts to increase labor supply and output, and that government spending acts to crowd out private consumption. The real intertemporal model allows us to move on from these basic insights and learn something new. First, the model shows how the intertemporal choices of consumers affect the economy's response to a change in government spending. An increase in *G* will act to increase the real interest rate, and this will introduce additional crowding-out effects on private spending working through both investment and consumption. Further, there will be an intertemporal substitution effect on labor supply as a result of the interest rate increase. Second, we will be able to study in detail the workings of expenditure multipliers, which can play an important role in macroeconomic policymaking. The multiplier is the ratio of the response of output to an initial change in government spending, for example.

We will model a temporary increase in government spending as an increase in *G*, the quantity of government purchases in the current period, leaving future government purchases, G', unchanged. When would the government choose to increase its expenditures on goods and services temporarily? An important example is a war. Typically, wars are known to be temporary (though their length can be uncertain), and the government commits spending to the war effort that will not remain in place when the war is over. Another example of an explicitly temporary change in government spending was the spending program contained in the American Recovery and Reinvestment Act (ARRA) of 2009.

We will suppose that government spending in the current period increases from G_1 to G_2, and we would first like to determine how large the resulting shift in the output demand curve will be. For convenience, assume that the marginal propensity to consume, *MPC*, is a constant, implying that the curve in Figure 11.18 is linear. This will also imply that the shift to the right in the output demand curve, which we will denote by Δ, will be the same for any real interest rate *r*.

The quantity Δ is the total change in the demand for goods, which will come from three sources: (i) the direct effect of the change in government spending, $G_2 - G_1$; (ii) the effect on consumption from the increase in taxes (in the present or the future) required to finance the government spending increase; and (iii) the effect on consumption from the increase in Δ, which the representative consumer will see as an increase in income. To determine the second effect, from the present-value government budget constraint,

Equation (11-18), the increase in the present value of taxes for the consumer must be equal to $G_2 - G_1$, the increase in government spending, and so the effect on the demand for consumption goods will be $-MPC(G_2 - G_1)$, since the marginal propensity to consume tells us how much the demand for consumption goods changes with a one-unit change in lifetime wealth. For the third effect, the change in demand for consumption goods is $MPC\Delta$, since an increase in current income of Δ units increases the demand for consumption goods by $MPC\Delta$ units. Then, the total increase in demand for goods is determined by

$$\Delta = G_2 - G_1 - MPC(G_2 - G_1) + MPC\Delta. \qquad (11\text{-}20)$$

Note that Δ appears on both sides of Equation (11-20), because an increase in Δ, through its effect on the demand for consumption goods, produces more demand for consumption goods—a multiplier effect. But how large is that multiplier? If we solve Equation (11-20) for Δ, we get

$$\Delta = G_2 - G_1.$$

Then, let m_d denote the **demand multiplier**, which is the ratio of Δ to the increase in government expenditure, so

$$m_d = \frac{G_2 - G_1}{G_2 - G_1} = 1,$$

and the demand multiplier is one. That is, total demand for goods increases by exactly the amount of the increase in government spending, and the shift to the right in the output demand curve is also the increase in government spending, $G_2 - G_1$.

Before the increase in current government purchases, G, in Figure 11.22, the economy is in equilibrium with a current real wage, w_1, current employment, N_1, current output, Y_1, and real interest rate, r_1. When G increases, this will have two effects, one on output supply and one on output demand. We have determined the effect on output demand, which is a shift to the right in the output demand curve, from Y_1^d to Y_2^d, where the horizontal shift is equal to the increase in G. Since lifetime wealth decreases due to the increase in the present value of taxes, leisure will decrease (leisure is a normal good) for the representative consumer, given the current real wage, and so the labor supply curve in Figure 11.22(a) shifts to the right from $N_1^s(r_1)$ to $N_2^s(r_1)$, and the output supply curve in Figure 11.22(b) shifts to the right from Y_1^s to Y_2^s.

To determine all the equilibrium effects by using the model, we start first with Figure 11.22(b). It is clear that current aggregate output must increase, as both the output demand and output supply curves shift to the right, and so Y increases from Y_1 to Y_2. It may appear that the real interest rate may rise or fall; however, there is strong theoretical support for an increase in the real interest rate. This is because the temporary increase in government spending should lead to only a small decrease in lifetime wealth for the consumer, which will produce a small effect on labor supply. Therefore, there should be only a small shift to the right in the Y^s curve, and the real interest rate will rise, as in Figure 11.22(b).

What is the **total government expenditure multiplier** here, by which we mean the ratio of the equilibrium increase in real output to the increase in government

Figure 11.22 A Temporary Increase in Government Purchases

The increase in G shifts the labor supply curve to the right, the output supply curve to the right, and the output demand curve to the right. The real interest rate rises, and aggregate output increases in equilibrium. There is an additional shift to the right in the labor supply curve because of the increase in r, so employment rises and the real wage falls in equilibrium.

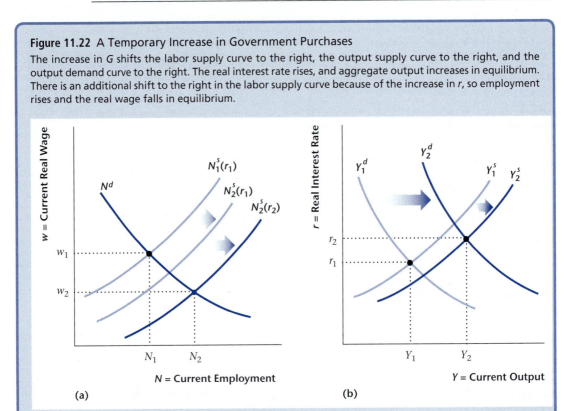

(a)

(b)

spending? Since the output demand curve in Figure 11.22(b) shifted to the right by the increase in government spending, the equilibrium increase in current output must be less than the increase in government spending. The total multiplier is less than one, and it will become smaller as the size of the wealth effect on labor supply falls (this makes the rightward shift in the output supply curve smaller), and as the intertemporal substitution effect of the real interest rate on labor supply falls (this makes the output supply curve steeper).

Some economists have argued that the government expenditure multiplier can be greater than one, particularly during a recession. These arguments typically rely on the existence of some form of economic inefficiency, for example sticky wages and prices, as in some forms of Keynesian analysis, or the failure of consumers to take account of the effects of the increase in future taxes needed to pay off the government debt. In Chapters 13 and 14, we will analyze Keynesian mechanisms, and show how this makes a difference.

What happens to current consumption in Figure 11.22? If the real interest rate did not change in equilibrium (e.g., if the output supply curves were horizontal), we know from the figure that real income would increase by an amount equal to the increase in government spending. If this occurred, then the change in the consumer's lifetime wealth would be zero, since the increase in the present value of taxes is equal to the increase in current income. As a result, current consumption would be unchanged.

However, in Figure 11.22(b) the real interest rate rises in equilibrium, so the representative consumer will substitute future consumption for current consumption, and therefore current consumption declines. As well, investment expenditures must decrease because of the increase in the real interest rate. Thus, both components of private expenditure (current consumption and investment) are crowded out by current government expenditure. Recall from Chapter 5, that when we analyzed the effects of an increase in government spending in a one-period model, without taking intertemporal substitution and investment into account, government spending crowded out only consumption expenditure. Since government spending is shown here to crowd out private investment expenditure, a further cost of government is that it reduces the economy's future productive capacity, as the future capital stock will be lower (than it otherwise would have been).

On the demand side of the goods market, it is the crowding out of private consumption and investment expenditure that causes the total government expenditure multiplier to be less than one here. On the supply side, output increases because of two effects on labor supply. First, just as in our Chapter 5 analysis, there is a negative wealth effect on leisure from the increase in lifetime tax liabilities. Second, the increase in the real interest rate makes future leisure cheaper relative to current leisure, and there is a further increase in labor supply.

The next step is to work through the effects of the increase in the real interest rate for the labor market. In Figure 11.22(a), given the initial interest rate r_1, the labor supply curve shifts from $N_1^s(r_1)$ to $N_2^s(r_1)$, because of the negative wealth effect arising from the increase in the present value of taxes. With an increase in the equilibrium real interest rate to r_2, the labor supply curve shifts further to the right, to $N_2^s(r_2)$. Therefore, the equilibrium real wage falls from w_1 to w_2.

What this analysis tells us is that increased temporary government spending, although it leads to higher aggregate output, comes at a cost. With higher current government spending, the representative consumer consumes less and takes less leisure, and he or she also faces a lower real wage rate. Further, current investment spending is lower, which implies that the capital stock will be lower in the future, and the future capacity of the economy for producing goods will be lower.

The Equilibrium Effects of a Decrease in the Current Capital Stock *K*

LO 11.7 Use the real intertemporal model to explain the effects of particular shocks to the economy.

Over time, through investment, a nation adds to its capital stock, and this generally occurs slowly, as investment expenditure is typically quite small relative to the total capital stock. Thus, increases in capital do not contribute much to short-run fluctuations in aggregate output and employment. However, sometimes major reductions in the aggregate capital stock occur over a short period of time. For example, a war can

THEORY CONFRONTS THE DATA

Government Expenditure Multipliers in the Recovery from the 2008–2009 Recession

Figure 11.23 shows the paths followed by real GDP, real consumption expenditures, and real government expenditures for the United States from the first quarter of 2007 to the fourth quarter of 2015. We have normalized each time series to equal 100 in the first quarter of 2007. In the figure, we can clearly see the effects of the most recent recession on GDP and consumption, with output and consumption falling from the last quarter of 2007 to the second quarter of 2009, and then recovering. But the recovery after the last recession was relatively weak, in that aggregate output grew on average at 2.13% per year from the second quarter of 2009 to the fourth quarter of 2015, a period over which consumption grew at an average rate of 2.24%. As a guidepost, average growth in real GDP has been about 3% on average since World War II, and GDP tends to grow at a higher rate than average during a recovery, so the most recent recovery has been quite sluggish.

A possible reason for the sluggish recovery has been low or negative growth in government expenditures on goods and services, as we can see in Figure 11.23. While government expenditures continued to grow through the 2008–2009 recession, in part as a result of the American Recovery and Reinvestment Act (ARRA) of 2009, by the fourth quarter of 2015, government spending was at about the same level as in the first quarter of 2007.

But how much higher would real GDP have been if government spending had not been cut after the ARRA expired? That is a question we could answer if we knew the total government expenditure multiplier. To get some feel for how large the government expenditure multiplier might be, we could consider a counterfactual experiment, supposing government expenditure had grown at a 3% annual rate (the same as the average growth rate in U.S. real GDP since World War II) from the end of the 2008–2009 recession in the second quarter of 2009, instead of at the rate of −1.15%, as actually transpired.

First, if the total government expenditure multiplier were equal to one, then the average growth rate of real GDP given the higher government expenditure would have been 2.96% since the second quarter of 2009 or 1.84% since the fourth quarter of 2007 (the beginning of the recession). If the total government expenditure multiplier were equal to two, then the average growth rate of real GDP given the higher government expenditure would have been 3.75% since the second quarter of 2009 or 2.48% since the fourth quarter of 2007.

Therefore, if we think that the last recession amounted to a negative level-adjustment in real GDP that we will never get back and that, post–2009, we are just on a lower growth path, then we might think that a government expenditure multiplier of one is about right. This requires that we also believe that a feasible growth rate for real GDP is about 3% per year. If the feasible growth rate for real GDP is now actually less than 3%, then the government expenditure multiplier could be much less than one. However, if we think that the feasible growth path for GDP is a 3% rate, and that it is feasible to recover the output lost during the last recession, then this would argue for a much higher total government expenditure multiplier, possibly above two. Thus, much depends on what the actual productive capacity of the economy is. In principle, this is something we can measure, given good theory and data.

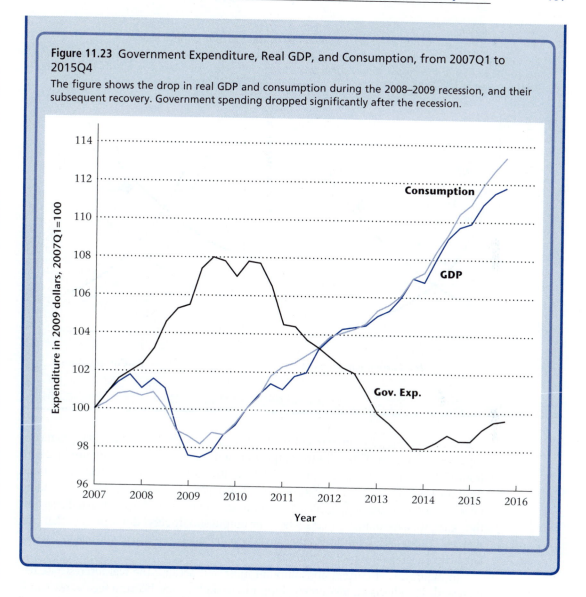

Figure 11.23 Government Expenditure, Real GDP, and Consumption, from 2007Q1 to 2015Q4

The figure shows the drop in real GDP and consumption during the 2008–2009 recession, and their subsequent recovery. Government spending dropped significantly after the recession.

leave a country with a much lower capital stock, as happened due to bombing in Germany, Great Britain, and Japan during World War II, and in Vietnam during the Vietnam War. The capital stock can also be reduced because of natural disasters such as floods and hurricanes.

In this subsection, we examine the effects of an experiment in our model in which the current capital stock K is reduced. Suppose that the representative firm begins the current period with a lower capital stock K. This affects both the supply and the demand for output. First, a decrease in K from K_1 to K_2 decreases the current marginal product of labor, which shifts the current demand for labor curve to the left from N_1^d to N_2^d in Figure 11.24(a). The output supply curve then shifts to the left, from Y_1^s to Y_2^s in Figure 11.24(b). Second,

Figure 11.24 The Equilibrium Effects of a Decrease in the Current Capital Stock

If the current capital stock falls—for example, because of a natural disaster—then the output demand curve shifts to the right and the output supply curve shifts to the left. The real interest rate rises, but current output may rise or fall.

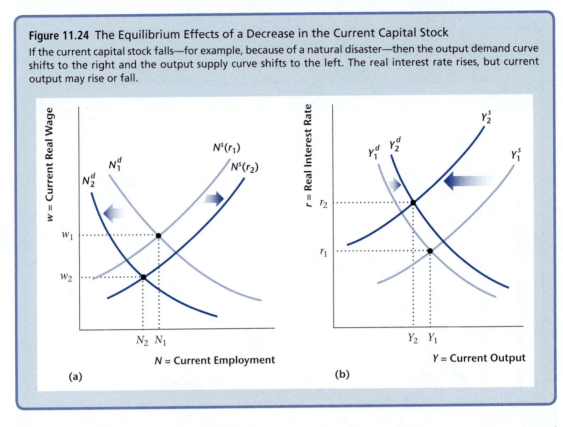

a decrease in K increases investment by the firm, because the future marginal product of capital will be higher. This shifts the output demand curve to the right in Figure 11.24(b), from Y_1^d to Y_2^d. The result is that, in equilibrium, in Figure 11.24(b), the real interest rate must rise from r_1 to r_2, but the effect on current aggregate output is ambiguous, depending on whether the output supply effect is larger or smaller than the output demand effect. In the figure, we have drawn the case where the output supply effect dominates, so that current real output falls. Empirically, there may be circumstances, such as with natural disasters, where aggregate output may not fall.

In Figure 11.24 current consumption must fall, because the real interest rate has increased. The effects on investment appear to be ambiguous, because the decrease in K causes investment to increase, while the increase in the equilibrium real interest rate causes investment to fall. However, investment must rise, because less capital would otherwise cause ever-decreasing investment, which would be inconsistent with the fact that the marginal product of capital rises as the quantity of capital falls. That is, as the quantity of capital falls, the marginal product of capital rises, making the return on investment very high, so that ultimately investment must increase if the capital stock decreases.

Because of the increase in the real interest rate, there is intertemporal substitution of leisure, with the representative consumer working harder in the current period for each current real wage w. Therefore, the labor supply curve shifts to the right in Figure 11.24(a) from $N^s(r_1)$ to $N^s(r_2)$. This reinforces the effect of the increase in labor demand on the real wage, and so the real wage must fall, from w_1 to w_2. The equilibrium effect on the quantity of labor is ambiguous, because the effect on labor demand and on labor supply work in opposite directions on the quantity of employment. In Figure 11.24(a), we show employment falling from N_1 to N_2.

Now, suppose that we interpret these results in terms of the macroeconomic effects of a natural disaster or a war that destroys part of the nation's capital stock. The model shows that there are two effects on the quantity of output. The lower quantity of capital implies that less output can be produced for a given quantity of labor input, which tends to reduce output. However, the lower quantity of capital acts to increase investment to replace the destroyed capital, which tends to increase output. Theoretically, it is not clear whether output increases or decreases, and there appear to be empirical cases in which the output supply and output demand effects roughly cancel, for example during and after large natural disasters such as the Mississippi floods in 1993, and Hurricane Katrina in 2005.

The Equilibrium Effects of an Increase in Current Total Factor Productivity *z*

LO 11.7 Use the real intertemporal model to explain the effects of particular shocks to the economy.

Temporary changes in total factor productivity are an important candidate as a cause of business cycles. Recall from Chapters 4, 5, and 7, that an increase in total factor productivity could result from good weather, a favorable change in government regulations, a new invention, a decrease in the relative price of energy, a more efficient allocation of factors of production across firms, or any other factor that results in more aggregate output being produced with the same factor inputs.

The experiment we examine here in our real intertemporal model is to increase current total factor productivity z, and then determine the effects of this change on current aggregate output, the real interest rate, current employment, the current real wage, current consumption, and investment. If current total factor productivity increases, the marginal product of labor goes up for each quantity of labor input, and so in Figure 11.25(a) the demand for labor curve shifts to the right, from N_1^d to N_2^d. Therefore, in Figure 11.25(b), the output supply curve shifts to the right, from N_1^s to N_2^s, and in equilibrium the quantity of output rises and the real interest rate must fall, from r_1 to r_2. The decrease in the real interest rate leads to increases in both consumption and investment.

In the labor market, the decrease in the real interest rate causes intertemporal substitution of leisure between the current and future periods, with current leisure increasing, and so the labor supply curve shifts to the left in Figure 11.25(a), from $N^s(r_1)$ to $N^s(r_2)$. In equilibrium, the real wage must increase from w_1 to w_2, but the net effect on the equilibrium quantity of employment is ambiguous. Empirically, however, the effect of the real interest rate on labor supply is small and, as in Figure 11.25(a), employment rises from N_1 to N_2.

When total factor productivity increases, this increases the current demand for labor, which raises the market real wage. With the real wage increase, workers are

Figure 11.25 The Equilibrium Effects of an Increase in Current Total Factor Productivity

When total factor productivity increases temporarily, the output supply curve shifts to the right in (b), with the real interest rate falling and aggregate output rising. Investment and consumption rise, and employment and the real wage increase in (a).

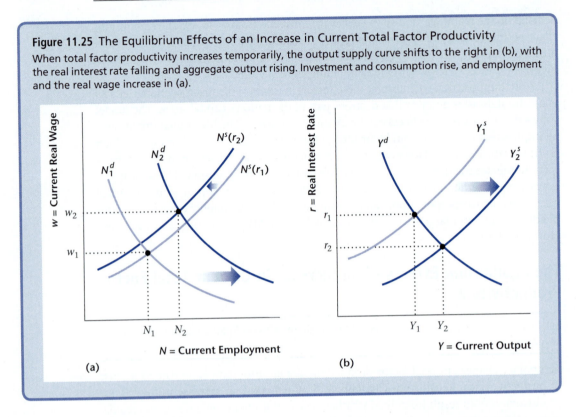

(a) (b)

willing to supply more labor, employment increases, and output increases. In the goods market, the increased supply of goods decreases the market real interest rate, which results in an increased demand for investment goods and consumption goods, so that the demand for goods rises to meet the increased supply of goods on the market. As well, the increase in current income increases consumption.

From Chapter 3, recall that some key business cycle facts are that consumption, investment, employment, the real wage, and average labor productivity are procyclical. Our real intertemporal model predicts these comovements in the data if the economy receives temporary shocks to total factor productivity. That is, because Figure 11.25 predicts that a temporary increase in total factor productivity increases aggregate output, consumption, investment, employment, and the real wage, the model predicts that consumption, investment, employment, and the real wage are procyclical, just as in the data. As well, the average product of labor must be higher when z increases, provided that N does not increase too much. We show this in Figure 11.26, where the average product of labor, Y/N, prior to the increase in z is the slope of AB, and the increase in z implies that labor productivity has risen to the slope of AD. In principle, average labor productivity could fall if N were to increase sufficiently in response to the increase in z, but this does not happen in quantitative versions of this type of model. Recall from Chapter 3 that the procyclicality of the average product of the labor is one of our business cycle facts.

Figure 11.26 The Effect on Average Labor Productivity of an Increase in z.

Average labor productivity is the ratio of aggregate output to employment, Y/N. Initially, average labor productivity is the slope of AB, and it rises to the slope of AD with the increase in z.

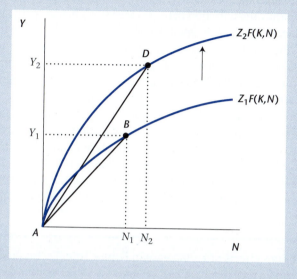

Thus, temporary shocks to total factor productivity are a candidate as a cause of business cycles, as in our model such shocks replicate the key business cycle facts from Chapter 3. Indeed, the proponents of real business cycle theory, which we study in detail in Chapter 13, argue that total factor productivity shocks are the most important cause of business cycles.

The Equilibrium Effects of an Increase in Future Total Factor Productivity, z': News About the Future and Aggregate Economic Activity

LO 11.7 Use the real intertemporal model to explain the effects of particular shocks to the economy.

The anticipation of future events can have important macroeconomic consequences in the present, as when an increase in total factor productivity is expected to happen in the future. For example, firms might learn of a new invention, such as the design for a new production process, which is not available currently but will come on line in the future. As we will show, this shock increases current investment, current output, and current employment, and reduces the real wage.

News about future events and the influence of this news has played an important role in macroeconomic theory. For example, Keynes had interest in the "animal spirits" of financial market investors and the influence of swings in investor sentiment on economic activity. Indeed, the stock market represents a forum in which people take bets on the future health of firms in the economy. Therefore, news that is informative about future productivity will tend to be reflected first in stock prices. In financial market theory, stock prices are typically the reflection of the average stock market participant's views on firms' future dividends, which are in good part determined by the future total factor productivity of firms. Empirical research in macroeconomics supports the view that news about future events is a key determinant of aggregate economic activity in the present.[1]

To capture the effect of news about future productivity, suppose in our model that everyone learns in the current period that z' will increase in the future. This implies that the future marginal product of capital increases for the representative firm, and so the firm wishes to invest more in the current period, which increases the demand for current goods, shifting the output demand curve to the right in Figure 11.27(b). In equilibrium, this implies that aggregate output increases from Y_1 to Y_2, and the real interest rate increases from r_1 to r_2. The increase in the real interest rate then causes current consumption to fall, but there is an opposing effect as consumption also tends

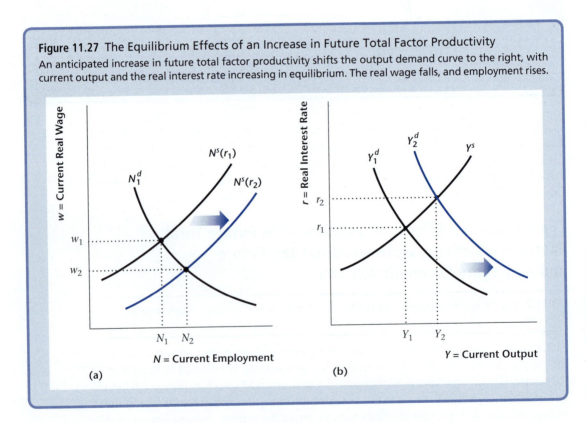

Figure 11.27 The Equilibrium Effects of an Increase in Future Total Factor Productivity
An anticipated increase in future total factor productivity shifts the output demand curve to the right, with current output and the real interest rate increasing in equilibrium. The real wage falls, and employment rises.

[1] P. Beaudry and F. Portier, 2006. " Stock Prices, News, and Economic Fluctuations," *American Economic Review* 96, 1293–1307; and M. Uribe and S. Schmitt-Grohe, 2008. " What's News in Business Cycles," NBER working paper 14215, National Bureau of Economic Research, Inc.

to rise because of the increase in current income and the anticipated increase in future income (because z' is expected to increase). As a result, consumption could rise or fall. In equilibrium, there are two effects on investment; the increase in z' causes investment to rise, and the increase in r causes it to fall. But investment must rise, as the initial shock to the economy works through a positive effect on investment.

What are the effects in the labor market? The increase in the real interest rate leads to a rightward shift of the labor supply curve, from $N^s(r_1)$ to $N^s(r_2)$ in Figure 11.27(a). Therefore, in equilibrium, the quantity of employment increases from N_1 to N_2, and the real wage falls from w_1 to w_2.

In anticipation of a future increase in total factor productivity, firms increase investment expenditure, as the marginal payoff to having a higher future capital stock has increased. The increase in the demand for investment goods raises the market real interest rate, which increases labor supply and employment and generates an increase in aggregate output. The increase in labor supply causes the real wage to fall.

THEORY CONFRONTS THE DATA

News, the Stock Market, and Investment Expenditures

The real intertemporal model tells us that news about future total factor productivity could potentially be an important factor affecting investment spending. If there are significant fluctuations in financial market views about the future, that is, waves of optimism and pessimism, then these fluctuations, through their effects on investment spending, could be very important for business cycles. We have shown that good news about future total factor productivity acts to increase investment, aggregate output, and employment, and bad news works in the opposite direction.

If news about future productivity is important for investment, then we should see this in economic data. In particular, financial theory tells us that stock prices act to aggregate information. That is, an individual stock price moves in a way that immediately incorporates all news about the future prospects of the individual firm that issued the stock. The stock simply represents a claim to the future dividends that the firm will pay, which will be determined by the performance of the firm in the future. A stock price index that averages all stock market prices then captures all of the news about the future prospects of all firms in the economy, and should include information about what is collectively known about what will happen to aggregate productivity in the future.

Therefore, if news about the future is an important determinant of aggregate investment, stock prices and investment expenditures should be highly positively correlated. In Figure 11.28, we show percentage deviations from trend in aggregate real investment spending and in a relative stock price, measured as the Standard and Poor's 500 stock price index divided by the

(Continued)

implicit GDP deflator, for the period 1957–2015. What we observe in the figure is a remarkably high degree of correlation between the two time series. Investment spending tracks the relative stock price remarkably closely. Further, stock prices tend to lead investment in the figure, which is consistent with our theory. News about the future can affect stock prices and investment plans simultaneously, but it takes time to build capital equipment, plants, and housing.

Therefore, stock prices should lead investment, just as we observe.

Figure 11.28 is consistent with the view that news about the future is a key determinant of investment spending. Therefore, since investment is a highly volatile component of GDP (e.g., much more volatile than consumption or government spending), fluctuations in sentiment about the future are likely a key source of business cycles.

Figure 11.28 Percentage Deviations from Trend in Investment and a Relative Stock Price Index, 1957–2015

Investment and the relative stock price index are highly positively correlated, with stock prices leading GDP. This is consistent with the view that fluctuations in news about the future are an important source of business cycles.

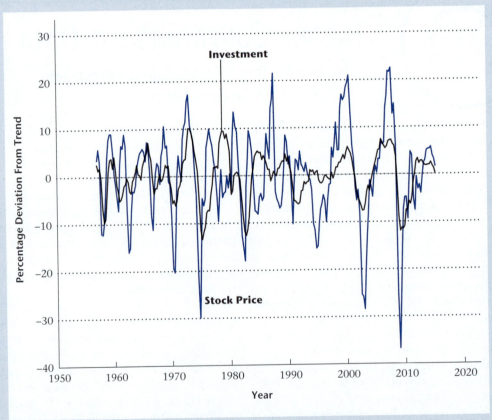

Credit Market Frictions and the Financial Crisis

LO 11.7 Use the real intertemporal model to explain the effects of particular shocks to the economy.

In Chapter 10, we analyzed the effects on credit markets of two types of financial frictions: asymmetric information and limited commitment. Early in this chapter we also studied how asymmetric information affects a firm's investment decision. Asymmetric information is important in credit markets, as financial institutions lending to consumers and firms can have difficulty distinguishing creditworthy borrowers from those who are not. This situation then makes borrowing more costly, even for good borrowers. All borrowers will face loan interest rates that are higher than the safe rates of interest at which financial institutions borrow, as financial institutions need to be compensated for the perceived default risk associated with lending. Limited commitment—the inability of economic agents to commit to repaying loans—can be mitigated when lending institutions require that borrowers post collateral. But then the quantity of loans extended in credit markets can be limited by the total value of collateralizable wealth.

A key feature of the financial crisis that led to the 2008–2009 recession was an increase in the importance of credit market frictions as the result of more severe asymmetric information and limited commitment problems. During the crisis, financial markets became more uncertain about the creditworthiness of would-be borrowers (the asymmetric information problem), and there was a large decrease in the value of collaterlizable wealth—housing wealth in particular (the limited commitment problem). Participants received critical news about a decrease in the value of assets held by financial institutions, firms, and consumers. We want to use our model to understand the macroeconomic effects of an increase in credit market frictions, and this analysis will help us organize our thinking about recent events.

In Figure 11.29, suppose the economy is initially in equilibrium with the real interest rate r_1, level of real income Y_1, real wage w_1, and level of employment N_1. In our model, the real interest rate, r, will denote the safe real rate of interest at which consumers and firms lend. However, borrowers may face a loan rate that is higher than r because of asymmetric information, or borrowers may not be able to borrow all they would like at the market interest rate because they are constrained by the value of available collateral. Decisions of borrowers are determined by a loan rate that is higher than r.

An increase in credit market frictions—due to asymmetric information and limited commitment—has two effects on consumers. First, the representative consumer's demand for consumption goods falls, shifting the output demand curve to the left from Y_1^d to Y_2^d. Second, more severe credit market frictions will cause the representative consumer to increase labor supply, shifting the labor supply curve to the right from $N_1^s(r_1)$ to $N_2^s(r_1)$, which causes the output supply curve to shift to the right from Y_1^s to Y_2^s. Thus the consumer, faced with tighter constraints on borrowing, and a higher effective loan rate, increases labor supply in an attempt to smooth consumption.

On net, the real interest rate must fall in Figure 11.29(b), but real output could rise or fall, depending on the relative strength of the output supply and output demand effects. It is more likely that the output demand effect is larger (labor supply should be

Figure 11.29 The Effect of More Severe Credit Market Frictions

The output demand curve shifts to the left because of a decrease in consumption demand, and labor supply increases, causing the output supply curve to shift to the right. The real interest rate must fall, and the presumption is that the output demand effect is larger than the output supply effect, so aggregate output and employment fall.

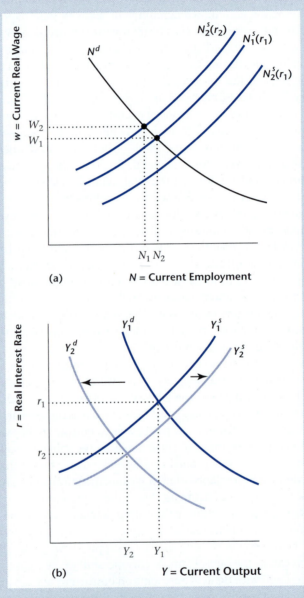

less responsive to credit market conditions than consumption demand), so that real output falls, as shown in the figure. As well, the effect of credit market frictions on firms will contribute to the shift in the output demand curve, by reducing the demand for investment goods.

In Figure 11.29, we show aggregate output falling, so consumption or investment must decrease, but the model does not tell us how much of the output decrease comes from a fall in investment expenditures and how much comes from a reduction in consumption expenditures. Indeed, it is theoretically possible for consumption or investment to increase, as the real interest rate has decreased. In the labor market, the decrease in the real interest rate causes the labor supply curve to shift to $N_2^s(r_2)$ in Figure 11.29(a) and, consistent with aggregate output falling, employment falls from N_1 to N_2. The real wage increases from w_1 to w_2.

The key effects of an increase in the severity of credit market frictions are the contraction in aggregate activity—less output and employment—and a lower real interest rate. In general, low safe real interest rates reflect a scarcity of safe assets (collateralizable wealth), and dysfunctional credit markets. Low real interest rates on government debt are an important feature of credit markets in the United States, post-financial crisis.

Sectoral Shocks and Labor Market Mismatch

LO 11.7 Use the real intertemporal model to explain the effects of particular shocks to the economy.

The 2008-2009 recession was unusual not only because of its causes, which are rooted in financial market phenomena, but also because of the unusual behavior of labor markets in the United States. We studied some of that unusual behavior, and the explanations for it, in Chapter 6. Relative to the search model of unemployment in Chapter 6, the real intertemporal model has less labor market detail—there is no search behavior, no unemployment, and no vacancies, for example—but it is much more developed in terms of savings and investment behavior, and the government policies we can study.

In this section, we will use the real intertemporal model to understand some of the effects of sectoral reallocation, and how this may be important for understanding the recent behavior of employment, output, and average labor productivity. One feature of the recent recession and, to a lesser extent, the two previous recessions in 1991–1992 and 2001, was the "jobless recovery." In the United States, employment grew sluggishly as the economy recovered, and this was coupled with unusually high growth in average labor productivity.

A **sectoral shock** is a disturbance to technology or preferences, which either changes relative total factor productivity in different sectors of the economy, or changes the relative demands for the goods and services produced in different sectors. These different sectors could be industries, or different geographical areas. For example, during the twentieth century, employment in the United States shifted dramatically from agriculture to manufacturing, and then from manufacturing to services. Also, in more recent times, automobile manufacturing employment has shifted from the north to the south. Finally, central to the recent recession was a decline in output and employment in the construction sector, relative to other sectors of the economy.

Sectoral shocks produce a reallocation of factors of production from declining sectors to growing sectors, and that reallocation can take time. In the course of adjusting to the sectoral shock, labor market mismatch can occur. For example, the skills required of workers in the growing sector of the economy may not match the skills of workers who are leaving the declining sector. As well, if the growing sector of the economy is geographically distant from the declining sector, workers who move from the declining sector to the growing sector will have to bear significant moving costs.

We will model a sectoral shock as a shock that has no effect on aggregate total factor productivity, but results in labor market mismatch. To capture this in our real intertemporal model, which is a competitive equilibrium model, we will add some "friction" to the labor market. Suppose that mismatch can be captured on the supply side of the labor market by a cost a_s that a worker bears if he or she enters the labor market. This cost is proportional to the quantity of labor supplied, so the effective wage a worker receives is $w - a_s$. The cost a_s captures the extra effort the worker must expend to find a job, given labor market mismatch. Similarly, on the demand side of the labor market, mismatch causes a firm to bear a cost a_d, which is proportional to the quantity of labor hired. Therefore, the effective wage the firm pays is $w + a_d$, where the cost a_d captures the extra recruiting effort required to hire workers in a labor market with mismatch.

The costs a_s and a_d are "wedges," which work like proportional taxes to distort the labor market. In other words, the difference between what the firm pays for labor, and what the worker receives is $a_s + a_d$, the sum of the two wedges, just as a proportional tax on labor income drives a wedge between what the firm pays and what the worker receives per hour worked.

In Figure 11.30, the sectoral shock, through the wedge a_s, shifts the labor supply curve in panel (a) to the left, from $N_1^s(r_1)$ to $N_2^s(r_1)$. The vertical shift in the curve is the quantity a_s. Similarly, the wedge a_d shifts the labor demand curve in panel (a) to the left, from N_1^d to N_2^d, with the vertical shift in the curve equal to a_s. Because of the shifts in the labor supply and labor demand curves, the output supply curve in panel (b) of the figure shifts to the left. Therefore, in terms of the effect in the current market for goods, this looks just like a negative total factor productivity (TFP) shock (see Figure 11.25). Aggregate output falls from Y_1 to Y_2, the real interest rate rises from r_1 to r_2, and consumption and investment expenditures fall. However, in the labor market in panel (b), while employment falls (as it would if TFP fell), the wage may rise or fall, depending on the elasticities of labor supply and demand, on a_s, and on a_d. In the figure, we show the case, after the labor supply curve settles down in equilibrium at $N_2^s(r_2)$, where the wage stays the same. Further, in Figure 11.31, average labor productivity rises, whereas it would fall if TFP fell, as in Figure 11.26. The average product of labor, Y/N, is initially the slope of AB, and it increases to the slope of AD after the sectoral shock.

The sectoral shock, even if it has no effect whatsoever on TFP, as in this example, adds friction to the labor market, and this friction reduces employment, aggregate output, consumption, and investment. Also, the average product of labor rises. Thus, sectoral shocks are a potential explanation for what might otherwise be a puzzling

Figure 11.30 The Effects of a Sectoral Shock

The sectoral shock, through a decrease in matching efficiency in the labor market, shifts the labor supply and labor demand curves to the left. This shifts the output supply curve to the left. The effects in the market for current goods is the same as for a total factor productivity decrease, but in the labor market the real wage could rise or fall.

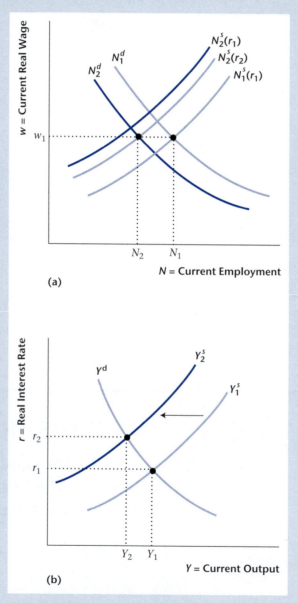

(a)

(b)

Figure 11.31 The Effects of a Sectoral Shock on Average Labor Productivity

Initially, average labor productivity is the slope of *AB*, and the sectoral shock increases average labor productivity to the slope of *AD*.

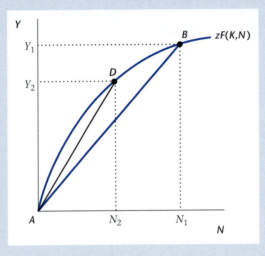

feature of the recent recession—labor productivity growing faster than would have been anticipated given the behavior of aggregate output.

Now that we have gained an understanding of the working of our real intertemporal model, we can go on to use this model further, adding money and nominal variables in Chapter 12, and then using the model as a basis for studying business cycles in Chapters 13 and 14.

THEORY CONFRONTS THE DATA

The Behavior of Real GDP, Employment, and Labor Productivity in the 1981–1982 and 2008–2009 Recessions

Some of the unusual behavior of the U.S. economy in the 2008–2009 recession relative to previous recessions can be illustrated by focusing on the 1981–1982 recession as a source of comparison, since that was the most recent severe recession. First, Figure 11.32 shows the path of real GDP in these two recessions, normalizing

GDP to 100 in the quarter the National Bureau of Economic Research denotes as the first quarter of the recession. The figure then tracks real GDP for the next 33 quarters for each recession. Note that the 2008–2009 recession is considerably longer and deeper than the 1981–1982 recession, and that growth in real GDP is much lower in the

Figure 11.32 Real GDP in Two Recessions

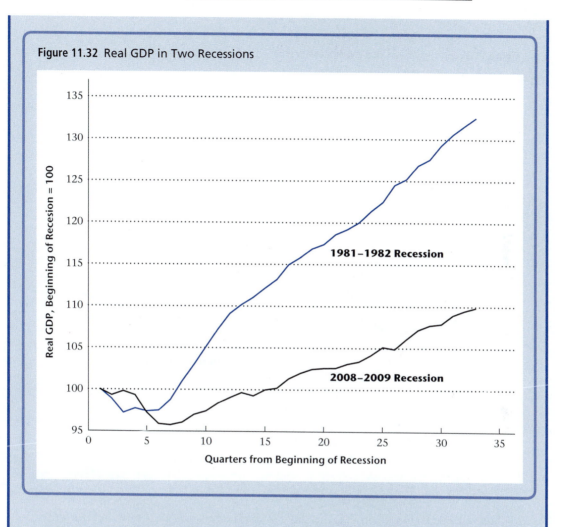

recovery phase of the 2008–2009 recession than in 1981–1982. After 12 quarters, real GDP had not recovered from the previous business cycle peak after the 2008–2009 recession, but was 10% greater than the business cycle peak at the same stage after the 1981–1982 recession.

Figure 11.33 is constructed in the same way as Figure 11.32, but we show aggregate employment instead of real GDP. Here, the difference between the two recessions is even more stark. In the 1981–1982 recession, the reduction in

employment was relatively small, employment began to grow six quarters after the recession began, and after 12 quarters employment was almost 5% higher than at the previous business cycle peak. In the 2008–2009 recession, the reduction in employment was very large. After 12 quarters employment had not yet begun to grow, and was still about 5% lower than at the previous business cycle peak.

Finally, Figure 11.34 is a similarly constructed chart for average labor productivity—the

(Continued)

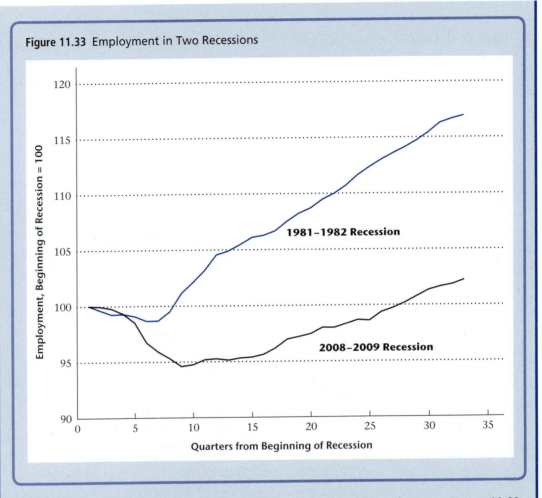

Figure 11.33 Employment in Two Recessions

ratio of real GDP to employment. This quantity behaves similarly in the two recessions and in the early part of the recovery, but the two time series diverge after that, with productivity growth much lower after the 2008–2009 recession.

A key observation from Figures 11.32–11.34 is that, during the 2008–2009 recession, average labor productivity grew at a much higher rate than we would have predicted—given past behavior of the time series, and given the behavior of real GDP in the 2008–2009 recession. Put another way, employment growth during the recession was much lower than in the average previous recession, given the behavior of real GDP.

The behavior we observe in Figures 11.32–11.34 is consistent with the existence of labor market mismatch, particularly during the recovery phase of the recession. As we showed in the previous section, labor market mismatch reduces both output and employment, but reduces employment proportionately more, so that average labor productivity increases. Thus, in combination with other shocks, labor market mismatch may have contributed in an important way to the behavior of aggregate economic variables during the recent recession. In Figure 11.34, the low growth in average labor productivity following the 2008–2009 recession likely reflects low total factor productivity growth.

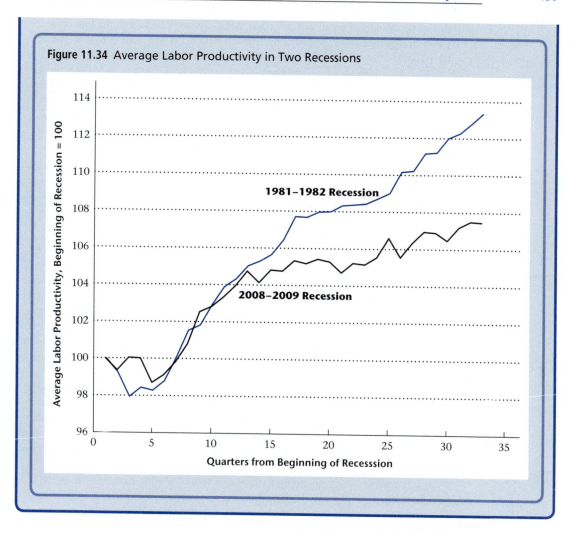

Figure 11.34 Average Labor Productivity in Two Recessions

Chapter Summary

- We developed a real intertemporal macroeconomic model that is useful for evaluating the macroeconomic effects of shocks to the economy, and that we can build on in later chapters. This model allows us to study the determinants of investment, consumption, aggregate output, the real interest rate, and employment, in an intertemporal setting.

- The model has two periods, the present and the future, and the representative consumer makes a work–leisure decision in each period and a consumption–savings decision in the current period. As the real interest rate increases, the consumer's demand for current consumption goods decreases, and his or her current labor supply increases. These effects are due to the intertemporal substitution of consumption and leisure between the present and the future in response to changes in the real interest rate.

- The representative firm produces output using labor and capital in each period. The firm's current demand for labor is determined by the usual marginal productivity condition (the marginal product of labor equals the real wage in the current period when the firm optimizes), and the firm invests in new capital in the current period until the net marginal product of capital in the future is equal to the real interest rate. An increase in the real interest rate leads to a decrease in the firm's optimal quantity of investment, and investment increases if the firm's initial quantity of capital decreases, if there is an anticipated increase in future total factor productivity, or if there is a decrease in credit market uncertainty.

- In equilibrium, the current goods market and the current labor market clear, and this implies that the credit market clears as well. For simplicity, we ignore markets in the future period.

- In the graphical representation of the model, there are two key elements: (1) output demand and supply, determining current aggregate output and the real interest rate; (2) current labor supply and current labor demand, determining current employment and the current real wage given the real interest rate.

- We conducted six experiments using the model:
  1. If current government purchases increase (a temporary increase in government spending), this increases the present value of taxes for the consumer, reducing lifetime wealth. Labor supply increases, and on net the demand for current goods rises by the amount of the increase in government spending. In equilibrium, current output rises, current employment rises, the current real wage falls, and the real interest rate increases given that a temporary increase in government purchases implies that the output supply effect is small. Consumption and investment are crowded out. The total government expenditure multiplier must be less than one, due to the crowding out of private expenditure by government spending.
  2. If the current capital stock decreases—for example, because of a natural disaster—then the optimal quantity of investment increases for the firm, given the real interest rate, so that output demand increases. Current output supply decreases, because the representative firm can produce less current output with a given input of labor. The real interest rate increases in equilibrium, but current aggregate output may rise or fall. If the output demand effect is small, then output falls.
  3. If current total factor productivity increases (a temporary increase in total factor productivity), then output supply increases, the real interest rate falls, and consumption and investment increase in the current period. Current employment may rise or fall, but it rises provided the interest rate effect on labor supply is small. The current real wage rises. These predictions of the model replicate some of the key business cycle facts from Chapter 3.
  4. An anticipated increase in future total factor productivity implies that the representative firm demands more investment goods, because the future marginal product of capital is expected to be higher. The demand for goods increases, causing the real interest rate and current aggregate output to rise. In the labor market, the real wage falls and employment rises, as the representative consumer substitutes leisure intertemporally in response to the real interest rate increase.
  5. An increase in the severity of credit market frictions shifts the output demand curve to the left, and increases labor supply, shifting the output supply curve to the right. The real interest rate must fall, and the presumption is that the labor supply effect is relatively small, so that aggregate output falls. Employment decreases, the real wage increases, and the effects on consumption and investment are ambiguous, though some expenditure quantity must fall.

6. A sectoral shock pushes a wedge between the effective wage that a firm pays and the effective wage a worker receives. In the goods market, the output supply curve shifts to the left, and output, consumption, and investment fall, with the real interest rate rising. In the labor market, employment falls, but the real wage may rise or fall. Average labor productivity rises, which is an important prediction relating to the recent recession.

Key Terms

Intertemporal substitution of leisure The substitution of leisure between the current and future periods in response to the market real interest rate. (p. 384)

Marginal propensity to consume The amount by which the demand for consumption goods increases when there is a one-unit increase in lifetime wealth. (p. 386)

Marginal cost of investment The profit forgone by the firm in the current period from investing in an additional unit of capital. (p. 392)

Marginal benefit from investment The future marginal product of capital plus $1 - d$, where d is the depreciation rate. (p. 392)

Net marginal product of capital The marginal product of capital minus the depreciation rate. (p. 393)

Optimal investment rule Rule stating that the firm invests until the future net marginal product of capital is equal to the real interest rate. (p. 393)

Optimal investment schedule A negative relationship between the firm's optimal quantity of investment and the market real interest rate. (p. 394)

Output supply curve A positive relationship between the quantity of output supplied by firms and the real interest rate. (p. 404)

Output demand curve A negative relationship between the quantity of output demanded (in the form of consumption expenditures, investment expenditures, and government expenditures) and the real interest rate. (p. 409)

Demand multiplier The ratio of the rightward shift in the output demand curve to the increase in government expenditure in the current period. (p. 415)

Total government expenditure multiplier The equilibrium ratio of the increase in real GDP to the increase in government expenditure. (p. 415)

Sectoral shock A disturbance to technology or preferences, which either changes relative total factor productivity in different sectors of the economy, or changes the relative demands for the goods and services produced in different sectors. (p. 429)

Questions for Review

All questions refer to the macroeconomic model developed in this chapter.

11.1 Explain how intertemporal substitution is important for current labor supply and for the current demand for consumption goods.

11.2 What are three factors that determine current labor supply?

11.3 What determines the current demand for labor?

11.4 What is the goal of the representative firm in the real intertemporal model?

11.5 What rule does the representative firm follow in determining its optimal level of investment?

11.6 How is optimal investment for the firm affected by an increase in the current capital stock?

11.7 How is optimal investment affected by an increase in future total factor productivity?

11.8 Explain how credit market uncertainty affects the investment decision of the firm.

11.9 What is the government's budget constraint in the real intertemporal model? Can the government run a deficit or run a surplus in the current period?

11.10　What are the factors that shift the output supply curve?

11.11　What are the factors that shift the output demand curve?

11.12　How are aggregate output and the real interest rate determined in competitive equilibrium?

11.13　What are the effects of a temporary increase in government purchases on the real interest rate, aggregate output, employment, the real wage, consumption, and investment?

11.14　What are the effects of a decrease in the current capital stock on the real interest rate, aggregate output, employment, the real wage, consumption, and investment?

11.15　What are the effects of an increase in total factor productivity on the real interest rate, aggregate output, employment, the real wage, consumption, and investment? Explain how these results relate to key business cycle facts and the causes of business cycles.

11.16　Determine the equilibrium effects of an anticipated increase in future total factor productivity in the real intertemporal model. Explain why these effects are different from the effects of an increase in current total factor productivity.

11.17　How do credit market frictions affect aggregate economic activity? Explain how tax policy can mitigate credit market frictions.

11.18　Explain how a sectoral shock is similar to, and different from, a total factor productivity shock.

Problems

1. **LO 3** What is the effect of an increase in d, the depreciation rate, on the representative firm's investment decision, and on its optimal investment schedule? Explain your results carefully.

2. **LO 3** Tom lives on an island and has 20 coconut trees in the current period, which currently produce 180 coconuts. Tom detests coconuts, but he can trade them with people on other neighboring islands for things that he wants. Further, Tom can borrow and lend coconuts with neighboring islands. In the coconut credit market, a loan of 1 coconut in the current period is repaid with 2 coconuts in the future period. Each period, Tom's trees produce, and then 10% of them die. If Tom plants a coconut in the ground in the current period, it will grow into a productive coconut tree in the future period. At the end of the future period, Tom can sell any remaining coconut trees for 1 coconut each. When Tom plants coconuts in the current period, he plants them in successively less fertile ground, and the less fertile the ground, the less productive is the coconut tree. For convenience, we assume here that fractions of coconuts can be produced by trees. Output in the future period, for given numbers of trees in

production in the future period, is given in the following table:

Trees in Production in the Future	Future Output of Coconuts
15	155
16	162
17	168
18	173
19	177
20	180
21	182
22	183.8
23	184.8
24	185.2
25	185.4

(a) Plot the level of output against the quantity of capital for the future period.

(b) Plot the marginal product of capital against the quantity of capital for the future period.

(c) Calculate Tom's present value of profits given each quantity of future trees.

(d) Calculate the net marginal product of capital for each quantity of future trees.

(e) Determine Tom's optimal quantity of investment, and explain your results.

3. **LO 3** The government wishes to bring about an increase in investment expenditures, and is considering two tax policies that policymakers think could bring this about. Under the first tax policy, firms would receive a subsidy in the current period of t per unit of current output produced. Policymakers reason that firms will use this subsidy for investment. The second policy under consideration is an investment tax credit, by which firms would receive a subsidy of s per unit of investment in the current period. Determine which tax policy would be more effective in accomplishing the government's goal of increasing current investment expenditures, and carefully explain your results.

4. **LO 3** Suppose that we modify the model of the firm's investment behavior by assuming that any capital the firm has remaining at the end of the period can be sold at the price p'_K (in our model we assumed the capital could be sold at a price of one, in terms of consumption goods).

(a) Determine how this change affects the optimal investment rule for the firm.

(b) Suppose that we interpret p'_K as the firm's stock price. If p'_K increases, what effect does this have on the firm's optimal investment schedule? What does this imply about the relationship between investment expenditures and stock prices?

5. **LO 5** Determine how the following affects the slope of the output demand curve, and explain your results:

(a) The marginal propensity to consume increases.

(b) The intertemporal substitution effect of the real interest rate on current consumption increases.

(c) The demand for investment goods becomes less responsive to the real interest rate.

6. **LO 7** The government decreases current taxes, while holding government spending in the present and the future constant.

(a) Using diagrams, determine the equilibrium effects on consumption, investment, the real

interest rate, aggregate output, employment, and the real wage. What is the multiplier, and how does it differ from the government expenditure multiplier?

(b) Now suppose that there are credit market imperfections in the market for consumer credit, for example due to asymmetric information in the credit market. Repeat part (a), and explain any differences in your answers in parts (a) and (b).

7. **LO 4** Determine how the following affect the slope of the output supply curve, and explain your results:

(a) The marginal product of labor decreases at a faster rate as the quantity of labor used in production increases.

(b) The intertemporal substitution effect of the real interest rate on current leisure decreases.

8. **LO 7** Suppose that there is a shift in the representative consumer's preferences. Namely, the consumer prefers, given the market real interest rate, to consume less current leisure and more current consumption goods.

(a) Determine the effects of this on current aggregate output, current employment, the current real wage, current consumption, and current investment.

(b) Explain your results. What might cause such a change in the preferences of consumers?

9. **LO 7** Suppose that there is a permanent increase in total factor productivity. Determine the implications of this for current macroeconomic variables, and show how the impact differs from the case where total factor productivity is expected to increase only temporarily. Explain your results.

10. **LO 7** Suppose that z' increases and that K increases at the same time. Show that it is possible for the real interest rate to remain constant as a result. What does this say about the model's ability to explain the differences between poor and rich countries and to explain what happens as a country's economy grows?

11. **LO 7** There is a temporary increase in the relative price of energy. Determine how the response of current aggregate output to this shock depends on the marginal propensity to consume, and explain carefully why you get this result.

12. **LO 7** Suppose that a country experiences destruction of part of its capital stock. Suppose also that the capital stock plays a role as collateral in credit contracts, so that the destruction of capital increases credit market frictions.
    (a) Determine how the net effects on macroeconomic variables differ from what is depicted in Figure 11.24.
    (b) Is there a government policy that can mitigate the effects of this capital destruction? What is it? Explain how it works.

13. **LO 7** A war breaks out that is widely expected to last only one year. Show how the effect of this shock on aggregate output depends on the size of the intertemporal substitution effect of the

real interest rate on current leisure, and carefully explain your results.

14. **LO 7** A macroeconomist suggests that, since aggregate output and employment have decreased, the government should increase expenditures on goods and services to increase both output and employment. Suppose that output and employment fell because of a sectoral shock.
    (a) Determine, using diagrams, what the net effects on output, employment, consumption, investment, the real interest rate, and the real wage would be of such a policy, combined with the sectoral shock.
    (b) Do you think such a policy is appropriate? Why or why not?

Working with the Data

Answer these questions using the Federal Reserve Bank of St. Louis's FRED database, accessible at http://research.stlouisfed.org/fred2/

1. Calculate the ratio of real investment expenditures to GDP, quarterly, for the period 1947–2015, and calculate the real interest rate as a three-month Treasury bill rate minus the inflation rate (be careful that you calculate the inflation rate as an annualized rate), then plot both of these variables as time series (you might want to be inventive about how you scale these variables). The theory of investment in this chapter predicts an optimal investment schedule that is a negative relationship between the investment and the real interest rate. Is this what you observe in the data? Explain.

2. Calculate the ratio of total real government purchases to real GDP, quarterly, from 1947 to 2015. Also calculate the real interest rate on a quarterly basis as a three-month Treasury bill rate minus the inflation rate. Plot these two variables as time series. The real intertemporal model predicts that a temporary increase in government spending increases the real interest rate. Do you observe anything in your chart that is consistent with that prediction? Why or why not?

3. Plot the relative price of housing (use the Case–Shiller 20-city home price index) and residential construction as a fraction of GDP. What do you observe? Is the theory of investment in this chapter consistent with your plots?

PART V

Money and Business Cycles

In this part, our first task is to integrate monetary factors into the real intertemporal model that was developed in Chapter 11. The resulting model, a monetary intertemporal model, is used in Chapter 12 to study the role of currency and the banking system in transactions, the effects of changes in the quantity of money, and monetary policy. In Chapters 13 and 14, we use the monetary intertemporal model to study the causes of business cycles and the role of fiscal and monetary policy over the business cycle. In Chapter 13, we examine two models of the business cycle with flexible wages and prices, and show how these models fit the key business cycle facts from Chapter 3. The implications of these models are also examined. Chapter 14 is devoted to the study of a New Keynesian sticky price model, which justifies a role for government intervention to smooth business cycles. The alternative business cycle models we study highlight the primary possible causes of business cycles that are important in practice.

Chapter 12

Money, Banking, Prices, and Monetary Policy

Learning Objectives

After studying Chapter 12, students will be able to:

12.1 Explain the functions of money, and how money is measured.

12.2 Construct the monetary intertemporal model.

12.3 Derive the Fisher relation.

12.4 Construct a competitive equilibrium in the monetary intertemporal model, and carry out equilibrium experiments using the model.

12.5 Demonstrate that money is neutral in the monetary intertemporal model.

12.6 List the factors that can shift money demand, and show how a shift in money demand affects economic variables in the monetary intertemporal model.

12.7 Show how conventional monetary policy is ineffective in a liquidity trap, and explain unconventional monetary policies.

Money is important for two reasons. First, the economy functions better with money than without it, because carrying out transactions by trading one kind of good for another is difficult and because using credit in some transactions is costly or impossible. Second, changes in the quantity of money in existence matter for nominal quantities—for example, the price level and the inflation rate—and can also affect real economic activity. The quantity of money in circulation is governed in most countries by the central bank, and the primary monetary policy decisions of the central bank concern how to set the level and growth rate of the money supply.

In this chapter, we will construct a monetary intertemporal model, which builds on the real intertemporal model in Chapter 11. In the monetary intertemporal model, consumers and firms choose among means of payment to carry out transactions. They use government-supplied currency for some transactions, and they also use the transactions services supplied by banks. In practice, these transactions services include the use of debit cards, credit cards, and checks, but for simplicity we represent these services with one type of payment instrument, a credit card. A key part of the model is that consumers and firms make choices about their usage of credit cards versus cash, and this is important for determining the demand for money. Building up a knowledge of the role of banks in the monetary system and in credit markets will add to our understanding of the role of financial factors in macroeconomics—a key contemporary issue. The monetary intertemporal model resulting from our work in this chapter will also serve as the basis for our study of business cycles in Chapters 13 and 14.

The first result we will derive using the monetary intertemporal model is the **neutrality of money**, under which a one-time change in the money supply has no real consequences for the economy. Consumption, investment, output, employment, the real interest rate, and economic welfare remain unaffected. The neutrality of money is a good starting point for examining the role of money in the economy, but most macroeconomists agree that money is neutral only in the long run and that, for various reasons, changes in the money supply will have real effects on the economy in the short run.

We then go on to show the features of a liquidity trap, in which monetary policy is ineffective. The liquidity trap has been a real concern for many central banks in the world following the 2008–2009 financial crisis. Given the ineffectiveness of conventional monetary policies in a liquidity trap, central banks have resorted to unconventional policies, including quantitative easing and negative nominal interest rates. We will discuss the efficacy of such policies.

What Is Money?

LO 12.1 Explain the functions of money, and how money is measured.

A traditional view of money is that it has three important functions. Namely, money is a **medium of exchange**, it is a **store of value**, and it is a **unit of account**. Money is a medium of exchange in that it is accepted in exchange for goods for the sole reason that it can in turn be traded for other goods, not because it is wanted for consumption purposes. Money is a store of value, like other assets such as stocks, bonds, housing, and so on, as it allows consumers to trade current goods for future goods. Finally, money is a unit of account because essentially all contracts are denominated in terms of money. For example, in the United States a typical labor contract is a promise to pay a specified number of U.S. dollars in exchange for a specified quantity of labor, and a typical loan contract is a promise to pay a specified number of U.S. dollars in the future in exchange for a specified quantity of U.S. dollars in the present. As well, U.S. firms keep their books in terms of U.S. dollars.

The distinguishing economic feature of money is its medium-of-exchange role. As mentioned above, there are other assets such as stocks, bonds, and housing that serve the store-of-value role that is served by money. However, there are difficulties in using these other assets in exchange. First, there is often imperfect information concerning the quality of assets. For example, it may be difficult to get the clerk in a convenience store to accept a stock certificate in exchange for a candy bar, as the clerk probably does not know the market value of the stock certificate, and it would be costly for him or her to sell the stock certificate. Second, some assets come in large denominations and are, therefore, difficult to use for small purchases. Even if the clerk in the convenience store knows the market value of a U.S. Treasury bill (a short-term debt instrument issued by the U.S. government), Treasury bills do not come in denominations less than $1,000, and so the clerk likely cannot make change for the purchase of a candy bar. Third, some assets take time to sell at their market value. For example, if I attempted to sell my house to the convenience store clerk, he or she would likely offer me much less for the house than I would receive if I searched the market for a buyer whose preferences best matched my house.

Measuring the Money Supply

As we discuss in more detail in Chapter 18, money has taken many forms historically. Money has circulated as commodity money (primarily silver and gold), circulating private bank notes (as was the case prior to the Civil War in the United States), commodity-backed paper currency (for example, under the gold standard), fiat money (for example, Federal Reserve notes in the United States), and transactions deposits at private banks. In the United States today, money consists mainly of objects that take the latter two forms, fiat money and transactions deposits at banks.

In modern developed economies, there are potentially many ways to measure the supply of money, depending on where we want to draw the line defining which assets satisfy the medium-of-exchange property and which do not. What is defined as money is somewhat arbitrary, and it is possible that we may want to use different definitions of money for different purposes. Table 12.1 shows measures of the standard **monetary aggregates** for March 2016, taken from the *Federal Reserve Bank of St. Louis FRED database*. A given monetary aggregate is simply the sum of a number of different assets for the U.S. economy.

The most narrowly defined monetary aggregate is M0, which is sometimes referred to as the **monetary base** or **outside money**. The monetary base consists entirely of liabilities of the **Federal Reserve System (the Fed)**, which is the central bank of the United States. The chief role of a central bank is to issue outside money. The liabilities making up M0 are U.S. currency outside the Fed and the deposits of depository institutions with the Fed. These deposits are typically referred to as reserves. The quantity of

Table 12.1 Monetary Aggregates, March 2016 (in $billions)	
M0	3898.4
M1	3180.7
M2	12660.7

Source: Data from FRED, Federal Reserve Bank of St. Louis, © Stephen D. Williamson.

M0 is called outside money, as it is the quantity of money outside of the banking system. The quantity of M1 is obtained by adding currency (outside the U.S. Treasury, the Fed, and the vaults of depository institutions), travelers' checks, demand deposits, and other transactions accounts at depository institutions. Thus, M1 is intended as a measure of the assets that are most widely used by the private sector in making transactions. An interesting feature of the numbers reported in Table 12.1 is that the monetary base in March 2016 was actually larger than M1, which was not a feature of the data before the 2008–2009 financial crisis. This state of affairs occurred because depository institutions were holding large quantities of reserves, but were not financing all of these reserve holdings with transactions accounts. The quantity of M2 is M1 plus savings deposits, small-denomination savings deposits, and retail money market mutual funds. These additional assets are not directly used in transactions, but they are easily exchanged for currency and transactions deposits, which can then be used in transactions.

The monetary aggregates are in principle important, as they can be useful indirect measures of aggregate economic activity that are available on a more timely basis than GDP. Further, there can be key regularities in the relationship between monetary aggregates and other aggregate variables, which can make monetary aggregates useful in economic forecasting and in policy analysis. Finally, the paths followed by monetary aggregates over time can be useful in evaluating the performance of the Fed. That said, monetary aggregates currently receive little attention from central bankers in the world, and for good reasons, which will be discussed later in this chapter and in Chapters 14 and 15.

A Monetary Intertemporal Model

LO 12.2 Construct the monetary intertemporal model.

Why do we use money in exchange? A useful analogy is that money is to economic exchange as oil is to an engine; money overcomes " frictions." Two important economic frictions that make money useful are the following. First, in modern economies, barter exchange—the exchange of goods for goods—is difficult. As Adam Smith recognized in his *Wealth of Nations,* specialization is key to the efficiency gains that come from economic development. Once economic agents become specialized in what they produce and what they consume, it becomes very time-consuming to trade what one has for what one wants through barter exchange. For example, if Sara specializes in giving economics lectures and wants to buy car repairs, to make a barter exchange she must not only find someone willing to repair her car—a **single coincidence of wants**—but the car repair person must also want to receive a lecture in economics—a **double coincidence of wants**. Clearly, Sara may have to spend a great deal of time and energy searching for a trading partner! The double coincidence problem was first studied by William Stanley Jevons in the nineteenth century.[1] Money solves the double-coincidence problem because, if everyone accepts money in exchange, then would-be buyers need only satisfy a single-coincidence problem to buy a good, which is much easier. Sara can sell economics lectures for money and then exchange this money for car repairs.

---

[1] See S. Jevons, 1910. *Money and the Mechanism of Exchange,* 23rd edition, London: Kegan Paul.

A second reason that money is useful in exchange is that there are circumstances where credit transactions may be difficult or impossible to make. For example, it would be unlikely that a street vendor in New York City would accept my personal IOU in exchange for a hot dog. Because the street vendor does not know me or my credit history, he or she cannot evaluate whether my IOU is good or not, and it would be costly for him or her to take legal action should I not be willing to pay off my IOU. While modern credit card systems solve some of the information problems connected with the use of personal credit in transactions, these systems are costly to operate, and there are sellers of goods who do not accept credit under any circumstances. Because money is easily recognizable, there are essentially no information problems associated with the use of money in exchange, other than the problems that arise from counterfeiting.

We will not include explicitly in our model the frictions that make money useful, as this would make things far too complicated for this level of analysis. It is important to keep these frictions in mind, however, and in Chapter 18 we will study a model that takes explicit account of the double-coincidence-of-wants problem in barter exchange. We will use that model to gain some insight into the fundamentals of the role of money in the economy. However, to study the issues in this chapter—the key determinants of the demand for money, monetary neutrality, and the basics of monetary policy—we will do pretty well without being explicit about monetary frictions.

Real and Nominal Interest Rates and the Fisher Relation

LO 12.3 Derive the Fisher relation.

In the monetary intertemporal model that we construct, there are many periods but, just as in the economic growth models studied in Chapters 7 and 8, our analysis is mainly in terms of an arbitrary *current period* and the following period, which we refer to as the *future period*. There are two primary assets, money and nominal bonds, and later we will introduce banks, which have some other assets and liabilities. For simplicity, the entire stock of outside money is assumed to consist of currency. We use money as the numeraire here (recall that the numeraire is the object in which all prices are denominated in an economic model) with P denoting the current price level, or the current price of goods in terms of money. Similarly, P' denotes the price level in the future period. A **nominal bond** is an asset that sells for one unit of money (e.g., one dollar in the United States) in the current period and pays off $1 + R$ units of money in the future period. Therefore, R is the rate of return on a bond in units of money, or the **nominal interest rate**. Nominal bonds can be issued by the government, by consumers, or by firms, and all bonds bear the same nominal interest rate, as we are assuming that no one defaults on their debts.

As in Chapters 9–11, the real rate of interest, r, is the rate of interest in terms of goods. The real interest rate is the real rate of return that someone receives when holding a nominal bond from the current period to the future period. The real interest rate can be determined from the nominal interest rate, and the **inflation rate** i, which is defined by

$$i = \frac{P' - P}{P}.$$

(12-1)

That is, the inflation rate is the rate of increase in the price level from the current period to the future period. Then, the real interest rate is determined by the **Fisher relation**, named after Irving Fisher, which is

$$1 + r = \frac{1 + R}{1 + i}. \tag{12-2}$$

To derive the Fisher relation, recall that $1 + R$ is the return in terms of money in the future period from giving up one unit of money in the current period to buy a nominal bond. In real terms, someone acquiring a nominal bond gives up $\frac{1}{P}$ goods in the current period and receives a payoff of $\frac{1+R}{P'}$ goods in the future period. Therefore, from Equation (12-1), the gross rate of return on the nominal bond, in real terms, is

$$1 + r = \frac{\dfrac{1+R}{P'}}{\dfrac{1}{P}} = \frac{1+R}{\dfrac{P'}{P}} = \frac{1+R}{1+i},$$

which gives us the Fisher relation, Equation (12-2).

Given a positive nominal interest rate on nominal bonds—that is, $R > 0$—the rate of return on nominal bonds exceeds the rate of return on money. The nominal interest rate on money is zero, and the real interest rate on money can be determined just as we determined the real interest rate associated with the nominal bond above. That is, if r^m is the real rate of interest on money, then as in Equation (12-2), we have

$$1 + r^m = \frac{1+0}{1+i} = \frac{1}{1+i},$$

and so if $R > 0$ then $r^m < r$, or the real interest rate on money is less than the real interest rate on the nominal bond. In our monetary intertemporal model, we need to explain why people are willing to hold money if they can receive a higher rate of return on the alternative asset, nominal bonds, when the nominal interest rate is positive.

The Fisher relation can be rewritten by multiplying each side of Equation (12-2) by $1 + i$ and rearranging to get

$$r = R - i - ir.$$

Then, if the nominal interest rate and the inflation rate are small, ir is negligible; for example, if the inflation rate is 10% and the real interest rate is 8%, then $i = 0.1$, $r = 0.08$, and $ir = 0.008$. We can say that, for small inflation rates and interest rates,

$$r \approx R - i; \tag{12-3}$$

that is, the real interest rate is approximately equal to the nominal interest rate minus the inflation rate. For example, if the nominal interest rate is 5%, or 0.05, and the inflation rate is 3%, or 0.03, then the real interest rate is approximately 2%, or 0.02.

While the Fisher relation, Equation (12-3), is just a definition—it defines the real interest rate—the **Fisher effect** is different. The Fisher effect posits a positive effect of inflation on the nominal interest rate or, in neo-Fisherian theory (discussed in Chapter 15), a positive effect of the nominal interest rate on inflation. The Fisher effect can be readily discerned in the data, as shown in Figure 12.1

In the figure, which is a scatter plot of the U.S. 3-month Treasury bill rate, versus the 12-month inflation rate for the period 1948–2015, we can readily see the positive correlation between the nominal interest rate and inflation. There is a wide scatter around the line, which is the best fit to the data; however, indicating that other factors than inflation matter for the level of the nominal interest rate. Empirically, there is a problem in measuring the real interest rate. Nominal interest rates on many different assets can be observed, but economic agents do not know the inflation rate that will be realized over the time they hold a particular asset. The correct inflation rate to use might be the one that an economic agent expects, but expectations cannot be observed. However, one approach to measuring the real rate of interest is to calculate it based on

Figure 12.1 The Nominal Interest Rate versus Inflation
The figure shows the nominal interest rate on 3-month U.S. Treasury bills and the corresponding real interest rate, calculated as the nominal interest rate minus the rate of change in the consumer price index.

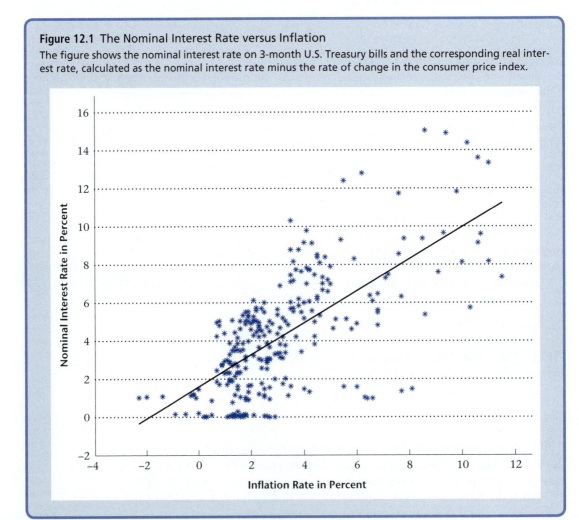

Equation (12-3), using the realized inflation rate for i. In Figure 12.2 we show data on the real interest rate, calculated as the nominal interest rate on 3-month Treasury bills, minus the inflation rate. Of note in Figure 12.2 is the variability in the real interest rate, and periods of persistently high and persistently low real interest rates. One feature of the data in Figure 12.2, which is a worldwide phenomenon, is the trend decrease in the real interest rate from the early 1980s until the end of the sample in 2015. The low levels of the real interest rate, particularly since the 2008–2009 recession, have been an issue for monetary policy, as will be discussed later in this chapter and in Chapter 15.

Banks and Alternative Means of Payment

In constructing the monetary intertemporal model, we need to modify the real intertemporal model of Chapter 11 to account for how transactions are carried out using currency supplied by the central bank and transactions services supplied by private

Figure 12.2 The Measured Real Interest Rate

The real interest rate has been highly variable, and has been persistently high and low. Of note is the long decline in the real interest rate from the early 1980s until 2015.

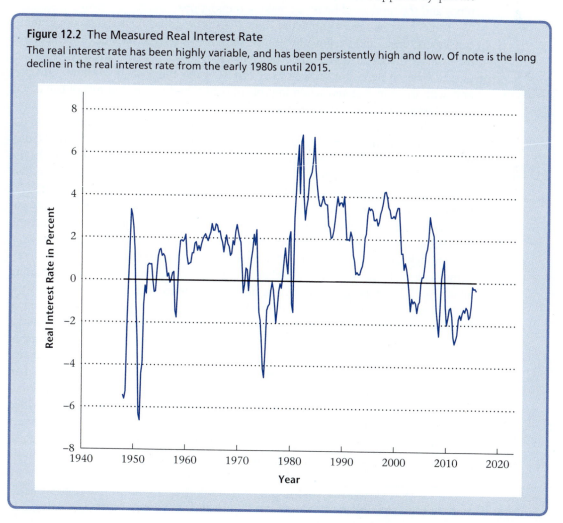

banks. For the analysis in this chapter and in Chapters 13 and 14, we do not have to alter how we model demand and supply in the labor market and goods market. However, we need to introduce a new market, the market for money. But we know that there are different definitions of " money," and that we might think of money in different ways depending on the task at hand. For this task—building our monetary intertemporal model—the money stock corresponds to currency—outside money not including bank reserves. The demand for money in the model will be determined, as we will show, by the behavior of the representative consumer and the representative firm, and the supply of money is determined by the central bank. As we will see, the demand for money is a quite different concept from the demand for a good or service. In contrast to goods and services, we want money not because it contributes directly to our happiness, but because it allows us to acquire the goods and services that ultimately make us happy. To understand the determinants of the demand for money, we need to be specific about how consumers and firms make choices between using currency and the services of banks in making transactions.

Banks have two roles in practice. First, they serve to facilitate transactions among consumers, firms, and the government. Second, banks serve as financial intermediaries that manage the savings of their depositors in a more efficient way than could be accomplished by each depositor on his or her own. For our purposes, it is simplest to deal only with the transactions-facilitating role of banks, and the second role of banks will be explored in some detail in Chapter 18.

The five primary alternatives to government-supplied currency that are in wide use in retail transactions are checks, debit cards, credit cards, prepaid cards, and ACH (automatic clearing house) transfers. The use of checks is declining at a high rate while the use of electronic means of payment is rising. Evidence from 2012 indicates that, of noncash transactions, 15% were carried out by check, 38% by debit card, 21% by credit card, 7% by prepaid card, and 18% by electronic ACH transfers.[2] It will be useful to start our analysis by thinking of credit cards as the only alternative to currency in transactions, and then show how we can generalize our thinking to include other means of payment.

Though different means of payment may all look essentially identical to a consumer—they all can be used in purchases of goods and services—there are important economic differences among them. The first key difference relates to whose liability the payments instrument represents. Currency is technically a liability of the central bank—all outstanding currency and coins in the United States show up as liabilities on the Federal Reserve System's balance sheet. However, when I use my debit card or pay with a check, I am transferring a private bank liability (part of my account balance with the bank) to someone else. When I use a credit card to make a transaction, then there is a somewhat complicated transfer of liabilities. At the time of the transaction, I have issued a liability—my IOU—in exchange for some goods and services provided by a retailer. The retailer then takes my IOU and exchanges it with a financial intermediary, Visa for example. Visa now has my IOU, and I eventually pay Visa to extinguish the IOU. With a prepaid card, I pay the card issuer for value on the card, effectively

---

[2]See "The 2013 Federal Reserve Payments Study," December 2013, *Federal Reserve System*, available at https://www.frbservices.org/files/communications/pdf/research/2013_payments_study_summary.pdf

making a loan to the card issuer, and then the card issuer pays off the loan as I spend the value on the card. An ACH transfer works much like a debit card transaction, except that the communication that needs to take place among the relevant parties to the transaction is different.

A second key difference among means of payment relates to the payment of interest on the liabilities in question. Currency is a liability that pays no interest, because this is impractical. However, until the time I make a debit card transaction or payment by check, I can earn interest on the bank deposit liability that I am going to transfer through use of the debit card or check. With credit card balances, the typical practice is for no interest to be paid on credit card debt extended during a monthly billing cycle, but interest is paid if the balance is carried over into the next month.

A third difference among means of payment is in the transactions costs involved. Government-supplied currency is a very low-tech means of payment, and exchange using currency is very low cost. Counterfeit currency may be a concern, but not if the government has done a good job of designing the currency to thwart counterfeiters and establish serious legal penalties for counterfeiting. Accepting payment using credit cards, debit cards, or checks is a more costly matter, typically involving electronic means for communicating with financial institutions or centralized credit agencies.

In our monetary intertemporal model, we will start by considering how payments by credit card would work as an alternative to currency in transactions. Suppose that goods can be purchased by consumers (who buy consumption goods C), firms (who purchase investment goods I) and the government (which purchases G) using currency or credit cards, and that firms sell goods at the same price P in terms of money, whether they are offered payment with currency or a credit card. Why do firms only accept currency and credit cards and not personal IOUs? This is because the information costs of checking an individual's credit history are too great. Monetary theorists would say that there is a lack of memory or recordkeeping on individuals in the credit system. Everyone recognizes government-supplied currency and Visa/Mastercard but few people know me or my creditworthiness.

Operating a credit card system is costly. The credit card issuer must set up a communication network, and must check the credit histories of individuals to whom it issues cards. Credit card holders must be billed every month, and debts collected. We will represent these costs by assuming that banks sell credit services for a price q, in units of goods, for each unit of real goods transacted using the credit card during the current period. As well, there exists a supply curve for credit card services $X^s(q)$ that denotes the quantity of credit card services (units of goods purchased with a credit card during the period) supplied given each price q. In Figure 12.3, the supply curve for credit card services is increasing because of the increasing marginal cost of supplying credit card services.

We will assume that when an economic agent buys some goods with a credit card, the economic agent acquires a debt with the bank that is paid off, at zero interest, at the end of the current period. If consumers, firms, or the government want to borrow (or lend) from one period to the next, they do so on the credit market at the market nominal interest rate R, with the borrowing and lending taking place at the beginning of the period.

Figure 12.3 The Supply Curve for Credit Card Services

The supply curve is upward-sloping as the profitability of extending credit balances increases as q increases, so banks increase quantity supplied.

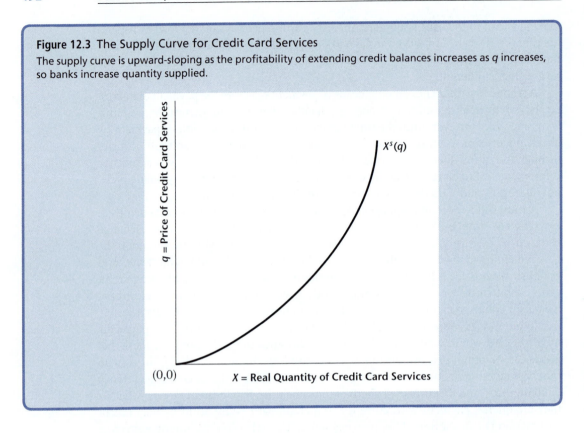

$X^s(q)$

q = Price of Credit Card Services

(0,0)

X = Real Quantity of Credit Card Services

Equilibrium in the Market for Credit Card Services, and the Demand for Money

To determine the demand for credit card services, we need to consider the behavior of consumers, firms, and government purchasing agents who are on the demand side of the goods market. Given that all of these economic agents want to collectively purchase Y units of goods, their decision relates to the quantity of goods they wish to purchase with credit cards, denoted by $X^d(q)$ (the demand for credit card services) relative to the remainder, $Y - X^d(q)$, which is the quantity of goods purchased with currency. We need to determine what $X^d(q)$ looks like and then, given the supply curve for credit card services in Figure 12.3, we can in turn determine the equilibrium quantity and price of credit card services.

Suppose that an economic agent considers buying one more unit of goods with credit, and one less unit of goods with currency. What are the costs and benefits, at the margin? The economic agent would then need to hold P fewer units of currency to make transactions during the current period, and this quantity could then be lent on the credit market, yielding $P(1 + R)$ units of money at the beginning of the future period. Thus, the marginal benefit is $P(1 + R)$ units of money at the beginning of the future period. However, the consumer must give up $P(1 + q)$ units of money at the end of the period in order to pay off the credit card debt and to pay the bank for its credit card services. Assume that any money available at the end of the period must be held as currency until the beginning of the next period. Thus, the marginal cost of buying one more unit of goods with a credit card is $P(1 + q)$, in units of money at the beginning of next period.

What does the economic agent want to do? This depends on the comparison between marginal benefit and marginal cost. If

$$P(1 + R) > P(1 + q), \qquad (12\text{-}4)$$

or $R > q$, then marginal benefit is greater than marginal cost, and the economic agent will purchase all goods with a credit card. However, if

$$P(1 + R) < P(1 + q), \qquad (12\text{-}5)$$

or $R < q$, then marginal benefit is less than marginal cost, and the economic agent will purchase all goods with currency. If $R = q$, then the agent is indifferent between using currency and a credit card. This implies that the demand curve for credit card services is as depicted in Figure 12.4. The demand curve is perfectly elastic at $q = R$. The equilibrium price for credit card services is therefore R, and the equilibrium quantity of credit card services is X^* in the figure.

Figure 12.4 Equilibrium in the Market for Credit Card Services
The demand curve for credit balances is horizontal at the price $q = R$, the equilibrium price of credit card services is $q = R$, and the equilibrium quantity is it X^*.

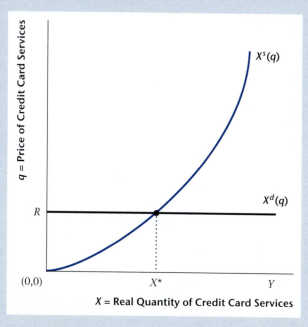

In Figure 12.5, consider what happens if the nominal interest rate rises from R_1 to R_2. In equilibrium the price of credit card services rises, and the quantity of credit card services rises from X_1^* to X_2^*. We can then write the equilibrium quantity of credit card services as $X^*(R)$, which is an increasing function of the nominal interest rate R, to capture the idea in Figure 12.5 that the equilibrium quantity of credit card services rises when the nominal interest rate rises. Effectively, this occurs because the opportunity cost of making a transaction with currency is higher the larger is the nominal interest rate. This implies that the quantity of goods purchased with currency is $Y - X^*(R)$ when the market for credit card services is in equilibrium, which means that the nominal quantity of currency that consumers, firms, and the government want to hold to make transactions is

$$M^d = P[Y - X^*(R)], \tag{12-6}$$

but since the function on the right-hand side of Equation (12-6) is increasing in Y and decreasing in R, it is simpler to write Equation (12-6) as

$$M^d = PL(Y, R), \tag{12-7}$$

Figure 12.5 The Effect of an Increase in the Nominal Interest Rate on the Market for Credit Card Services

An increase in the nominal interest rate from R_1 to R_2 shifts the demand curve for credit balances up from X_1^d to X_2^d. The equilibrium price of credit card balances increases from R_1 to R_2 and the equilibrium quantity increases from X_1^* to X_2^*.

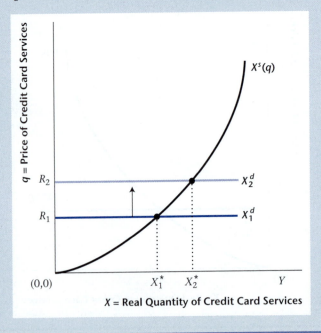

where the function L is increasing in real income, Y, and decreasing in the nominal interest rate, R. Note that if we include an analysis of the use of debit cards and checks as well, the demand for currency will take the same form as in Equation (12-6). The use of debit cards or checks in transactions involves the transfer of ownership of an interest-bearing bank liability. Thus, the use of debit cards and checks must rise with the nominal interest rate, as a higher nominal interest rate implies a lower cost of using debit cards and checks relative to currency.

The function $PL(Y, R)$ in Equation (12-7) is a nominal money demand function, though it would be quite misleading to think of the money demand function as being much like the demand function for a good or service. In our model, the money demand function is derived as an equilibrium relationship given the choices of banks concerning the supply of credit card services, and the choices of consumers, firms, and the government concerning how they will use cash and credit cards in making transactions.

The nominal demand for money is proportional to the price level, as the quantity that matters to consumers and firms in their choice of means of payment is the real quantity of money, M^d/P. Money demand increases with real income as consumers and firms wish to engage in a larger real volume of transactions as real income rises, and the capacity of the banking system to supply alternative means of payment is limited. Finally, money demand falls as the nominal interest rate rises, because a higher nominal interest rate increases the opportunity cost of holding cash, and so consumers and firms are more inclined to use alternative means of payment such as credit cards and debit cards.

Taking the approximate Fisher relation Equation (12-3) as an equality (that is, assuming the real interest rate and the inflation rate are small) implies that we can substitute $r + i$ for R in Equation (12-7), to get

$$M^d = PL(Y, r + i).\tag{12-8}$$

For most of the analysis that we do in this chapter and in Chapters 13 and 14, we look at economic experiments that do not deal with the effects of changes in long-run inflation. That is, most of the experiments we consider in these chapters leave the inflation rate i unaffected. When i is constant in Equation (12-8), it is harmless to set it to zero for convenience, which implies that Equation (12-8) becomes

$$M^d = PL(Y, r).\tag{12-9}$$

With Y and r given, the function on the right-hand side of Equation (12-9) is linear in P with slope $L(Y, r)$, and we depict this function in Figure 12.6. If real income increases, for example from Y_1 to Y_2, then in Figure 12.7 the money demand curve shifts to the right from $PL(Y_1, r)$ to $PL(Y_2, r)$. We would obtain the same type of rightward shift in the money demand curve if the real interest rate r were to decrease.

Government

We have to expand on our treatment of government from Chapter 10 to take into account the ability of the government to issue money. For our purposes, it is convenient to assume that there is a single institution in our model called the government, which is responsible for both fiscal and monetary policy. Therefore, the government

Figure 12.6 The Nominal Money Demand Curve in the Monetary Intertemporal Model

Nominal money demand is a straight line and it shifts with changes in real income Y and the real interest rate r.

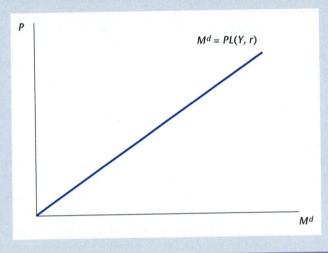

Figure 12.7 The Effect of an Increase in Current Real Income on the Nominal Money Demand Curve

The current nominal money demand curve shifts to the right with an increase in current real income Y. The curve shifts in the same way if there is a decrease in the real interest rate r.

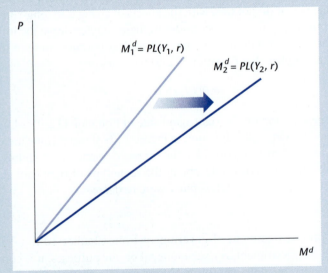

entity in this model is essentially what we would get if we merged the U.S. Treasury with the Federal Reserve System and placed them both under the control of the Congress. In the United States, the Federal Reserve System, which is the monetary authority, is essentially independent of the Treasury, which is the federal fiscal authority controlled by the U.S. government. The arrangement between the central bank and the federal government varies considerably across countries. In some countries, such as the United States, the central bank has considerable independence, while in other countries it does not.

In the current period, the government purchases G goods and pays the nominal interest and principal on the government debt outstanding from the last period, $(1 + R^-)B^-$, where B^- is the quantity of one-period nominal bonds issued by the government in the previous period, which come due in the current period, with each of these bonds bearing a nominal interest rate of R^-. Current government purchases and the interest and principal on government debt, which sum to total current government outlays, are financed through taxation, the issue of new bonds, and by printing money. The government budget constraint in the current period is, therefore, given by

$$PG + (1 + R^-)B^- = PT + B + M - M^-. \tag{12-10}$$

The government budget constraint, Equation (12-10), is expressed in nominal terms, with the left-hand side denoting total government outlays during the period, and the right-hand side denoting total government receipts. On the right-hand side, PT denotes nominal taxes, B denotes government bonds issued in the current period, which come due in the future period, and the final term, $M - M^-$, is the change in the nominal money supply, where M is the total quantity of money outstanding in the current period, and M^- is the previous period's money supply.

Adding money creation, $M - M^-$, to the government budget constraint is an important step here over the kinds of models we considered in Chapters 5, 9, 10, and 11, where we did not take account of the monetary transactions that take place in the economy. We are now able to consider the effects of monetary policy and how monetary and fiscal policy interact.

Competitive Equilibrium—The Complete Monetary Intertemporal Model

LO 12.4 Construct a competitive equilibrium in the monetary intertemporal model, and carry out equilibrium experiments using the model.

In the monetary intertemporal model there are three markets to consider—the market for current goods, the market for current labor, and the money market. As in the real intertemporal model studied in Chapter 11, equilibrium in the credit market is implied by equilibrium in these three other markets. The markets for current goods and current labor operate exactly as in the real intertemporal model, so the only important difference here from the model of Chapter 11 is the addition of the money market. In adding money to the model, we needed to analyze the behavior of banks, consumers, and firms in the market for credit card balances. However, in the work we did above, we showed how all of that behavior can be summarized in a money demand function.

Figure 12.8 The Current Money Market in the Monetary Intertemporal Model
The figure shows the current nominal demand for money curve M^d and the money supply curve M^s. The intersection of these two curves determines the equilibrium price level, which is P^* in the figure.

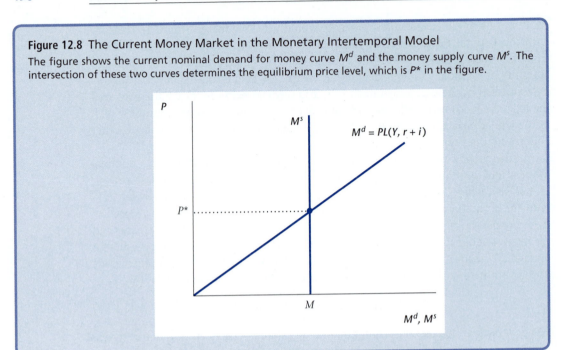

In the new market we need to include in the model the market for money; we will assume that the money supply M^s is determined exogenously by the government as $M^s = M$. Then for the money market to be in equilibrium, the nominal quantity of money supplied equals the quantity of money demanded, or

$$M = PL(Y, r). \tag{12-11}$$

In Figure 12.8 we illustrate the workings of the money market, with the nominal money demand curve M^d being upward-sloping and linear in P, as we saw previously. Here, we have added the money supply curve, which is a vertical line at the quantity M, because the money supply is exogenous. The intersection of the nominal money demand and nominal money supply curves determines the price level P. In the figure, the equilibrium price level is P^*.

Next, integrating the money market into the real intertemporal model of Chapter 11, we show in Figure 12.9 how the endogenous variables in the monetary intertemporal model are determined. In Figure 12.9(b), we depict equilibrium in the current goods market, where the output demand curve Y^d and the output supply curve Y^s jointly determine the equilibrium real interest rate r^* and the equilibrium quantity of aggregate output, Y^*. Then, in Figure 12.9(a), given the equilibrium real interest rate r^*, which determines the position of the labor supply curve $N^s(r^*)$, the labor demand curve N^d and the labor supply curve $N^s(r^*)$ jointly determine the equilibrium real wage w^* and the equilibrium quantity of employment, N^*. Then, in Figure 12.9(c), the equilibrium quantity of output, Y^*, and the equilibrium real interest rate r^* determine the position of the money demand curve M^d. Then, the money demand curve and the money supply curve in Figure 12.9(c) determine the equilibrium price level P^*.

Figure 12.9 The Complete Monetary Intertemporal Model

In the model, the equilibrium real interest rate r and equilibrium current aggregate output Y are determined in panel (b). Then, the real interest rate determines the position of the labor supply curve in panel (a), where the equilibrium real wage w and equilibrium employment N are determined. Finally, the equilibrium price level P is determined in the money market in panel (c), given the equilibrium real interest rate r and equilibrium output Y.

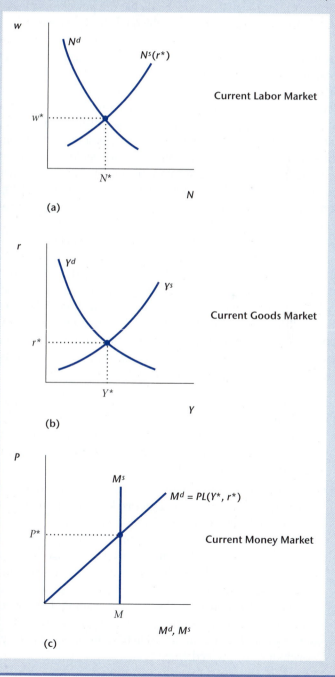

A Level Increase in the Money Supply and Monetary Neutrality

LO 12.5 Demonstrate that money is neutral in the monetary intertemporal model.

A government, through its central bank, has the power to increase the money supply by several different means. Historically, the power of a government to print money has been important, as the issue of new money can finance transfers to the private sector, can involve changing the quantity of interest-bearing assets held by the private sector, and can finance government expenditures. In this section, we would like to determine the effects on current macroeconomic variables of a one-time increase in the money supply. As we will see, a change in the level of the money supply of this sort is **neutral**, in that no real variables change, but all nominal quantities change in proportion to the change in the money supply. The neutrality of money is an important concept in monetary economics, and we want to understand the theory behind it and what it means in practice.

In the experiment we perform in the model, we suppose that the money supply is fixed at the quantity $M = M_1$ until the current period, as in Figure 12.10. Until the current period, everyone anticipates that the money supply remains fixed at the quantity M_1 forever. During the current period, however, the money supply increases from M_1 to M_2 and then remains at that level forever. What could cause such an increase in the money supply? From the government budget constraint, Equation (12-10), the change in the money supply in the current period, $M - M^- = M_2 - M_1$, is positive, and so this positive change in the money supply in the current period needs to be offset by some other term in Equation (12-10). Because the nominal interest rate from the previous period, R^-, and the quantity of bonds issued by the government in the previous period, B^-, were determined last period based on the expectation that the quantity of money in circulation would be M_1 forever, only the other terms in Equation (12-10) could be affected. There are three possibilities:

1. The government could reduce current taxes T. The money supply increase, therefore, is reflected by a decrease in taxes on the household, which is the same as an increase in transfers. Milton Friedman referred to this method of increasing the money stock as a "**helicopter drop**," because it is much like having a government helicopter fly over the countryside spewing money.

2. The government could reduce the quantity of bonds, B, that it issues during the current period. This is an **open market operation**, which in practice is carried out when the fiscal authority issues interest-bearing government debt, and then the monetary authority—the central bank—purchases some of this debt by issuing new money. An **open market purchase** is an exchange of money for interest-bearing debt by the monetary authority, and an **open market sale** is the sale of interest-bearing debt initially held by the monetary authority in exchange for money. In the case we examine here, where the money supply increases, there is an open market purchase. The day-to-day control of the money supply is accomplished in the United States mainly through open market operations by the Fed.

Figure 12.10 A Level Increase in the Money Supply in the Current Period
The figure shows a one-time increase in the money supply from M_1 to M_2.

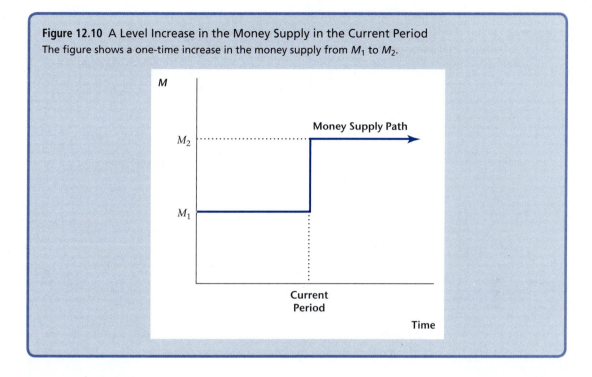

3. The government could temporarily increase the quantity of government spending, G, in the current period. Thus, the government would be printing money in order to finance government spending. When the government does this, it collects **seigniorage**. Seigniorage originally referred to the profit made by a seigneur, or ruler, from issuing coinage, but it has come to take on a broader meaning as the revenue earned by the government from issuing money. Seigniorage is also referred to as the revenue from the **inflation tax**, because the extra money that the government prints in general increases prices. Historically, seigniorage has been an important revenue-generating device. In the United States, seigniorage was a key source of revenue for the federal government during the Civil War and during World War I.

   For our purposes, it is most convenient for now to suppose that the money supply increase occurs through the first aforementioned method—a lump-sum transfer of money to the representative consumer. What happens in equilibrium when the money supply increases in the current period from M_1 to M_2? Here, because the level of the money supply does not matter for labor supply, labor demand, and the demand and supply of goods, the equilibrium determination of N, Y, r, and w in Figure 12.11 is unaffected by the current money supply M. That is, there a **classical dichotomy**: The model solves for all the real variables (output, employment, the real interest rate, and the real wage) in the labor market and the goods market in Figure 12.11, and the price level is then determined, given real output, in the money market. Real activity is

Figure 12.11 The Effects of a Level Increase in *M*—The Neutrality of Money

A level increase in the money supply in the monetary intertemporal model from M_1 to M_2 has no effects on any real variables, but the price level increases in proportion to the increase in the money supply. Money is neutral.

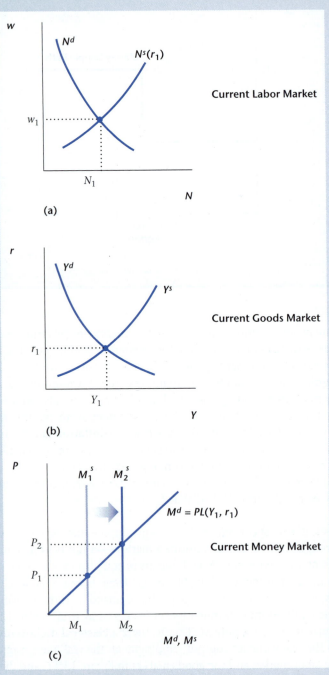

(a) Current Labor Market

(b) Current Goods Market

(c) Current Money Market

completely separated from nominal variables (the money supply, the price level). In Figure 12.11(b), the real interest rate and current real output are given by r_1 and Y_1, respectively, and in Figure 12.11(a), the equilibrium real wage and level of employment are w_1 and N_1, respectively.

In the model, we want to investigate the effects of having a money supply of M_2 from the current period on, rather than a money supply of M_1. In Figure 12.11 there is no effect on real activity, because the labor market and goods market are unaffected by the level of the money supply. However, there is an effect on the price level. In Figure 12.11(c), the money supply curve shifts to the right because of the increase in the money supply from M_1 to M_2. The money demand curve is unaffected, because Y does not change and r does not change. As a result, the price level increases in equilibrium from P_1 to P_2. Further, we can say something about how much the price level increases. Because $M = PL(Y, r)$ in equilibrium (money supply equals money demand) and because Y and r are unaffected by the increase in M, P must increase in proportion to M, so that $\frac{M}{P} = L(Y, r)$ remains unchanged. That is, if M increases by 10%, then P increases by 10%, so that the real money supply $\frac{M}{P}$ is unaffected. Note that the level increase in the money supply causes a level increase in the price level. There is only a one-time increase in the inflation rate (the rate of change in the price level), from the previous period to the current period, and no long-run increase in the inflation rate.

In this model, then, money is neutral. Money neutrality is said to hold if a change in the level of the money supply results only in a proportionate increase in prices, with no effects on any real variables. Thus, a change in the level of the money supply does not matter here. This does not mean, however, that money does not matter. In this model, if there were no money, then no goods could be consumed, because money is necessary to acquire these goods. In the real world, even if money were neutral, we know that if we eliminated money, then people would have to use more cumbersome means, such as barter, for making transactions. This would be much less efficient, and, in general, people would be worse off.

Is monetary neutrality a feature of the real world? In one sense, it almost obviously is. Suppose that the government could magically add a zero to all Federal Reserve notes. That is, suppose that overnight all \$1 bills become \$10 bills, all \$5 bills become \$50 bills, and so on. Suppose further that this change was announced several months in advance. It seems clear that, on the morning when everyone wakes up with their currency holdings increased by 10 times, all sellers of goods would have anticipated this change and would have increased their prices by 10 times as well, and that there would be no real change in aggregate economic activity. Though this thought experiment helps us understand the logic behind monetary neutrality, real-world increases in the money supply do not occur in this way, and there is in fact much debate about the extent of money neutrality in the short run.

There is broad agreement, however, that money is neutral in the long run. If the central bank engineers an increase in the money supply, after a long period of time it will make no difference to anyone whether the money supply increase ever occurred. Economists have different views, however, about what the long run means in practice. Do the effects of central bank actions on real economic variables essentially disappear after three months, six months, two years, or ten years? This all depends on the reason for the short run non-neutrality of money. For example, in Chapter 14 we will study a New Keynesian model in which the short run is the period of time over which prices sticky.

Shifts in Money Demand

LO 12.6 List the factors that can shift money demand, and show how a shift in money demand affects economic variables in the monetary intertemporal model.

In the monetary intertemporal model, the demand for money is determined by the choices of consumers and firms concerning the means of payment to be used in transactions, and the choices of banks concerning the supply of credit card services. Any factor that affects either the demand or supply of credit card services will bring about a shift in the demand for money.

Here, we will focus on the effects of a shift in the supply of credit card services. In Figure 12.12, suppose that the supply curve for credit card services shifts to the left from $X_1^s(q)$ to $X_2^s(q)$. Such a shift could be caused, for example, by a widespread power failure that shuts down communications between some retailers and credit card issuers. As a result, while the price of credit card balances remains constant at $q = R$, the market quantity of credit balances falls from X_1^* to X_2^*. Therefore, the equilibrium quantity

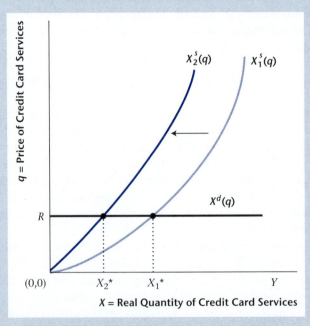

Figure 12.12 A Shift in the Supply of Credit Card Services

A decrease in the supply of credit card services does not change the equilibrium price, but equilibrium quantity falls.

of credit card services, $X^*(R)$, decreases for each R. Recall that the nominal demand for money is given by

$$M^d = PL(Y, R) = P[Y - X^*(R)],$$

so the demand for money is now higher for each P, Y, and R.

We will again set $i = 0$, so the nominal interest rate equals the real interest rate, or $R = r$. Then, in Figure 12.13, the demand for money increases and the money demand curve shifts to the right, from $PL_1(Y, r)$ to $PL_2(Y, r)$. Now, Y and r are determined in the goods market and labor market, and they are unaffected by what happens to the supply and demand for money. Thus, the price level falls from P_1 to P_2. Because the real demand for money has risen, the real money supply (M/P) must rise to meet the increased demand, and this can only happen if P falls.

What would cause shifts in the supply and demand curves for credit card services, other than our power failure example, leading to shifts in the money demand function?

1. *New information technologies that lower the cost for consumers of accessing bank accounts.* In 1970, banks did not provide ATM machines, ACH transfers, or debit cards. A typical transactions account could typically be accessed only by going to the bank or by making a transaction with a check. ATM machines dramatically reduced the cost of communicating with banks. As well, a typical debit card or ACH transaction, handled electronically, can be done at much lower cost than a transaction involving a check, which requires depositing the

Figure 12.13 A Shift in the Demand for Money
The money demand curve shifts to the right, causing a decrease in the equilibrium price level P, from P_1 to P_2.

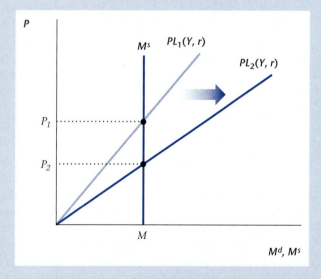

check in the bank and routing it through the check-clearing system. Thus, replacing the use of checks with debit cards and ACH transfers has reduced the cost of banking. Online banking is another technological development that has lowered the cost of banking transactions and reduced the demand for money. In the context of our model, we can think of these advances as reducing the average length of time between trips to replenish cash balances, which tends to reduce the average quantity of cash that each individual holds. For example, the wider availability of ATMs and debit cards may mean that an individual will switch to visiting the ATM once every two days, withdrawing $40 each time, and holding an average cash balance of $20, from visiting the ATM once per week, withdrawing $140 each time, and holding an average cash balance of $70.

2. *New financial instruments that lower the cost of banking.*   An example of such an instrument is a *sweep account*. These are accounts offered by banks that are held by businesses (and some consumers) and that automatically minimize the money balances held in transactions accounts by making transfers in and out of interest-earning accounts. For a bank, a transactions account is more costly to offer, in part because it is subject to reserve requirements (discussed in Chapter 18), so reducing total balances in transactions accounts will lower costs for banks. Sweep accounts therefore lower the cost of banking and reduce the demand for money.

3. *A change in government regulations.*   An example is the Depository Deregulation and Monetary Control Act of 1980, which permitted depository institutions (banks, savings and loan institutions, and credit unions) to pay interest on transactions accounts. This acted to lower the cost of banking and to reduce the demand for money.

4. *A change in the perceived riskiness of banks.*   If consumers and firms perceive that holding a banking deposit is a more risky proposition, for example if they think that banks could fail and they might lose their deposits, then consumers and firms may forego dealing with the banking system and simply conduct transactions using currency. During the Great Depression in the United States, and around the world during the recent financial crisis, the perceived instability of banks made households more uncertain about the value of their bank deposits, and there was an increase in the demand for currency. This therefore increased the demand for money. Bank riskiness is currently not an issue for small depositors in banks, because of government-provided deposit insurance, but it potentially matters for large depositors. We will discuss this further in Chapter 18.

5. *Changes in hour-to-hour, day-to-day, or week-to-week circumstances in the banking system.*   There are times of the day, times of the week, or times of the month when the volume of financial transactions is particularly high or particularly low. For example, the volume of transactions among banks and other financial institutions tends to increase as financial traders get close to the end of the financial trading day. As the volume of transactions rises, the marginal cost of making financial transactions rises, due to congestion. In our model, this works as a shift to the left in the supply curve for credit card balances. Many such

effects are predictable, but there are sometimes unpredictable shocks to the financial system, such as the failure of a large financial institution, or a breakdown in the financial network because of a power failure or terrorist attack. Such failures and breakdowns tend to increase the demand for money.

THEORY CONFRONTS THE DATA

Instability in the Money Demand Function

Are shifts in the money demand function a big deal in practice? To answer this question, we will look at the demand for M1 in the United States for the period 1959–2015. In order to get started, we have to choose a specific function that we can use to try to fit the data. We will assume that

$$L(Y, R) = Ye^{aR},$$

where e is approximately equal to 2.72, and is the base for the natural logarithms. The parameter a satisfies $a < 0$, and is what we want to choose so that this money demand function fits the data as closely as possible. This form for the money demand function implies that money demand is proportional to real income, so that the size of the economy is irrelevant to the real quantity of money that each person wishes to hold.

From Equation (12-7), the equilibrium condition for the money market, we obtain

$$M = PYe^{aR},$$

or, if we rewrite the above equation and take natural logarithms on both sides of the equation,

$$\log\left(\frac{M}{PY}\right) = -aR.$$

Suppose that our theory of money demand is a good one, that we have chosen a good functional form for the money demand function, and that there are only random shifts in the money demand function. Then a negatively sloped straight line should do a good job of fitting the data on the log of the ratio of money to nominal GDP and the nominal interest rate.

If we take M to be the measured quantity of M1 over the period 1959–2015, PY to be measured nominal GDP, and R to be the short-term Treasury bill rate, then we obtain the scatter plot in Figure 12.14. In the figure, we measure the nominal interest rate in percentage terms on the vertical axis, and the natural log of the ratio of money to nominal GDP on the horizontal axis. The points in the figure are identified separately as those for the period 1959–1979 (dark blue) and those for the period 1980–2015 (light blue).

The money demand function fits quite well in Figure 12.14 for the period 1959–1979. A straight line fits the points for 1959–1979 closely, and there is a small amount of variability around that line. However, after 1980, what had seemed to be a stable money demand function began to shift dramatically. Indeed, if we mechanically fit a straight line to the points for 1980–2015, that straight line would be upward-sloping, which would make no sense in terms of our theory of money demand.

Of course we know a lot about factors that could have affected money demand in dramatic ways since 1980. There has been growth in the use of ATMs, debit cards, and credit cards, for example, and major changes in regulations,

(Continued)

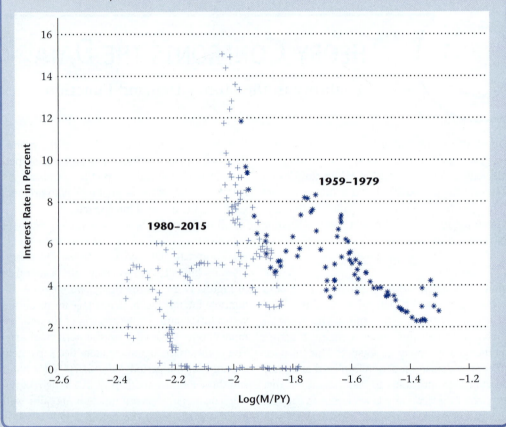

Figure 12.14 Instability in Money Demand
The figure shows the money demand relationship for the period 1959–1979 (dark blue) and for 1980–2015 (light blue). In the early period, there appears to be a stable money demand relationship, but not in the later period.

particularly the Monetary Control Act of 1980. Indeed, the 1980–2015 points in the figure would be best-fit by a positively sloped line because the nominal interest rate fell during this period during times when other factors were causing money demand to fall. Thus, falling money demand coincided with falling nominal interest rates, in spite of the fact that the falling nominal interest rate was causing the quantity of money demanded to increase.

Money demand instability was a critical problem that led to central banks abandoning some monetarist ideas that were popular in the 1970s and 1980s. The instability we can see in Figure 12.14 was a problem not only in the United States, but in other countries as well. Monetarism, best represented by the ideas of Milton Friedman, took as a cornerstone the notion that the demand for money was stable and could be captured by a simple function of a few variables. Given the stable money demand function, monetarists recommended that central banks conduct and evaluate policy according to the observed behavior of the money stock. The fact that money demand is unstable, and became increasingly so after 1980, caused a drift away from monetarist ideas.

Conventional Monetary Policy, the Liquidity Trap, and Unconventional Monetary Policy

LO 12.7 Show how conventional monetary policy is ineffective in a liquidity trap, and explain unconventional monetary policies.

The modern era in monetary policy in the United States began with the term of Fed Chair Paul Volcker, which ran from August 1979 to August 1987. Volcker incorporated the ideas of **monetarists**, such as Milton Friedman, into Fed policymaking. Monetarists argue that the job of controlling the price level and inflation should be assigned to the central bank, and that the best way to control inflation is for the central bank to commit to a target for the growth rate in the money supply.

By the later 1970s, there was wide recognition that inflation rates were too high, and in the early 1980s, Volcker proceeded to reduce inflation by reducing money supply growth. This project was a success in terms of its stated goal—reducing inflation. But, after inflation had been brought down, in the mid-1980s, money growth targeting did not appear to be working as an ongoing approach to monetary policy implementation. Why? In order for money supply control to work well as an approach to controlling the price level and inflation, the money demand function should be fairly stable. But, as discussed earlier in "Theory Confronts the Data: Instability in the Money Demand Function," money demand has been highly unstable since 1980. An unstable money demand function means that there is a weak relationship between money growth and inflation, in which case money growth targeting is a bad idea.

Since the 1980s, the Fed has developed a monetary policy framework of nominal interest rate targeting. At each of the eight Federal Open Market Committee meetings each year, the FOMC—the monetary policy decision-making committee of the Fed—chooses a target for the federal funds rate, a key short-term market interest rate, which then helps determine all other interest rates. The New York Federal Reserve Bank then intervenes in financial markets so as to come as close as possible to this interest rate target. This approach works well, as it tends to absorb shocks that occur in financial markets—shifts in the money demand function—in the very short run, between FOMC meetings.

In meeting its goals, which we will discuss in more detail in Chapters 14 and 15, a central bank may encounter a problem: that there is a limit to how low the nominal interest rate can go. Typically, economists have argued that this lower bound on the nominal interest rate is zero. As the argument goes, when the **zero lower bound** is encountered, the nominal interest rate cannot go lower, as if it did, there would exist an **arbitrage opportunity** in financial markets. That is, people would prefer to hold currency, which always earns zero interest in nominal terms, rather than interest-bearing assets. But this is inconsistent with equilibrium in financial markets.

Then, at the zero lower bound, following this conventional argument, outside money issued by the central bank and government bonds become perfect substitutes. The money market then works as in Figure 12.15, where instead of the supply of nominal liquidity being the money supply M, it is now $M + B$, where B is the nominal

Figure 12.15 A Liquidity Trap

When the nominal interest rate is zero, money and government debt become perfect substitutes, so open market operations cannot affect the price level.

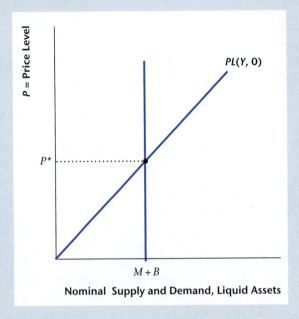

stock of liquid government debt (by "liquid" we mean easily tradeable in financial markets). The money demand function when the nominal interest rate is zero is $L(Y,0)$, and so the price level P^* in the figure is determined by money demand at the zero lower bound and the nominal stock of money plus liquid government debt.

But then, in Figure 12.15, if the central bank conducts a typical open market operation at the zero lower bound, which is a swap of money for short-term government debt, this does not affect the total $M + B$, and therefore has no effect on the price level. This is a **liquidity trap**, first identified by John Maynard Keynes in *The General Theory of Employment, Interest, and Money*, published in 1936.

Since the 2008–2009 recession, many central banks in the world, including the Fed, have encountered the zero lower bound, or something close to it. For example, from late 2008 until December 2015, the Fed's target for the federal funds rate was set in a range of 0–0.25%. In achieving their goals, the world's central banks in some cases decided that further "easing" of monetary policy at the zero lower bound was important, and some of them resorted to unconventional means to accomplish such easing. **Unconventional monetary policy** typically refers to intervention by central banks in financial markets that does not involve typical changes in a short-term nominal interest rate target. The unconventional policies that have been tried by central banks include **quantitative easing** and **negative nominal interest rates**, which we will discuss in turn.

Quantitative Easing

In a quantitative easing (QE) intervention by the central bank, rather than purchasing short-term government securities (for example U.S. Treasury bills, which mature in less than a year), the central bank purchases long-term government securities (Treasury bonds and notes, which mature in more than a year). The theory is that, in doing this, the central bank is making the stock of government debt held by the public more liquid. If this works, then in Figure 12.15 this is like increasing M and reducing B but by a less than offsetting amount (because the stock of debt held by the public is now more liquid), so that $M + B$ increases and the price level goes up.

The Fed did extensive QE from the time of the 2008–2009 recession until late 2014. For the Fed, QE involved not only outright purchases of long-maturity Treasury securities, but also purchases of mortgage-backed securities, and swaps of shorter-maturity Treasury securities for longer-maturity securities. Other central banks in the world, including the Bank of Japan, the Swiss National Bank, the Swedish Riksbank, the Bank of England, and the European Central Bank, have done QE, and some of those QE programs were operating on a continuing basis as of early 2016.

Whether QE has the desired effects, or has any effect, is debatable. Some empirical evidence indicates that QE announcements by the central bank can move financial market prices in the desired directions, but evidence to support the idea that QE influences inflation or real economic activity is scarce. For example, a massive QE program that began in Japan in April 2014 has, as of March 2016, had no apparent effect on inflation.[3]

Negative Nominal Interest Rates

Economists have come to realize that the **effective lower bound** on nominal interest rates is not zero at all, but something lower. This is because holding currency in large quantities may be a poor alternative to holding interest-bearing assets. But how can the nominal interest rate be negative? Why would I ever have to pay a lender to take my money? The answer is that currency can be a very inconvenient alternative to holding assets such as Treasury bills and bank reserves bearing negative interest. For example, if the 3-month Treasury bill rate were negative, I may not prefer to hold currency, as there is a chance that my currency will be stolen (Treasury bills are issued as individual electronic accounts with the U.S. Treasury), and currency in large quantities takes up space and is hard to use in large payments (e.g., payments of thousands or millions of dollars). Thus, there may be extra convenience associated with Treasury bills relative to currency.

Some central banks in the world have experimented with negative nominal interest rates, and have shown that rates can in fact go below zero. Central banks that have pushed nominal interest rates below zero include the Swedish Riksbank, the European Central Bank, the Swiss National Bank, and the Bank of Japan. There is no public evidence that the Fed has ever considered pushing short-term nominal interest rates below zero.

Negative nominal interest rates have been used by central banks primarily to help increase inflation. But, as we will discuss in Chapter 15, neo-Fisherians argue that lower nominal interest rates ultimately just make inflation lower.

---

[3]See S. Williamson, 2014. "Monetary Policy in the United States: A Brave New World?" *Federal Reserve Bank of St. Louis Review* 96, No. 2,111–122, Second Quarter; S. Williamson, 2015. "Monetary Policy Normalization in the United States," *Federal Reserve Bank of St. Louis Review* 97, No. 2, 87–108, Second Quarter.

MACROECONOMICS IN ACTION:

Quantitative Easing in the United States

By late 2008, in the midst of the global financial crisis, the Fed's federal funds rate target had essentially reached zero. But, as part of its crisis intervention, the Fed wanted to do more to intervene in financial markets, and began to experiment with unconventional monetary policy. The first quantitative easing program, often called QE1, was initiated in early 2009. As can be seen in Figure 12.16, this resulted in an increase in the total quantity of assets held. This increase was accounted for mostly by purchases of mortgage-backed securities (MBS in the figure), and in a minor way by purchases of long-term Treasury securities (Treasury notes and bonds in the figure).

Another part of the Fed's postfinancial crisis intervention program was to reduce its holdings of short-term Treasury bills ("bills" in the Figure 12.16), eventually to zero by 2012. Whereas Treasury bills were typically an important part of Fed securities holdings before 2008, accounting for 30% to 40% of total securities holdings, this was not the case by mid-2008. The elimination of Treasury bill holdings by the Fed, along with increases in the average maturity of the long-term Treasury securities it held, acted to increase dramatically the average maturity of the Fed's securities portfolio.

In part in response to a slow recovery in real GDP from the 2008–2009 recession, the Fed continued with its QE operations in the form of QE2 (late 2010 into 2011), which consisted (see Figure 12.16) of purchases of long-term Treasury securities, and QE3 (late 2012 to fall 2014) under which the Fed purchased both mortgage-backed securities and long-term Treasury securities.

Thus, from 2007 until the end of 2014, the securities holdings of the Fed had increased by more than five-fold, and the average maturity of those securities had increased significantly. What are the issues this raises?

1. Was QE effective? As with any macroeconomic policy, this is difficult to evaluate. There appeared to be announcement effects of QE in the United States; for example, the interest rates on long-maturity Treasury bonds seemed to go down in response to QE, as Fed policymakers said they should. But evidence that QE had any influence on the Fed's ultimate goals—inflation, unemployment, GDP, for example—is scarce.

2. Does QE give the Fed a "large footprint?" If QE works, then it may act to favor some credit market participants relative to others. For example, if purchases of mortgage-backed securities work, then this will lower mortgage interest rates. But this may mean that other interest rates in credit markets go up; interest rates on corporate bonds, for example. So, while mortgage borrowers may be better off, firms borrowing long term may be worse off. The fact that the Fed could act to favor some borrowers over others might act to politicize the Fed, which would be detrimental to its independence.

3. Could the Fed become insolvent? Insolvency happens for a private financial institution when the value of its liabilities exceeds the value of its assets. But this can never happen to the Fed, as its liabilities (currency and reserves) are not promises to deliver anything in the future. However,

Figure 12.16 Securities Held by the Fed

"Total" denotes total securities held outright by the Fed. Of that quantity, "bills" denote Treasury bills, and "MBS" are mortgage-backed securities. From 2007 until 2014, the Fed purchased a large quantity of securities, and increased the average maturity of the securities in its portfolio. The three major asset purchase programs, shown in the figure, are QE1, QE2, and QE3.

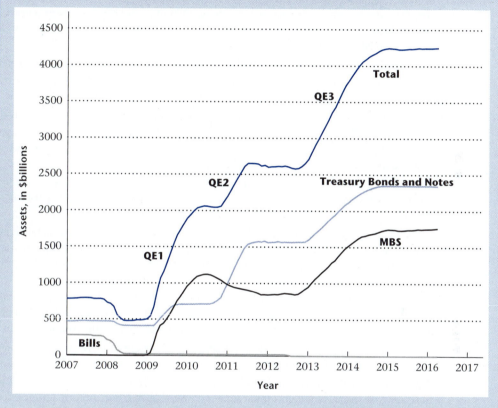

the Fed could find itself in a position where it earns zero or negative profits. In any year, any profits the Fed makes are rebated to the Treasury, and the Fed has been making large profits since the 2008–2009 recession because of its large securities holdings, as shown in Figure 12.16. But, suppose short-term interest rates go up further. Then the Fed's large quantity of interest-bearing reserves, which financed the large increase in its securities holdings, would become a greater cost for the Fed. And if short-term interest rates rise sufficiently, then the Fed's profits would become negative, and it could no longer make transfers to the U.S. Treasury. Economically, this is of no consequence, as if the Fed had not purchased the large quantity of assets that it did, the U.S. Treasury would be paying the interest on its own debt, instead of the Fed paying interest on its reserves. But a situation in which the Fed was no longer earning profits could be damaging for the Fed, from a political point of view.

Chapter Summary

- Money has three functions in the economy—it is a medium of exchange, a store of value, and a unit of account.

- The key measures of money are the monetary aggregates, which are the sums of quantities of assets having the functions of money. The monetary base, or M0, is the narrowest monetary aggregate, and it consists only of liabilities of the Federal Reserve System, in particular currency and the reserves of depository institutions. Other broader monetary aggregates, which include bank deposits and other assets, are M1 (broader than M0), M2 (broader than M1), and M3 (broader than M2).

- The monetary intertemporal model builds on the real intertemporal model of Chapter 9 by including supply and demand in the market for money. Money in the model is currency, which economics agents use, along with credit cards, to make transactions.

- The demand for money is determined by first determining the equilibrium price and quantity of credit card balances. Credit balances are supplied by banks.

- The real demand for money increases when real income increases, since more money is required to execute more transactions when GDP is higher.

- The real demand for money falls when the nominal interest rate increases, as this increases the opportunity cost of holding money, so that households economize on money balances and use noncash alternatives (credit cards) to a greater extent.

- In the monetary intertemporal model, money is neutral in the sense that an increase in the level of the money supply leaves real variables—employment, output, consumption, the real interest rate, the real money supply, and the real wage—unaffected and causes only a proportionate increase in all money prices.

- Shifts in money demand can occur because of new information technologies, new financial instruments, changes in government regulations, changes in the perceived riskiness of banks, and changes in the hour-to-hour or week-to-week circumstances of the banking system.

- Money demand shifts can be a particular problem for monetary policy, especially if monetary policy is guided by monetarist principles.

- The nominal interest rate cannot fall below its effective lower bound, which was once thought to be zero, but negative nominal interest rates are feasible, and have occurred in practice. At the effective lower bound, there is a liquidity trap. When they encounter the effective lower bound, some central banks resort to unconventional monetary policy, which includes quantitative easing (QE) and negative nominal interest rates.

Key Terms

Neutrality of money Money is neutral if a change in its level has no real effects and causes only a proportionate increase in the price level. (p. 443)

Medium of exchange A property of money; a medium of exchange is accepted in transactions for the sole reason that it can in turn be exchanged for other goods and services. (p. 443)

Store of value A property of money that is shared with other assets that permit current goods and services to be traded for future goods and services. (p. 443)

Unit of account The object in an economy in which prices and contracts are denominated. (p. 443)

Monetary aggregates These are measures of the money supply; each is the sum of a number of different types of assets in the economy. (p. 444)

Monetary base The quantity of M0, consisting of U.S. currency outside the Federal Reserve System and the deposits of depository institutions with the Fed. (p. 444)

Outside money This is identical to the monetary base. (p. 444)

Federal Reserve System (the Fed) The central bank of the United States. (p. 444)

Single coincidence of wants Situation in which two people meet and one person has what the other wants. (p. 445)

Double coincidence of wants Situation in which two people meet and the first person has what the second person wants and the second has what the first wants. (p. 445)

Nominal bond A bond for which the payoff is defined in terms of money. (p. 446)

Nominal interest rate If R is the nominal interest rate on an asset, then if 1 unit of money is exchanged for a given quantity of the asset in the current period, then this quantity of the asset pays off $1 + R$ units of money in the next period. (p. 446)

Inflation rate The rate of change in the price level. (p. 446)

Fisher relation Condition stating that $1 + r = \frac{1+R}{1+i}$, where r is the real interest rate from the current period to the future period, R is the nominal interest rate from the current period to the future period, and i is the rate of inflation between the current period and the future period. (p. 447)

Fisher effect A positive effect of inflation on the nominal interest rate. (p. 447)

Neutral Describes a government policy that has no real effects. (p. 460)

Helicopter drop Milton Friedman's thought experiment, which corresponds to an increase in the money supply brought about by transfers. (p. 460)

Open market operation A purchase or sale of interest-bearing government debt by the central bank. (p. 460)

Open market purchase An open market operation in which interest-bearing government debt is purchased by the central bank, increasing the money supply. (p. 460)

Open market sale An open market operation in which interest-bearing government debt is sold by the central bank, decreasing the money supply. (p. 460)

Seigniorage Revenue generated by the government through printing money. (p. 461)

Inflation tax Inflation arising when the government prints money to extract seigniorage; this effectively taxes the private sector. (p. 461)

Classical dichotomy Situation in an economic model where real variables are determined by real factors, and the money supply determines only the price level. (p. 461)

Monetarist An adherent of ideas shared by Milton Friedman, who argued for money supply targeting as a monetary policy rule. (p. 469)

Zero lower bound The theoretical limit of zero below which the nominal interest rate cannot pass. (p. 469)

Arbitrage opportunity Exists if some financial market participant can buy and sell assets in such a way as to make an immediate profit. (p. 469)

Liquidity trap A state of the world in which the short-term nominal interest rate is zero, and open market operations have no effect on any quantities or prices. (p. 470)

Unconventional monetary policy Actions by the central bank that are not related to conventional changes in the nominal interest rate target. (p. 470)

Quantitative easing (QE) An attempt by the central bank to lower long-term interest rates by purchasing long-maturity assets when there is a liquidity trap. (p. 470)

Negative nominal interest rates (p. 470)

Effective lower bound The actual level of the nominal interest rate when currency becomes as attractive as assets bearing negative interest. (p. 471)

Questions for Review

12.1　What are the three functions of money?

12.2　List three monetary aggregates and the assets that these monetary aggregates include.

12.3　Why is money used in exchange when people could carry out transactions by trading goods or using credit?

12.4　How are the real interest rate, the nominal interest rate, and the inflation rate related to one another?

12.5　What is the real rate of interest on money?

12.6   What are the alternatives to using currency in transaction in the monetary intertemporal model?

12.7   What determines the demand for money in the monetary intertemporal model?

12.8   What are the effects of an increase in the money supply in the monetary intertemporal model?

12.9   What are three ways the government could bring about a change in the money supply?

12.10   Explain how money can be nonneutral in the short run.

12.11   How does conventional monetary policy work?

12.12   What is a liquidity trap, and how does monetary policy work in a liquidity trap?

12.13   List two unconventional monetary policy actions, and explain how each is supposed to work.

12.14   Why might the effective lower bound not be zero?

Problems

1. **LO 4** In the monetary intertemporal model, show that it is possible to have an equilibrium where money is not held and only credit cards are used in transactions. Is there such a thing as a price level in this equilibrium? Does monetary policy work? If so, how? Explain your results and what they mean for actual economies.

2. **LO 4** The government decides that the use of credit cards is bad, and introduces a tax on credit card balances. That is, if a consumer or firm holds a credit card balance of X (in real terms), he or she is taxed tX, where t is the tax rate. Determine the effects on the equilibrium price and quantity of credit card balances, the demand for money, and the price level, and explain your results.

3. **LO 4** Suppose that the nominal interest rate is zero; that is, $R = 0$.
   (a) What is the equilibrium quantity of credit card balances?
   (b) In what sense does the economy run more efficiently with $R = 0$ than with $R > 0$?
   (d) Explain your results in parts (a) and (b). Discuss the realism of these predictions.

4. **LO 4** In the monetary intertemporal model, suppose that the money supply is fixed for all time. Determine the effects of a decrease in the capital stock, brought about by a war or natural disaster, on current equilibrium output, employment, the real wage, the real interest rate, the nominal interest rate, and the price level. Explain your results.

5. **LO 4, 6** A new technological innovation comes on line. What are the current effects on aggregate output, consumption, investment, employment, the real wage, the real interest rate, the nominal interest rate, and the price level? Explain your results. Also explain how they fit the key business cycle facts in Chapter 3.

6. **LO 4, 6** Suppose that there is an increase in the number of ATM machines in service. What are the effects of this innovation on the demand for money and on the price level?

7. **LO 4, 6** Suppose that we allow for the fact that cash can be stolen, but assume that a stolen credit card cannot be used, as it is instantly cancelled, so no one steals credit cards. Determine the effects this has on the quantity and price of credit card balances, the demand for money, and the price level. Explain your results.

8. **LO 7** Suppose that, in a liquidity trap, bank reserves are less liquid than government debt. If the central bank conducts an open market purchase of government debt, what will be the effect on the price level? Use a diagram, explain your results, and discuss.

9. **LO 7** Suppose that the central bank can influence expectations about inflation, by promising to increase the money supply in the future. In a liquidity trap, what effect does this have? Use a diagram to illustrate your results, and explain.

Working with the Data

Answer these questions using the Federal Reserve Bank of St. Louis's FRED database, accessible at http://research.stlouisfed.org/fred2/

1. Plot the monetary base (M0) along with your choice of price index (consumer price index, implicit GDP deflator, for example). How do you square what you see in the chart with the long-run neutrality of money? Discuss.

2. Plot the ratio of M2 to nominal GDP, and the 3-month Treasury bill rate. Do you see evidence of a money demand relationship? Explain.

3. Plot rates of growth (over a year) in M1 and in real GDP. What do you see in your chart? Can you make sense of what you see by using the theory developed in this chapter?

Business Cycle Models with Flexible Prices and Wages

Learning Objectives

After studying Chapter 13, students will be able to:

13.1 Construct the real business cycle model, explain how it matches the key business cycle facts, and use the model to analyze other problems.

13.2 Show how the real business cycle model could be consistent with the observed comovements of money and output.

13.3 Discuss criticisms of the real business cycle model.

13.4 Construct the Keynesian coordination failure model, explain how it matches key business cycle facts, and use the model to analyze other problems.

13.5 Discuss criticisms of the Keynesian coordination failure model.

13.6 Explain how the business cycle models in this chapter are, or are not, consistent with the observed behavior of U.S. time series during the 2008–2009 recession.

John Maynard Keynes's *A General Theory of Employment, Interest, and Money*,[1] published in 1936, changed how economists thought about business cycles and the role of government policy. By the 1960s, Keynesian thought had come to dominate macroeconomics. At that time, most macroeconomists accepted Keynesian business cycle models as capturing the behavior of the economy in the short run. There appeared to be broad agreement that money was not neutral in the short run, and most macroeconomists viewed this nonneutrality as arising from the short-run inflexibility of wages and prices. In Old Keynesian macroeconomic models—the Keynesian models that existed before

---

[1]See J. M. Keynes, 1936. *The General Theory of Employment, Interest, and Money*, London: Macmillan.

the 1980s—price and wage inflexibility were the key to the mechanism by which shocks to the economy could cause aggregate output to fluctuate. In the Old Keynesian view, the fact that prices and wages are slow to move to their efficient values implies that there is a role for monetary and fiscal policy in stabilizing the economy in response to aggregate shocks.

By the 1960s, the main disagreements in macroeconomics were between monetarists and Keynesians. Monetarists tended to believe that monetary policy was a more effective stabilization tool than fiscal policy, but they were skeptical about the ability of government policy to fine-tune the economy; some monetarists argued that the short run over which policy could be effective was very short indeed. Keynesians believed that monetary policy was unimportant relative to fiscal policy and that government policy should take an active role in guiding the economy along a smooth growth path. It may have seemed at the time that all the theoretical issues in macroeconomics had been resolved, in that most everyone agreed that the Old Keynesian model was a satisfactory model of the macroeconomy, and all that remained was for empirical work to sort out the disagreements between monetarists and Keynesians.

This view changed dramatically, however, with the advent of the rational expectations revolution in the early 1970s. Some important early contributors to the rational expectations revolution were Robert Lucas, Thomas Sargent, Neil Wallace, and Robert Barro. Two key principles coming out of the rational expectations revolution were:

1. Macroeconomic models should be based on microeconomic principles; in other words, they should be grounded in descriptions of the preferences, endowments, technology, and optimizing behavior of consumers and firms.

2. Models with flexible wages and prices can be productive vehicles for studying macroeconomic phenomena.

There was some resistance to following these two principles, but there was wide acceptance, at least of the first principle, by the 1980s. It became clear as well, with respect to the second principle, that the flexibility of wages and prices does not automatically rule out an active role for government policy, and that Keynesian ideas can be articulated in flexible-wage-and-price models.

In this chapter, we study two models of the business cycle, which were each developed as models with optimizing consumers and firms, and with flexible prices and wages. These models are the real business cycle model, and the Keynesian coordination failure model. These two models differ in terms of what is important in causing business cycles and the role implied for government policy. However, we will show that we can describe each of these models by building on the monetary intertemporal model of Chapter 12 in straightforward ways. We will show how well each model matches the business cycle facts discussed in Chapter 3, and discuss each model's shortcomings.

Chapter 14 will be devoted to studying a New Keynesian model, which captures the key elements of modern Keynesian thought in a sticky price framework. We treat this model separately, as there are some critical differences in how our basic framework operates when we include sticky prices.

Why is it necessary to study two different business cycle models? As we discussed in Chapter 3, business cycles are remarkably similar in terms of the comovements among macroeconomic time series. However, business cycles can have many causes, and fiscal and monetary policymakers are constantly struggling to understand what macroeconomic shocks are driving the economy and what this implies for future aggregate activity. Each business cycle model we study allows us to understand one or a few features of the economy and some aspects of the economy's response to macroeconomic shocks. Putting all of these features into one model would produce an unwieldy mess that would not help us understand the fundamentals of business cycle behavior and government policy.

Different business cycle models, however, sometimes give contradictory advice concerning the role of government policy. Does this mean that business cycle theory has nothing to say? The contradictory advice that different business cycle models give concerning the role of government policy reflects the reality of macroeconomic policymaking. Policymakers in federal and state governments and in central banks often disagree about the direction in which policy should move. To make persuasive arguments, however, policymakers have to ground those arguments in well-articulated macroeconomic models. This chapter shows, in part, how we can evaluate and compare macroeconomic models and come to conclusions about their relative usefulness.

The Real Business Cycle Model

LO 13.1 Construct the real business cycle model, explain how it matches the key business cycle facts, and use the model to analyze other problems.

Real business cycle theory was introduced by Finn Kydland and Edward Prescott[2] in the early 1980s. Kydland and Prescott asked whether or not a standard model of economic growth subjected to random productivity shocks (that is, "real" shocks, as opposed to monetary shocks) could replicate, qualitatively and quantitatively, observed business cycles. Kydland and Prescott were perhaps motivated to pursue this question by the observation, as shown in Figure 13.1, that the detrended Solow residual (a measure of total factor productivity z) closely tracks detrended real GDP. Thus, productivity shocks appear to be a potential explanation for business cycles.

Recall that many factors can lead to changes in total factor productivity. Essentially, any change implying that an economy can produce more aggregate output with the same factor inputs is an increase in total factor productivity—an increase in z in our model. Factors that increase z include good weather, technological innovations, the easing of government regulations, and decreases in the relative price of energy.

The version of the real business cycle model we study here is the monetary intertemporal model from Chapter 12. Though Kydland and Prescott studied a model where there was no role for money, Thomas Cooley and Gary Hansen showed, in a real

---

[2]See F. Kydland and E. Prescott, 1982. "Time to Build and Aggregate Fluctuations," *Econometrica* 50, 1345–1370.

Figure 13.1 Solow Residuals and GDP

The Solow residual (the colored line), a measure of total factor productivity, tracks aggregate real GDP (the black line) quite closely.

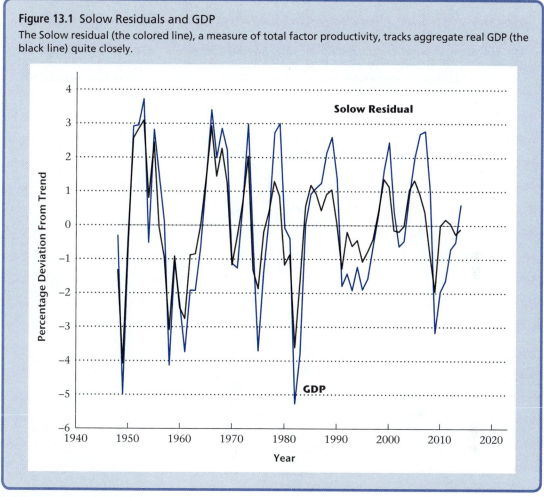

business cycle model with monetary exchange, that adding money made little difference to the results.[3]

The Solow residual, as observed in Figure 13.1, is a persistent variable. When it is above (below) trend, it tends to stay there. This tells us that total factor productivity shocks are persistent, so that when there is a current increase in z, we would expect future total factor productivity z' to be higher as well. This implies that, in analyzing how the real business cycle model reacts to a total factor productivity shock, we need to combine the results of two different shocks from Chapter 12, a shock to z and a shock to z'.

Suppose that there is a persistent increase in total factor productivity in the monetary intertemporal model, so that there are increases in z and z', current and future total factor productivity, respectively. In Figure 13.2 we show the equilibrium effects.

---

[3]See T. Cooley and G. Hansen, 1989. "The Inflation Tax in a Real Business Cycle Model," *American Economic Review* 79, 733–748.

Figure 13.2 Effects of a Persistent Increase in Total Factor Productivity in the Real Business Cycle Model

With a persistent increase in total factor productivity, the output supply curve shifts to the right because of the increase in current total factor productivity, and the output demand curve shifts to the right because of the anticipated increase in future total factor productivity. The model replicates the key business cycle facts.

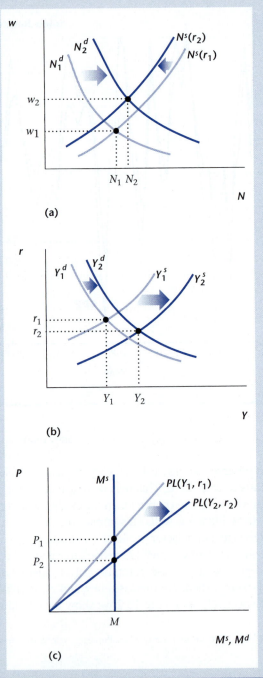

The increase in current total factor productivity, z, increases the marginal product of labor for each quantity of labor input, so that the labor demand curve shifts rightward from N_1^d to N_2^d in Figure 13.2(a), and this shifts the output supply curve rightward from Y_1^s to Y_2^s in Figure 13.2(b). There are additional effects because of the anticipated increase in future total factor productivity z'. First, the demand for investment goods increases, as the representative firm anticipates an increase in the future marginal productivity of capital. Second, the representative consumer anticipates that higher future total factor productivity implies higher future income, so that lifetime wealth increases and the demand for consumption goods goes up. Both of these factors cause the output demand curve Y^d to shift rightward from Y_1^d to Y_2^d.

In equilibrium, in Figure 13.2(b), aggregate output must rise, but it may seem that the real interest rate may rise or fall, depending on whether the shift in output demand dominates the shift in output supply, or vice versa. However, the real interest rate will fall for the following reasons. The consumer now expects that current and future income will be higher because of the positive and persistent productivity shock. However, because the shock is in part temporary (i.e., the increase in z' is not as large as the increase in z), consumers are expecting their real income to fall. The consumer wishes to smooth consumption over time, and so he or she tries to save more so as to consume less in the current period and more in the future, but this has the effect of driving down the market real interest rate, from r_1 to r_2 in Figure 13.2(b). Current consumption expenditures then increase because of the decrease in the real interest rate, the increase in current real income, and the increase in future real income stemming from the increase in future total factor productivity. Current investment rises because of the decrease in the real interest rate and the increase in future total factor productivity. In the money market, in Figure 13.2(c), because equilibrium real output rises and the real interest rate falls, money demand increases, and the nominal money demand curve shifts rightward from $PL(Y_1, r_1)$ to $PL(Y_2, r_2)$. Therefore, in equilibrium, the price level falls from P_1 to P_2. In the labor market, in Figure 13.2(a), the labor supply curve shifts leftward from $N^s(r_1)$ to $N^s(r_2)$ because of the fall in the real interest rate. However, as in Chapter 11, the labor supply curve shifts less than the labor demand curve, since the intertemporal substitution effect on labor supply from the change in the real interest rate is relatively small. Hence, current equilibrium employment rises from N_1 to N_2, and the current real wage rises from w_1 to w_2. In Figure 13.3, we show the response of average labor productivity, as in Chapter 11. Initially employment is N_1 and output is Y_1, and average labor productivity is the slope of AB. After the increase in current and future total factor productivity, employment increases to N_2 and output to Y_2, with average labor productivity being the slope of AD in the figure. Thus, average labor productivity increases. We could have drawn the figure so that employment increased sufficiently that the slope of AD was smaller than the slope of AB. However, Figure 13.3 is consistent with the results from Kydland and Prescott's model, where N would increase in this circumstance but not enough that Y/N would decrease.

Therefore, as shown in Table 13.1, the real business cycle model qualitatively explains essentially all of the key business cycle regularities. Consumption, investment, employment, the real wage, and average labor productivity are procyclical. Perhaps more importantly, the real business cycle model can also quantitatively replicate some important observations about business cycles, as can be shown if a more sophisticated version of

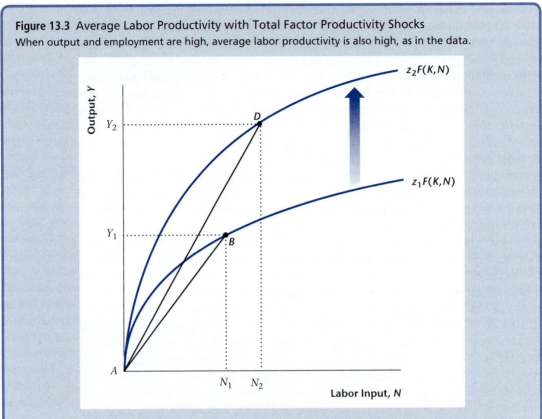

Figure 13.3 Average Labor Productivity with Total Factor Productivity Shocks

When output and employment are high, average labor productivity is also high, as in the data.

Table 13.1 Data versus Predictions of the Real Business Cycle Model with Productivity Shocks

Variable	Data	Model
Consumption	Procyclical	Procyclical
Investment	Procyclical	Procyclical
Employment	Procyclical	Procyclical
Real Wage	Procyclical	Procyclical
Average Labor Productivity	Procyclical	Procyclical

this model is put on a computer and simulated. The model can explain the fact that consumption is less variable than output and that investment is more variable than output. Further, it can approximately replicate the observed relative variabilities in consumption, investment, output, and employment, which were discussed in Chapter 3.[4]

---

[4]See E. Prescott, Fall 1986. "Theory Ahead of Business Cycle Measurement," *Federal Reserve Bank of Minneapolis Quarterly Review* 10, 9–22.

Real Business Cycles and the Behavior of Nominal Variables

LO 13.2 Show how the real business cycle model could be consistent with the observed comovements of money and output.

In the real business cycle model, money is neutral; level changes in M have no effect on real variables and cause a proportionate increase in the price level. In the United States, in earlier time periods, there were strong regularities in the comovements between money supply measures and real GDP, and between the price level and real GDP. Over the last 40 years, roughly, these strong regularities have either disappeared or become more muted. However, we would like a business cycle model to explain these phenomena. Why were there strong regularities, and why did they disappear?

With respect to comovements between the money supply and real economic activity, the following were once strong regularities in U.S. data, for example as documented by Milton Friedman and Ann Schwartz in *A Monetary History of the United States, 1867–1960* (Princeton University Press, Princeton NJ). Friedman and Schwartz found that, in the 1867-1960 U.S. data:

1. The nominal money supply is procyclical.
2. The nominal money supply tends to lead real GDP.

As we show, however, the real business cycle model can be made consistent with these two facts through some straightforward extensions.

First, in the real business cycle model, the procyclicality of the nominal money supply can be explained by way of **endogenous money**. In practice, the money supply is not determined exogenously by the monetary authority but responds to conditions in the economy. Endogenous money can explain the procyclicality of money in two ways, supposing that business cycles are caused by fluctuations in z. First, if our money supply measure is M1, M2, or some broader monetary aggregate, then part of the money supply consists of bank deposits. When aggregate output increases, all sectors in the economy, including the banking sector, tend to experience an increase in activity at the same time. An increase in banking sector activity is reflected in an increase in the quantity of bank deposits and, therefore, in an increase in M1, M2, and the broader monetary aggregates, and we observe the money supply increasing when total factor productivity increases.

Second, the money supply could increase in response to an increase in z because of the response of monetary policy. Suppose that the central bank wishes to stabilize the price level. When there is a persistent increase in total factor productivity, this causes an equilibrium increase in Y, and the real interest rate falls, as we showed above. In Figure 13.4 output increases from Y_1 to Y_2 and the real interest rate falls from r_1 to r_2, so that the nominal money demand curve shifts rightward from $PL(Y_1, r_1)$ to $PL(Y_2, r_2)$. If the central bank did nothing, the price level would fall from P_1 to P_2. However, because the central bank wishes to stabilize the price level, it increases the money supply from M_1 to M_2, shifting the money supply curve from M_1^S to M_2^S. As a result, the money supply is procyclical, as it increases when output increases, in response to the persistent total factor productivity increase.

Figure 13.4 Procyclical Money Supply in the Real Business Cycle Model with Endogenous Money

A persistent increase in total factor productivity increases aggregate real income and reduces the real interest rate, causing money demand to increase. If the central bank attempts to stabilize the price level, this increases the money supply in response to the total factor productivity shock.

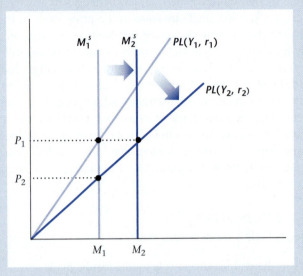

Fact (2) above, that the nominal money supply tends to lead real GDP, appears to be a particular problem, because this might be viewed as strong evidence that money supply fluctuations cause the fluctuations in real GDP. Indeed, this was the interpretation given to fact (2) by Milton Friedman and Anna Schwartz.[5] However, the weak link in Friedman and Schwartz's interpretation of the data is that **statistical causality** need not tell us anything about true causality. A variable a statistically causes a variable b if current a helps predict future b. For example, every year we observe birds flying south before the onset of winter, and so the flight patterns of birds statistically predict the winter. However, birds flying south do not cause winter; it is winter that is causing the birds to fly south.

There is an explanation for the tendency of money to lead output that is analogous to the example of birds flying south for the winter. There are two reasons that productivity shocks could cause money to lead output, again through the process of endogenous money. First, the banking sector tends to lead other sectors of the economy, as banks provide loans for real activity that will occur at a later date. When bank loans increase, so do bank deposits, as a bank borrows by way of bank deposits to finance its lending. Thus, bank deposits tend to be procyclical and to lead real GDP, and, therefore, M1, M2, and broader monetary aggregates tend to lead real GDP. Second, if the monetary authority is trying to stabilize prices, and it uses all available information

---

[5]See M. Friedman and A. Schwartz, 1963. *A Monetary History of the United States, 1867–1960*, Cambridge, MA: National Bureau of Economic Research.

efficiently, it can predict an increase in output due to an increase in z before the output increase is observed. Because an increase in the money supply may take time to affect prices, the monetary authority may want to act on this information before the increase in output and the decrease in the price level actually occur. Thus, money can lead real GDP because of preemptive monetary policy actions.

These ideas can also give us an explanation for why the price level is negatively correlated with real GDP, but this correlation has become negligible in absolute value, as shown in Chapter 3. If, as has been the case since at least 1979 in the United States, the central bank takes more seriously a goal of targeting the price level, the real business cycle model tells us that we should see a low correlation between the price level and real GDP. Indeed, in Figure 13.4, the central bank is successful in pegging the price level in the face of productivity shocks, and what we would observe in the data is zero correlation between the price level and real GDP, as the price level will never move.

Implications of Real Business Cycle Theory for Government Policy

Now that we know how the real business cycle model works and have discussed how it fits the data, we can explore what the model implies for government policy. In the basic real business cycle model, there is no role for government stabilization policy. First, level changes in the money supply are neutral, and so attempts to smooth out business cycles through monetary policy actions have no effect. Second, because all markets clear, and there are no inefficiencies (for example, distorting taxes or externalities) in the basic model that government policy should correct, there is also no reason that the government should vary its spending in response to fluctuations in total factor productivity. Government spending can have an effect on output, but the level of such spending should be set according to the appropriate long-run role of the government in providing public goods (goods and services, such as national defense, that cannot or should not be provided by the private sector), not to smooth short-run fluctuations in aggregate GDP. In the basic real business cycle model, business cycles are essentially optimal responses of the economy to fluctuations in total factor productivity, and nothing should be done about them. Given the first fundamental theorem of welfare economics, from Chapter 5, if the allocation of resources in the economy is Pareto optimal, there is no need for the government to intervene, unless we think the government should redistribute income and wealth.

Though there is no role for government in the basic real business cycle model, other more elaborate versions of this model explain a role for government arising from the need to correct market failures and distortions.[6] For example, in practice all taxes are distorting. Income taxes distort labor supply decisions because firms and workers face different effective wage rates, and sales taxes distort consumer purchasing patterns because firms and consumers do not face the same effective prices for all goods. Over time, it is efficient for the government to smooth out these distortions, or welfare losses, that arise from taxation. This can tell us that tax rates should be smooth over time, which then implies that the government should let total tax revenues rise in booms and fall in recessions, as tax revenue increases with income if the income tax rate is constant.

---

[6] See T. Cooley, 1995. *Frontiers of Business Cycle Research,* Princeton, NJ: Princeton University Press.

This is a kind of countercyclical government policy, which may look like it is intended to stabilize output but is actually aimed at smoothing tax distortions.

Critique of Real Business Cycle Theory

LO 13.3 Discuss criticisms of the real business cycle model.

The real business cycle model clearly does a good job of fitting the key business cycle facts. Real business cycle theory is also internally consistent, and it helps focus our attention on how government policy should act to correct market failures and distortions, rather than on attempting to correct for the fact that prices and wages may not be set efficiently over short periods of time, as in some Keynesian models.

Real business cycle theory certainly has shortcomings, however, in its ability to explain business cycles. One problem is that the assessment of whether or not real business cycle theory fits the data is based on using the Solow residual to measure total factor productivity. There is good reason to believe that there is a large cyclical error in how the Solow residual measures total factor productivity z, and that the close tracking of detrended GDP by the Solow residual in Figure 13.1 might be at least partly explained by measurement error. During a boom, the aggregate capital stock is close to being fully utilized. Most machinery is running full time, and many manufacturing plants are in operation 24 hours per day. Further, the workers who are operating the plant and equipment are very busy. These workers are under pressure to produce output, because demand is high. There are few opportunities to take breaks, and overtime work is common. Thus, workers are being fully utilized as well. Alternatively, in a temporary recession, the aggregate capital stock is not fully utilized, in that some machinery is sitting idle and plants are not running 24 hours per day. Further, during a temporary recession, a firm may not wish to lay workers off (even though there is not much for them to do), because this may mean that these workers would get other jobs and the firm would lose workers having valuable skills that are specific to the firm. Thus, workers employed at the firm during a recession might not be working very hard—they might take long breaks and produce little. In other words, the workforce tends to be underutilized during a recession, just as the aggregate capital stock is. This phenomenon of underutilization of labor during a recession is sometimes called **labor hoarding**.

The underutilization of capital and labor during a recession is a problem for the measurement of total factor productivity, because during recessions the capital stock and the labor input would be measured as being higher than they actually are. Thus, in terms of measurement, we could see a drop in output during a recession and infer that total factor productivity dropped because the Solow residual decreased. But output may have dropped simply because the quantity of inputs in production dropped, with no change in total factor productivity.

To see how this works, consider the following example. Suppose that the production function is Cobb–Douglas with a capital share in output of 30%, as we assumed in calculating Solow residuals in Chapter 7. That is, the production function takes the form

$$Y = zK^{0.3}N^{0.7},$$ (13-1)

where Y is aggregate output, z is total factor productivity, K is the capital stock, and N is employment. Now, suppose that initially $z = 1$, $K = 100$, and $N = 50$, so that from Equation (13-1) we have $Y = 61.6$, and capital and labor are fully utilized. Then, suppose that a recession occurs that is not the result of a drop in total factor productivity, so that $z = 1$ as before. Firms still have capital on hand equal to 100 units, and employment is still 50 units, and so measured capital is $K = 100$ and measured employment is $N = 50$. However, suppose only 95% of the capital in existence is actually being used in production (the rest is shut down), so that actual capital is $K = 95$. Further, suppose the employed workforce is being used only 90% as intensively as before, with workers actually putting in only 90% of the time working that they were formerly. Thus, actual employment is $N = 45$. Plugging $z = 1$, $K = 95$, and $N = 45$ into Equation (13-1), we get $Y = 56.3$. Now, if we mistakenly used the measured capital stock, measured employment, and measured output to calculate the Solow residual, we would obtain

$$\hat{z} = \frac{56.3}{(100)^{0.3}(50)^{0.7}} = 0.915,$$

where $\hat{z}$ is the Solow residual or measured total factor productivity. Therefore, we would measure total factor productivity as having decreased by 8.5%, when it really had not changed at all. This shows how decreases in the utilization of factors of production during recessions can lead to biases in the measurement of total factor productivity and to biases in the evaluation of the importance of total factor productivity shocks for business cycles.

A Keynesian Coordination Failure Model

LO 13.4 Construct the Keynesian coordination failure model, explain how it matches key business cycle facts, and use the model to analyze other problems.

The equilibrium theory of the business cycle that we have discussed thus far in this chapter—real business cycle theory—implies that the government has no role in stabilizing the economy. However, this does not mean that all equilibrium theories of the business cycle imply skepticism about the role of the government in smoothing business cycles. Some modern Keynesians adopt an approach to macroeconomics very similar to that of classical economists, in assuming that prices and wages are fully flexible and that all markets clear. Some of these modern Keynesians explore an idea that one can find in Keynes's *General Theory*, the notion of **coordination failure**. In macroeconomics, coordination failures were first studied rigorously by Peter Diamond in the early 1980s,[7] and later contributions were by Russell Cooper and Andrew John,[8]

---

[7] See P. Diamond, 1982. "Aggregate Demand in Search Equilibrium," *Journal of Political Economy* 90, 881–894.

[8] R. Cooper and A. John, 1988. "Coordinating Coordination Failures in Keynesian Models," *Quarterly Journal of Economics* 103, 441–463.

MACROECONOMICS IN ACTION

Business Cycle Models and the Great Depression

The Great Depression was a unique event in U.S. macroeconomic history. The Great Depression began in 1929, and real GDP declined for about four years, decreasing by 31% from 1929 to 1933. It then took another seven years for real GDP to recover to its 1929 level. Relative to the average post–World War II recession, the length and size of the decline in output during the Great Depression were very large, and the recovery took a particularly long time. In the average post–World War II recession, GDP declined by 2.9% after about one year and then recovered in one-and-a-half years. Was the Great Depression essentially a larger-scale version of a recession that otherwise looks much like a typical post–World War II recession, or do standard macroeconomic theories of the business cycle fail to explain the behavior of the U.S. economy during the Great Depression? In an article in the *Federal Reserve Bank of Minneapolis Quarterly Review*, Harold Cole and Lee Ohanian set out to answer this question.[9]

Cole and Ohanian look at several business cycle theories, including the real business cycle model and the Keynesian sticky wage model (related to the sticky price model that we will study in Chapter 14), to see how well these models fit the data for the Great Depression. The Keynesian sticky wage model does not fare very well. During the Great Depression, there was a large decline in the money supply. In a

typical Keynesian sticky wage model, this would reduce the price level, and then, given a sticky nominal wage, the real wage would rise, and this would cause firms to hire less labor, with output decreasing. In the manufacturing sector, real wages increased while output was declining from 1929 to 1933, but outside of manufacturing the real wage fell precipitously over this period, and nonmanufacturing real wages were still much below trend in 1939. These data do not appear to be consistent with broad-based stickiness in nominal wages being a major influence during the Great Depression.

Cole and Ohanian find that shocks to total factor productivity can explain the decline in aggregate output from 1929 to 1933, but cannot explain the slow recovery. Similar results are obtained for the money surprise model. Estimated total factor productivity shocks and money surprises during the Great Depression predict that the recovery should have happened much earlier than it did.

Thus, the problem with standard theories of the business cycle, when confronted with the Great Depression, is primarily in explaining the long and weak recovery. What is Cole and Ohanian's alternative explanation for the length of the recovery during the Great Depression? They conjecture that regulation was the culprit. The National Industrial Recovery Act of 1933 suspended U.S. antitrust laws and permitted more collusion among firms, particularly in the manufacturing sector. More collusion among firms in an industry tends to reduce output, raise prices, and lower investment—all features consistent with the Great Depression.

---

[9]See H. Cole and L. Ohanian, Winter 1999. "The Great Depression in the United States from a Neoclassical Perspective," *Federal Reserve Bank of Minneapolis Quarterly Review* 23, 2–24.

Jess Benhabib and Roger Farmer,[10] and Roger Farmer and Jang-Ting Guo.[11] The basic idea in coordination failure models is that it is difficult for private sector workers and producers to coordinate their actions, and there exist **strategic complementarities**, which imply that one person's willingness to engage in some activity increases with the number of other people engaged in that activity.

An example of an activity with a strategic complementarity is a party. If Paul knows that someone wishes to hold a party and that only a few other people will be going, he will probably not want to go. However, if many people are going, this will be much more fun, and Paul will likely go. Paul's potential enjoyment of the party increases with the number of other people who are likely to go. We might imagine that there are two possible outcomes (equilibria) here. One outcome is that no one goes, and another is that everyone goes. These are equilibria because, if no one goes to the party, then no individual would want to go, and if everyone goes to the party, then no individual would want to stay at home. If Paul could coordinate with other people, then everyone would certainly agree that having everyone go to the party would be a good idea, and they could all agree to go. However, without coordination, it is possible that no one goes.

If we use the party as an analogy to aggregate economic activity, the willingness of one producer to produce may depend on what other producers are doing. For example, if Jennifer is a computer software producer, the quantity of software she can sell depends on the quantity and quality of computer hardware that is sold. If more hardware is sold, it is easier for Jennifer to sell software, and if Jennifer sells more software, it is easier to sell hardware. Computer hardware and computer software are complementary. Many such complementarities exist in the economy, and different producers find it difficult to coordinate their actions. Thus, it is possible that there may be **multiple equilibria** for the aggregate economy, whereby output and employment might be high, or output and employment might be low. Business cycles might simply be fluctuations between these high and low equilibria, driven by waves of optimism and pessimism.

To formalize this idea in an economic model, we start with the notion that there are aggregate increasing returns to scale, which implies that output more than doubles if all inputs double, as discussed in Chapter 4. Until now, we have assumed constant returns to scale, which implies that the marginal product of labor is diminishing when the quantity of capital is fixed. Increasing returns to scale at the aggregate level can be due to the strategic complementarities that we discussed above. We can then have increasing returns to scale at the aggregate level in a situation where, for each individual firm, there are constant returns to scale in production. With sufficient aggregate increasing returns to scale, the aggregate production function, fixing the quantity of capital, can be convex, as in Figure 13.5. Then, because the slope of the production function in the figure increases with the labor input, the marginal product of labor for the aggregate economy is increasing rather than decreasing. Because the aggregate

---

[10]See J. Benhabib and R. Farmer, 1994. "Indeterminacy and Increasing Returns," *Journal of Economic Theory 63,* 19–41.

[11]See R. Farmer and J. Guo, 1994. "Real Business Cycles and the Animal Spirits Hypothesis," *Journal of Economic Theory 63,* 42–72.

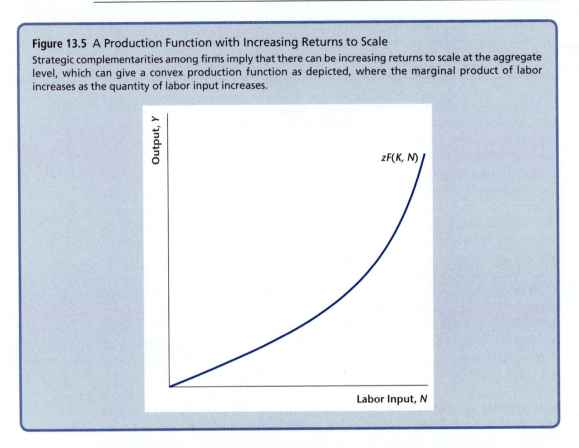

Figure 13.5 A Production Function with Increasing Returns to Scale

Strategic complementarities among firms imply that there can be increasing returns to scale at the aggregate level, which can give a convex production function as depicted, where the marginal product of labor increases as the quantity of labor input increases.

demand for labor is just the aggregate marginal product of labor schedule, this implies that the aggregate labor demand curve N^d can be upward sloping as in Figure 13.6.

Now, for the coordination failure theory to work, the aggregate labor demand curve must have a greater slope than the labor supply curve, as in Figure 13.7. To repeat the exercise from Chapter 11 where we derived the output supply curve Y^s, suppose that the real interest rate is r_1, with the labor supply curve $N^s(r_1)$ in Figure 13.8(c). Then the equilibrium quantity of employment would be N_1 and output would be Y_1, from the production function in Figure 13.8(b). Therefore, an output-real interest rate pair implying equilibrium in the labor market is (Y_1, r_1) in Figure 13.8(a). Now, if the real interest rate is higher, say r_2, then the labor supply curve shifts rightward to $N^s(r_2)$ in Figure 13.8(c), because workers wish to substitute future leisure for current leisure. As a result, the equilibrium quantity of employment falls to N_2 and output falls to Y_2. Thus, another point on the output supply curve in Figure 13.8(a) is (Y_2, r_2), and the Y^s curve is downward-sloping.

The Coordination Failure Model: An Example

We now consider a simple example that shows some of the key insights that come from coordination failure models. Suppose that the downward-sloping Y^s curve and the downward-sloping Y^d curve intersect at just two places (though this need not be the case; there could be more than two intersections, or there could be only one), as in

Figure 13.6 Aggregate Labor Demand with Sufficient Increasing Returns to Scale

With sufficient increasing returns to scale, the aggregate labor demand curve slopes upward, as the aggregate marginal product of labor increases with aggregate employment.

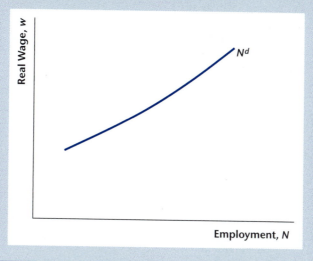

Figure 13.7 The Labor Market in the Coordination Failure Model

With sufficient increasing returns, the labor demand curve is steeper than the labor supply curve, which is required for the coordination failure model to work.

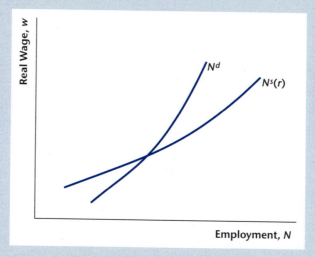

Figure 13.8 The Output Supply Curve in the Coordination Failure Model

The figure shows the construction of the output supply curve Y^s in the coordination failure model. An increase in the real interest rate shifts the labor supply curve to the right, reducing employment and output.

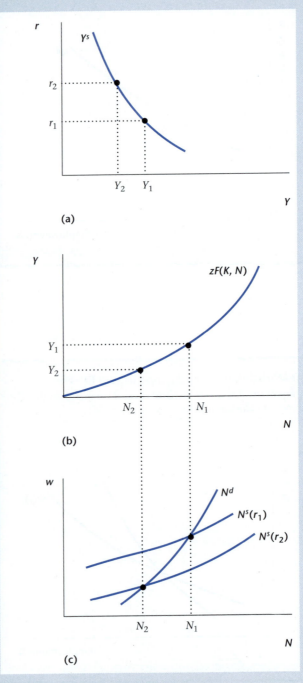

Figure 13.9b. Here, the economy could be in one of two equilibria. In the first, the "bad equilibrium," output is Y_1, the real interest rate is r_1, the price level is P_1, the real wage is w_1, and employment is N_1. In the second, the "good equilibrium," output is Y_2, the real interest rate is r_2, the price level is P_2, the real wage is w_2, and employment is N_2. In a more explicit version of this model, which would have a description of consumers' preferences, consumers would be better off in the good equilibrium with high output and employment than in the bad equilibrium with low output and employment.

Will the economy be in the good equilibrium or the bad equilibrium? There is certainly nothing to prevent the bad equilibrium from arising. Even though everyone prefers the good equilibrium, the bad equilibrium could arise if everyone is pessimistic and expects bad things to happen. Similarly, the good equilibrium arises if everyone is optimistic. In this model, business cycles could result if consumers and firms are alternately optimistic and pessimistic, so that the economy alternates between the good equilibrium and the bad equilibrium. This seems much like what Keynes referred to as "animal spirits," the waves of optimism and pessimism that he viewed as being an important determinant of investment.

In the coordination failure model, it is possible that extraneous events that are completely unrelated to economic fundamentals (technology, preferences, and endowments) can "cause" business cycles. Macroeconomists sometimes call such extraneous events **sunspots**, in analogy to the irregular occurrence of dark spots observed on the sun, because a dark spot on the sun does not affect production possibilities, preferences, or available resources (i.e., anything fundamental) on earth. However, sunspots are in principle observable to everyone. Therefore, if workers and firms all treat the observation of a sunspot as a sign of optimism, then the economy goes to the good equilibrium when a sunspot is observed, and it goes to the bad equilibrium when no sunspot is observed. It then appears that sunspots are causing business cycles. The behavior of the stock market is perhaps most indicative of the presence of "sunspot behavior," in that there is much more variability in stock prices than can be explained by fluctuations in fundamentals (the earnings potential of firms). Alan Greenspan, the former chairman of the Federal Reserve Board, once referred to the stock market as being under the influence of "irrational exuberance." Sunspot behavior in the economy need not literally be driven by sunspots, but by events with no connection to anything fundamentally important to preferences, endowments, and technology.

Predictions of the Coordination Failure Model

From Figure 13.9, the good equilibrium has a low real interest rate, a high level of output, a low price level, a high level of employment, and a high real wage. The bad equilibrium has a high real interest rate, a low level of output, a high price level, a low level of employment, and a low real wage. Thus, given the low (high) real interest rate, the good (bad) equilibrium has a high (low) level of consumption and investment. Therefore, if business cycles are fluctuations between the good and bad equilibrium, then, as in Table 13.2, consumption, investment, and employment are procyclical, and the real wage is procyclical, just as observed in the data. As well, in Figure 13.10 average labor productivity (the slope of a ray from the origin to the relevant point on the production function) must be procyclical, as it is higher in the good equilibrium than

Figure 13.9 Multiple Equilibria in the Coordination Failure Model

Because the output supply curve is downward-sloping in the coordination failure model, there can be two equilibria, as in this example. In one equilibrium, aggregate output is low and the real interest rate is high; in the other, aggregate output is high and the real interest rate is low.

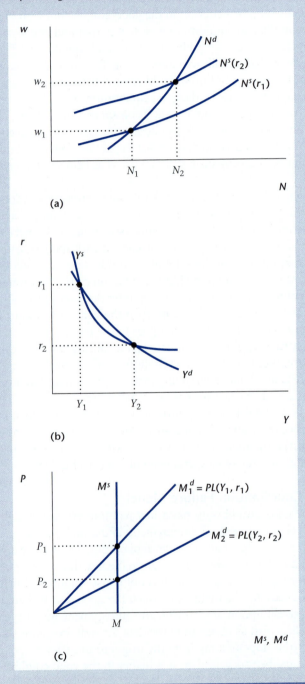

Table 13.2 Data versus Predictions of the Coordination Failure Model

Variable	Data	Model
Consumption	Procyclical	Procyclical
Investment	Procyclical	Procyclical
Employment	Procyclical	Procyclical
Real Wage	Procyclical	Procyclical
Average Labor Productivity	Procyclical	Procyclical

Figure 13.10 Average Labor Productivity in the Keynesian Coordination Failure Model

In the good (bad) equilibrium, output is high (low), employment is high (low), and average labor productivity is high (low).

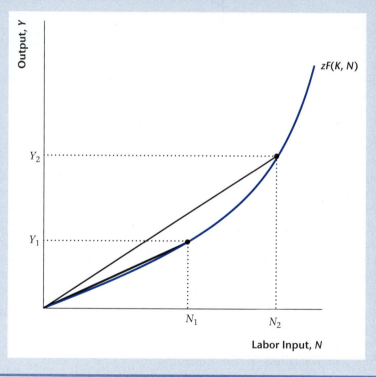

in the bad equilibrium. Further, Roger Farmer and Jang-Ting Guo have shown that a version of the coordination failure model does essentially as well as the real business cycle model in quantitatively replicating U.S. business cycle behavior.[12]

---

[12]See R. Farmer and J. Guo, 1994. "Real Business Cycles and the Animal Spirits Hypothesis," *Journal of Economic Theory* 63, 42–72.

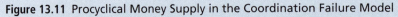

Figure 13.11 Procyclical Money Supply in the Coordination Failure Model

If the money supply is a sunspot variable in the coordination failure model, then money may appear to be nonneutral because people believe it to be. When the money supply is high (low), everyone is optimistic (pessimistic), and output is high (low).

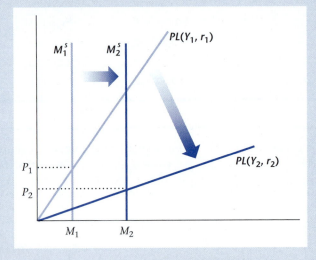

Though money is neutral in the coordination failure model, as it is in the real business cycle model, the coordination failure model can explain why the nominal money supply has been procyclical at times in the past. Suppose that the money supply fluctuates between M_1 and M_2, where $M_2 > M_1$. Also, suppose that money acts as a sunspot variable. That is, when consumers and firms observe a high money supply, they are optimistic, and when they observe a low money supply, they are pessimistic. Therefore, when the money supply is high, the economy is in the good equilibrium, and when the money supply is low, the economy is in the bad equilibrium, and people's expectations are self-fulfilling. In Figure 13.11, we can still have the price level moving countercyclically, provided money supply does not fluctuate too much. In the good equilibrium, nominal money demand is $PL(Y_2, r_2)$, and in the bad equilibrium, nominal money demand is $PL(Y_1, r_1)$. Money supply increases in the good equilibrium from M_1 to M_2, and the price level falls from P_1 to P_2. Here, though money is actually neutral, it can appear to be causing business cycles.

Policy Implications of the Coordination Failure Model

In terms of how they match the data, the coordination failure and real business cycle models are essentially indistinguishable. However, the two models have very different policy implications. In the real business cycle model, decreases in output and employment are just optimal responses to a decline in total factor productivity, while in the coordination failure model, the good equilibrium is in principle an opportunity available in the aggregate economy when the bad equilibrium is realized. Thus, if we believe this model, then government policies that promote optimism would be beneficial. For

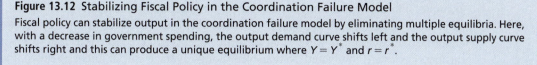

Figure 13.12 Stabilizing Fiscal Policy in the Coordination Failure Model

Fiscal policy can stabilize output in the coordination failure model by eliminating multiple equilibria. Here, with a decrease in government spending, the output demand curve shifts left and the output supply curve shifts right and this can produce a unique equilibrium where $Y = Y^*$ and $r = r^*$.

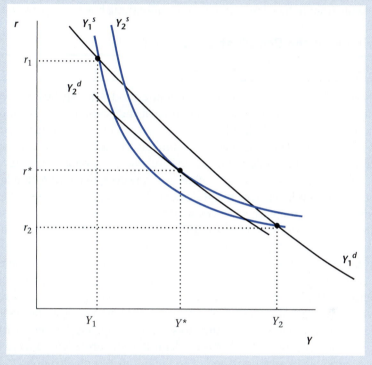

example, encouraging statements by public officials, such as the treasury secretary or the chairman of the Federal Reserve Board, could in principle bump the economy from the bad equilibrium to the good equilibrium.

Policy could also be designed to smooth business cycles or to eliminate them altogether in the coordination failure model. As an example, consider Figure 13.12, where there are initially two equilibria, a bad equilibrium where the real interest rate is r_1 and the level of output is Y_1, and a good equilibrium where the real interest rate is r_2 and the level of output is Y_2. Then, suppose that the government reduces current government spending G. Recall from Chapter 11 that a decrease in current government spending reduces the present value of taxes, causing a decrease in current labor supply. Here, this shifts the output supply curve to the right (not to the left as in Chapter 11) from Y_1^s to Y_2^s in the figure. Further, recall from Chapter 11 that we know that a decrease in G shifts the output demand curve leftward from Y_1^d to Y_2^d. If the government reduces G by just the right amount, then there is only one equilibrium, where $Y = Y^*$ and $r = r^*$, as in the figure. Effectively, the bad equilibrium gets better and the good equilibrium gets worse, because of the decrease in G, and there are no business cycles. It is not clear whether eliminating business cycles in this manner is advantageous. For example, if in the absence of the decrease in *G* the economy was in the good equilibrium most of the time, then average welfare could go down when business cycles are eliminated. It could be, however, that there are benefits from reduced uncertainty when business cycles are eliminated, so that even though average output might go down, the benefits from reduced uncertainty from smoothing business cycles could be beneficial.

Critique of the Coordination Failure Model

LO 13.5 Discuss criticisms of the Keynesian coordination failure model.

The key insight of the coordination failure model is that business cycles can result simply from self-fulfilling waves of optimism and pessimism. As mentioned previously, the existence of these self-fulfilling expectations appears to be most evident in the case of the stock market, where it seems difficult to explain the wild gyrations that occur daily as being the result of changes in fundamental economic factors.

There are some potential weaknesses, however, in coordination failure theories of the business cycle. First, a critical element of the coordination failure theory is that there exist sufficient increasing returns to scale in aggregate production that the aggregate labor demand curve slopes upward and is steeper than the aggregate labor supply curve. If aggregate production is subject to constant returns to scale or decreasing returns to scale, then this theory is a nonstarter. In practice, the measurement of returns to scale in aggregate production is very imprecise. Some researchers claim to find evidence of increasing returns in the data, but others do not. A good reference for this issue is the work by Harold Cole and Lee Ohanian.[13] At best, the evidence supporting the existence of increasing returns to scale at the aggregate level is weak.

Second, a problem with this model is that the underlying shocks that cause business cycles are expectations, and expectations are essentially unobservable. This makes it difficult to use the theory to understand historical recessions and booms.

Business Cycle Theories and the 2008–2009 Recession

LO 13.6 Explain how the business cycle models in this chapter are, or are not, consistent with the observed behavior of U.S. time series during the 2008–2009 recession.

During and following the global financial crisis and the recession of 2008–2009, macroeconomists came under criticism, in some cases from other economists. For example, Paul Krugman, winner of the 2008 Nobel Prize in Economics, argued that macroeconomists had failed dramatically, not only in giving no warning of the impending financial crisis, but in focusing their research efforts during the rational expectations revolution on models that could not explain an event like the 2008–2009 recession.[14] To what extent are such criticisms warranted?

---

[13]See H. Cole and L. Ohanian, Summer 1999. "Aggregate Returns to Scale: Why Measurement Is Imprecise," *Federal Reserve Bank of Minneapolis Quarterly Review* 23, 19–28.

[14]See P. Krugman, 2009. "How Did Economists Get It So Wrong?" *New York Times Magazine*, September 2, 2009, http://www.nytimes.com/2009/09/06/magazine/06Economic-t.html.

We know from our study of the two business cycle models in this chapter that it is hard to choose between these two models based on how they fit the aggregate time series data. Both models are roughly consistent with observed regularities in the comovements in the data. So, how do the models do in fitting the 2008–2009 recession? In Figure 13.13, we show the Solow residual and real GDP for the period 2005–2012, a period long enough to include the recession, along with the lead-in to the recession, and the recovery. In the figure, each time series is normalized to 100 at the beginning of 2005. The figure shows a drop in the Solow residual coinciding with a drop in real GDP, which is consistent with a real business cycle explanation of the 2008–2009 recession. However, if the decrease in the Solow residual accurately measures a drop in total factor productivity (TFP), then the magnitude of the decline in TFP does not seem consistent with TFP playing an important role in the recession. In Figure 13.1, TFP tends to be less variable on

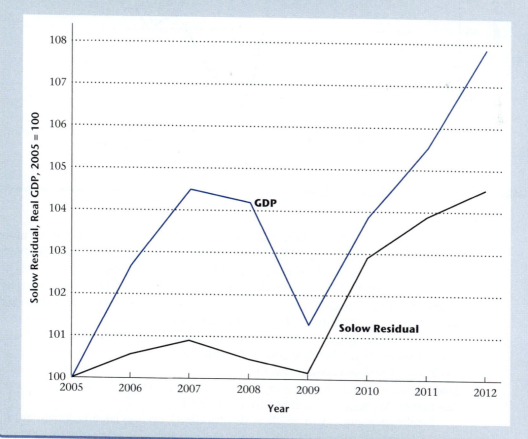

Figure 13.13 The Solow Residual and Real GDP, 2005–2012

During the 2008–2009 recession, total factor productivity appears to have dropped only a small amount, and so does not seem to have been a key contributing factor to the recession. Time series are normalized to 100 as of the first quarter of 2005.

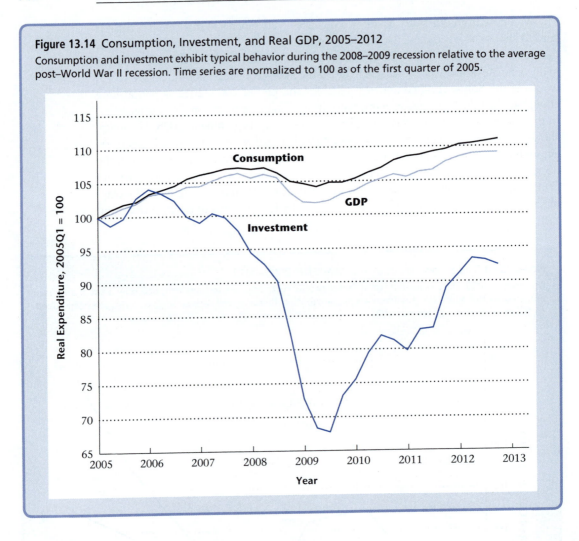

Figure 13.14 Consumption, Investment, and Real GDP, 2005–2012

Consumption and investment exhibit typical behavior during the 2008–2009 recession relative to the average post–World War II recession. Time series are normalized to 100 as of the first quarter of 2005.

average than GDP, but only by a small amount. Further, as discussed previously in this chapter, the Solow residual could be biased as a measure of TFP, and the drop we observe in TFP during the 2008–2009 recession could just be measurement error.

Next, Figure 13.14 shows a fairly typical pattern of consumption and investment behavior during a recession (again, all time series are normalized to 100 at the beginning of 2005). Consumption declines less than real GDP, and behaves in a smooth fashion, while the decline in investment is much larger than the decline in real GDP. These time series are therefore consistent with the average behavior we characterized in Chapter 3, and also consistent with what the two models in this chapter predict. But, from Figure 13.13 we have reason to doubt that the 2008–2009 recession is a real business cycle phenomenon driven by a TFP shock.

Finally, in Figure 13.15 we show the price level, average labor productivity, and real GDP for the period 2005–2012, again normalizing each time series to 100 in the

Figure 13.15 The Price Level, Average Labor Productivity, and Real GDP, 2005–2012

The price level dropped below trend, and average labor productivity was higher at the end of the 2008–2009 recession than at the beginning. Both of these facts are inconsistent with the two business cycle theories studied in this chapter. Time series are normalized to 100 as of the first quarter of 2005.

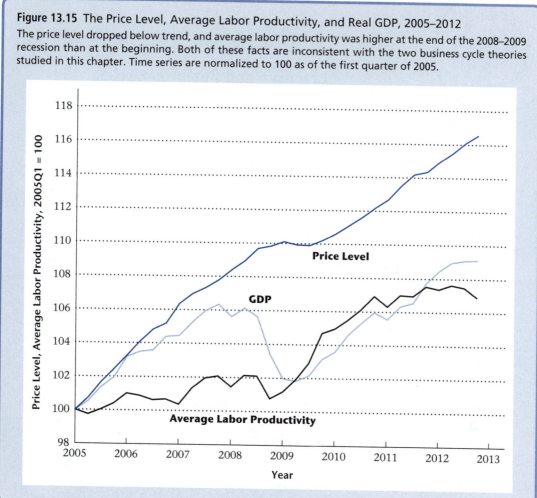

first quarter of 2005. The price level declines modestly from trend during the recession, which is consistent with neither business cycle theory we have examined in this chapter. In both business cycle models, output declines and the real interest rate rises during a recession, which reduces money demand and increases the price level. Further, when the recession ends in mid-2009, average labor productivity is actually higher than at the beginning of the recession in early 2008. This is inconsistent with both theories in that each predicts procyclical average labor productivity. So, according to the theories, since real GDP went down, average labor productivity should have gone down as well.

The behavior of average labor productivity in the 2008–2009 recession highlights one difference in the behavior of aggregate time series from the typical post–World War II recession. Anecdotally, of course, the 2008–2009 recession was an unusual event in that it is typically ascribed to financial factors. If that is the case, then the business cycle models of this chapter have neglected important features of the economy. While

MACROECONOMICS IN ACTION
Uncertainty and Business Cycles

Features of the 2008–2009 recession, including the weak recovery in some parts of the world, particularly the United States and Europe, have generated much interest in the role of uncertainty in the recession, and in previous recessions as well. Aggregate uncertainty can come from the private sector, the public sector, or both.

With respect to the private sector, aggregate economic activity could be depressed because economic agents have observed events that cause them to be more pessimistic about future productivity growth, for example. From Chapter 11, we know that a decline in anticipated future productivity reduces current investment expenditures and current real GDP. An increase in uncertainty can have the same effects, as firms become more cautious and less likely to invest. The recent financial crisis in itself could have caused more uncertainty, as economic agents may have revised their beliefs about the future volatility of the aggregate economy.

The public sector can also generate its own uncertainty. If firms are uncertain about future taxes and future regulatory constraints, these firms could be more reluctant to hire workers or to invest. Also, workers could react to higher uncertainty about future tax rates by working less, or by investing less in their own training.

A working paper by Nicholas Bloom, Max Floetotto, and Nir Jaimovich[16], studies an extension of a real business cycle model that allows for these types of uncertainty. In their model, firms can be uncertain about factors that affect their own productivity, and about factors affecting aggregate productivity. Because it is costly for firms to adjust their capital and labor inputs, a higher degree of uncertainty will cause firms to be cautious, because they do not want to invest more today or hire more workers, if it is likely they will have to reverse these decisions in the future. Thus, recessions tend to be associated with a higher degree of uncertainty in their model.

Bloom, Floetetto, and Jaimovich find strong empirical evidence that increased uncertainty is a regular feature of all recessions, and not only of the 2008–2009 recession. Further, an increase in uncertainty will tend to be associated with a lower Solow residual. Thus, some of what we are measuring as decreases in total factor productivity in a recession could actually be a symptom of higher uncertainty.

With respect to uncertainty created by the government, there has been much public speculation about the uncertainty created by economic policymakers, but little empirical evidence to go on. However, two researchers at the Cleveland Federal Reserve Bank, Mark Schweitzer and Scott Shane,[17] find evidence that uncertainty about economic policy has a significant negative effect on the behavior of small businesses.

Thus, we can say in general that economic uncertainty has been important for business cycle activity, and particularly for the 2008–2009 recession. The evidence is strong that

---

[16]N. Bloom, M. Floetotto, and N. Jaimovich, 2011. "Really Uncertain Business Cycles," working paper, Stanford University.

[17]M. Schweitzer and S. Shane, 2011. "Economic Policy Uncertainty and Small Business Expansion," Cleveland Federal Reserve Bank Economic Commentary, http://cleveland-fed.org/research/commentary/2011/2011-24.cfm.

private sector factors play an important role in aggregate uncertainty. However, while economic policy could potentially create a good deal of uncertainty, there is no overwhelming evidence that it has been important for the 2008–2009 recession.

behavior in credit markets—what we studied in Chapter 9—was important in building up these models, both business cycle models have no credit market frictions. For example, features like asymmetric information, limited commitment, and the role of collateral—as studied, for example, in Chapter 10—are not a part of real business cycle theory or Keynesian coordination failure theory.

Some economists—Paul Krugman, for example—have attempted to make the case that a wholesale revamping of macroeconomics was in order in light of the financial crisis. However, macroeconomists have certainly not thrown out their toolkit and started over in the years following the financial crisis, and for good reason. While much was learned in the financial crisis and after, in 2008 there was also much off-the-shelf economic theory that only needed to be brought into the foreground to help make sense of what was going on. Indeed, Christiano et al. (2014) argue that a sufficiently rich macroeconomic model, incorporating conventional economic theory—particularly credit frictions—can successfully account for the behavior of U.S. time series during the 2008–2009 recession.[15]

This completes our study of business cycle models with flexible prices and wages. In Chapter 14 we will analyze a New Keynesian model with sticky prices.

Chapter Summary

- In this chapter, we constructed two different equilibrium models of the business cycle, and we evaluated these models in terms of how they fit the data, their policy predictions, and their plausibility.

- The first model studied in this chapter is the real business cycle model, in which business cycles are explained by persistent fluctuations in total factor productivity. The real business cycle model is consistent with all the business cycle facts from Chapter 3, and endogenous money can explain the regularities in the behavior of the nominal money supply relative to real aggregate output.

- The basic real business cycle model has no role for government policy, since business cycles are simply optimal responses to fluctuations in total factor productivity.

- The real business cycle model is not always successful in explaining historical business cycle events, and there are measurement problems in using the Solow residual as a measure of total factor productivity.

- The second model studied here is the Keynesian coordination failure model, which is based on the existence of strategic complementarities giving rise to increasing returns to scale at the

---

[15]L. Christiano, M. Eichenbaum, and M. Trabandt, 2014. "Understanding the Great Recession," NBER working paper \#20040.

aggregate level. This implies that there can be multiple equilibria, and we considered an example in which the model had two equilibria: a good equilibrium with high output, consumption, investment, employment, and real wage, and a low real interest rate and price level; and a bad equilibrium with low output, consumption, investment employment, and real wage, and a high real interest rate and price level. The economy could then fluctuate between these two equilibria, with fluctuations driven by waves of optimism and pessimism.

- Money is neutral in the Keynesian coordination failure model, but it could be a sunspot variable that produces optimism and pessimism, thus making it appear that money is not neutral.

- The coordination failure model does as well as the real business cycle model in fitting the data. The role for government policy in the coordination failure model could be to produce optimism, and there may be a role for fiscal policy in smoothing out business cycles.

- During the 2008–2009 recession, the decline in total factor productivity was small, the price level fell relative to trend, and average labor productivity rose. Thus, the recent recession appears inconsistent with the business cycle theories in this chapter.

Key Terms

Endogenous money The concept that the money supply is not exogenous but depends on other aggregate economic variables because of the behavior of the banking system and the central bank. (p. 485)

Statistical causality When an economic variable a helps predict the future values of an economic variable b, we say that a statistically causes b. (p. 486)

Labor hoarding The process by which firms may not lay off workers during a recession, even though those workers are not as busy on the job as they might be. (p. 488)

Coordination failure A situation in which economic agents cannot coordinate their actions, producing a bad equilibrium. (p. 489)

Strategic complementarities Relationships in which actions taken by others encourage a particular firm or consumer to take the same action. (p. 491)

Multiple equilibria The presence of more than one equilibrium in an economic model. (p. 491)

Sunspot An economic variable that has no effect on aggregate production possibilities or on consumers' preferences. (p. 495)

Questions for Review

13.1 What were the two main principles introduced in the rational expectations revolution?
13.2 Why is it useful to study different models of the business cycle?
13.3 What causes output to fluctuate in the real business cycle model?
13.4 Why is money neutral in the real business cycle model?
13.5 How can the real business cycle model explain the behavior of the money supply over the business cycle?
13.6 Should the government act to stabilize output in the real business cycle model?
13.7 Does the real business cycle model fit the data?
13.8 What are the important shortcomings of the real business cycle model?
13.9 Describe an example of a coordination failure problem.
13.10 What causes business cycles in the coordination failure model?
13.11 Why is money neutral in the coordination failure model?
13.12 Does the coordination failure model fit the data?

13.13 Which is the better macro model, the real business cycle model or the coordination failure model? Explain.

13.14 In what ways was the 2008–2009 recession consistent or inconsistent with the two business cycle theories in this chapter?

13.15 Does the 2008–2009 recession mean that macroeconomists have failed and should start over?

Problems

1. **LO 1** In the real business cycle model, suppose that government spending increases temporarily. Determine the equilibrium effects of this. Could business cycles be explained by fluctuations in *G*? That is, does the model replicate the key business cycle facts from Chapter 3 when subjected to temporary shocks to government spending? Explain carefully.

2. **LO 1** Suppose that temporary increases in government spending lead to permanent increases in total factor productivity, perhaps because some government spending improves infrastructure and makes private firms more productive. Show that temporary shocks to government spending of this type could lead to business cycles that are consistent with the key business cycle facts, and explain your results.

3. **LO 1** In the real business cycle model, suppose that firms become infected with optimism and they expect that total factor productivity will be much higher in the future.
   (a) Determine the equilibrium effects of this.
   (b) If waves of optimism and pessimism of this sort cause GDP to fluctuate, does the model explain the key business cycle facts?
   (c) Suppose that the monetary authority wants to stabilize the price level in the face of a wave of optimism. Determine what it should do, and explain.

4. **LO 4** Suppose that money plays the role of a sunspot variable in the coordination failure model, so that the economy is in the bad equilibrium when the money supply is low and in the good equilibrium when the money supply is high. Explain what the monetary authority could do to make consumers better off. Compare this prescription for monetary policy with the one coming from the money surprise model, and discuss.

5. **LO 4** In the coordination failure model, suppose that consumers' preferences shift so that they want to consume less leisure and more consumption goods. Determine the effects on aggregate variables in the good equilibrium and in the bad equilibrium, and explain your results.

6. **LO 1** Suppose that there is a natural disaster that destroys some of the nation's capital stock. The central bank's goal is to stabilize the price level. Given this goal, what should the central bank do in response to the natural disaster? Explain with the aid of diagrams.

7. **LO 1, 4** Suppose that the central bank observes a drop in real GDP, but does not know what caused this drop.
   (a) How would the central bank respond if it believed that GDP dropped because of a decline in total factor productivity, and that real business cycle theory is correct?
   (b) How would the central bank respond if it believed that GDP dropped because of a wave of pessimism, and that the Keynesian coordination failure model is correct?
   (c) Explain your answers to (a) and (b) with the aid of diagrams.

8. **LO 1** Suppose there is a liquidity trap, as studied in Chapter 12. In the real business cycle model, what does this imply about the comovements we should observe between money, the price level, and output? Discuss, with the aid of a diagram.

9. **LO 4** Suppose a liquidity trap, as studied in Chapter 12. We know that conventional monetary policy does not matter in a liquidity trap. However, show that, in the coordination failure model, monetary policy could act as a signal that coordinates private actions on a good equliibrium. Use a diagram, and discuss your results.

Working with the Data

Answer these questions using the Federal Reserve Bank of St. Louis's FRED database, accessible at http://research.stlouisfed.org/fred2/

1. Plot the percentage changes in quarterly real GDP and in quarterly M2. Is there a tendency for changes in M2 to precede changes in the same direction in real GDP? Comment on what you see in your chart.

2. Plot the monetary base and real GDP for the period 2007–2015. Do you see any connection? Discuss.

3. Plot a measure of the real interest rate, measured as the difference between the 3-month Treasury bill rate and the 12-month CPI inflation rate, and real GDP, for the period 2005–2012. Is what you observe consistent with the business cycle models in this chapter? Discuss.

Chapter 14

New Keynesian Economics: Sticky Prices

Learning Objectives

After studying Chapter 14, students will be able to:

14.1 Construct the New Keynesian model with sticky prices.

14.2 Demonstrate that money is not neutral in the New Keynesian model.

14.3 Show how government policy—both monetary and fiscal policy—works in the New Keynesian sticky price model.

14.4 Show the implications of the New Keynesian model for what we should see in the data, assuming optimal monetary policy.

14.5 Construct a liquidity trap equilibrium in the New Keynesian model, and show how negative interest rate policy works.

14.6 Explain the criticisms of New Keynesian models.

Keynesian ideas have been with us since Keynes wrote his *General Theory*[1] in 1936. Keynesians argue that wages and prices are imperfectly flexible or "sticky" in the short run, with the result that supply may not equal demand (in the usual sense) in all markets in the economy at each point in time. The implication, as Keynesians argue, is that government intervention through fiscal and monetary policy can improve aggregate economic outcomes by smoothing out business cycles.

Business cycle models based on these Keynesian ideas have been very influential among both academics and policymakers, and continue to be so. The basic formal modeling framework underlying these models was developed by Hicks in the late 1930s[2] in his "IS-LM" model and popularized in Paul Samuelson's textbook in the

---

[1]See J. M. Keynes, 1936. "The General Theory of Employment, Interest, and Money," London, Macmillan.

[2]J. Hicks, 1937. "Mr. Keynes and the Classics: A Suggested Interpretation," *Econometrica* 5, 147–159.

1950s. In the 1960s, large-scale versions of these Keynesian business cycle models were fit to data and used in policy analysis.

Since the 1960s, Keynesians have adapted their models and ideas to the newer methods and ideas coming from other schools of thought in macroeconomics. In the 1960s and 1970s, monetarist approaches, represented primarily by the work of Milton Friedman, were in part adopted by Keynesians in what was called the "neoclassical synthesis." In the 1980s, the influence of equilibrium models with optimizing consumers and firms, of the type studied in Chapter 12, were influential in the development of Keynesian "menu cost" models, which explained sticky prices as arising from the costs to firms of changing prices.[3] More recently, Keynesian models with sticky prices have been constructed that have as their core a basic real business cycle framework but incorporate sticky prices.[4] Those who work in this research program call it "New Keynesian Economics," and argue that it represents the newest synthesis of ideas in macroeconomics.

The primary feature that makes a Keynesian macroeconomic model different from the models we have examined thus far is that some prices and wages are not completely flexible—that is, some are "sticky." That some prices and wages cannot move so as to clear markets will have important implications for how the economy behaves and for economic policy. The New Keynesian model studied in this chapter is essentially identical to the monetary intertemporal model in Chapter 12, except that the price level is not sufficiently flexible for the goods market to clear in the short run. Given the failure of the goods market to clear, the New Keynesian model will have far different properties from the monetary intertemporal model, but constructing the model will be a straightforward extension of our basic monetary intertemporal framework.

Though Keynesian models certainly have some strong adherents, they have many detractors as well.[5] Part of what we will do in this chapter is to critically evaluate the New Keynesian model, just as we evaluated flexible-price-and-wage business cycle models in Chapter 13. However, as we will show, if policymakers are doing their jobs correctly in the New Keynesian world, then the data will not allow us to discriminate between the New Keynesian model and a real business cycle model.

In contrast to the monetary intertemporal model in Chapter 12, the New Keynesian model will have the property that money is not neutral. When the monetary authority increases the money supply, there will be an increase in aggregate output and employment. In general, monetary policy can then be used to improve economic performance and welfare. Keynesians typically believe strongly that the government should play an active role in the economy, through both monetary and fiscal policy and Keynesian business cycle models support this belief.

---

[3]L. Ball and N. G. Mankiw, 1994. "A Sticky-Price Manifesto," *Carnegie-Rochester Conference Series on Public Policy* 41, 127–151.

[4]R. Clarida, J. Gali, and M. Gertler, 1999. "The Science of Monetary Policy: A New Keynesian Perspective," *Journal of Economic Literature* 37, 1661–1707; M. Woodford, 2003. *Money, Interest, and Prices*, Princeton, NJ: Princeton University Press.

[5]See R. Lucas, 1980. "Methods and Problems in Business Cycle Theory," *Journal of Money, Credit, and Banking* 12, 696–715; S. Williamson, 2008. "New Keynesian Economics: A Monetary Perspective," *Economic Quarterly*, 94, Federal Reserve Bank of Richmond, 197–218.

In line with how most central banks in the world currently operate, in the New Keynesian model the central bank will use the market interest rate as its policy target. As we will show, however, what the central bank controls directly is the money supply, so any target for the market interest rate must be supported with appropriate money supply control. Once we treat the market interest rate as the central bank's policy target, we will eliminate a feature of traditional Keynesian textbook analysis, Hicks's "LM curve," which was included in these traditional models to summarize money demand, money supply, and equilibrium in the money market.

In our New Keynesian model, we will show how active monetary and fiscal policy can smooth out business cycles by reacting to extraneous shocks to the economy. Given well-informed fiscal and monetary authorities that can act very quickly, there is little difference between monetary and fiscal policy in terms of their ability to stabilize aggregate output. However, the active use of fiscal policy in stabilizing the economy will matter for the division of aggregate spending between the public and private sectors.

The New Keynesian Model

LO 14.1 Construct the New Keynesian model with sticky prices.

Our New Keynesian model will have very different properties from the basic monetary intertemporal model that we constructed in Chapter 12. However, there is only one fundamental difference in the New Keynesian model: The price level is sticky in the short run and will not adjust quickly to equate the supply and demand for goods.

Why might goods prices be sticky in the short run? Some Keynesians argue that it is costly for firms to change prices, and even if these costs are small, this could lead firms to fix the prices for their products for long periods of time. Consider a restaurant, which must print new menus whenever it changes its prices. Printing menus is costly, and this causes the restaurant to change prices infrequently. Given that prices change infrequently, there may be periods when the restaurant is full and people are being turned away. If menus were not costly to print, the restaurant might increase its prices under these circumstances. Alternatively, there may be periods when the restaurant is not full and prices would be lowered if it were not for the costs of changing prices. The restaurant example is a common one in the economic literature on sticky price models. Indeed, sticky price models are sometimes referred to as **menu cost models**.

In typical New Keynesian models, it is assumed that, among the many firms in the economy, some will change their prices during any given period of time, and some will not. This could be modeled the hard way, by assuming a fixed cost for a firm associated with changing its price. Then, a firm will change its price only when the firm's existing price deviates enough from the optimal price, making it profit-maximizing for the firm to bear the menu cost and shift to the optimal price. An easier approach is to simply assume that a firm receives an opportunity at random to change its price. Every period, the firms that are lucky receive this opportunity and change their prices, while the unlucky firms are stuck charging the price they posted in the previous period.

Whichever way sticky prices are modeled, this tends to lead to forward-looking behavior on the part of firms. Whenever a firm changes its price, it knows that it may be charging this price for some time into the future, until it can change its posted price again. Thus, in making its price-setting decision the firm will attempt to forecast the shocks that are likely to affect future market conditions and the firm's future profitability. While this forward-looking behavior can play an important role in New Keynesian economics, we will need to simplify here by assuming that all firms charge the price P for goods in the current period, and that this price is sticky and will not move during the period in response to shifts in the demand for goods.

In Figure 14.1, we display the basic apparatus for the New Keynesian model, which includes the same set of diagrams we used for the basic monetary intertemporal model in Chapter 12, with the addition of the production function. That is, the labor market is in panel (a) of the figure, the goods market in panel (b), the money market in panel (c), and the production function in panel (d).

Start with panel (c), the money market. Here, the price level is fixed at P^*, which is the sticky price charged by all firms. Assume that this price was set in the past and firms cannot change it during the current period. Then, in panel (b), r^* is the interest rate target of the central bank. Here we assume, as in Chapter 12, that the anticipated inflation rate is a constant—zero for convenience—so that the Fisher relation tells us that the nominal interest rate R is identical to the real interest rate r. In practice we know that central banks typically target a nominal interest rate, which is consistent with what the central bank does in the model, where setting r is the same as setting R.

Given the interest rate target r^*, output is determined by the output demand curve in Figure 14.1(b), so aggregate output is Y^*. Note that, in Keynesian models with sticky prices or wages, in line with the tradition of Hicks, what we have called the output demand curve, Y^d, is typically called the IS curve. Thus, we have labeled the output demand curve "$Y^d(IS)$" in Figure 14.1(b).

Given the level of output Y^*, and the interest rate r^*, in the money market in 14.1(c), the quantity of money demanded is $PL(Y^*, r^*)$, so in order to hit its target market interest rate of r^*, given the price level P^*, the central bank must supply M^* units of money. From the production function in panel (d), firms hire the quantity of labor N^*, which is just sufficient to produce the quantity of output demanded in the goods market, Y^*. In the labor market in panel (a), the labor supply curve is $N^s(r^*)$, determined by the equilibrium real interest rate r^*. The real wage w^* is the wage rate at which the quantity of labor that consumers are willing to supply is N^*.

A critical feature of the model is that some markets clear, while others do not. The money market clears in Figure 14.1(c), since the central bank needs to supply a sufficient quantity of money, that money demand equals money supply at the central bank's target interest rate r^*, given the fixed price level P^* and the level of output Y^*. The goods market need not clear, however. In panel (b), firms would like to supply the quantity of output Y_1 at the interest rate r^*, but firms actually produce only the quantity demanded, which is Y^*. If firms could, they would lower prices, but prices are rigid in the short run. Note that the quantity of output Y_m is the market-clearing level of output that would be determined in the monetary intertemporal model. The market-clearing interest rate r_m is sometimes referred to as the **natural rate of interest** in the New Keynesian literature. As well, New Keynesians call the difference between the market-clearing level of output and actual level of output, $Y_m - Y^*$, the **output gap**.

Figure 14.1 The New Keynesian Model

Given the fixed price level $P*$ and the target interest rate $r*$, output is $Y*$, determined by the output demand (*IS*) curve, and the central bank must supply $M*$ units of money to hit its interest rate target. Firms hire $N*$ units of labor at the real wage $w*$. The natural rate of interest is r_m, and the output gap is $Y_m - Y*$.

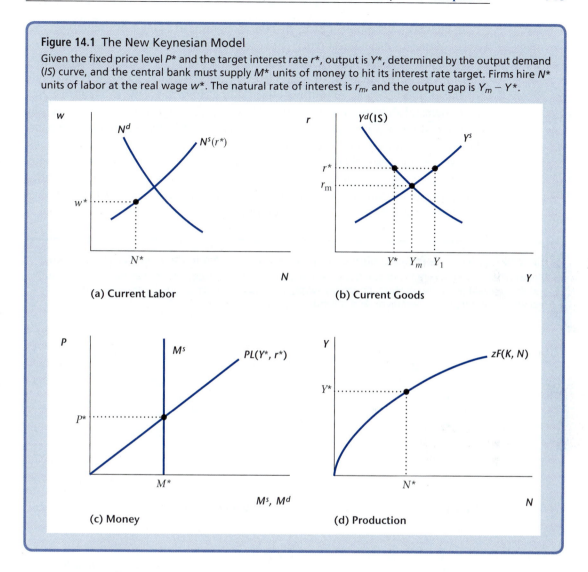

(a) Current Labor

(b) Current Goods

(c) Money

(d) Production

In the New Keynesian model, the labor market need not clear in the short run. In particular, in Figure 14.1(a), at the market real wage $w*$, firms would like to hire more labor than $N*$, but firms know that if they hired more labor they would not be able to sell the larger amount of produced output at the price $P*$.

The Nonneutrality of Money in the New Keynesian Model

LO 14.2 Demonstrate that money is not neutral in the New Keynesian model.

Given our short-run New Keynesian model, we can proceed with an experiment, which will illustrate how money fails to be neutral in this model.

In Figure 14.2, suppose initially that the economy is in a long-run equilibrium with level of output Y_1, real interest rate r_1, price level P_1, employment N_1, and real wage w_1, given the money supply M_1. Then, the central bank lowers its interest rate target to r_2, implying that output increases to Y_2 in Figure 14.2(b), as firms supply the extra output demanded since the price of output is fixed in the short run at P_1. In Figure 14.2(c), money demand shifts to the right from $PL(Y_1, r_1)$ to $PL(Y_2, r_2)$, as real income has risen and the real interest rate has fallen, both of which act to increase money demand. Therefore, to support the lower nominal interest rate target, the central bank must increase the money supply to M_2. In the labor market in Figure 14.2(a), the labor supply curve shifts to the left from $N^s(r_1)$ to $N^s(r_2)$, as a result of intertemporal substitution in response to the lower interest rate. Therefore, the real wage must rise so as to induce consumers to supply the extra labor required to produce the higher level of output.

Figure 14.2 A Decrease in the Central Bank's Interest Rate Target in the New Keynesian Model
Money is not neutral with sticky prices. A decrease in the interest rate target results in an increase in output, and the central bank must increase the money supply to achieve its interest rate target. Employment, the real wage, consumption, investment, and the money supply all increase.

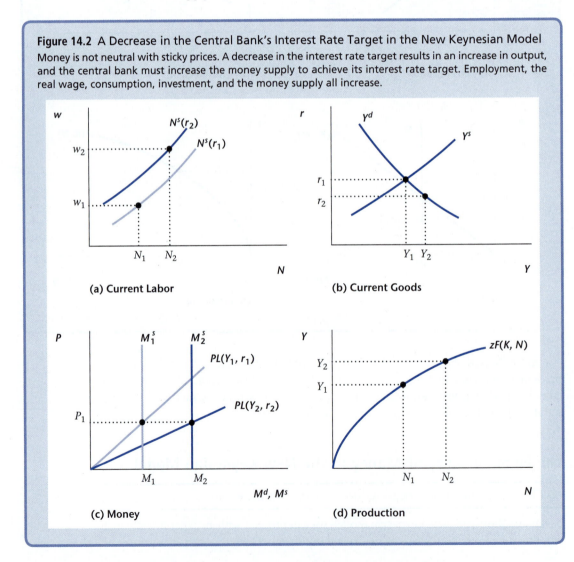

(a) Current Labor

(b) Current Goods

(c) Money

(d) Production

Another way to view this is that the central bank increases the money supply, which results in an excess supply of money at the interest rate r_1, and so the interest rate falls so as to equate money supply and demand. The decrease in the real interest rate then increases the demand for consumption goods and investment goods, and so firms supply the extra output given that prices are fixed in the short run. Money is not neutral, because the increase in the money supply has real effects; the real interest rate falls, real output increases, the real wage increases, and employment increases. Keynesians think of money as having these real effects through the above-described **Keynesian transmission mechanism for monetary policy**. That is, an increase in the money supply has its first effects in financial markets; the real interest rate falls to equate money demand with the increased money supply, and this acts to increase the demand for goods.

Most Keynesians regard money as being neutral in the long run. Although Keynesians argue that money is not neutral in the short run because of sticky prices (or wages), they also believe that prices will eventually adjust so that supply equals demand in the goods and labor markets, in which case money will be neutral, just as in the monetary intertemporal model we studied in Chapter 12.

The Role of Government Policy in the New Keynesian Model

LO 14.3 Show how government policy—both monetary and fiscal policy—works in the New Keynesian sticky price model.

In macroeconomics, some important disagreements focus on the issue of whether the government should act to smooth out business cycles. This smoothing, or what is sometimes referred to as **stabilization policy**, involves carrying out government actions that will increase aggregate real output when it is below trend and decrease it when it is above trend. Using government policy to smooth business cycles may appear to be a good idea. For example, we know that a consumer whose income fluctuates will behave optimally by smoothing consumption relative to income, so why shouldn't the government take actions that will smooth aggregate real income over time? As we saw in Chapter 13, this logic need not apply when considering the rationale for government policy intervention with respect to macroeconomic events. For example in a real business cycle model, stabilization policy must be detrimental, as business cycles are just optimal responses to aggregate productivity shocks.

Keynesians tend to believe that government intervention to smooth out business cycles is appropriate, and the New Keynesian model provides a justification for this belief. We will start by considering a situation where an unanticipated shock has hit the economy, causing the price level to be higher than its equilibrium level in the goods market, as in Figure 14.3. Alternatively, the central bank's interest rate target r_1 is too high, so there exists a positive output gap of $Y_2 - Y_1$ in Figure 14.3 or, in other words, a situation where firms would like to supply more output than is demanded given the price level P_1 and the interest rate target r_1.

After the shock has hit the economy, the allocation of resources is not economically efficient. Recall from Chapter 5 that the first fundamental theorem of welfare economics implies that a competitive equilibrium is Pareto-optimal, but in Figure 14.3 the economy is not in a competitive equilibrium, as initially the quantity of output demanded is not equal to the quantity of output that firms would like to supply. One response of the government to the economic inefficiency caused by the shock to the economy would be to do nothing and let the problem solve itself. Since the price level P_1 is initially above its long-run equilibrium level, with the quantity of goods demanded less than what firms would like to supply, the price level will tend to fall over time. If the central bank does nothing, this means that it does not change the quantity directly under its control, which is the quantity of money. The money supply remains fixed at M_1, as in Figure 14.3(b). Then, as the price level falls over time, money demand must increase, so the central bank's interest rate target must fall until ultimately, in the long run, the interest rate target is r_2, output is Y_2, and the price level is P_2, as in Figure 14.4, and the economy is again in equilibrium and operating efficiently.

Keynesian macroeconomists argue that the long run is too long to wait. In Figure 14.3 suppose alternatively, that instead of doing nothing in response to the shock to the economy, the central bank immediately reduces its interest rate target from r_1 to r_2. To hit this lower interest rate target requires that the central bank increase the money supply from M_1 to M_2 in Figure 14.3. This immediately closes the output gap and restores economic efficiency in the short run. The price level is P_1 and the level of output is Y_2.

Note that after the increase in the money supply, the economy is in exactly the same situation, in real terms, as it would have been in the long run if the central bank did nothing and allowed the price level to fall. The only difference is that the price level

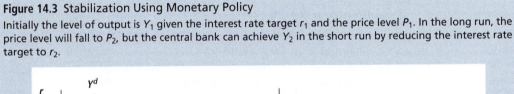

Figure 14.3 Stabilization Using Monetary Policy
Initially the level of output is Y_1 given the interest rate target r_1 and the price level P_1. In the long run, the price level will fall to P_2, but the central bank can achieve Y_2 in the short run by reducing the interest rate target to r_2.

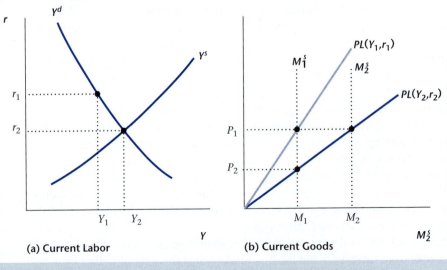

is higher in the case where the central bank intervenes. The advantage of intervention is that an efficient outcome is achieved faster than if the central bank let events take their course.

The return to full employment could also be achieved through an increase in government expenditures, G, but with some different results. In Figure 14.4, we show a similar initial situation to Figure 14.3, where initial output is Y_1, which is less than the quantity of output that firms want to supply given the price level P_1 and the interest rate target r_1. Now, suppose that the central bank maintains its interest rate target at r_1, in anticipation that the government fiscal authority will increase government spending to correct the inefficiency problem that exists in the short run. If the government increases government purchases, G, by just the right amount, then the output demand curve shifts to the right from Y_1^d to Y_2^d and the output supply curve shifts to the right from to Y_1^s to Y_2^s (recall our analysis from Chapter 11, where we analyzed the effects of temporary increases in G). In Figure 14.4(b), the price level is sticky in the short run at P_1, and the increase in output shifts the money demand curve to the right from $PL(Y_1, r_1)$ to $PL(Y_2, r_1)$, and so to maintain its interest rate target the central bank increases the money supply from M_1 to M_2.

Now, note the differences in final outcomes between Figures 14.3 and 14.4. Recall from Chapter 11 that the entire increase in output from Y_1 to Y_2 in Figure 14.4 is due to the increase in government spending, as the interest rate is unchanged. That is, the fiscal policy response to the shock results in no increase in consumption or investment,

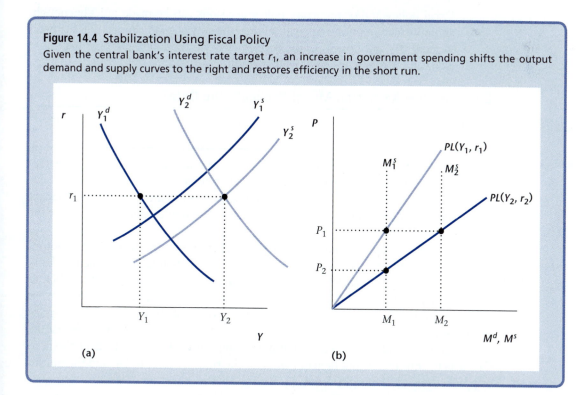

Figure 14.4 Stabilization Using Fiscal Policy
Given the central bank's interest rate target r_1, an increase in government spending shifts the output demand and supply curves to the right and restores efficiency in the short run.

(a)

(b)

with the only component of spending that increases being government spending, with output increasing one-for-one with government spending. After government intervention, output is higher in Figure 14.4 than in Figure 14.3, but with monetary policy intervention, consumption and investment are higher in Figure 14.4 than in Figure 14.3 because of the decrease in the target central bank interest rate. Thus, the key difference that fiscal policy intervention makes, relative to monetary policy intervention to stabilize the economy, is that output needs to change more in response to fiscal policy in order to restore efficiency, and the composition of output is different with fiscal policy, with a greater emphasis on public spending relative to private spending, compared to what happens with monetary policy intervention.

Whether fiscal or monetary policy is used to smooth business cycles, the New Keynesian model provides a rationale for stabilization policy. If shocks kick the economy out of equilibrium, because of a failure of private markets to clear in the short run, fiscal or monetary policymakers can, if they move fast enough, restore the economy to equilibrium before self-adjusting markets achieve this on their own. Thus, the important elements of the Keynesian view of government's role in the macroeconomy are as follows:

1. Private markets fail to operate smoothly on their own, in that not all wages and prices are perfectly flexible, implying that supply is not equal to demand in all markets, and economic efficiency is not always achieved in a world without government intervention.

2. Fiscal policy and/or monetary policy decisions can be made quickly enough, and information on the behavior of the economy is good enough that the fiscal or monetary authorities can improve efficiency by countering shocks that cause a deviation from a full-employment equilibrium.

Does the New Keynesian Model Replicate the Data?

LO 14.4 Show the implications of the New Keynesian model for what we should see in the data, assuming optimal monetary policy.

Though the New Keynesian model can be used to analyze the effects of monetary policy, the model was developed primarily as a tool to aid in the formulation of monetary policy. And since monetary policy is not neutral in the short run in this model, it is important to incorporate endogenous policy into the model to understand how the model may or may not fit the data.

Specifically, suppose that the central bank acts to minimize the size of the output gap in response to shocks that hit the economy. As well, assume that the central bank can observe aggregate shocks perfectly. For example, consider a persistent shock to total factor productivity (TFP) identical to what we considered in Chapter 13, in studying the real business cycle model, as in Figure 13.2. In Figure 14.5, the price level is sticky at P_1, and initial output is Y_1, with initial interest rate r_1. Assume that the output gap is initially zero. The initial money supply is M_1. The persistent shock to TFP acts to shift the output demand curve to the right from Y_1^d to Y_2^d, and the output supply curve to the right from Y_1^s to Y_2^s. In the absence of any government

Figure 14.5 Persistent Total Factor Productivity Shocks with an Optimal Monetary Policy Response

If the central bank responds optimally to the productivity shock, the data can behave in the same manner as data produced by a real business cycle model.

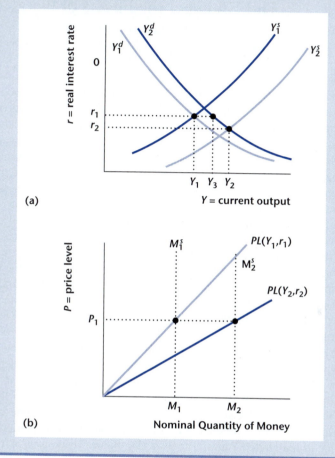

(a)

(b)

intervention, the central bank's interest rate target stays at r_1, and output increases to Y_3. Therefore, there is an output gap equal to $Y_2 - Y_3 > 0$. So, aggregate output is inefficiently low.

If the central bank behaves optimally in response to the persistent TFP shock, it will act to achieve a zero output gap. It does this by reducing its interest rate target to r_2, which the central bank accomplishes through an increase in the money supply from M_1 to M_2. Thus, output will increase to Y_2 in response to the persistent TFP shock. Monetary policy effectively acts to accommodate the shock by expanding the money supply and lowering market interest rates.

But, if the central bank were behaving optimally in this fashion, what would we observe? If the economy were being continually buffeted by TFP shocks, then output would be fluctuating in an efficient manner because the central bank optimally

MACROECONOMICS IN ACTION

The Timing of the Effects of Fiscal and Monetary Policy

While the effects of fiscal and monetary policies are instantaneous in the New Keynesian model, in practice it takes time to formulate policy, and it takes time for policy to affect the economy. First, policymakers do not have complete information. The national income accounts, employment data, and price data are time-consuming to compile, and policymakers in the federal government and at the Fed have good information only for what was happening in the economy months previously. Second, when information is available, it may take time for policymakers to agree among themselves concerning a course of action. Finally, once a policy is implemented, there is a time lag before the policy has its effects on aggregate economic activity. The awkward lags in macroeconomic policymaking were recognized at least as early as 1948, by Milton Friedman.[6]

While the first stage of policymaking (information collection) is essentially the same for fiscal and monetary policy, it is generally recognized that the second stage (decision making) takes much longer for fiscal policy than for monetary policy in the United States. The congressional process of passing a budget can take months, while the Federal Open Market Committee, the decision-making body of the Fed, meets every six weeks, and it can make decisions between these meetings if necessary. For the third stage in the timing of the effects of fiscal and monetary policy—that is, the lag between a policy decision and when its effects

are realized in the economy—it is not clear whether fiscal or monetary policy takes longer. For fiscal policy, the results will depend on whether the fiscal policy changes are due to taxes or government spending. Tax changes can in principle have their effects quickly. For example, the government can send out checks in the mail at short notice, with essentially immediate effects on consumption/savings decisions. However, new spending takes longer to allocate, and for public works projects there are long lags in getting the projects off the ground. With regard to monetary policy, one of the points of Milton Friedman and Anna Schwartz's study of the role of money in the U.S. economy, *A Monetary History of the United States, 1867–1960*, is that the lag between a monetary policy action and its effects is "long and variable." That is, it can take a long time for monetary policy to have its effects, perhaps six months to a year, and this length of time is always uncertain.

Factors relating to time-consuming policymaking and implementation came into play in the policy responses of the U.S. federal government and the Fed to the 2008 financial crisis and the ensuing 2008–2009 recession. For monetary policy, some viewed the Fed as being overly complacent and oblivious to the problems developing in the mortgage market, beginning with the decline in the price of housing in 2006. However, with the developing recession in 2008 and the financial crisis in the fall of 2008, the Fed acted quickly to reduce the target federal funds rate and to implement other measures to intervene in credit markets. Whether the Fed did the right things or did too much continues to be a subject of debate, but the ability of the central

---

[6]M. Friedman, 1948. "A Monetary and Fiscal Framework for Economic Stability," *American Economic Review* 38, 245–264.

bank to act quickly was certainly evident in its response to the financial crisis.

With respect to fiscal policy, two main programs were put in effect. The first was the Emergency Economic Stabilization Act of 2008 (EESA), which authorized $700 billion for the Troubled Asset Relief Program (TARP). The act was passed by Congress in October 2008 and was a very unusual fiscal policy program. The act gave the secretary of the Treasury a great deal of discretion in implementing the legislation, in consultation with the Federal Reserve chairman. Originally, the intention appeared to be for the federal government to buy up "troubled assets," for which organized markets had essentially shut down. These assets would be purchased from financial institutions, including banks. In this respect, this program looked more like monetary policy than fiscal policy, in that the federal government would essentially be issuing its own debt to finance the purchase of assets, and therefore be acting as a financial intermediary. Ultimately, the program evolved into a scheme to "bail out" banks and other financial institutions. Funds were transferred by the federal government to financial institutions in exchange for equity claims, with some restrictions then placed on the terms of hiring and employee compensation of these financial institutions. The goal of the program was to temporarily stabilize financial markets, and to encourage lending by banks and other financial institutions. This program was certainly implemented much more quickly than is typically the case for fiscal policy programs, though the program has frequently been criticized as poorly thought-out and as a simple redistribution from taxpayers to the financial sector of the economy. Whether it has had its intended effects is debatable.

The second key fiscal policy program was the American Recovery and Reinvestment Act (ARRA). This act of Congress was passed in February 2009, and included a range of government expenditure, tax, and transfer programs. Of all the monetary and fiscal policy interventions carried out in response to the financial crisis and the 2008–2009 recession, this program was the one most strongly motivated by traditional Keynesian economics and the one also most clearly subject to Milton Friedman's concerns about policy timing issues. Though the ARRA was quickly put together and passed by Congress (a concern in itself, as little thought was given to the economic efficiency of the components of the program), much of the spending authorized by the program did not take place until late 2009, 2010, and even in 2011. Although the last recession turned out to be much more prolonged, and the recovery much weaker than anticipated, that was not known when the ARRA was implemented. One concern of Friedman's was that attempts to stabilize the economy through government policy could actually contribute to instability, if, for example, stimulative policy is put into place and the economy continues to be "stimulated" long after the problem has gone away. However, some Keynesian economists have argued that the problem with the ARRA was that the program was smaller than what was actually needed.

Even if we believe that stabilizing the economy through the use of fiscal and monetary policy is appropriate, as the New Keynesian model tells us, there is still much that can go wrong. Guiding the economy can be much like trying to steer a car with a faulty steering mechanism; one has to see the bumps and curves in the road well in advance to avoid driving into the ditch or otherwise having a very uncomfortable ride. These concerns led some economists, for example Milton Friedman, to encourage abstinence from stabilization policy altogether. Friedman argued that well-intentioned stabilization policy could do more harm than good, as the lags in policy could lead to stimulative action being taken when tightening the screws on the economy would be more appropriate, and vice versa.

accommodates these shocks. Indeed, the data this model produces for employment, consumption, investment, and real GDP, would look just like the data produced by the real business cycle model in Chapter 13. The only difference would be in the behavior of nominal variables—the price level and the money supply. But if, in the real business cycle model the central bank acts to stabilize the price level, as in Figure 13.4 in Chapter 13, then the data produced by the New Keynesian model and the real business cycle model will be exactly the same. Thus we may not be able to distinguish statistically between a world in which prices are sticky and the central bank behaves optimally to minimize the output gap, and a world in which prices are perfectly flexible and the central bank acts to stabilize prices.

This is just an example of a fundamental difficulty in macroeconomics. The fact that policy is endogenous—it reacts in real time to events in the economy—serves to confound the effects of policy and macroeconomic shocks in the data we observe. This makes it difficult to test macroeconomic theory using the standard aggregate time series observations.

The Liquidity Trap and Sticky Prices

LO 14.5 Construct a liquidity trap equilibrium in the New Keynesian model, and show how negative interest rate policy works.

As discussed in Chapter 12, a liquidity trap can occur when the nominal interest rate reaches zero (or possibly lower). In Figure 14.6, suppose initially that the output gap is zero, with level of aggregate output Y_1 and real interest rate r_1. Also suppose that the nominal interest rate is initially zero. That is, if i denotes the anticipated inflation rate, then $r_1 + i = 0$, and we have assumed so far, for convenience, that $i = 0$, so $r_1 = 0$. In Figure 14.6, the nominal quantity of money is M_1, the nominal quantity of government debt is B_1, and open market operations by the central bank—swaps of money for short-term government debt—will have no effect on the total quantity of liquid assets $M_1 + B_1$ and, because money and short-term government debt are perfect substitutes at the zero lower bound on the nominal interest rate, monetary policy will have no effect.

In Figure 14.6, given the initial equilibrium (Y_1, r_1), suppose there is an increase in credit market frictions, as occurred in the 2008–2009 financial crisis, as represented in Chapter 11, Figure 11.29. Then, the output demand curve shifts to the left from Y_1^d to Y_2^d, and the output supply curve shifts to the right from Y_1^s to Y_2^s. Thus, in Figure 14.6, the central bank would like to lower the real interest rate to r_2 so as to eliminate the output gap that would otherwise arise, but because of the liquidity trap it cannot do this. Therefore, the real interest rate will stay at r_1, and output will fall from Y_1 to Y_2. As a result, because of the liquidity trap, the effect of the increase in credit market frictions is larger than it would have been if the central bank could respond optimally by lowering market interest rates.

The liquidity trap problem that arises in New Keynesian models potentially provides a rationale for the unconventional monetary policies discussed in Chapter 12. For example, perhaps the lower bound on the nominal interest rate is not zero, but some lower negative number—the effective lower bound. Then, if r_2 were greater than

Figure 14.6 Liquidity Trap

Initially at (Y_1, r_1) the nominal interest rate is zero. If an increase in credit market frictions occurs, and the nominal interest rate is constrained by the zero lower bound, then output falls to Y_2. But, if the central bank can implement negative nominal interest rates, it may be possible to lower the real interest rate to r_2 and to achieve output level Y_3.

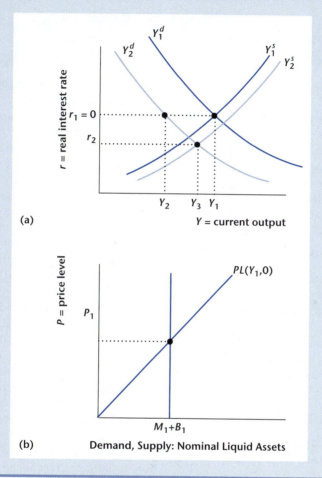

(a)

(b)   **Demand, Supply: Nominal Liquid Assets**

this effective lower bound, the central bank could in fact lower the market real interest rate to r_2, and reduce the output gap to zero, with output at the level Y_3. A potential problem is that we have left some important elements out of our model. In particular, there might be concerns that negative interest rates could produce inefficiencies in the banking system, because banks cannot lower the interest rates on their deposit accounts to compete with zero-interest currency. As well, negative nominal interest rates could encourage consumers and firms to hold more zero-interest currency than is socially efficient. We will discuss the potential effects of other unconventional monetary policies in Chapter 15.

MACROECONOMICS IN ACTION

New Keynesian Models, the Zero Lower Bound, and Quantitative Easing

The model presented in this chapter is a simplification of New Keynesian models that are used by economists and central bankers. Those models have a more elaborate dynamic structure than we have shown here and typically include a monetary policy rule that explains how the central bank's nominal interest rate target evolves over time. One such monetary policy rule is the Taylor rule, named after John Taylor, currently at Stanford University.

The Taylor rule is included in most New Keynesian models, and Taylor rules have been successfully fit to the data. One such rule is described in a newsletter from the Federal Reserve Bank of San Francisco, by Glenn Rudebusch.[7] Following Rudebusch's approach, we capture the behavior of the Fed before the financial crisis by fitting a Taylor rule to the data for 1988–2007. Our estimated Taylor rule then takes the form

$$R = 2.0 + 1.2i - 1.5gap, \qquad (14\text{-}1)$$

where R is the actual federal funds rate, i is the inflation rate, measured as the 12-month percentage increase in the personal consumption expenditure deflator, and gap is the output gap, which is the difference between the unemployment rate and the "natural rate of unemployment," as measured by the Congressional Budget Office. This Taylor rule says that, if the inflation rate were to increase by one percentage point, then

the central bank should tighten by increasing the target nominal interest rate by 1.2 percentage points. However, if the unemployment rate were to increase by one percentage point relative to the natural rate of unemployment, then the central bank should ease by reducing the target nominal interest rate by 1.5 percentage points.

Figure 14.7 shows the actual federal funds rate and the rate predicted by the Taylor rule in Equation (14-1). Note that the Taylor rule was estimated to fit the data for 1988–2007, and then was used to provide predicted values for the period from 2008 to 2016Q1. By the first quarter of 2009, the Taylor rule estimated that the federal funds rate should be negative, and the predicted value generated by the Taylor rule would go as low as −5% in the third quarter of 2009, and then increase to 1.2% by first quarter 2012. Thus, the New Keynesian interpretation of what we see in the figure is that, for the period from first quarter 2009 to first quarter 2011, recommended policy was thwarted by the zero lower bound—the liquidity trap case.

So what is to be done when monetary policy hits the zero lower bound? As was discussed in this chapter, the central bank has no power to ease policy through a reduction in its target interest rate, so one possibility is for the central bank to do nothing and let fiscal policy take the lead. But there are other policies the central bank might pursue other than changes in its policy rate, particularly during a financial crisis. One such policy is for the central bank to step into its role as lender of last resort to financial institutions, which is part of what the Fed did during the financial crisis.

---

[7]See G. Rudebusch, 2009. "The Fed's Monetary Policy Response to the Current Crisis," http://www.frbsf.org/publications/economics/letter/2009/el2009-17.html.

As we discussed in Chapter 12, the Fed also engaged in quantitative easing (QE), during the period 2009–2012. These programs more than quadrupled the asset holdings of the U.S. central bank over a more than five year period beginning in early 2009. Recall that quantitative easing involves open market purchases of long-term government debt or other long-maturity assets, rather than the purchase of short-term government debt as in conventional monetary policy.

One argument that was used for QE during the financial crisis was based on pictures like Figure 14.7. Assuming that monetary policy was being conducted appropriately before the financial crisis, the fitted Taylor rule tells us how the central bank's policy rate should be set in a way consistent with past behavior. Figure 14.7 tells us that the federal funds rate should have been negative from first quarter 2009 to first quarter 2011. But the federal funds rate cannot be negative, so if the Fed could somehow ease policy in

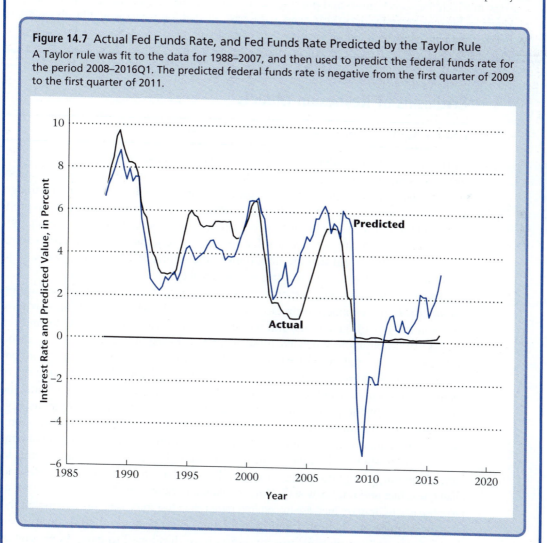

Figure 14.7 Actual Fed Funds Rate, and Fed Funds Rate Predicted by the Taylor Rule

A Taylor rule was fit to the data for 1988–2007, and then used to predict the federal funds rate for the period 2008–2016Q1. The predicted federal funds rate is negative from the first quarter of 2009 to the first quarter of 2011.

(Continued)

another way, that would be appropriate, according to this argument. Fed officials argued that they could reduce long-term interest rates by purchasing long-term assets and thereby reduce the output gap.

What is wrong with that argument? Unfortunately, the New Keynesian models that formed the framework that was guiding many central bankers did not have the financial details necessary to evaluate the effects of QE and to find out whether it would work as intended. This is one way in which macroeconomists and policymakers possibly took excessive risks during and following the financial crisis, in implementing

policies that were not well understood. This experience points out a need for more macroeconomic research on central banking and the effects of various kinds of central bank asset purchases on market interest rates and economic activity.

An interesting feature of Figure 14.7 is that the predicted fed funds rate rose above zero in 2011, well before the Fed actually increased the target range for the fed funds rate, from 0–0.25% to 0.25%–0.50% in December of 2015. Thus, if the Fed had behaved as it had in the past, the fed funds rate would be above 3% in early 2016.

Criticisms of Keynesian Models

LO 14.6 Explain the criticisms of New Keynesian models.

Critics of Keynesian models argue that these models fall short in some respects. For example, some economists argue that the theory underlying sticky wage and sticky price models is poor or nonexistent. Typically these models do not capture the underlying reasons for wage and price stickiness—the stickiness is simply assumed. To properly understand why wages might be sticky and exactly how this matters for macroeconomic activity, some argue that we need to be explicit in our theories about the features of the world that are important to the setting of wages and prices and to show how a model with such features explains reality.

Menu cost models were a response to the criticisms by classical economists of Keynesian models. In those models, firms face explicit costs of changing prices, firms maximize profits in the face of these costs, and the result is that prices are in fact sticky and the models have implications much like those of our New Keynesian model. However, menu cost models have certainly not been immune from criticism. Some economists point out that the costs of changing prices are minuscule compared with the short-run costs of changing the quantity of output. Consider the case of a restaurant. On the one hand, the cost of changing menu prices is the cost of making a few keystrokes on a computer keyboard and then running off a few copies of the menu on the printer in the back room. Indeed, a restaurant will be printing new menus frequently anyway, because restaurant patrons tend to spill food on the menus. On the other hand, if the restaurant wants to increase output in response to higher demand, it will have to move in more tables and chairs, and hire and train new staff. Why would the restaurant want to change output in response to a temporary increase in demand rather than just increasing prices temporarily?

These questions help in framing the debate as to how we should improve on the business cycle models macroeconomists have developed to date. As we saw in

MACROECONOMICS IN ACTION
How Sticky Are Nominal Prices?

Casual observation tells us that some prices appear to be quite sticky. For example, the prices of newspapers and magazines tend to remain fixed for long periods of time. As well, there are some prices that clearly change frequently. The prices of fresh vegetables change week-to-week in the supermarket, and the prices of gasoline posted by gas stations can change on a daily basis. However, to evaluate the importance of Keynesian sticky price models, it is important to quantify the degree of price stickiness for a broad array of consumer goods. If there is little actual price stickiness for the average good or service in the economy, then price stickiness will be relatively unimportant in contributing to business cycles and the nonneutrality of money. As well, we would like to know whether the pattern of price changes we observe in the economy is consistent with the type of price stickiness that Keynesian theorists typically build into their models.

Until recently, economists had not gathered comprehensive evidence on the nature of price changes across the economy's goods and services. However, Mark Bils and Peter Klenow gained access to Bureau of Labor Statistics data on the prices of goods and services that were heretofore unavailable to researchers.[8] Their findings are surprising. Bils and Klenow found that, for half of the goods and services in their data set, prices changed every 4.3 months or less, which is a much lower frequency of price changes than indicated by previous studies. While this does not entirely preclude significant effects from the sticky price mechanism for business cycles and the nonneutrality of money, it raises questions about previous results in Keynesian macroeconomics that would have exaggerated Keynesian sticky price effects.

Another feature of the data that Bils and Klenow find is that the rates of change in prices for particular goods and services are far more variable than is consistent with sticky price models. In a typical sticky price model, of the type in common use by Keynesian researchers, a shock to the economy that causes prices to increase will lead to staggered price increases over time, as individual firms do not coordinate their price increases. As a result, the rate of change in the price of an individual good or service should be persistent over time, and not very volatile, but this is not so in the data.

The work of Bils and Klenow points to some key faults in the sticky price models typically used in practice. Their work does not definitively resolve issues about the value of Keynesian business cycle models relative to the alternatives. However, Bils and Klenow have cast some doubt on whether the sticky price mechanism is of key importance in understanding business cycles and how monetary policy works.

[8]M. Bils, and P. Klenow, 2004. "Some Evidence on the Importance of Sticky Prices," *Journal of Political Economy* 112, 947–985.

Chapter 13, models with flexible wages and prices in general have quite different implications for the role of fiscal and monetary policy than does the New Keynesian model, with some equilibrium models implying that government intervention is detrimental. However, in the Keynesian coordination failure model (which has flexible wages and prices) active government stabilization policy could be justified. We can learn something useful about the causes and consequences of business cycles from all of these models, but taken together, there is much scope for improvement. For example, the 2008–2009 financial crisis deepened our understanding of the role played by financial markets in economic activity, but perhaps macroeconomists have done too little to integrate that understanding into our core macroeconomic models.

Now that we have gained an understanding of how New Keynesian models work, we can go on in the next chapter to study the role of inflation, in Keynesian and non-Keynesian contexts.

Chapter Summary

- A New Keynesian model was constructed in which the price level is sticky in the short run, and the central bank manipulates the money supply so as to maintain a target interest rate. Otherwise, the model is identical to the monetary intertemporal model of Chapter 12. Price stickiness implies that the goods market and labor market need not clear in the short run, though the money market does clear.

- Monetary policy is not neutral in the New Keynesian model. A decrease in the central bank's target interest rate, brought about by an increase in the money supply, will increase output, employment, consumption, investment, and the real wage.

- Under either monetary policy shocks or shocks to the demand for investment goods, the New Keynesian model replicates most of the key business cycle facts from Chapter 3, but the price level is not countercyclical in the model and average labor productivity is countercyclical rather than procyclical, as it is in the data.

- Though some markets do not clear in the short run and the economy does not achieve a Pareto-optimal outcome, in the long run prices will adjust so that economic efficiency holds. Keynesian economists argue that the long run is too long to wait, and that better results can be achieved through monetary and fiscal policy intervention in the short run, in response to shocks to the aggregate economy.

- Aggregate stabilization through monetary policy has different effects from fiscal policy stabilization. Monetary policy stabilization achieves the same result that would occur in the long run when prices adjust, in terms of real economic variables, but fiscal policy stabilization alters the mix of public versus private spending in the goods market. If monetary policy is behaving optimally, the Keynesian sticky price model delivers predictions about the data that can be identical to a real business cycle model. This illustrates that distinguishing empirically among business cycle theories may be daunting.

- The nominal interest rate cannot fall below zero, which may constrain monetary policy. At the zero lower bound, there is a liquidity trap and monetary policy is ineffective. However, expansionary fiscal policy works in a liquidity trap just as it does away from the zero lower bound.

- Some find the assumptions made in sticky price and sticky wage Keynesian models implausible, and empirical evidence on the behavior of individual prices seems inconsistent with elements of Keynesian models.

Key Terms

Menu cost models Sticky price models with explicit costs of changing prices. (p. 511)

Natural rate of interest The real interest rate that would be determined in equilibrium when all prices and wages are flexible. (p. 512)

Output gap The difference between actual aggregate output and the efficient level of aggregate output. (p. 512)

Keynesian transmission mechanism for monetary policy The real effects of monetary policy in the Keynesian model. In the model, money is not neutral, because an increase in the money supply causes the real interest rate to fall, increasing the demand for consumption and investment, and causing the price level to increase. The real wage then falls, the firm hires more labor, and output increases. (p. 515)

Stabilization policy Fiscal or monetary policy justified by Keynesian models, which acts to offset shocks to the economy. (p. 515)

Questions for Review

14.1   Are Keynesian business cycle models currently being used? If so, what for?

14.2   What is the key difference between the New Keynesian model and the models studied in Chapter 12?

14.3   Which markets clear in the New Keynesian model, and which do not?

14.4   How is monetary policy determined in the New Keynesian model? What is the central bank's target, and what does the central bank control directly?

14.5   Why is monetary policy not neutral in the New Keynesian model? What are the effects of a change in the central bank's target interest rate?

14.6   How does the New Keynesian model fit the key business cycle facts from Chapter 3?

14.7   What happens in the long run in the New Keynesian model?

14.8   How do Keynesians justify intervention in the economy through monetary and fiscal policy?

14.9   How does monetary policy stabilization differ from fiscal policy stabilization?

14.10 What happens when the money supply increases in a liquidity trap?

14.11 In the New Keynesian model, does a liquidity trap imply that no economic policy can close a positive output gap?

14.12 What are the faults of the New Keynesian model?

Problems

1. **LO 1** Suppose government spending increases temporarily in the New Keynesian model.
   (a) What are the effects on real output, consumption, investment, the price level, employment, and the real wage?
   (b) Are these effects consistent with the key business cycle facts from Chapter 3? What does this say about the ability of government spending shocks to explain business cycles?

2. **LO 3** In the New Keynesian model, suppose that supply is initially equal to demand in the goods market and that there is a negative shock to the demand for investment goods, because firms anticipate lower total factor productivity in the future.
   (a) Determine the effects on real output, the real interest rate, the price level, employment, and the real wage if the government did nothing in response to the shock.
   (b) Determine the effects if monetary policy is used to stabilize the economy, with the goal of the central bank being zero economic efficiency.
   (c) Determine the effects if government spending is used to stabilize the economy, with the

goal of the fiscal authority being economic efficiency.

(d) Explain and comment on the differences in your results among parts (a), (b), and (c).

3. **LO 3** Suppose that the goal of the fiscal authority is to set government spending so as to achieve economic efficiency, while the goal of the monetary authority is to achieve stability of the price level over the long run. Assume that the economy is initially in equilibrium and that there is then a temporary decrease in total factor productivity. Show that there are many ways in which the fiscal and monetary authority can achieve their separate goals. What could determine what fiscal and monetary policy settings are actually used in this context? Discuss.

4. **LO 3** Some macroeconomists have argued that it would be beneficial for the government to run a deficit when the economy is in a recession, and a surplus during a boom. Does this make sense? Carefully explain why or why not, using the New Keynesian model.

5. **LO 3** In the New Keynesian model, how should the central bank change its target interest rate in response to each of the following shocks? Use diagrams and explain your results.
   (a) There is a shift in money demand.
   (b) Total factor productivity is expected to decrease in the future.
   (c) Total factor productivity decreases in the present.

6. **LO 3** In the New Keynesian model, suppose that in the short run the central bank cannot observe aggregate output or the shocks that hit the economy.

However, the central bank would like to come as close as possible to economic efficiency. That is, ideally the central bank would like the output gap to be zero. Suppose initially that the economy is in equilibrium with a zero output gap.
   (a) Suppose that there is a shift in money demand. That is, the quantity of money demanded increases for each interest rate and level of real income. How well does the central bank perform in relative to its goal? Explain using diagrams.
   (b) Suppose that firms expect total factor productivity to increase in the future. Repeat part (a).
   (c) Suppose that total factor productivity increases in the current period. Repeat part (a).
   (d) Explain any differences in your results in parts (a)–(c), and explain what this implies about the wisdom of following an interest rate rule for the central bank.

7. **LO 1** Suppose that consumption expenditures and investment expenditures are very inelastic with respect to the real interest rate. What does this imply about the power of monetary policy relative to fiscal policy in closing a positive output gap? Explain your results with the aid of diagrams.

8. **LO 5** Suppose that the central bank could convince the public to expect more inflation in the future. If the economy is currently in a liquidity trap, what effects would this have? Use a diagram, and explain your results.

9. **LO 5** If there is a liquidity trap, what will happen in the long run as prices adjust? Use a diagram, and discuss.

Working with the Data

Answer these questions using the Federal Reserve Bank of St. Louis's FRED database, accessible at http://research.stlouisfed.org/fred2/

1. Plot monthly percentage changes in the consumer price index, and in the Standard and Poor's stock price index. How does the behavior of an index of the prices of goods and services differ from the behavior of an index of asset prices? Discuss.

2. Plot the difference between real GDP and potential real GDP, as measured by the Congressional Budget Office. What could this difference measure? Explain what you see in the chart.

3. Plot the federal funds rate, and the difference between the unemployment rate and the natural rate of unemployment (Congressional Budget Office measure). What do you observe, and how do you explain this?

Chapter 15

Inflation: Phillips Curves and Neo-Fisherism

Learning Objectives

After studying Chapter 15, students will be able to:

15.1 Construct the basic New Keynesian model with inflation, and demonstrate how it works.

15.2 Show how there is a trade-off between the goals of the central bank in the basic New Keynesian model.

15.3 Demonstrate the problem a central bank faces when the real interest rate is low, and show how this might be solved with forward guidance by the central bank.

15.4 Construct the New Keynesian model under rational expectations, and show what happens in the model in response to changes in the nominal interest rate.

15.5 Show the perils of Taylor rules given the Taylor principle, and the benefits of neo-Fisherian monetary policy.

Introduction

Beginning in Chapter 12, we analyzed macroeconomic models in which we can determine the price level, and in Chapters 12–14 we examined the effects of monetary policy and macroeconomic shocks on the price level. But, a key practical policy concern is the rate of inflation—the rate of increase over time in the price level. Thus, it is important that we show how inflation is typically modeled by macroeconomists, and to analyze the benefits and drawbacks of these approaches.

The costs of inflation are well-documented. For example, Thomas Sargent studied four countries that experienced extremely high inflation—hyperinflations—in Europe during the 1920s.[1] In some instances that he studied the rate of inflation reached 10,000% per year, for example. Such high rates of inflation cause obvious disruptions in economic activity. People do not want to hold cash for any period of time as it depreciates rapidly in value, and it is difficult to carry on business because prices may be changing daily or hourly. There are some modern instances of very high inflation; for example, Venezuelan inflation approached 200% at the end of 2015, but such experiences might seem mild relative to extreme hyperinflations.

In the United States, the 1970s and early 1980s was a period of relatively high inflation, with the 12-month rate of increase in the consumer price index peaking at close to 15% in 1980. At the time, this rate of inflation was thought to be intolerably high, and the Fed, under chair Paul Volcker, acted to reduce inflation. This project was successful in that, since late 1982, inflation as measured by the consumer price index has rarely been above 5%.

But why is inflation costly? There are costs associated with unanticipated inflation, and with anticipated inflation. Unanticipated inflation matters for economic decision making as, for example, if inflation is unexpectedly high, then this will tend to redistribute income from lenders to borrowers. Lenders get a bad deal, as the real interest rate is lower than they expected—a good deal for borrowers. Thus, if inflation is uncertain, this creates uncertainty for participants in credit markets, and makes these markets function poorly. Further, high inflation uncertainty tends to be associated with high rates of average inflation, so in principle bringing inflation down to a low level should reduce uncertainty.

A high rate of anticipated inflation causes consumers and firms to economize more than they otherwise would on currency, which does not bear interest. In anticipation that currency will be depreciating in value at a high rate, consumers and firms will bear more costs—more trips to the ATM, for example—and this will matter for economic activity. We will analyze such costs in Chapter 18. While these anticipated costs of inflation may matter qualitatively in theory, in practical terms they are thought to be small. Further, with currency falling out of favor as a means of payment (in favor of debit cards, credit cards, and other electronic payment instruments), these small costs are falling over time.

A perhaps more important cost of anticipated inflation, in Keynesian economics, is the cost associated with sticky wages and prices. For example, if firms change their prices at infrequent intervals, and there is a high rate of inflation, relative prices will tend to be out of line with the optimal relative prices that would efficiently allocate resources in the economy. With higher rates of inflation, relative prices get more out of line, with increasing welfare costs, and firms may resort to changing prices at higher frequency, thus incurring greater management costs.

In this chapter, the anticipated costs arising from sticky prices will be our primary concern. We will extend the New Keynesian sticky price model of Chapter 14, and use

---

[1]See T. Sargent, 1982. "The Ends of Four Big Inflations," in *Inflation: Causes and Effects*, edited by Robert Hall, Cambridge, MA: National Bureau of Economic Research.

it to study inflation determination and the role of monetary policy in controlling inflation. An important element in this extension of the New Keynesian model will be the Phillips curve.

In the 1950s, A. W. Phillips noticed, in data for the United Kingdom,[2] that there was a negative relationship between the rate of change in nominal wages and the unemployment rate. Other researchers found that such a relationship existed in data for other countries. Further, because the rate of change in nominal wages is highly positively correlated with the rate of change in other money prices, and the unemployment rate is highly negatively correlated with the deviation of aggregate economic activity from trend, it should not be surprising that if there is a negative correlation between the rate of change in nominal wages and the unemployment rate, there is also a positive correlation between the inflation rate and the deviation of aggregate economic activity from trend. Indeed, the term Phillips curve has come to denote any positive correlation between aggregate economic activity and the inflation rate.

In some macroeconomic theories,[3] the Phillips curve is simply a correlation that we might see in the data at some times, but not at other times. In such theories, the Phillips curve is unstable, and can shift with anticipations about future inflation, and with changes in economic policy rules. However, in New Keynesian macroeconomic theory, the Phillips curve has had a resurgence, and plays an important role in the theory. Many central banks have embraced New Keynesian models, in part because they rationalize traditional central banking approaches to controlling inflation.

In this chapter, we first explore a basic New Keynesian model that incorporates a Phillips curve and determines inflation. In this model, we treat anticipated inflation as exogenous. The model shows how there are trade-offs in a central bank's goals with respect to inflation and real economic activity. The model has the property that an increase in the central bank's nominal interest rate target reduces inflation; if the central bank thinks the inflation rate is too high (low), then it should increase (decrease) its nominal interest rate target.

We study what happens when monetary policy is constrained by the zero lower bound on the nominal interest rate. That is, the central bank could encounter a situation in which inflation and output are deemed to be too low. Such a situation would normally dictate lowering the central bank's nominal interest rate target, but if the nominal interest rate is already at zero, this cannot be done. In such circumstances, an unconventional monetary policy approach—forward guidance—can work to accomplish the central bank's goals. Such a policy works by promising higher inflation in the future, so as to increase inflation and output today.

We extend the New Keynesian model by incorporating rational expectations—the idea that consumers and firms use information efficiently. This will involve modeling more explicitly how the economy evolves dynamically over time, and allows us to explore neo-Fisherian ideas, in a *New Keynesian rational expectations model (NKRE model)*.

---

[2]See A.W. Phillips, 1958. "The Relationship Between Unemployment and the Rate of Change of Money Wages in the United Kingdom, 1861–1957," *Economica* 25, 283–299.

[3]R. Lucas, 1972. "Expectations and the Neutrality of Money," *Journal of Economic Theory* 4, 103–124.

Recall from Chapter 12 that the Fisher effect is a positive association between the nominal interest rate and inflation. If we observed this correlation in the data (which we do, as shown in Chapter 12) we might infer that, if the central bank were to increase its nominal interest rate, this should increase inflation. Conventional central banking practice and our basic New Keynesian model with exogenous anticipated future inflation would say this is wrong. But, we can show in our NKRE model that this is correct. This is the basic neo-Fisherian principle: raising the nominal interest rate increases inflation.

In our analysis with the NKRE model, we show how typical central banking policy rules can go astray. Further, we show how neo-Fisherian monetary policy rules bring about efficient inflation control.

Inflation in a Basic New Keynesian Model

LO 15.1 Construct the basic New Keynesian model with inflation, and demonstrate how it works.

In modern Keynesian sticky price models, a Phillips curve is derived from the microeconomic behavior of price-setting firms. In a typical New Keynesian setting, firms engage in **Calvo pricing**,[4] in that each firm has a random opportunity to change its price each period. That is, firms face a menu cost (a cost of changing prices, as discussed in Chapter 14), determined each period, which is either zero or infinite. So, if a given firm has an opportunity to set its price at a particular point in time, it knows that this opportunity may not happen again until some date (randomly determined) in the future. Thus, in setting its price, the firm needs to make a forecast of how likely a price-setting opportunity is to arise in the future, and what it will do in the future if the price-setting opportunity arises, and if it does not. A key assumption—and part of much traditional Keynesian economics—is that, if a firm cannot change its price in the current period, its output is demand-determined. That is, the firm serves all demand for its product, given the sticky price that it cannot change.

This price-setting behavior, and demand-determined output, implies that, if future inflation is higher than firms expected, then firms have made an error in setting their prices, which will tend to be lower for the firms that cannot change their prices than for the firms that can. Thus, the sticky-price firms will see a surge in demand, and output will go up. This is the Phillips curve relation: unexpectedly high inflation implies higher output. This translates into a Phillips curve that we can write as

$$i = a(Y - Y_m) + bi'. \tag{15-1}$$

In Equation (15-1), i is the current inflation rate, Y_m is the efficient level of output, and i' is the anticipated future rate of inflation. Assume that $a > 0$, and $0 < b < 1$. Thus,

---

[4]G. Calvo 1983. "Staggered Prices in a Utility-Maximizing Framework," *Journal of Monetary Economics* 12, 383–398.

the higher is current inflation, the smaller is the output gap $(Y_m - Y)$, as firms that cannot change their prices are producing more output than expected. As well, the higher is anticipated future inflation, the higher is current inflation, as firms that can change their prices will increase them more to account for projected future inflation. But this latter effect is less than one-for-one: a 1% increase in the anticipated future inflation rate increases current inflation by less than 1%.

Recall from Chapter 12 that the Fisher relation, which defines the real interest rate, can be written

$$r = R - i',$$ (15-2)

so the real interest is the nominal interest rate minus anticipated future inflation. We can then extend the New Keynesian sticky price model in Chapter 14 so that it determines inflation using the Phillips curve relationship, Equation (15-1). Further, we can depict the New Keynesian model in a simpler way, to capture the essentials we need, in Figure 15.1. In panel (a) of the figure is the output demand curve (or IS curve, using New Keynesian language), $Y^d(IS)$, and the Phillips curve defined by Equation (15-1) is in panel (b), denoted by PC. In panel (a), r^* is the natural rate of interest; if $r = r^*$, then output is at its efficient level.

In Figure 15.1, anticipated inflation i' is exogenous, and the nominal interest rate R is determined exogenously by the central bank. Then, output Y_1 in the figure is determined in panel (a), given equation (15-2). Given the equilibrium solution for Y_1, the Phillips curve in panel (b), denoted by PC, determines inflation i in equilibrium.

Monetary Policy Goals

LO 15.2 Show how there is a trade-off between the goals of the central bank in the basic New Keynesian model.

Many modern central banks have an inflation target, as does the Fed. Thus, suppose in our model that the central bank has determined a target rate of inflation i^* that maximizes aggregate economic welfare. So, any departures from the inflation target - on the high side or the low side - will reduce economic welfare. We will not model the details of why i^* is optimal, and why low inflation and high inflation can be bad, but will take these things as given. Further, assume that the marginal cost of a departure from the inflation target increases as the size of the departure increases. For example, if the optimal inflation rate is 2%, then a 1% increase in the inflation is more costly if the actual inflation rate is 10% than if it is 3%.

Central banks also care about real economic activity. For example, the U.S. Congress has given the Fed a **dual mandate**, which specifies that the Fed should care about price stability, and about "maximum employment." The Fed has interpreted price stability to mean a 2% inflation target, but "maximum employment" is a rather vague guideline. However, in the context of our model, the central bank's target for aggregate economic activity should be the efficient level of aggregate output, $Y = Y_m$. That is, the government in our model should specify that the second part of the dual mandate

Figure 15.1 The Basic New Keynesian Model

Panel (a) depicts the output demand curve (or IS curve), while panel (b) is the Phillips curve. The central bank determines the nominal interest rate, which determines output in panel (a). Then, given equilibrium output, current inflation is determined in panel (b) by the Phillips curve.

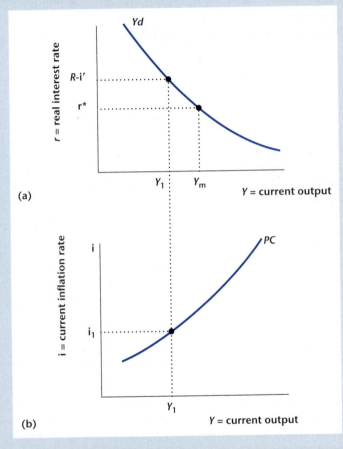

(after price stability) for the central bank should be an output gap equal to zero. This is the same as a target for the real interest rate of r^*, the natural rate of interest.

So, the optimum for the central bank is $i = i^*$ and $r = r^*$, but it may not be possible to achieve this optimum—the central bank may face trade-offs. For example, in Figure 15.2, suppose that the economy is initially in equilibrium at A, with the real interest rate r_1^* and inflation rate i^*. Then, suppose that the natural rate of interest declines to r_2^*, in this case because of a shift to the right in the output supply curve; for example, because of a temporary increase in total factor productivity. With anticipated future inflation unchanged, if the central bank keeps the nominal interest rate at its initial value, the equilibrium will stay at point A, which implies that the central bank continues to achieve its inflation target. But at point A the real interest rate is above the

Figure 15.2 A Decrease in the Natural Rate of Interest

The economy is initially in equilibrium at point A. The natural interest rate falls. The central bank could stay at A and achieve its inflation target, or go to B and achieve a zero output gap. But a point like D, which trades off the two goals of the central bank, is optimal.

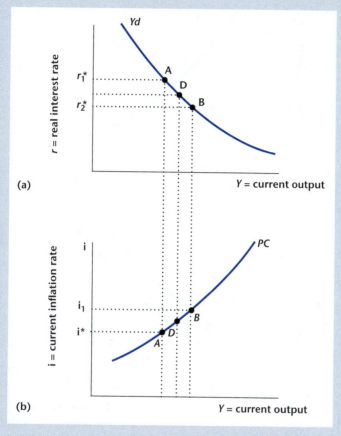

new natural rate r_2^*, so the central bank is not achieving its output target—there is a positive output gap.

A possibility for the central bank is to lower the nominal interest rate so that $R - i' = r_2^*$, in which case the equilibrium will be at point B in Figure 15.2. This implies that the central bank is hitting its output target, but not its inflation target, as $i_1 > i^*$. Given our assumptions about the losses from being away from its target, the central bank's optimal policy is a point intermediate between A and B, point D, where it is achieving neither target, but is optimally trading off the losses of deviations from the two targets.

Alternatively, suppose in Figure 15.3 that the economy is initially in equilibrium with output demand curve Y^d and Phillips curve PC_1, so that in equilibrium $r = r^*$ and $i = i^*$.

Figure 15.3 An Increase in Anticipated Future Inflation

The initial equilibrium is at point A. Similar to Figure 15.2, the best response of the central bank is a point like D, which trades off the central bank's two goals.

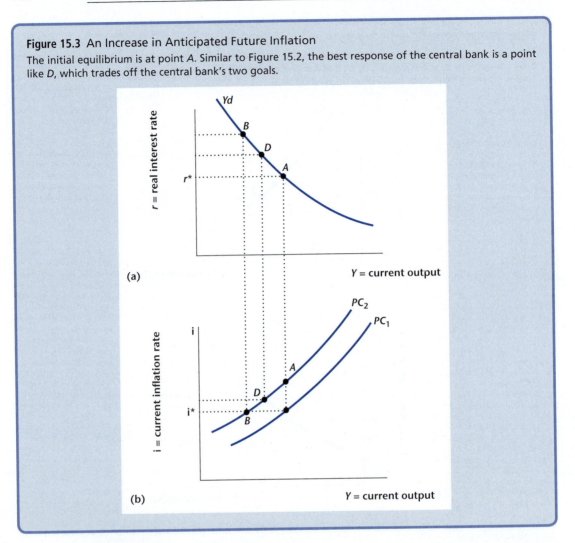

Then, suppose that the anticipated future inflation rate rises from i_1' to i_2'. This shifts the Phillips curve up to PC_2. In this circumstance the central bank could just increase the nominal interest rate one-for-one with the increase in anticipated inflation, so that $R - i_2' = r^*$. In this case, the equilibrium will be at A, so that the central bank is hitting its output target (the output gap is zero), but inflation is greater than the inflation target.

Another option for the central bank in Figure 15.3 is to increase the nominal interest rate even more than one-for-one in response to the increase in anticipated inflation, to reach B. Then, the central bank would be achieving its inflation target, but there would be a positive output gap. Just as in Figure 15.2, an optimal choice for the central bank is an intermediate point such as D, in which the central bank is missing its inflation target on the high side, and there is a positive output gap. Note that point D implies that the central bank increased the nominal interest rate more than one-for-one in response to the increase in anticipated inflation.

THEORY CONFRONTS THE DATA
The Phillips Curve

The Phillips curve first made an appearance in macroeconomic thought in the 1950s, when A. W. Phillips pointed out a negative correlation between the rate of change in nominal wages and the unemployment rate, for U.K. data. By the 1960s, some macroeconomists had taken to treating the Phillips curve as a structural relationship, representing a policy menu. That is, given the reasoning at the time, it was thought that central banks could achieve permanently lower unemployment, at the cost of permanently higher inflation.[5]

However, Milton Friedman reasoned that there could be no long-run Phillips curve trade-off, and Robert Lucas provided a theoretical foundation for this claim.[6] Lucas's theory showed how the Phillips curve could shift with inflation expectations and with monetary policy rules, and thus be unstable over time. Thus, by the 1970s, it appeared that the Phillips curve had been debunked as a useful element in macroeconomic policymaking. However, New Keynesian models, developed beginning in the 1990s, included the Phillips curve as a key element in the theory, and provided support for the idea that firms faced with costs of setting their prices could produce the Phillips curve correlation in the data.[7]

The Phillips curve is not something that is immediately discernible in the data, unlike the Fisher relation, shown in Figure 12.1, Chapter 12. For example, if we plot the inflation rate for the period 1949–2016 for the United States against a measure of the output gap—the Congressional Budget Office's natural rate of unemployment minus the unemployment rate—a Phillips curve is not discernible. We show the scatter plot in Figure 15.4. The Phillips curve, if it were stable over time, would appear as a positively sloped relationship in the scatter plot, but all we see is a cloud.

But over the period 1949–2016 represented in the data in Figure 15.4, inflation expectations should not have been constant, as inflation increased until the 1970s, and then decreased over time. What if we examine a period when we could argue that expected inflation was roughly constant? Figure 15.5 shows the path of the inflation rate and our measure of the output gap over the period 2009Q2, which marked the end of the 2008–2009 recession, and 2016Q1. In the figure, the line connects points from the beginning of the sample period to the end, from left to right, over a period when the unemployment rate was falling relative to the natural rate.

By 2009, the Fed had gained a solid reputation for achieving low and stable inflation, so we could argue that expected inflation was relatively stable over the period 2009Q2 to 2016Q1. Thus, in Figure 15.5, the line should trace out an upward-sloping Phillips curve. But it does not. For much of the period, particularly from the peak in the inflation rate of close to 3% in 2011Q3, unemployment and inflation were both falling. The Phillips curve correlation over this period has the wrong sign.

(Continued)

---

[5]Paul Anthony Samuelson and Robert M. Solow, 1960. "Analytical Aspects of Anti-inflation Policy," *American Economic Review* 50(2), 177–194.

[6]M. Friedman, 1968. "The Role of Monetary Policy," *American Economic Review* 58, 1–17; R. Lucas, 1972, "Expectations and the Neutrality of Money," *Journal of Economic Theory* 4, 103–124.

[7]See M. Woodford, 2003. *Interest and Prices*, Princeton, NJ: Princeton University Press.

Figure 15.4 A Phillips Curve?

Data for 1949–2016 shows no discernible Phillips correlation.

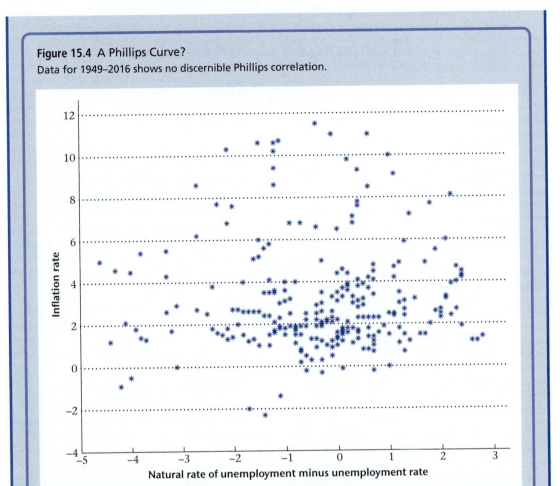

In general, the Phillips curve is not a strong relationship in macroeconomic data, if it exists at all. For example, recent econometric work suggests that the Phillips curve correlation in the data, while it may have the right sign, is not large.[8]

[8] O. Blanchard, 2015. "The U.S. Phillips Curve: Back to the 1960s?" Peterson Institute for International Economics, *Policy Brief*, PB16-1, https://piie.com/publications/pb/pb16-1.pdf.

(Continued)

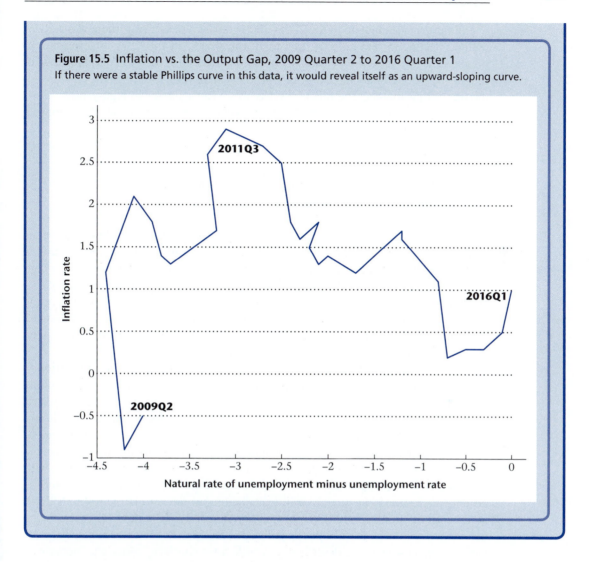

Figure 15.5 Inflation vs. the Output Gap, 2009 Quarter 2 to 2016 Quarter 1

If there were a stable Phillips curve in this data, it would reveal itself as an upward-sloping curve.

Low Real Interest Rates and the Zero Lower Bound

LO 15.3 Demonstrate the problem a central bank faces when the real interest rate is low, and show how this might be solved with forward guidance by the central bank.

From Chapter 11, the natural rate of interest—the equilibrium real interest rate if prices were perfectly flexible—is determined by the intersection of the output demand and supply curves. Thus, the determinants of the natural real rate of interest, on the output demand side, are the factors determining the consumption/savings behavior of consumers, factors determining the investment decisions of firms, and government spending on goods and services. The determinants of the real interest rate on the output supply side are current total factor productivity, the capital stock, and factors affecting labor supply.

In the years leading up to the 2008–2009 global financial crisis, there was a documented decline in real rates of interest in the world. In the U.S., for example, in Figure 12.2 in Chapter 12 we can observe a trend decline in the short-term real rate of interest beginning in about 1980. As well, there were further declines in real rates of interest during and after the financial crisis, as we can again see in Figure 12.2.

What were the causes of this long-term decline in real interest rates? Economists have suggested at least three, which are

1. The global "savings glut."
2. A dearth of investment opportunities, or "secular stagnation."
3. An increase in financial market frictions.

First, Ben Bernanke has argued that an unusually high level of household savings in the world acted to reduce real interest rates—the **savings glut**.[9] What he has in mind is mainly a high level of savings in Asia—China in particular. From Chapter 9, a high level of savings could result from a shift in consumers' preferences; for example, if consumers care more about the future they will save more and consume less in the present, given their lifetime wealth and the market real interest rate. Then, in the real intertemporal model of Chapter 11, this serves to shift the output demand curve to the left, and reduce the natural real rate of interest.

Second, Lawrence Summers has developed the concept of **secular stagnation**.[10] Summers argues that investment opportunities are much less attractive, particularly after the financial crisis. In our model we could ascribe this to a decline in anticipated future total factor productivity, which reduces the demand for investment goods and shifts the output demand curve to the left, reducing the natural real rate of interest.

Finally, there was an increase in financial market frictions during the financial crisis, along with stiffer financial regulation after the 2008–2009 financial crisis, with these two factors having similar effects in credit markets. As we studied in Chapter 11, greater financial market frictions will shift the output demand curve to the left and increase labor supply, shifting the output supply curve to the right. As a result, the natural rate of interest falls. In public policy discussions, the increase in financial market frictions is sometimes described as a "safe asset shortage," since the increase in financial market frictions causes a flight to the safety of safe assets such as government debt and high-grade corporate debt and asset-backed securities.[11] With the increase in demand for such assets relative to supply, consumers and firms are willing to hold these safe assets at lower rates of return; that is, real interest rates fall.

So, suppose that the natural rate of interest has declined. In our basic New Keynesian model, what implications might this have? In Figure 15.6, we show a situation in

---

[9]See B. Bernanke, 2015. "Why Are Interest Rates So Low, Part 3: The Global Savings Glut," http://www.brookings.edu/blogs/ben-bernanke/posts/2015/04/01-why-interest-rates-low-global-savings-glut.

[10]L. Summers, 2016. "The Age of Secular Stagnation: What It Is and What to Do About It," *Foreign Affairs*, March–April issue.

[11]See D. Andolfatto and S. Williamson, 2015. "Scarcity of Safe Assets, Inflation, and the Policy Trap," *Journal of Monetary Economics* 73, 70–92.

Figure 15.6 A Liquidity Trap: The Zero Lower Bound
The nominal interest rate cannot go below zero, with a positive output gap and inflation below its target.

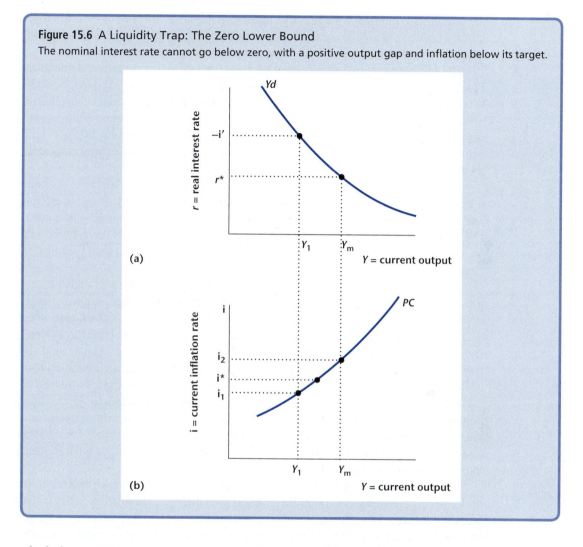

which the nominal interest rate is set at zero by the central bank, implying that the real interest rate is $r = -i'$. But, even with a nominal interest rate equal to zero, the market real interest rate is higher, in the figure, than the natural rate of interest, r^*. This implies that there is a positive output gap, equal to $Y_m - Y_1$. As well, in the configuration shown in Figure 15.6, the actual inflation rate i_1 is lower than the optimal inflation rate i^*, which is lower than the inflation rate i_2, which is the hypothetical equilibrium inflation rate we would see if in fact the real interest rate could fall to r^*.

Figure 15.6 depicts a problem for conventional monetary policy. Under normal conditions, the central bank can adjust the nominal interest rate to achieve the optimal trade-off between its two goals—optimal inflation and zero output gap. But in the case depicted in the figure, inflation is below the inflation target, and there is a positive output gap. This would normally dictate that the central bank should lower its nominal interest rate target, since this would move the inflation rate toward its target, and reduce the output gap. But, since the nominal interest rate is at its lower bound, it can go no lower. This was exactly the conundrum that many central banks in the world—including the Fed—saw themselves in after the 2008–2009 financial crisis.

Though conventional monetary policy is stymied by the situation depicted in Figure 15.6, it is possible that unconventional alternatives exist. Indeed, Michael Woodford,[12] among others, has suggested that **forward guidance** would be an effective unconventional policy action in a situation where the zero lower bound restricts conventional monetary policy actions. Forward guidance is a commitment by the central bank to take an action in the future that may not be optimal for the central bank once the future arrives.

To see how forward guidance works, consider Figure 15.7, which depicts the same initial situation as in Figure 15.6. That is, in Figure 15.7, initially the nominal interest rate is set at zero by the central bank, and anticipated future inflation is i'_1. The initial Phillips curve is PC_1, and in equilibrium the level of output is Y_1 and the inflation rate is i_1 Thus, there is a positive output gap initially, and inflation is lower than the inflation target, which is i^*.

Forward guidance in this context is a promise by the central bank of higher future inflation than would otherwise be optimal for the central bank. Thus, suppose that i'_1 is the optimal level of inflation that the central bank would choose in the future when the natural rate of interest has risen so that the zero lower bound is no longer a problem. If the central bank promises that inflation in the future will be even higher, and the public believes the central bank will keep this promise, then anticipated inflation rises to i'_2, which shifts the Phillips curve up to PC_2 and lowers the real rate of interest to $-i'_2$. Thus, with the nominal interest rate still at zero, output increases to Y_2, and inflation increases to i_2, which is greater than the inflation target. If the central bank commits to the right amount of inflation in the future, then this will achieve the optimal trade-off for the central bank between its current inflation and output goals, and its future inflation and output goals.

But, in using forward guidance, commitment by the central bank is essential. In the future, the central bank may be tempted to reduce inflation below what it had promised, because in the future the past is gone, and the current level of inflation would be viewed as excessive. But, if the central bank does not fulfill its promise, then it is unlikely that the central bank's promises will be believed if it decides it wants to use forward guidance again.

This is much like the problem faced by a teacher and his or her students. Suppose that an ideal outcome for both the teacher and the students is that the students learn the course material. At the beginning of the course, the teacher promises the students that he or she will conduct a final exam at the termination of the course. If the teacher has credibility, then the students believe that he or she will conduct the exam, and they learn the course material. But once the exam date arrives, the teacher and students will all be better off if the exam is not held. The students do not have to sit for the exam, and the teacher does not have to spend tedious hours grading exam papers. If the

---

[12]M. Woodford, 2012. "Methods of Policy Accommodation at the Interest Rate Lower Bound," presented at the Federal Reserve Bank of Kansas City Symposium on "The Changing Policy Landscape," Jackson Hole, WY, August 31, 2012, http://www.columbia.edu/~mw2230/JHole2012final.pdf.

Figure 15.7 Forward Guidance at the Zero Lower Bound

A promise of higher inflation in the future shifts the Phillips curve, reduces the output gap, and increases inflation.

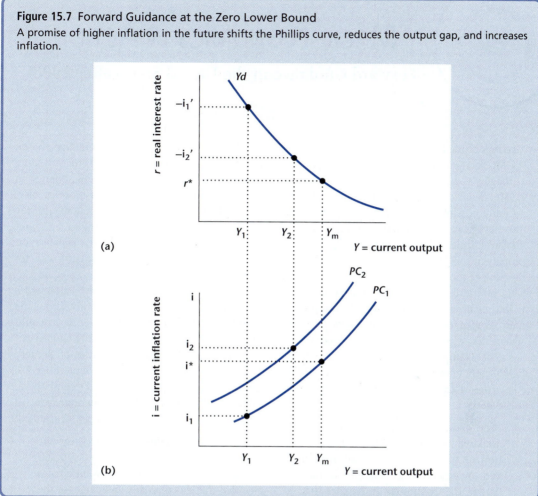

teacher has no means for committing to holding the exam, the students will understand that the teacher's promise is empty, and they will not learn the course material. This is why, in practice, educational institutions typically regard a course syllabus as a firm commitment akin to a legal contract, from which a teacher cannot deviate.

In practice, central banks may find it difficult to adhere to explicit commitments. Indeed, the promises made in policy statements may be too vague to have any force—they may commit the central bank to nothing at all. But, some central banks have explicit commitment mechanisms built into their relationship with the government. For example, in New Zealand, the governor of the Reserve Bank of New Zealand (RBNZ, New Zealand's central bank) writes a policy targets agreement (PTA) with the government of New Zealand. Since 1991, the PTA has specified an explicit target for the inflation rate.[13] This

---

[13]"Explaining New Zealand's Monetary Policy," Reserve Bank of New Zealand, http://www.rbnz.govt.nz/-/media/ReserveBank/Files/Publications/Factsheets%20and%20Guides/factsheet-explaining-new-zealands-monetary-policy.pdf

MACROECONOMICS IN ACTION

Forward Guidance in the United States after 2008

Meetings of the Federal Open Market Committee (FOMC) of the Fed take place eight times per year, at roughly 6-week intervals. At each meeting the FOMC decides on a target for the federal funds rate, and possibly on elements of unconventional monetary policy—quantitative easing or forward guidance. Indeed, forward guidance has played a prominent role in Fed policy since late in 2008, at the peak of the financial crisis. Forward guidance was communicated in public statements by the FOMC chair and other Fed officials, but the primary vehicles for forward guidance were the policy statements issued after each FOMC meeting.[14]

One example of forward guidance is in the FOMC policy statement of December 16, 2008.[15] After a description of the FOMC's current actions, it is stated:

> "The Federal Reserve will employ all available tools to promote the resumption of sustainable economic growth and to preserve price stability. In particular, the Committee anticipates that weak economic conditions are likely to warrant exceptionally low levels of the federal funds rate for some time."[16]

This paragraph is about what the FOMC plans for the future, and therefore constitutes forward guidance. But, as a commitment, it is rather vague. The FOMC does not tell us what the "available tools" are that it might employ. And it tells us it plans to keep interest rates low, but gives no hint as to what "some time" might mean.

By March 18, 2009, the language in the FOMC statement had changed from "for some time" to "an extended period." This change in wording made the meaning a bit more precise, suggesting that the federal funds rate would stay low for a long time, without saying much about how long that might be. While the clarification seemed encouraging, the commitment was not very solid.

On August 9, 2011, the FOMC attached a calendar date to its forward guidance about the path for the federal funds rate, saying it would remain low "at least through mid-2013." This calendar guidance was extended further, on January 5, 2012, to "late 2014," and on September 13, 2012, to "mid-2015." Then, on December 12, 2012, the FOMC abandoned calendar forward guidance about the federal funds rate, and stated:

> " . . . the Committee decided to keep the target range for the federal funds rate at 0 to 1/4 percent and currently anticipates that this exceptionally low range for the federal funds rate will be appropriate at least as long as the unemployment rate remains above 6-1/2 percent, inflation between one and two years ahead is projected to be no more than a half percentage point above the Committee's 2 percent longer-run goal, and longer-term inflation expectations continue to be well anchored. The Committee views these thresholds as consistent with its earlier date-based guidance. In determining how long to maintain a highly accommodative stance of monetary policy, the Committee will also consider other information, including additional measures of labor market conditions,

---

[14]These policy statements can be found on the Board of Governors website, at http://www.federalreserve.gov/monetarypolicy/fomccalendars.htm.

[15]http://www.federalreserve.gov/newsevents/press/monetary/20081216b.htm.

[16]December 16, 2008, FOMC statement, Federal Reserve.

indicators of inflation pressures and inflation expectations, and readings on financial developments. When the Committee decides to begin to remove policy accommodation, it will take a balanced approach consistent with its longer-run goals of maximum employment and inflation of 2 percent."[17]

So, there are a lot more words in that paragraph, meant to describe what the FOMC will do with the federal funds rate target in the future. What do those words mean? The FOMC seemingly intended to lay out a contingent plan, which is somewhat more consistent with sound macroeconomics, in that the future plans were actually tied to the state of the economy, and not to a particular calendar date. But what did the FOMC intend to do when the unemployment rate crossed the 6.5% threshold, provided inflation was lower than 2.5%, and inflation expectations were well-anchored? And what exactly does anchored mean, as regards inflation expectations? Is this something we can measure, or what? The Committee was going to take a "balanced approach" sometime in the future, but what would it be balancing, and why? Perhaps this wordy paragraph raises more questions than it answers.

By March 19, 2014, the FOMC was anticipating that the unemployment rate would soon cross the 6.5% threshold, as it did in April 2014. The part of the March 19, 2014, FOMC statement regarding federal funds rate forward guidance reads:

> "To support continued progress toward maximum employment and price stability, the Committee today reaffirmed its view that a highly accommodative stance of monetary policy remains appropriate. In determining how long to maintain the current 0 to 1/4 percent target range for the federal funds rate, the Committee will assess progress—both realized and expected— toward its objectives of maximum

employment and 2 percent inflation. This assessment will take into account a wide range of information, including measures of labor market conditions, indicators of inflation pressures and inflation expectations, and readings on financial developments. The Committee continues to anticipate, based on its assessment of these factors, that it likely will be appropriate to maintain the current target range for the federal funds rate for a considerable time after the asset purchase program ends, especially if projected inflation continues to run below the Committee's 2 percent longer-run goal, and provided that longer-term inflation expectations remain well anchored."[18]

Basically, this statement says that the FOMC was not yet ready to increase its target for the federal funds rate. But when would it be ready? Apparently, when it could look at all the data and deem that the state of the economy warranted an increase in interest rates. But it is unclear from this paragraph what would tip the balance. Apparently, the FOMC would look at all available information and make a decision, which is not actually saying much, other than that this would be a "considerable time" in the future.

Ultimately, the FOMC decided to increase its target range for the federal funds rate from 0–0.25% to 0.25%–0.50% on December 16, 2015, after about seven years of close-to-zero nominal interest rates—unprecedented since the modern era of independent Fed policymaking began in 1951. In December 2015, the unemployment rate was at 5%, well below the 6.5% threshold that it had set three years earlier.

What are we to make of this seven-year period of Fed experimentation with forward guidance? From macroeconomic theory, we know that commitment by the policymaker is important if forward guidance is to work, and that

---

[17]December 12, 2012, the FOMC statement, Federal Reserve.

[18]March 19, 2014 FOMC statement, Federal Reserve.

(Continued)

forward guidance should be clear, simple, and easy to understand. If those are our standards for success, then the experiment was a failure.

The Fed's forward guidance certainly did not constitute a commitment. First, the statements were often vague—what does "considerable time" or "extended period" mean? Second, when forward guidance specified a specific threshold—for example, 6.5% for the unemployment rate—it was unclear what would

happen after the threshold was crossed. Further, when action was ultimately taken, this seemed to bear no relation to the previously specified 6.5% threshold.

Finally, we could hardly say that the Fed was communicating in a clear, simple, and easy-to-understand fashion. Over time, the Fed's policy statements became more convoluted and confusing—unhelpful, to say the least. Perhaps we can sometimes say more with less.

represents a firm commitment, in that the governor of the RBNZ can in principle be dismissed if he or she fails in meeting the terms of the PTA. However, to date the PTA does not specify anything as specific as forward guidance at the zero lower bound.

Neo-Fisherism, and a New Keynesian Rational Expectations (NKRE) Model

LO 15.4 Construct the New Keynesian model under rational expectations, and show what happens in the model in response to changes in the nominal interest rate.

The traditional view of central bankers is that, if a higher (lower) rate of inflation is desired, then this can be achieved through a reduction (increase) in the nominal interest rate target. That is, if inflation is greater (lower) than the central bank's inflation target, the central bank should raise (lower) the nominal interest rate target. The traditional view is captured in the basic New Keynesian model that we have worked with thus far in this chapter.

Neo-Fisherians assert that traditional central bankers have inflation control wrong. That is, a neo-Fisherian central banker would increase (decrease) the nominal interest rate when inflation is below (above) the central banker's inflation target. This idea may at first seem radical, but we can show how this works by being more explicit about how our New Keynesian model works.

To be specific, suppose for simplicity that there are no aggregate shocks in the present or at any time in the future. This allows us to focus our attention on inflation, its causes, and how inflation changes over time in response to monetary policy. We can write the output demand relationship as

$$Y - Y' = -\frac{1}{d}(R - i' - r^*). \tag{15-3}$$

In Equation (15-3), Y' denotes the anticipated future demand for goods, and $1/d$ is the intertemporal elasticity of substitution, a measure of the representative consumer's willingness to substitute consumption intertemporally, with $d > 0$. Equation (15-3) states that the difference between the current demand for goods and the future demand for goods depends on the difference between the real interest rate, $R - i'$, and the natural real rate of interest r^*. The natural rate of interest is another name for the representative consumer's rate of time preference, which is the rate at which the consumer discounts future utility relative to utility today. If the real rate of interest is higher than the natural rate of interest, the demand for future goods is higher than for goods in the present, as the representative consumer will substitute consumption in the future for consumption in the present.

Next, we will simplify the Phillips curve specification by setting $b = 0$ in Equation (15-1) to get

$$i = a(Y - Y_m). \tag{15-4}$$

This implies that, when firms set their prices, they do not do so in a forward-looking fashion that accounts for anticipated inflation. This does not matter for anything important in our analysis, and it makes the math much easier.

A key assumption we will now make is **rational expectations**, which has been an organizing principle in macroeconomics since the 1970s. In general terms, rational expectations modeling assumes that the people who live in the models do the best they can in forecasting future economic variables, given their knowledge of the world they live in. If we assume in our model that the consumers and firms in the model world have full knowledge of how the economy works, then rational expectations means that, in equilibrium, their forecasts are on average correct. In models in which there are unpredictable aggregate shocks, rational expectations implies that people do not make systematic errors—they cannot be fooled on a regular basis. But, since we are assuming in our model that there are no shocks, in equilibrium rational expectations implies that anticipated future inflation is equal to actual inflation in the future period, and anticipated future output is equal to actual future output. In equilibrium, the people in our model will not be surprised.

The next step is to solve for an equilibrium in this model. In Equations (15-3) and (15-4), r^* and Y_m are exogenous, and we will assume that these two variables are constant for all time. Then, Equations (15-3) and (15-4) show the relationship among current output, current inflation, future output and future inflation, given the nominal interest rate R, which is set by the central bank. Like the Malthusian model and the Solow growth model in Chapter 7, this New Keynesian model is a dynamic model, and an equilibrium consists of inflation rates and output levels that start at the beginning of time, and continue forever, and that solve the two Equations (15-3) and (15-4) at each date.

To simplify, note that Equation (15-4) must also hold in the future period, so

$$i' = a(Y' - Y_m). \tag{15-5}$$

Then, substitute for Y and Y' respectively, in Equation (15-3), using Equations (15-4) and (15-5), and solve this equation with i' on the left-hand side of the equation, obtaining

$$i' = \frac{a(R - r^*)}{a + d} + \frac{di}{a + d}. \tag{15-6}$$

Then, an equilibrium is an initial inflation rate i_0 and a sequence of inflation rates determined by Equation (15-6). That is, start with $i = i_0$ on the right-hand side of Equation (15-6), which determines future inflation i', which is inflation in the next period. Then, plug this value into the right-hand side of Equation (15-6) for i, which determines inflation in the next period, and so on.

In Figure 15.8, we depict Equation (15-6), with current inflation on the horizontal axis, and future inflation on the vertical axis. If R, the nominal interest rate, is constant forever then, as in the dynamic economic growth models we studied in Chapter 7, there is a steady state, which is point A in the figure, where the equation defined by Equation (15-6) intersects the 45 degree line along which $i = i'$. Once inflation reaches its steady state value, it will stay there forever, given a constant nominal interest rate.

But, something that differs in this dynamic model from the growth models in Chapter 7 is that there is nothing to tie down the initial inflation rate i_0, given a constant nominal interest rate. This is a property common to monetary models in macroeconomics—an **indeterminacy problem**. That is, given a constant nominal interest rate, there are many equilibria. For example, the steady state A in Figure 15.8 is an equilibrium, but there are also many equilibria that have an initial inflation rate away from the steady state, but that converge to the steady state in the long run. One of these equilibria is depicted in the figure, in which the inflation rate increases from an initial value below the steady state, and ultimately converges to the steady state. The indeterminacy problem matters for monetary policy. In general we would like economic policies to produce predictable outcomes, otherwise it is difficult or impossible to make policy recommendations.

Though the equilibrium is indeterminate given a constant nominal interest rate, there is a unique steady state—point A in Figure 15.8. This is the unique long-run equilibrium. If we solve for the steady state by setting $i' = i$ in Equation (15-6) and solve for i, we obtain

$$i = R - r^*, \tag{15-7}$$

which is the **long-run Fisher relation**. That is, in the long-run the inflation rate is equal to the nominal interest rate minus the natural rate of interest. Thus, in the long run, it must be the case that an increase in the nominal interest rate results in a one-for-one increase in the inflation rate. As we noted in Chapter 12, the Fisher effect is a positive relationship between inflation and the nominal interest rate. In this instance, the Fisher effect is causal, running from the nominal interest rate to inflation. That is, the central bank sets the nominal interest rate, and in the long run a higher nominal interest rate *causes* the inflation rate to be higher. In this model, this long-run Fisher effect is one-for-one, though there are some factors in other more complicated economic models that could yield a long-run effect of monetary policy on the natural rate of interest r^*.

This is the first neo-Fisherian insight: in the long run, a higher nominal interest rate causes higher inflation. This is clearly very different from the short-run result that we obtained in the New Keynesian model when future anticipated inflation was

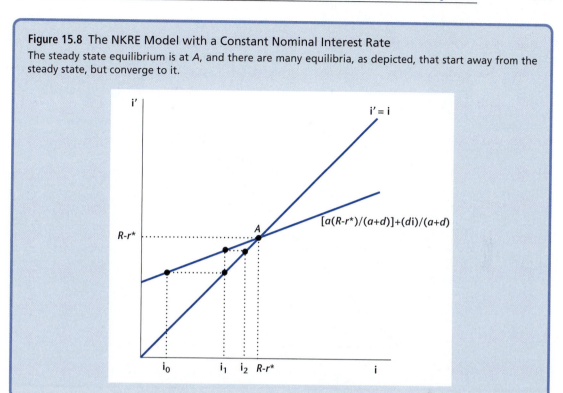

Figure 15.8 The NKRE Model with a Constant Nominal Interest Rate

The steady state equilibrium is at *A*, and there are many equilibria, as depicted, that start away from the steady state, but converge to it.

exogenous. In that context, a higher nominal interest rate increased the real interest rate, which reduced output, which in turn reduced inflation via the Phillips curve (a higher output gap means lower inflation). What is different here? With rational expectations, a higher nominal interest rate implies a higher real interest rate, which causes intertemporal substitution: the representative consumer demands more goods in the future relative to the present. But this does not mean that current output goes down, it means that future output goes up. With higher future output, future inflation goes up due to a Phillips curve effect (lower output gap in the future), and ultimately inflation increases to the point where the long-run Fisher relation, Equation (15-7), holds.

But what happens in the short run under rational expectations if the nominal interest rate goes up? Suppose in Figure 15.9 that the economy is initially in a long-run equilibrium with a nominal interest rate R_1, at point *A* in the figure. Then, the nominal interest rate increases to R_2, which implies that the solution given by Equation (15-6) shifts up from D_1 to D_2 in Figure 15.7, so that the steady state shifts to point *B*. Then, the inflation rate will follow a path as shown in the figure. In the period after the nominal interest rate goes up, the inflation rate is i_1. Then, in the period after that the inflation rate i_2, and so on. In Figure 15.10, we show the same process, with time on the horizontal axis and inflation on the vertical axis. The central bank increases the nominal interest rate in period T, and then the inflation rate rises over time to its new

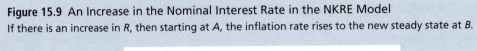

Figure 15.9 An Increase in the Nominal Interest Rate in the NKRE Model
If there is an increase in R, then starting at A, the inflation rate rises to the new steady state at B.

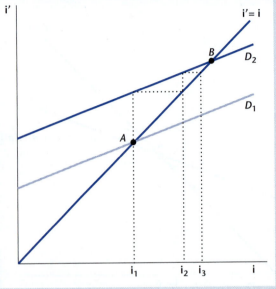

steady state. On the path to the new steady state, the increase in inflation induced by the increase in the nominal interest rate is not one-for-one, but in the long run it is.

The key point is that, in Figures 15.9 and 15.10, the inflation rate never decreases below what it would have otherwise been, even in the short run, when the nominal interest rate is increased by the central bank. This is our second neo-Fisherian result: If the central bank wants the inflation rate to go up, it needs to increase the nominal interest rate—*even in the short run.* That this is a property of the New Keynesian model, which is widely used by central bankers who appear to believe that increasing nominal interest rates reduces inflation, is perhaps surprising.[19]

Neo–Fisherism and Taylor Rules

LO 15.5 Show the perils of Taylor rules given the Taylor principle, and the benefits of neo-Fisherian monetary policy.

In 1993, John Taylor proposed a rule for monetary policy, specifying that central banks should set the nominal interest rate in response to current inflation and

---

[19]Also see J. Cochrane, 2016. "Do Higher Interest Rates Raise or Lower Inflation?" working paper, Hoover Institution, http://faculty.chicagobooth.edu/john.cochrane/research/papers/fisher.pdf; and S. Williamson, 2016. "The Road to Normal: New Directions in Monetary Policy," *Federal Reserve Bank of St. Louis Annual Report 2016,* https://www.stlouisfed.org/annual-report/2015/the-road-to-normal.

Figure 15.10 An Increase in the Nominal Interest Rate in the NKRE Model, Part II

This figure shows the same process as in Figure 15.9, but with time on the horizontal axis, and inflation on the vertical axis.

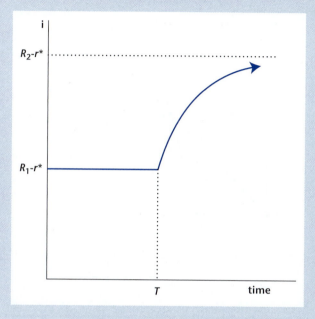

the output gap.[20] Taylor argued that such a rule should perform well in implementing the Fed's dual mandate. For our purposes, it will be convenient to ignore the response of the nominal interest rate target to the output gap, as we want to focus on the behavior of inflation in response to the policy rule. In our model, Taylor's 1993 rule, simplified, takes the form

$$R = \max[0, hi + (1 - h)i^* + r^*]. \tag{15-8}$$

In Equation (15-8) h is a parameter which, in principle, could be any real number—it could be positive or negative. Recall that i^* is the central bank's inflation target. In the equation, the max operator takes the maximum of the two arguments in the operator, to take account of the zero lower bound. For example, if the inflation rate i is such that the second argument in the max operator is negative, then the central bank will set $R = 0$. In the case where $h > 1$, which is what Taylor recommended, the Taylor rule takes the form shown in Figure 15.9. In this case, the Taylor rule, Equation (15-8), says

$$R = 0, \text{ if } i \le \frac{h-1}{h}i^* - \frac{r^*}{h},$$

[20]J. Taylor, 1993. "Discretion vs. Policy Rules in Practice," *Carnegie-Rochester Conference Series on Public Policy* 39, 195–214.

Figure 15.11 A Taylor Rule Under the Taylor Principle

There are two steady states, one at A in which the central bank achieves its inflation target, and one at B where the central bank gets stuck at the zero lower bound with too-low inflation.

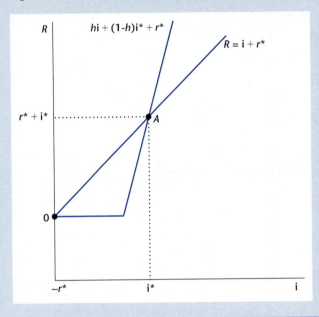

and

$$R = hi + (1 - h)i^* + r^*, \text{ if } i \geq \frac{h - 1}{h}i^* - \frac{r^*}{h}.$$

Why does the Taylor rule take the form it does in Equation (15-8)? If we use the long-run Fisher relation, Equation (15-7), to substitute for the nominal interest rate in Equation (15-8), in the long run there is always a solution for which $i = i^*$. That is, the Taylor rule, Equation (15-8), guarantees that there is a long-run steady state in which the central bank meets its inflation target. In Figure 15.11, this desired steady state is point A. However, when $h > 1$, as is the case in Figure 15.11, there is another steady state in which $R = 0$ and $i = -r^*$. This is an undesired steady state in which the inflation rate is lower than the central bank's inflation target and the central bank is stuck at the zero lower bound.

To explore this further, we want to take the Taylor rule, Equation (15-8), and use it to substitute for R in Equation (15-6). To do the substitution, note that the max operator has the property that $x + max(y, z) = max(x + y, x + z)$, for any x, y, z, and $xmax(y, z) = max(xy, xz)$, for any x, y, z. We obtain

$$i' = max\left[-\frac{ar^*}{a + d} + \frac{di}{a + d}, \frac{(ah + d)i}{a + d} + \frac{a(1 - h)i^*}{a + d}\right]. \tag{15-9}$$

Figure 15.12 Inflation Dynamics Under the Taylor Principle

This illustrates Taylor rule perils. There are many equilibria converging to the undesired steady state at *B*, in which inflation perpetually undershoots the inflation target.

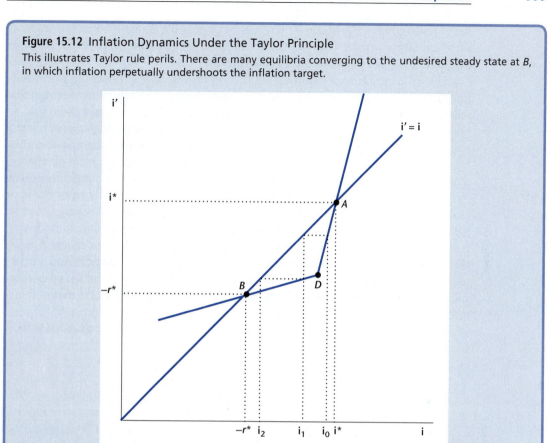

Equation (15-9) is depicted in Figure 15.12, where point *A* is the desired steady state in which the central bank achieves its inflation target, and *B* is the steady state in which $i = -r^*$ and the central bank undershoots its inflation target forever. Point *D* is a critical point for which higher inflation rates imply a positive nominal interest rate, and lower inflation rates imply a nominal interest rate of zero.

A key feature in Figure 15.12 is that there are many equilibria with initial inflation rates near the steady state *A* that diverge from this steady state. Indeed, there are many equilibria like the one depicted in Figure 15.12 that converge to the undesired steady state. That is, the desired steady state is an unstable steady state for which initial inflation rates near that steady state diverge from it, while the undesired steady state is stable.

In the Taylor rule, Equation (15-8), $d > 1$ is called the **Taylor principle**, as this is what Taylor recommended. Taylor's logic seemed to have been that a more-than-one-for-one response of the nominal interest rate to higher inflation would increase the real interest rate, reduce output, and increase the output gap, which would reduce inflation by a Phillips curve mechanism. But, as we can see in Figure 15.12, the Taylor principle has an indeterminacy problem—there are many possible equilibria. Further, many of these equilibria involve convergence to the zero lower bound, and perpetually low inflation. These are **perils of the Taylor rule.**[21]

Thus, a central banker following the Taylor principle, $d > 1$, under the Taylor rule, Equation (15-8), can get stuck at the zero lower bound. The central banker sees that inflation is too low, that is $i = -r^* < i^*$, and the central banker is convinced that, to raise inflation, the nominal interest rate must go down. But, since the nominal interest rate is at the zero lower bound, it cannot go lower. This is not just a theoretical curiosity, as many central banks in the world, as of early 2016, face the problem of inflation that is below their inflation targets, with nominal interest rates at or close to zero. The "solution" these central banks typically choose is to keep the nominal interest rate at or close to zero, and resort to some or several forms of unconventional "easing"; that is, some combination of quantitative easing, negative nominal interest rates, and forward guidance. Central banks typically do not suggest, in spite of what our model tells us, that raising the nominal interest rate would be a cure for too-low inflation. And, important to note, it is not only our New Keynesian model that has neo-Fisherian properties. Indeed, essentially all mainstream macroeconomic models predict that higher nominal interest rates set by the central bank cause higher inflation.

But if the Taylor principle is a poor choice for a monetary policy rule, what works? Consider the following monetary policy rule:

1. If $i < i^*$, then

$$R = r^* + \frac{(a + d)i^*}{a} - \frac{d}{a}i. \tag{15-10}$$

2. If $i \geq i^*$, then

$$R = r^* - \frac{d}{a}i^* + \frac{(a + d)i'}{a}. \tag{15-11}$$

This policy rule says that, if inflation is currently below the central bank's inflation target, the central bank follows the rule given by Equation (15-10), which says that the central bank responds to lower inflation with a higher nominal interest rate. Thus, Equation (15-10) is a neo-Fisherian rule. If the central bank sees current inflation that is at or above the inflation target, then it responds with the rule given by Equation (15-11), which says that the central bank sets the nominal interest rate higher, the higher is anticipated future inflation.

If we substitute the rules given by Equations (15-10) and (15-11) into Equation (15-6), then we can determine what this policy rule will imply for inflation. If we do this, we obtain

1. If $i < i^*$, then $i' = i^*$.
2. If $i \geq i^*$, then $i = i^*$.

[21]J. Benhabib, S. Schmitt-Grohe, and M. Uribe, 2001. "The Perils of Taylor Rules," *Journal of Economic Theory* 96, 40–69.

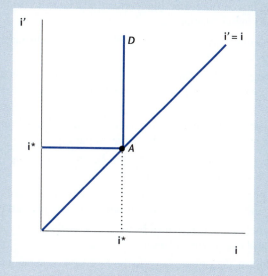

Figure 15.13 Inflation Under a Neo-Fisherian Monetary Policy Rule

Inflation can be lower than the inflation target for one period, then it returns to the target and stays there forever.

In Figure 15.13, the relationship between i and i' is given by D, with a right angle at the point $i = i' = i^*$. Thus, in equilibrium, the initial inflation rate is indeterminate, though we can say that $i_0 \leq i^*$.[22] But after the initial period, the inflation rate goes to the central bank's inflation target and stays there.

Why does this policy rule work so well? The first part of the rule, according to which the central bank responds to too-low current inflation with higher nominal interest rates, assures that the inflation rate—through a Fisher effect—is returned to the target in the next period if inflation is too low. If inflation is potentially too high, the central bank keeps the inflation rate at the target by fending off any incipient inflation that might occur in the future. It does this by offsetting any potential increases in future inflation with more-than-one-for-one increases in the nominal interest rate. This serves to hold output constant and, through the Phillips curve effect, hold inflation constant at its target level.

Neo-Fisherism is new, and not widely accepted. But, as we showed, neo-Fisherism is not a new theory. Indeed, understanding neo-Fisherism just involves recognizing the properties of widely used macroeconomic models, and the implications for macroeconomic policy can be dramatic.

This ends our examination of New Keynesian models, the Phillips curve, and inflation. In the next two chapters we will explore some issues in open economy macroeconomics.

---

[22]Note that the indeterminacy of the initial inflation rate is not a problem that the central bank can solve. This is just a general property of these models—controlling the nominal interest rate essentially controls future inflation, not current inflation, in New Keynesian models.

Chapter Summary

- The Keynesian sticky price model is extended to determine inflation, by including a Phillips curve.
- In the Phillips curve relationship, current inflation is determined by the output gap and the anticipated future inflation rate.
- A higher output gap reduces current inflation, while a higher anticipated future rate of inflation increases current inflation.
- In the basic New Keynesian model, with exogenous anticipated future inflation, a higher nominal interest rate target for the central bank increases the output gap and reduces current inflation.
- In the basic New Keynesian model, a higher future rate of anticipated inflation increases the current rate of inflation and reduces the output gap.
- The natural real interest rate can be low because of a savings glut, secular stagnation, or an increase in financial market frictions.
- A low natural real interest rate can lead to a situation where the central bank is at the zero lower bound on the nominal interest rate, and the actual real interest rate is too high.
- If the central bank is constrained by the zero lower bound, it can resort to forward guidance—a promise of high future inflation.
- Neo-Fisherian ideas are explored in the New Keynesian rational expectations (NKRE) model.
- In the NKRE model, an increase in the nominal interest rate increases the inflation rate one-for-one in the long run.
- Even in the short run, in the NKRE model, the central bank increases the inflation rate by increasing the nominal interest rate.
- Standard Taylor rules under the Taylor principle cause an indeterminacy problem, and the central bank can get stuck at the zero lower bound with too-low inflation.
- A neo-Fisherian monetary policy rule that increases the nominal interest rate when inflation is low has good properties—the central bank can hit its inflation target forever in the NKRE model.

Key Terms

Calvo pricing A modeling approach under which a firm receives a random opportunity to change its price each period. (p. 534)

Dual mandate The directive given to the Fed by Congress, which dictates that the Fed should be concerned with price stability and maximum employment. (p. 535)

Savings glut A high supply of savings in the world economy, which tends to reduce world real interest rates. (p. 542)

Secular stagnation A dearth of investment opportunities, that acts to reduce the real interest rate. (p. 542)

Forward guidance A promise by the central bank to take a future action. (p. 544)

Neo-Fisherians Macroeconomists who argue that increasing the nominal interest rate will increase inflation in the short run, and in the long run. (p. 548)

Rational expectations A modeling strategy under which the people in a macroeconomic model efficiently forecast future variables—implies that people cannot be systematically fooled. (p. 549)

Indeterminacy problem A problem for policy in that, given the policymakers policy rule, there are multiple equilibria. (p. 550)

Long-run Fisher relation In the long run, an increase in the nominal interest rate leads to a one-for-one increase in the inflation rate. (p. 550)

Taylor principle If, in the Taylor rule, the nominal interest rate increases more than one-for-one with the inflation rate, the Taylor rule satisfies the Taylor principle. (p. 555)

Perils of the Taylor rule The Taylor principle produces an indeterminacy problem, and can cause the central banker to get stuck at the zero lower bound with too-low inflation. (p. 556)

Questions for Review

15.1   Explain why the Phillips curve relationship in the basic New Keynesian model takes the form it does.

15.2   What is the effect of an increase in the central bank's nominal interest rate target in the basic New Keynesian model?

15.3   What is the effect of an increase in anticipated future inflation in the basic New Keynesian model?

15.4   What three factors have been suggested for the decline in real interest rates in the world?

15.5   If there is a decline in the natural rate of interest, what problem can this create for monetary policy?

15.6   How does forward guidance help the central bank deal with a low natural real rate of interest?

15.7   What is the basic neo-Fisherian idea?

15.8   Explain the concept of rational expectations.

15.9   If the nominal interest rate increases permanently, what effect does this have in the NKRE model in the long run?

15.10   What is the form of the standard Taylor rule?

15.11   What is the Taylor principle, and how does the Taylor principle go awry?

15.12   Explain how the neo-Fisherian monetary policy rule acts to achieve good economic results.

Problems

1. **LO 1** In the basic New Keynesian model, suppose that there is an increase in the future marginal product of capital.

   (a) Suppose that the central bank does nothing. What will be the effect on current inflation and on output?

   (b) Suppose the economy initially has inflation equal to the central bank's inflation target, and an output gap of zero. When the shock occurs, what should the central bank do?

   (c) Explain your results in parts (a) and (b) with the aid of diagrams.

2. **LO 2** Suppose initially that inflation is at the central bank's target and the output gap is zero. Then, government spending goes down. Deter-

mine, with the aid of diagrams, how the degree of price stickiness affects the central bank's optimal response, and explain your results.

3. **LO 3** Suppose that the natural rate of interest has gone down, and that the central bank is constrained by the zero lower bound, with inflation below the central bank's target, and a positive output gap. Further, suppose that if government spending goes up permanently, that higher future government spending will increase anticipated future inflation (by a Phillips curve effect in the future).

   (a) What will be the multiplier effect of government spending on output, assuming that the nominal interest rate stays at zero?

(b) Explain your results, with the aid of diagrams.

4. **LO 4, 5** In the NKRE model, suppose a Taylor rule as in Equation (15-8), with $-\frac{d}{a} < h < 1$. What does this imply for: (i) steady state equilibria; (ii) the whole set of equilibria that we could see? Explain with the aid of a diagram.

5. **LO 4, 5** Now, suppose in the NKRE model that the central bank follows a Taylor rule as in Equation (15-8), and $h < -\frac{d}{a}$. Show what this implies for steady state equilibria, and for the whole set of equilibria that can arise, and explain your results with the aid of a diagram.

6. **LO 4, 5** Suppose, in the NKRE model, that from time 0 until time *T-1*, the natural rate of interest is r_1^*, where $r_1^* < -i^*$, and from time *T* on the natural rate of interest is $r_2^* > 0$. Also, suppose that the central bank can achieve its inflation target from period *T* onward, and that the central bank sets the nominal interest rate to zero from time 0 until time *T-1*.

(a) What will happen to inflation and output from period 0 until period *T-1*. Explain with the aid of a diagram.

(b) What can the central bank do about the problem that arises in part (a)? Discuss.

Working with the Data

Answer these questions using the Federal Reserve Bank of St. Louis's FRED database, accessible at http://research.stlouisfed.org/fred2/

1. Plot the federal funds rate and the 12-month CPI inflation rate from 1980 to the end of the sample, both as time series, and as a scatter plot. What do you notice?

2. When people discuss the "Volcker disinflation," that is, the period when Fed chair Paul Volcker acted to reduce inflation, they will typically argue that Volcker reduced inflation by raising the nominal interest rate. Plot the federal funds rate and the CPI inflation rate over Volcker's term, August 1979 to August 1987, and explain what you see.

3. Plot the inflation rate vs. the unemployment rate in scatter plots for decade-long periods: 1950–1959, 1960–1969, 1970–1979, 1980–1989, 1990–1999, and 2000–2009. What do you observe? Explain.

PART VI

International Macroeconomics

Because of globalization—the continuing integration of world markets in goods, services, and assets—international factors are increasingly important for the performance of the domestic economy and for the conduct of fiscal and monetary policy. In this part, we study models of open economies in which there is trade between the domestic economy and the rest of the world. We use these models in Chapter 16 to study the determinants of the current account surplus, the implications of current account deficits, and international indebtedness. In Chapter 17, we examine the role of money in the world economy, the determination of exchange rates, the effects of fixed and flexible exchange rates, and the implications of shocks occurring abroad for domestic business cycles.

Chapter 16

International Trade in Goods and Assets

Learning Objectives

After studying Chapter 16, students will be able to:

16.1 Construct the first two-period small open economy (SOE) model.

16.2 Show how the first two-period SOE model explains the determinants of the current account balance.

16.3 Modify the first two-period SOE model to incorporate credit market imperfections and the possibility of national default on debt, and show how this model illustrates the determinants of default.

16.4 Construct the second two-period SOE model with production and investment, and show how this model is used to understand the links between international trade and domestic macroeconomic activity.

Our goal in this chapter is to extend some of the models developed in Chapters 9, 10, and 11, so that they can address issues in international macroeconomics. Until now, we have looked at closed-economy macroeconomic issues using closed-economy models, but for many interesting macroeconomic problems, we must do our analysis in an open-economy context. This chapter is confined to issues relating to real international macroeconomics. In Chapter 17, we address the monetary side of international interaction.

During the twentieth and twenty-first centuries, international trade has become increasingly important for three reasons. First, the costs of transporting goods and assets across international boundaries have fallen dramatically, permitting a freer flow of international trade. Second, government-imposed barriers to trade, such as import quotas, tariffs, and restrictions on international financial activity, have been relaxed. A relaxation of trade restrictions was carried out under the General Agreement on Tariffs and Trade

(GATT) between 1947 and 1995, when the GATT framework was replaced by the World Trade Organization. Trade restrictions have also been reduced through regional agreements, for example, the North American Free Trade Agreement (NAFTA), signed in 1992, and the European Union (EU). Third, world financial markets, particularly credit markets, have become more highly developed, with a freer flow of assets across countries. Given the increasing importance of trade in the world economy, there is much to be gained from understanding its implications for domestic macroeconomic activity.

In this chapter, we study the importance for domestic aggregate economic activity of trade with the rest of the world in goods and assets. We are interested particularly in how the current account surplus and domestic output, employment, consumption, and investment are affected by events in the rest of the world. To study this, we extend some of the models we have worked with in Chapters 9, 10, and 11.

Throughout this chapter, we confine our attention to small open-economy models, which are models in which actions by consumers and firms in the domestic economy have no collective effect on world prices. Some countries are clearly small relative to the rest of the world, such as New Zealand, Singapore, and Luxembourg, and for these countries it is clear that the small open-economy assumption is quite realistic. However, for large countries such as the United States, which play a particularly important role in the world economy, the assumption of price-taking on world markets is perhaps less plausible. There are three reasons that we study small open-economy models here and use them to explain events in large open economies (the United States in particular). The first is that small open-economy models are relatively simple to work with; for example, it is easy to modify closed-economy models in constructing small open-economy models. Second, many of the conclusions we derive from small open-economy models are identical to the ones we would obtain in more complicated large open-economy models. Third, as time passes, the small open-economy assumption becomes more realistic for a country such as the United States. Given development in the rest of the world, GDP in the United States relative to GDP in the rest of the world falls, and it becomes a closer approximation to the truth that the United States is a price-taker in world goods and asset markets.

In this chapter, we study two small open-economy models that build, respectively, on the two-period model in Chapter 9 and the real intertemporal model in Chapter 11. In the first model, we can approach the decisions of a single country concerning the choice of consumption, government spending, and the current account surplus, in exactly the same way we considered the consumption–savings decision of an individual in Chapter 9. An important idea is that international borrowing and lending permits the smoothing of aggregate consumption over time for the domestic economy, just as a single consumer can smooth consumption by borrowing and lending. The model is extended to allow for default, using some of the ideas about credit market frictions from Chapter 10. We show a nation's decision to default on its debt to the rest of the world depends on the size of the debt, the interest rate, and what the nation has to lose in the future from defaulting.

In the second model, we include investment and production, so that we can study the relationships among domestic consumption, output, investment, government spending, and the current account balance. We study the role of domestic investment in determining the current account deficit and address the extent to which a current account deficit is good or bad for a nation's welfare.

A Two-Period Small Open-Economy Model: The Current Account

LO 16.1 Construct the first two-period small open economy (SOE) model.

LO 16.2 Show how the first two-period SOE model explains the determinants of the current account balance.

For convenience, we will work with a model of a **small open economy (SOE)**. In a small open economy, economic agents are price takers with respect to the rest of the world. They treat prices in other countries and interest rates on world credit markets as given. This is a reasonable assumption to make, even if we are interested in modeling the United States. The United States is becoming smaller over time, in terms of its contribution to world GDP and, even though the United States may have significant effects on world prices, taking these effects into account would not matter much for the issues we want to tackle in this chapter and the next one.

We want to start in the this section by developing a simple model that can explain some of the determinants of the current account surplus. We know from Chapter 2 that a current account surplus must always be reflected in an excess of domestic savings over domestic investment and by an increase in the net claims of domestic residents on foreign residents. Thus, to analyze the current account, we need a model where, at the minimum, consumers make borrowing and lending and consumption–savings decisions. A useful model of borrowing and lending and consumption–savings decisions is the two-period model we developed in Chapter 9. Here, we modify that model by having a single representative consumer, capturing the average behavior of all domestic consumers, and we allow borrowing and lending between domestic and foreign residents.

We suppose that there is a single representative consumer in the SOE, and that this consumer lives for two periods, the current and future periods. For the representative consumer, income is exogenous in both periods, with Y denoting current real income and Y' future real income. The consumer also pays lump-sum taxes to the SOE government of T in the current period and T' in the future period. Because this economy is small and open, the actions of the representative consumer do not affect the world real interest rate, and so we assume that the consumer in the SOE can borrow and lend as much as he or she wishes at the world real interest rate r. Just as in Chapter 9, the representative consumer's lifetime budget constraint is

$$C + \frac{C'}{1+r} = Y - T + \frac{Y' - T'}{1+r}. \tag{16-1}$$

Private saving in the current period is then given by $S^p = Y - T - C$. Government spending in the current and future periods is G and G', respectively, and these quantities are exogenous, just as in Chapter 9. The government then sets current and future taxes on the representative consumer, T and T', respectively, to satisfy the government's present-value budget constraint

$$G + \frac{G'}{1+r} = T + \frac{T'}{1+r}. \tag{16-2}$$

Then, the quantity of government saving is given by $S^g = T - G$, and in this economy, where there is no investment, the current account surplus in the current period, from Chapter 2, is

$$CA = S - I = (S^p + S^g) - 0 = Y - C - G. \tag{16-3}$$

From the consumer's lifetime budget constraint, Equation (16-1), and the present-value budget constraint for the government, Equation (16-2), we get

$$C + G + \frac{C' + G'}{1+r} = Y + \frac{Y'}{1+r}, \tag{16-4}$$

which is the **national present-value budget constraint** for the SOE, which states that the present value of consumption plus government spending must equal the present value of national income. Also, given the definition of the current account surplus from Equation (16-3), we can write the nation's budget constraints for the current and future periods, respectively, as

$$C + G + CA = Y \tag{16-5}$$

$$C' + G' = (1 + r)CA + Y'. \tag{16-6}$$

In this model, it is useful to think of the representative consumer making choices over consumption bundles $(C + G, C' + G')$. Suppose that private consumption and government consumption are perfect substitutes in the current and future periods, and that the representative consumer can choose both private consumption and government consumption, through private decisions and the electoral process, respectively. Although the control of electors over public expenditures and government saving is imperfect in practice, for our purposes making the strong assumption that the representative consumer controls perfectly what the government does will be very useful.

In Figure 16.1, the representative consumer has indifference curves that represent preferences over consumption bundles $(C + G, C' + G')$, and the consumer optimizes by choosing the point on AB, which is the national present-value budget constraint, Equation (16-4). The optimum is point D.

Figure 16.1 allows us to treat the determination of the current account surplus, CA, in the same way we would treat the determination of savings for an individual consumer. From our analysis in Chapter 9, it is straightforward to derive the following results.

- *The current account surplus rises with an increase in current income.* Recall from Chapter 9 that an increase in current income increases current consumption and future consumption, and current consumption increases by less than the increase

Figure 16.1 A Two-Period Small Open-Economy Model

The representative consumer chooses current private consumption plus government consumption in the present and the future, given the world real interest rate. The optimal choice is at point D, and the current account surplus is $CA = Y - C - G$.

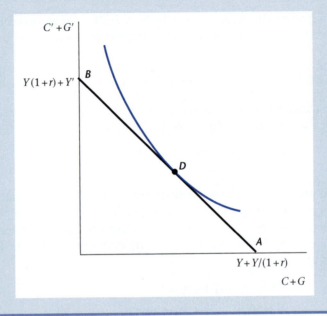

in current income, because the consumer wishes to smooth consumption over his or her lifetime. In our model, $C + G$ will increase when Y increases, but by less than the increase in Y, so that $CA = Y - C - G$ increases. An increase in Y, therefore, leads to an increase in the current account surplus. Because of the consumption-smoothing motive, a country that experiences an increase in current income saves more by lending abroad, and this is reflected in an increase in the current account surplus.

- *The current account surplus falls with an increase in future income.* Recall from Chapter 9 that, for an individual consumer, an increase in future income increases current and future consumption, and reduces savings. In our model, an increase in Y' will increase $C + G$ and $C' + G'$, and CA must fall, as $CA = Y - C - G$, and Y is unchanged.

- *Changes in taxes have no effect on the current account surplus, everything else held constant.* Given the Ricardian equivalence theorem from Chapter 9, changes in taxes have no effect on aggregate consumption, because consumers simply adjust savings to account for the change in their future tax liabilities. Private saving and government saving change by equal and opposite amounts, and the current account surplus does not change. However, as in Chapter 10, if there are significant credit market imperfections, then a change in current taxes in general affects current consumption, and this matters for the current account surplus.

- *If* $CA < 0$, *then an increase in the real interest rate increases CA.* Recall from Chapter 9 that the effect of a change in the real interest rate on current consumption for an individual consumer depends on whether the representative consumer is initially a net borrower or a net lender. If the consumer is a net borrower, the income and substitution effects work in the same direction, and an increase in the real interest rate causes a decrease in current consumption and an increase in savings. Similarly, if the current account surplus is negative, so that the country as a whole is borrowing from the rest of the world, then an increase in r reduces $C + G$ and increases the current account surplus.

- *If* $CA > 0$, *then an increase in the real interest rate has an ambiguous effect on CA.* Recall from Chapter 9 that, if an individual consumer is a net lender, then an increase in the real interest rate could increase or decrease savings, depending on the strength of opposing income and substitution effects. In this model, an increase in r could cause $C + G$ to rise or fall, so CA could rise or fall.

The key insight that comes from this model is that the current account surplus is in part a reflection of consumption-smoothing for the nation as a whole. Just as an individual consumer can smooth consumption relative to income by borrowing and lending in the domestic credit market, a country can smooth private and government consumption relative to GDP by borrowing and lending in the world credit market.

Credit Market Imperfections and Default

LO 16.3 Modify the first two-period SOE model to incorporate credit market imperfections and the possibility of national default on debt, and show how this model illustrates the determinants of default.

National indebtedness to the rest of the world is important, particularly in times of financial stress, such as the global financial crisis of 2008–2009. For any country, national indebtedness consists of both private and sovereign debt. Sometimes problems with private and sovereign debt are difficult to disentangle. For example, during the global financial crisis, the focus was on private debts and the financial condition of private financial institutions. Those financial market stresses in turn were related to the subsequent sovereign debt problems of European countries, in particular, Greece, Spain, Italy, and Portugal, which came to the fore after the important events of the financial crisis.

To address the determinants of national indebtedness, and why this indebtedness can be problematic, we have to think carefully about default. Thus, it is important that we deal explicitly with credit market frictions, which were covered in Chapter 10. We can use some of that apparatus here to organize our thinking about borrowing and lending between an individual country and the rest of the world.

We will adapt the model from the previous section to include a limited commitment friction, allowing a country, if it chooses, to walk away from its debts to the rest of the world. Suppose that, at the beginning of the current period, the nation's (private sector and government) debt to the world is B. Assume that B can be positive (the

THEORY CONFRONTS THE DATA

Is a Current Account Deficit a Bad Thing?

It may seem that a current account deficit is undesirable, because if a country runs a current account deficit, it is borrowing from the rest of the world and accumulating debt. However, just as is the case for individual consumers, lending and borrowing is the means by which a nation smooths consumption. If a given country runs current account deficits when aggregate income is low and runs current account surpluses when aggregate income is high, this allows the residents of that country to smooth their consumption over time. This state of affairs is preferable to one in which the country always has a current account surplus of zero and consumption is as variable as income.

Thus, there are good reasons for expecting that countries should run current account surpluses in good times and current account deficits in bad times. Government policy aimed at correcting this tendency could be counterproductive. But do countries actually smooth consumption over time as theory predicts? In Figure 16.2 we show the deviations from trend in real GDP and the ratio of the current account surplus to GDP for the United States over the period 1999–2015. For real GDP, the deviations are percentage deviations from trend, and for the current account surplus ratio

these are the deviations from trend, multiplied by 100 to scale the time series. In the figure, there is a tendency for the current account surplus to be above (below) trend when real GDP is below (above) trend, so that deviations from trend in GDP and the current account surplus are negatively correlated. This is the opposite of consumption smoothing, in that the United States tended to export goods and lend more abroad when output was low, and to borrow more abroad when output was high.

Why would the data not exhibit obvious evidence of consumption smoothing when economic theory tells us that nations should smooth consumption by lending (borrowing) abroad when income is high (low)? A potential explanation may be that the timing and severity of business cycles in the rest of the world and in the United States are similar. For example, the data in Figure 16.2 are consistent with consumption smoothing if business cycles coincided in the United States and the rest of the world, but the upturns and downturns were more severe in the rest of the world. Then, the United States could in equilibrium be lending to other countries when its own output was low and borrowing from other countries when its own output was high.

country starts as a net debtor) or negative (the country starts as a net creditor). In the current period, the nation's budget constraint is

$$C + G = Y + \frac{B'}{1 + r} - B, \qquad (16\text{-}7)$$

and the future period national budget constraint is

$$C' + G' = -B' + Y'. \qquad (16\text{-}8)$$

Figure 16.2 Deviations from Trend in the Current Account Surplus and GDP

In U.S. data for 1999–2015, there does not appear to be evidence of national consumption smoothing, as deviations from trend in the current account surplus and GDP are negatively correlated. This may be the result of synchronization in business cycles across countries.

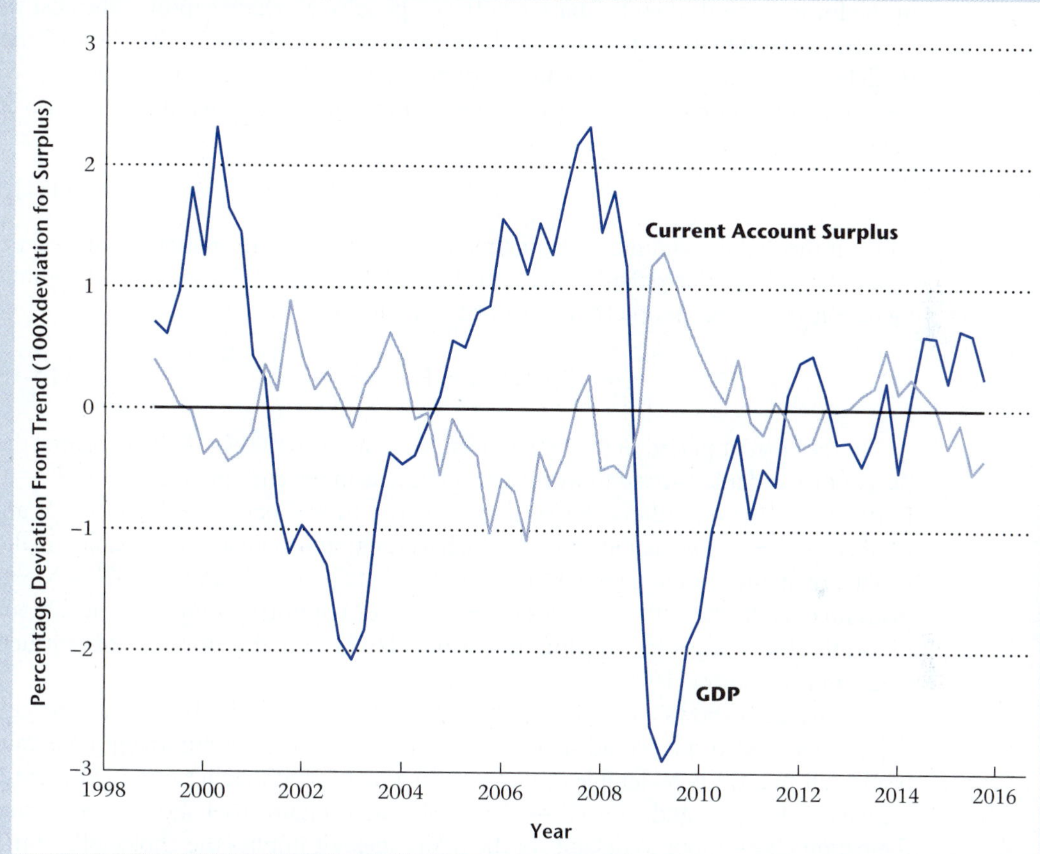

In Equation (16-7), B' is the nation's indebtedness at the beginning of the future period. Thus, if the indebtedness of the nation is $\frac{B'}{1+r}$ at the end of the current period, and the world interest rate is r, then the size of the debt at the beginning of the future period is B'. The current account surplus in the current period is the quantity $CA = B - \frac{B'}{1+r}$, which is minus the change in national indebtedness in the current period. As in the previous subsection, we can collapse the two budget constraints (16-7) and (16-8) into a single national present-value budget constraint

$$C + G + \frac{C' + G'}{1+r} = Y - B + \frac{Y'}{1+r}. \tag{16-9}$$

Limited commitment means that the nation can default on its debt either in the future period or the current period. In contrast to our limited commitment framework in Chapter 10, a government cannot post collateral against its debts. But a country can face an implicit penalty for default, in that it will have difficulty in borrowing in world credit markets in the future if it defaults today. In our model, if default occurs in the future period, then the nation suffers a penalty v, which captures the cost the country will suffer from being denied access to credit markets in the "future" (not modeled) that exists beyond the future period. As in Chapter 10, world lenders will not lend in the current period to the extent that the country would default on its debts, so

$$-B' \le v, \tag{16-10}$$

which is the limited commitment constraint that implies that the nation's indebtedness cannot be so large that default will occur. Using Equation (16-7), the limited commitment constraint, Equation (16-10), can be rewritten as

$$C + G \le Y - B + \frac{v}{1+r}. \tag{16-11}$$

In the current period, if the nation defaults on its current debt, B, then assume that the country is denied access to world credit markets in the current period, with $B' = 0$. Further, the nation suffers the penalty v in the future period, so $C + G = Y$ and $C' + G' = Y' - v$. The nation chooses whichever option—default or no default—makes it better off in the current period. Default implies that $C + G = Y$, and $C' + G' = Y' - v$. With no default, the nation chooses $(C + G, C' + G')$ optimally subject to the national present-value budget constraint, Equation (16-9) and the limited commitment constraint, Equation (16-11).

Figure 16.3 shows a case where the nation chooses default. An optimal choice if default does not occur would be point B, where the limited commitment constraint binds, but point A is preferable to B as it is on a higher indifference curve. At point B, we have $C + G = Y$ and $C' + G' = Y' - v$. Similarly, Figure 16.4 shows a case where the nation chooses not to default. In the figure, default implies the choice of A, but B is preferred to A, and at B there is no default.

In the case we have depicted in Figures 16.3 and 16.4, where the limited commitment constraint binds if there is no default, it is straightforward to show what affects the nation's decision to default. If the nation does not default, and the limited commitment constraint binds, then Equation (16-11) holds as an equality. Then, from Equations (16-9) and (16-11), private plus government consumption in the current and future periods is, respectively,

$$C + G = Y - B + \frac{v}{1+r}$$

$$C' + G' = Y' - v.$$

But if default occurs in the current period, then $C + G = Y$, and $C' + G' = Y' - v$. Therefore, consumption is the same in the future period whether default occurs or not.

Figure 16.3 Default Is Chosen

If default were not chosen, the nation chooses B, where the limited commitment constraint binds. But A (default) is preferable to B, as it is on a higher indifference curve.

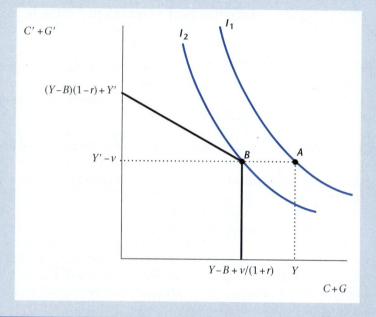

Figure 16.4 Default Is not Chosen

In contrast to Figure 16.3, in this figure not defaulting (point B) is preferable to defaulting (point A).

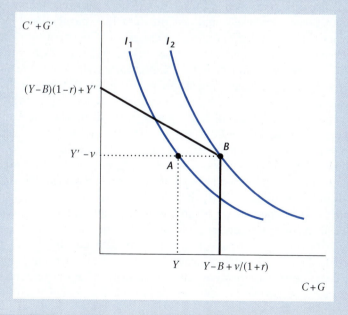

THEORY CONFRONTS THE DATA
Greece and Sovereign Default

An important step for Greece was entering the Euro area in 2001, at which point Greece fell under the umbrella of the European Central Bank, and began using the Euro. In Figure 16.5, we can see one of the effects of membership in the Euro area. In the figure, we compare bond yields on 10-year government securities in Greece relative to Germany, which has an excellent record of fiscal prudence, with German government debt rated highly on world credit markets. Prior to Greece entering the Euro area, Greek government debt traded at a higher yield than German government debt. That is, prior to 2001, participants in world credit markets charged the Greek government higher interest rates than they charged to the German government. This reflected a perception that Greece might either default on its debt with higher probability, or that the Greek central bank could produce unexpected inflation, so as to reduce the real value of its nominal debt. But, inflating away the value of a country's debt is essentially implicit default, so the higher yield on Greek government debt before 2001 reflects a default premium.

But, after 2001, Greek government bond yields converged roughly to German government bond yields, as we see in Figure 16.5. Clearly, financial market participants thought, as of 2001, that Greek debt was about as safe as German debt, likely because it was perceived that membership in the Euro area would somehow discipline the Greek government's external borrowing.

This state of affairs continued until the 2008–2009 financial crisis when, as we see in Figure 16.5, the yield on Greek government debt began to rise. By 2011 and 2012, the situation had become dire. In June 2012, international creditors were willing to lend to Germany for 10

years at an interest rate of 1.3%, but would only lend to Greece if the Greek government promised them an interest rate of about 28%. What happened?

In Figure 16.6, we show the ratio of government debt to GDP for a group of six countries, including Greece, for the period 1990–2012. For Greece, government debt rose rapidly from 107% of GDP in 2007, before the financial crisis, to 170% of GDP in 2011. Consistent with our model, a high level of government debt for Greece produced a situation in which the government of Greece was perceived to be likely to default, which increased the interest rates faced by the Greek government, which according to our model, would further increase the chances of default. Indeed, the Greek government could not meet its debt payments, and received assistance from the International Monetary Fund, the European Union, and the European Central Bank. Given the outcome, we could also make the case that membership in the Euro area reduced the Greek government's incentives to avoid default, since Greece would rationally expect to be bailed out in the event that its debt was in trouble. In terms of our model, this is essentially a reduction in v, which would tend to increase the likelihood of default.

But our model does not capture everything we see in Figure 16.6. Greece certainly had a much higher debt level than Australia, for which the debt to GDP ratio in 2012 was 28%. But debt levels in Germany, Canada, and the United States were certainly not low, at 82%, 85%, and 103% of GDP, respectively, in 2012. And Japan had a debt to GDP ratio of 238% in 2012—much higher than in Greece. But participants in world credit markets appear to think that a sovereign

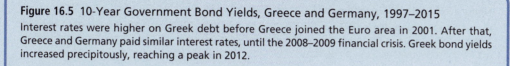

Figure 16.5 10-Year Government Bond Yields, Greece and Germany, 1997–2015

Interest rates were higher on Greek debt before Greece joined the Euro area in 2001. After that, Greece and Germany paid similar interest rates, until the 2008–2009 financial crisis. Greek bond yields increased precipitously, reaching a peak in 2012.

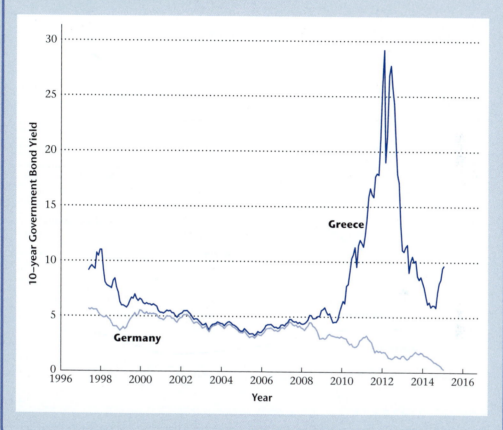

default in Germany, Canada, the United States, and Japan is extremely unlikely, as all these countries can borrow at very low interest rates. Why are these countries different from Greece?

In our model, it is only the size of the government debt that matters, but a key element in sovereign default in practice is a country's ability to service its debt. For example, if a government has difficulty in collecting tax revenue, or in controlling government expenditures on goods and services and transfer payments, it may have difficulty making the interest payments on its debt. The difficulty arises, basically, from weak enforcement of tax laws, and general corruption.

(*Continued*)

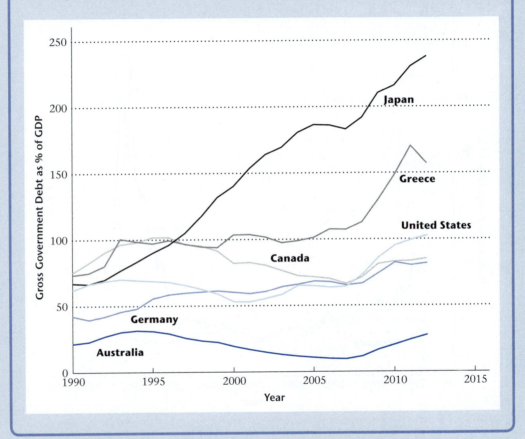

Figure 16.6 Ratio of Government Debt to GDP

Greek debt increased from 107% of GDP in 2007 to a peak of 170% in 2011. But the debt ratios in Germany, Canada, the United States, and particularly Japan, were not low, though these countries are not perceived to be likely to default.

As a result, the nation's default decision is determined by which option implies the higher level of current consumption. Default will occur if $Y - B + \dfrac{v}{1+r} < Y$, or simplifying, if

$$B > \frac{v}{1+r}. \tag{16-12}$$

Inequality Equation (16-12) tells us that default is more likely if the current value of the nation's indebtedness is higher, as an increase in B increases the left-hand side of Equation (16-12). As well, if the national cost of defaulting is larger, then default is less likely to occur, in that an increase in v increases the right-hand side of Equation (16-12).

Finally, a higher world real interest rate reduces the right-hand side of Equation (16-12) and makes default more likely.

Thus, our model is roughly consistent with the history of sovereign defaults in the world. Countries tend to default that have accumulated a lot of debt to the rest of the world, and default tends to be associated with high interest rates. As well, we can find cases where it seems clear that poor incentives, that is, a small value of v, will tend to produce sovereign default. We will explore these ideas further, for the case of Greece, in the next Theory Confronts the Data section.

Production, Investment, and the Current Account

LO 16.4 Construct the second two-period SOE model with production and investment, and show how this model is used to understand the links between international trade and domestic macroeconomic activity.

While the previous model yields some useful insights concerning the role of the current account in national consumption smoothing, and can be extended to include default, it is important to understand more completely the relationship between the current account surplus and events in the domestic economy. In this section, we study a model based on the real intertemporal model in Chapter 11, which includes production and investment behavior.

In this model, just as in the previous one, the SOE faces a given world real interest rate. As in Chapter 11, output supply is given by the upward-sloping curve Y^s in Figure 16.7. Here, however, we assume that goods can be freely traded with foreign countries, and so from the income–expenditure identity $Y = C + I + G + NX$, the demand for goods also includes net exports, NX. In Figure 16.7, the world real interest rate is r^*, which then determines the domestic demand for consumption goods and investment goods. If total domestic demand, $C + I + G$, exceeds the domestic supply of goods at the world real interest rate, then goods are imported and net exports are negative; and if domestic demand is less than the domestic supply of goods at the world real interest rate, then goods are exported and net exports are positive. The equilibrium quantity of net exports is the quantity NX, which yields a downward-sloping output demand curve Y_1^d that intersects the Y^s curve in Figure 16.7 at the world real interest rate r^*. We have depicted a case in Figure 16.7, where $NX > 0$; that is, if there were no trade in goods with the rest of the world, then the output demand curve would be Y_2^d, to the left of Y_1^d, and the domestic real interest rate would be r_c. In general, it could be the case that $r^* < r_c$ or $r^* > r_c$. Given the world real interest rate r^*, the quantity of aggregate output produced in the SOE is Y_1, but in this case the domestic demand for goods, $C + I + G$, is less than Y_1. The domestic demand for goods, $C + I + G$, is sometimes referred to as **absorption**, as this is the quantity of aggregate output that is absorbed by the domestic economy. The quantity NX is then the current account surplus, or net exports. Recall from Chapter 2 that the current account surplus is net exports plus net factor payments from abroad, but net factor payments from abroad equal zero in this model. In Figure 16.7, the SOE has a positive current account surplus; that is, $NX > 0$ which implies that the SOE is accumulating assets from the rest of the world.

Figure 16.7 A Small Open-Economy Model with Production and Investment

The world real interest rate, determined on world credit markets, is r^*. Net exports adjust so that the Y^d curve intersects the Y^s curve at the world real interest rate. Here, $NX > 0$, and in the absence of trade, the domestic real interest rate would be r_c.

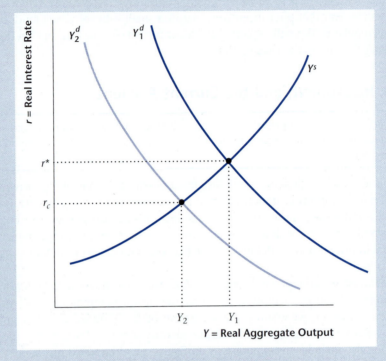

The Effects of an Increase in the World Real Interest Rate

Because the model here is essentially identical to the real intertemporal model with a real interest rate that is fixed on world credit markets, it is straightforward to use the model to analyze the effects of particular shocks to the domestic economy. The output demand curve and output supply curve shift in the same ways in response to shocks as in the real intertemporal model of Chapter 11, with the only modification in the analysis being that NX adjusts so that the output demand curve intersects the output supply curve at the world real interest rate r^*. The first experiment we carry out is to look at the effects in the model of an increase in the world real interest rate. Such a change could have many causes; it could result from, for example, a negative total factor productivity shock in other countries (recall our analysis of domestic total factor productivity shocks from Chapter 11).

Suppose, in Figure 16.8, that the world real interest rate increases from r_1 to r_2. Then the current account surplus increases causing the output demand curve to shift to the right from Y_1^d to Y_2^d. Domestic investment must decrease, as the real interest rate increases, but domestic consumption may rise or fall as there is a negative effect from the increase in r and a positive effect from the increase in Y.

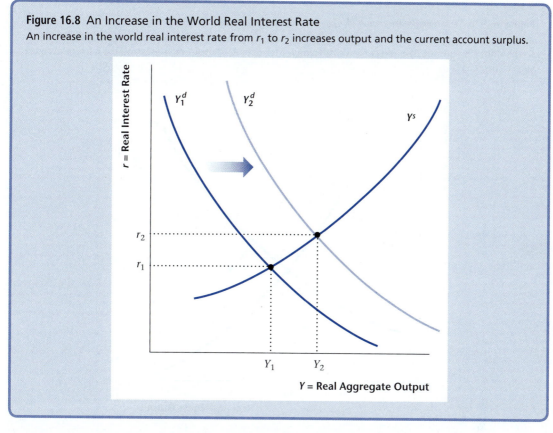

Figure 16.8 An Increase in the World Real Interest Rate

An increase in the world real interest rate from r_1 to r_2 increases output and the current account surplus.

These results have the interesting implication that a negative total factor productivity shock abroad, which would *decrease* foreign output and cause the world real interest rate to rise, also causes an *increase* in domestic output. Therefore, a foreign shock of this sort, when transmitted to the domestic economy, does not cause output in the domestic economy and in the rest of the world to move together.

Government Expenditure and the Current Account

For our second experiment, we consider the effects of increases in domestic government expenditure. Suppose that there is an increase in G, a temporary increase in government spending. Just as in Chapter 11, there is a negative income effect on leisure for the representative consumer, because of the increase in the present value of taxes, and so labor supply increases, shifting the output supply curve rightward from Y_1^s to Y_2^s in Figure 16.9. There is a shift to the right in the output demand curve resulting from the net increase in output demand caused by the increase in G. The current account surplus then adjusts so that the output demand curve ultimately shifts from Y_1^d to Y_2^d (see Figure 16.9). As in Chapter 11, the initial shift in the output supply curve is small relative to the shift in the output demand curve (because the increase in government spending is temporary, so that the effects on lifetime wealth are small). The current account surplus, therefore, must decrease.

Figure 16.9 A Temporary Increase in Government Spending

An increase in current government spending shifts the output demand curve and the output supply curve to the right (the output demand curve shifts to a greater extent). Output increases and the current account surplus decreases.

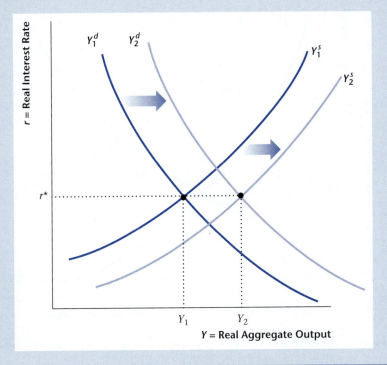

It is useful to compare our results to what happened in the closed-economy real intertemporal model in Chapter 11. Note that the real interest rate does not increase in the open economy, as the interest rate is determined on world markets. As a result, there is no crowding out of investment and consumption as a result of an interest rate increase. Further, consumption actually increases here (rather than decreasing, as in the real intertemporal model), since real income increases while the real interest rate stays constant. Crowding out does occur, but it is crowding out of net exports, since the current account surplus has gone down. We have thus seen one way in which results can change in important ways when we take account of open-economy factors. While it is true in general that government spending crowds out private activity, this crowding-out occurs in different ways in an open economy.

The Effects of Increases in Current and Future Total Factor Productivity

Earlier in this text, we have studied how total factor productivity matters for domestic real aggregate activity. In Chapter 11, we showed that an increase in current total factor productivity in a closed economy increases labor demand, and it leads to increases in the real wage, employment, and output, and a decrease in the real interest rate. An anticipated increase in future total factor productivity increases the current demand for investment goods and consumption goods in a closed economy, and it increases current aggregate output and the real interest rate. In an SOE, some of these results are somewhat different, as the real interest rate is determined on the world credit market. We are also able to determine the effects of total factor productivity shocks on the current account.

Suppose first that current total factor productivity increases. Recall from Chapter 11 that this causes a shift to the right in the output supply curve. In Figure 16.10 the output supply curve shifts from Y_1^s to Y_2^s. Then, the current account surplus increases, shifting the output demand curve to the right from Y_1^d to Y_2^d. As a result, aggregate output increases from Y_1 to Y_2, and there is an increase in the current account surplus. Domestic consumption increases because of the increase in real income, but given that the real interest rate is unchanged there is no effect on investment. In a closed economy, the real interest rate falls when total factor productivity increases, causing increases in C and I. However, the real interest rate is determined on world markets here, and so an increase in total factor productivity in the domestic economy has no effect on the real interest rate. Typically, though, different countries

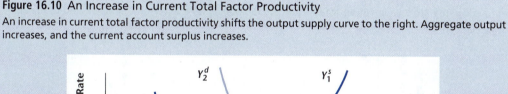

Figure 16.10 An Increase in Current Total Factor Productivity

An increase in current total factor productivity shifts the output supply curve to the right. Aggregate output increases, and the current account surplus increases.

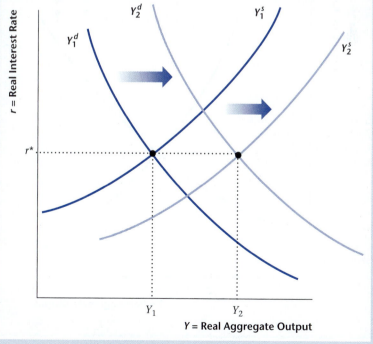

simultaneously experience increases in total factor productivity at the same time, as changes in production technology tend to be transmitted across international borders. Therefore, an increase in total factor productivity domestically would also tend to be associated with a decrease in the world real interest rate and increases in domestic consumption and investment.

Next, suppose that an increase in future total factor productivity is anticipated. Recall from Chapter 11 that this implies that the representative firm expects an increase in the future marginal product of capital, which causes an increase in the demand for investment goods. Further, the representative consumer anticipates higher future income as the result of the increase in future total factor productivity, and this causes an increase in the demand for current consumption goods. The increase in the demand for current consumption and investment goods shifts the output demand curve in Figure 16.11 rightward, but there is a corresponding decrease in the current account surplus so that demand equals supply for domestically produced goods. In equilibrium, aggregate output remains fixed at Y_1, but the current account surplus falls.

The above analysis predicts that an investment boom, driven by optimism about future total factor productivity, reduces the current account surplus. This is broadly

Figure 16.11 An Increase in Future Total Factor Productivity

An anticipated increase in future total factor productivity shifts the output demand curve to the right. Aggregate output remains unchanged, and the current account surplus declines.

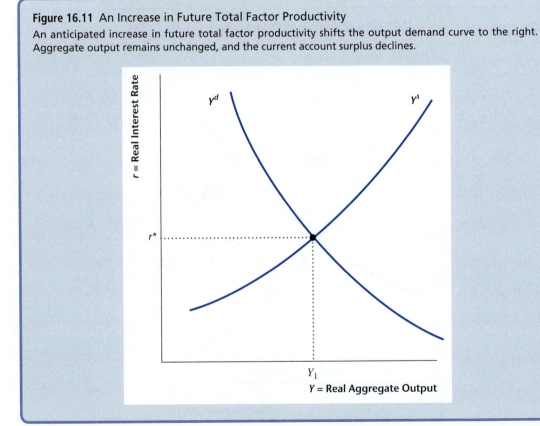

consistent with what happened in the United States in the 1990s, when investment expenditures in the United States were driven in part by the "dot-com" boom.

This chapter explored the real macroeconomic implications of having trade in goods and assets among nations. In Chapter 17, we integrate money into the second model that we studied in this chapter so as to understand the determination of nominal exchange rates, the importance of flexible and fixed exchange rates, and why capital controls are important for macroeconomic activity.

Chapter Summary

- In this chapter we studied the implications of international trade in goods and assets for domestic welfare, output, consumption, investment, and the current account surplus. We constructed two small open-economy models and showed how these models can be used to understand the importance of openness for the domestic economy. In a small open economy (SOE), domestic residents are price-takers with respect to the rest of the world.

- The first model we considered was a two-period model of an SOE, where we treat the determination of the current account surplus using the same approach that we used in Chapter 9 to understand individual saving behavior. We treat the representative consumer as if he or she can choose consumption and government spending in the current and future periods, with exogenous income in both periods. The current account surplus is then just the nation's desired savings, determined by borrowing and lending in world credit markets.

- In the model, the current account surplus increases when current income increases and when future income falls. Taxation has no effect on the current account surplus, due to Ricardian equivalence. An increase in the world real interest rate will increase the current account surplus if the surplus is initially negative. However, if the current account surplus is initially positive, an increase in the real interest rate could make the current account surplus go up or down, depending on opposing substitution and income effects.

- Current account deficits need not be a bad thing, as this implies borrowing abroad, which helps domestic consumers to smooth their consumption over time.

- We extended the first model in this chapter to address problems related to credit frictions, international indebtedness, and default. A country is more likely to default on its debt. The larger the debt is, the higher the world real interest rate, and the lower the cost to defaulting.

- In the second small open-economy model, we allowed for the determination of production and investment, with the domestic economy facing an interest rate determined on world markets. Here, the current account surplus is the difference between domestic output and absorption, where absorption is the domestic demand for goods, or consumption plus investment plus government spending.

- An increase in the world real interest rate increases domestic output, reduces absorption, and increases the current account surplus.

- A temporary increase in government spending increases domestic absorption and decreases the current account surplus.

- An increase in current total factor productivity increases domestic output and increases the current account surplus, whereas an anticipated increase in future total factor productivity causes no change in current aggregate output and reduces the current account surplus.

Key Terms

Small open economy (SOE) An economy that trades with the rest of the world, and for which the collective actions of domestic consumers and firms have negligible effects on prices on world markets. (p. 564)

National present-value budget constraint In the first model in this chapter, this constraint states that the present value of private consumption and government consumption is equal to the present value of income, for the nation as a whole. (p. 565)

Absorption Consumption plus investment plus government expenditures; the quantity of domestically produced goods absorbed through domestic spending. (p. 575)

Questions for Review

16.1 What is a small open economy?

16.2 Why is it appropriate to use a small open-economy model to explain events in the United States?

16.3 In the first model in this chapter, what are the determinants of the current account surplus, and how does each of these determinants affect it?

16.4 Why could it be a good thing for a country to run a current account deficit?

16.5 What can constrain borrowing in world markets by an individual country?

16.6 What makes a country more likely to default on its international debt?

16.7 What are the effects of an increase in the world real interest rate on output, absorption, and the current account surplus?

16.8 What are the effects of a temporary increase in government expenditure on output, absorption, and the current account surplus?

16.9 What are the effects of an increase in current and future total factor productivity on output, absorption, and the current account surplus?

16.10 How do we explain the post–1990 behavior of investment expenditures and the current account surplus in the United States?

Problems

1. **LO 1, 2** Assume a two-period model where national income is 100 in the current period, and 120 in the future period. The world real interest rate is assumed to be 10% per period. The representative consumer always wishes to set current consumption plus government spending equal to future consumption plus government spending $(C + G = C' + G')$, which implies perfect-complements preferences.

   (a) Determine consumption plus government spending in the current and future periods, and the current account surplus. Draw a diagram to illustrate your results.

   (b) Now, suppose that the world real interest rate increases to 20% per period. Again, determine consumption plus government spend-

   ing in the current and future periods and the current account surplus, and show these in your diagram.

   (c) Explain the difference in your results in parts (a) and (b).

2. **LO 1, 2** Use the first model in this chapter to answer this question. Suppose that governments in the rest of the world impose a tax on lending to foreigners. Determine how this affects consumption plus government spending in the present and the future, and the current account surplus. Explain your results.

3. **LO 3** Suppose in the first model in this chapter that there is a limited commitment friction and the possibility the nation could default in the cur-

rent or future periods. Suppose that, if the nation does not default, then the limited commitment constraint does not bind. Could default still be preferred in the current period to not defaulting? Explain, with the aid of a diagram.

4. **LO 1, 2** Suppose, as in Chapter 9, that in the first model in this chapter there is limited commitment in the credit relationships between the small open economy and the rest of the world. There is some portion of the nation's capital stock, denoted by K_c, which is collateralizable on world markets. This collateralizable capital is illiquid in the current period and is valued at price p on world markets in the future period. Assume that borrowing by the SOE on world markets is limited by the value of collateralizable wealth in the future period. Now, suppose that p falls. How does this affect consumption in the SOE in the present and the future, and the current account surplus? Explain your results with the aid of diagrams.

5. **LO 4** Use the second model in this chapter, with production and investment, to answer this question. The government in a small open economy is concerned that the current account deficit is too high. One group of economic advisers to the government argues that high government deficits cause the current account deficit to be high and that the way to reduce the current account deficit is to increase taxes. A second group of economic advisers argues that the high current account deficit is caused by high domestic investment and proposes that domestic investment should be taxed, with these investment taxes returned to consumers as lump-sum transfers.
   (a) Which advice should the government take if its goal is to reduce the current account deficit? Explain.
   (b) Is the government's goal of reducing the current account deficit sensible? Why or why not? What will happen if the government takes the advice that achieves its goal, as in part (a)?

6. **LO 4** In Chapter 13, we studied how persistent total factor productivity shocks in a closed economy can provide an explanation for business cycles. In the second model studied in this chapter, with production and investment, determine the effects of a persistent increase in total factor productivity on domestic output, consumption, investment, and the current account surplus. Are the predictions of the model consistent with what you observe in Figure 16.2? Explain why or why not.

7. **LO 4** Suppose, in the second model in this chapter, with production and investment, that there is an increase in credit market frictions, as studied in Chapter 11. What are the effects on aggregate output and the current account surplus? Comment on these effects, as they relate to U.S. experience during the financial crisis and the 2008–2009 recession.

Working with the Data

Answer these questions using the Federal Reserve Bank of St. Louis's FRED database, accessible at http://research.stlouisfed.org/fred2/

1. Plot the current account surplus and net exports. How much difference is there between the two time series? Comment on the significance of this.

2. The models in this chapter assume that interest rates are determined on world markets. If this were true in practice, there should not be much difference between the federal funds rate and the overnight LIBOR rate, based on the U.S. dollar. Plot these two time series and comment on what you observe.

Chapter 17

Money in the Open Economy

Learning Objectives

After studying Chapter 17, students will be able to:

17.1 Explain the differences between the real exchange rate and the nominal exchange rate, and discuss the purchasing power parity relationship.

17.2 Explain the institutional arrangements behind fixed and flexible exchange rates, and discuss the role of the International Monetary Fund.

17.3 Construct the monetary small open-economy (SOE) model with a flexible exchange rate, and use the model to analyze shocks to the economy and macroeconomic policy.

17.4 Construct the monetary SOE with a fixed exchange rate, and use the model to analyze shocks to the economy, monetary and fiscal policy, and exchange rate devaluation.

17.5 Explain balance of payments accounting and the role of the capital account.

17.6 Explain how capital controls work and their macroeconomic effects.

17.7 Construct the Keynesian sticky price open economy model, and use the model to analyze the effects of monetary and fiscal policy, and macroeconomic shocks.

Many issues in international macroeconomics can be well understood without the complication of monetary exchange in the picture, as we saw in Chapter 16. However, there are also many intriguing issues in international finance—particularly those involving the determination of nominal exchange rates, the effects of having flexible or fixed exchange rates, the transmission of nominal macroeconomic shocks among countries, the effects of capital controls, and the role of international financial institutions—that we need monetary models to understand. In this chapter, we build on the second small open-economy model we studied in Chapter 16 to integrate money into a monetary small open-economy model that can address some key issues in international monetary economics.

We will first consider purchasing power parity, or the law of one price, which is a cornerstone of the flexible-price version of the monetary small open-economy model in this chapter. Purchasing power parity would hold if the prices of all goods in the world economy were equal, corrected for nominal exchange rates, where a nominal exchange rate is the price of one currency in terms of another. While there are economic forces that result in a long-run tendency toward purchasing power parity, in reality there can be fairly large and persistent deviations from purchasing power parity, as we will show. However, although purchasing power parity may not be the best approximation to reality in the short run, it proves to be very useful in simplifying the basic model used in this chapter. The New Keynesian sticky price model introduced later in this chapter will feature deviations from purchasing power parity.

The monetary small open-economy model we construct and put to work in this chapter builds on the second small open-economy model from Chapter 16, in that the goods markets in the two models are identical. The model of this chapter also has much in common with the monetary intertemporal model in Chapter 12. In particular, the monetary small open-economy model features a classical dichotomy, in that nominal variables—in this case, the price level and the nominal exchange rate—are determined independently of real variables. Further, money is neutral. This is a useful starting point for international monetary economics, because adding some of the frictions that we considered in the business cycle models of Chapters 13 and 14—sticky prices and coordination failures—involves straightforward extensions of this basic framework. At the end of the chapter, we include one extension—sticky prices—in a New Keynesian framework.

The first experiments we carry out with the model in this chapter emphasize the effects of shocks from abroad under flexible and fixed nominal exchange rates. A flexible exchange rate is free to move according to supply and demand in the market for foreign exchange, whereas under a fixed exchange rate the domestic government commits in some fashion to supporting the nominal exchange rate at a specified value. A flexible exchange rate has the property that monetary policy can be set independently in the domestic economy, and the domestic price level is not affected by changes in foreign prices. Under a fixed exchange rate, however, the domestic central bank cannot control its money supply independently, and price level changes originating abroad are essentially imported to the domestic economy. Flexible and fixed exchange rate regimes each have their own advantages and disadvantages, as we discuss.

We examine the effects of capital controls on the behavior of the domestic economy. Capital controls are restrictions on the international flow of assets, and these controls tend to dampen the fluctuations that result from some shocks to the economy. Capital controls are detrimental, however, in that they reduce economic efficiency.

Finally, we study a New Keynesian sticky price open-economy model that is an extension of the basic framework. The approach we take is much like what we did for a closed economy in Chapter 14. With sticky prices, money is not neutral, and purchasing power parity does not hold in the short run. Just as in closed-economy models, sticky prices imply a role for stabilization policy. Output gaps may exist that fiscal or monetary policy can close, but the exchange rate regime matters in an important way for the potency of monetary versus fiscal policy.

The Nominal Exchange Rate, the Real Exchange Rate, and Purchasing Power Parity

LO 17.1 Explain the differences between the real exchange rate and the nominal exchange rate, and discuss the purchasing power parity relationship.

The basic model we work with in this chapter is a monetary small open-economy model, which builds on the second small open-economy model of Chapter 16 and the monetary intertemporal model in Chapter 12. Key variables in this model are the nominal exchange rate and the real exchange rate, which are defined in this section. Further, in this section we derive the purchasing power parity relationship, which determines the value of the real exchange rate.

In the model in this chapter, just as in the monetary intertemporal model, all domestically produced goods sell at a price P, in terms of domestic currency. Foreign-produced goods sell at the price P^*, in terms of foreign currency. In the model, there is a market for foreign exchange, on which domestic currency can be traded for foreign currency, and we let e denote the price of one unit of foreign currency in terms of domestic currency. Thus, e is the **nominal exchange rate**. If a domestic resident holding domestic currency wished to buy goods abroad, assuming that foreign producers of goods accept only foreign currency in exchange for their goods, one unit of foreign goods costs eP^* in units of domestic currency. This is because the domestic resident must first buy foreign currency with domestic currency, at a price of e, and then buy foreign goods with foreign currency at a price of P^*. To give an example, suppose that a book in England costs five British pounds, and that the exchange rate between U.S. dollars and British Pounds is two U.S. dollars per British Pound, that is, $e = 2$. Then, the cost of the book in U.S. dollars is $2 \times 5 = 10$.

Because the price of domestic goods in domestic currency is P, and the price of foreign goods in terms of domestic currency is eP^*, the **real exchange rate** (or the terms of trade), which is the price of foreign goods in terms of domestic goods, is

$$\text{Real exchange rate} = \frac{eP^*}{P}.$$

Suppose that it is costless to transport goods between foreign countries and the domestic country and that there are no trade barriers, such as government-set import quotas and tariffs (import taxes). Then, if $eP^* > P$, it would be cheaper to buy goods domestically than abroad, so that foreign consumers would want to buy domestic goods rather than foreign goods, and this would tend to increase P. Alternatively, if $eP^* < P$, then foreign goods would be cheaper than domestic goods, and so domestic consumers would prefer to purchase foreign goods rather than domestic goods, in which case P would tend to fall. Thus, with no transportation costs and no trade barriers, we should expect to observe that

$$P = eP^*, \tag{17-1}$$

and this relationship is called **purchasing power parity (PPP)**. This relationship is also called the **law of one price**, as, if it holds, the price of goods is the same, in terms of domestic currency, at home and abroad. If PPP holds, then the real exchange rate is 1.

In the real world, we would not in general expect PPP to hold exactly if we measure P and P^* as the price levels in two different countries. Any measure of the price level, such as the consumer price index or the implicit GDP price deflator, includes the prices of a large set of goods produced and consumed in the economy. Some of these goods are traded on world markets, such as agricultural commodities and raw materials, while other goods are only traded domestically, such as local services like haircuts. While we would expect that there would be a tendency for the law of one price to hold for goods that are traded internationally, we would not expect it to hold for nontraded goods. For example, crude oil can be shipped at relatively low cost over large distances by pipeline and in large oil tankers, and there is a well-organized world market for crude oil, so that crude oil sells almost anywhere in the world at close to the same price (plus transport costs). However, there is not a world market in haircuts, as the cost of traveling to another country for a haircut is in most cases very large relative to the cost of the haircut. The law of one price should hold for crude oil but not for haircuts.

In general, there are strong economic forces that tend to make market prices and nominal exchange rates adjust so that PPP holds. For example, if PPP does not hold, then even if there are large costs of transporting goods across countries, consumers would want to move to where goods are relatively cheaper, and firms would want to move their production where goods are relatively more expensive, and ultimately we would expect PPP to hold over the long run. Unless it is very difficult to move goods, labor, and capital across international borders, purchasing power parity should hold, at least as a long-run relationship. Though PPP may be a poor description of short-run reality, as we show in the next section, and the adjustment to PPP may be quite slow, it simplifies some of our models considerably to make the PPP assumption, and this simplification allows us to focus our analysis. However, at the end of the chapter, we will consider a New Keynesian sticky price model, in which purchasing power parity does not hold in the short run.

Flexible and Fixed Exchange Rates

LO 17.2 Explain the institutional arrangements behind fixed and flexible exchange rates, and discuss the role of the International Monetary Fund.

In addition to PPP, another important component of the monetary small open-economy model is the exchange rate regime. As we show, a key determinant of how the domestic economy responds to shocks, and an important factor for the conduct of domestic monetary and fiscal policy, is the set of rules for government intervention in foreign exchange markets. Roughly speaking, the polar extremes in foreign exchange market intervention are a **flexible exchange rate regime** and a **fixed exchange rate regime**. Currently, there are countries in the world that conform closely to an idealized flexible

THEORY CONFRONTS THE DATA

The PPP Relationship for the United states and Canada

A case where we might expect relatively small deviations from PPP involves the relationship between the United States and Canada. Historically, there has been a high volume of trade between these two countries. The United States and Canada signed a free trade agreement in 1989, which was replaced in 1992 by the North American Free Trade Agreement (NAFTA), which included Mexico. An earlier trade agreement was the Canada–U.S. Auto Pact, signed in 1965, which permitted the shipment of autos and auto parts across the Canada–U.S. border by manufacturers. Given the close proximity of Canada and the United States, and natural north–south transportation links, transportation costs between the United States and Canada are quite low. Not only are goods easy to move between these two countries, but NAFTA now permits freer movement of labor across the Canada–U.S. border as well. Capital is also relatively free to move between these two countries. Therefore, there are especially strong forces in place in the U.S.–Canada case that would cause us to be surprised if PPP did not apply, at least approximately.

In Figure 17.1 we show the real exchange rate, $\frac{eP^*}{P}$, for Canada versus the United States for the years 1951–2015. Here, e is the price of Canadian dollars in terms of U.S. dollars, P^* is the Canadian consumer price index, and P is the CPI in the United States. The real exchange rate has been scaled for convenience, so that its value is 100 in January 1951. Purchasing power parity predicts that the real exchange rate in the figure should be constant, but it is certainly not. In the figure, the real exchange rate has fluctuated significantly. The fluctuations are not small short-run fluctuations around a constant value but are more persistent in nature. Indeed, there appears to be no tendency for the real exchange rate to fluctuate more closely around some long-run value after the free trade agreement in 1989. If there are such large deviations from PPP for Canada and the United States, we should expect PPP relationships between the United States and other countries of the world to be even more loose in the short run.

exchange rate regime, others that fix the exchange rate, and some countries that mix the two approaches.

Under a flexible or floating exchange rate, there is no intervention by the domestic fiscal or monetary authorities to specifically target the nominal exchange rate e. If the nominal exchange rate is truly flexible, it is free to move in response to market forces. Some countries with flexible exchange rates are Japan, Sweden, the United Kingdom, Australia, New Zealand, Canada, and the United States. For reasons we discuss ahead, essentially all countries care about short-run movements in their nominal exchange rate, and they therefore intervene from time to time, through monetary and fiscal policy, to influence the value of the nominal exchange rate, even under a flexible exchange rate regime.

There are several different important fixed exchange rate systems, which can be roughly characterized as **hard pegs** and **soft pegs**. Under a hard peg, a country

Figure 17.1 The Real Exchange Rate for Canada versus the United States
Purchasing power parity predicts that the real exchange rate should be a constant, but there have been large and persistent deviations from PPP in this case.
Source: Data from Statistics Canada and Bureau of Labor Statistics, © Stephen D. Williamson.

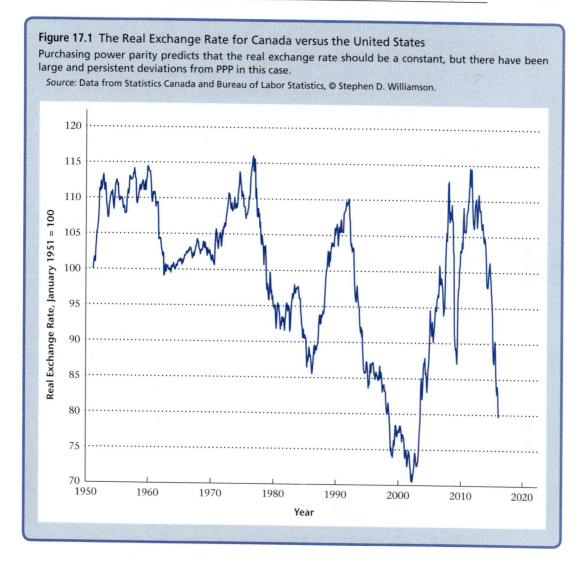

commits to a fixed nominal exchange rate relative to some other currency for the indefinite future. With a soft peg, there is no long-term commitment to a particular value for the exchange rate, but the exchange rate can be fixed relative to another currency for long periods of time, with periodic **devaluations** (increases in the nominal exchange rate e) and **revaluations** (decreases in e).

A hard peg can be implemented in basically three different ways. First, a country could abandon its national currency and **dollarize**. Dollarization essentially involves using the currency of another country as the national medium of exchange. For example, Ecuador currently uses the U.S. dollar as its national currency, though dollarization can refer to a situation in which a country uses a currency other than the U.S. dollar. A disadvantage of dollarizing is that a country relinquishes its ability to collect seigniorage (discussed in Chapter 12); that is, it cannot print money to finance government spending.

The second way to implement a hard peg is through the establishment of a **currency board**. With a currency board, there is a centralized institution, which could be the country's central bank, that holds interest-bearing assets denominated in the currency of the country against which the nominal exchange rate is being fixed. This institution then stands ready to exchange domestic currency for foreign currency at a specified fixed exchange rate, and it can buy and sell interest-bearing assets in order to carry out these exchanges. A country that currently uses a currency board is Hong Kong, which fixes its nominal exchange rate relative to the U.S. dollar. Under a currency board, a country maintains its ability to collect seigniorage.

Finally, a third approach to implementing a hard peg is through mutual agreement among countries to a common currency, as in the **European Monetary Union (EMU)**, which was established in 1999. Most European countries are EMU members, with some notable exceptions such as the United Kingdom. The common currency of the EMU is the **Euro**, and the supply of Euros is managed by the **European Central Bank (ECB)**. The rules governing the operation of the ECB specify how the seigniorage revenue from the printing of new Euros is to be split among the EMU members.

Soft pegs involve various degrees of commitment to a fixed exchange rate or to target bands for the exchange rate. For example, under the **European Monetary System (EMS)**, which was established in 1979 and preceded the EMU, member European countries committed over the short run to target their exchange rates within specified ranges. In this arrangement, coordination was required among the EMS members, and there were periodic crises and changes in target bands for exchange rates. Another soft peg was the **Bretton Woods arrangement**, the rules for which were specified in an agreement negotiated at Bretton Woods, New Hampshire, in 1944. The Bretton Woods arrangement governed post–World War II international monetary relations until 1971. Under Bretton Woods, the United States fixed the value of the U.S. dollar relative to gold, by agreeing to exchange U.S. dollars for gold at a specified price. All other countries then agreed to fix their exchange rates relative to the U.S. dollar. This was, thus, a modified gold standard arrangement. For reasons we discuss later in this chapter, soft peg arrangements have tended to be unstable; the arrangements typically collapse and are replaced by alternative systems, as was the case with the EMS and the Bretton Woods arrangement.

A key international monetary institution that plays an important role in exchange rate determination is the **International Monetary Fund (IMF)**, the framework for which was discussed at Bretton Woods in 1944, with the IMF established in 1946. The IMF currently has 189 member countries, and it performs a function that is in some ways similar to the one carried out by a central bank relative to the domestic banks under its supervision. Namely, the IMF plays the role of a **lender of last resort** for its member countries, just as a central bank is a lender of last resort for domestic financial institutions (as we discuss in Chapter 18). The IMF stands ready to lend to member countries in distress, though IMF lending comes with strings attached. Typically, IMF lending is conditional on a member country submitting to a program set up by the IMF, which typically specifies corrective policy actions.

A Monetary Small Open-Economy Model with a Flexible Exchange Rate

LO 17.3 Construct the monetary small open-economy (SOE) model with a flexible exchange rate, and use the model to analyze shocks to the economy and macroeconomic policy.

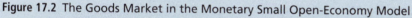

Now that we have discussed some of the institutional arrangements governing the determination of exchange rates, we can proceed to work with a monetary small open-economy model in which there is international monetary interaction. This model is in part based on the monetary intertemporal model in Chapter 12. This is a small open-economy model that essentially involves adding a money market to the second real small open-economy model in Chapter 16. In this model, we assume for now that the exchange rate is flexible, and we study the properties of a fixed exchange rate system in the next section.

In Figure 17.2 we show the goods market for the monetary small open-economy model, which is identical to the goods market for the third real small open-economy

Figure 17.2 The Goods Market in the Monetary Small Open-Economy Model

The goods market in this model is identical to the goods market in the real small open-economy model with investment in Chapter 14. The world real interest rate is r^*, and equilibrium real output is Y_1. The current account surplus adjusts so that the Y^d curve intersects the Y^s curve at the world real interest rate r^*.

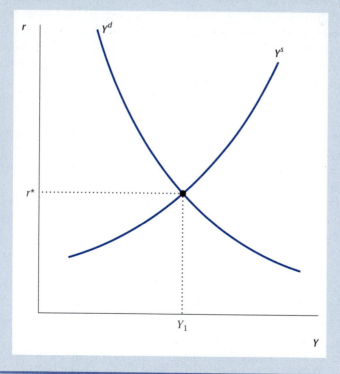

model of Chapter 16. The curve Y^d is the output demand curve, which is downward sloping because of the negative effect of the real interest rate on the demand for consumption and investment goods, and Y^s is the output supply curve, which is upward sloping because of the intertemporal substitution effect of the real interest rate on labor supply. The output supply and output demand curve shift as the result of factors discussed in detail in Chapter 16. Just as in Chapter 16, the small open-economy assumption implies that domestic firms and consumers are collectively price-takers on world markets. In equilibrium, the income expenditure identity holds, so that $Y = C + I + G + NX$. Given that the domestic economy is, as a whole, a price-taker on world markets, any output not absorbed domestically as C, I, or G is exported (if net exports are positive) or any excess of domestic absorption over domestic output is purchased abroad (if net exports are negative).

We assume that PPP holds, so that

$$P = eP^*, \tag{17-2}$$

where P is the domestic price level, e is the price of foreign exchange in terms of domestic currency, and P^* is the foreign price level. Though we know from above that the PPP relationship typically does not hold in the short run, assuming PPP simplifies our model greatly and essentially implies that we are ignoring the effects of changes in the terms of trade, which would cloud some of the issues we want to discuss here. Later in this chapter we will modify this model by including sticky prices, which will imply that PPP does not hold. Here, given the assumption of a small open economy, events in the domestic economy have no effect on the foreign price level P^*, and so we treat P^* as exogenous. However, the domestic price level P and the exchange rate e are endogenous variables. The exchange rate is flexible, in that it is determined by market forces, as we show below.

Next, we want to determine how the money market works in our equilibrium model. As in Chapter 12, money demand is given by

$$M^d = PL(Y, r^*), \tag{17-3}$$

where $L(Y, r^*)$ denotes the demand for real money balances, which depends positively on aggregate real income Y and negatively on the real interest rate. Here, recall that the domestic real interest rate is identical to the world real interest rate r^*, and we are assuming no long-run money growth, so that the domestic inflation rate is zero and the real interest rate is equal to the nominal interest rate given the Fisher relation (see Chapter 12). Now, given the PPP relation, Equation (17-2), we can substitute in Equation (17-3) for P to get

$$M^d = eP^* L(Y, r^*).$$

We take the nominal money supply to be exogenous, with $M^s = M$. In equilibrium, money supply equals money demand, so that $M^s = M^d$, or

$$M = eP^* L(Y, r^*). \tag{17-4}$$

In Figure 17.3, money demand and money supply are on the horizontal axis, while e, the exchange rate, is on the vertical axis. Then, given Y and r^*, money demand M^d is

Figure 17.3 The Money Market in the Monetary Small Open-Economy Model with a Flexible Exchange Rate

With a flexible exchange rate, and given purchasing power parity, the equilibrium nominal exchange rate is e_1, determined by the intersection of the nominal money supply and nominal money demand curves.

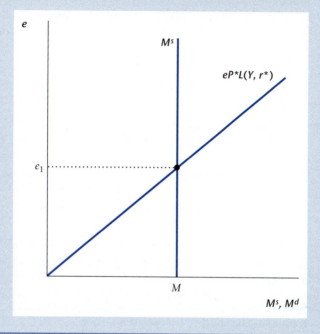

a straight line through the origin in the figure, while money supply M^s is a vertical line at $M^s = M$. The intersection of the supply and demand curves for money then determines the nominal exchange rate e, so that the equilibrium exchange rate in the figure is e_1. Once we have determined e, we have also determined the domestic price level P from the PPP Equation (17-2).

Thus, in this model, the nominal exchange rate is determined by the nominal demand for money relative to the nominal supply of money. Because the nominal exchange rate is a nominal variable, this seems natural. Movements in the exchange rate are caused either by a shift in money demand or a shift in money supply.

The Neutrality of Money with a Flexible Exchange Rate

Now that we have set up the model, we can proceed to study its properties. Just as in the monetary intertemporal model we studied in Chapter 12, this model features a classical dichotomy, in that real variables (the level of output, the current account surplus, consumption, and investment) are determined independently of nominal variables (the domestic price level P and the nominal exchange rate e). In Figure 17.3, the nominal exchange rate is determined by the supply and demand for money, and the level of the nominal exchange rate has no bearing on real variables.

If the central bank increases the money supply, say from M_1 to M_2 in Figure 17.4, this has the effect of shifting the money supply curve rightward from M_1^s to M_2^s. In equilibrium, the nominal exchange rate increases from e_1 to e_2, and there is no effect on the level of real output, the real interest rate (which is the real interest rate on world markets, r^*), consumption, investment, or the current account surplus. Because the price of foreign currency has risen in terms of domestic currency, we say that there is a **depreciation** of the domestic currency. Ultimately, because Equation (17-4) implies that

$$\frac{M}{e} = P^* L(Y, r^*),$$

and because P^*, Y, and r^* remain unaffected by the change in the money supply, $\dfrac{M}{e}$ remains unchanged. Thus, the nominal exchange rate increases in proportion to the money supply; for example, if the money supply increased by 5%, the nominal exchange rate would also increase by 5%. Further, because PPP holds, or $P = eP^*$, and because P^* is fixed, the price level P also increases in proportion to the increase in the money supply.

Thus, money is neutral in this model economy with a flexible exchange rate. There are no real effects of an increase in the nominal money supply, but all money prices,

Figure 17.4 An Increase in the Money Supply in the Monetary Small Open-Economy Model with a Flexible Exchange Rate

Money is neutral in the monetary small open-economy model with a flexible exchange rate. An increase in the money supply causes the nominal exchange rate and the price level to increase in proportion to the increase in the money supply, with no effect on real variables.

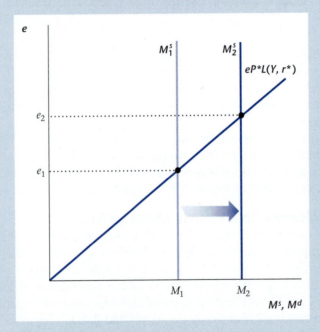

including the nominal exchange rate, increase in proportion to the increase in the money supply. While most macroeconomists adopt the view that money is neutral in the long run in an open economy, there are differences of opinion about the short-run neutrality of money and the explanations for any nonneutralities of money, just as in closed-economy macroeconomics. Later in this chapter, we explore one possible source of monetary nonneutralities—sticky prices.

A Nominal Shock to the Domestic Economy from Abroad: P^* Increases

We would like to use the monetary small open-economy model to investigate how the domestic economy is affected by events in the rest of the world. The first example we consider is the case of an increase in the price level in the rest of the world, which is essentially a nominal shock to the domestic economy. We see that a flexible exchange rate system has an insulating property with respect to increases in the foreign price level. That is, the nominal exchange rate adjusts to exactly offset the increase in the foreign price level, and there are no effects on the domestic price level or domestic real variables. In particular, the temporary foreign inflation resulting from the increase in the foreign price level is not imported to the domestic economy.

Suppose that P^* increases from P_1^* to P_2^*, perhaps because central banks in foreign countries increase the quantity of foreign money in circulation. Then, in Figure 17.5, the money demand curve shifts rightward from $eP_1^*L(Y, r^*)$ to $eP_2^*L(Y, r^*)$. In equilibrium, there is no effect on real variables, but the nominal exchange rate falls from e_1 to e_2, so that there is an **appreciation** of the domestic currency. Because $P = eP^*$, from Equation (17-4) we have

$$\frac{M}{P} = L(Y, r^*),$$

and because M, Y, and r^* remain unchanged, P is also unchanged. Therefore, no domestic variables were affected by the price level change in the rest of the world. In particular, the appreciation of the domestic currency was just sufficient to offset the effect of the increase in P^* on the domestic price level. That is, the flexible exchange rate insulated the domestic economy from the nominal shock from abroad. This is certainly a desirable property of a flexible exchange rate regime. Under flexible exchange rates, the domestic price level, and by implication the domestic inflation rate, is determined by the quantity of domestic money supplied by the domestic central bank, and it is not influenced by how monetary policy is conducted by foreign central banks.

A Real Shock to the Domestic Economy from Abroad

As an experiment to determine how real domestic variables, the nominal exchange rate, and the price level respond to a real disturbance transmitted from abroad, we examine the effects of an increase in the world real interest rate. Such a shock could result, for example, from a decrease in total factor productivity in the rest of the world (recall our analysis of the effects of total factor productivity shocks from Chapter 10). As we show, a flexible exchange rate cannot shield the domestic economy from the effects of a change in the world real interest rate; the nominal exchange rate appreciates (e falls), and the price level falls.

Figure 17.5 An Increase in the Foreign Price Level in the Monetary Small Open-Economy Model with a Flexible Exchange Rate

If the foreign price level increases, this shifts the nominal money demand curve to the right, with the nominal exchange rate falling from e_1 to e_2 in equilibrium. The decrease in the nominal exchange rate exactly offsets the increase in the foreign price level, and there is no effect on the domestic price level.

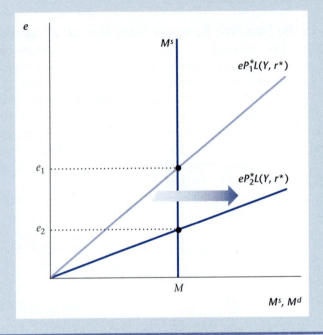

In Figure 17.6 the world real interest rate increases from r_1^* to r_2^*. The real effects of this are the same as we considered for the second real small open-economy model in Chapter 16. In Figure 17.6(a), the current account surplus increases, shifting the output demand curve to the right until it comes to rest at Y_2^d. Output increases from Y_1 to Y_2 because of the increase in labor supply that results from intertemporal substitution of leisure by the representative consumer. The increase in the real interest rate causes domestic consumption expenditures and investment expenditures to fall, though the increase in current income causes consumption to rise. On net, consumption may rise or fall. Total domestic absorption, $C + I + G$, may rise or fall, but any increase in absorption is smaller than the increase in domestic output, so that the current account surplus rises.

The nominal effects of the increase in the world real interest rate depend on how the demand for money changes. The increase in the real interest rate causes the demand for money to fall, while the increase in domestic output causes the demand for money to rise. It is not clear whether $L(Y_2, r_2^*) < L(Y_1, r_1^*)$ or $L(Y_2, r_2^*) > L(Y_1, r_1^*)$. However, if real money demand is much more responsive to real income than to the interest rate, then money demand will rise, and the money demand curve in Figure 17.6(b) shifts to

Figure 17.6 An Increase in the World Real Interest Rate with a Flexible Exchange Rate

Under a flexible exchange rate, if the world real interest rate increases, this causes real output to rise, and the money demand curve shifts to the right, assuming money demand is much more responsive to real income than to the real interest rate. The nominal exchange rate decreases in equilibrium.

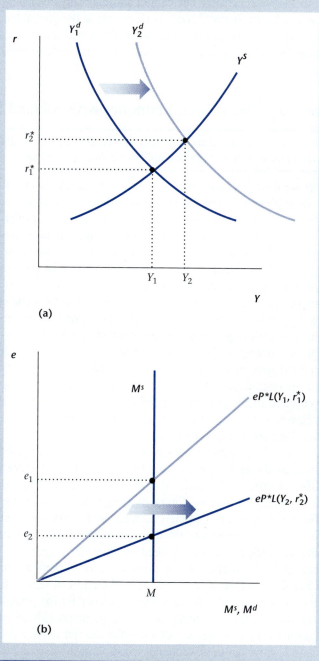

(a)

(b)

the right. In equilibrium, the exchange rate appreciates, with the nominal exchange rate decreasing from e_1 to e_2. As purchasing power parity holds—that is, $P = eP^*$, with P^* constant—P falls in proportion to the decrease in e. Thus, the increase in the world real interest rate leads to an exchange rate appreciation and a decrease in the price level. Clearly, the flexible exchange rate cannot automatically insulate the domestic economy from real shocks that occur abroad. For example, if the central bank wished to stabilize the price level in the face of the increase in the world real interest rate, it would have to increase the money supply in response to the increase in money demand resulting from the shock.

A Monetary Small Open Economy with a Fixed Exchange Rate

LO 17.4 Construct the monetary SOE with a fixed exchange rate, and use the model to analyze shocks to the economy, monetary and fiscal policy, and exchange rate devaluation.

Now that we have studied how the economy behaves under a flexible exchange rate regime, we explore how real and nominal variables are determined when the exchange rate is fixed. The type of fixed exchange rate regime we consider is a type of soft peg, where the government fixes the nominal exchange rate for extended periods of time, but might devalue or revalue the domestic currency at some times.

Under the fixed exchange rate regime we model, the government chooses a level at which it wants to fix the nominal exchange rate, which is e_1 in Figure 17.7. The government must then, either through its central bank or some other authority, stand ready to support this exchange rate. For simplicity, we suppose that the fixed exchange rate is supported through the government standing ready to exchange foreign currency for domestic currency at the fixed exchange rate e_1. To see how this happens, consider the simplified government balance sheet in Table 17.1. This is a consolidated balance sheet for the central bank and the fiscal authority. To support a fixed exchange rate, the government must act to buy or sell its foreign exchange reserves (think of this as foreign currency) for outside money (domestic currency) in foreign exchange markets, whenever there are market forces that would tend to push the exchange rate away from the fixed value the government wants it to have. For example, if there are forces tending to increase the exchange rate and, thus, cause a depreciation of the domestic currency, the government should sell foreign currency and buy domestic currency to offset those forces. If there are forces pushing down the exchange rate (appreciation), the government should buy foreign currency and sell domestic currency.

With a fixed exchange rate, the domestic central bank necessarily loses control over the domestic stock of money. To see this, consider Figure 17.7, where the nominal exchange rate is fixed at e_1. If the domestic central bank attempted to increase the money supply above M, its current value, the effect of this would be to put upward pressure on the exchange rate. Given the tendency for the price of foreign currency to rise in terms of domestic currency as a result, participants in foreign exchange markets would want to trade domestic currency for foreign currency, and the government would have to carry out these exchanges to support the fixed exchange rate. This would tend to reduce the stock of domestic money in circulation, and the attempt by the

Figure 17.7 The Money Market in the Monetary Small Open-Economy Model with a Fixed Exchange Rate

With a fixed exchange rate, the money supply is endogenous. Given the fixed exchange rate e_1, the money supply M is determined so that the money supply curve M^s intersects the money demand curve for an exchange rate equal to e_1.

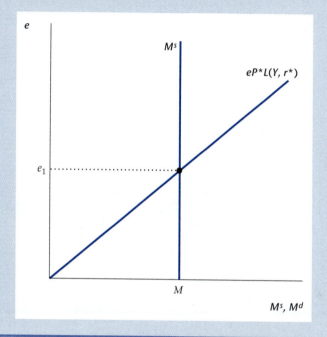

Table 17.1 A Simplified Government Balance Sheet

Assets	Liabilities
Foreign Exchange Reserves	Outside Money
	Interest-Bearing Government Debt

central bank to increase the money supply would be completely undone by actions in the foreign exchange market to support the fixed exchange rate. The money supply would remain at M, with the exchange rate and the domestic price level P unchanged. Similarly, if the domestic central bank attempted to engineer a reduction in the money supply below M, this would put downward pressure on the exchange rate, participants in the foreign exchange market would want to exchange foreign currency for domestic currency, and the government would be forced to exchange domestic currency for foreign currency, thus increasing the supply of money. The money supply could, therefore, not be reduced below M. The implication of this is that, under a fixed exchange

Figure 17.8 An Increase in the Foreign Price Level in the Monetary Small Open-Economy Model with a Fixed Exchange Rate

With a fixed exchange rate, an increase in the foreign price level shifts the money demand curve to the right, which causes the domestic money supply to increase. The domestic price level increases in proportion to the increase in the foreign price level.

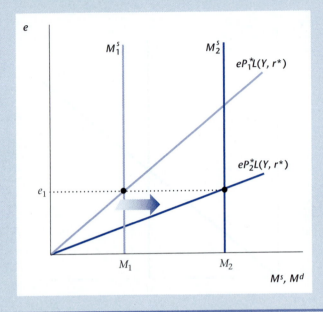

rate regime, the supply of money cannot be determined independently by the central bank. But once the government fixes the exchange rate, the domestic money supply is determined.

A Nominal Foreign Shock Under a Fixed Exchange Rate

Suppose that the foreign price level increases when the domestic economy is under a fixed exchange rate. In Figure 17.8, P^* increases from P_1^* to P_2^*. As a result, the demand for money shifts rightward from $eP_1^* L(Y,r^*)$ to $eP_2^* L(Y,r^*)$. This increase in the demand for money results in downward pressure on the exchange rate, so that domestic currency becomes more attractive relative to foreign currency. On foreign exchange markets, the government must exchange domestic currency for foreign currency, and this leads to an increase in the domestic money supply from M_1 to M_2. Because $P = eP^*$, and the exchange rate is fixed, the domestic price level increases in proportion to the increase in the foreign price level. Thus, under a fixed exchange rate regime, in contrast to the flexible exchange rate regime, the domestic economy is not insulated from nominal shocks that occur abroad. When the foreign price level changes, this price level change is imported, and the domestic price level increases in proportion. Because domestic monetary policy is not independent under a fixed exchange rate, the domestic central bank is forced to adopt the world's inflation rate domestically.

A Real Foreign Shock Under a Fixed Exchange Rate

Now, we consider the effects of an increase in the world real interest rate from r_1^* to r_2^*, just as we did for the case of a flexible exchange rate. In Figure 17.9(a), as under the flexible exchange rate regime, the real effects of the interest rate increase are an increase in domestic output from Y_1 to Y_2, a decrease in investment, an increase or decrease in consumption, and an increase in current account surplus. Assuming that the effect of the increase in real income on money demand is much larger than that of the increase in the real interest rate, the demand for money shifts rightward in Figure 17.9(b), from $eP^* L(Y_1, r_1^*)$ to $eP^* L(Y_2, r_2^*)$. Then, with the exchange rate fixed at e_1, the domestic money supply must rise from M_1 to M_2. Because $P = eP^*$ and e and P^* do not change, the domestic price level does not change. Thus, a fixed exchange rate can insulate the domestic price level from real shocks that occur abroad. The same result could be achieved under a flexible exchange rate, but this would require discretionary action by the domestic central bank, rather than the automatic response that occurs under a fixed exchange rate.

Exchange Rate Devaluation

Under a fixed exchange rate regime, a devaluation of the domestic currency (an increase in the fixed exchange rate e) might be a course the government chooses in response to a shock to the economy. In this section, we show how a temporary reduction in domestic total factor productivity would lead to a reduction in foreign exchange reserves that the government may not desire. In this case, the decrease in foreign exchange reserves can be prevented by a devaluation of the domestic currency. The total factor productivity shock also causes a decrease in the current account surplus, but the devaluation has no effect in offsetting this current account change.

Suppose in Figure 17.10 that the domestic economy is initially in equilibrium with the output demand curve Y_1^d and the output supply curve Y_1^s determining domestic output Y_1 in panel (a), given the world real interest rate r^*. In Figure 17.10(b), the exchange rate is fixed at e_1 at first, nominal money demand is initially $eP^* L(Y_1, r^*)$, and the money supply is M_1. Now, suppose that there is a temporary negative shock to domestic total factor productivity. This shifts the output supply curve leftward from Y_1^s to Y_2^s in Figure 17.10(a), as in Chapter 11. The current account surplus falls, shifting the output demand curve to the left, until it comes to rest at Y_2^d. In equilibrium, output falls to Y_2, domestic absorption falls because of the decrease in consumption (as income falls), and the current account surplus falls as well. In Figure 17.10(b), the money demand curve shifts leftward to $eP^* L(Y_2, r^*)$ with the fall in real income. If the government were to continue to support the fixed nominal exchange rate at e_1, this would imply, given the fall in the demand for the domestic currency, that the government would have to sell foreign currency on the foreign exchange market and buy domestic currency. This implies that the money supply would contract from M_1 to M_2.

Suppose, however, that the government does not wish to sell any of its foreign exchange reserves or that it does not have the foreign exchange reserves to sell, when the demand for domestic money falls. The government can avoid selling foreign exchange by fixing the exchange rate at e_2 in Figure 17.10(b). This implies that the money supply remains fixed at M_1, and there is a devaluation in the exchange rate, as the price of foreign currency has risen relative to domestic currency.

Figure 17.9 An Increase in the World Real Interest Rate with a Fixed Exchange Rate

Under a fixed exchange rate, an increase in the world real interest rate causes an increase in real output and a shift to the right in nominal money demand. The money supply increases to accommodate the increase in money demand, and the domestic price level remains unchanged.

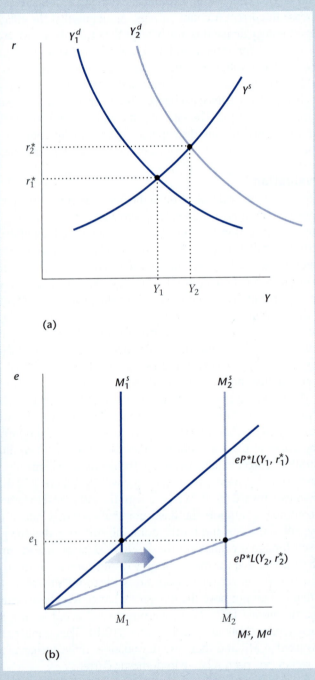

Figure 17.10 A Devaluation in Response to a Temporary Total Factor Productivity Shock

A temporary decrease in total factor productivity shifts the output supply curve to the left, reducing output and the current account surplus. The nominal money demand curve shifts to the left. If the government wants to avoid a loss in foreign exchange reserves, it can increase the fixed exchange rate from e_1 to e_2 and devalue the domestic currency.

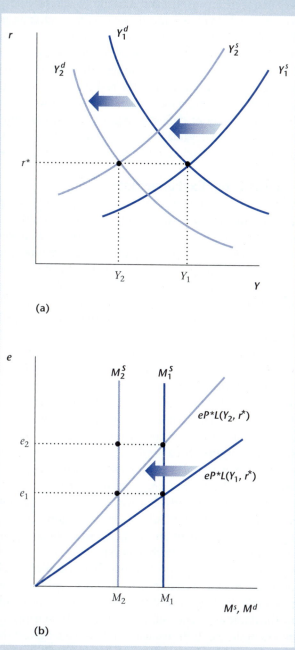

An important point is that the devaluation of the domestic currency has no effect here on the current account deficit. We might think that a devaluation would make domestic goods cheaper relative to foreign goods, thus increasing the real exchange rate, and that this would cause imports to fall, exports to rise, and the current account deficit to fall. While this might be true in the short run in some types of Keynesian analysis with sticky prices (but there are income and substitution effects to be concerned with, in terms of the effect on the current account deficit), with purchasing power parity there is no effect on the real exchange rate. Ultimately, if the government determined that the current account deficit that results here is a problem—for example, if the current account deficit is caused by excessive government spending—then this is a real problem that should be corrected through real means. That is, the real current account deficit could be reduced through a reduction in government spending, which we know from Chapter 13 can reduce the current account deficit in Figure 17.10(a). Trying to reduce the current account deficit through a devaluation in the domestic currency essentially involves trying to make a real change through nominal means, which cannot work in the long run.

Flexible Versus Fixed Exchange Rates

Governments face important choices concerning exchange rate policy, and a key choice is whether a flexible or fixed exchange rate regime should be adopted. What are the arguments for the adoption of flexible versus fixed exchange rates? In the previous subsections, we have seen that the exchange rate regime affects how the domestic economy is insulated from shocks from abroad. When a country's central bank seeks to stabilize the price level, our analysis tells us that if nominal shocks from abroad are important, then a flexible exchange rate is preferable to a fixed exchange rate, because a flexible exchange rate absorbs a shock to the foreign price level and stabilizes the domestic price level. Alternatively, if real shocks from abroad are important, then a fixed exchange rate is preferable to a flexible exchange rate, as this acts to prevent the domestic price level from moving in response to real shocks from abroad, because the domestic money supply acts as a shock absorber. Thus, in this respect, whether a particular country should choose a fixed or flexible exchange rate depends on its circumstances. It is possible that a particular country might want to move from a fixed to a flexible exchange rate over time and then back again.

It is sometimes argued that a flexible exchange rate allows the domestic central bank to implement a monetary policy independent of what happens in the rest of the world. In our model, with a flexible exchange rate, the domestic government can set the domestic money supply independently, but with a fixed exchange rate, the money supply is not under the control of the domestic government. However, giving the domestic central bank the power to implement an independent monetary policy is useful only if the central bank can be trusted with this power. Some central banks, such as those in the United States, Canada, and parts of Europe, have excellent track records in controlling the rate of inflation after World War II. In other countries, the track record is not so good, for example, in Argentina. If the central bank is weak, in that it has difficulty in controlling the domestic money supply, then a fixed exchange rate can be a very important commitment device. If the exchange rate is fixed against the currency of a country with a strong central bank, then this implies, given PPP, that the weak-central-bank country essentially adopts the monetary policy of the strong-central-bank country. With a fixed exchange rate, the price level of the domestic economy is tied to the foreign price level, which is essentially determined by foreign monetary policy.

In conclusion, there is no clear case for flexible versus fixed exchange rates in all circumstances. For the United States, where the central bank is relatively independent of political pressures and appears to be well focused on controlling inflation, a flexible exchange rate seems appropriate. The Federal Reserve System appears to be sufficiently trustworthy relative to foreign central banks that allowing the Fed to pursue a monetary policy geared to U.S. interests seems advisable. However, for other countries, particularly some in Latin America and Africa, a fixed exchange rate regime makes good sense.

There are many long-standing instances of fixed exchange rates that we take for granted. For example, rates of exchange between different denominations of Federal Reserve notes have always been fixed in the United States. Why should it necessarily be the case that five one-dollar bills trade for one five-dollar bill in all circumstances in the United States? This is because the Federal Reserve always stands ready to trade one five-dollar bill for five ones; essentially, the Fed maintains fixed exchange rates among notes of different denominations. Further, all of the regional Federal Reserve Banks in the United States issue different notes that are clearly marked according to the Federal Reserve Bank of issue (check your wallet, and you will see that this is true; for example, I9 denotes the ninth Federal Reserve district—a note issued by the Minneapolis Federal Reserve Bank). Why should a one-dollar bill issued by the Kansas City Federal Reserve Bank trade one-for-one for a one-dollar bill issued by the Richmond Federal Reserve Bank? The answer is that all Federal Reserve Banks stand ready to exchange all Federal Reserve notes at their face value for other Federal Reserve notes. Again, the Fed maintains fixed exchange rates in this respect.

Essentially all countries maintain fixed exchange rates within their borders. There is a national currency that is accepted as legal tender, and typically this currency circulates nationally as a medium of exchange, though in some countries foreign currencies, in particular U.S. dollars, circulate widely. What then determines the natural region, or **common currency area**, over which a single currency dominates as a medium of exchange? Clearly, a common currency area need not be the area over which there is a single political or fiscal authority. In the United States, each state has the power to tax state residents, but the states cede monetary authority to the Federal Reserve System, for which the central decision-making power resides with the Board of Governors in Washington, D.C. In the EMU, member countries maintain their fiscal independence, but monetary policy is in the hands of the ECB. An advantage of having a large trading area with a common currency is that this simplifies exchange; it is much easier to write contracts and trade across international borders without the complications of converting one currency into another or bearing the risk associated with fluctuating exchange rates. However, in joining a **currency union** such as the EMU, a country must give up its monetary independence to the group. The formation of the EMU clearly has created tensions among EMU members, concerning matters that include the choice of the leaders of the European Central Bank and the monetary policy stance this central bank should take. Great Britain, which has the world's oldest central bank, the Bank of England, chose not to join the EMU so as to maintain its monetary independence.

Recently, the fact that EMU members have independent fiscal policies has become a key issue that may cause the EMU to disintegrate. Southern European members of the EMU, particularly Greece, Spain, and Italy, have unsustainable external debt burdens that make default increasingly likely for those countries (see Chapter 16). Coordination between the fiscal authority in a country and the central bank is important to making the monetary system work. When there are multiple independent fiscal authorities within an economy with a single central banking authority, coordination between the fiscal authorities and the central bank may ultimately be impossible, so that arrangements like the EMU (at least in its current form) may be unworkable.

MACROECONOMICS IN ACTION

Sovereign Debt and the EMU

Sovereign debt is the debt issued by a government that is held by foreigners. The potential for default on sovereign debt has become an important issue, which threatens the existence of the European Monetary Union.

In Chapter 16, we considered a model of explicit default by a country on its external debt, where the external debt was modeled as the debt of the government and the private sector to foreigners. That model gives us some basic understanding of the factors driving sovereign default. In particular, in the Chapter 16 model without money, and with the potential for default, we showed that a country would be more likely to default on its debt the larger the size of the debt, the larger the interest rate on this debt, and the smaller the costs of defaulting.

Some of the principles of sovereign debt are discussed in a survey paper by Jonathan Eaton and Raquel Fernandez.[1] There is a sense in which the relationship between a sovereign debtor and that sovereign's creditors is much like the relationship between a private debtor and creditors who live in the same country. Sovereign debt will take the form of promises to pay, in units of a

particular currency, at specific dates in the future, just as for domestic debt. Creditors are taking bets on the ability of the debtor to pay in the future, and the credit relationship may be subject to credit market frictions—asymmetric information and limited commitment. What makes sovereign debt different, however, is that creditors do not have the same potential for recourse as with domestic credit arrangements. For example, in the United States, there is well-established and enforced bankruptcy law which prescribes what will happen should a debtor fail to make good on promised payments. There is also a domestic legal structure that governs collateral—when and how it can be seized, for example. With sovereign debt, there are typically no courts to appeal to and collateral arrangements are essentially impossible, as the sovereign cannot credibly post an asset as collateral and guarantee that a creditor can seize it in the future in the event of nonpayment.

Suppose that we focus just on the limited commitment problem with respect to sovereign debt. We might want to ask why there would be any lending to sovereign governments at all. Why would a sovereign government have any incentive to repay its debts? If the sovereign government will not repay its debts, why would anyone lend to it? Potentially, a sovereign government will make

---

[1]J. Eaton and R. Fernandez, 1995. "Sovereign Debt," in *Handbook of International Economics*, 1st ed., vol. 3, G. Grossman and K. Rogoff, eds., pp. 2031–2077, Elsevier.

good on promises to pay off debt if there is a threat, typically implicit, that credit will be denied in the future should the sovereign default. The sovereign then repays the debt because the value of access to future credit markets is greater than what is gained from defaulting. But such a punishment is hard to carry out, particularly as it may require coordination among many creditors. However sovereign debt does in fact exist. Indeed, international financial institutions are active in lending to governments, and there is a thriving international market in government bonds. Therefore, sovereign debtors must indeed face the threat of serious consequences should they choose to default.

Short of outright default on its outstanding debt, there are other options open to a government which is having difficulty meeting its debt obligations to foreign creditors. Creditors could forgive some of the debt, reasoning that it would be more costly for default to occur and to sort out the losses than to just accept the loss and renegotiate the debt contract. Debt can also be rescheduled. For example, it may be feasible for the sovereign to meet its debt payments if short-maturity debt is converted into long-maturity debt. Finally, it is possible for a government to implicitly default on its debt through monetary policy. If a government issues debt denominated in its own currency and the central bank engages in expansionary monetary policy—increasing the money supply—then the price level and the exchange rate will rise, and reduce the value of the government's debt payments in units of other currencies. Thus, it is possible for the government to inflate away its debt payments through an unanticipated expansion in the money supply. Such an approach might actually be much more efficient—for debtors and creditors alike—than outright default.

The problem with implicit default through expansionary monetary policy is that governments may have difficulty committing to *not* implicitly defaulting. Any central bank would like to have a reputation as an institution that is committed to low inflation. Once such a reputation is gained, then international creditors understand that implicit default is unlikely, and the government

can borrow internationally at low interest rates. If a government is expected to implicitly default with high probability, then international debtors will lend to that government only at high interest rates, reflecting a default (inflation) premium.

The sovereign debt problems that developed after the financial crisis, with respect to Greece and other EMU member countries, related to debt that was denominated in terms of Euros. Greek debt had risen to a level, and interest rates had reached levels, such that it was impossible for the Greek government to meet its external debt obligations. If Greece were a country with its own central bank, then implicit default might have been the most desirable option. Greece could have engineered a monetary expansion, with an ensuing increase in Greek prices and a decrease in the value of Greek currency relative to other currencies in the world, thus reducing the real value of the Greek debt. However, Greece is an EMU member, and the European Central Bank determines monetary policy for the EMU. For other EMU countries, particularly Germany, the loss in credibility for the ECB as a low-inflation central bank would be too costly. Thus, for some EMU members, particularly Greece, Italy, and Spain, a Euro monetary expansion would be a good thing. For Germany, an implicit default on German debt would not be of sufficient benefit, relative to the loss in credibility of a monetary expansion. Thus, the EMU members were in conflict, principally because of their different fiscal circumstances.

In general, a monetary union is very difficult to sustain unless there is some means for the members of the union to jointly constrain their fiscal policies. The United States is a kind of monetary union (the states of the United States share a currency) in which the states are constrained to balance their budgets. This constraint on the states' fiscal behavior is an important feature that sustains the United States as a monetary union. For the EMU, some type of enforceable fiscal constraints on the behavior of EMU members is essential for EMU survival. Such constraints would act to eliminate conflicts among EMU members concerning monetary policy decisions.

Capital Controls

A useful application of the monetary small open-economy model is to the problem of the role of capital controls in the international economy. Capital controls refer broadly to any government restrictions on the trade of assets across international borders. We show here that capital controls can reduce movements in the nominal exchange rate in response to some shocks under a flexible exchange rate regime, and they can reduce fluctuations in foreign exchange reserves under a fixed exchange rate regime. We argue, however, that capital controls are, in general, undesirable, because they introduce welfare-decreasing economic inefficiencies.

The Capital Account and the Balance of Payments

LO 17.5 Explain balance of payments accounting and the role of the capital account.

To understand capital controls, we have to first understand the accounting practices behind the **capital account**. The capital account is part of the **balance of payments**, which includes the current account and the capital account. The capital account includes all transactions in assets, in which entries in the capital account where a foreign resident purchases a domestic asset are recorded as a positive amount—a **capital inflow**—and entries where a domestic resident purchases a foreign asset are recorded as a negative amount—a **capital outflow**. For example, if a British bank lends to a U.S. firm, this is a capital inflow, as the loan to the U.S. firm is an asset for the British bank. If a U.S. automobile manufacturer builds a new plant in Britain, this is a capital outflow for the United States, and it is part of **foreign direct investment** in Britain. Foreign direct investment is distinct from **portfolio inflows and outflows**, which are capital account transactions involving financial assets, including stocks and debt instruments. A helpful rule of thumb in counting asset transactions in the capital account is that the transaction counts as a capital inflow if funds flow into the domestic country to purchase an asset, and as an outflow if funds flow out of the domestic country to purchase an asset.

The balance of payments is defined to be the current account surplus plus the capital account surplus. That is, letting BP denote the balance of payments, and KA the capital account surplus, we have

$$BP = KA + CA,$$

where CA is the current account surplus. A key element in balance of payments accounting is that the balance of payments is always zero (though it is not measured as such because of measurement error), so that

$$KA = -CA.$$

Therefore, the capital account surplus is always the negative of the current account surplus. If the current account is in deficit (surplus), then the capital account is in surplus (deficit). We have not discussed the capital account until now for this reason—the capital account surplus is just the flip side of the current account surplus, so that when we know the current account surplus, we know exactly what the capital account surplus is.

The balance of payments is always zero, because any transaction entering the balance of payments always has equal and opposite entries in the accounts. For example, suppose that a U.S. firm borrows the equivalent of $50 million in British pounds from a British bank so that it can purchase $50 million worth of auto parts in Britain to ship to the United States. The loan from the British bank enters as a capital inflow, because the British bank has accumulated a U.S. asset, and so there is an entry of $+$50 million in the capital account for the United States. Next, when the auto parts are purchased and imported into the United States, this enters as $-$50 million in the current account. Thus, in this, as in all cases, the net effect on the balance of payments is zero. The offsetting entries associated with a given transaction need not be in the current account and the capital account, but in some cases could be all in the current account or all in the capital account.

The Effects of Capital Controls

LO 17.6 Explain how capital controls work and their macroeconomic effects.

In practice, capital controls can be imposed in terms of capital inflows or capital outflows, and they sometimes apply to foreign direct investment and sometimes to portfolio inflows and outflows. For example, restrictions on capital outflows were introduced in Malaysia in 1998 after the Asian crisis, and Chile used controls on capital inflows extensively from 1978 to 1982 and from 1991 to 1998. In both cases, the capital controls were in terms of portfolio inflows and outflows. Countries sometimes also restrict foreign direct investment, which is a control on capital inflows. Controls on foreign direct investment are sometimes put in place because of concern (perhaps misplaced) over the foreign ownership of the domestic capital stock.

What are the macroeconomic effects of capital controls? Essentially, capital controls alter the way in which the domestic economy responds to a shock. For example, suppose that there is a temporary negative shock to domestic total factor productivity under a flexible exchange rate. In Figure 17.11(a), suppose that the output demand curve is Y_1^d and the initial output supply curve is Y_1^s, and assume that initially the current account surplus is zero, with output equal to Y_1 at the world real interest rate r^*. In Figure 17.11(b), the initial money demand curve is $eP^*L(Y_1, r^*)$ and the initial nominal exchange rate is e_1, given the nominal money supply M.

Now, suppose there is a temporary decrease in domestic total factor productivity, which shifts the output supply curve leftward to Y_2^s in Figure 17.11(a). With no capital controls in place, this implies that the current account surplus falls (with the current account then running a deficit), shifting the output demand curve to the left until it comes to rest at Y_2^d. Real output falls to Y_2 from Y_1, and consumption falls because of the decrease in income. In Figure 17.11(b), nominal money demand shifts leftward to $eP^*L(Y_2, r^*)$, and there is an exchange rate depreciation, with the nominal exchange rate increasing to e_2.

Now, assume an extreme form of capital controls where the government prohibits all capital inflows and outflows. This implies that the capital account surplus must be zero in equilibrium, and so the current account surplus must be zero as well. With a temporary decrease in domestic total factor productivity in Figure 17.11, the domestic real interest rate rises to r_1, which is above the world real interest rate r^*. In equilibrium, foreign investors would like to purchase domestic assets, as the return on domestic

Figure 17.11 A Temporary Total Factor Productivity Shock, with and Without Capital Controls
With a temporary decrease in total factor productivity, under a flexible exchange rate there is a larger decrease in aggregate output and the current account surplus and a larger increase in the nominal exchange rate in the case without capital controls.

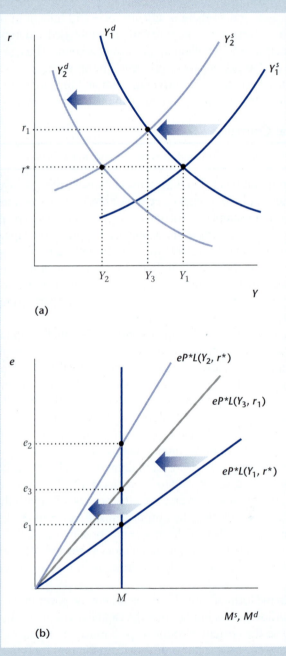

(a)

(b)

assets is greater than it is in the rest of the world, but they are prohibited from doing so. Thus, in this case, real output decreases to Y_3 in equilibrium. Assuming that money demand is much more responsive to real income than to the real interest rate, the money demand curve shifts to the left in Figure 17.11(b), though by less than it does in the case with no capital controls. The nominal exchange rate rises to e_3.

The results are that the nominal exchange rate increases by a smaller amount when capital controls are in place than when they are not, output falls by a smaller amount, and there is a smaller change in the current account deficit. Thus, capital controls tend to dampen aggregate fluctuations in output, the current account surplus, and the nominal exchange rate resulting from shocks of this type to the economy. If a country is concerned about the effects of fluctuations in the nominal exchange rate under a flexible exchange rate regime (for reasons that are not modeled here), capital controls tend to mitigate this problem, at least if the major source of shocks is temporary changes in total factor productivity. This solution is quite costly, however, as it produces an economic inefficiency. As in Chapter 5, the equilibrium allocation of resources is Pareto optimal in this model in the absence of capital controls. With no capital controls, in this example, the domestic economy would face a lower real interest rate after the total factor productivity shock, and this means that lenders would be worse off and borrowers better off. Though some would win and some would lose from getting rid of capital controls, there would in general be an average gain in welfare.

Under a fixed exchange rate, Figure 17.11(a) still applies, but the money market works as in Figure 17.12. The nominal exchange rate is assumed to be fixed at e_1. Initially, the money supply is M_1, and in the absence of capital controls, the money supply declines to M_2, but with capital controls there is a decline in the money supply only to M_3. Here, fluctuations in the money supply are smaller with capital controls, which implies that foreign exchange reserves drop by a smaller amount with capital controls. Therefore, with capital controls in place a government can better support a fixed exchange rate, if exhausting the stock of foreign exchange reserves on hand is potentially a problem without controls. Again, though, capital controls come at a cost in lost economic efficiency.

MACROECONOMICS IN ACTION

Do Capital Controls Work in Practice?

With regard to how capital controls work in practice, we are primarily interested in two questions: (1) Can capital controls be effectively enforced, so that they have the intended effects? (2) How large are the economic inefficiencies that capital controls cause? In an article in the *Journal of*

Economic Perspectives, Sebastian Edwards sets out to answer these questions, using the example of Chile.[2]

Edwards argues that there is little support by economists for restrictions on capital outflows, but that some economists have pointed to Chile as an example of how restrictions on capital inflows appeared to have worked well in practice. One aim of his article is to dismiss these latter arguments by studying the details of what happened in Chile, where controls on capital inflows were in place from 1978 to 1982 and from 1991 to 1998. These restrictions mainly applied to portfolio inflows of short-maturity securities, and they took the form of reserve requirements on these inflows. That is, if a foreigner purchased short-term, interest-bearing Chilean assets (a capital inflow), then a fraction of the value of these assets would have to be held as a noninterest-bearing deposit with the central bank of Chile. This had the same effect as would a tax on short-term capital inflows, as the noninterest-bearing deposits could otherwise be held in interest-bearing form.

What were the effects of the capital controls in Chile? Edwards finds that apparently many investors learned how to avoid the controls.

While capital inflows appeared to have shifted somewhat toward longer-term inflows from shorter-term inflows, the shift was not that large, and investors seemed to have found many clever schemes for disguising short-term capital inflows as long-term ones. Edwards argues that the severe effects of the capital controls were on small- and medium-sized Chilean firms, which faced much higher costs of borrowing.

Thus, the conclusion of Edwards's article is that the welfare costs of capital controls are small on average, mainly because the controls are ineffective, but the costs are large for some groups in the population. Edwards argues that capital controls should be phased out in countries where they still exist. However, he argues that in some cases this phaseout should be gradual. The inefficiencies caused by capital controls may in some cases be small relative to the potential inefficiencies arising from a poorly regulated banking system. If restrictions on capital inflows are relaxed quickly, then domestic banks can borrow more easily abroad so as to finance domestic lending. However, if domestic banks are improperly regulated (as we study in more depth in Chapter 18), then they take on too much risk, and this problem can be exacerbated in a wide-open international lending environment. The relaxation of capital controls sometimes needs to be coupled with improvements in the regulation of domestic financial institutions.

---

[2]S. Edwards, 1999. "How Effective Are Capital Controls?" *Journal of Economic Perspectives* 13, 65–84.

A New Keynesian Sticky Price Open–Economy Model

LO 17.7 Construct the Keynesian sticky price open economy model, and use the model to analyze the effects of monetary and fiscal policy, and macroeconomic shocks.

The open-economy model with flexible wages and prices that was constructed in this chapter can be modified to include sticky prices, in a manner similar to our modification of the monetary intertemporal model of Chapter 12 that gives us the New Keynesian sticky price model in Chapter 14. To start, we will assume that P and P^* are fixed exogenously, so that the prices charged for domestic and foreign goods are sticky in terms of their own currency. In this sticky price model, the purchasing power parity relationship, Equation (17-1), will not hold in general.

Figure 17.12 A Total Factor Productivity Shock Under a Fixed Exchange Rate, with and Without Capital Controls

Under a fixed exchange rate, capital controls dampen the reduction in the money supply that occurs when there is a temporary decline in total factor productivity.

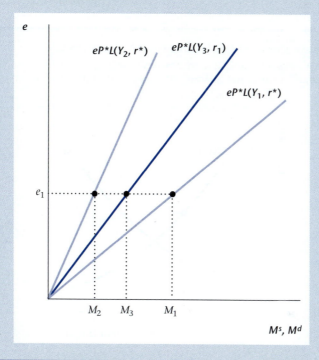

In this model, we will assume that goods produced domestically and goods produced in other countries are not perfect substitutes for consumers. We will let $NX\left(\dfrac{eP^*}{P}\right)$ denote the demand for net exports, which is increasing in $\dfrac{eP^*}{P}$, the real exchange rate or terms of trade. An increase in $\dfrac{eP^*}{P}$ increases the relative price of goods produced abroad to goods produced domestically, which implies that domestic and foreign consumers will substitute domestic goods for foreign goods, which reduces the demand for imports and increases the demand for exports, thus increasing the demand for net exports. Thus, since an increase in net exports shifts the output demand curve to the right, increases in $\dfrac{eP^*}{P}$ will shift the output demand curve to the right.

Flexible Exchange Rate

In Figure 17.13, the price level P_1 is fixed, and the real interest rate r^* is exogenous, as it is determined on world markets. In equilibrium, money supply is equal to money demand in panel (b) of the figure, which requires that output, Y, adjust to Y_1, so that money demand is just sufficient to clear the money market. In panel (a) of the figure, how does output adjust? As in the New Keynesian model in Chapter 14, output is determined by the output demand curve. In the closed-economy model in Chapter 14,

Figure 17.13 The New Keynesian Model with a Flexible Exchange Rate

In the money market in panel (b), Y adjusts so that money supply equals money demand. Then, in panel (b), the exchange rate adjusts so that the quantity of output demanded is equal to Y_1 at the world real interest rate r^*.

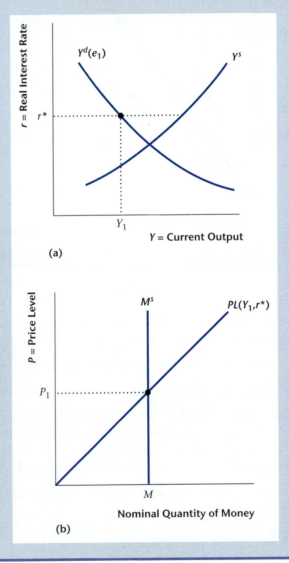

(a)

(b)

output depends on goods demanded at the market real interest rate, but in this model, the quantity of goods demanded depends on the fixed world real interest rate r^* and on the exchange rate, as we have indicated by denoting the output demand curve $Y^d(e)$. In panel (a), the nominal exchange rate adjusts to its equilibrium value e_1, which is the exchange rate at which Y_1 goods are demanded at the world real interest rate r^*.

Monetary Policy in the New Keynesian Model with a Flexible Exchange Rate What does monetary policy do in this open-economy fixed-price context? In Figure 17.14, suppose that the economy is initially in equilibrium with aggregate income Y_1 and exchange rate e_1, where the nominal exchange rate determines the position of the output demand curve $Y^d(e)$, so that the level of income Y induces money demand so that the money market clears in panel (b) of the figure. The example has been constructed so that there is initially an output gap, equal to $Y_2 - Y_1$.

It is possible for the central bank to act to close the output gap in Figure 17.14, but the central bank cannot do this by changing the market real interest rate, which is fixed on world markets at r^*. Instead, the central bank increases the money supply from M_1 to M_2, which causes an exchange rate depreciation. The nominal exchange rate increases from e_1 to e_2, which increases the real exchange rate (purchasing power parity does not hold), and increases net export demand, shifting the output demand curve to the right to $Y^d(e_2)$. If the central bank engineers a sufficiently large increase in the money supply, then output increases to Y_2, which shifts the money demand curve to the right in panel (b) of the figure and closes the output gap in panel (a) of the figure.

In this open-economy context, money is not neutral, just as in the closed-economy New Keynesian model. However the effects of monetary policy are transmitted in this model through changes in the nominal exchange rate rather than through changes in the real interest rate.

Fiscal Policy In Figure 17.15, we show the effects of an increase in current government spending G in the New Keynesian model. In this case, the increase in G will shift the output supply curve to the right from Y_1^s to Y_2^s. The increase in G increases the demand for goods, but output is essentially determined by the money supply in panel (b) of the figure. As a result, there must be an exchange rate appreciation, with the exchange rate falling from e_1 to e_2. Net exports fall, and the output demand curve remains fixed at $Y^d(e_1)$. Thus, fiscal policy cannot reduce the output gap under a flexible exchange rate. More government spending simply crowds out an equal quantity of net exports.

Fixed Exchange Rate

In a fixed exchange rate regime, the money market will clear through adjustment of the money supply, rather than through adjustment of money demand (by way of income and the nominal exchange rate). Monetary policy is completely ineffective, as it must be passive to support the fixed exchange rate, but fiscal policy matters. In Figure 17.16, output is initially Y_1, with a fixed exchange rate e_1 and money supply M_1. There is an output gap, which fiscal policy can close through an increase in G, which shifts the output demand curve to the right to $Y_2^d(e_1)$ from $Y_1^d(e_1)$, and shifts the output supply

Figure 17.14 Monetary Policy in the New Keynesian Model with a Flexible Exchange Rate
An increase in the money supply causes e to fall, increasing net exports and closing the output gap.

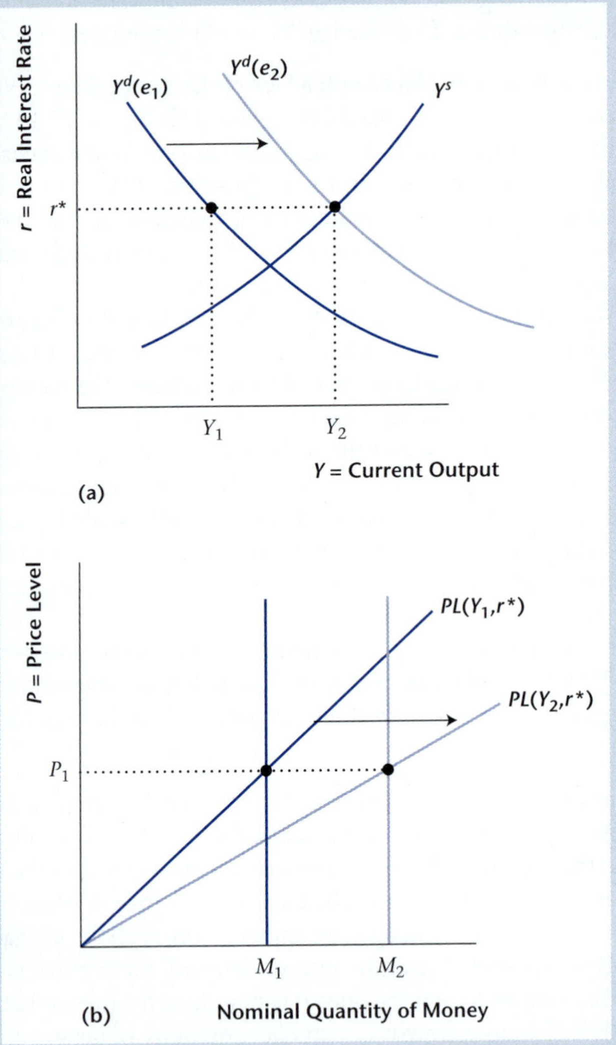

(a)

(b)

curve to the right from Y_1^s to Y_2^s. An appropriate increase in G eliminates the output gap, and the money supply increases from M_1 to M_2.

This New Keynesian model has properties that are much like the properties of the classic Mundell–Fleming (MF) model. The MF model was written down in a somewhat different form from what we have here, but gave similar policy results. In particular monetary policy under a fixed exchange rate and fiscal policy under a flexible exchange

Figure 17.15 An Increase in Current Government Spending in the New Keynesian Model with a Flexible Exchange Rate

An increase in G has no effect on output, but the exchange rate appreciates and reduces net exports.

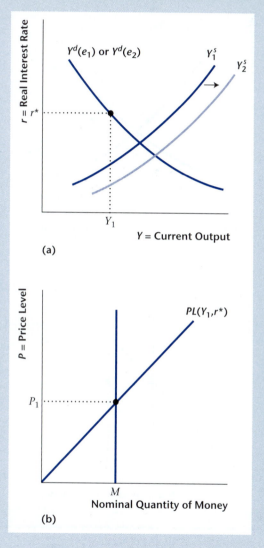

(a)

(b)

rate are ineffective stabilization tools, while monetary policy under a flexible exchange rate and fiscal policy under a fixed exchange rate are effective.

While there are many more interesting issues to study in international macro-economics, this chapter ends our discussion of this topic in this book. In Part VII, we move on to study topics in money, banking, and inflation—in-depth issues in closed-economy macroeconomics.

Figure 17.16 An Increase in G in the New Keynesian Model with a Fixed Exchange Rate

An increase in G can eliminate the output gap.

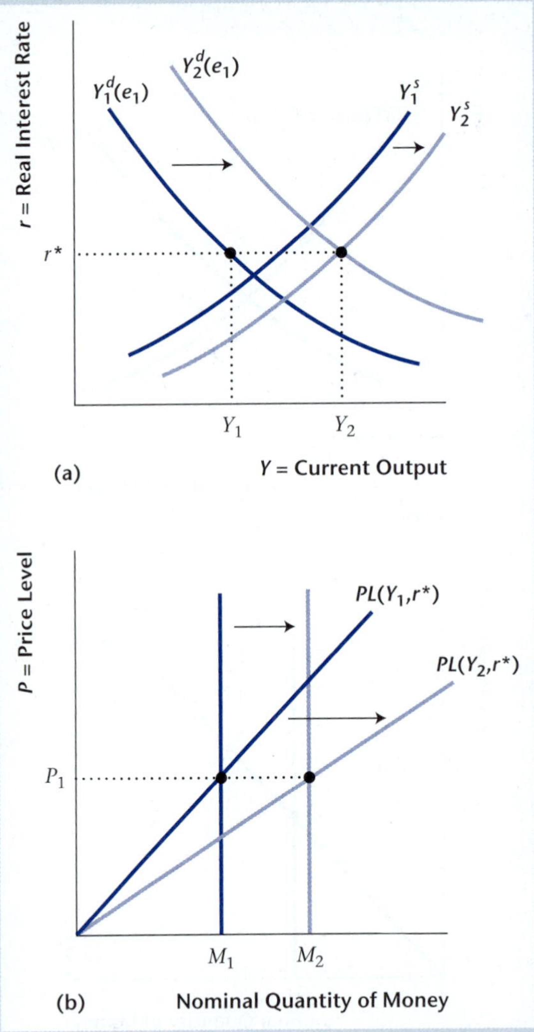

(a)

(b)   Nominal Quantity of Money

Chapter Summary

- We first studied purchasing power parity, or the law of one price, which predicts that prices are equated across countries in terms of the same currency. While there can be large and persistent deviations from purchasing power parity in practice, there are strong economic forces that move prices and exchange rates toward purchasing power parity over the long run. The purchasing power parity assumption is very useful in the basic model studied in this chapter.

- In the monetary small open-economy model, the real interest rate and the foreign price level are determined on world markets.

- Under a flexible exchange rate, money is neutral, and the domestic economy is insulated from nominal shocks from abroad, in that no real or nominal domestic variables are affected by a change in the foreign price level. The nominal exchange rate moves in equilibrium to absorb completely a shock to the foreign price level. However, the flexible exchange rate does not insulate the domestic price level against real shocks from abroad.

- A fixed exchange rate causes the domestic price level to increase in proportion to an increase in the foreign price level, but the fixed exchange rate regime insulates the domestic price level from foreign real shocks. Under a fixed exchange rate regime, a devaluation of the domestic currency might occur if the government's foreign exchange reserves are depleted. A devaluation raises the domestic price level.

- Whether a flexible exchange rate regime is preferred to a fixed exchange rate regime depends on a country's circumstances, but a flexible exchange rate regime implies that domestic monetary policy can be independent, whereas a fixed exchange rate regime implies that the domestic economy adopts the monetary policy of a foreign central bank.

- Capital controls involve restrictions on capital inflows and outflows, which are items in the capital account, where the asset transactions for a nation are added up. The balance of payments surplus is the sum of the capital account surplus and the current account surplus, and the balance of payments surplus is always zero.

- Capital controls can dampen fluctuations in output, the current account surplus, and the exchange rate (under a flexible exchange rate) or the money supply (under a fixed exchange rate), but these controls reduce economic efficiency. In practice, capital controls appear not to have been very effective, and in this sense they have not had large effects on efficiency.

- A New Keynesian model was developed, as an extension of the basic model in this chapter. In that model, the domestic and foreign price levels are exogenous, as is the world real interest rate. Output is determined by output demand, as in the New Keynesian sticky price model in Chapter 14, but in the open-economy model, the nominal exchange rate moves to equilibrate the money market.

- In the New Keynesian model, money is not neutral. An increase in the money supply increases the nominal exchange rate and the real exchange rate, and increases output under a flexible exchange rate. Government spending is ineffective in closing the output gap when the exchange rate is flexible.

- In the New Keynesian model, monetary policy is ineffective as a stabilization tool with a fixed exchange rate, but fiscal policy is potent under this exchange rate regime.

Key Terms

Nominal exchange rate The price of foreign currency in terms of domestic currency, denoted by e in the model of this chapter. (p. 586)

Real exchange rate The price of foreign goods in terms of domestic goods, or $\frac{eP^*}{P}$ in our model. (p. 586)

Purchasing power parity (PPP) $P = eP^*$, where P is the domestic price level, P^* is the foreign price level, and e is the exchange rate. (p. 587)

Law of one price The same thing as PPP, except that P refers to the price of a particular good or service, and P^* is the price of that good or service in the other country. (p. 587)

Flexible exchange rate regime A system under which a nation's nominal exchange rate is determined by market forces. (p. 587)

Fixed exchange rate regime A system under which the domestic government supports the value of the exchange rate at a specified level in terms of a foreign currency or currencies. (p. 587)

Hard pegs Exchange rate systems where there is a firm commitment to a fixed exchange rate, either through dollarization or a currency board. (p. 588)

Soft pegs Exchange rate systems where the government commits to a fixed exchange rate for periods of time, but sometimes changes the value at which the exchange rate is fixed. (p. 588)

Devaluations Increases in the price of foreign exchange in terms of domestic currency. (p. 588)

Revaluations Decreases in the price of foreign exchange in terms of domestic currency. (p. 588)

Dollarize For a nation to abandon its own currency and adopt the currency of another country as its medium of exchange. (p. 588)

Currency board An institution that fixes the exchange rate by holding foreign-currency-denominated interest-bearing assets and committing to buying and selling foreign exchange at a fixed rate of exchange. (p. 588)

European Monetary Union (EMU) An organization of European countries, established in 1999, which shares a common currency, the Euro. (p. 588)

Euro The currency shared by the members of the EMU. (p. 588)

European Central Bank The central bank of the EMU countries. (p. 588)

European Monetary System (EMS) A cooperative exchange rate system in place among European countries from 1979 until 1999. (p. 588)

Bretton Woods arrangement A worldwide cooperative exchange rate system, in place from 1946 to 1971, under which the price of gold was fixed in terms of U.S. dollars, and there were fixed exchange rates for all other currencies in terms of the U.S. dollar. (p. 589)

International Monetary Fund (IMF) An international monetary institution established in 1946, which was intended as a lender of last resort for its member countries, which now number 183. (p. 590)

Lender of last resort A centralized institution that lends to economic agents in distress; examples are central banks, which lend to domestic banks, and the IMF, which lends to its member countries. (p. 590)

Depreciation (of the exchange rate) A rise in the price of foreign currency in terms of domestic currency. (p. 594)

Appreciation (of the exchange rate) A fall in the price of foreign currency in terms of domestic currency. (p. 595)

Common currency area A region over which a single currency dominates as a medium of exchange. (p. 605)

Currency union A group of countries that agrees to become a common currency area. (p. 605)

Capital account The component of the balance of payments in which all international asset transactions between the domestic economy and foreign countries are added up. (p. 608)

Balance of payments A system of accounts for a country for adding up all international transactions in goods and assets. (p. 608)

Capital inflow The purchase of a domestic asset by a foreign resident, recorded as a positive entry in the capital account. (p. 608)

Capital outflow The purchase of a foreign asset by a domestic resident, recorded as a negative entry in the capital account. (p. 608)

Foreign direct investment A capital inflow that involves the acquisition of a new physical asset by a foreign resident. (p. 608)

Portfolio inflows and outflows Capital account transactions involving international transactions in financial assets. (p. 608)

Questions for Review

17.1   Does purchasing power parity hold in practice in the short run? Why or why not? Does it hold in the long run? Why or why not?

17.2   What countries in the world have flexible exchange rates? Which have fixed exchange rates?

17.3   What are the different systems for fixing the exchange rate? Describe how each works.

17.4 Describe the role of the International Monetary Fund.

17.5 In the model constructed in this chapter, what are the effects on the domestic economy of an increase in the foreign price level under a flexible exchange rate and under a fixed exchange rate?

17.6 In the model in this chapter, what are the effects on the domestic economy of an increase in the world real interest rate under a flexible exchange rate and under a fixed exchange rate?

17.7 In the model, is money neutral under a flexible exchange rate? Explain why or why not. Can we say that money is neutral under a fixed exchange rate? Explain.

17.8 Explain why domestic monetary policy is not independent under a fixed exchange rate.

17.9 What are the effects of a devaluation of the domestic currency under a fixed exchange rate?

17.10 List the key pros and cons of fixed versus flexible exchange rate regimes.

17.11 Give two examples of fixed exchange rates within the United States.

17.12 What are the advantages and disadvantages of a common currency area or currency union?

17.13 If the capital account surplus is positive, what can we say about the current account surplus?

17.14 Give two examples of countries where capital controls were imposed.

17.15 What do capital controls imply for the response of the economy to shocks?

17.16 Are capital controls a good idea? Why or why not?

17.17 Are capital controls effective in practice? Explain.

17.18 Why is money nonneutral in the New Keynesian open-economy model?

17.19 How does the exchange rate regime matter for stabilization policy in the New Keynesian model?

Problems

1. **LO 3, 4** Suppose that there is a cost to carrying out transactions in the foreign exchange market. That is, to purchase one unit of foreign currency requires $e(1 + a)$ units of domestic currency, where e is the nominal exchange rate and a is a proportional fee. Suppose that a decreases. What will be the equilibrium effects under a flexible exchange rate regime, and under a fixed exchange rate regime? Explain your results.

2. **LO 3, 4** In the equilibrium small open-economy model, suppose that total factor productivity increases temporarily.
   (a) If the exchange rate is flexible, determine the effects on aggregate output, absorption, the current account surplus, the nominal exchange rate, and the price level.
   (b) Repeat part (a) for the case of a fixed exchange rate. If the goal of the domestic government is to stabilize the price level, would it be preferable to have a fixed exchange rate or a flexible exchange rate regime when there is a change in total factor productivity?
   (c) Now, suppose that under a flexible exchange rate regime, the domestic monetary authority controls the money supply so as to stabilize the price level when total factor productivity increases. Explain the differences between the outcome in this case and what happens in part (b) with a fixed exchange rate.

3. **LO 3, 4** Suppose in the model that government expenditures increase temporarily. Determine the effects on aggregate output, absorption, the current account surplus, the nominal exchange rate, and the price level. What difference does it make if the exchange rate is flexible or fixed?

4. **LO 3, 4** Suppose that better transaction technologies are developed that reduce the domestic demand for money. Use the monetary small open-economy model to answer the following:

(a) Suppose that the exchange rate is flexible. What are the equilibrium effects on the price level and the exchange rate?

(b) Suppose that the exchange rate is flexible, and the domestic monetary authority acts to stabilize the price level. Determine how the domestic money supply changes and the effect on the nominal exchange rate.

(c) Suppose that the exchange rate is fixed. Determine the effects on the exchange rate and the price level, and determine the differences from your results in parts (a) and (b).

5. **LO 6** Consider a country with a flexible exchange rate, and which initially has a current account surplus of zero. Then, suppose there is an anticipated increase in future total factor productivity.

(a) Determine the equilibrium effects on the domestic economy in the case where there are no capital controls. In particular, show that there will be a current account deficit when firms and consumers anticipate the increase in future total factor productivity.

(b) Now, suppose that the government dislikes current account deficits, and that it imposes capital controls in an attempt to reduce the current account deficit. With the anticipated increase in future total factor productivity, what will be the equilibrium effects on the economy? Do the capital controls have the desired effect on the current account deficit? Do capital controls dampen the effects of the shock to the economy on output and the exchange rate? Are capital controls sound macroeconomic policy in this context? Why or why not?

6. **LO 3** Suppose a flexible exchange rate. There is an increase in the degree of uncertainty in credit markets, which affects firms but not consumers, as considered in Chapter 9.

(a) Determine the effects on aggregate output, the price level, the exchange rate, and the real interest rate. Explain your results.

(b) Does this help to explain features of the financial crisis? Discuss.

7. **LO 6** The domestic central bank increases the supply of money under a flexible exchange rate

regime, leading to a depreciation of the nominal exchange rate. If the government had imposed capital controls before the increase in the money supply, would this have had any effect on the exchange rate depreciation? Explain your results and comment on their significance.

8. **LO 6** Suppose that capital controls take the form of a total ban on capital inflows, but all capital outflows are permitted. Also suppose that initially the current account surplus is zero. Determine the effects of a temporary increase in total factor productivity, and of a temporary decrease in total factor productivity under a flexible exchange rate. Carefully explain how and why your results differ in the two cases.

9. **LO 7** Suppose in the New Keynesian open-economy model, that there is an increase in future total factor productivity.

(a) Under a flexible exchange rate, what are the equilibrium effects? Should economic policy respond to the change in future productivity? If so, how?

(b) Now suppose that there is a fixed exchange rate. Repeat part (a).

(c) Explain your results.

10. **LO 7** Suppose in the New Keynesian open-economy model, that there is a positive output gap. There is also a liquidity trap at the world level, in that $r^* = 0$. Is there anything that economic policy can do to close the output gap? If so, what? Explain.

11. **LO 7** Suppose in the New Keynesian open-economy model that there is an increase in the world real interest rate r*.

(a) With the aid of a diagram, determine what happens when the exchange rate is flexible.

(b) Repeat part (a) for the case of a fixed exchange rate.

(c) What are your policy conclusions? Discuss.

12. **LO 7** It has been argued that Greece, which effectively has a fixed exchange rate with the rest of the EMU, would have done better after the 2008–2009 recession if it were not part of the EMU, and instead had a flexible exchange rate. Does this argument make sense? Why or why not? Discuss, with the aid of diagrams.

Working with the Data

Answer these questions using the Federal Reserve Bank of St. Louis's FRED database, accessible at http://research.stlouisfed.org/fred2/

1. Plot $\dfrac{eP^*}{P}$, where P^* is the consumer price index in the UK, e is the price of British pounds in terms of U.S. dollars, and P is the U.S. consumer price index. What do you observe in the plot? Discuss.

2. Plot the ratio of M2 in the United States to M2 in Canada, and the price of a Canadian dollar in U.S. dollars. What do you observe? Is this consistent with the models in this chapter?

3. What is more variable, the Canada/U.S. exchange rate or the UK/U.S. exchange rate? Does this mean that we are closer to having a fixed exchange rate regime with one of these countries?

PART VII

Money, Banking, and Inflation

In this part, we deal with some in-depth topics. In Chapter 18, we study at a more detailed level the role of money in the economy, the forms that money has taken historically, the effects of long-run inflation on aggregate activity and economic welfare, and the role of banks and other financial intermediaries in the economy.

Chapter 18

Money, Inflation, and Banking: A Deeper Look

> **Learning Objectives**
>
> After studying Chapter 18, students will be able to:
>
> **18.1** List the current and historic alternative forms of money, and explain their importance.
>
> **18.2** Explain the absence-of-double-coincidence problem, and show how this idea can be captured formally.
>
> **18.3** Show the long-run effects of inflation in the monetary intertemporal model, with a cash-in-advance approach.
>
> **18.4** State the Friedman rule, and explain what this implies for optimal monetary policy and inflation in the long run.
>
> **18.5** State the key properties of assets, and explain the role of financial intermediaries.
>
> **18.6** Construct the Diamond–Dybvig model, and derive its implications.
>
> **18.7** Explain the role of deposit insurance, and discuss the too-big-to-fail problem.

In the monetary analysis we have done so far in this book, particularly in Chapters 12–15 and 17, we made some basic assumptions about how currency and credit cards are used in transactions to derive a demand function for money, and proceeded from there. This allowed us to understand the effects of changes in the quantity of money, the role of money in the business cycle, and how money influences foreign exchange rates. In this chapter, we wish to gain a deeper understanding of the functions of money in the economy, to understand the long-run effects of inflation on aggregate economic activity and economic welfare, and to study the role of banks and other financial intermediaries in the economy.

In this chapter we first discuss how historical monetary systems worked, and we study the basic role of money in the economy in overcoming the difficulty of carrying out exchange using only commodities. Then, we use a modified version of the monetary intertemporal model developed in Chapter 12 and use this model to study the long-run effects of inflation. In our model, higher long-run inflation is caused by higher growth in the money supply, reflected in a higher long-run nominal interest rate, through the Fisher effect. We see that higher rates of money growth and inflation tend to reduce employment and output. This is because inflation erodes the purchasing power of money in the period between when labor income is earned and when it is spent. Thus, inflation tends to distort labor supply decisions. We show that an optimal long-run inflation policy for a central bank is to follow a **Friedman rule**, according to which the money supply grows at a rate that makes the rate of return on money identical to the rate of return on alternative assets and drives the nominal interest rate to zero. We discuss the relationship between Friedman rules in theory and practice.

Finally, we examine the role of banks and other financial intermediaries in the economy. A **financial intermediary** is any financial institution that borrows from one large group of people and lends to another large group of people, transforms assets in some way, and processes information. Banks and other depository institutions are financial intermediaries that are of particular interest to macroeconomists for two reasons. First, some of the liabilities depository institutions issue are included in measures of the money supply and compete with currency as media of exchange. Second, depository institutions interact closely with the central bank and are typically on the receiving end of the first-round effects of monetary policy.

We study a simple model of a bank, which is the Diamond–Dybvig banking model. This model shows how banks supply a kind of insurance against the need to make transactions using liquid assets, why bank runs can occur (as happened in the Great Depression and before the existence of the Federal Reserve System), and why government-provided deposit insurance might prevent bank runs. We discuss the incentive problem that deposit insurance creates for banks. Finally, we examine the too-big-to-fail doctrine, and its role in the financial crisis.

Alternative Forms of Money

LO 18.1 List the current and historic alternative forms of money, and explain their importance.

In Chapter 12, we discussed how money functions as a medium of exchange, a store of value, and a unit of account, with the key distinguishing feature of money being its medium-of-exchange property. Though all money is a medium of exchange, historically there have been many different objects that have performed this role. The most important forms of money have been commodity money, circulating private bank notes, commodity-backed paper currency, fiat money, and transactions deposits at private banks. We discuss each of these in turn.

Commodity money: This was the earliest money, in common use in Greek and Roman civilizations and in earlier times, and it was typically a precious metal, for example, gold, silver, or copper. In practice, commodity money systems involved having the government operate a mint to produce coins from precious metals, which then circulated as money. Control over the mint by the government was important, because the ability to issue money provided an important source of seigniorage revenue for the government. Commodity money systems, however, had several problems. First, the quality of any commodity is difficult to verify. For example, gold can be adulterated with other cheaper metals, so that there is an opportunity for fraud in the production of commodity money. Also, in the exchange of commodity monies, bits could be clipped off coins and melted down, with the hope that this would go undetected. Second, commodity money is costly to produce. For example, gold has to be dug out of the ground, minted, and then reminted when the coins wear out. Third, the use of a commodity as money diverts it from other uses. Gold and silver, for example, can also be used as jewelry and in industrial applications. In spite of these three problems, at the time commodity monies were used there were no good alternatives, mainly because any laws against the counterfeiting of paper currency would have been difficult or impossible to enforce. What may seem paradoxical is that the high cost of producing a commodity money was a virtue. To avoid inflation, the quantity of money must be in limited supply, and one characteristic of gold and silver that made them function well as commodity monies is their scarcity.

Circulating private bank notes: In the **Free Banking Era** in the United States (1837–1863), and earlier, banks chartered by state governments issued pieces of paper that were exchanged hand-to-hand, much as currency is today. A system of note issue by private banks was also in place in Canada before 1935.[1] A problem during the Free Banking Era was that there were thousands of banks issuing notes, so that it was very difficult for a person offered a note in a particular location to evaluate its quality. For example, a storekeeper in Boston offered a note issued by a New Orleans bank may not have known whether this was an insolvent bank that might ultimately not redeem the note or if the New Orleans bank indeed even existed. Some characterize the Free Banking Era as chaotic, but the efficiency of free banking is an issue that is much debated by economic historians.[2]

---

[1]See S. Williamson, 1989. "Restrictions on Financial Intermediaries and Implications for Aggregate Fluctuations: Canada and the United States 1870–1913," in *NBER Macroeconomics Annual 1989*, Olivier Blanchard and Stanley Fischer, eds., pp. 303–340, Cambridge, MA: MIT Press; and B. Champ, B. Smith, and S. Williamson, 1996. "Currency Elasticity and Banking Panics: Theory and Evidence," *Canadian Journal of Economics* 29, 828–864.

[2]See, for example, B. Smith and W. Weber, 1999. "Private Money Creation and the Suffolk Banking System," *Journal of Money, Credit and Banking* 31, 624–659; and A. Rolnick and W. Weber, 1983. "New Evidence on the Free Banking Era," *American Economic Review* 73, 1080–1091.

Commodity-backed paper currency: In this type of monetary system, there is government-issued paper currency, but the currency is backed by some commodity, as for example under the **gold standard**. The United States operated under the gold standard before 1933. Under the rules of the gold standard, the U.S. government stood ready to exchange currency for gold at some specified price, so that government currency was always redeemable in gold. Effectively this was a commodity money system, but it saved on some of the costs of a commodity money, in that consumers did not have to carry large quantities of the commodity (in this case gold) around when they wanted to make large purchases.

Fiat money: This is at least part of the monetary system in place in most modern economies. In the United States, fiat currency is the stock of Federal Reserve notes issued by the Fed. Fiat money consists of pieces of paper that are essentially worthless in that, for example, most people do not value U.S. Federal Reserve notes for their color or for the pictures on them. However, U.S. Federal Reserve notes are valued in that they can be exchanged for consumable goods. Why is fiat money accepted in exchange for goods? We accept fiat money because we believe that others will accept this money in exchange for goods in the future. This notion of the value of money supported by belief is intriguing, and it is part of what excites those who study monetary economics.

Transactions deposits at private banks: In the United States, widespread deposit banking and the use of checks in transactions was mainly a post–Civil War phenomenon, and the U.S. financial system (and similarly the financial systems in most developed economies) has evolved to the point where much of the total volume of transactions is carried out through banks. With a bank deposit that can be transferred with a debit card or by writing a check, consumers can make purchases without the use of fiat money. A debit card or check transaction is a message that specifies that a given quantity of value is to be debited from the account of the person writing the check or using the debit card and credited to the account of the person on the other end of the transaction. If the accounts of the buyer and the seller are in different banks, then, for the correct accounts to be debited and credited, the transaction needs to be cleared through an interbank transaction. In the United States, most domestic transactions between financial institutions are cleared by means of **Fedwire**, a payments system operated by the Federal Reserve System.

Some readers may be concerned that we have not mentioned credit cards as a form of money. There is a good reason we have not done this—money and credit are fundamentally different. When a credit card purchase is made, the vendor of goods or services extends credit to the purchaser, and then this credit is transferred to the credit card issuer (Visa, Mastercard, or American Express, for example). The credit extended is not money in the sense that currency or a bank deposit is money, because the issuer of credit cannot use what is effectively an IOU of the purchaser as a medium of exchange. However, forms of credit, particularly credit cards, are a substitute for money in making transactions, and, therefore, they are important in terms of how we think about the monetary system. Indeed, in Chapter 12, we modeled the demand for credit card balances as an important component to explain the demand for money.

MACROECONOMICS IN ACTION

Commodity Money and Commodity-Backed Paper Money, Yap Stones, and Playing Cards

A commodity money system that appears unusual on the surface but has several features common to other commodity money systems is the exchange of so-called Yap stones on the island of Yap in Micronesia, as studied by the anthropologist William Henry Furness III in 1903.[3] On the island of Yap, there were large stones that served as money and measured from 1 foot to 12 feet in diameter.[4] These stones were quarried from limestone deposits on another island about 400 miles from Yap and transported back by boat. What the Yap stones had in common with other commodity monies, such as gold and silver, was scarcity. It was quite costly in time and effort to create a new Yap stone, and the value of the stones increased with the difficulty in acquiring them, which might include weathering storms on the trip back to Yap. What seems different about the Yap stones as a commodity money is that they were extremely difficult to move around; an attractive feature of gold and silver as commodity monies was that the quantities required to make moderate-sized transactions were extremely portable. However, the Yap islanders did not typically move the Yap stones when transactions were made. Yap stones were most often used to make large land transactions and to make large gifts, but the stones themselves usually stayed in a fixed location. It was well known to most of the small population of Yap who owned which stones, and a transaction involving a Yap stone was public

knowledge, but there was no written record of ownership. Thus, it appears that exchange was actually carried out on the island of Yap using commodity-backed money. What changed hands in a transaction was the record of the ownership of the stone, which was stored in the collective memories of the islanders, and the stones were just the backing for the currency, which was not physical objects at all, but an entry in public memory.

Yap stones had much in common with the earliest known paper money used in North America, in New France, in 1685. There had been difficulties in keeping coins minted in France in circulation in New France (now the province of Quebec in Canada), as the coins were often used in payment for imports from France and, thus, left the colony. Therefore, the coins constantly had to be replenished by shipments from France in the form of payments to the troops in New France. In 1685, the shipment of coins was late in arriving from France, and De Meulles, the Intendant (governor of the colony) of New France authorized the issue of playing card money. De Meulles requisitioned the playing cards in the colony, and the cards were issued, signed by him in different denominations, as payment to the troops. These playing cards were essentially IOUs, which promised payment in coin when the shipment arrived from France. The playing cards then circulated as a medium of exchange in New France, and they were subsequently retired, as promised. These cards were then issued repeatedly in later years, but ultimately the government of France lost interest in its colony in New France, and the shipments of coins did not arrive from France in

---

[3]W. Furness, 1910. *The Island of Stone Money: Yap and the Carolines*, Philadelphia and London: J. P. Lippincott Co.

[4]See M. Bryan, February 2004. "Island Money," Federal Reserve Bank of Cleveland Commentary.

the quantities promised, so the IOUs that the playing cards represented could not be honored in full. There were problems with inflation, because of the temptation to issue the playing card money in excess of the promises that the Intendant could actually keep.[5]

---

[5] See http://collections.ic.gc.ca/bank/english/emar76.htm for a description and photograph of card money in New France from the Bank of Canada currency museum.

Like the ownership rights to the Yap stones that circulated on the island of Yap, playing card money in New France was a commodity-backed money. However, the New France playing card monetary system seems to have been less successful than the Yap system, because the commodity backing of the playing card money was uncertain (due to the inability of public officials to keep their promises), whereas the existence of the Yap stones was well known to essentially everyone on the island of Yap.

Money and the Absence of Double Coincidence of Wants: The Role of Commodity Money and Fiat Money

LO 18.2 Explain the absence-of-double-coincidence problem, and show how this idea can be captured formally.

Now that we know something about what objects have served as a medium of exchange, we consider in more detail what it means for some object to be a medium of exchange, which is the distinctive function of money. In this section, we consider a model that formalizes why money is useful as a medium of exchange. This model helps us understand the role of the two simplest types of money, commodity money and fiat money.

A fundamental question in monetary economics is why market exchange is typically an exchange of goods for money (monetary exchange) rather than of goods for goods (barter exchange). Jevons[6] argued that money helped to solve a problem of an **absence of double coincidence of wants** associated with barter exchange. To understand the double-coincidence-of-wants problem, imagine a world where there are many goods and people are specialized in what they wish to produce and consume. For example, suppose person I produces corn but wants to consume wheat. If person I meets another person II who has wheat, that would be a single coincidence of wants, because II has what I wants. However, II may not want corn in exchange for her wheat. If II wanted to consume corn, there would be a double coincidence of wants, because I wants what II has and II wants what I has. Barter exchange can only take place if there is a double coincidence. Searching for a trading partner is costly in time and resources (for example, hauling corn from place to place looking for a double coincidence of wants), particularly if there are many goods in the economy, so that there are many would-be sellers to search among. It would be much easier if, in selling corn, person I only needs to satisfy a single coincidence of wants; that is, find a person who wants corn. This would be the case if everyone accepted some object, called money. Then, in selling corn in exchange

---

[6] See S. Jevons, 1910. *Money and the Mechanism of Exchange*, 23rd ed., London: Kegan Paul.

for wheat, all person *I* needs to do is to sell corn for money in a single-coincidence meeting, then sell money for wheat in another single-coincidence meeting.

To see how this might work, consider the following simple economy, depicted in Figure 18.1. This is an example from the work by Nobuhiro Kiyotaki and Randall Wright,[7] who formalized Jevons's notion of the role of money using modern dynamic methods. There are three types of people in this economy. Type *I* people consume good 1 and produce good 2, type *II* people consume good 2 and produce good 3, and type *III* people consume good 3 and produce good 1. There are many people of each type in the economy, and everyone lives forever, with people meeting each other pairwise and at random each period. That is, each person meets one other person each period, and that other person is someone he or she bumps into at random. If the people in this economy each produce their good, and then wait until they meet another person with whom they can engage in a barter exchange, everyone will wait forever to trade, because this economy has an absence of double coincidence of wants. This is the simplest type of example in which there are no possible pairwise meetings where a double coincidence of wants occurs.

Figure 18.1 An Absence-of-Double-Coincidence Economy

In the model there are three types of people. A type *I* person consumes good 1 and produces good 2, a type *II* person consumes good 2 and produces good 3, and a type *III* person consumes good 3 and produces good 1.

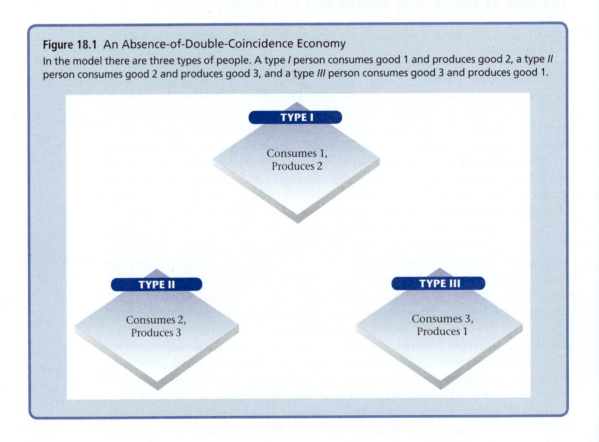

[7]N. Kiyotaki and R. Wright, 1989. "On Money as a Medium of Exchange," *Journal of Political Economy* 97, 927–954.

How might trade be accomplished here? One solution would be for people to use a commodity money. Suppose, for example, that good 1 can be stored at a relatively low cost. Then good 1 might be used as a commodity money, in that type *II* people accept good 1 in exchange for good 3 when meeting type *III* people. Why does type *II* accept good 1 even though it is not something he or she consumes? This is because type *II* knows that type *I* accepts good 1 in exchange for good 2 (this is a double-coincidence trade). Good 1 in this example is then a commodity money—a medium of exchange—as it is accepted in exchange by people who do not ultimately consume it. We show the equilibrium patterns of trade in Figure 18.2.

Another solution to the absence-of-double-coincidence problem would be the introduction of a fourth good, fiat money, which no one consumes but is acceptable to everyone in exchange for goods. A possible equilibrium pattern of exchange is shown in Figure 18.3. Here, when types *I* and *II* meet, *II* buys good 2 with money; when *I* and *III* meet, *I* buys good 1 with money; and when *III* and *II* meet, *III* buys good 3 with money. Thus, money circulates clockwise in Figure 18.3, and goods are passed counterclockwise.

For this model to say something interesting about the conditions under which commodity money would be useful, and when a fiat money system would be better

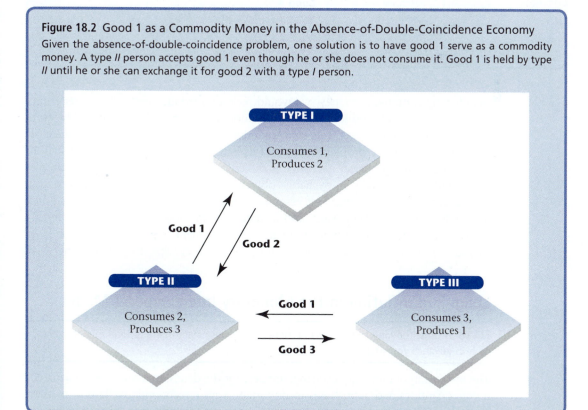

Figure 18.2 Good 1 as a Commodity Money in the Absence-of-Double-Coincidence Economy
Given the absence-of-double-coincidence problem, one solution is to have good 1 serve as a commodity money. A type *II* person accepts good 1 even though he or she does not consume it. Good 1 is held by type *II* until he or she can exchange it for good 2 with a type *I* person.

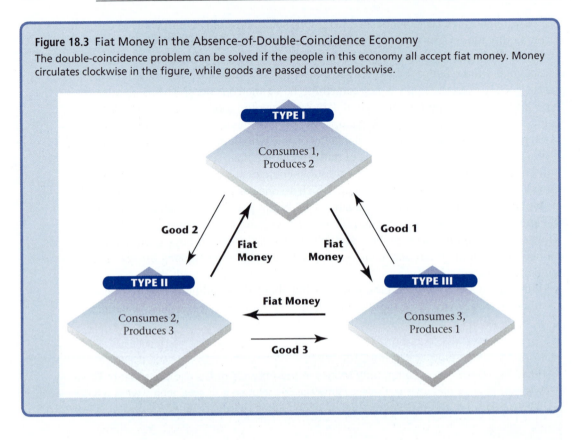

Figure 18.3 Fiat Money in the Absence-of-Double-Coincidence Economy
The double-coincidence problem can be solved if the people in this economy all accept fiat money. Money circulates clockwise in the figure, while goods are passed counterclockwise.

than having commodity money, we would have to introduce costs of counterfeiting, the resource costs of producing commodity money, and so forth. This would be quite complicated to do. However, this simple model captures the essentials of the absence-of-double-coincidence problem and why this helps to make money socially useful in promoting exchange. Barter exchange is difficult, in fact impossible in this example, unless individuals accept in exchange objects that they do not consume. That is, a medium of exchange—money—is essential in allowing people to exchange what they do not want for what they want, and it, therefore, increases welfare. In fact, in this example the institution of money is a Pareto improvement (recall our discussion from Chapter 5), because it increases welfare for everyone over what it would be otherwise.

Long-Run Inflation in the Monetary Intertemporal Model

LO 18.3 Show the long-run effects of inflation in the monetary intertemporal model, with a cash-in-advance approach.

The institution of monetary exchange matters for the determination of real macroeconomic quantities and contributes in important ways to economic welfare in modern economies. Once this institution is in place, however, the money supply can change in ways that have no consequences at all for real macroeconomic variables or for welfare. Though short-run monetary nonneutralities might arise because of sticky prices (studied in Chapters 12 and 14, and 15), for example in the long run money is neutral (as we showed in Chapter 12), in that a one-time level increase in the stock of money only changes prices in proportion and has no long-run effects on real variables.

Though money is neutral in the long run, in that a change in the *level* of the money supply has no long-run real effects, changes in the *growth rate* of the money supply are not neutral. It should not be surprising, because an increase in the level of the money supply causes an increase in the price level, that an increase in the rate of growth in the money supply causes an increase in the rate of growth in the price level; that is, an increase in the inflation rate. By modifying the monetary intertemporal model we constructed in Chapter 12, we are able to show why money growth and inflation are costly in terms of lost aggregate output and misallocation of resources. Further, we determine an optimal prescription for monetary growth, often referred to as the Friedman rule for monetary policy, after Milton Friedman. The Friedman rule for optimal money growth is that money should grow at a rate that implies that the nominal interest rate is zero. It turns out that the optimal money growth rate and the implied optimal inflation rate are negative.

There are many factors that can cause changes in the price level, some of which we have explored in Chapters 12 to 14. For example, a change in total factor productivity changes equilibrium aggregate output Y and the equilibrium real interest rate r, and this shifts the money demand curve and causes a change in the price level. In Chapter 15, we studied inflation in the context of a New Keynesian sticky-price model. However, those models are designed to capture only the effects of inflation on sticky-price distortions, and leave out the factors that we will explore here. The causal link between money growth and inflation was emphasized by Milton Friedman and Anna Schwartz in *A Monetary History of the United States 1867–1960*.[8]

However, particularly since 1980, the empirical relationship between money supply growth and inflation has weakened, as was emphasized in Chapter 12. Thus, as shown in Figure 12.2 in Chapter 12, a more reliable long-run relationship tied to inflation is the Fisher effect, according to which the nominal interest rate and the inflation rate are positively related in the data. As we will show in what follows, the Fisher effect is a key element in our model—higher money growth induces higher inflation, which also raises the nominal interest rate in the long run.

We will simplify the monetary intertemporal model in Chapter 12 so as to make it a more conventional type of **cash-in-advance** model. Such models have been widely used in macroeconomic research, with the initial theory developed in part by Robert Lucas.[9]

In our cash-in-advance model, the representative consumer comes into the period with some money and some bonds, the central bank can then intervene by injecting

---

[8]M. Friedman and A. Schwartz, 1960. *A Monetary History of the United States 1867–1960*, Princeton, NJ: Princeton University Press.

[9]See R. Lucas, 1980. "Equilibrium in a Pure Currency Economy," in J. Kareken and N. Wallace, editors, *Models of Monetary Economies*, Minneapolis, MN: Federal Reserve Bank of Minneapolis, pp. 131–145.

money into the economy (or taking money out of the financial system) through open market operations, and the consumer can then trade on financial markets. Then, the consumer purchases goods, but must pay for them with money. Income earned during the current period cannot be spent until the future period.

To understand the effects of long-run inflation, we allow the money supply to grow forever at a constant rate in our model. We suppose that the government permits the money supply to grow by making lump-sum transfers to the representative household each period, with the money supply growing according to

$$M' = (1 + x)M, \tag{18-1}$$

where M' is the future money supply, M is the current money supply, and x is the growth rate of the money supply from the current period to the future period. For simplicity, we suppose that the economy looks exactly the same in every period, in that total factor productivity, real government spending, and consumer preferences are identical in every period. The only exogenous variable that changes over time is the money supply, which grows according to Equation (18-1). This implies that all of the endogenous variables in the model, except the price level, remain the same for all time. That is, the real wage, employment, aggregate output, the real interest rate, and the inflation rate are constant for all time. In the current period, money supply is equal to money demand in equilibrium, and so from Chapter 12, we have

$$M = PL(Y, r + i). \tag{18-2}$$

Recall from Chapter 12 that, on the left-hand side of Equation (18-2), M is the nominal money supply and, on the right-hand side of Equation (18-2), $PL(Y, r + i)$ is nominal money demand. From the Fisher relation, recall that $r + i$ (the real interest rate plus the inflation rate) is equal (approximately) to the nominal interest rate. It must also be the case in equilibrium that money supply is equal to money demand in the future period, so that

$$M' = P'L(Y', r' + i'), \tag{18-3}$$

where P' is the price level in the future period, Y' is the future aggregate output, r' is the future real interest rate, and i' is the future inflation rate. Then, from Equations (18-2) and (18-3), we have

$$\frac{M'}{M} = \frac{P'L(Y', r' + i')}{PL(Y, r + i)}. \tag{18-4}$$

But in equilibrium, aggregate output, the real interest rate, and the inflation rate remain constant over time, which implies that $Y' = Y$, $r' = r$, and $i' = i$. This then gives $L(Y', r' + i') = L(Y, r + i)$, so that the real demand for money is the same in the future and current periods. Then, from Equation (18-4), we get

$$\frac{M'}{M} = \frac{P'}{P},$$

so that the growth rates of the money supply and the price level are the same in equilibrium. This implies, from Equation (18-1), that the inflation rate is given by

$$i = \frac{P'}{P} - 1 = \frac{M'}{M} - 1 = x,$$

so that the inflation rate is equal to the money growth rate. The equality of the money growth rate and the inflation rate is special to this situation in which real variables remain constant over time. From Equation (18-4), if the real demand for money changes over time, so that $L(Y', r' + i') \neq L(Y, r + i)$, then the money growth rate is not equal to the inflation rate. However, it is still true that the inflation rate will increase as the money growth rate increases.

We wish to determine the effects of an increase in x on output, the real interest rate, employment, and the real wage in the monetary intertemporal model. To do this, we first need to understand how inflation affects labor supply and the demand for current consumption goods in this cash-in-advance model. Since consumption goods are purchased using money acquired by the representative consumer before the goods market opens and the consumer receives his or her wage income after goods are purchased, wage income must be held in the form of money before it is spent in the future period. Just as in Chapter 9, when the representative consumer optimizes, he or she sets the marginal rate of substitution of current consumption goods for future consumption goods equal to $1 + r$, or

$$MRS_{C,C'} = 1 + r. \tag{18-5}$$

As well, because current wages cannot be spent on consumption goods until the future period, the effective real wage for the consumer is $\frac{Pw}{P'}$, which is the current nominal wage divided by the future price level. Therefore (recall Chapter 4), when the consumer optimizes, he or she sets the marginal rate of substitution of current leisure for future consumption equal to $\frac{Pw}{P'}$ or

$$MRS_{l,C'} = \frac{Pw}{P'}. \tag{18-6}$$

Now, because Equations (18-5) and (18-6) tell us how the consumer substitutes at the optimum between current and future consumption and between current leisure and future consumption, we can derive from these two equations a marginal condition for substitution at the optimum between current leisure and current consumption. That is, at the optimum it must be the case that

$$MRS_{l,C} = \frac{MRS_{l,C'}}{MRS_{C,C'}} = \frac{Pw}{P'(1 + r)},$$

from Equations (18-5) and (18-6). Therefore, from the Fisher relation in Chapter 12, we have

$$MRS_{l,C} = \frac{w}{1 + R}, \tag{18-7}$$

where R is the nominal interest rate. To understand the marginal condition, Equation (18-4), it helps to run through how the consumer would substitute between current consumption and current leisure, which is roundabout because of the cash-in-advance constraint. If the consumer wishes to supply one extra unit of time during the current period as labor, he or she earns additional real wages of w, which then must be held over to the future period, when their value in terms of future consumption goods is $\frac{Pw}{P'}$. To consume more current goods, the consumer can borrow against this amount in the credit market before he or she arrives in the goods market. The real quantity that can be borrowed is $\frac{Pw}{P'(1+r)} = \frac{w}{1+R}$, which then must be the relative price of current leisure for current consumption.

Given Equation (18-7), a higher nominal interest rate R causes substitution away from consumption goods and toward leisure. Equation (18-4) then tells us that, from the approximate Fisher relation $R = r + i$, given the real interest rate r and the real wage w, and assuming that substitution effects dominate income effects, an increase in the inflation rate i causes substitution from consumption goods to leisure.

In Figure 18.4 we show the effects in the current period of an increase in the money growth rate from x_1 to x_2, which takes place for all periods, and is anticipated by everyone. In equilibrium the inflation rate in every period then increases from x_1 to x_2, given our analysis above where we showed that the money growth rate equals the inflation rate in equilibrium. The increase in the inflation rate causes substitution by the representative consumer from consumption goods to leisure. This causes the labor supply curve to shift to the left in Figure 18.4(a), which in turn shifts the output supply curve to the left in Figure 18.4(b). As well, because the consumer substitutes away from consumption goods, the output demand curve shifts to the left in Figure 18.4(b). Then, in Figure 18.4(b), it is not clear whether the real interest rate rises or falls. For simplicity, we show the case where the output demand and output supply effects on the real interest rate just cancel, so that the real interest rate does not change. This also implies that investment and the capital stock are unaffected (assume that we are in a steady state where the capital stock is constant over time), which also greatly simplifies matters.

In Figure 18.4, equilibrium output falls from Y_1 to Y_2, employment falls from N_1 to N_2, and the real wage rises from w_1 to w_2. In the figure the real interest rate remains constant, so that investment expenditures are unaffected, but consumption must fall as real income has decreased. From the approximate Fisher relation, $R = r + i$, where R is the nominal interest rate. Therefore, because r is constant, and i increases from x_1 to x_2, the nominal interest rate increases by the amount of the money growth rate increase. This is the Fisher effect, which was discussed in Chapter 12. Also, given equilibrium in the money market,

$$\frac{M}{P} = L(Y, r + i), \tag{18-8}$$

real output Y has decreased, r is the same, and i has increased; therefore, real money demand on the right-hand side of Equation (18-8) has decreased, and so the current real money supply on the left-hand side of Equation (18-8) must also decrease. Higher

Figure 18.4 The Long-Run Effects of an Increase in the Money Growth Rate

An increase in the money growth rate increases the inflation rate, which shifts the labor supply curve to the left, the output supply curve to the left, and the output demand curve to the left. The real wage rises, employment falls, and output falls. The real interest rate may rise or fall, but for simplicity we show the case where it stays constant.

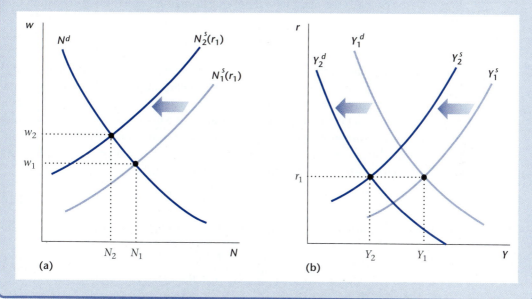

money growth and inflation causes the consumer to hold a smaller quantity of real cash balances in equilibrium.

Though money is neutral in this economy, in that a change in the level of the money supply has no real effects, a change in the growth rate of the money supply is not neutral. If a change in the money growth rate had no real effects, we would say that money was **superneutral**. However, money is not superneutral here, as an increase in the money growth rate leads to decreases in consumption, output, and employment. These effects occur because higher money growth leads to higher inflation, which affects the consumer's decisions concerning how much to work in the current period and how much and what to consume. Higher inflation increases the nominal interest rate, which is the opportunity cost of holding money for transactions purposes. As a result, the household economizes on money balances. The resulting costs of inflation are lost output and consumption.

Optimal Monetary Policy: The Friedman Rule

LO 18.4 State the Friedman rule, and explain what this implies for optimal monetary policy and inflation in the long run.

At this point, we would like to demonstrate the key economic inefficiencies that result from inflation, and then show how these inefficiencies can be corrected by the appropriate long-run monetary policy. Recall from Chapter 5 that economic efficiency is achieved when the allocation of resources in an economy is Pareto optimal; that is, when there is no way to rearrange production or the allocation of goods so that someone is better off and no one worse off. A key condition for Pareto optimality that we derived in Chapter 5 was that the marginal rate of substitution of leisure for consumption must be equal to the marginal rate of transformation of leisure for consumption; that is,

$$MRS_{l,C} = MRT_{l,C}. \tag{18-9}$$

This condition applies at the Pareto optimum because it is efficient for the rate at which the consumer is just willing to substitute leisure for consumption to be equal to the rate at which leisure can be converted into consumption goods using the production technology. In this model, as in the model of Chapter 5, the marginal rate of transformation of leisure for consumption is equal to the marginal product of labor, MP_N. In a competitive equilibrium, profit maximization by the representative firm implies that $MP_N = w$, so it is also true in a competitive equilibrium that

$$MRT_{l,C} = w. \tag{18-10}$$

Therefore, substituting for w in Equation (18-7) using Equation (18-10) gives

$$MRS_{l,C} = \frac{MRT_{l,C}}{1+R}. \tag{18-11}$$

Therefore, because Equation (18-11) holds in competitive equilibrium in this model, Equation (18-9) does not hold, and so the competitive equilibrium is not Pareto optimal, in general, as long as the nominal interest rate is positive, or $R > 0$. That is, a positive nominal interest rate drives a "wedge" between the marginal rate of substitution and the marginal rate of transformation, thus, creating an inefficiency. The fact that the nominal interest rate is positive implies that too much leisure is consumed, too little output is produced, consumption is too low, and real money balances are too low.

    We know that an increase in the money growth rate x causes an increase in the nominal interest rate, so that higher money growth, which is associated with higher inflation, implies a larger wedge separating the marginal rate of substitution from the marginal rate of transformation. If the money growth rate and inflation were reduced, then it appears that this would promote economic efficiency, but what would be the best money growth rate for the government to set? Clearly, if the nominal interest rate were reduced to zero, then the marginal rate of substitution would be equal to the marginal rate of transformation in Equation (18-11). What is the money growth rate x that would drive the nominal interest rate to zero? Because in equilibrium the nominal interest rate is $R = r + x$, if $R = 0$, it is optimal for the money growth rate to be $x = -r$. Because the real interest rate is positive ($r > 0$), at the optimum, $x < 0$ and the money supply decreases over time. Further, if the money supply is decreasing over time, there is **deflation**, because the inflation rate is $i = x = -r < 0$. Thus, it is optimal for the government to generate a deflation that continues forever, implying that the nominal interest rate is zero in every period.

The fact that the optimal monetary policy drives the nominal interest rate to zero is of prime importance in understanding why this policy works to maximize welfare. A positive nominal interest rate on bonds implies that the representative consumer economizes too much on money balances in favor of holding bonds. The consumer also consumes too small a quantity of goods and too much leisure. If the nominal interest rate is driven to zero through deflation, giving money a higher real return, then the household becomes indifferent between holding bonds and money, and this is optimal.

This type of optimal deflationary monetary policy is called a Friedman rule, after Milton Friedman.[10] In practice, the Friedman rule means that the nominal interest rate on riskless securities should always be zero. This does not mean that all nominal interest rates should be zero (this would be impossible), but that the nominal interest rate on short-term government debt (for example, U.S. Treasury bills) should be zero.

There are alternative ways, in principle, to implement a Friedman rule, other than engineering a deflation to support a nominal interest rate of zero. If central banks could pay interest on money at a rate equal to the interest rate on government debt, this would also solve the problem. Paying interest on circulating currency is impractical, but it is easy for central banks to pay interest on reserves, which also serve as money, as reserves are essentially checking accounts with the central bank. Indeed, part of the motivation for a change in the Federal Reserve Act that permitted the payment of interest on reserves beginning in October 2008 was the idea that this change would increase economic efficiency.

Though the Friedman rule is probably the most robust policy conclusion that comes from monetary economics, it has never found much favor in the central banks of the world. Central banks that target inflation typically choose a positive target rate. A target inflation rate of 2% is common. But recently, many central banks in the world, including those in Sweden, Denmark, the Euro area, the United Kingdom, and Switzerland, have had nominal interest rate targets close to zero, or below it, and have experienced low rates of inflation. The most extreme case is Japan, where nominal interest rates have been close to zero for more than 20 years, and the inflation rate over that period has averaged about zero. Are these regimes examples of the Friedman rule at work? That is certainly not the stated intention of the central banks in these countries, which appear to want higher inflation. Perhaps some central banks are just confused, as we outlined in Chapter 15.

Our cash-in-advance model tells us that anticipated inflation is costly. High inflation reduces output and employment, and a reduction in economic welfare. But how high are those costs in practice? Some research indicates that, at low levels of inflation, say below 10% per annum, the gains from reducing inflation are very small. Indeed, Thomas Cooley and Gary Hansen[11] conclude that, in a monetary model similar to the one we have studied here, the welfare loss from an inflation rate of 10% per annum is about 0.5% of consumption for the average consumer, and the welfare loss from a

---

[10] See "The Optimum Quantity of Money," in M. Friedman, 1969. *The Optimum Quantity of Money and Other Essays,* pp. 1–50, Hawthorne, NY: Aldine Publishing.

[11] See T. Cooley and G. Hansen, 1989. "The Inflation Tax in a Real Business Cycle Model," *American Economic Review* 79, 733–748.

MACROECONOMICS IN ACTION

Should the Fed Reduce the Inflation Rate to Zero or Less?

Our monetary intertemporal model tells us that the optimal rate of inflation is negative, which implies that the Fed should engineer a rate of growth in the money supply that would give permanent deflation. However, as we pointed out, no central bank appears to have attempted to bring about a deflation. At most, some policy-makers are willing to recommend that the infla-tion rate be reduced to zero, so that the price level will remain constant over time.

In the United States, the goals for the Fed are specified in the Employment Act of 1946, later amended in the Full Employment and Balanced Growth Act of 1978. The latter act is popularly known as the Humphrey–Hawkins (HH) Act. The HH Act is typically interpreted as giving the Fed a "dual mandate," to promote "maximum employment," and "price stability." The instruc-tions from the Congress to the Fed contained in the HH Act are rather vague, particularly as these instructions contain no quantitative information. It is generally recognized that the dual mandate means that the Fed should care about real eco-nomic variables, such as unemployment rate, real GDP, and employment—the first part of the mandate. It should also care about inflation—the second part of the mandate. However, the HH Act says nothing, for example, about what level of the unemployment rate would be most desir-able, or what the inflation rate should be.

The dual mandate is an unusual framework among those that constrain central banks in the more developed countries of the world. To the extent that central banks are mandated to do any-thing, it is typically to control inflation by way of an inflation target, as in Australia, Canada, New Zealand, the United Kingdom, and the

Euro zone, for example. The Fed's "Statement of Longer-Run Goals and Monetary Policy Strategy," first written in January 2012 and last amended in January 2016, states that " . . . inflation at the rate of 2 percent, as measured by the annual change in the price index for personal consump-tion expenditures, is most consistent over the longer run with the Federal Reserve's statutory mandate. The Committee would be concerned if inflation were running persistently above or below this objective."[12] This states how the Fed intends to implement its dual mandate over the longer run, in terms of the "price stability" part of the mandate. The Fed thinks that a reasonable target for inflation is 2% per year, as measured by the personal consumption deflator, which is derived as part of national income accounting. The personal consumption deflator is closely related to the consumer price index (CPI), but is thought to give a more accurate measure of inflation than the CPI.

Why do Fed officials think that 2% is the appropriate inflation rate, and not −2%, 0%, or 10%, for example? The Fed has never provided specific reasons for its 2% target, but perhaps there are sound economic reasons that would back up the "2% inflation rule." Suppose that we start with the Friedman rule. The basic reasoning behind the Friedman rule is instructive, though perhaps we do not want to take the rule seriously as a literal prescription for monetary policy. The Friedman rule tells us that inflation causes an

---

[12]"Monetary Policy Report," Board of Governors of the Federal Reserve System, February 10, 2016, Federal Reserve.

intertemporal distortion—it distorts the relative price of future goods in terms of current goods. That distortion causes resources to be misallocated (for example, people put too much effort into economizing on their money balances) and will in general imply that less inflation is better.

But there are other distortions associated with money and inflation that we may need to be concerned about. First, New Keynesian analysis tells us that relative price distortions can arise from sticky prices and wages. In product markets, if firms change their prices infrequently in a staggered fashion, and the inflation rate is high, then relative prices can get out of line with what is economically efficient, resulting in a loss in aggregate economic welfare. In labor markets, staggered wage setting by firms can similarly result in wage distortions and the misallocation of labor across firms. In general, for these distortions it will be just as bad if there is deflation (an inflation rate less than zero) as inflation, so these types of relative price distortions will make price stability (zero inflation) desirable.

Second, there are various types of costs associated with the operation of a monetary system. In the United States, for example, it is costly to maintain the stock of currency. Paper currency wears out and must be replaced, and the currency must be designed to thwart counterfeiters. As well, counterfeiting itself involves a social cost, in that the time and effort people devote to counterfeiting generates no social benefits. Finally, currency is a medium of exchange that permits transactions to occur in private, and privacy is very useful for criminals. Counterfeit goods are typically sold for cash; recreational drugs are sold for cash; bribes are made with cash. Without currency, any number of criminal activities would be more costly, and we would therefore have less of those activities. Thus, some of the costs associated with a currency system are social costs—currency makes crime less costly. Inflation can then be beneficial, in the sense that it acts like a user fee, taxing users of currency, and taxing activities that are socially costly—counterfeiting and other illegal activities. In this sense, more inflation is better than less.

So, if we take all of the costs and benefits of inflation into account, what does this tell us the optimal inflation rate should be? Is it 2%? A Friedman rule rate might perhaps imply a long-run inflation rate of −2%, though experience in Japan over the last 20 years might suggest that inflation with a long-run nominal interest rate of zero might be closer to 0%. And, if we take New Keynesian relative price distortions seriously, we might think of 0% inflation as optimal. But if in addition we take account of the factors that should make us want to tax currency transactions with higher inflation, a 2% optimal inflation rate starts to look plausible. However, without completely quantifying all of the relevant factors, we cannot say that 2% looks better than 0% or 5%, say. Economists have done some work on measuring the costs of inflation, but we perhaps know less than we should about guiding the central bank's choice of an optimal inflation rate.

monetary rule with 0% inflation versus the Friedman rule rate of deflation is about 0.14% of consumption for the average consumer.

Though most macroeconomic models tell us that the welfare losses from moderate inflations are quite small, the costs of extremely high rates of inflation—that is, **hyperinflations**—are clearly very large. Some prominent hyperinflations occurred in Austria, Hungary, Germany, and Poland in the early 1920s following World War I. For example, the inflation rate in Austria averaged 10,000% per annum between January 1921 and August 1922. Typically, hyperinflations occur because the government is unwilling or unable to finance large government outlays through taxation or borrowing, and so it must resort to seigniorage. For example, the German hyperinflation following World War I occurred in part because the German government financed large war reparations to other European countries by printing money at a very high rate. The key to stopping a hyperinflation, as Thomas Sargent points out,[13] is gaining control over fiscal policy by reducing the government deficit.

Financial Intermediation and Banking

LO 18.5 State the key properties of assets, and explain the role of financial intermediaries.

The purpose of this section is to study the place of banks and other financial intermediaries in the monetary system. Earlier in this chapter we discussed the historical importance of currency issued by private banks and how in modern economies much of transactions activity takes place using bank deposits. The role that banks and other financial intermediaries play in the economy is intimately related to the properties that different assets have, and so in the following subsection we discuss the characteristics of assets and their economic importance.

Properties of Assets

The four most important properties of assets are rate of return, risk, maturity, and liquidity; we discuss each of these in turn.

Rate of return: The rate of return on an asset is the payoff on the asset over some specified period of time divided by the initial investment in the asset, minus one. For example, the one-period rate of return on an asset that is bought at price q_t in period t, sold at price q_{t+1} in period $t + 1$, with a payout (say a dividend on a stock) of d in period $t + 1$, would be

$$r_t^a = \frac{q_{t+1} + d}{q_t} - 1.$$

Everything else held constant, consumers prefer assets that bear higher rates of return.

Risk: In modern finance theory, the risk that matters for a consumer's behavior is the risk that an asset contributes to the consumer's entire portfolio, where a portfolio is the entire set of assets the consumer holds. For example, a set of stocks might be quite risky on an individual basis, in that their rates of return fluctuate a great deal over time. However, when all these stocks are held together in a well-diversified portfolio, the entire portfolio may not be very risky. For instance, holding all of one's wealth in shares of Joe's Restaurant might be quite risky, but holding shares in all the restaurants in town might not be very risky at all. Even though diversifying one's portfolio by holding many different assets reduces risk, because the rates of return

---

[13] See "The Ends of Four Big Inflations," in T. Sargent, 1993. *Rational Expectations and Inflation*, 2nd ed., New York: Harper Collins, pp. 43–116.

on some assets can go up while other rates of return go down, there is a limit to the risk reduction that can be gained from diversification. Risk that cannot be diversified away is aggregate or macroeconomic risk, and it is the amount of this **nondiversifiable risk** present in a particular asset that matters for economic behavior. Here, we assume that consumers are **risk-averse**, so that, everything else held constant, a consumer prefers to hold assets with less nondiversifiable risk.

Maturity: Maturity refers to the time it takes for an asset to pay off. For some assets, maturity is a straightforward concept. For example, a 91-day U.S. Treasury bill is a security issued by the U.S. government that pays its face value 91 days from the date of issue, so maturity in this case is 91 days. For some other assets, however, this is not so clear, as in the case of a long-maturity bond. Many bonds provide for coupon payments, which are amounts the bearer receives at fixed intervals until the bond matures, when it pays its face value. Thus, a 30-year bond that provides for coupon payments at monthly intervals does not have a maturity of 30 years, but something less than that, because the payoffs on the asset take place during the 30-year period until all payoffs are received. All other things held constant, a consumer prefers a short-maturity asset to a long-maturity asset. Short-maturity assets imply more flexibility in meeting unanticipated needs for funds, and even if a consumer is certain that the funds will not be needed until far in the future (suppose the consumer is saving for a child's education, for example), it is possible to meet this need by holding a string of short-maturity assets rather than a long-maturity asset.

Liquidity: The final asset characteristic is liquidity, which is a measure of how long it takes to sell an asset for its market value, and of how high the costs are of selling the asset. Because money is widely acceptable in exchange and can, therefore, essentially be sold for its market value instantaneously, it is the most liquid asset. A good example of an illiquid asset is a house, which can often take weeks to sell, with a high transaction fee paid to an intermediary—the real estate agent—to find a buyer. Liquidity is important to an asset holder, because investors face uncertainty about when they want to purchase goods or assets. For example, consumers may face unforeseen expenses such as medical bills, or they may want to take advantage of an unanticipated investment opportunity. All else held constant, consumers prefer more liquidity to less liquidity.

Financial Intermediation

Now that we know something about the properties of assets, we can examine the role of financial intermediaries in the monetary system.

A financial intermediary is defined by the following characteristics:

1. It borrows from one group of economic agents and lends to another.
2. The group of economic agents it borrows from is large, and so is the group it lends to. That is, a financial intermediary is well diversified.
3. It transforms assets. That is, the properties of its liabilities are different from the properties of its assets.
4. It processes information.

Examples of financial intermediaries are insurance companies, mutual funds, and depository institutions. The economic role that these intermediaries play is intimately related to their four defining characteristics. Suppose that we consider depository institutions as an example. Depository institutions include commercial banks, thrift institutions (savings and loan associations and mutual savings banks), and credit unions. These institutions exist in part because of difficulties in getting ultimate borrowers and ultimate lenders together. To see why this is so, consider how the borrowing and lending done by a depository institution would take place in the absence of this institution. An individual wanting to borrow to start up a business, for example, would have to first find a lender willing to loan him or her the funds. Even if the would-be borrower were well known to the would-be lender, the would-be lender may not have good information on the would-be borrower's ability to repay the loan, and some time and effort would have to be forgone to acquire this information. Further, given that the loan required is sizable, the would-be borrower might have to approach several would-be lenders to finance the business startup, and each of these would-be lenders would have to incur information costs to ascertain the riskiness of lending to the would-be borrower. Supposing the loan is made, each of the lenders would bear some risk, given that there is always some chance that the borrower will not repay the loan. Further, unless the lenders had the means to enforce the loan contract, the borrower might try to abscond with the loan without repaying, even though he or she could repay. Finally, after the loan is made, it would be difficult for the lender to sell the loan to someone else should he or she require funds at short notice. That is, the loan is illiquid, in part because it has a long maturity, supposing that it will take a long period of time for the borrower's business to become profitable. In fact, the funds required to start up the business might be very large relative to the monthly profit the business will yield. As a result, the maturity of the loan may be so long that few would-be lenders would want to tie up funds for this length of time. To summarize, there are six potential problems with direct lending from ultimate lenders to ultimate borrowers, without the benefit of a financial intermediary:

1. Matching borrowers with lenders is costly in time and effort.
2. The ultimate lenders may not be skilled at evaluating credit risks.
3. Because several lenders would often be required to fund any one borrower, there would be replication of the costs required to evaluate credit risk.
4. Because lenders economize on information costs by lending to few borrowers, lending is risky.
5. Loans tend to be illiquid.
6. Loans tend to have longer maturities than lenders would like.

Without financial intermediaries, few loans would be made, and the only lending would be to the least risky borrowers. However, in our running example, consider what a depository institution can do to alleviate the aforementioned six difficulties. First, the depository institution is a well-defined place of business, and people know where to go if they wish to borrow or lend, and so this eliminates the search costs involved in getting borrowers and lenders together. Second, the depository institution is specialized in evaluating credit risks, and so can do this at a lower cost per loan than would be the case for an unspecialized individual. That is, there are economies of scale in acquiring information. Third, because the financial intermediary pools the funds of many lenders, it can avoid the replication of costs that occurs when there is direct lending. Fourth, because the financial intermediary is well diversified with respect to both its assets and liabilities, it can transform risky, illiquid, long-maturity assets into relatively safe, liquid, short-maturity liabilities.

Taking a depository institution specializing in business lending as an example, each business loan may be risky, illiquid, and of long maturity. However, because the depository institution holds many business loans (it is well diversified on the asset side of its balance sheet), the payoff on the bank's entire asset portfolio is relatively predictable, because the fraction of business loans that default should be predictable. Further, even though all the assets of the depository institution are illiquid and of long maturity, the institution's liabilities can be liquid and of short maturity because of the diversification of its liabilities. That is, suppose that the depository institution has many depositors, all holding transactions accounts. An individual depositor could decide to make withdrawals and deposits or to make debit card transactions at random times, but taken as a group, the behavior of depositors is predictable. Thus, though a transactions deposit is highly liquid and has as short a maturity as the depositor might wish for, the institution can make highly illiquid and long-maturity loans based on its ability to predict the aggregate behavior of a large number of depositors.

The Diamond–Dybvig Banking Model

LO 18.6 Construct the Diamond–Dybvig model, and derive its implications.

This banking model was developed in the early 1980s by Douglas Diamond and Philip Dybvig.[14] It is a simple model that captures some of the important features of banks and helps to explain why bank runs might occur (as they did historically) and what role the government might have in preventing bank runs.

In the model, there are three periods: 0, 1, and 2. There are N consumers, where N is very large, and each consumer is endowed with one unit of a good in period 0, which can serve as an input to production. The production technology takes one unit of the input good in period 0 and converts this into $1 + r$ units of the consumption good in period 2. However, this production technology can also be interrupted in period 1. If interruption occurs in period 1, then one unit of consumption goods can be obtained for each unit of the good invested in period 0. If production is interrupted, then nothing is produced in period 2.

A given consumer might wish to consume early—in period 1—or to consume late—in period 2. However, in period 0, individual consumers do not know whether they are early or late consumers; they learn this in period 1. In period 0, each consumer knows that they have a probability t of being an early consumer and probability $1 - t$

---

[14] D. Diamond and P. Dybvig, 1983. "Bank Runs, Liquidity, and Deposit Insurance," *Journal of Political Economy* 91, 401–419.

of being a late consumer, and in period 1, tN consumers learn that they are early consumers and $(1 - t)N$ consumers learn that they are late consumers. We have $0 < t < 1$.
For example, if $t = \frac{1}{2}$ then a consumer has equal probabilities of being an early or late
consumer, as if consuming early or late were determined by the flip of a coin.

The production technology captures liquidity in a simple way. That is, using the
production technology is much like investing in a long-maturity asset that could be
sold with some loss before it matures. For a consumer, the possibility that he or she
might consume early captures the idea that there exist random needs for liquid assets;
that is, unforeseen circumstances when transactions need to be made. In practice we
make many transactions over the course of a day or a week, and not all of these transactions are anticipated. For example, one might see a book in a store window and wish
to purchase it, or one might be caught in an unexpected rainstorm and need to buy an
umbrella, and so forth.

Whether consumption takes place early or late, the utility (or pleasure) that the
consumer receives is given by $U(c)$, where U is a utility function and c is consumption.
The utility function is concave, as in Figure 18.5, because the marginal utility of consumption declines as consumption increases. The **marginal utility of consumption**,
MU_c, is given by the slope of the utility function. For example, in Figure 18.5 the MU_c,
when $c = c^*$, is given by the slope of a tangent to the utility function at point A.

Figure 18.5 The Utility Function for a Consumer in the Diamond–Dybvig Model
The utility function is concave, and the slope of the function is the marginal utility of consumption, MU_c.

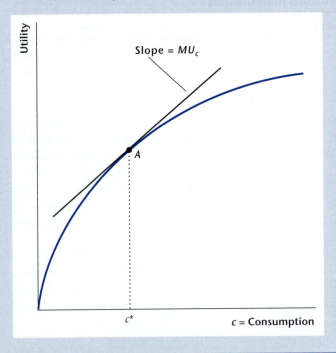

Given the world that an individual consumer lives in here, he or she needs to make decisions under uncertainty in period 0. In economics, a productive approach to modeling consumer choice under uncertainty is to assume that a consumer maximizes expected utility, which here is

$$\text{Expected Utility} = tU(c_1) + (1-t)U(c_2),$$

where c_1 is consumption if the consumer needs to consume early and c_2 is consumption if the consumer is a late consumer. That is, expected utility is a weighted average of utilities that occur if the particular events happen (early or late consumption), where the weights are the probabilities that the particular events occur, which in this case are t and $1-t$.

We can represent a consumer's expected utility preferences in terms of indifference curves, with c_1 (early consumption) on the horizontal axis and c_2 (late consumption) on the vertical axis in Figure 18.6. As in Chapters 4 and 9, these indifference curves are downward sloping and convex. The marginal rate of substitution of early consumption for late consumption for the consumer is given by

$$MRS_{c_1,c_2} = \frac{tMU_{c_1}}{(1-t)MU_{c_2}}, \tag{18-12}$$

where MRS_{c_1,c_2} is minus the slope of an indifference curve in Figure 18.6. When $c_1 = c_2$, so that early consumption and late consumption are equal, we have $MU_{c_1} = MU_{c_2}$ (if consumption is the same, the marginal utility of consumption must also be the same). From Equation (18-12) we have

$$MRS_{c_1,c_2} = \frac{t}{(1-t)},$$

when $c_1 = c_2$. Therefore, in Figure 18.6, an important property of the indifference curves is that, along the line $c_1 = c_2$, the slopes of each of the indifference curves is $\frac{-t}{1-t}$.

Suppose that each consumer must invest independently. On his or her own, what would a consumer do? Clearly, he or she invests all of his or her one unit of endowment in the technology in period 0. Then, in period 1, if he or she is an early consumer, then he or she interrupts the technology and is able to consume $c_1 = 1$. If he or she is a late consumer, then the technology is not interrupted and the consumer gets $c_2 = 1 + r$ in period 2 when the investment matures. What we would like to show is that a bank can form that allows all consumers to do better than this.

A Diamond–Dybvig Bank   In this model, a bank is an institution that offers deposit contracts to consumers. These deposit contracts allow consumers to withdraw c_1 units of goods from the bank in period 1 if they wish or to leave their deposit in the bank until period 2 and receive c_2 units of goods then. In period 1, consumers are served in sequence by the bank; that is, if a consumer wishes to withdraw his or her deposit in period 1, he or she is randomly allocated a place in line. We assume that the bank cannot tell the difference between early consumers and late consumers. While an early consumer would

Figure 18.6 The Preferences of a Diamond–Dybvig Consumer

The figure shows the indifference curves for a Diamond–Dybvig consumer, who has preferences over early consumption and late consumption.

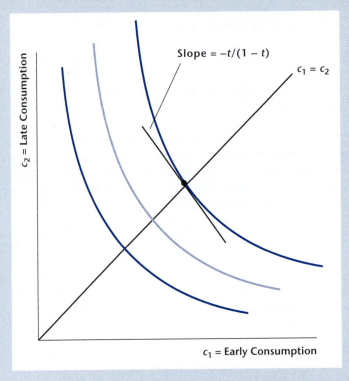

$c_1 = $ Early Consumption

not want to pose as a late consumer by not withdrawing early, as this could only make him or her worse off, it is possible that there might be circumstances in which a late consumer might want to withdraw early. We suppose that a late consumer who withdraws in period 1 can store goods until period 2 and then consume them.

What determines the deposit contract (c_1, c_2) that the bank offers? We suppose that there is one bank in which all consumers make their deposits and that this bank behaves competitively. There is free entry into banking, implying that the bank earns zero profits in equilibrium. The bank makes each depositor as well off as possible, while earning zero profits in periods 1 and 2, because if it did not behave in this way, then some other bank could enter the market offering an alternative deposit contract and attract all consumers away from the first bank. Because all consumers deposit in the bank in period 0, the bank has N units of goods to invest in the technology in period 0. In period 1, the bank must choose the fraction x of the investment to interrupt so that it can pay c_1 to each depositor who wishes to withdraw at that time. Supposing that only early consumers show up at the bank to withdraw in period 1, we must have

$$Ntc_1 = xN,$$ (18-13)

or the total quantity of withdrawals equals the quantity of production interrupted. Then, in period 2, the quantity of uninterrupted production matures, and this quantity is used to make payments to those consumers who chose to wait, who we are supposing are only the late consumers. Then, we have

$$N(1 - t)c_2 = (1 - x)N(1 + r). \tag{18-14}$$

That is, the total payout to the late consumers (on the left-hand side of Equation (18-14)) is equal to the total return on uninterrupted production (on the right-hand side of Equation (18-14)). If we substitute in Equation (18-14) for x using Equation (18-13) and simplify, we get

$$tc_1 + \frac{(1 - t)c_2}{1 + r} = 1, \tag{18-15}$$

and Equation (18-15) is like a lifetime budget constraint for the bank that governs how the deposit contract (c_1, c_2) can be set. We can rewrite the bank's lifetime budget constraint in slope-intercept form as

$$c_2 = -\frac{t(1 + r)}{1 - t}c_1 + \frac{1 + r}{1 - t}, \tag{18-16}$$

and the bank's lifetime budget constraint is depicted in Figure 18.7; in the figure, points A, B, and D lie on the constraint. The constraint has a vertical intercept of $\frac{1 + r}{1 - t}$, which is the maximum payout to late consumers if the bank does not interrupt any of its production, and the horizontal intercept is $\frac{1}{t}$, which is the maximum amount that could be withdrawn by early consumers in the case where all production is interrupted by the bank. The slope of the bank's lifetime budget constraint is $\frac{-t(1 + r)}{1 - t}$. The equilibrium deposit contract offered by the bank is at point A in Figure 18.7, where an indifference curve for the consumer is tangent to the bank's lifetime budget constraint. The equilibrium deposit contract has two important properties, which are:

1. The equilibrium deposit contract, at point A in Figure 18.7, lies to the northwest of point B, which is the point on the bank's lifetime budget constraint where the bank's payouts to early and late consumers are the same. We know from above that at point B the marginal rate of substitution of early consumption for late consumption is $\frac{-t}{1 - t}$, and so an indifference curve running through point B is less steep than the lifetime budget constraint of the bank. Therefore, A must lie to the northwest of B in the figure. The importance of this observation is that late consumers consume more than early consumers, given the equilibrium deposit contract; that is $c_2 > c_1$. Thus, if all other late consumers do not withdraw, any individual late consumer prefers not to withdraw in period 1. A late consumer is not tempted to pose as an early consumer if other late consumers do not do this.

2. The equilibrium deposit contract, at point A in Figure 18.7, lies to the southeast of point D, which is what the consumer would choose in the absence of the

Figure 18.7 The Equilibrium Deposit Contract Offered by the Diamond–Dybvig Bank

Point A, where there is a tangency between the bank's lifetime budget constraint and the consumer's indifference curve, is the equilibrium deposit contract. Point B would have equal consumption for early and late consumers, and point D is what the consumer could achieve in the absence of the bank.

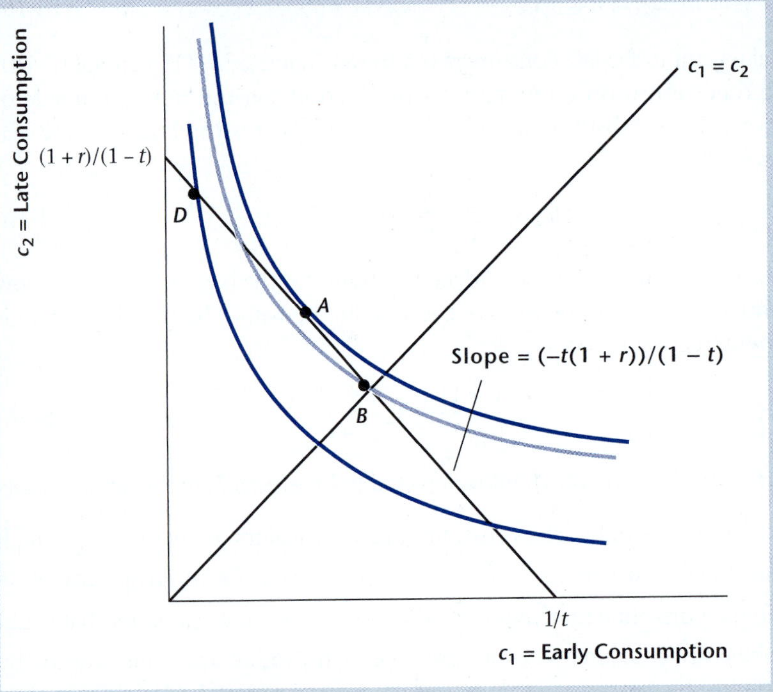

bank. By substituting in the bank's lifetime budget constraint, Equation (18-15), the deposit contract $(1, 1 + r)$ (point D in the figure) satisfies this constraint, so that the consumption profile chosen by the consumer in the absence of the bank is a choice open to the bank as well. To guarantee that point D lies to the northwest of point A in the figure requires an extra assumption, essentially that there is enough curvature in the utility function depicted in Figure 18.5. Without getting into the technical details concerning why this makes sense, we simply assume here that D lies to the northwest of A in the figure. The reason this is important is that it guarantees that $c_1 > 1$ and $c_2 < 1 + r$, so that there is a sense in which the bank provides insurance against the event that the consumer needs liquidity in period 1 to make a transaction (to consume). By accepting the banking contract, the consumer is able to consume more in period 1 than he or she could otherwise, at the expense of lower consumption in period 2.

The Diamond–Dybvig bank has some of the properties of financial intermediaries that we mentioned above. While it does not lend but instead holds assets directly, and it does not process information, the bank in this model borrows from a large number of depositors (it is well diversified), and it carries out an asset transformation. The fact that the bank is well diversified is important for its role in transforming assets. That is, because the bank holds the deposits of a large number of depositors, the number of depositors who wish to withdraw is predictable, and so the bank need only interrupt that fraction of production required to satisfy the withdrawal needs of the early consumers. The bank holds illiquid assets and is able to convert these assets into liquid deposits, providing depositors with a type of insurance against the need for liquid assets.

Bank Runs in the Diamond–Dybvig Model The fact that the Diamond–Dybvig bank supplies consumers with insurance against the need for liquidity also leaves the bank open to bank runs. Given the banking contract at point A in Figure 18.7, where $c_1 > 1$ and $c_2 < 1 + r$, there is a *good equilibrium* where each early consumer lines up at the bank to withdraw their deposit in period 1, each late consumer waits to withdraw until period 2, and everyone is happy. Given these circumstances, no late consumer has the incentive to withdraw in period 1, as $c_1 < c_2$ at point A in Figure 18.7, so withdrawing early would only make a late consumer worse off. However, suppose that a late consumer believes that all other late consumers will go to the bank to withdraw in period 1. Because all early consumers withdraw in period 1, the individual late consumer then believes that everyone else will go to the bank in period 1. Because $c_1 > 1$ at point A in Figure 18.7, even if the bank liquidates all of its assets in period 1, which yields the quantity N in consumption goods, it cannot satisfy total withdrawal demand, which is $(N - 1)c_1$ (recall that N is large, so that $(N - 1)c_1 > N$ at point A in the figure). Thus, the individual late consumer is faced with two choices. He or she can run to the bank and hope to get a place close to the front of the line, in which case he or she gets c_1, while risking the chance of being too close to the rear of the line, in which case he or she gets nothing. If he or she chooses to wait until period 2 to withdraw, there will definitely be nothing left. Therefore, the choice is clear; if a late consumer anticipates in period 1 that everyone else will run to the bank to withdraw their deposit, he or she will want to do it as well. Thus, there is a *bad equilibrium*, which is a **bank run**. Everyone runs to the bank in period 1; some consume c_1, but others consume nothing. This outcome is no better for some consumers (the early consumers who manage to get to the bank before it runs out of funds) and is worse for everyone else than the good equilibrium.

The Diamond–Dybvig model, thus, has multiple equilibria, much like the Keynesian coordination failure model we studied in Chapter 13. Multiple equilibria are used here to explain why bank runs have occurred historically. In the United States, before the establishment of the Federal Reserve System in 1914, there were recurring **banking panics** during the **National Banking Era** (1863–1913). During these panic episodes, which were typically triggered by the failure of a large financial institution or institutions, there were large deposit withdrawals from banks that sometimes appeared to be contagious. As well, widespread bank runs occurred during the Great Depression in the United States. The Diamond–Dybvig model provides an explanation for why an otherwise sound bank could experience a bank run and fail. According to the logic of the model, because a bank provides a liquidity transformation service to consumers, this leaves it open to bank runs. Because bank deposits are liquid, if all depositors show up at the bank in the anticipation that the bank will fail, then their expectations are self-fulfilling, and the bank will indeed fail.

Deposit Insurance

LO 18.7 Explain the role of deposit insurance, and discuss the too-big-to-fail problem.

A potential solution to the problem of bank runs is government-provided deposit insurance. In the Diamond–Dybvig model, if the government steps in and guarantees each depositor that they will receive the quantity c_2 given by the banking contract at point A in Figure 18.7, then no late consumer would have a reason to run to the bank. This leaves aside the question of who the government will tax if it has to make good on its deposit insurance guarantees. However, in the model the bad equilibrium will never occur with deposit insurance in place, so the government will never have to make any payouts related to its insurance program. The model tells us that promises by the government can serve to prevent a bad outcome.

In the United States, deposits in depository institutions are insured up to $250,000 by the Federal Deposit Insurance Corporation (FDIC). This means that, if a depository institution fails, the depositors are guaranteed that they will receive the value of their deposits up to $250,000. The FDIC was established in 1934, mainly in response to the failure of about one-third of all depository institutions during the Great Depression.

The main cost of deposit insurance is that it creates a **moral hazard** problem, and this problem is something that is not taken into account in the Diamond–Dybvig banking model. Moral hazard arises in essentially all insurance situations, because the insured individual tends to take less care in preventing the event against which he or she is insured. For example, if the owner of a car is completely insured against damages to his or her car, he or she takes less care in driving in parking lots, and, therefore, is more likely to have an accident. It is difficult for the insurance company to correct for this problem, because the amount of care taken by the driver of the car is hard to observe. Moral hazard can explain the existence of deductibles in insurance contracts, which require the insured party to bear the cost of small losses.

For a depository institution, moral hazard arises because deposit insurance encourages the depository institution to take on more risk. This happens because the riskiness of a bank's assets is difficult to observe and because with deposit insurance the depositors have no interest in whether the depository institution is risky or not. Therefore, though deposit insurance can prevent the failures of sound depository institutions that might occur because of self-fulfilling panics, it could produce more failures because of the increased riskiness of banks. Thus, the existence of deposit insurance requires that the regulators of depository institutions impose restrictions on depository institution activities to assure that these institutions do not take on too much risk.

Another element of moral hazard in the U.S. monetary system results from the **too-big-to-fail doctrine**. This represents the belief that the regulators of the U.S. financial system would not tolerate losses by depositors at any large depository institution in the country, because of the fear that such losses would lead to widespread financial panic. Given that large banks know that all or most of the holders of their liabilities are implicitly insured against loss, these large banks have an even greater incentive than small banks to take on too much risk.

MACROECONOMICS IN ACTION

Banks, Nonbank Financial Intermediaries, Too-Big-to-Fail, and Moral Hazard

The United States has a colorful history of financial crises and governmental responses to those crises. The repeated banking panic episodes of the National Banking Era, following the Civil War, resulted in the Federal Reserve Act (1913), and the establishment of the Federal Reserve System in 1914. The failure of about one-third of U.S. banks during the Great Depression led to the legislation that introduced deposit insurance and the separation of banking and stock market activity in the United States. In the late 1980s, the savings and loan crisis (the failure of many savings and loan depository institutions due to excessive risk-taking) led to reforms of deposit insurance and bank regulation. These are only some examples of an at-times chaotic U.S. financial and banking history.

The intervention by the U.S. Treasury and the Fed in the financial system beginning in the fall of 2008 was unprecedented in scale. The two key interventions were (i) the Emergency Economic Stabilization Act of 2008 (EESA) and (ii) a very large increase in the monetary base by the Fed. The ESSA gave the Treasury considerable discretion to allocate up to $700 billion through the Troubled Asset Relief Program (TARP). Ultimately, intervention through this program amounted to an injection of funds to banks and other financial intermediaries in exchange for federal government equity participation in those financial institutions. The increase in the monetary base by the Fed was used to purchase large quantities of assets not typically found on the Fed's balance sheet, including loans to nonbank financial intermediaries and mortgage-backed securities.

What was the nature of the financial crisis that the U.S. Treasury and the Fed were responding to, and what were its causes? The crisis had the following elements:

1. In most countries of the world where organized mortgage lending exists, mortgage loans are made by banks that hold and service the loans until they mature. The mortgage market in the United States is unusual. Currently, most mortgages in the United States are originated by brokers who negotiate the terms of the loan with the borrower, and who then sell the loan to another financial institution. This institution could be a government agency, such as FNMA or FHLMC ("Fannie Mae," the Federal National Mortgage Association and "Freddie Mac," the Federal Home Loan Mortgage Corporation, respectively), which finances purchases of mortgages by issuing debt, or a private financial intermediary that repackages these mortgages as *mortgage-backed securities*. A mortgage-backed security is an asset that is a claim to the payoffs (or some part of the payoffs) on an underlying portfolio of mortgages. Mortgage-backed securities are tradeable on financial markets. With financial innovation, mainly after 2000, mortgage originators began lending to increasingly risky borrowers in the so-called *subprime mortgage market*. The financial institutions that purchased these mortgages and repackaged them as mortgage-backed securities, and the rating agencies that certified

(Continued)

the quality of the mortgage-backed securities, seemed assured that the underlying mortgages were sound, or at least that their payoffs were very predictable, given the diversification involved. However, the prices of houses began to fall widely across the United States in 2006, and this led to a large increase in the default rates on subprime mortgages. These mortgages appeared not to be so sound after all, and it became clear that there were severe incentive problems in the mortgage market—mortgage brokers were doing a poor job of screening borrowers, as they would be well paid for their work whether the mortgages ultimately paid off or not, and someone else would be left holding the bag.

2. Some investment banks and *shadow banks* that were heavy investors in mortgage-backed securities were carrying on activities that looked much like conventional banking. These investment banks would purchase mortgage-backed securities, and finance these purchases through a sequence of short-term *repurchase agreements*, which are short-term collateralized loans. In these repurchase agreements, it was the mortgage-backed securities themselves that served as collateral for the loans. This type of financial intermediation looks somewhat like what a bank does, as the assets on the investment banks' balance sheets were long-maturity, while the liabilities were short-maturity. A difference from a conventional bank is that mortgage-backed securities are by nature liquid—they can be sold at any time on organized markets. However, the assets held by a traditional bank are illiquid.

3. An important recent financial innovation was the *credit default swap*, which is essentially insurance on a debt contract. Suppose for example that Lehman Brothers (a now-defunct investment bank) issued debt in order to purchase mortgage-backed securities. Someone, say the holder of this debt, could purchase a credit default swap at some price from American International Group (an insurance company), for example. If Lehman Brothers were to default on its debt, then American International Group would guarantee the specified payoffs on the debt for the debtholder who had purchased the credit default swap. Holding the credit default swap in conjunction with the underlying debt essentially insures the debtholder against the event that the debt issuer defaults. However, someone could purchase a credit default swap and not hold the underlying debt, and thus be taking a bet on whether the debt issuer would default.

4. Once it became clear (for most investors, mainly in 2008) that the ultimate payoffs on subprime mortgages were not going to be as high as expected, the mortgage-backed securities that represented packages of these mortgages fell in price. Investment banks such as Bear Stearns and Lehman Brothers found it increasingly difficult to borrow short term to finance their holdings of mortgage-backed securities, hence there was pressure to sell these securities. This further reduced the market prices of mortgage-backed securities, and ultimately led to the failure of Lehman Brothers in the fall of 2008. Once Lehman Brothers failed, financial market participants learned that American

International Group (AIG) was the issuer of a large quantity of credit default swaps that would have to be paid out. At this point, there was the potential that AIG could fail, along with some other large financial institutions, including investment banks and the largest U.S. banks, principally Citigroup and Bank of America. It was in this context that the U.S. Treasury and the Fed intervened in such a massive way.

What was the rationale for this dramatic policy intervention, and what were the alternatives? It will be useful to frame the arguments in terms of (i) *the interventionist view* and (ii) *the laissez-faire view.*

The interventionist view is perhaps best summarized in then-Fed Chairman Ben Bernanke's speech at the August 2009 Policy Conference at Jackson Hole, Wyoming.[15] Bernanke argued that the financial intervention by the Treasury and the Fed was essentially staving off a repeat of the Great Depression. According to Bernanke, there were elements of the financial crisis that looked much like a Diamond–Dybvig bank run, though in this case a run on nonbank financial institutions that were not protected by deposit insurance. Indeed, the liabilities of these institutions were not deposits, but typically short-term repurchase agreements. However, the argument is that the flight of lenders from short-term lending was much like a bank run or classic liquidity crisis. At risk, according to Bernanke, was the whole financial sector, through interrelationships of borrowing, lending, and elaborate financial arrangements that were difficult for anyone to understand in full. Should one large financial institution fail, the others would soon follow, according to the interventionist view. The correct response to the problem, in the Fed's view was (i) to intervene in conventional ways through

open market operations, reducing the fed funds rate essentially to zero; (ii) to lend generously by way of the Fed's discount window, not only to banks, but to other financial institutions as well; and (iii) to have the Fed act essentially as a mortgage banker, issuing outside money and holding mortgage-backed securities.

The other piece of financial intervention, the TARP funds authorized through the ESSA, was another means to prevent the failure of large financial institutions. By "recapitalizing" banks and other financial institutions with government funds, it was thought that banks would begin lending more (lending in credit markets tightened dramatically in mid-to late 2008), and the failure of these large financial institutions would be forestalled.

The laissez-faire view is that the Fed and the Treasury overdid their intervention—a view held not only outside policy circles, but also by some dissenters within the Federal Reserve System in particular. In the laissez-faire view, some intervention in response to the crisis may have been called for, but the Fed should have restricted its activities to conventional types of central bank intervention—lending exclusively to banks, and open market operations in short-term government securities. According to this view, activities such as the purchase of mortgage-backed securities by the Fed are at best ineffective and at worst misallocate credit in the economy. Laissez-faire economists would argue that large financial institutions should be allowed to fail. If not, serious moral hazard problems set in—these institutions come to expect that they can take on large amounts of risk, reap the benefits when times are good, and let taxpayers make up the difference when times are bad. Indeed, one could view the whole financial crisis as stemming from the too-big-to-fail doctrine. Large financial institutions engaged in some very risky activities knowing that, in the seemingly unlikely event that house prices should fall, setting off a chain reaction of defaults on credit arrangements, the government would intervene and bail out the losers. These

---

[15]See http://www.federalreserve.gov/newsevents/speech/bernanke20090821a.htm.

(Continued)

large institutions were then ultimately correct in their assumptions about how the federal government and the Fed would behave.

Which view is correct, the interventionist view, or the laissez-faire view? It is impossible to know for sure, without re-running history in the absence of the massive policy interventions. Ben Bernanke insists that his astute intervention prevented a second Great Depression. But others argue that, if financial intervention had been more modest, and large financial institutions had been permitted to fail, the 2008–2009 recession may have been somewhat more severe, but the potentially larger long-term costs of the too-big-to-fail doctrine and ensuing moral hazard problems could have been avoided.

MACROECONOMICS IN ACTION

Bank Failures and Banking Panics in the United States and Canada

Canada and the United States are in many ways economically similar, but they have very different banking systems.[16] The two countries have also had very different historical experiences with banking panics and bank failures, and this represents a challenge to the Diamond–Dybvig banking model.

While the United States has a unit banking system, with thousands of small banks that typically serve small geographical areas, along with a few large banks, Canada has a branch banking system, with only a handful of commercial banks that branch nationally. On the one hand, the United States has had a network of regulations designed to keep banks small, and it is relatively

easy to open a new bank. On the other hand, in Canada banks are typically not prevented from becoming large, and it requires federal legislation for a bank to obtain a charter and open for business.

United States banking history has many episodes of widespread bank failures and banking panics, as we have discussed. There were recurrent banking panics during the National Banking Era in the United States, from 1863 to 1913. The Federal Reserve System, established in 1914, was supposed to correct the institutional problems that caused banking panics, but missteps in monetary policy in the Great Depression contributed to a situation in which about one-third of U.S. banks failed between 1929 and 1933.

Before the establishment of the Canadian central bank, the Bank of Canada, in 1935, there were no banking panics of note in Canada. Canada was a latecomer to deposit insurance, introducing it in 1967, but in spite of this there were few bank failures before that time. No commercial banks failed in the Great Depression in Canada, and the most recent bank failure before

---

[16] The material here relies heavily on S. Williamson, 1989. "Restrictions on Financial Intermediaries and Implications for Aggregate Fluctuations: Canada and the United States, 1870–1913," in O. Blanchard and S. Fischer, eds., *NBER Macroeconomics Annual 1989*, Cambridge, MA: NBER; and B. Champ, B. Smith, and S. Williamson, 1996. "Currency Elasticity and Banking Panics: Theory and Evidence," *Canadian Journal of Economics* 29, 828–864.

1985 was the failure of the Home Bank in 1923. The most recent commercial bank failures were those of the Northland Bank and the Canadian Commercial Bank in 1985. From January to August 2009, about 80 banks failed in the United States, while there were zero failures in Canada.

Why have the experiences with bank failures and panics been so different in Canada and the United States? This seems hard to explain using the Diamond–Dybvig banking model, where bank runs arise simply because banks are performing a useful intermediation service; in this sense U.S. banks and Canadian banks are no different. The evidence points to two factors (not included in the Diamond–Dybvig banking model) that appear to be important in explaining these differences between the United States and Canada. First, in the period before 1935, much of the circulating currency in Canada was issued by commercial banks (see the discussion earlier in this chapter). This private currency was viewed by the public as being quite safe. At times of the year when the demand for currency was particularly high (typically during the fall harvest) relative to bank deposits, it was easy for the chartered banks to convert deposit liabilities into notes in circulation by printing more notes to issue when depositors chose to withdraw. In periods of high demand for currency in the United States between 1863 and 1913, a panic could result, but this was averted in Canada because of the note-issuing ability of Canadian commercial banks. Bank failures are also averted in Canada by the fact that Canadian banks are relatively large and well diversified geographically. One of the reasons for the failures of the Northland Bank and Canadian Commercial Bank in 1985 was that these banks did most of their lending in one western province of Canada, which exposed them to the risks associated with local shocks. In this case the local shock was a sharp drop in the prices of oil and natural gas that caused a reduction in local asset prices, resulting in borrowers at these banks defaulting on their loans. Small U.S. banks, which are typically not well diversified geographically, are exposed to the same kind of risk and, thus, are more likely to fail than a well-diversified Canadian branch bank.

One might think that the negative effects of the too-big-to-fail doctrine would be in evidence in Canada, with its large banks, but there appears to be no history in Canada of the government or the central bank propping up ailing banks. Indeed, Canada's banking system is viewed as one of the world's safest. Why is this so? In Canada, banks are regulated differently. First, Canada does not have the confusing, conflicting, and overlapping regulatory structure involving several different financial regulators that the United States does. Second, Canadian banks are in some ways more tightly regulated (though they have more flexibility in terms of how they offer financial services). In particular, entry into the banking system is more difficult in Canada, and banks are required to hold higher levels of capital in Canada than in the United States. Canadian regulations, while they reduce competition among Canadian banks, give these banks a larger cushion against losses, and make them fundamentally sounder.

Chapter Summary

- Money functions as a medium of exchange, a store of value, and a unit of account. Historically, the objects that have played the role of money are commodity money, circulating private bank notes, commodity-backed paper currency, fiat money, and transactions deposits at private banks.

- We considered a simple model capturing the absence-of-double-coincidence-of-wants problem that can exist in barter economies where people only have goods to trade. In the model,

commodity money or fiat money can overcome the double-coincidence problem by providing a universally acceptable medium of exchange.

- A modified, cash-in-advance version of the monetary intertemporal model from Chapter 12 was used to study the effects of long-run inflation. A higher money growth rate causes an increase in the rate of inflation, an increase in the nominal interest rate, and decreases in output, consumption, and employment.

- A positive nominal interest rate represents a distortion that drives a wedge between the marginal rate of substitution of leisure for consumption and the marginal rate of transformation of leisure for consumption.

- An optimal long-run monetary policy in the monetary intertemporal model is for the central bank to follow a Friedman rule, whereby the money growth rate and the inflation rate are equal to minus the real interest rate. This implies that the nominal interest rate is zero at the optimum.

- In the Diamond–Dybvig banking model, a bank provides its depositors with insurance against the event that they need liquid assets to make transactions. The bank converts illiquid assets into liquid deposits.

- In the Diamond–Dybvig model, there is a good equilibrium where all early consumers withdraw their deposits from the bank early and all late consumers withdraw late. There is also a bad equilibrium (a bank run) where all consumers choose to withdraw early, and the bank fails. The bank run equilibrium can be prevented through government-provided deposit insurance.

- There is a moral hazard problem associated with deposit insurance, in that an unregulated bank with insured deposits takes on too much risk. According to the too-big-to-fail doctrine, the implicit insurance of the deposits and other liabilities of large banks makes these banks especially prone to the moral hazard problem.

Key Terms

Friedman rule An optimal rule for monetary policy, whereby the money supply grows at a rate that implies a zero nominal interest rate. (p. 627)

Financial intermediary Any financial institution that borrows from one large group of people and lends to another large group of people, transforms assets in some way, and processes information. (p. 627)

Free Banking Era The period 1837–1863 in the United States characterized by the issuance of currency by many private banks. (p. 628)

Gold standard An arrangement whereby a country stands ready to exchange its money for gold at a fixed price. (p. 629)

Fedwire A payments system operated by the Federal Reserve System through which transactions between financial institutions are cleared. (p. 629)

Absence of double coincidence of wants Situation in which there are two would-be trading partners, but it is not true that each has the good the other wants. (p. 631)

Cash-in-advance A type of macroeconomic model in which it is assumed that money balances on hand are required to buy some class of goods. (p. 635)

Superneutral Describes money in the situation where a change in the money supply growth rate has no real effects. (p. 639)

Deflation Decrease in the price level over time. (p. 640)

Hyperinflations Situations where the inflation rate is extremely high. (p. 643)

Nondiversifiable risk Risk that an individual cannot diversify away by holding a large portfolio of assets. (p. 645)

Risk-averse Describes an individual who does not like risk. (p. 645)

Marginal utility of consumption The slope of the utility function, or the marginal increase in utility (happiness) resulting from a one-unit increase in consumption. (p. 648)

Bank run A situation where a bank's depositors panic and simultaneously attempt to withdraw their deposits. (p. 653)

Banking panics Situations where bank runs are widespread. (p. 653)

National Banking Era The period in the United States between 1863 and 1913. (p. 653)

Moral hazard The tendency of insured individuals to take less care to prevent a loss against which they are insured. (p. 654)

Too-big-to-fail doctrine The doctrine according to which U.S. regulatory agencies should intervene to prevent the failure of any large financial institution. (p. 654)

Questions for Review

18.1 What are five forms that money has taken historically?

18.2 What do Yap stones and the playing card money of New France have in common? What is different about these two forms of money?

18.3 How does an absence of double coincidence of wants make money socially useful?

18.4 What are the effects of an increase in the money supply growth rate in the monetary intertemporal model?

18.5 What are the costs of anticipated inflation?

18.6 Should the monetary authority manipulate the money supply to hold the price level constant over time?

18.7 Why don't real-world central banks want to follow the Friedman rule?

18.8 List four properties of assets, and explain why these properties are important.

18.9 What are the four defining characteristics of a financial intermediary?

18.10 What are three types of financial intermediaries?

18.11 What is unusual about depository institutions relative to other financial intermediaries?

18.12 In the Diamond–Dybvig banking model, why does a consumer do better by depositing in a bank rather than investing on his or her own?

18.13 What features of real-world banks does a Diamond–Dybvig bank have?

18.14 Why are there two equilibria in the Diamond–Dybvig banking model? How do the two equilibria compare?

18.15 How can bank runs be prevented?

18.16 Explain what moral hazard is and why and how deposit insurance and the too-big-to-fail doctrine induce a moral hazard problem.

Problems

1. **LO 2** Consider the absence-of-double-coincidence economy depicted in Figure 18.1. Determine who would trade what with whom if good 2 were used as a commodity money. Explain your results.

2. **LO 2** As an alternative to the economy depicted in Figure 18.1, suppose that there are three types of people, but now the person who consumes good 1 produces good 3, the person who consumes good 2 produces good 1, and the person who consumes good 3 produces good 2.

    (a) Determine who trades what with whom if good 1 is used as a commodity money, and

    compare this with what happens when good 1 is used as a commodity money in the economy in Figure 18.1. Explain.

    (b) Determine who trades what with whom if fiat money is used in exchange, and commodity money is not used. Explain.

3. **LO 3** In the monetary intertemporal model, suppose the central bank issues money in exchange for capital, and rents this capital out to firms each period, thus earning the market real interest rate r on the capital. Over time, as the central bank earns interest on its capital holdings, it uses these

returns to retire money from the private economy. What are the long-run effects? Is the outcome economically efficient? Explain your results.

4. **LO 3** Suppose, in the monetary intertemporal model, that the government can pay interest on money, financing this interest with lump-sum taxes on consumers. If the nominal interest rate on money is the same as the nominal interest rate on bonds, determine the effects in the model, illustrating this in a diagram. Explain your results.

5. **LO 4** Suppose that consumers are concerned about theft, and so they are willing to use banks for some of their transactions even if the nominal interest rate is zero. Further, suppose that, the more currency consumers hold, the more people are encouraged to steal, as theft is now more profitable. How would the Friedman rule for monetary policy be altered under these circumstances?

6. **LO 4** Suppose that there are shocks to total factor productivity that cause aggregate output to fluctuate. What does this imply for the Friedman rule; that is, how should the central bank conduct monetary policy optimally? Discuss.

7. **LO 4** How would we modify the Friedman rule in the context of a New Keynesian sticky price model like the one in Chapter 14, assuming that monetary policy is the only policy that can be used to close output gaps? Explain.

8. **LO 5** Consider the following assets: (i) a work of art; (ii) a United States Treasury bill; (iii) a share in Microsoft; (iv) a loan to a close relative; (v) a loan to General Motors. For each asset, answer the following questions:
   (a) Does the asset have a high rate of return or a low rate of return (on average)?
   (b) Is the asset high risk or low risk?
   (c) Is the asset a long-maturity asset or a short-maturity asset?
   (d) Is the asset highly liquid, less liquid, somewhat illiquid, or highly illiquid?
   (e) Explain why the asset has the above four properties.
   (f) Which of the properties of money (medium of exchange, store of value, unit of account) does the asset have? Would we consider it money and why or why not?

9. **LO 6** In the Diamond–Dybvig banking model, suppose that the banking contract includes a suspension of convertibility provision according to which the bank allows only the first tN depositors in line in period 1 to withdraw their deposits. Will there still be a bank run equilibrium? Carefully explain why or why not.

10. **LO 6** In the Diamond-Dybvig banking model, suppose that, instead of a bank, consumers can trade shares in the production technology. That is, each consumer invests in the production technology in period 0. Then, if the consumer learns that he or she is an early consumer in period 1, he or she can either interrupt the technology or can sell their investment at a price p. A consumer who learns that he or she is a later consumer in period 1 can purchase shares in investment projects at a price p, and can interrupt his or her production technology in order to acquire the goods required to buy shares.
   (a) Determine what p is in equilibrium, and what each consumer's quantity of early and late consumption is, in a diagram like Figure 18.7.
   (b) Do consumers do better or worse than they would with a banking system? Do they do better than they would with no banks and with no trading in shares?
   (c) Explain your results.

11. **LO 6** Alter the Diamond–Dybvig model in the following way. Suppose that there are two assets, an illiquid asset that returns $1 + r$ units of consumption goods in period 2 for each unit invested in period 0, and a liquid asset that returns one unit of consumption goods in period 1 for each unit invested in period 0. The illiquid asset production technology cannot be interrupted in period 1. The model is otherwise the same as outlined in this chapter.
   (a) Determine a consumer's lifetime budget constraint when there is no bank, show this in a diagram, and determine the consumer's optimal consumption when an early consumer and when a late consumer in the diagram.
   (b) Determine a bank's lifetime budget constraint, show this in your diagram, and determine the optimal deposit contract for the bank in the

diagram. Are consumers who deposit in the bank better off than in part (a)? Explain why or why not.

(c) Is there a bank run equilibrium? Explain why or why not.

12. **LO 7** Explain how moral hazard arises in each of the following situations:

(a) A mother promises her daughter that she will help her with her homework during the coming school year but only if the daughter has difficulty with her homework.

(b) An individual's house is insured against damage by fire for its full value.

(c) An individual is appointed to manage an investment portfolio for a group of coworkers.

(d) The same individual in part (c) is appointed to manage the investment portfolio, and the government guarantees that all investors in the group will receive a 5% return per year. That is, the government will make up the difference if the return on the portfolio falls below 5% in a given year.

Working with the Data

Answer these questions using the Federal Reserve Bank of St. Louis's FRED database, accessible at http://research.stlouisfed.org/fred2/

1. Answer the following questions:
   (a) Plot the quarterly percentage increases in the consumer price index and in M1.
   (b) Calculate percentage increases in the consumer price index and in M1 for annual data. How does this chart compare to the one you constructed in part (a)? Explain.

2. Plot the three-month Treasury bill interest rate, the interest rate on a 10-year Treasury note, and the interest rate on a 3-month certificate of deposit. What do you observe? How do the properties of assets explain the regularities in this interest rate data?

3. Plot the 3-month Treasury bill interest rate and the rate of inflation over the previous year in a time series plot. To what extent does the nominal interest rate reflect the actual inflation rate? Is this consistent with the predictions of the monetary intertemporal model in this chapter? Explain.

Appendix

Mathematical Appendix

This appendix provides more formal treatments of some of the models in the book, and it is intended for students with a knowledge of calculus and more advanced algebraic techniques who wish to study some of the topics of this book in more depth. The appendix assumes an understanding of mathematical methods in economics at the level of Alpha C. Chiang and Kevin Wainwright's *Fundamental Methods of Mathematical Economics,* McGraw Hill/Irwin, New York, 2004. We proceed by working through results for selected models from selected chapters.

Chapter 4 Consumer and Firm Behavior

Chapter 4 dealt with the representative consumer's and representative firm's optimization problems in the closed-economy one-period model. We set up the consumer's and firm's problems and derive the main results of Chapter 4 formally.

The Representative Consumer

The representative consumer's preferences are defined by the utility function $U(C, l)$, where C is consumption and l is leisure, with $U(\cdot, \cdot)$ a function that is increasing in both arguments, strictly quasiconcave, and twice differentiable. These properties of the utility function imply that indifference curves are downward-sloping and convex and that the consumer strictly prefers more to less. The consumer's optimization problem is to choose C and l so as to maximize $U(C, l)$ subject to his or her budget constraint—that is,

$$\max_{C, l} U(C, l)$$

subject to

$$C = w(h - l) + \pi - T,$$

and $C \geq 0$, $0 \leq l \leq h$, where w is the real wage, h is the quantity of time the consumer has available, π is dividend income, and T is the lump-sum tax. This problem is a constrained optimization problem, with the associated Lagrangian

$$L = U(C, l) + \lambda[w(h - l) + \pi - T - C],$$

where λ is the Lagrange multiplier.

We assume that there is an interior solution to the consumer's problem where $C > 0$ and $0 < l < h$. This can be guaranteed by assuming that $U_1(0, l) = \infty$ (i.e., the derivative of the utility function with respect to the first argument goes to infinity in the limit as consumption goes to zero) and $U_2(C, 0) = \infty$. These assumptions imply that $C > 0$ and $l > 0$ at the optimum. In a competitive equilibrium, we cannot have $l = h$, as this would imply that nothing would be produced and $C = 0$. Given an interior solution to the consumer's problem, we can characterize the solution by the first-order conditions from the problem of choosing C, l, and λ to maximize L. These first-order conditions are (differentiating L with respect to C, l, and λ, respectively, and setting each of these first derivatives equal to zero)

$$U_1(C, l) - \lambda = 0, \tag{A-1}$$

$$U_2(C, l) - \lambda w = 0, \tag{A-2}$$

$$w(h - l) + \pi - T - C = 0. \tag{A-3}$$

In Equations (A-1) and (A-2), $U_i(C, l)$ denotes the first derivative with respect to the ith argument of $U(\cdot, \cdot)$, evaluated at (C, l). From Equations (A-1) and (A-2), we can obtain the condition

$$\frac{U_2(C, l)}{U_1(C, l)} = w, \tag{A-4}$$

which is the optimization condition for the consumer that we showed graphically in Chapter 4, Figure 4.5. Equation (A-4) states that the marginal rate of substitution of leisure for consumption (on the left side of the equation) is equal to the real wage (on the right side) at the optimum. For our purposes, we can rewrite Equation (A-4) as

$$U_2(C, l) - wU_1(C, l) = 0, \tag{A-5}$$

and then (A-3) and (A-5) are two equations determining the optimal choices of C and l given w, π, and T.

In general, we cannot obtain explicit closed-form solutions for C and l from Equations (A-3) and (A-5) without assuming an explicit form for the utility function $U(\cdot, \cdot)$, but we can use comparative statics techniques to determine how C and l change when any of w, π, or T changes. To do this, we totally differentiate (A-3) and (A-5), obtaining

$$-dC - wdl + (h - l)dw + d\pi - dT = 0, \tag{A-6}$$

$$[U_{12} - wU_{11}]dC + [U_{22} - wU_{12}]dl - U_1dw = 0. \tag{A-7}$$

In Equation (A-7), U_{ij} denotes the second derivative with respect to the ith and j^{th} arguments of $U(\cdot, \cdot)$. Now, it is useful to write (A-6) and (A-7) in matrix form, as

$$\begin{bmatrix} -1 & -w \\ U_{12} - wU_{11} & U_{22} - wU_{12} \end{bmatrix} \begin{bmatrix} dC \\ dl \end{bmatrix} = \begin{bmatrix} -(h - l)dw - d\pi + dT \\ U_1 dw \end{bmatrix}. \qquad \text{(A-8)}$$

Then, we can solve for the derivatives of interest by using Cramer's rule.

First, consider the effects of a change in dividend income π. Using Cramer's rule, from Equation (A-8) we get

$$\frac{dC}{d\pi} = \frac{-U_{22} + wU_{12}}{\nabla}, \qquad \text{(A-9)}$$

$$\frac{dl}{d\pi} = \frac{U_{12} - wU_{11}}{\nabla}, \qquad \text{(A-10)}$$

where

$$\nabla = -U_{22} + 2wU_{12} - w^2 U_{11}.$$

Now, ∇ is the determinant of the bordered Hessian associated with the constrained optimization problem for the consumer, and the quasi-concavity of the utility function implies that $\nabla > 0$. This, however, does not allow us to sign the derivatives in (A-9) and (A-10). Our assumption from Chapter 4 that consumption and leisure are normal goods is equivalent to the conditions $-U_{22} + wU_{12} > 0$ and $U_{12} - wU_{11} > 0$. Thus, given normal goods, we have $\frac{dC}{d\pi} > 0$ and $\frac{dl}{d\pi} > 0$, so that the quantities of consumption and leisure chosen by the consumer increase when dividend income increases. It is straightforward to show that $\frac{dC}{dT} = -\frac{dC}{d\pi}$ and $\frac{dl}{dT} = -\frac{dl}{d\pi}$, so that the effects of a decrease in taxes are equivalent to the effects of an increase in dividend income.

Next, we can derive the effects of a change in the real wage, again using Cramer's rule to obtain, from Equation (A-8),

$$\frac{dC}{dw} = \frac{wU_1 + (h - l)(-U_{22} + wU_{12})}{\nabla}, \qquad \text{(A-11)}$$

$$\frac{dl}{dw} = \frac{-U_1 + (h - l)(U_{12} - wU_{11})}{\nabla}. \qquad \text{(A-12)}$$

Now, assuming that consumption is a normal good, we have $-U_{22} + wU_{12} > 0$, and because $\nabla > 0$ and $U_1 > 0$ (utility increases as consumption increases), we know from (A-11) that $\frac{dC}{dw} > 0$, so that consumption increases when the real wage increases. However, we cannot determine the sign of $\frac{dl}{dw}$ from (A-12) because of the opposing income and substitution effects of a change in the real wage on leisure. It is possible to separate algebraically the income and substitution effects in Equation (A-12) by determining the response of leisure to a change in the real wage, holding utility constant. This gives a substitution effect, which can be expressed as

$$\frac{dl}{dw}(subst) = \frac{-U_1}{\nabla} < 0,$$

so that the substitution effect is for leisure to fall and hours worked to rise when the real wage increases. This implies that, from (A-12), the income effect is

$$\frac{dl}{dw}(inc) = \frac{dl}{dw} - \frac{dl}{dw}(subst) = \frac{(h-l)(U_{12} - wU_{11})}{\nabla} > 0,$$

assuming that leisure is a normal good, which implies that $U_{12} - wU_{11} > 0$. Therefore, the income effect is for leisure to increase when the real wage increases. In general, without putting additional restrictions on the utility function, we do not know the sign of $\frac{dl}{dw}$.

The Representative Firm

We assumed in Chapter 4 that the production function for the representative firm is described by

$$Y = zF(K, N^d),$$

where Y is output, z is total factor productivity, $F(\cdot, \cdot)$ is a function, K is the capital stock, and N^d is the firm's labor input. The function $F(\cdot, \cdot)$ is assumed to be quasi-concave, strictly increasing in both arguments, homogeneous of degree one or constant-returns-to-scale, and twice differentiable. We also assume that $F_2(K, 0) = \infty$ and $F_2(K, \infty) = 0$ to guarantee that there is always an interior solution to the firm's profit-maximization problem, where $F_2(K, N^d)$ is the first derivative with respect to the second argument of the function $F(\cdot, \cdot)$. The firm's profit-maximization problem is to choose the labor input N^d so as to maximize

$$\pi = zF(K, N^d) - wN^d,$$

subject to $N^d \geq 0$, where π is the difference between revenue and labor costs in terms of consumption goods. That is, the firm solves

$$\max_{N^d}(zF(K, N^d) - wN^d). \tag{A-13}$$

The restrictions on the function $F(\cdot, \cdot)$ imply that there is a unique interior solution to problem (A-13), characterized by the first-order condition

$$zF_2(K, N^d) = w, \tag{A-14}$$

which states that the firm hires labor until the marginal product of labor $zF_2(K, N^d)$ equals the real wage w.

We can determine the effects of changes in w, z, and K on labor demand N^d through comparative statics techniques. Totally differentiating Equation (A-14), which determines N^d implicitly as a function of w, z, and K, we obtain

$$zF_{22}dN^d - dw + F_2dz + zF_{12}dK = 0.$$

Then, solving for the appropriate derivatives, we have

$$\frac{dN^d}{dw} = \frac{1}{zF_{22}} < 0,$$

$$\frac{dN^d}{dz} = \frac{-F_2}{zF_{22}} > 0,$$

$$\frac{dN^d}{dK} = \frac{-zF_{12}}{zF_{22}} > 0.$$

We can sign the above derivatives because $F_{22} < 0$ (the marginal product of labor decreases as the quantity of labor increases), $F_2 > 0$ (the marginal product of labor is positive), and $F_{12} > 0$ (the marginal product of labor increases as the capital input increases). These are restrictions on the production function discussed in Chapter 4. Because $\frac{dN^d}{dw} < 0$, the labor demand curve is downward sloping. Further, $\frac{dN^d}{dz} > 0$ and $\frac{dN^d}{dK} > 0$ imply that the labor demand curve shifts to the right when z or K increases.

Problems

1. Suppose that the consumer's preferences are given by the utility function $U(C, l) = \ln C + \alpha \ln l$, where $\alpha > 0$. Determine the consumer's choice of consumption and leisure and interpret your solutions.

2. In the consumer's choice problem, show that at least one good must be normal.

3. Suppose that the firm's production technology is given by $Y = zF(K, N) = zK^\alpha N^{1-\alpha}$, where $0 < \alpha < 1$. Determine the firm's demand for labor as a function of z, K, α, and w, and interpret.

4. Suppose that the firm's production technology is given by $Y = z \min(K, \alpha N)$, where $\alpha > 0$. As in Problem 3, determine the firm's demand for labor as a function of z, K, α, and w, and interpret.

Chapter 5 A Closed–Economy One-Period Macroeconomic Model

Here, we show formally the equivalence between the competitive equilibrium and the Pareto optimum in the one-period model and then determine, using comparative statics, the equilibrium effects of a change in government spending and in total factor productivity.

Competitive Equilibrium

In a competitive equilibrium, the representative consumer maximizes utility subject to his or her budget constraint, the representative firm maximizes profits, the government budget constraint holds, and the market on which labor is exchanged for consumption goods clears. From the previous section, the two equations describing consumer optimization are the budget constraint, Equation (A-3), or

$$w(h - l) + \pi - T - C = 0, \tag{A-15}$$

and Equation (A-5), or

$$U_2(C, l) - wU_1(C, l) = 0. \tag{A-16}$$

Optimization by the representative firm implies Equation (A-14), or

$$zF_2(K, N^d) = w, \tag{A-17}$$

and profits for the firm are

$$\pi = zF(K, N^d) - wN^d. \tag{A-18}$$

The government budget constraint states that government spending is equal to taxes; that is,

$$G = T. \tag{A-19}$$

Finally, the market-clearing condition is

$$h - l = N^d, \tag{A-20}$$

or the supply of labor is equal to the demand for labor. Equations (A-15) to (A-20) are six equations that solve for the six endogenous variables C, l, N^d, T, π, and w, given the exogenous variables z and G. To make this system of equations more manageable, we can simplify as follows. First, using Equations (A-18) to (A-20) to substitute for π, T, and N^d in Equation (A-15), we obtain

$$C = zF(K, h - l) - G. \tag{A-21}$$

Then, substituting in Equation (A-18) for N^d using Equation (A-20), and then in turn for w in Equation (A-16) using Equation (A-18), we obtain

$$U_2(C, l) - zF_2(K, h - l)U_1(C, l) = 0. \tag{A-22}$$

Equations (A-21) and (A-22) then solve for equilibrium C and l. Then, the real wage w can be determined from (A-17), after substituting for N^d from (A-20), to get

$$w = zF_2(K, h - l). \tag{A-23}$$

Finally, aggregate output is given from the production function by

$$Y = zF(K, h - l).$$

Pareto Optimum

To determine the Pareto optimum, we need to ask how a fictitious social planner would choose consumption and leisure so as to maximize welfare for the representative consumer, given the production technology. The social planner solves

$$\max_{C, l} U(C, l)$$

subject to

$$C = zF(K, h - l) - G.$$

To solve the social planner's problem, set up the Lagrangian associated with the constrained optimization problem above, which is

$$L = U(C, l) + \lambda[zF(K, h - l) - G - C].$$

The first-order conditions for an optimum are then

$$U_1(C, l) - \lambda = 0, \tag{A-24}$$

$$U_2(C, l) - \lambda z F_2(K, h - l) = 0, \tag{A-25}$$

$$zF(K, h - l) - G - C = 0. \tag{A-26}$$

From Equations (A-24) and (A-25), we obtain

$$U_2(C, l) - zF_2(K, h - l)U_1(C, l) = 0. \tag{A-27}$$

Now, Equations (A-26) and (A-27), which solve for the Pareto-optimal quantities of leisure l and consumption C, are identical to Equations (A-21) and (A-22), so that the Pareto-optimal quantities of leisure and consumption are identical to the competitive equilibrium quantities of leisure and consumption. As a result, the competitive equilibrium and the Pareto optimum are the same thing in this model, so the first and second welfare theorems hold.

Equation (A-27) can be written (suppressing arguments for convenience) as

$$\frac{U_2}{U_1} = zF_2,$$

which states that the marginal rate of substitution of leisure for consumption is equal to the marginal product of labor (the marginal rate of transformation) at the optimum.

Comparative Statics

We would like to determine the effects of changes in G and z on equilibrium C, l, Y, and w. To do this, we totally differentiate Equations (A-26) and (A-27), obtaining

$$-dC - zF_2 dl + F dz - dG = 0,$$

$$(U_{12} - zF_2 U_{11})dC + (U_{22} + zF_{22}U_1 - zF_2 U_{12})dl - F_2 U_1 dz = 0.$$

Then, putting these two equations in matrix form, we get

$$\begin{bmatrix} -1 & -zF_2 \\ U_{12} - zF_2 U_{11} & U_{22} + zF_{22}U_1 - zF_2 U_{12} \end{bmatrix} \begin{bmatrix} dC \\ dl \end{bmatrix} = \begin{bmatrix} -Fdz + dG \\ F_2 U_1 dz \end{bmatrix}. \tag{A-28}$$

Using Cramer's rule to determine the effects of a change in government spending G, from (A-28) we then get

$$\frac{dC}{dG} = \frac{U_{22} + zF_{22}U_1 - zF_2 U_{12}}{\nabla},$$

$$\frac{dl}{dG} = \frac{-U_{12} + zF_2 U_{11}}{\nabla},$$

where

$$\nabla = -z^2 F_2^2 U_{11} + 2zF_2 U_{12} - U_{22} - zF_{22}U_1.$$

Here, ∇ is the determinant of the bordered Hessian associated with the social planner's constrained optimization problem, and the quasi-concavity of the utility function and the production function guarantees that $\nabla > 0$. To sign the derivatives above, in equilibrium $zF_2 = w$, from Equation (A-17). This then implies, given our assumption that consumption and leisure are normal goods, that $U_{22} - zF_2U_{12} < 0$ and $-U_{12} + zF_2U_{11} < 0$ (recall our discussion from the previous section); because $F_{22} < 0$ (the marginal product of labor declines as the labor input increases), we have $\frac{dC}{dG} < 0$ and $\frac{dl}{dG} < 0$, so that consumption and leisure decline when government purchases increase because of negative income effects. For the effect on the real wage w, because $w = zF_2(K, h - l)$, we have

$$\frac{dw}{dG} = -zF_{22}\frac{dl}{dG} < 0,$$

and so the real wage decreases. For the effect on aggregate output, because $Y = C + G$, we have

$$\frac{dY}{dG} = \frac{dC}{dG} + 1 = \frac{-z^2F_2^2U_{11} + zF_2U_{12}}{\nabla} > 0,$$

as leisure is assumed to be normal, implying $zF_2U_{11} - U_{12} < 0$.

Now, to determine the effects of a change in z, again we use Cramer's rule in conjunction with Equation (A-28), obtaining

$$\frac{dC}{dz} = \frac{-F(U_{22} + zF_{22}U_1 - zF_2U_{12}) + F_2^2zU_1}{\nabla},$$

$$\frac{dl}{dz} = \frac{-F_2U_1 + F(U_{12} - zF_2U_{11})}{\nabla}.$$

Here, because consumption is a normal good, $U_{22} - zF_2U_{12} < 0$, and given $F_{22} < 0$, $F > 0$, and $U_1 > 0$, we have $\frac{dC}{dz} > 0$ and consumption increases with an increase in total factor productivity, as we showed diagrammatically in Chapter 5, Figure 5.9. However, we cannot sign $\frac{dl}{dz}$ as there are opposing income and substitution effects. We can separate out the income and substitution effects on leisure by determining the response of leisure to a change in z holding utility constant. This gives a substitution effect, which is

$$\frac{dl}{dz}(subst) = \frac{-F_2U_1}{\nabla},$$

so that the substitution effect is for leisure to decrease and employment ($= h - l$) to increase. The income effect of the change in z is then

$$\frac{dl}{dz}(inc) = \frac{dl}{dz} - \frac{dl}{dz}(subst) = \frac{F(U_{12} - zF_2U_{11})}{\nabla} > 0,$$

because leisure is a normal good. Therefore, an increase in z has a positive income effect on leisure.

Problems

1. For the closed-economy, one-period model, suppose that $U(C, l) = \ln C + \beta l$, and $F(K, N) = zK^\alpha N^{1-\alpha}$, where $\beta > 0$ and $0 < \alpha < 1$. Determine consumption,

employment, output, leisure, and the real wage in a competitive equilibrium, and explain your solutions.

2. For the closed-economy, one-period model, suppose that $U(C, l) = \min(C, \beta l)$, and $F(K, N) = \alpha K + \delta N$, where $\beta > 0$, $\alpha > 0$, and $\delta > 0$. Determine consumption, employment, output, leisure, and the real wage in a competitive equilibrium, and explain your solutions. Also draw a diagram with the consumer's preferences and the production possibilities frontier, and show the competitive equilibrium in this diagram.

Chapter 6 Search and Unemployment

One-Sided Search Model

In this section, we formally set up the one-sided search model of unemployment from Chapter 6, derive some of the results for that model, and construct an illustrative example. For this model, an elementary knowledge of probability is useful.

In the one-sided search model, the infinite-lived worker has preferences given by

$$E_0 \sum_{t=0}^{\infty} \left(\frac{1}{1+r}\right)^t U(C_t),$$

where E_0 is the expectation operator conditional on information known in period 0, r is the subjective discount rate, C_t is consumption, and $U(\cdot)$ is the period utility function, which is strictly increasing, continuous, and strictly concave. Here, because the worker faces uncertainty, we have assumed that he or she is an expected-utility maximizer.

A worker who is employed at a job paying the real wage w supplies one unit of labor during the period and consumes his or her labor earnings (we assume no savings). There is a probability s, where $0 < s < 1$, that the worker will be separated from his or her job and become unemployed at the end of the period. We will use dynamic programming methods (discussed in more detail in the next section of this appendix) to solve the unemployed agent's optimization problem. Let $V_e(w)$ denote the value of being employed at the real wage w, and V_u the value of being unemployed, where both values are calculated as of the end of the current period. Then, the Bellman equation for an employed worker is

$$V_e(w) = \frac{1}{1+r}[U(w) + sV_u + (1-s)V_e(w)] \tag{A-29}$$

that is, the value of being employed at the end of the current period is the current discounted value of the utility from employment next period plus the expected value at the end of the period, given the separation rate s.

Next, a worker who is unemployed receives the unemployment insurance benefit b at the beginning of the period, and then with probability p receives a wage offer, which is a random draw from the probability distribution $F(w)$, which has the associated probability density function $f(w)$. Assume that $w \in [0, w_1]$, where $w_1 > 0$. The unemployed worker must decide whether to accept a given wage offer or turn it down. Thus, the value of unemployment is given by

$$V_u = \frac{1}{1+r}\left\{U(b) + (1-p)V_u + p\int_0^{w_1} max[V_u, V_e(w)]f(w)dw\right\}, \qquad \text{(A-30)}$$

so that the value of being unemployed at the end of the current period is equal to the discounted value of the utility from consuming the unemployment benefit plus the probability of remaining unemployed times the value of remaining unemployed plus the probability of receiving a job offer times the expected value of the job offer.

Equations (A-29) and (A-30) can be simplified, respectively, as follows:

$$rV_e(w) = U(w) + s[V_u - V_e(w)], \qquad \text{(A-31)}$$

$$rV_u = U(b) + p\int_0^{w_1} max[0, V_e(w) - V_u]f(w)dw. \qquad \text{(A-32)}$$

From Equation (A-31), we can solve for $V_e(w)$ to get

$$V_e(w) = \frac{U(w) + sV_u}{r+s},$$

so that $V_e(w)$ inherits the properties of $U(w)$—that is, it is strictly increasing, continuous, and strictly concave. This implies that the worker accepts any wage offer greater than or equal to w^* and rejects any offer less than w^*, where w^* solves

$$V_e(w^*) = V_u.$$

That is, w^* is the reservation wage, at which the worker is just indifferent between accepting the job offer and remaining unemployed.

To determine the unemployment rate, the flow of workers from employment to unemployment must be equal to the flow from unemployment to employment in the steady state, or

$$s(1 - u) = p[1 - F(w^*)]u.$$

Solving for the unemployment rate u, we obtain

$$u = \frac{s}{p[1 - F(w^*)] + s}.$$

An example shows how the model works. Suppose that, conditional on receiving a wage offer, an unemployed worker receives a wage offer w_2 with probability π and a wage offer of zero with probability $1 - \pi$, where $0 < \pi < 1$. Then, conjecturing that a wage offer of w_2 is always accepted and a wage offer of zero is always turned down, Equations (A-31) and (A-32) in this case give

$$rV_e = U(w_2) + s[V_u - V_e],$$
$$rV_u = U(b) + p\pi(V_e - V_u),$$

where V_e is the value of being employed at the real wage w_2. Then, solving the above two equations for V_e and V_u, we get

$$V_e = \frac{(p\pi + r)U(w_2) + sU(b)}{r(s + p\pi + r)},$$

$$V_u = \frac{(s + r)U(b) + p\pi U(w_2)}{r(s + p\pi + r)}$$

with

$$V_e - V_u = \frac{U(w_2) - U(b)}{s + p\pi + r}.$$

Therefore, we have $V_u > 0$, so that a wage offer of zero will be turned down as conjectured, even if the unemployment insurance benefit b is zero. Further, the wage offer of w_2 will be accepted if and only if $w_2 \geq b$, that is, if the wage on the job is higher than the unemployment insurance benefit. The unemployment rate is

$$u = \frac{s}{p\pi + s}$$

but if $b > w_2$, then no one would accept jobs, and we would have $u = 1$ and everyone would be unemployed. This is an extreme example of how an increase in the unemployment insurance benefit can increase the unemployment rate.

Problem

1. Suppose in the one-sided search model that an unemployed worker receives a wage offer with probability π. Then, conditional on receiving a wage offer, the offer is w_2 with probability α_2, w_3 with probability α_3, and zero with probability $1 - \alpha_2 - \alpha_3$, where $0 < w_2 < w_3$. Determine under what conditions an unemployed worker would turn down a wage offer of w_2, accepting a wage offer of w_3, and under what conditions an unemployed worker would accept any wage offer greater than zero. Interpret these conditions.

Two-Sided Search Model

In this section, we will extend the two-sided search model in Chapter 6 to a dynamic setting, so that it corresponds more closely to the search models studied by Diamond, Mortensen, and Pissarides. Useful references are Christopher Pissarides's book[1] or the survey article by Richard Rogerson, Robert Shimer, and Randall Wright.[2]

In the model, there are infinite-lived workers and firms. Time is indexed by $t = 0, 1, 2, \ldots$. Each worker has preferences given by

$$E_0 \sum_{t=0}^{\infty} \left(\frac{1}{1+r}\right)^t c_t,$$

[1] C. Pissarides, 1990. *Equilibrium Unemployment Theory*, Basil-Blackwell, Cambridge, MA.

[2] R. Rogerson, R. Shimer, and R. Wright, 2005. "Search Theoretic Models of the Labor Market: A Survey," *Journal of Economic Literature* 43, 959–988.

where E_0 is the expectation operator conditional on information in period 0, r is the worker's discount rate, and c_t is consumption in period t. A firm has preferences

$$E_0 \sum_{t=0}^{\infty} \left(\frac{1}{1+r}\right)^t (\pi_t - x_t),$$

where π_t denotes the firm's profits in period t, and x_t is effort in posting vacancies.

Throughout, we will confine attention to a steady state, in which all variables are constant for all time. Let Q denote the number of workers who are unemployed and searching for work, and A the number of active firms posting vacancies. Then, as in Chapter 6, the number of matches that occur between workers and firms is

$$M = em(Q, A), \tag{A-33}$$

where the function on the right side of (A-33) is the matching function, e is matching efficiency, and $m(\cdot, \cdot)$ is strictly increasing in both arguments and homogeneous of degree 1.

Let W_u and $W_e(w)$ denote the values of being unemployed and of being employed, for a worker, which are the expected utilities from that date forward of being in the unemployed or employed state, respectively. The value of being employed depends on the wage w. Similarly, let $J(w)$ denote the value to a firm of being matched with a worker, and let V denote the value to a firm of posting a vacancy.

When a worker and firm match, they have to bargain over the wage, w. Nash bargaining theory tells us that the wage solves

$$\max_w [(W_e(w) - W_u)^a (J(w) - V)^{1-a}], \tag{A-34}$$

where a denotes the worker's bargaining power, $W_e(w) - W_u$ is the worker's surplus from the match, and $J(w) - V$ is the firm's surplus. The first-order condition for an optimum, from (A-34) gives

$$W_e'(w)a[J(w) - V] + J'(w)(1 - a)[W_e(w) - W_u] = 0. \tag{A-35}$$

Using dynamic programming (see the next section for more on dynamic programming, if you are unfamiliar with the techniques), the value of a match for a worker and a firm, respectively, are determined by the following Bellman equations:

$$rW_e(w) = w + \delta[W_u - W_e(w)], \tag{A-36}$$

$$rJ(w) = z - w + \delta[V - J(w)], \tag{A-37}$$

where δ is the separation rate—the exogenous rate at which matches break up. Solving these two equations for $W_e(w)$ and $J(w)$ and then differentiating gives us

$$W_e'(w) = -J'(w) = \frac{1}{r + \delta},$$

so if we substitute in the first-order condition (A-35) for $W_e'(w)$ and $J'(w)$ and simplify, we get

$$W_e - W_u = a(J - V + W_e - W_u). \tag{A-38}$$

In Equation (A-38), we have dropped the arguments from the value functions, as values will be constant in the steady state. Equation (A-38) tells us that Nash bargaining implies that the worker's surplus from the match is a constant fraction of the total surplus from the match.

Next, the Bellman equation determining the value of unemployment for a worker is

$$rW_u = b + em(1, j)(W_e - W_u), \tag{A-39}$$

where b is the unemployment insurance benefit, and $j = \frac{A}{Q}$ is labor market tightness. A firm posting a vacancy bears a cost in terms of effort k, so the value of posting a vacancy is given by the Bellman equation

$$rV = -k + em\left(\frac{1}{j}\right)(J - V). \tag{A-40}$$

In equilibrium, firms will post vacancies until

$$V = 0, \tag{A-41}$$

as the opportunity cost of posting a vacancy is zero for a firm.

To solve for the steady state in this model, first define the total surplus in a match by

$$S = J - V + W_e - W_u.$$

Then, use Equations (A-36)–(A-41) to obtain two equations that solve for total surplus S and labor market tightness, j:

$$S = \frac{z - b}{r + \delta + aem(1, j)} \tag{A-42}$$

$$S = \frac{k}{(1 - a)em\left(\frac{1}{j}\right)}. \tag{A-43}$$

Then, given the solution for S and j, we can work backward to determine J, W_e, W_u, and w using Equations (A-36)–(A-41). Then, letting E denote the number of employed workers, in the steady state, we must have

$$\delta E = em(1, j)Q, \tag{A-44}$$

as the flow of workers from employment to unemployment must equal the flow of workers from unemployment to employment in the steady state. We can use Equation (A-44) to solve for the unemployment rate

$$u = \frac{Q}{Q + E} = \frac{\delta}{\delta + em(1, j)},$$

and the vacancy rate from Equation (A-44) is

$$v = \frac{A}{E + A} = \frac{j\delta}{em(1, j) + j\delta}.$$

Problems

1. Determine the effects of an increase in the separation rate δ on $w, j, u,$ and v.

2. Show how to determine the size of the labor force, $Q + E$, using the same approach as in Chapter 6.

3. Determine the effects of an increase in matching efficiency, e, on $w, j, u,$ and v.

Chapters 7 and 8 Economic Growth

In this section, we work out explicitly the effects of changes in the savings rate, the labor force growth rate, and total factor productivity on the steady state quantity of capital per worker and output per worker in the Solow growth model. We omit an algebraic analysis of the Malthusian growth model, as this is very straightforward. We determine the golden rule for capital accumulation in the Solow model. Finally, we develop a growth model where consumption–savings decisions are made endogenously. In solving this model, we provide some detail about dynamic programming techniques, which were used in the previous section, and will be used again later in this appendix.

Explicit Results for the Solow Growth Model

Recall from Chapter 7 that the aggregate quantity of capital in the Solow growth model evolves according to

$$K' = (1 - d)K + I, \tag{A-45}$$

where K' is future period capital, d is the depreciation rate, K is current period capital, and I is current period investment. In equilibrium, saving is equal to investment, and so $sY = I$, where s is the savings rate and Y is aggregate income. Further, the production function is given by $Y = zF(K, N)$, where z is total factor productivity and N is the labor force, so that substituting in Equation (A-45), we have

$$K' = (1 - d)K + zF(K, N). \tag{A-46}$$

Then, dividing the right and left sides of Equation (A-46) by N, using the relationship $N' = (1 + n)N$, which describes labor force growth, with N' denoting the future labor force and n the population growth rate, and rewriting in the form of lowercase variables that denote per-worker quantities, we have

$$k' = \frac{szf(k)}{1 + n} + \frac{(1 - d)k}{1 + n}. \tag{A-47}$$

Equation (A-47) then determines the evolution of the per-worker capital stock from the current period to the future period, where k is the current stock of capital per worker, k' is the stock of future capital per worker, and $f(k)$ is the per-worker production function.

In the steady state, $k' = k = k^*$, where $k*$ is the steady state quantity of capital per worker, which, from Equation (A-47), satisfies

$$szf(k^*) - (n + d)k^* = 0. \qquad \text{(A-48)}$$

Now, to determine the effects of changes in s, n, and z on the steady state quantity of capital per worker, we totally differentiate Equation (A-48) getting

$$[szf'(k^*) - n - d]dk^* + szf(k^*)ds - k^* dn + sf(k^*)dz = 0. \qquad \text{(A-49)}$$

Then, solving for the appropriate derivatives, we obtain

$$\frac{dk^*}{ds} = \frac{-zf(k^*)}{szf'(k^*) - n - d} > 0,$$

$$\frac{dk^*}{dn} = \frac{k^*}{szf'(k^*) - n - d} < 0,$$

$$\frac{dk^*}{dz} = \frac{-sf(k^*)}{szf'(k^*) - n - d} > 0.$$

Here, capital per worker increases with increases in s and z, and decreases with an increase in n. We get these results because $szf'(k^*) - n - d < 0$ in the steady state. Because output per worker in the steady state is $y^* = zf(k^*)$, for each of these experiments, steady state output per worker moves in the same direction as steady state capital per worker.

In the steady state, the quantity of consumption per worker is

$$c^* = zf(k^*) - (n + d)k^*.$$

Now, when the savings rate changes, the response of consumption per worker in the steady state is given by

$$\frac{dc^*}{ds} = \left[zf'(k^*) - n - d \right] \frac{dk^*}{ds}.$$

Though $\frac{dk^*}{ds} > 0$, the sign of $zf'(k^*) - n - d$ is ambiguous, so that consumption per worker could increase or decrease with an increase in the savings rate. The golden rule savings rate is the savings rate s_{gr} that maximizes consumption per worker in the steady state. The golden rule steady state quantity of capital per worker solves the problem

$$\max_{k*}[zf(k*) - (n + d)k*],$$

letting k_{gr}^* denote this quantity of capital per worker, k_{gr}^* solves

$$zf'(k_{gr}^*) - n - d = 0,$$

and then s_{gr} is determined from Equation (A-48) by

$$s_{gr} = \frac{(n+d)k_{gr}^*}{zf(k_{gr}^*)}.$$

For example, if $F(K, N) = K^\alpha N^{1-\alpha}$, where $0 < \alpha < 1$ (a Cobb–Douglas production function), then $f(k) = k^\alpha$, and we get

$$k_{gr}^* = \left(\frac{z\alpha}{n+d}\right)^{\frac{1}{1-\alpha}},$$

$$s_{gr} = \alpha.$$

Problem

1. Suppose in the Solow growth model that there is government spending financed by lump-sum taxes, with total government spending $G = gY$, where $0 < g < 1$. Solve for steady state capital per worker, consumption per worker, and output per worker, and determine how each depends on g. Can g be set so as to maximize steady state consumption per worker? If so, determine the optimal fraction of output purchased by the government, g^*, and explain your results.

Optimal Growth: Endogenous Consumption–Savings Decisions

In this model, we relax the assumption made in the Solow growth model that the savings rate is exogenous and allow consumption to be determined optimally over time. The model we develop here is a version of the optimal growth theory originally developed by David Cass and Tjalling Koopmans.[3] In this model, the second welfare theorem holds, and so we can solve the social planner's problem to determine the competitive equilibrium. We set the model up as simply as possible, leaving out population growth and changes in total factor productivity; but, these features are easy to add.

There is a representative infinitely lived consumer with preferences given by

$$\sum_{t=0}^{\infty} \beta^t U(C_t), \tag{A-50}$$

where β is the subjective discount factor of the representative consumer, with $0 < \beta < 1$, and C_t is consumption in period t. Throughout, t subscripts denote the time period. The period utility function $U(\cdot)$ is continuously differentiable, strictly increasing, strictly concave, and bounded. Assume that $\lim_{C \to 0} U'(C) = \infty$. Each period, the consumer is endowed with one unit of time, which can be supplied as labor.

The production function is given by

$$Y_t = F(K_t, N_t),$$

---

[3]See D. Cass, 1965. "Optimum Growth in an Aggregative Model of Capital Accumulation," *Review of Economic Studies* 32, 233–240; and T. Koopmans, 1965. "On the Concept of Optimal Growth," in *The Econometric Approach to Development Planning*, T. Koopmans ed., pp. 225–287. North Holland, Amsterdam.

where Y_t is output, K_t is the capital input, and N_t is the labor input. The production function $F(\cdot, \cdot)$ is continuously differentiable, strictly increasing in both arguments, homogeneous of degree one, and strictly quasi-concave. Assume that $F(0, N) = 0$, $\lim_{K\to 0} F_1(K, 1) = \infty$, and $\lim_{K\to\infty} F_1(K, 1) = 0$.

The capital stock obeys the law of motion

$$K_{t+1} = (1 - d)K_t + I_t, \tag{A-51}$$

where I_t is investment and d is the depreciation rate, with $0 \leq d \leq 1$, and K_0 is the initial capital stock, which is given. In equilibrium, we have $N_t = 1$ for all t, and so it is convenient to define the function $H(K_t)$ by $H(K_t) = F(K_t, 1)$. The resource constraint for the economy is

$$C_t + I_t = H(K_t), \tag{A-52}$$

or consumption plus investment is equal to the total quantity of output produced. It is convenient to substitute for I_t in Equation (A-52) using (A-51) and to rearrange, obtaining a single constraint

$$C_t + K_{t+1} = H(K_t) + (1 - d)K_t. \tag{A-53}$$

We can think of the resources available in period t to the social planner on the right-hand side of Equation (A-53) as being period t output plus the undepreciated portion of the capital stock, which is then split up (on the left-hand side of the equation) between period t consumption and the capital stock for period $t + 1$.

The social planner's problem for this economy is to determine consumption and the capital stock in each period so as to maximize Equation (A-50) subject to the constraint Equation (A-53). Again, the solution to this problem is equivalent to the competitive equilibrium solution. The social planner solves

$$\max_{\{C_t, K_{t+1}\}_{t=0}^{\infty}} \sum_{t=0}^{\infty} U(C_t), \tag{A-54}$$

given K_0 and (A-53) for $t = 0, 1, 2, \ldots \infty$.

Now, the problem of solving Equation (A-54) subject to (A-53) may appear quite formidable, as we need to solve for an infinite sequence of choice variables. However, dynamic programming techniques essentially allow us to turn this infinite-dimensional problem into a two-dimensional problem.[4] To see how this works, note from the right side of (A-53) that the current capital stock K_t determines the resources that are available to the social planner at the beginning of period t. Thus, K_t determines how much utility the social planner can give to the consumer from period t on. Suppose that the social planner knows $v(K_t)$, which is the maximum utility that the social planner could provide for the representative consumer from period t on. Then, the problem that the social planner would solve in any period t would be

$$\max_{C_t, K_{t+1}} [U(C_t) + \beta v(K_{t+1})]$$

---

[4]For more detail about dynamic programming methods in economics, see N. Stokey, R. Lucas, and E. Prescott, 1989. *Recursive Methods in Economic Dynamics,* Harvard University Press, Cambridge, MA.

subject to

$$C_t + K_{t+1} = H(K_t) + (1 - d)K_t.$$

That is, the social planner chooses current period consumption and the capital stock for the following period so as to maximize the sum of current period utility and the discounted value of utility from the next period on, subject to the resource constraint. Now, because the problem of the social planner looks the same in every period, it is true that

$$v(K_t) = \max_{C_t, K_{t+1}} [U(C_t) + \beta v(K_{t+1})] \tag{A-55}$$

subject to

$$C_t + K_{t+1} = H(K_t) + (1 - d)K_t. \tag{A-56}$$

Then, Equation (A-55) is called a Bellman equation, or functional equation, and it determines what $v(\cdot)$ is. We call $v(K_t)$ the value function as this tells us the value of the problem at time t to the social planner as a function of the state variable K_t. Given the assumptions we have made, there is a unique function $v(\cdot)$ that solves the Bellman equation. There are some circumstances where we can obtain an explicit solution for $v(\cdot)$ (see the problem at the end of this section), but in any case the dynamic programming formulation of the social planner's problem, Equation (A-55) subject to (A-56), can be convenient for characterizing solutions, if we assume that $v(\cdot)$ is differentiable and strictly concave (which it is here, given our assumptions).

We can simplify the problem above by substituting for C_t in the objective function (A-55) using the constraint (A-56), getting

$$v(K_t) = \max_{K_{t+1}} \{U[H(K_t) + (1 - d)K_t - K_{t+1}] + \beta v(K_{t+1})\}. \tag{A-57}$$

Then, given that the value function $v(\cdot)$ is concave and differentiable, we can differentiate on the right side of (A-57) to get the first-order condition for an optimum, which is

$$U'[H(K_t) + (1 - d)K_t - K_{t+1}] + \beta v'(K_{t+1}) = 0. \tag{A-58}$$

Now, to determine $v'(K_{t+1})$, we apply the envelope theorem in differentiating Equation (A-57), obtaining

$$v'(K_t) = [H'(K_t) + 1 - d]U'[H(K_t) + (1 - d)K_t - K_{t+1}].$$

Then, we update one period, and substitute for $v'(K_{t+1})$ in (A-58), getting

$$-U'[H(K_t) + (1-d)K_t - K_{t+1}] + \beta[H'(K_{t+1}) + 1 - d] \times U'[H(K_{t+1}) + (1-d)K_{t+1} - K_{t+2}] = 0. \tag{A-59}$$

Now, we know that, in this the model, the quantity of capital converges to a constant steady state value, K^*. Equation (A-59) can be used to solve for K^* by substituting $K_{t+1} = K_t = K^*$ in (A-59), which gives, after simplifying,

$$-1 + \beta[H'(K^*) + 1 - d] = 0, \tag{A-60}$$

or

$$H'(K^*) - d = \frac{1}{\beta} - 1$$

in the optimal steady state. That is, in the optimal steady state, the net marginal product of capital is equal to the subjective discount rate of the representative consumer.

In the model, the savings rate is given by

$$s_t = \frac{I_t}{Y_t} = \frac{K_{t+1} - (1 - d)K_t}{H(K_t)},$$

and so in the steady state the savings rate is

$$s^* = \frac{dK^*}{H(K^*)}.$$

In this model, because the savings rate is optimally chosen over time, choosing a "golden rule savings rate" makes no sense. Indeed, the steady state optimal savings rate in this model does not maximize steady state consumption. Steady state consumption would be maximized for a value of the steady state capital stock K^* such that $H'(K^*) = d$, but this is different from the optimal steady state capital stock determined by Equation (A-60).

Problem

1. In the optimal growth model, suppose that $U(C_t) = \ln C_t$ and $F(K_t, N_t) = K_t^\alpha N_t^{1-\alpha}$, with $d = 1$ (100% depreciation).

    (a) Guess that the value function takes the form $v(K_t) = A + B \ln K_t$, where A and B are undetermined constants.

    (b) Substitute your guess for the value function on the right side of Equation (A-57), solve the optimization problem, and verify that your guess was correct.

    (c) Solve for A and B by substituting your optimal solution from part (b) on the right side of Equation (A-57) and equating coefficients on the left- and right sides of the equation.

    (d) Determine the solutions for K_{t+1} and C_t as functions of K_t, and interpret these solutions.

Chapter 9 A Two-Period Model

In this section, we formally derive the results for individual consumer behavior, showing how a consumer optimizes by choosing consumption and savings over two periods and how the consumer responds to changes in income and the market real interest rate.

The Consumer's Optimization Problem

The consumer has preferences defined by a utility function $U(c, c')$, where c is current period consumption, c' is future consumption, and $U(\cdot, \cdot)$ is strictly quasi-concave, increasing in both arguments, and twice differentiable. To guarantee an interior solution to the consumer's problem, we assume that the marginal utilities of current and future consumption each go to infinity in the limit as current and future consumption go to zero, respectively. The consumer chooses c and c' to maximize $U(c, c')$ subject to the consumer's lifetime budget constraint, that is,

$$\max_{c,c'} U(c, c')$$

subject to

$$c + \frac{c'}{1+r} = y + \frac{y'}{1+r} - t - \frac{t'}{1+r},$$

where y is the current income, y' is the future income, t is the current tax, and t' is the future tax. The Lagrangian associated with this constrained optimization problem is

$$L = U(c, c') + \lambda\left(y + \frac{y'}{1+r} - t - \frac{t'}{1+r} - c - \frac{c'}{1+r}\right),$$

where λ is the Lagrange multiplier. Therefore, the first-order conditions for an optimum are

$$U_1(c, c') - \lambda = 0, \tag{A-61}$$

$$U_2(c, c') - \frac{\lambda}{1+r} = 0, \tag{A-62}$$

$$y + \frac{y'}{1+r} - t - \frac{t'}{1+r} - c - \frac{c'}{1+r} = 0. \tag{A-63}$$

Then, in Equations (A-61) and (A-62), we can eliminate λ to obtain

$$U_1(c, c') - (1 + r)U_2(c, c') = 0, \tag{A-64}$$

or rewriting Equation (A-64),

$$\frac{U_1(c, c')}{U_2(c, c')} = 1 + r,$$

which states that the intertemporal marginal rate of substitution (the marginal rate of substitution of current consumption for future consumption) is equal to one plus the real interest rate at the optimum.

For convenience, we can rewrite Equation (A-63) as

$$y(1 + r) + y' - t(1 + r) - t' - c(1 + r) - c' = 0. \tag{A-65}$$

Then, Equations (A-64) and (A-65) determine the quantities of c and c' the consumer chooses given current and future incomes y and y', current and future taxes t and t', and the real interest rate r.

Comparative Statics
To determine the effects of changes in current and future income and the real interest rate on current and future consumption and savings, we totally differentiate Equations (A-64) and (A-65), obtaining

$$[U_{11} - (1 + r)U_{12}]dc + [U_{12} - (1 + r)U_{22}]dc' - U_2dr = 0,$$
$$- (1 + r)dc - dc' + (y - t - c)dr + (1 + r)dy + dy' - (1 + r)dt - dt' = 0;$$

these two equations can be written in matrix form as

$$\begin{bmatrix} U_{11} - (1 + r)U_{12} & U_{12} - (1 + r)U_{22} \\ -(1 + r) & -1 \end{bmatrix} \begin{bmatrix} dc \\ dc' \end{bmatrix}$$

$$= \begin{bmatrix} U_2dr \\ -(y - t - c)dr - (1 + r)dy - dy' - (1 + r)dt - dt' \end{bmatrix}. \tag{A-66}$$

First, we determine the effects of a change in current income y. Applying Cramer's rule to (A-66), we obtain

$$\frac{dc}{dy} = \frac{(1 + r)[U_{12} - (1 + r)U_{22}]}{\nabla},$$

$$\frac{dc'}{dy} = \frac{(1 + r)[-U_{11} + (1 + r)U_{12}]}{\nabla},$$

where

$$\nabla = -U_{11} + 2(1 + r)U_{12} - (1 + r)^2U_{22}.$$

Given our restrictions on the utility function, ∇, which is the determinant of the bordered Hessian associated with the consumer's constrained optimization problem, is strictly positive. Further, assuming current and future consumption are normal goods, we have $U_{12} - (1 + r)U_{22} > 0$ and $-U_{11} + (1 + r)U_{12} > 0$, and so $\frac{dc}{dy} > 0$ and $\frac{dc'}{dy} > 0$. Thus, an increase in current income causes increases in both current and future consumption. Saving in the current period is given by $s = y - c - t$, so that

$$\frac{ds}{dy} = 1 - \frac{dc}{dy} = \frac{-U_{11} + (1 + r)U_{12}}{\nabla} > 0,$$

because the assumption that goods are normal gives $-U_{11} + (1 + r)U_{12} > 0$. Therefore, saving increases in the current period when y increases.

To determine the effects of a change in future income y', we again apply Cramer's rule to Equation (A-66), getting

$$\frac{dc}{dy'} = \frac{1}{1 + r}\frac{dc}{dy} > 0,$$

$$\frac{dc'}{dy'} = \frac{1}{1 + r}\frac{dc'}{dy} > 0,$$

so that the effects of a change in y' are identical qualitatively to the effects of a change in y, except that the derivatives are discounted, using the one-period discount factor $\frac{1}{1 + r}$. The effect on saving is given by

$$\frac{ds}{dy'} = -\frac{dc}{dy'} < 0,$$

and so saving decreases when future income increases.

Finally, to determine the effects of a change in the real interest rate r on current and future consumption, we again apply Cramer's rule to Equation (A-66), getting

$$\frac{dc}{dr} = \frac{-U_2 + [U_{12} - (1+r)U_{22}](y - t - c)}{\nabla},$$

$$\frac{dc'}{dr} = \frac{(1+r)U_2 - [U_{11} - (1+r)U_{12}](y - t - c)}{\nabla}.$$

The signs of both of these derivatives are indeterminate, because the income and substitution effects may be opposing. As above, we can separate the income and substitution effects by determining the responses of c and c' to a change in r holding utility constant. The substitution effects are

$$\frac{dc}{dr}(subst) = \frac{-U_2}{\nabla} < 0,$$

$$\frac{dc'}{dr}(subst) = \frac{(1+r)U_2}{\nabla} > 0,$$

so that the substitution effect is for current consumption to decrease and future consumption to increase when the real interest rate increases. The income effects are

$$\frac{dc}{dr}(inc) = \frac{dc}{dr} - \frac{dc}{dr}(subst) = \frac{[U_{12} - (1+r)U_{22}](y - t - c)}{\nabla},$$

$$\frac{dc'}{dr}(inc) = \frac{dc'}{dr} - \frac{dc'}{dr}(subst) = \frac{[U_{11} - (1+r)U_{12}](y - t - c)}{\nabla}.$$

Here, the assumption that goods are normal gives $U_{12} - (1+r)U_{22} > 0$ and $U_{11} - (1+r)U_{12} < 0$, and so given this assumption the signs of the income effects are determined by whether the consumer is a lender or a borrower, that is, by the sign of $y - t - c$. If the consumer is a lender, so that $y - t - c > 0$, then the income effects are for current consumption and future consumption to increase. However, if $y - t - c < 0$, so the consumer is a borrower, then the income effect is for current consumption to decrease and future consumption to decrease.

Because savings is $s = y - c - t$, the effect on savings of a change in the real interest rate is determined by the effect on current consumption, namely,

$$\frac{ds}{dr} = -\frac{dc}{dr}.$$

Problems

1. Suppose that $U(c, c') = \ln c + \beta \ln c$, where $\beta > 0$. Determine consumption in the current and future periods for the consumer, and interpret your solutions in terms of income and substitution effects.

2. Suppose that $U(c, c') = \ln c + \beta \ln c$, where $\beta > 0$, and assume that the consumer lends at the real interest rate r_1 and borrows at the interest rate r_2, where $r_1 < r_2$. Under what conditions is the consumer (a) a borrower, (b) a lender, and (c) neither a borrower nor a lender? Explain your results.

Chapter 11 A Real Intertemporal Model with Investment

There is not much to be gained from analyzing the model developed in this chapter algebraically. It is possible to linearize the model so as to make it amenable to an explicit solution, but to do analysis with this linearized model requires a good deal of tedious algebra. For this chapter, we confine attention to a formal treatment of the representative firm's investment problem.

The current and future production functions for the firm are given, respectively, by

$$Y = zF(K, N) \tag{A-67}$$

and

$$Y' = z'F(K', N'), \tag{A-68}$$

where Y and Y' are current and future outputs, respectively, z and z' are current and future total factor productivities, K and K' are current and future capital stocks, and N and N' are current and future labor inputs. The capital stock evolves according to

$$K' = (1 - d)K + I, \tag{A-69}$$

where d is the depreciation rate and I is investment in capital in period 1. The current value of profits for the firm is

$$V = Y - I - wN + \frac{Y' - w'N' + (1 - d)K}{1 + r}, \tag{A-70}$$

where w is the current real wage, w' is the future real wage, and r is the real interest rate. We can substitute in Equation (A-70) for Y, Y', and K' using Equations (A-67) to (A-69) to obtain

$$V = zF(K, N) - I - wN + \frac{z'F[(1 - d)K + I', N'] - w'N' + (1 - d)[(1 - d)K + I]}{1 + r}. \tag{A-71}$$

The objective of the firm is to choose N, N', and I to maximize V. The first-order conditions for an optimum, obtained by differentiating Equation (A-71) with respect to N, N', and I, are

$$\frac{\partial V}{\partial N} = zF_2(K, N) - w = 0, \tag{A-72}$$

$$\frac{\partial V}{\partial N'} = \frac{z'F_2[(1 - d)K + I, N'] - w'}{1 + r} = 0, \tag{A-73}$$

$$\frac{\partial V}{\partial I} = -1 + \frac{z'F_1[(1 - d)K + I, N'] + 1 - d}{1 + r} = 0. \tag{A-74}$$

Equations (A-72) and (A-73) state, respectively, that the firm optimizes by setting the marginal product of labor equal to the real wage in the current period and in the future period. We can simplify Equation (A-74) by writing it as

$$z'F_1[(1 - d)K + I, N'] - d = r, \tag{A-75}$$

or the firm chooses investment optimally by setting the future net marginal product of capital equal to the real interest rate, given N'. To determine how changes in z', K, d, and r affect the investment decision, given future employment N', we totally differentiate Equation (A-75), getting

$$z'F_{11}dI + z'(1-d)F_{11}dK + F_1dz - (z'KF_{11} + 1)dd - dr = 0.$$

Then, we have

$$\frac{dI}{dr} = \frac{1}{z'F_{11}} < 0,$$

so that investment declines when the real interest rate increases;

$$\frac{dI}{dK} = d - 1 < 0$$

so that investment is lower the higher the initial capital stock K is;

$$\frac{dI}{dz'} = \frac{-F_1}{z'F_{11}} > 0,$$

so that investment increases when future total factor productivity increases; and

$$\frac{dI}{dd} = \frac{z'KF_{11} + 1}{z'F_{11}},$$

which has an indeterminate sign, so that the effect of a change in the depreciation rate on investment is ambiguous.

Problem

1. Suppose that the firm produces output only from capital. Current output is given by $Y = zK^\alpha$, and future output is given by $Y' = z'(K')^\alpha$, where $0 < \alpha < 1$. Determine investment for the firm, and show how investment depends on the real interest rate, future total factor productivity, the depreciation rate, and α. Explain your results.

Chapter 12 Money, Banking, Prices, and Monetary Policy

Here, we develop an explicit cash-in-advance model, which is somewhat different from the model laid out in Chapter 12. This model can also be used to get some of the results in Chapter 18, with regard to the long-run effects of inflation, in a more formal setting. In this model there is no investment or capital, and all consumption goods are purchased with cash. There are no credit purchases. However, we can use this model to work out in detail many of the results from Chapters 12 and 17 that deal with the monetary intertemporal model, and more.

In the cash-in-advance model there is a representative consumer, who lives forever and has preferences given by the utility function

$$\sum_{t=0}^{\infty} \beta^t [U(C_t) - V(N_t)], \tag{A-76}$$

where β is the subjective discount factor, with $0 < \beta < 1$, C_t is consumption in period t, N_t is labor supply in period t, $U(\cdot)$ is a strictly increasing and strictly concave function with $U'(0) = \infty$, and $V(\cdot)$ is a strictly increasing and strictly convex function with $V'(0) = 0$. Assume that $U(\cdot)$ and $V(\cdot)$ are twice continuously differentiable.

For simplicity we do not have capital or investment in the model, to focus on the key results, and the production function is given by

$$Y_t = zN_t, \tag{A-77}$$

where Y_t is output in period t and z is the marginal product of labor. The linear production function has the constant-returns-to-scale property.

Within any period t, timing works as follows. At the beginning of the period, the representative consumer has M_t units of money carried over from the previous period, B_t nominal bonds, and X_t real bonds. Each nominal bond issued in period t is a promise to pay one unit of money in period $t + 1$, and each real bond issued in period t is a promise to pay one unit of the consumption good in period $t + 1$. With nominal and real bonds in the model, we can determine explicitly the nominal and real interest rates. A nominal bond issued in period t sells for q_t units of money, while a real bond sells for s_t units of period t consumption goods.

At the beginning of the period, the asset market opens, the consumer receives the payoffs on the bonds held over from the previous period, and the consumer can exchange money for nominal and real bonds that come due in period $t + 1$. The consumer must also pay a real lump-sum tax of T_t at this time. After the asset market closes, the consumer supplies N_t units of labor to the firm and buys consumption goods on the goods market, but he or she must purchase these consumption goods with money held over after the asset market closes. Consumption goods are sold at the money price P_t in period t. Therefore, the representative consumer must abide by the cash-in-advance constraint

$$P_tC_t + q_tB_{t+1} + P_ts_tX_{t+1} + P_tT_t = M_t + B_t + P_tX_t. \tag{A-78}$$

When the goods market closes, the consumer receives his or her labor earnings from the representative firm in cash. The consumer then faces the budget constraint

$$P_tC_t + q_tB_{t+1} + P_ts_tX_{t+1} + P_tT_t + M_{t+1} = M_t + B_t + P_tX_t + P_tzN_t, \tag{A-79}$$

where M_{t+1} is the quantity of money held by the consumer at the end of the period and z is the real wage in period t, which must be equal to the constant marginal product of labor in equilibrium.

Letting $\overline{M}_t$ denote the supply of money at the beginning of period t, the government budget constraint is given by

$$\overline{M}_{t+1} - \overline{M}_t = -P_tT_t, \tag{A-80}$$

and the government sets taxes so that the money supply grows at a constant rate α. That is, we have $\overline{M}_{t+1} = (1 + \alpha)\overline{M}_t$ for all t. This then implies, from Equation (A-80), that

$$\alpha\overline{M}_t = -P_tT_t. \tag{A-81}$$

Now, it is convenient to scale the constraints (A-78) and (A-79) by multiplying by $\frac{1}{M_t}$ and letting lowercase letters denote scaled nominal variables, for example, $p_t = \frac{P_t}{M_t}$. Then, we can rewrite Equations (A-78) and (A-79) as

$$p_t C_t + q_t b_{t+1}(1 + \alpha) + p_t s_t X_{t+1} + p_t T_t = m_t + b_t + p_t X_t \qquad \text{(A-82)}$$

and

$$p_t C_t + q_t b_{t+1}(1+\alpha) + p_t s_t X_{t+1} + p_t T_t + m_{t+1}(1+\alpha) = m_t + b_t + p_t X_t + p_t z N_t. \quad \text{(A-83)}$$

The representative consumer's problem is to choose C_t, N_t, b_{t+1}, X_{t+1}, and m_{t+1} in each period $t = 0, 1, 2, \ldots, \infty$, to maximize Equation (A-76) subject to the constraints (A-82) and (A-83). We can simplify the problem by formulating it as a dynamic program. Letting $v(m_t, b_t, X_t; p_t, q_t, s_t)$ denote the value function, the Bellman equation associated with the consumer's problem is

$$\overset{v(m_t,\, b_t,\, X_t;\, p_t,\, q_t,\, s_t)}{= \underset{C_t,\, N_t,\, b_{t+1},\, X_{t+1},\, m_{t+1}}{\max}} [U(C_t) - V(N_t) + \beta v(m_{t+1}, b_{t+1}, X_{t+1}; p_{t+1}, q_{t+1}, s_{t+1})],$$

subject to Equations (A-82) and (A-83). Letting λ_t and μ_t denote the Lagrange multipliers associated with the constraints (A-82) and (A-83), the first-order conditions for an optimum are

$$U'(C_t) - (\lambda_t + \mu_t)p_t = 0, \qquad \text{(A-84)}$$

$$-V'(N_t) + \mu_t p_t z = 0, \qquad \text{(A-85)}$$

$$-q_{t+1}(1 + \alpha)(\lambda_t + \mu_t) + \beta \frac{\partial v}{\partial b_{t+1}} = 0, \qquad \text{(A-86)}$$

$$-p_t s_t(\lambda_t + \mu_t) + \beta \frac{\partial v}{\partial X_{t+1}} = 0, \qquad \text{(A-87)}$$

$$-(1 + \alpha)\mu_t + \beta \frac{\partial v}{\partial m_{t+1}} = 0. \qquad \text{(A-88)}$$

We can also derive the following envelope conditions by differentiating the Bellman equation and applying the envelope theorem:

$$\frac{\partial v}{\partial b_t} = \lambda_t + \mu_t; \qquad \text{(A-89)}$$

$$\frac{\partial v}{\partial X_t} = p_t(\lambda_t + \mu_t); \qquad \text{(A-90)}$$

$$\frac{\partial v}{\partial m_t} = \lambda_t + \mu_t. \qquad \text{(A-91)}$$

Now, we can use the envelope conditions, Equations (A-89) to (A-91), updated one period, to substitute for the derivatives of the value function in Equations (A-86) to

(A-88), and then use Equations (A-84) and (A-85) to substitute for the Lagrange multipliers in Equations (A-86) to (A-88), obtaining

$$\frac{-q_t(1+\alpha)U'(C_t)}{p_t} + \beta\frac{U'(C_{t+1})}{p_{t+1}} = 0, \tag{A-92}$$

$$-s_tU'(C_t) + \beta U'(C_{t+1}) = 0, \tag{A-93}$$

$$\frac{-(1+\alpha)V'(N_t)}{p_tz} + \beta\frac{U'(C_{t+1})}{p_{t+1}} = 0. \tag{A-94}$$

Next, the market-clearing conditions are

$$m_t = 1, \quad b_t = 0, \quad X_t = 0,$$

for all t; that is, money demand equals money supply, the demand for nominal bonds equals the zero net supply of nominal bonds, and the demand for real bonds equals the zero net supply of these bonds as well, in each period. Substituting the market-clearing conditions in Equations (A-82) and (A-83) and using Equation (A-81) to substitute for T_t, we obtain

$$p_tC_t = 1 + \alpha, \tag{A-95}$$

$$C_t = zN_t. \tag{A-96}$$

Equations (A-95) and (A-96) state, respectively, that all money is held in equilibrium at the beginning of the period by the representative consumer and is used to purchase consumption goods and that in equilibrium all output produced is consumed.

Now, there is an equilibrium where $C_t = C$, $N_t = N$, $p_t = p$, $q_t = q$, and $s_t = s$, for all t, and we can use Equations (A-92) to (A-96) to solve for C, N, p, q, and s. We obtain

$$q = \frac{\beta}{1+\alpha}, \tag{A-97}$$

$$s = \beta, \tag{A-98}$$

$$(1+\alpha)V'(N) - \beta zU'(zN) = 0, \tag{A-99}$$

$$C = zN, \tag{A-100}$$

$$p = \frac{1+\alpha}{C}. \tag{A-101}$$

Here, Equations (A-97) and (A-98) give solutions for q and s, respectively, while Equation (A-99) solves implicitly for N. Then, given the solution for N, we can solve recursively for C and p from Equations (A-100) and (A-101). We can solve for the Lagrange multiplier λ using Equations (A-84), (A-85), (A-95), (A-96), and (A-99), to get

$$\lambda = \frac{CU'(C)}{1+\alpha}\left(1 - \frac{\beta}{1+\alpha}\right) = \frac{CU'(C)}{1+\alpha}(1-q). \tag{A-102}$$

Now, note that the nominal interest rate is determined by the price of the nominal bond q, as $R = \frac{1}{q} - 1$, so that the nominal interest rate is positive as long as $q < 1$. From

Equation (A-97), the nominal interest rate is positive when $\alpha > \beta - 1$, that is, as long as the money growth rate is sufficiently large. The Lagrange multiplier associated with the cash-in-advance constraint is positive, that is, $\lambda > 0$ if and only if $q < 1$. Thus, a positive nominal interest rate is associated with a binding cash-in-advance constraint.

From Equation (A-97), the nominal interest rate is

$$R = \frac{1+\alpha}{\beta} - 1.$$

The real interest rate is $\frac{1}{s} - 1$; from Equation (A-98) this is

$$r = \frac{1}{\beta} - 1,$$

which is the representative consumer's subjective rate of time preference. Further, the inflation rate is

$$i = \frac{P_{t+1}}{P_t} - 1 = \frac{P_{t+1}\overline{M}_{t+1}}{P_t\overline{M}_t} - 1 = \alpha,$$

so that the inflation rate is equal to the money growth rate. Now, from the above, it is clear that the Fisher relation holds, as

$$1 + r = \frac{1+R}{1+i}.$$

The effects of money growth on real variables can be obtained by totally differentiating Equation (A-99) with respect to N and α and solving to obtain

$$\frac{dN}{d\alpha} = \frac{-V'}{(1+\alpha)V'' - \beta z^2 U''} < 0;$$

thus, employment declines with an increase in the money growth rate, and because $Y = C = zN$ in equilibrium, output and consumption also decline. This effect arises because inflation distorts intertemporal decisions. Period t labor income is held as cash and not spent on consumption until period $t + 1$, and it is, therefore, eroded by inflation. Higher inflation then reduces labor supply, output, and consumption.

What is the optimal rate of inflation? To determine a Pareto optimum, we solve the social planner's problem, which is to solve

$$\max_{\{C_t, N_t\}_{t=0}^{\infty}} \sum_{t=0}^{\infty} \beta^t [U(C_t) - V(N_t)]$$

subject to $C_t = zN_t$ for all t. The solution to this problem is characterized by the first-order condition

$$zU'(zN^*) - V'(N^*) = 0,$$

where N^* is optimal employment in each period t. In equilibrium, employment N is determined by Equation (A-99), and equilibrium employment is equal to N^* for the case where $\alpha = \beta - 1$. The optimal money growth rate $\beta - 1$ characterizes a Friedman rule, as this implies from Equation (A-97) that the nominal interest rate is zero and that the inflation rate is $\beta - 1$, so that the rate of return on money is $\frac{1}{\beta} - 1$, which is identical to the real interest rate r. From Equation (A-102), the cash-in-advance constraint does not bind when $\alpha = \beta - 1$, because $\lambda = 0$. Thus, a Friedman rule relaxes the cash-in-advance constraint and causes the rates of return on all assets to be equated in equilibrium.

Problem

1. Suppose in the monetary intertemporal model that $U(C) = 2C^{\frac{1}{2}}$ and $V(N) = (\frac{1}{2})N^2$. Determine closed-form solutions for consumption, employment, output, the nominal interest rate, and the real interest rate. What are the effects of changes in z and α in equilibrium? Explain your results.

Chapter 18 Money, Inflation, and Banking: A Deeper Look

We work through formal results for two models here, which are a Kiyotaki–Wright monetary search model and the Diamond–Dybvig banking model. The results on money growth using the monetary intertemporal model are derived in the previous section.

A Kiyotaki–Wright Monetary Search Model

Here, we develop a version of the Kiyotaki–Wright random matching model to show how fiat money can overcome an absence-of-double-coincidence-of-wants problem. This model is closely related to the one constructed by Alberto Trejos and Randall Wright in an article in the *Journal of Political Economy*,[5] and it generalizes the model of Chapter 17 to a case where there are n different goods rather than three. To work through this model requires an elementary knowledge of probability.

In the model, there are n different types of consumers and n different goods, where $n \geq 3$. Each consumer is infinite-lived and maximizes

$$E_0 \sum_{t=0}^{\infty} \left(\frac{1}{1+r}\right)^t U_t,$$

where E_0 is the expectations operator conditional on information at $t = 0$, r is the consumer's subjective discount rate, and U_t is the utility from consuming in period t, where $U_t = 0$ if nothing is consumed. Given that the consumer faces uncertainty, we have assumed that he or she is an expected-utility maximizer. A consumer of type i produces good i and consumes good $i + 1$, for $i = 1, 2, 3, \ldots, n - 1$, and a type n consumer produces good n and consumes good 1. If $n = 3$, then this is the same setup we considered in Chapter 15. In this n-good model, there is an absence-of-double-coincidence problem, as no two consumers produce what each other wants.

---

[5]See A. Trejos and R. Wright, 1995. "Search, Bargaining, Money, and Prices," *Journal of Political Economy* 103, 118–141.

Goods are indivisible, so that when a good is produced, the consumer produces only one unit. At $t = 0$, a fraction M of the population is endowed with one unit of fiat money each, and fiat money is also indivisible. Further, a consumer can hold at most one unit of some object at a time, so that at the end of any period a consumer is holding one unit of a good, one unit of money, or nothing. It is costless to produce a good and costless to hold one unit of a good or money as inventory.

At the end of period 0, each consumer not holding money produces a good, and then he or she holds this in inventory until period 1. In period 1, consumers are matched two-by-two and at random, so that a given consumer meets only one other consumer during period 1. Two consumers who meet inspect each other's goods and announce whether they are willing to trade. If both are willing, they trade, and any consumer receiving his or her consumption good in a trade consumes it (this is optimal), receives utility $u > 0$ from consumption, and produces another good. Then consumers move on to period 2 and so on. No two consumers meet more than once, because there are infinitely many consumers in the population. We assume that there are equal numbers of each type of consumer, so that the fraction of the population who are of a given type is $\frac{1}{n}$. Then, in any period, the probability that a consumer meets another consumer of a particular type is $\frac{1}{n}$.

What can be an equilibrium in this model? One equilibrium is where money is not valued. That is, if no one accepts money, then no one wants to hold it, and because of the absence-of-double-coincidence problem, there is no exchange and everyone's utility is zero. If no one has faith that money has value in exchange, then this expectation is self-fulfilling. A more interesting equilibrium is one where everyone accepts money. Here, we let μ denote the fraction of the population that holds money in equilibrium, V_g denotes the value of holding a good in equilibrium, and V_m is the value of holding money. Though there are n different goods, the optimization problems of all consumers are identical in equilibrium, and so the value of holding any good is the same for each consumer. The Bellman equations associated with a consumer's optimization problem are

$$V_g = \frac{1}{1+r}\left[(1-\mu)V_g + \mu\left(1-\frac{1}{n}\right)V_g + \mu\frac{1}{n}(V_m - V_g)\right], \quad \text{(A-103)}$$

$$V_m = \frac{1}{1+r}\left[(1-\mu)\left(1-\frac{1}{n}\right)V_m + (1-\mu)\frac{1}{n}(u + V_g) + \mu V_m\right]. \quad \text{(A-104)}$$

In Equation (A-103), the value of holding a good at the end of the current period is equal to the discounted sum of the expected payoff in the following period. In the following period, the consumer meets another agent with a good with probability $1 - \mu$, in which case trade does not take place, and the consumer is holding a good at the end of the next period and receives value V_g. With probability $\mu(1 - \frac{1}{n})$, the consumer meets another consumer with money who does not wish to purchase the consumer's good, and again trade does not take place. With probability $\mu\frac{1}{n}$, the consumer meets a consumer with money who wants his or her good, trade takes place, and the consumer is holding money at the end of the next period. In Equation (A-104), a consumer with money does not trade with another consumer who has money or with another consumer who has a good that he or she does not consume. However, with probability $(1 - \mu)\frac{1}{n}$ the consumer meets another consumer with his or her consumption good, in which case trade takes place, the consumer gets utility u from consuming the good, and then he or she produces another good.

We can solve for V_g and V_m from Equations (A-103) and (A-104), which give

$$V_g = \frac{\mu(1 - \mu)u}{rn(1 + rn)},$$

$$V_m = \frac{(rn + \mu)(1 - \mu)u}{rn(1 + rn)},$$

so that

$$V_m - V_g = \frac{(1 - \mu)u}{1 + rn} > 0.$$

Therefore, the value of holding money is greater than the value of holding a good, so that everyone accepts money (as conjectured) in equilibrium. Further, consumers who have money in any period prefer to hold it rather than produce a good, and so we have $\mu = M$ in equilibrium.

The values of V_g and V_m are the utilities that consumers receive from holding goods and money, respectively. As $V_g > 0$ and $V_m > 0$, everyone is better off in an economy where money is used than in one where it is not used.

Problem

1. Suppose a search economy with the possibility of double coincidences; that is, assume that when an agent produces a good, that she cannot consume it herself. In a random match where two agents meet and each has the good that they produced, the first agent has what the second consumes with probability x, the second has what the first consumes with probability x, and each has what the other consumes with probability x^2.

   (a) In this economy, show that there are three equilibria: a barter equilibrium where money is not accepted, an equilibrium where an agent with a good is indifferent between accepting and not accepting money, and an equilibrium where agents with goods always accept money.

   (b) Show that x needs to be sufficiently small before having money in this economy actually increases welfare over having barter, and explain this result.

The Diamond–Dybvig Banking Model

There are three periods, 0, 1, and 2, and an intertemporal technology that allows one unit of the period 0 good to be converted into $1 + r$ units of the period 2 good. The intertemporal technology can be interrupted in period 1, with a yield of one unit in period 1 for each unit of input in period 0. If production is interrupted in period 1, there is no return in period 2. Goods can be stored from period 1 to period 2 with no depreciation. There is a continuum of consumers with unit mass, and each consumer maximizes expected utility

$$W = tU(c_1) + (1 - t)U(c_2),$$

where c_i is the consumer's consumption if he or she consumes in period i, for $i = 1, 2$, and t is the probability that the consumer consumes early. Here, t is also the fraction of agents who are early consumers. We assume that t is known in period 0, but consumers do not know their type (early or late consumer) until period 1. Each consumer is endowed with one unit of goods in period 0.

Suppose that there are no banks, but consumers can trade investment projects in period 1, with one project selling for the price p in terms of consumption goods. Then, each consumer chooses to invest all of one's goods in the technology in period 0, and in period 1 a consumer must decide how much of the investment to interrupt and how many investment projects to buy and sell. In period 1, an early consumer wants to sell the investment project if $p > 1$ and will want to interrupt the investment project and consume the proceeds if $p < 1$. The early consumer is indifferent if $p = 1$. A late consumer in period 1 wants to interrupt the investment project and purchase investment projects if $p < 1$, chooses to hold the investment project if $p > 1$, and is indifferent if $p = 1$. The equilibrium price is, therefore, $p = 1$, and in equilibrium fraction t of all projects is interrupted in period 1, early consumers each consume $c_1 = 1$, and late consumers consume $c_2 = 1 + r$. Expected utility for each consumer in period 0 is

$$W_1 = tU(1) + (1 - t)U(1 + r).$$

Now, suppose that there is a bank that takes deposits from consumers in period 0, serves depositors sequentially in period 1 (places in line are drawn at random), and offers a deposit contract (d_1, d_2), where d_1 is the amount that can be withdrawn in period 1 for each unit deposited, and d_2 is the amount that can be withdrawn in period 2 for each unit deposited. Assume that all consumers deposit in the bank in period 0. Then, the bank chooses d_1, d_2, and x, the quantity of production to interrupt, to solve:

$$\max[tU(d_1) + (1 - t)U(d_2)] \tag{A-105}$$

subject to

$$td_1 = x, \tag{A-106}$$

$$(1 - t)d_2 = (1 - x)(1 + r), \tag{A-107}$$

$$d_1 \leq d_2. \tag{A-108}$$

Here, Equation (A-106) is the bank's resource constraint in period 1, Equation (A-107) is the resource constraint in period 2, and Equation (A-108) is an incentive constraint, which states that it must be in the interest of late consumers to withdraw late rather than posing as early consumers and withdrawing early.

Ignoring the constraint (A-108), substituting for d_1 and d_2 using the constraints (A-106) and (A-107) in the objective function (A-105), the first-order condition for an optimum is

$$U'\left(\frac{x}{t}\right) = (1+r)U'\left(\frac{(1-x)(1+r)}{1-t}\right). \tag{A-109}$$

with $d_1 = \frac{x}{t}$ and $d_2 = \frac{(1-x)(1+r)}{1-t}$. Equation (A-109) then implies that $d_1 < d_2$ so that Equation (A-108) is satisfied. Further, if we assume that $\frac{-cU''(c)}{U'(c)} > 1$, then Equation (A-109) implies that $d_1 > 1$ and $d_2 < 1 + r$. Thus, under this condition, the bank provides consumers with insurance against the need for liquid assets in period 1, and the bank gives consumers higher expected utility than when there was no bank ($d_1 = 1$ and $d_2 = 1 + r$ if the bank chooses $x = t$).

However, there also exists a bank-run equilibrium. That is, if a late consumer expects all other consumers to run to the bank in period 1, he or she will want to do it as well.

Problems

1. Suppose that consumers can meet and trade in period 1 instead of going to the bank in sequence. Show that, given the banking contract (d_1, d_2), there could be Pareto-improving trades that early and late consumers could make in period 1 that would undo the banking contract, so that this would not constitute an equilibrium. Discuss your results.

2. Show that, if $U(c) = \ln c$, then there is no need for a bank in the Diamond–Dybvig economy, and explain this result.

Index

Page numbers with *f* indicate figures; those with *t* indicate tables.

Notation

a = capital share in national income

a = worker's bargaining power (Chapter 6)

a = fraction of defaulting borrowers in the credit market (Chapter 10)

a = coefficient on the output gap in the Phillips curve (Chapter 15)

b = unemployment insurance payment (Chapter 6)

b = productivity of labor in producing human capital (Chapter 8)

b = coefficient on inflation expectations in the Phillips curve equation (Chapter 15)

c = individual current consumption

d = depreciation rate

$1/d$ = intertemporal elasticity of substitution (Chapter 15)

e = matching efficiency (Chapter 6)

$em(Q, A)$: matching function (Chapter 6)

e = nominal exchange rate (Chapter 16)

f = per worker production function

g = function describing the relationship between current population and future population in the Malthusian growth model

h = time available to the consumer

h = coefficient on inflation in the Taylor rule (Chapter 15)

i = inflation rate

i' = anticipated inflation rate

i^* = inflation target

j = labor market tightness

k = capital per worker

l = leisure

l = land per worker (Chapter 7)

n = labor force growth rate

p = price of housing (Chapter 10)

p = job offer rate (Chapter 6)

p_c = probability of finding work for a consumer

p_f = probability for a firm of finding a match with a worker

q = price of credit card balances

r = real interest rate

r^* = world real interest rate

r^* = natural rate of interest (Chapters 14 and 15)

r_1 = real interest rate at which consumers can lend

r_2 = real interest rate at which consumers can borrow

s = savings rate (Chapters 7 and 8)

s = separation rate (Chapter 6)

t = tax rate (Chapter 5)

t = current lump sum tax paid by the individual (Chapter 9)

t = fraction of early consumers (Chapter 17)

U = unemployment rate (Chapter 6)

u = time spent producing consumption goods (Chapter 8)

v = vacancy rate

v = loss from default (Chapter 16)

w = real wage

we = lifetime wealth

x = money growth rate

y = individual current income

z = total factor productivity

A = number of active firms

B = bonds issued by the government

C = aggregate consumption

CA = current account surplus

D = government deficit

E = employment

G = government expenditures